ADRIAN PIPER

TO THE MEMORY OF SOL LEWITT

ADRIAN PIPER

A SYNTHESIS OF INTUITIONS 1965–2016

CHRISTOPHE CHERIX
CORNELIA BUTLER
DAVID PLATZKER

THE MUSEUM OF MODERN ART
NEW YORK

DIRECTORS' FOREWORD

Adrian Piper's achievements are varied and countless—as well as being an accomplished artist, she is also a philosopher and a writer of consummate skill—and an expansive exhibition of her work has long been overdue. *Adrian Piper: A Synthesis of Intuitions, 1965–2016*, an exhibition of unprecedented reach and depth, has been in the making for more than five years, and we are excited to be sharing with our public a body of work that is as relevant and critical today as it was when she began her career, in the 1960s.

From the beginning, Adrian's work has tackled complex subjects with the utmost precision. As such, her voice has been critical to the success of this retrospective of her work. She has been a true partner and collaborator from its inception to the design of the installations at our institutions. She has graciously shared her archives, insight, and brilliance with us along the way, pushing us to rethink our institutional mantras while at the same time trusting us to realize her vision. We are immensely grateful for her continued support, without which neither our presentations nor this publication would have been possible. They are the product of a journey marked by lively dialogue and a tireless determination from everyone involved.

Adrian has also helped us to realize the beautiful and powerful traveling show *Adrian Piper: Concepts and Intuitions, 1965–2016*, which will be presented at the Hammer Museum and Haus der Kunst. These two representations of her work elaborate on Adrian's profound body of work, and reflect on her undeniable mark in Europe and the United States.

At The Museum of Modern Art, the show is made possible by Hyundai Card, with essential support provided by The Modern Women's Fund and Lannan Foundation, as well as The Friends of Education of The Museum of Modern Art, Marilyn and Larry Fields, Marieluise Hessel Artzt, and the MoMA Annual Exhibition Fund. We are deeply grateful to them all. The Hammer Museum wishes to thank Board Chair Marcy Carsey, Board President Michael Rubel, and the Hammer Board of Directors for their ongoing leadership and support. Haus der Kunst would like to thank its shareholders, Freestate of Bavaria, and the Gesellschaft der Freunde Haus der Kunst e.V., as well as its major supporter, the Alexander Tutsek Foundation.

With *Adrian Piper: A Synthesis of Intuitions, 1965–2016* and *Adrian Piper: Concepts and Intuitions, 1965–2016*, we hope to cement Adrian's critical role in the history of the art of our times and to broaden our audience's knowledge of her lasting contribution to the field. It has been a tremendous honor to work alongside her, with her team in Berlin, and with all our colleagues in New York, Los Angeles, and Munich. Thank you, Adrian.

Glenn D. Lowry, Director, The Museum of Modern Art, New York
Ann Philbin, Director, Hammer Museum, Los Angeles
Okwui Enwezor, Director, Haus der Kunst, Munich

ARTIST'S ACKNOWLEDGMENTS

None of us realized what we were in for when we started. I certainly was not prepared for the curators' persuasive demonstration, at our first meeting four years ago, that they already knew more about my work than I did. And perhaps they were not prepared for me to show up at that meeting with the APRA Foundation Berlin's Exhibition and Loan Agreement in hand. Since then, working on this exhibition with the entire staff of The Museum of Modern Art has been the most profoundly fulfilling collaboration of my life. My gratitude to each and every member of the MoMA team, and my awe and respect for the level of quality, scholarship, and professionalism at which MoMA regularly operates, know no bounds.

The very first to whom I owe that debt of gratitude is MoMA's Prime Mover, Glenn Lowry (whom I have occasionally confused with God), without whose unstinting support this exhibition would not have occurred, and without whose creative contributions it would not have been what it is. Glenn's openness, his willingness to experiment, to ask questions and test boundaries, and to rethink settled expectations, procedures, and habits have been absolutely crucial to the new ground this historic retrospective breaks and the wide variety of entrenched assumptions it violates. Fellow artists, listen up: this man is not a suit.

The idea for the retrospective first took root in Connie Butler's resourceful and wide-ranging imagination, where it germinated quietly for several years. Connie's committed participation, experienced judgment and deft interventions in our extended planning process, from near and afar, created and reinforced the firm and stable foundation of curatorial integrity on which the final form of this exhibition is based. It was fertilized by David Platzker's careful and detailed research, and his conscientious organization of the resulting wealth of information. I thank him for suggesting *Adrian Piper: A Reader* as a companion volume to this catalogue; and the authors who contributed to that publication—Diarmuid Costello, Jörg Heiser, Kobena Mercer, Nizan Shaked, Vid Simoniti, and Elvan Zabunyan—for the refreshingly original and varied approaches to my work they have provided. Together with the curators' profoundly innovative essays in this catalogue, all of them undergird this retrospective with a strong, reliable, and veridically well-anchored intellectual framework of the highest quality. The retrospective blossomed into maturity under the judicious leadership of Christophe Cherix. His careful and considered curatorial decisions, wise guidance, and confident coordination of the entire undertaking from inception to completion; his reassuring presence, in the background as well as in the foreground; and his always steady hand on the wheel have steered this project with inimitable grace, skill, and sensitivity. Okwui Enwezor was unable to contribute an essay to this catalogue, for reasons beyond anyone's control. But his presence is felt in its very existence. I am immensely grateful to him for bringing my work to the attention of a larger public in documenta 11 and in the 56th Venice Biennale. At this level of artistic collaboration, it is extremely difficult to draw a line between artist and curator or artist and administrator. I can only think of all of these good people, with very great affection, as co-conspirators.

All good co-conspirators have a network of allies who provide the specialized knowledge, competence, and devotion to the job that ensures that the job gets done at a standard of performance of which everyone can be proud. From the beginning, Tessa Ferreyros has given enormous energy, skill, and devotion to gathering, collating, and systematizing all of the information we have needed at each stage of the process. She has been not only MoMA's representative to my team at APRA but also the medium through which virtually all communications between these two institutions have been transmitted or coordinated. I did not begin to really comprehend what was at stake in this exhibition until I encountered Mack Cole-Edelsack's brilliant, detailed architectural scale model representing the way my retrospective would look when installed in MoMA's Sixth Floor and Marron Atrium. The dexterity and resourcefulness with which he engineered the reconstruction of the space and the placement of work within it gave me a powerful sense of the full scale of the curators' achievement. It left me speechless. I am also deeply indebted to Josh Higgason for his masterful fabrication of a recent major work, *Mauer*, which will be seen at MoMA for the first time. Ramona Bronkar Bannayan, with the assistance of Jennifer Cohen, generously shared with me her wealth of experience in long-term planning and administering the logistics of what has been a particularly challenging and demanding show by every measure. Wendy Woon tolerated my inept incursions into her area of specialization—museum education—with great patience and good humor, and contributed liberally to my own continuing adult education along the way. Stuart Comer materialized to work his magic at several crucial junctures, and this exhibition has benefited tremendously from his involvement. Lizzie Gorfaine undertook the difficult work of realizing my performances within the MoMA context. Peter Oleksik demonstrated the full scope of his technological prowess through the tolerance and sympathy with which he approached my stubbornly low-tech media installations. The expertise and dedication of MoMA's Publications Department is evident in every page of this catalogue. I have been privileged to work closely with Emily Hall, Chris Hudson, and Hannah Kim on it and the accompanying reader and installation brochure. I am immensely indebted to Emily for her rigor, precision, and unyielding pursuit of lucid prose, and to Chris for his heroic patience, tolerance, good judgment, and sense of humor at every step of the publication process. Hannah Kim joined the design process at precisely that moment at which we have been best able to appreciate her very considerable talent, resourcefulness, and quick thinking.

The only support team that even begins to measure up to MoMA's is my own. Aude Pariset's steady presence, persistence, and technological sophistication have contributed crucially to every aspect of our activities and planning for this exhibition from the beginning. Sophie Mattheus put her wealth of prior curatorial, administrative, and organizational experience to work the minute she joined the team, and has guided to successful completion the most challenging exhibition project we will ever face. Levno von Plato has contributed finely honed analytical skills, fortitude, and commitment to conquering the paperwork required at each step of our administrative procedures. Elise Lammer's help and support in launching this project in its early stages greatly benefited its later stages. Katharina Roeck Martinelli's superb restorations and Viola Eickmeier's exceptional refabrications restored to me a vivid memory of early periods of my productivity. And Timo Ohler's exceptional photography is the source of many of the most beautiful images in this catalogue. The human and technological resources of the digital-engineering team at Concept AV in Berlin provided invaluable and expeditious support at every stage, often with virtually no advance warning.

A selection of works from this exhibition will travel to the Hammer Museum and the Haus der Kunst under the name *Adrian Piper: Concepts and Intuitions, 1965–2016*. I am deeply grateful to Ann Philbin and Ulrich Wilmers for their enthusiasm and commitment in taking on this exhibition, and not least of all for their patience and fortitude in weathering the vicissitudes of our protracted process of planning its traveling schedule.

Among the gallerists whose cooperation was essential to the success of this project, I owe a special debt of thanks first and foremost to Dominique Lévy and Begum Yasar for their unstinting support and generosity at every level. I am also grateful to Emi Fontana, Elizabeth Dee, Thomas Erben, and Paula Cooper for their cooperation. All of the lenders to this exhibition have contributed immensely to its success, and my appreciation for their generosity is very great. Special thanks is due to Sabine Breitwieser, Director first of the Generali Foundation and then of the Museum der Moderne Salzburg, who has for many years managed the Generali's extensive collection of my work according to the highest curatorial and custodial standards. Other collectors to whom I am deeply grateful include Beth Rudin DeWoody, Nicola Ferraro, Lonti Ebers, and Peter Norton. There are many more individuals I could name here whose contributions to and participation in this project have been absolutely crucial. But I hope I have said enough to make clear that it has been a fully collaborative endeavor at every stage and at every level. I am merely the front man.

Adrian Piper
Berlin, January 27, 2018

CURATORS' ACKNOWLEDGMENTS

Since the early 1960s Adrian Piper has been producing uncompromising and groundbreaking work that has profoundly shaped contemporary art. Spanning five decades, *Adrian Piper: A Synthesis of Intuitions, 1965–2016*, and the traveling exhibition *Adrian Piper: Concepts and Intuitions, 1965–2016*, recognize the artist's significant influence, surveying the full range of diverse media in which she has contributed. The scope of such a monumental retrospective would not have been possible without the dedicated exhibition teams at The Museum of Modern Art, New York; the Hammer Museum, Los Angeles; and Haus der Kunst, Munich.

First and foremost, the staff at the Adrian Piper Research Archive Foundation Berlin (APRA) has been instrumental in realizing this exhibition over the past four years. We thank Aude Pariset, Registrar, for her continued support and, more recently, Levno von Plato, Archivist, and Sophie Mattheus, Assistant Director. We also thank Elise Lammer, the former Exhibitions Assistant at APRA, for her early contributions to the project.

At MoMA we wish to wholeheartedly acknowledge the generosity of Gwen and Peter Norton who decisively advocated on behalf of Adrian's art at the Museum and donated two seminal works to the collection in 2011. We are also deeply grateful for the support of our Trustees, including Agnes Gund, President Emeritus and Chairman of the Board of MoMA PS1; Jerry I. Speyer, Chairman; Marie-Josée Kravis, President; Marlene Hess, Vice Chairman; and Donald B. Marron, President Emeritus, for his leadership as Chairman of the Committee on Drawings and Prints. These Trustees, along with the generous assistance of Donald L. Bryant, Jr.; Eileen and Michael Cohen; Lonti Ebers; Carol and Morton Rapp; and Candace King Weir, in addition to The Committee on Drawings and Prints, The Friends of Education of The Museum of Modern Art, and The Modern Women's Fund, have helped us demonstrate our commitment to Adrian's work, through their abundant support toward acquisitions in multiple departments. And we heartily reiterate the thanks of our directors to all the sponsors of the exhibition.

Our sincere appreciation goes to the many private and public lenders who have shared their work for this exhibition, including Adrian Piper Research Archive Foundation Berlin; Konrad Baumgartner; Neal Benezra, Director, San Francisco Museum of Modern Art; Sabine Breitwieser, Artistic and Managing Director, Museum der Moderne Salzburg; Antonia Lotz, Curator, The Generali Foundation and Collection, Salzburg; John Campione; Alan Cravitz and Shashi Caudill; Elizabeth Dee Gallery, New York; Lisa Dorin, Interim Director, Williams College Museum of Art; Lonti Ebers; Thomas Erben; Nathalie Ergino, Director, Collection Institut d'art contemporain, Rhône-Alpes; Katharina Faerber; Simona and Francesco Fantinelli; Rothier Faria Collection; Marilyn and Larry Fields; Sandra Q. Firmin, Director and Chief Curator, University of Colorado Art Museum, Boulder; Louise Fishman; Lisa Fischman, the Ruth Gordon Shapiro '37 Director, Davis Museum of Wellesley College; Emi Fontana; Alison Gass, the Dana Feitler Director, Smart Museum Of Art, The University of Chicago; Sherri Geldin, Director, Wexner Center for the Arts, Ohio State University; Annette Gentz and Pascal Decker; Thelma Golden, Director and Chief Curator, The Studio Museum in Harlem; Madeleine Grynsztejn, Pritzker Director, Museum of Contemporary Art, Chicago; Saralyn Reece Hardy, Marilyn Stokstad Director, Spencer Museum of Art, the University of Kansas; The Heithoff Family Collection; Udo Kittelmann, Director, and Dr. Sven Beckstette, Curator Staatliche Museen zu Berlin, Nationalgalerie; Liz and Eric Lefkofsky; Margaret and Daniel S. Loeb; Thomas J. Loughman, Director and C.E.O., Wadsworth Atheneum; Paul and Karen McCarthy; Gregory R. Miller and Michael Wiener; Mott-Warsh Collection, Flint, Michigan; Dona Nelson; Eileen Norton; Tricia Y. Paik, the Florence Finch Abbott Director, Mount Holyoke College Art Museum; J-E Van Praet; Anne Pasternak, the Shelby White and Leon Levy Director, Brooklyn Museum; Rennie Collection, Vancouver; Lawrence R. Rinder, Director, University of California, Berkeley Art Museum and Pacific Film Archive; Silvia Rocciolo and Eric Stark, Curators, The New School Art Collection, New York; James Rondeau, President and the Eloise W. Martin Director, Art Institute of Chicago; Beth Rudin DeWoody; Richard and Ellen Sandor Family Collection; Stephen Schiffer; Siemens Fotosammlung; Lila Silverman and Jon Hendricks, The Gilbert B. and Lila Silverman Collection, Detroit; Gary Tinterow, Director, Museum of Fine Arts, Houston; Sara M. and Michelle Vance Waddell; Philippe Vergne, the Maurice Marciano Director, Museum of Contemporary Art, Los Angeles; Olga Viso, former Director, and Siri Engberg, Senior Curator and Director of Exhibitions Management, Visual Arts, Walker Art Center, Minneapolis; Collection Sands and Robin Murray-Wassink; Candace King Weir; Lesley C. Wright, Director, and Daniel Strong, Associate Director and Curator of Exhibitions, Faulconer Gallery, Grinnell College; and the many lenders who wish to remain private.

This publication could not have been realized without the unwavering dedication and commitment of the Department of Publications at The Museum of Modern Art, New York. We thank Christopher Hudson, Publisher; Don McMahon, Editorial Director; Marc Sapir, Production Director; Cerise Fontaine, Department Manager; Hannah Kim, Senior Marketing and Production Coordinator, for her first-rate management of the images and design; and Editor Emily Hall for her unflappable and expert handling of the authors' texts and for being a conduit for the artist's voice in this process. These individuals were all crucial in bringing the catalogue to fruition, while Adam Michaels and Siiri Tännler of Inventory Form & Content produced a beautiful design that beautifully communicates Adrian's multifaceted work.

MoMA's Director, Glenn D. Lowry, championed the exhibition through its many stages, providing unwavering support and guidance along the way and critical leadership when essential. The direct involvement of Ramona Bannayan, Senior Deputy Director for Exhibitions and Collections, was essential for our exhibition's success. We are grateful for the dedication of James Gara, Chief Operating Officer and Assistant Treasurer; Kathy Halbreich, former Associate Director and now Curator and Advisor to the Director of the Laurenz Foundation; Peter Reed, Senior Deputy Director for Curatorial Affairs; and Todd

Bishop, Senior Deputy Director for External Affairs. Many thanks are also due to Quentin Bajac, The Joel and Anne Ehrenkranz Chief Curator of Photography; Stuart Comer, Chief Curator, Department of Media and Performance Art; Rajendra Roy, The Celeste Bartos Chief Curator of Film; Martino Stierli, The Philip Johnson Chief Curator of Architecture and Design; and Ann Temkin, The Marie-Josée and Henry Kravis Chief Curator of Painting and Sculpture.

Every member of MoMA's exhibitions team has played a valuable role in the New York presentation. Their tireless, kind, and patient dedication to the project was truly remarkable and made the seemingly impossible possible. A special thanks to the meticulous and skilled management of Jennifer Cohen, Associate Director of Exhibition Planning and Administration, and Maya Taylor, Department Assistant, Exhibition Planning and Administration, along with Cate Griffin, Exhibition Manager, and Erik Patton, Director, Exhibition Planning and Administration and Senior Administration and Planning Expansion Project Manager.

We have been grateful for the talent and boundless expertise of Mack Cole-Edelsack, Senior Design Manager, who traveled to Berlin multiple times to work directly with Adrian on realizing a complicated installation with absolute finesse, and his colleagues in the Exhibition Design and Production department, led by Lana Hum, Director, with contributions from Michele Arms, Assistant Production Manager, and Harry Harris, Department Coordinator. Our graditude also goes to Patty Lipshutz, General Counsel and Secretary to the Board, and Nancy Adelson, Deputy General Counsel, who creatively solved the many questions and concerns that arose, and to Jessica Nilsen, Associate Registrar, Exhibitions, for coordinating the safe delivery of art from near and far with her colleagues Caitlin Kelly, Senior Registrar Assistant, and Sacha Eaton, Associate Registrar. Our thanks to Lizzie Gorfaine, Assistant Director, Performance and Live Programs Producer, and Kate Scherer, Assistant Performance Coordinator, Exhibition Planning and Administration, who expertly handled the many performative works in the show, and Aaron Louis, Director of Audio Visual, and his team, who set the stage for Adrian's multifaceted installations. Matias Pacheco, Senior Manager of Client Services, Information Technology, and Chiara Bernasconi, Assistant Director, Digital Media, brought their skills as well to the exhibition's installation. We extend our thanks to Athena Holbrook, Collection Specialist, Department of Media and Performance Art; to Kurt Heumiller, Studio Production Manager, and Paul Abbey, Preparator, from the Imaging and Visual Resources department; to Tom Krueger, Assistant Manager, Art Handling and Preparation; and to former MoMA Photographer Peter Butler and Gregg Deering of Atelier 4 for their last-minute assistance imaging the final works for inclusion in this publication.

Our colleagues in MoMA's Department of Graphic Design and Advertising created a cohesive voice for the exhibition's didactic material. They are Ingrid H. Y. Chou, Associate Creative Director; with Damien Saatdjian, Art Director; Eva Bochem-Shur, Senior Graphic Designer; and Claire Corey, Production Manager. Thank you to Robert Kastler, Director of Imaging and Visual Resources, and his associates; and to Peter Perez, Frame Shop Foreman, Exhibition Design and Production, for his kind and knowledgeable insight, also to his staff for framing works and preparing gallery labels and signage. Thanks also to Sarah Wood, Assistant Manager, Art Handling and Preparation, and all of our art handlers under Rob Jung's leadership as Manager, Art Handling and Preparation.

We also thank Michelle Elligott, Chief of Archives, Library, and Research Collections; Michelle Harvey, Rona Roob Museum Archivist; and Librarian Jennifer Tobias for their eagerness in fielding research questions over the last five years; Wendy Woon, The Edward John Noble Foundation Deputy Director for Education; Pablo Helguera, Director, Adult and Academic Education; Sara Bodinson, Director, Interpretation, Research, and Digital Learning; Sarah Kennedy, Assistant Director, Learning Programs and Partnerships; Jess Van Nostrand, Assistant Director, Exhibition Programs and Gallery Initiatives; Adelia Gregory, Associate Educator, Public Programs and Gallery Initiatives; Francesca Rosenberg, Director of Community and Access Programs, Lara Schweller, Coordinator, Community and Access Programs; Maria Marchenkova, Assistant Editor, Publications, each for helping us with our educational programming and making this exhibition accessible to all. And thanks to Audrey Stoltz, Assistant Director, Visitor Services; Tunji Adeniji, Director of Facilities and Safety, Daniel Platt, Director of Security; Tyrone Wyllie, Associate Director of Security; and their entire highly dedicated teams; for all their efforts to welcome visitors to the exhibition and ensure the safety of our guests and the works on view. Our thanks to Kate Lewis, The Agnes Gund Chief Conservator, The David Booth Conservation Center and Department; Laura Neufeld, Assistant Conservator; Erika Mosier, Conservator; LeeAnn Daffner, Photography Conservator; Peter Oleksik, Associate Conservator; Amy Brost, Assistant Media Conservator, for overseeing all aspects of the exhibition's conservation needs. To Maggie Lyko, Director, Affiliate/Donor Programs, and Director, Special Programming and Events, and to Jessie Cappello, Events Coordinator, Special Programming and Events, go our thanks for organizing the exhibition's opening events. Thanks also to Rebecca Stokes, Director, Digital Initiatives, External Affairs; Meg Montgoris, Publicist, Communications; Margaret Doyle, former Director of Communications; and former Chief Communications Officer Kim Mitchell for helping us advance this exhibition to the public with the grace it deserves. Thanks to Laura Coppelli, Associate Director, Human Resources, for skillfully managing our staffing needs.

The exhibition and publication were made possible by the entire staff of the Department of Drawings and Prints at The Museum of Modern Art, New York: John Prochilo, Department Manager, and Alex Diczok, Assistant to the Chief Curator, provided vital organizational support. We thank Ana Torok, Curatorial Assistant, for her assistance with research and exhibition support. We would like to extend our gratitude to Department Assistants Emily Manges and Kiko Aebi, who seamlessly handled a multitude of requests; to our Preparators Jeff White and David Moreno; to Sydney Briggs, our

Department's dedicated Associate Registrar, Collections; to Jane Cavalier, Curatorial Assistant, for her indispensable assistance at the end; to Emily Cushman, Collection Specialist, who accommodated many rushed photography requests with the help of Robert Gerhardt, Collections Photographer in Imaging and Visual Resources; and to Emily Edison, Collection Specialist, Acquisitions and Loans, and Heidi Hirschl Orley, Curatorial Expansion Project Manager. We would also like to thank the many seasonal interns who have participated in this project over the past four years, including Carey Gibbons, Isabelle Rose, Alymamah Rashed, and Sila Ulug. We give special thanks to our former Louise Bourgeois Intern, Jennie Waldow, for her contributions during the initial stages of this exhibition's research, and to Curatorial Assistant Tara Keny, who lent her expertise to the catalogue during the final critical moments, as well as to Ashley James, former Museum Research Consortium Fellow, who provided a thoughtfully considered voice to our exhibition texts. We would also like to thank Jodi Hauptman, Senior Curator, for her sage advice during our work on this exhibition.

The Hammer Museum has been a partner since the project's inception. Director Ann Philbin advocated bringing Adrian's work to Los Angeles from the beginning, and we thank her and Deputy Director, Curatorial Affairs, Cynthia Burlingham for their unfailing support. Director, Exhibition and Publication Management, Melanie Crader has expertly coordinated every detail of administration and installation of the project at the Hammer with Director, Registration and Collections Management, Portland McCormick; Chief Preparator, Jason Pugh; and Assistant Director, Exhibition Design and Production, Peter Gould, who designed the installation. Assistant Curator Erin Christovale was an integral part of coordinating and activating the exhibition. Director, Public Programs, Claudia Bestor provided dynamic evening programs and events that brought the exhibition to life for a broader audience.

Haus der Kunst extends immense thanks to its entire team, without whose professional work and tireless engagement this exciting project could not have been realized: to the members of the curatorial team for their valuable input, with Julienne Lorz, Sabine Brantl, Anna Schneider, Daniel Milnes, and most particularly to Chief Curator Ulrich Wilmes; to Melissa Klein and Isabella Krelder, for managing the director's and curatorial offices; to External Affairs, with Tina Anjou, Elena Heitsch, Teresa Lengl, Iris Ludwig, and Andrea Weniger, as well as Anne Leopold and Sylvia Clasen and the entire team of the Children's and Youth Programs; and to interim Commercial Managing Director Dr. Stefan Gros and our former Finance Director Marco Graf von Matuschka and Moritz Petersen, for managing the finances and administration. Special thanks go Tina Köhler and Registrar Cassandre Schmid for the organization and coordination required to bring the show to Munich, and to all the members of their team: Conservators Susanne von der Groeben and Marjen Schmidt, Installers Elena Carvajal, Tanja Eiler, Moritz Friedrich, Martin Hast, Marzieh Kermani, Oh-Seok Kwon, Christian Leitna, Thomas Silberhorn, Tim Wolff, and Technical Director Anton Köttl and the members of his team, including Markus Brandenburg, Hans-Peter Frank, and Roland Roppelt.

The exhibition and this catalogue would not have been possible without the fervent commitment of Tessa Ferreyros, Curatorial Assistant, who has helped realize the project from its inception four years ago. Her invaluable, patient, and intelligent contributions to the exhibition history, bibliography, chronology, and every aspect of this complex exhibition have been instrumental to the realization of this project.

The curators would also like to acknowledge and thank Rhea Anastas, Paula Cooper and Steven Henry of Paula Cooper Gallery, Elizabeth Dee and the staff of her gallery, Elyse Goldberg, Dan Graham, Jean-Noël Herlin, Susan Inglett, Dominique Lévy and Begum Yasar of Lévy Gorvy gallery, Andrea Miller-Keller, the late Kynaston McShine, Gregory R. Miller, Amy O'Neill, Amy Baker Sandback, Susanna Singer, Lawrence Weiner, and Martha Wilson for their advice, insight, and counsel.

Most of all, we would like to thank Adrian Piper. The exhibition and publications have been produced through an utter and true collaboration with you. Your guidance has thoroughly reshaped our understanding of your practice and has provided us with invaluable insights and fresh means of exploring your life and art. Your dedication to every step of this project has made it possible for us to bring your work to a broad audience with intimate clarity and immeasurable depth.

Christophe Cherix
The Robert Lehman Foundation Chief Curator of Drawings and Prints
The Museum of Modern Art

David Platzker
Former Curator
Drawings and Prints
The Museum of Modern Art

Connie Butler
Chief Curator
Hammer Museum

WHO CALLS THE TUNE?

IN AND OUT OF *THE HUMMING ROOM*

CHRISTOPHE CHERIX

When I am alone in the solitude of my study or studio,
I am completely out of the closet: I move back and forth
easily among art, philosophy, and yoga (my third hat).
It's the only time I feel completely free to be who I am.
So I will go to almost any lengths to protect my privacy.
If I lose that, I lose everything.
—Adrian Piper[1]

An installation of contemporary art calls for its curator to focus on a work of art in relation both to the artist's practice and to visitors to the exhibition, so that two logics apply simultaneously: one remarkably singular, carrying the artist's structures of thought, and the other multiple by definition, as various as the perceptions of the public that will see it. An exhibition that has managed to remain faithful to the artist's vision while also attending to viewers is *Do It*, an itinerant and ongoing project that started in 1993 as a conversation between a curator, Hans Ulrich Obrist, and two artists, Christian Boltanski and Bertrand Lavier. The art for this exhibition exists primarily as instructions dictated by artists, and it is up to the curators at each venue to fabricate the works according to the requirements of their specific space as well as to the idiosyncrasies of their given public—thus the injunction, "Do it!" The different iterations of *Do It* have revealed, however, that the initial injunction might have meant different things to those who first conceived the show: to the curators it has suggested the freedom to interpret and carry out the instructions of the artists, while to some of the artists it has suggested direct engagement with the public. Indeed, most of the artists involved with *Do It* have chosen participatory works—works that ask viewers to take part in the art itself, either by being directly asked to do so or by interacting with the work more spontaneously—such as Felix Gonzalez-Torres's proposal for a sculpture made of candies that visitors could take and eat.

Adrian Piper was invited to participate in *Do It* in 2012, and for it she designed a participatory work titled *The Humming Room*, made up of an empty room guarded by a security officer (fig. 1).[2] On the work's origins, and the particular events that triggered its conception, Piper has noted,

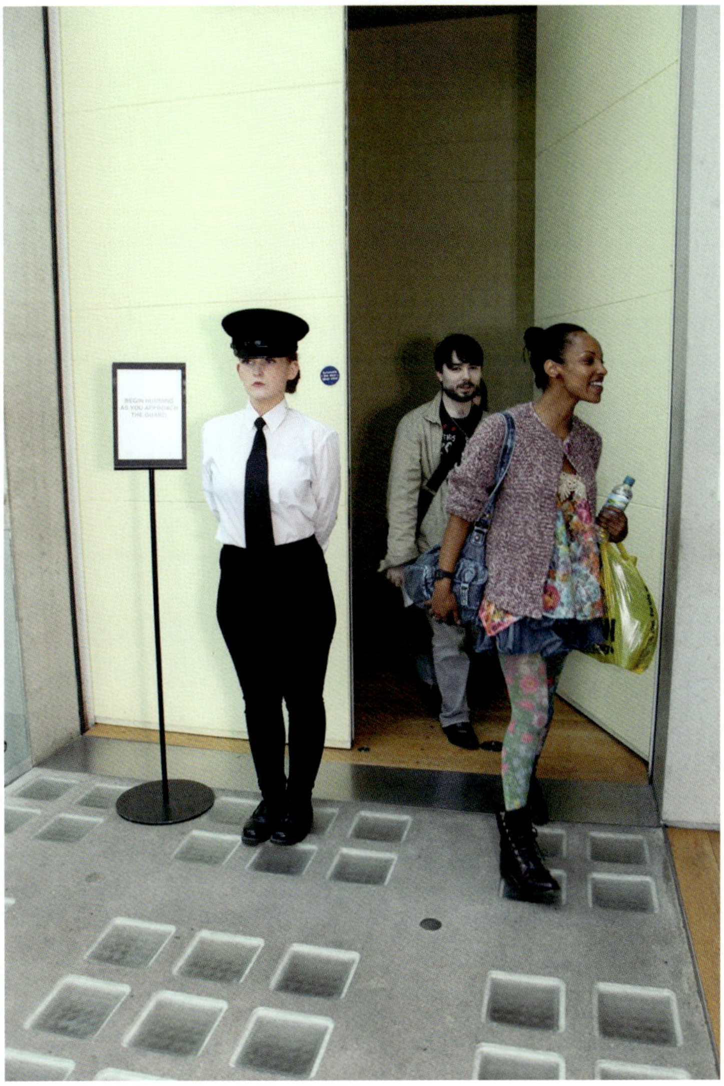

Fig. 1
***The Humming Room.* 2012**
Voluntary group performance. Full-time museum guard, empty room equipped to echo, and two text signs, one above the door and one adjacent
Dimensions variable
Installation view in *Do It 2013*, Manchester Art Gallery, U.K., July 5–21, 2013
Collection Adrian Piper Research Archive Foundation Berlin

> *The Humming Room* was conceived in direct response to Hans Ulrich's invitation, and it came up in my mind very quickly after I heard from him. It emerged fully formed, POP! out of my subconscious. I didn't have to think or reason my way to it at all. But I do think the particular events going on in my life at that time had an influence on it, definitely. I had been having very friendly communications with an academic institution on my side of the Atlantic that had expressed an interest in further affiliation, and this presented a conflict. On the one hand, I was very flattered because it was so highly ranked in the world of academia; on the other hand, my prior experiences of the dysfunctionality of highly ranked academic institutions (I talk about some of these in [the memoir] *Escape to Berlin*) had produced a very pronounced aversive reaction to the very thought of any such affiliation. Then I realized that of course my designated identity as African American was enhancing my attractiveness, and that was also part of a very familiar

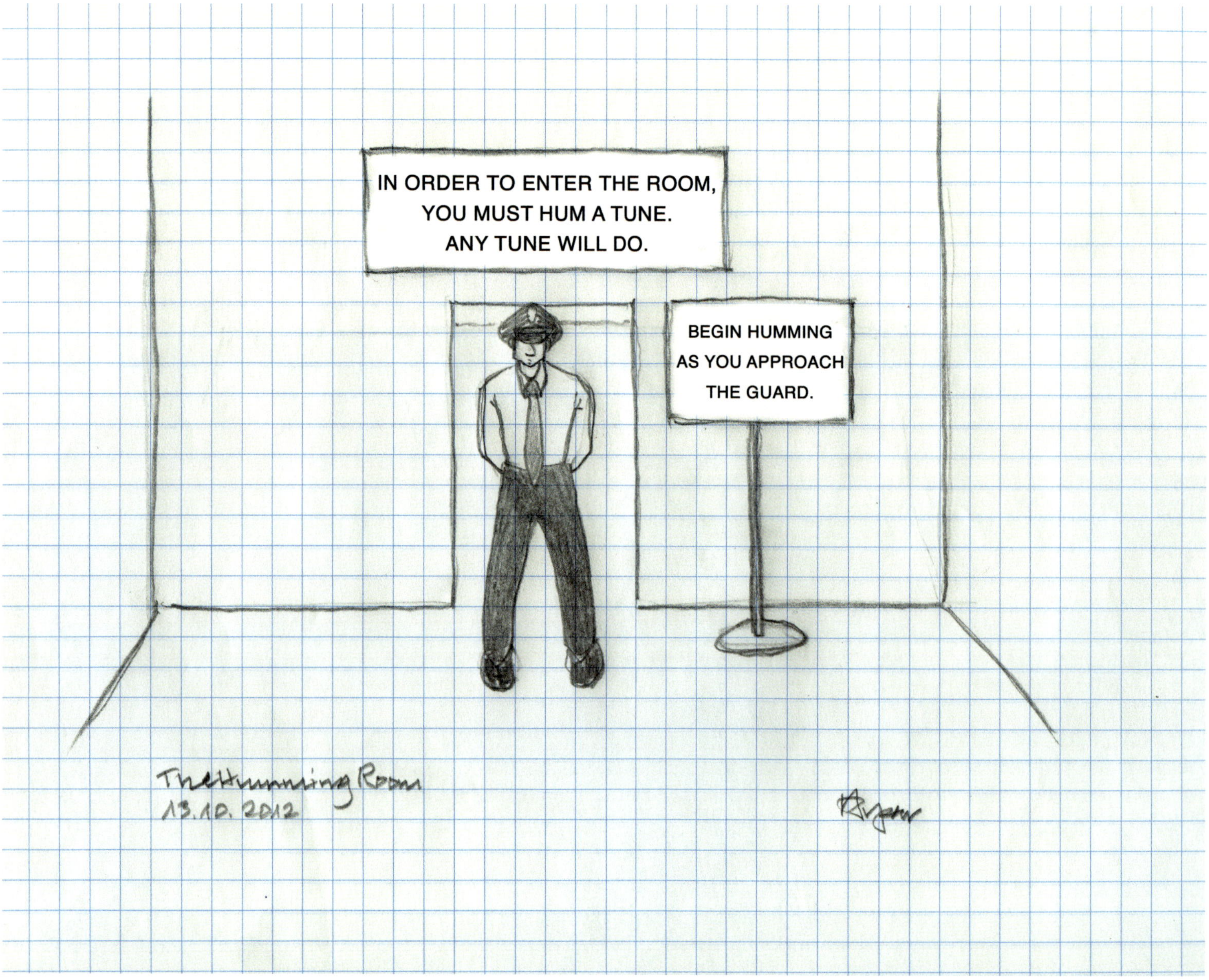

Fig. 2
The Humming Room. 2012
Exhibition instruction. Pencil on graph paper with digital additions
8½ × 11 in. (21.6 cm × 27.9 cm)
Collection Adrian Piper Research Archive Foundation Berlin

> dysfunctional pattern I had previously experienced. My piece *Thwarted Projects, Dashed Hopes, A Moment of Embarrassment* (fig. 3) came up in my mind on the heels of that realization. That piece had an incredibly liberating effect on me. It made me laugh at myself, at all such institutions, at their dysfunctionality, and at their pretensions to authority. So when I received Hans Ulrich's invitation, I was in a very happy, jubilant place. Psychologically, I had just detached myself from any dependence on such authority for my sense of self-worth. I was feeling free and humorous. That was the soil in which *The Humming Room* took root. It was a perfect expression of my state of mind at that moment, a joyous celebration of my final release from a whole set of needs, desires, anxieties, and ambitions connected with institutional validation.[3]

Any visitor who wishes to enter *The Humming Room* is given the following instructions, also printed above the door to the room: "IN ORDER TO ENTER THE ROOM, YOU MUST HUM A TUNE. ANY TUNE WILL DO." Right at the entrance, visitors are met with a paradoxical proposition—an obligation that can be fulfilled any way they wish. "Any tune will do" allows everyone—of all ages and backgrounds, with or without prior knowledge of the artist's work—creativity and personal interaction in an otherwise apparently inflexible framework. "I firmly believe," Piper added,

> that everyone is creative and everyone is potentially an artist. All children are artists. I believe that they stop drawing or painting or singing or dancing in response to social pressure—from their family or peers or figures of institutional authority, who force them to shut up in order to fit in. But just because their creative impulses to self-expression are suppressed doesn't mean that they are extinguished. They're still there, waiting for some context that will give them permission to emerge.[4]

A freestanding stanchion, reminiscent of border-control signage, next to *The Humming Room*'s entrance informs visitors to "BEGIN HUMMING AS YOU APPROACH THE GUARD." No material record of this work is meant to outlast any specific installation, other than a sketch Piper drew at the time of its creation (fig. 2), the primary function of which was instructional, for the curators. Everything else—the guard, the room, the signage—has changed at each subsequent presentation of the work. What is distinctive about *The Humming Room*, beyond the preposterous nature of its directive, is its ephemerality and ever-changing nature. It seems safe to say that there will never be identical tunes hummed simultaneously in any of the empty rooms. The work is also characterized by how it cancels out the very possibility of an audience: because visitors must hum while they are in the room, they automatically become performers of the work. They carry out the artist's directions but without the artist's being physically present. For this reason, only a participating audience can experience *The Humming Room*; the work forces those who enter to cross the mirror between artist and public. Visitors thus take on, for a brief moment, the role of the artist. They are free to forget where they are, what brought them there, and even who it was who gave

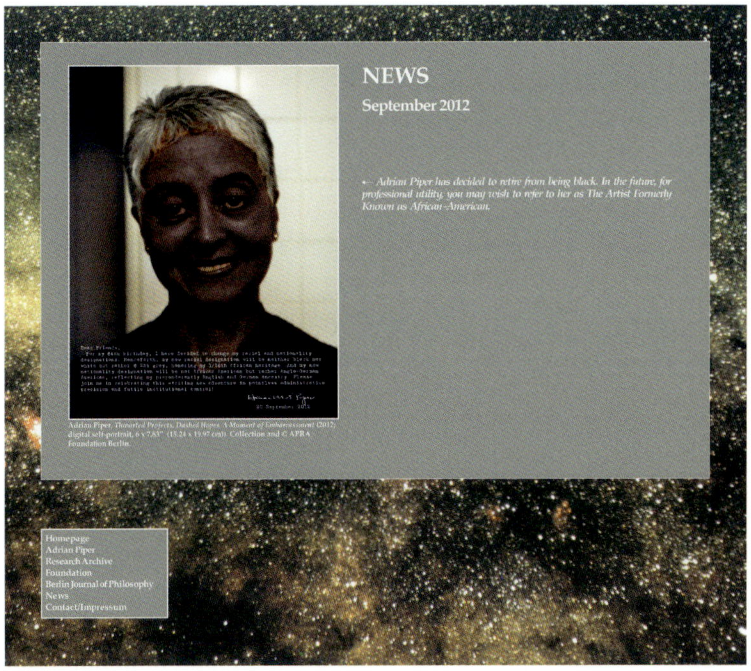

Fig. 3
Thwarted Projects, Dashed Hopes, A Moment of Embarrassment. 2012
Digital file
Dimensions variable
Collection Adrian Piper Research Archive Foundation Berlin

them such mysterious instructions. Until they exit the room, the agency is all theirs: their private tunes to hum, their sole encounters to stumble upon, and their own show to run.

Adrian Piper: A Synthesis of Intuitions, 1965–2016, the artist's 2018 retrospective at The Museum of Modern Art, New York, will be the first time in MoMA's history that the work of a living artist will occupy the entirety of its sixth-floor special-exhibitions gallery. And in this presentation, *The Humming Room* will undergo a slight but significant change. Rather than inhabiting a separate room, as it has in various iterations of *Do It*, the only times it had been staged until now, *The Humming Room* will be positioned two-thirds of the way into the vast spaces of the show—slightly altering the strict chronological order of the works up to that point—as an obligatory passageway, the only way to get from the first two-thirds of the exhibition to the last. This placement doubles the inconvenience of failing to agree to the terms of the work: uncooperative visitors exclude themselves not only from *The Humming Room* but from the rest of the exhibition—which they will either have to miss entirely or else gain access to by backtracking and reentering at the other end. But for both the visitors who do go through and those who do not, the concept of authority might suddenly signify differently—as arbitrary, perhaps, or as ridiculous as the instruction to hum a tune. On this particular placement of the work, Piper has recalled,

> The suggestion to situate *The Humming Room* two-thirds of the way through the exhibition, and to require viewers to pass through it in order to access the final third of the show, was Glenn [Lowry]'s brilliant idea. As soon as he described it, I realized that we had to do it. The work that precedes it is from the 1990s, a period in which I was battling American society literally every day, to protect my civil rights as an American citizen and as a high-functioning professional, as well as the singularity of my personal identity and the value of my work. I was acutely aware of being on the receiving end of repressive forces from many different directions, and all of this found expression in the work of that period. People often say about it, "Why's she so angry? She can pass for white!"—as though somehow that were cause for less anger rather than more. But if you take the aggressiveness and confrontationality of the work as a measure of the aggressiveness and confrontationality of the racist and misogynistic attacks I was fighting, it becomes clear that the work is a fully proportional and justifiable reaction to them. This reaction is what viewers of this work are required to deal with and absorb as they move through this part of the exhibition, regardless of whether they themselves have racist and misogynistic attitudes or not! It's a very intense and difficult journey for any viewer. It's why I refer to this section of the exhibition as the Corridor of Pain. Following it with the empty, inviting, cheerful space of *The Humming Room* provides an open environment for relaxed improvisation, a kind of pressure valve that allows viewers to let off steam, to release the anger and tension and anxiety that always build up in reaction to the work of the 1990s, by humming. Instead of shouting or having a heart attack or punching one of the guards or posting a virulent message on social media or writing a scathing review in order to release that anger, viewers can transform it into a tune that they like and that they can hum as long and as loud as need be, until that dark cloud of pent-up emotion floats up on the air and dissipates into music. This interlude makes it so much easier to perceive clearly and on its own terms the more recent work of the 2000s, which moves beyond those issues—in the same way and at the same time that I was moving beyond American society and preparing to emigrate to Germany. In a way *The Humming Room* is like the departure hall at airport check-in, where you sit and wait and make ready to leave; you let go of the preoccupations attached to where you've been, in order to refocus your attention on where you're going. In the final third of the exhibition, you find out where I'm going, and where that more recent work is taking you.[5]

Piper's work has confronted viewers in similar ways in earlier pieces, notably in *Food for the Spirit* (1971) **(fig. 4 and pages 186–93)**, a sequence of fourteen gelatin silver prints showing a mirror reflection of Piper holding a camera pointed at herself, in the mirror, and at the viewer: always in the same pose, with or without clothing, in various degrees of darkness. The work came about during a summer when Piper was obsessively studying Immanuel Kant's *Critique of Pure Reason* and felt herself in danger of disappearing:

> I rigged up a camera and tape recorder next to the mirror so that every time the fear of losing myself overtook me and drove me to the "reality check" of the mirror, I was able both to record my physical appearance objectively, and also record myself on tape repeating the passage in the *Critique* that was currently driving me to self-transcendence.[6]

But in the photographs Piper seems to stare as much at us as at herself, so that the work ultimately feels less about depicting the artist than about bringing us into the work. When we lock gazes with the artist, we become the object of her camera. The photographs become an improbable mirror image of the viewer on the verge of disappearance not only literally, into the darkness of the room, but also metaphorically, forcing us back on to the question of how, often unconsciously, we differentiate ourselves. Captured by the camera pointed toward us but perhaps not resembling the person represented in the image facing us, we nevertheless, despite all evidence, become her reflection, and she becomes ours.

From very early on in Piper's practice, the relationship between viewers—exhibition visitors, passersby, or fixed audience—and artwork has been paramount. Piper belongs to a generation of artists who emerged in New York right after the advent of what is called (much too reductively) Minimalism, in which works of art exist through their spatial surroundings, often completed by the viewer's physical engagement with them. In many ways Piper, in parallel with artists such as Hanne Darboven, Dan Graham, and Vito Acconci, liberated themselves from Minimalism by pushing its logic further. Some of them rejected the object altogether. By not necessarily

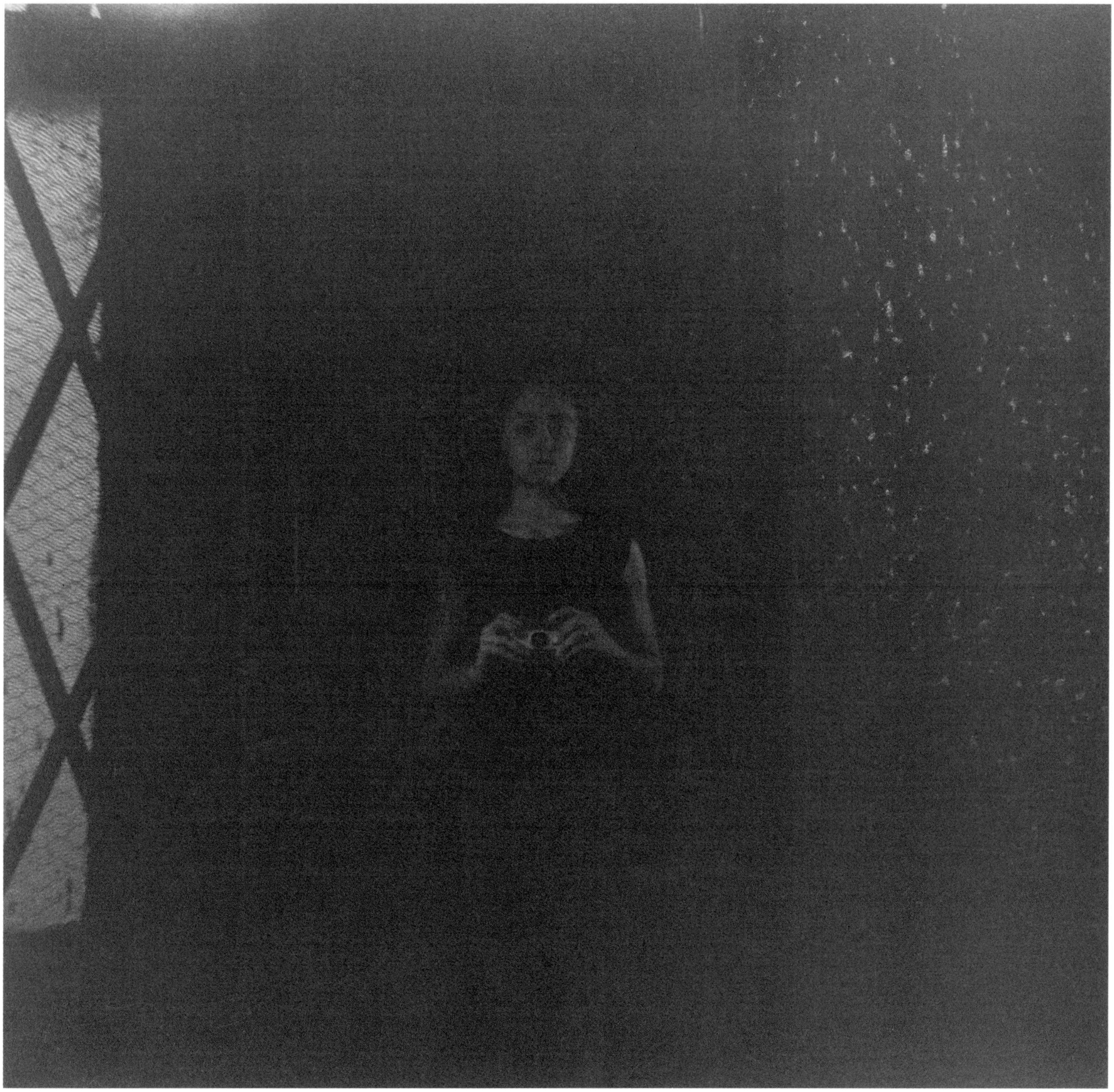

Fig. 4
Food for the Spirit #8. 1971
Gelatin silver print (printed 1997)
14 9/16 × 14 13/16 in. (37 × 37.7 cm)
The Museum of Modern Art, New York. The Family of Man Fund
Detail: one of fourteen

producing material things to be looked at or by shifting their focus to things not always understood as objects—such as, in Piper's work, a sheet of paper—this generation moved away from the museum and the gallery and explored new venues for art, such as the pages of magazines, the street, and the theater.

One particularly telling example is *Untitled Performance at Max's Kansas City* (figs. 5, 6 and pages 178, 179), Piper's first public performance. It was realized on May 2, 1970, in the eponymous New York bar, a popular gathering place for artists and musicians, as part of *The Saturday Afternoon Show*, a one-hour group exhibition of performance-based works, organized by the American poet Hannah Weiner. The artist walked around the bar wearing long gloves, high boots, earplugs, a nose plug, a long-sleeved shirt, and a blindfold.[7] Piper, in this performance, isolated herself completely from her surroundings, unable to see, touch, hear, and smell, putting herself deliberately in a particularly vulnerable situation that was reinforced by her youth, gender, and sheer presence in a bar infamous for its regular brawls. One of the work's most striking aspects was the way in which it wholly disconnected performer from (unsuspecting) audience and questioned its own existence. Did the work exist only in the perception of the bar patrons who, with a sense of disbelief, watched someone clearly not inebriated but entirely alienated from her environment, occasionally stumbling over the furniture or onto people? Or did it lie in the mind of the performer anxiously moving around an utterly foreign space, struggling to grasp the world around her, constantly juggling so as not to lose track of time? The experiences could not be farther apart, with performer and audience sharing only the fact of being—either literally or metaphorically—kept in the dark. As *The Humming Room* does, *Untitled Performance at Max's Kansas City* throws into question the roles of the viewer and the performer/artist, and their relationship.

Untitled Performance at Max's Kansas City is a profoundly disenchanted work. It doesn't lead to a moment of truth or reconciliation, in which the performer ultimately reconnects with the audience by, for example, removing her blindfold and earplugs. The artist presents herself at a complete remove from the public, numb to the environment around her, as if the very roles of art in a modern society—such as promoting social change and anticipating future progress—were relegated to a distant past or place. The work ultimately posits the viewer and the artist as inseparable, irreconcilable, as if head and tail of a single coin.

In the same *Saturday Afternoon Show*, Acconci—the poet, artist, and coeditor of the experimental magazine *0 TO 9*, to which Piper had previously contributed—performed *Rubbing Piece* (1970) (fig. 7), which became one of his most notorious works. The performance, Acconci explained, consisted in "sitting alone at a booth, during the ordinary activity at the restaurant. Rubbing my left forearm for an hour, gradually producing a sore."[8] The historian Nick Kaye, who approached Conceptual art through the lens of performance and media installation, noted about this work that

> in his notes to the performance, [Acconci] recounts a logic in which as artist, he becomes "Performer as producer (I give myself the sore); performer as consumer (I receive

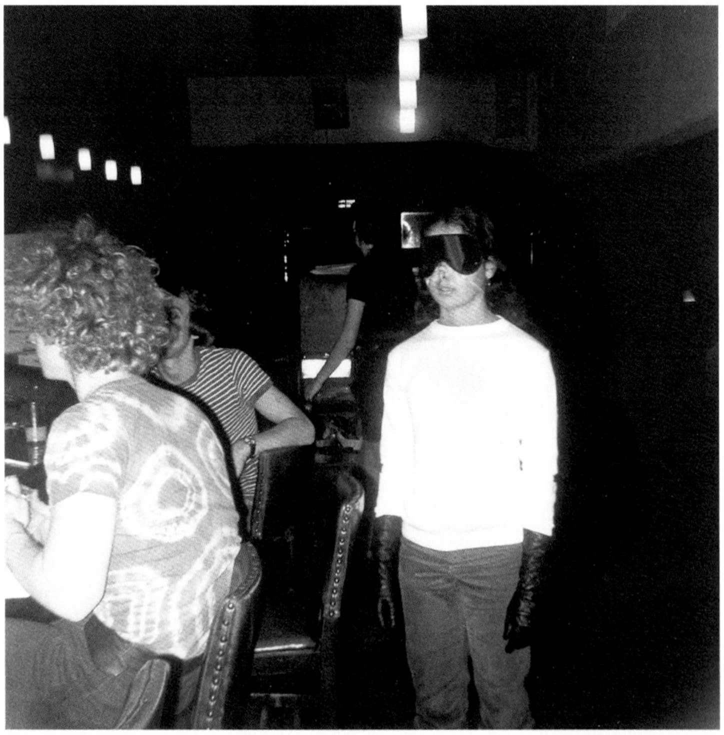

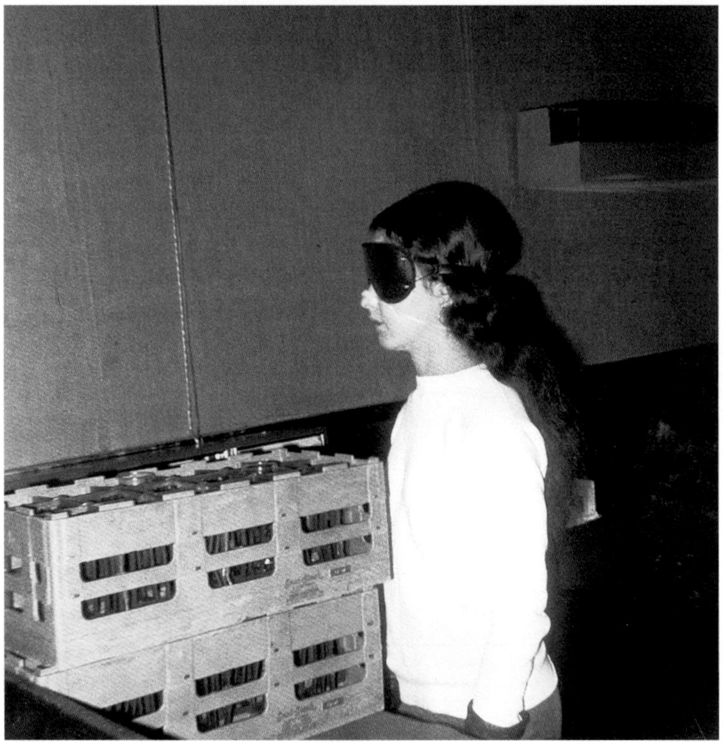

Figs. 5, 6
Untitled Performance at Max's Kansas City. 1970
Documentation of the performance. Four gelatin silver prints
Each 3⁹⁄₁₆ × 3⁹⁄₁₆ in. (9 × 9 cm)
Photograph by Rosemary Mayer
Collection Adrian Piper Research Archive Foundation Berlin
Details:
photograph #4
photograph #2

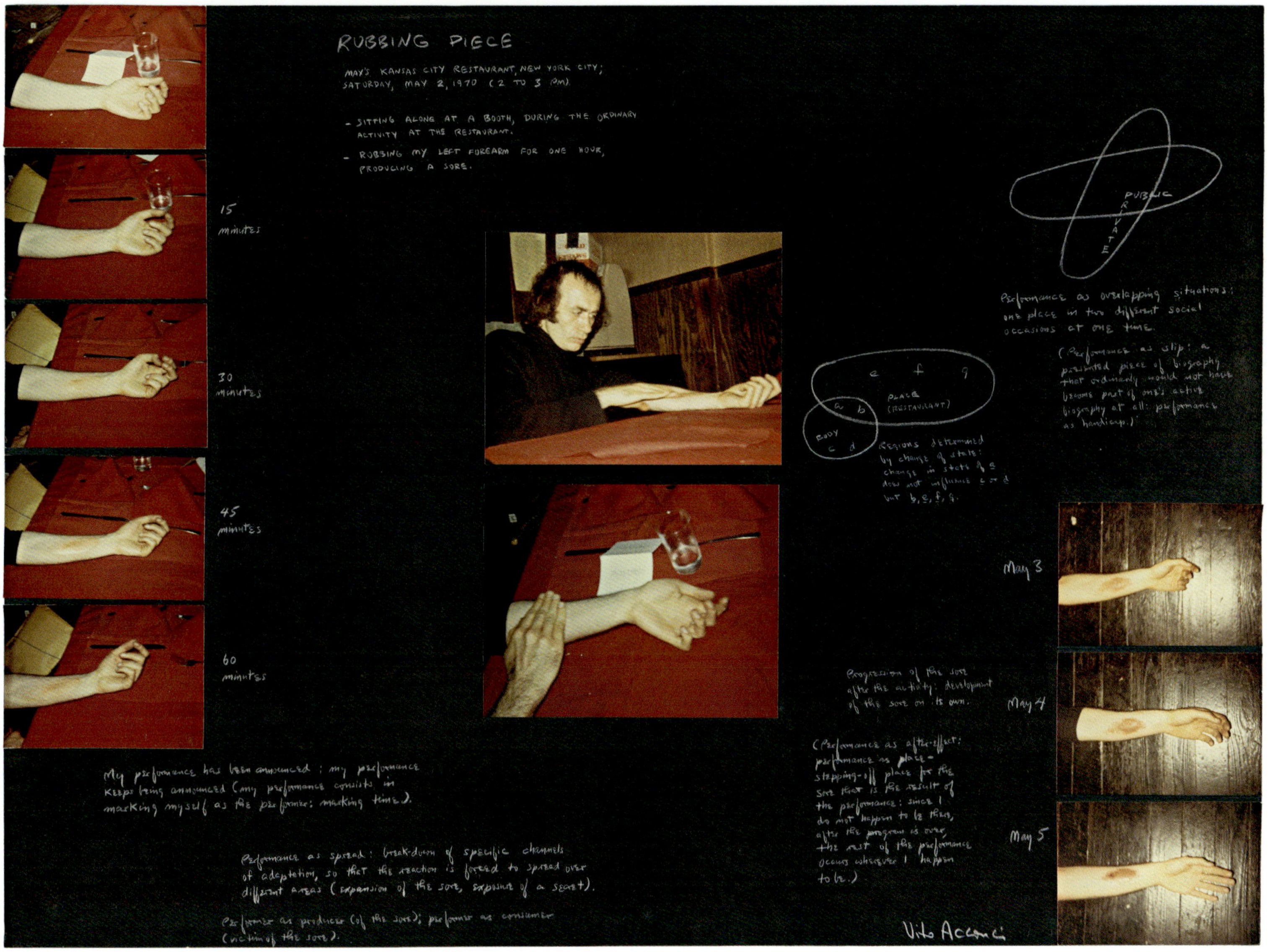

Fig. 7
Vito Acconci
Rubbing Piece. 1970
Ten silver dye bleach prints and colored pencil on board
Overall 29¹⁵⁄₁₆ × 40³⁄₁₆ in. (76 × 102 cm)
The Museum of Modern Art, New York. Partial gift of the Daled Collection and partial purchase through the generosity of Maja Oeri and Hans Bodenmann, Sue and Edgar Wachenheim III, Agnes Gund, Marlene Hess and James D. Zirin, Marie-Josée and Henry R. Kravis, and Jerry I. Speyer and Katherine G. Farley

> the sore)" and in which "rather than do an act that takes place elsewhere, my body can be a place on which an event is enacted." Here, Acconci acts out his body as the material and place of the artwork, proposing that his performance "consists in marking myself as performer: marking time." In the process, Acconci . . . works toward imbrications of public and private activities and spaces. In this private action in a public space, Acconci suggests, he creates "a piece of biography that ordinarily would not have become part of one's active biography at all," where the exposure of the sore amounts to the "exposure of a secret." Indeed, this exposure of a private act in a public work, Acconci supposes, produces "performance as overlapping situations: one place in two different social occasions at one time."[9]

In a single hour at Max's Kansas City, two groundbreaking performances took place, remarkably different and at the same time similar. Both used the body as material and simultaneously included and excluded their audience (in neither of them was the public allowed to participate), but one—Acconci's—clearly marks time and opens a private sphere, while the other—Piper's—rejects time and any incursion of the audience into the artist's private life.

Much later, in the 2000s, Piper would articulate her relationship to the viewer in a very different manner, not only with works such as *The Humming Room* but also with *The Probable Trust Registry: The Rules of the Game #1–3* (figs. 8, 9 and pages 308, 309), a participatory performance conceived and first shown in a gallery setting—at Elizabeth Dee Gallery, in New York, in 2013—and two years later at the Venice Biennale, for which she received the Golden Lion award for the fair's best artist. As for *The Humming Room*, the work entirely relies on audience participation; unlike *Untitled Performance at Max's Kansas City,* it aims to establish direct rapport within the public and between the visitors and the artist. The work comprises three desks at which visitors may sign an electronic contract pledging a personal commitment to three things: "I will always mean what I say," "I will always be too expensive to buy," and "I will always do what I say I am going to do." The relationship between *The Probable Trust Registry* and *The Humming Room*, according to Piper, is that

> in some ways [they] are in harmony; in other ways they are in counterpoint. I am not aware of any causal influence between them. But both probably arise from my jaded attitude toward institutional authority. *The Probable Trust Registry* is in a way my response to the despair induced by recognizing, at a deep level, that the human institutions that are supposed to civilize and prepare us for a stable community anchored in shared interests and values are not working, and never have worked, because institutional professions of commitment to those values almost always mask a bottomless pit of need to accumulate, preserve, and extend personal power. As usual, self-interest trumps (you will pardon the pun) impartiality and greed trumps the common good. *The Probable Trust Registry* reminds us that there is more to human nature than that, and of what the benefits would be if each and every one of us were

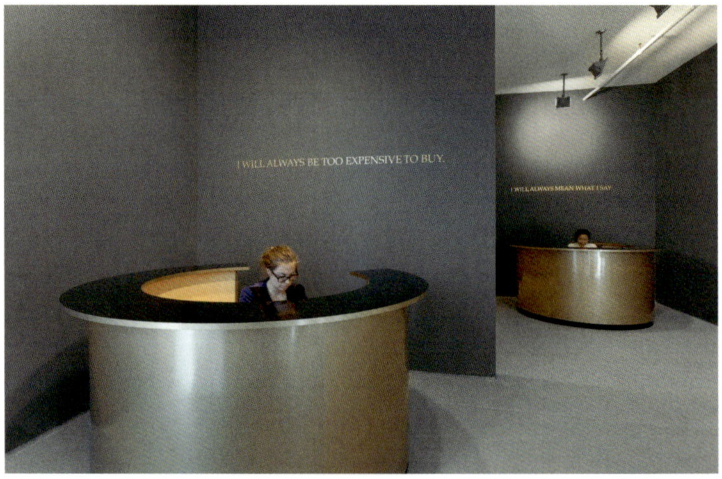

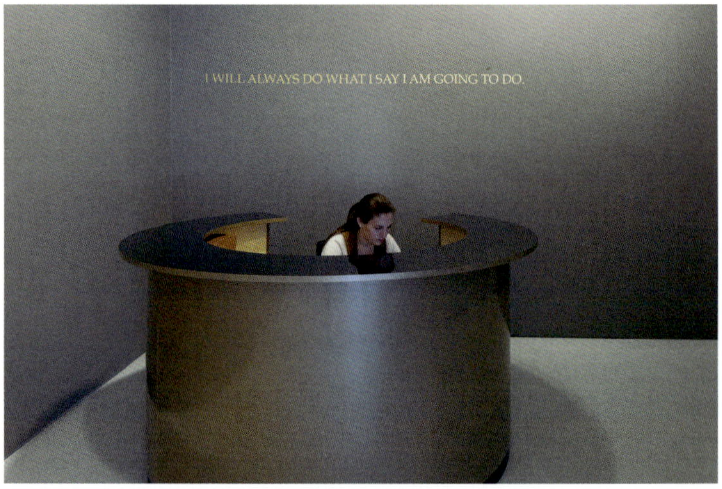

Figs. 8, 9
The Probable Trust Registry: The Rules of the Game #1–3. 2013
Installation and participatory group performance. Embossed gold vinyl text on three walls with 70% gray paint, three circular gold reception desks with stools, computer system, contracts, registry of contact data for signatories, three administrators, and self-selected members of the public
Each desk 6 ft. 1/16 in. (183 cm) diam. × 53 in (160 cm) high; installation dimensions variable
Installation views in *Adrian Piper: The Probable Trust Registry*, Elizabeth Dee Gallery, New York, May 3–31, 2014
Hamburger Bahnhof–Museum fur Gegenwart, Nationalgalerie, Staatliche Museen, Berlin

> willing to put greed on hold, just for one minute, just for this action right now, for the sake of the common good, and it offers each participant the opportunity to explore those other parts of human nature.
>
> I think *The Humming Room* can be viewed as offering an alternative path into that exploration, by poking gentle fun at institutional authority rather than despairing over its corruptions. After all, institutional representatives are just trying to do their jobs the best way they can, no matter how ridiculous or incompetent they may look to a detached observer—just like the guard who orders us to hum a tune, any tune, as a condition of admission to the room. But both pieces are similar in that each creates a new kind of elite: of those who are willing to make a public commitment to live by their principles as best they can in the case of *The Probable Trust Registry*, and of those who are willing to take the risk of spontaneous self-expression in the case of *The Humming Room*. In that respect, both also bear a relationship to *The Order of Celestial Laughter*, which creates an elite of humorous humility. These are some elites worth joining.

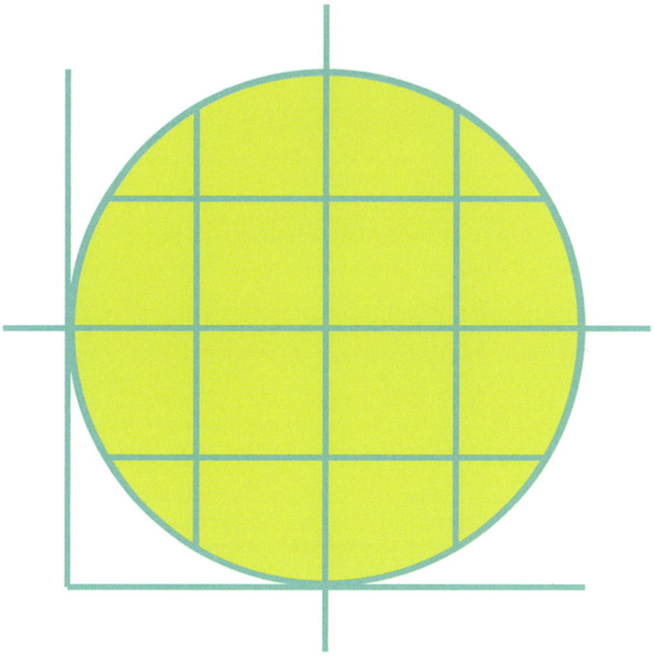

Fig. 10
Logo of *The Order of Celestial Laughter*. 2017
Participatory group performance
No spatiotemporal dimensions
Collection Adrian Piper Research Archive Foundation Berlin

The Order of Celestial Laughter (2017) **(fig. 10)** is, like the other two works, a participatory group performance, but it is one that exists solely in the mind of its participants rather than in performative acts such as signing a contract or executing an instruction. *The Order of Celestial Laughter*'s membership—which, as it is in *The Probable Trust Registry*, is disclosed only to its members but, contrarily to it, is open exclusively by invitation—shares, according to the artist, "the rare capacity to laugh at themselves" while making sure to stay away from any form of "ridicule, mockery, scorn, or contempt."[10] In the 2000s Piper's work has consistently attempted, through varied approaches, to bring audiences together, to rally communities around common values and ideas. In parallel with the astonishing development of social media, Piper has pushed her work into a new frontier, vaulting it into a world in which customary notions of networks, communication, and civil engagement are being redefined.

Like *The Order of Celestial Laughter*, *The Humming Room* is full of irony, but it is also a work full of happiness, humor, and the potential for self-enjoyment, a trait that is intermittently woven into the fabric of Piper's work. The sadness brought on by the current state of our society—a feeling that was particularly acute when *The Humming Room* was made, in a year marked by senseless massacres, in the United States, of children and moviegoers—has never been for Piper an excuse for surrendering to melancholy. Humor can be a powerful tool for addressing difficult issues, such as the exercise of institutional power and its potential abuses. The artist, poet, and filmmaker Marcel Broodthaers, in spite of his own melancholic tendencies, also confronted the economic structures and critical authorities of his time and place—the late 1960s and early 1970s in postwar Belgium—with a blend of provocation and light humor.[11] Among the many examples that come to mind is an untitled work referred to as "General with cigar," from 1970 **(figs. 11, 12)**, a work involving not a simple instruction but a single gesture—the sticking of a cigar into the mouth

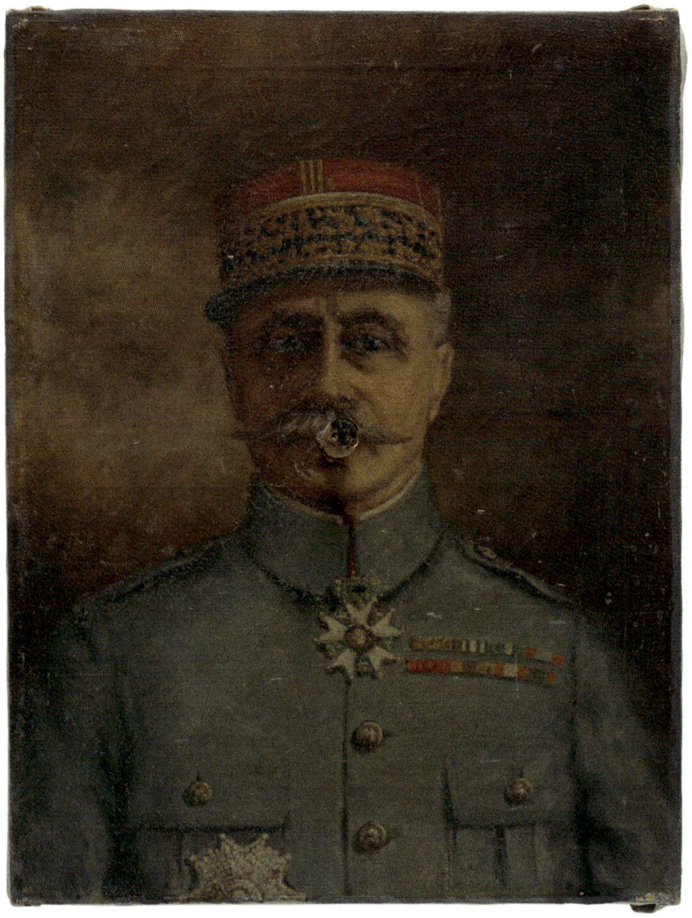

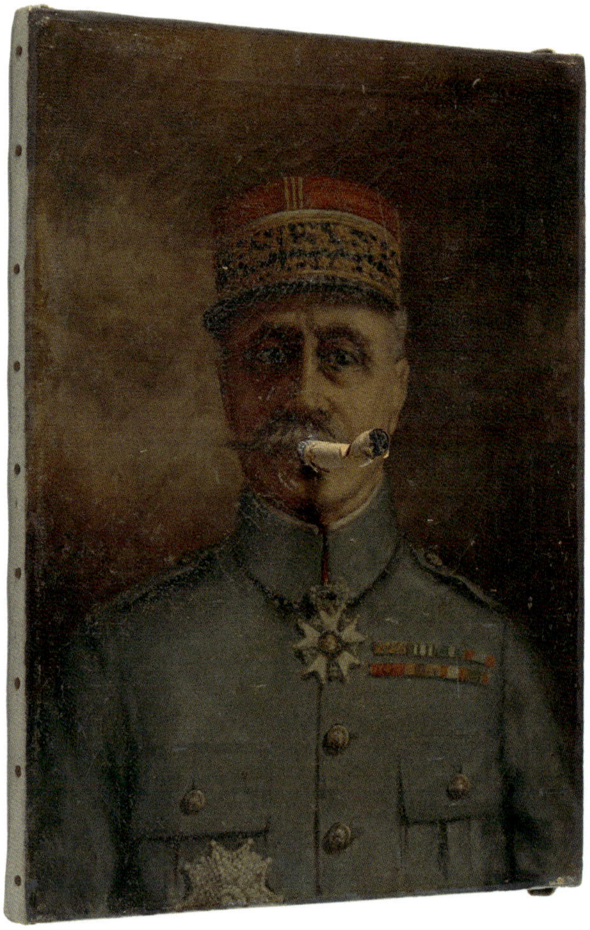

Figs. 11, 12
Marcel Broodthaers
Untitled (General with cigar). 1970
Found oil painting and cigar (recto and angled view)
15¾ × 11¹³⁄₁₆ × 2¾ in. (40 × 30 × 7 cm)
The Museum of Modern Art, New York. Partial gift of the Daled Collection and partial purchase through the generosity of Maja Oeri and Hans Bodenmann, Sue and Edgar Wachenheim III, Agnes Gund, Marlene Hess and James D. Zirin, Marie-Josée and Henry R. Kravis, and Jerry I. Speyer and Katherine G. Farley

of a painted portrait of a military general that the artist had bought at a flea market. Broodthaers later recalled of this work,

> I made a little hole in the general's pinched mouth so as to insert a cigar butt. In this object-portrait, there is a fortunate tonal harmony. The paint is brown, sort of pissy, and so is the cigar butt. Not just any cigar would suit any general's mouth . . . the caliber of the cigar, the shape of the mouth.[12]

The Humming Room takes a radically different approach. In contrast with Broodthaers's symbolical silencing of the general, Piper aims to liberate the voices of visitors:

> The voice occupies a special position in the range of creative human capabilities. It is the only instrument we can play without the involvement of some external object, such as a violin or a paintbrush or a computer. That gives it a direct and immediate link to our fundamental impulse of self-expression, which enables a greater degree of spontaneity in self-expression than with any other instrument. At the same time, when we hum, we tame that instrument in a manner that produces a clearly modulated sound, but without needing to undergo the rigorous training that many other instruments require. For that reason it is pleasurable and fulfilling in a modest but special way. Sometimes when people have not been using their voice in that way for a long time—perhaps even not since childhood—they have to be coaxed into remembering its power as an instrument of creative experience. They may even be intimidated, by hearing the extraordinary performance of a great opera or jazz singer, into thinking that they don't have that power at all, if they ever did. But of course they did, and still do. For people who know this, and hum regularly, *The Humming Room* will offer an opportunity to revel in the enjoyment of exercising their instrument. But for people who don't know it, they'll find out—that is, if they want to get through to the last room of the exhibition in the right sequence. For those people, perhaps they will, indeed, remember the tune they hummed as the moment they were forced to rediscover their own creative voice.[13]

Music and rhythm have been an intrinsic part of Piper's life, beginning when she was seven years old, with piano lessons and

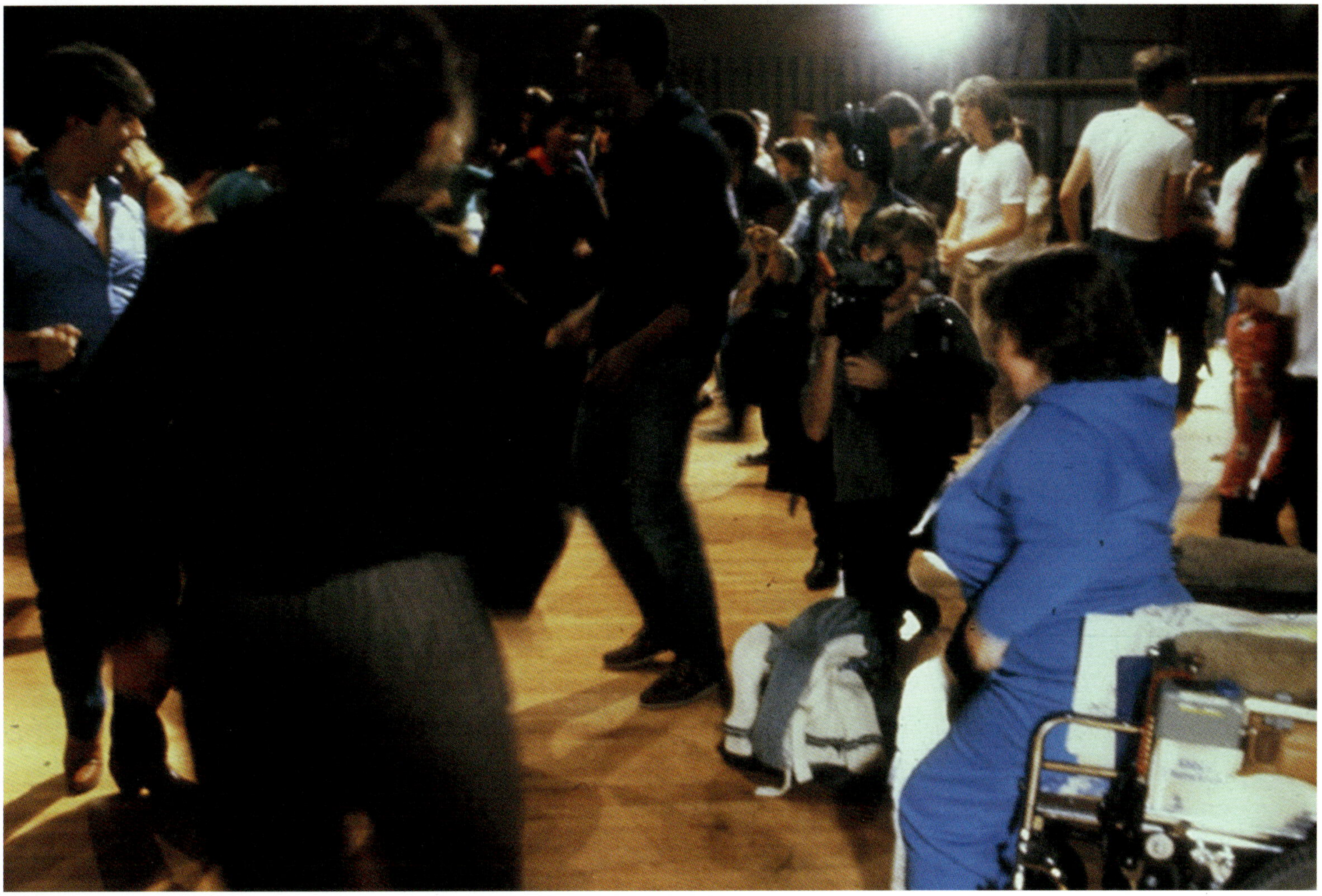

Fig. 13
Funk Lessons. 1983–84
Documentation of the group performance at University of California, Berkeley, November 6, 1983. Color photograph
Collection Adrian Piper Research Archive Foundation Berlin

ballet lessons, and leading to wide involvement with all kinds of music, both as performer and composer.[14] Rosemary Mayer, the artist and a close friend of Piper, who documented a number of the *Catalysis* works in now-iconic photographs, recalled *Aretha Franklin Catalysis* (1971–72):

> Piper has performed her *Aretha Franklin Piece* several times this past year. The piece began with Piper's memorizing "Respect" until she could hear the entire song in her mind at will. The piece itself involved her listening to the song in her mind and simultaneously dancing to it. She dances a mixture of the Bugaloo, the Jerk, the Lindy, the Strut and the Twist with lots of improvisation. Piper performed the piece unannounced, while waiting in line at the bank, at a bus stop, and in a public library.[15]

The *Aretha Franklin Piece* opened the way for Piper's first performance for an audience, *Some Reflective Surfaces* (1975–76) (page 216). In it, Piper, sporting glasses and crossing genders as well as races in ambiguous attire and whiteface makeup, appeared facing the audience under a spotlight. Various recordings played over the course of the work—the artist recalling her experience as a discotheque dancer; Franklin's "Respect," as Piper danced against the projection of a film of her and some of her graduate-school classmates dancing; and, finally, an eruptive voice-over of a man shouting at dancers to perform with more elegance.[16]

In an earlier performance, *Bach Whistled* (1970), which in many ways prefigured *The Humming Room*, Piper whistled along with recordings of Johann Sebastian Bach's Concertos in D minor, A minor, and C major, such that, as the artist has written, "at the beginning the whistling is relatively strong, clear, and on key. As the performance progresses, it becomes weaker, flatter, and more like plaintive cheeping."[17] The performance *Funk Lessons* (1983–84) (fig. 13) conveys both musicality and direct engagement with the viewer; as the curator Maurice Berger has recalled,

> *Funk Lessons* took the form of a participatory scholarly demonstration. The artist was the instructor; audience members were her students. She distributed a photocopied bibliography and a list of some of the characteristics of funk dance and music. She began by attempting to free her students of their presumptions

> and misperceptions about funk music, elucidating both its fact and its fiction. . . . Finally, the students practiced dance movements with musical accompaniment. Because Piper did not want to intimidate her audience, she attempted to design a "comfortable and safe" format for people to explore their apprehensions about the music and their ability to soul dance. . . . Still, individual audience reactions ranged from enmity and resistance to euphoria. Successful performances ended up as a jubilant dance party; failed ones degenerated into an atmosphere of confusion and resentment.[18]

Funk Lessons, like *The Humming Room*, recruited the public to be its performers (although unlike *The Humming Room*, it was videotaped). In the former, Piper also clearly opened the discourse to the issue of race, but this is directed primarily at the performing students and only secondarily to any future viewers of the film. The continued existence of *Funk Lessons* as a work of art is supported only by its documentation; Piper does not wish it to be enacted again, as it was conceived not as a performance but rather as an action in the world. The video allows *Funk Lessons* to reconnect with an art environment, but the particularity of the work, as it was for *Untitled Performance at Max's Kansas City*, was to exist outside the realm of art. *Funk Lessons* presented the powerful notion that an artwork can be constituted by an artist leading the public through a process, a groundbreaking idea that supposes nothing less than a renegotiation of the role of the artist, who is cast here as an enlightened educator or, as the critic Robert Storr has said, "as an agent of social change."[19] In contrast to early twentieth-century artists, whose options were to oppose, support, or turn a blind eye to the transformation of the society around them, Piper's generation shared the belief that art can provide an adequate platform for activism, and that art itself could be an agent of social change, but few of the artists whose history is interwoven with the advent of Conceptual art have kept such a belief alive through the years. In the early 1970s Conceptual art found its way into the commercial world, irrevocably distancing itself from the public it had hoped to reach, but Piper has never compromised her mission. Her work—in contrast with that of most of her peers, and despite the expectations of the art world—as it changes, continues to challenge society as *it* changes. One can only hope that future historians will prove her right: that it did make a difference in our world.

While *The Humming Room* further articulates ideas that had already been present in Piper's work, it also points toward a web of conceptual practices that emerged in the late 1950s and ripened through the 1960s and '70s. It is not, for example, the first artwork to use humming as a mode of self-expression. In 1965 the American artist Bob Sheff made a work called *Hum* **(fig. 14)**, which was published around 1968 in *Flux Year Box 2*, a box, designed by George Maciunas, containing a number of editioned works (small publications, games, films, instructions) by artists associated with the Fluxus movement. *Hum* took the form of an instruction piece typeset on a piece of paper:

> [And] if you don't know much about music but you really like a tune you can HUM, then now is high time to
>
> HUM.
>
> -instructions-
> Detach a paper, lick lips, bend paper across its longest part, attach to both sprongs of comb between and
> HUM.
> If you run out of paper or don't have a comb, take one of those candy boxes which have a large cellophane transparency, bend one end very slightly, blow and
> HUM.
> And when you don't have any of these go right ahead and
> HUM.
>
> In genuine expression, HUM can be done by any number of people.[20]

Sheff specifically opens the possibility for *HUM* to be performed by a group—like many Fluxus works of that period—which anticipates the way in which Piper, without knowing of Sheff's piece, later defined *The Humming Room*: a work that can be performed by more than one person at a time, even though humming is a largely solitary practice.

The idea that a space can be filled with something other than objects finds a historical counterpart in Yves Klein's 1958 exhibition at Galerie Iris Clert, Paris, which bore the lengthy title *La Spécialisation de la sensibilité à l'état de matière première en sensibilité picturale stabilisée* (The specialization of sensibility in the raw material state into stabilized pictorial sensibility), often simply referred to as *Le Vide* (The void). The short title is, however, misleading in French: the exhibition was not meant to be empty (another meaning of the French word *vide*) but to be filled by an immaterial void, in which the visitors of the show could submerge themselves. *The Humming Room*, also an immersive environment activated by its viewers, builds on such an idea, despite Piper's limited knowledge of Klein's work at the time.[21] For both Klein and Piper the relation to viewers is critical, even if for the latter both method and message are approached from a much more straightforward point of view:

> I put work into the world for two reasons: first, because I feel compelled to; and second, as an act of communication. I have done work in which I myself am the target of communication, where there is something I can only clarify to myself by putting it outside my mind, out in the world with its own material boundaries. But the temptation is always there to take that process of self-inquiry a step further: Now that *I* have gotten clear about that idea or image or thing that was in my mind, what will be its relation to other minds? Will it clarify something for them, too? Will they experience it as I do, or in a completely different way? This is part of how I discover who I am, simultaneously with my discovery of who others are: the work enables us to find out what we have in common and what differentiates us from one another, through our similar or dissimilar responses to it. At this point, every work is nothing without the visitors who view it. Any work that exists in its own space implicitly invites us all into a shared space in which we experience it.[22]

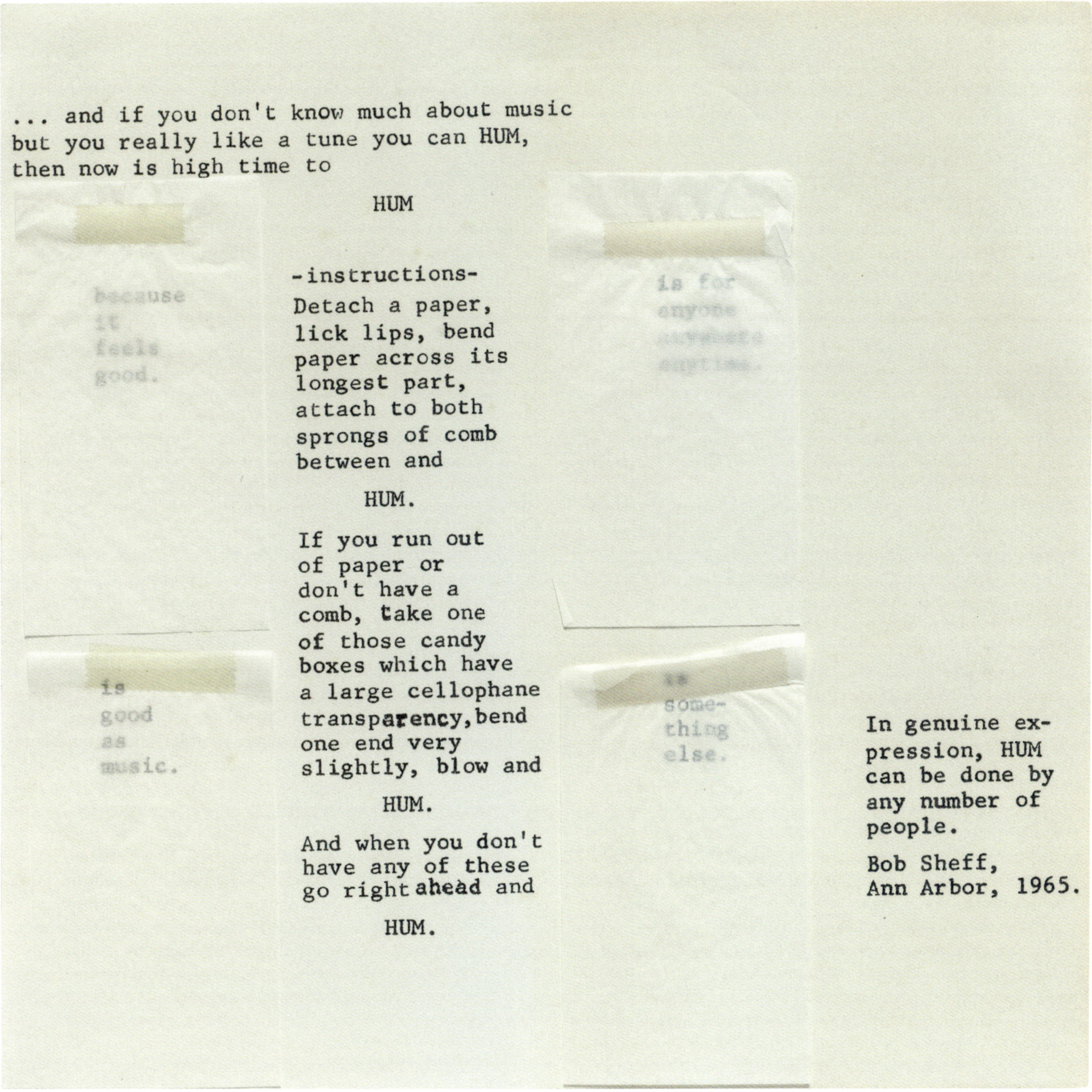

Fig. 14
Bob Sheff
Hum (1965), from *Flux Year Box 2*. c. 1968
Cigarette papers and pressure-sensitive tape on mimeographed paper
6¾ × 6¹¹⁄₁₆ in. (17.2 × 17 cm)
The Museum of Modern Art, New York. The Gilbert and Lila Silverman
Fluxus Collection Gift

Uncanny similarities persist, however, between *The Humming Room* and *Le Vide*, such as Piper's placement of a security officer in front of the installation's door, echoing the two uniformed Republican Guards posted by Klein in front of the gallery on opening night. Klein had also hired two additional guards in order to restrict attendance in the exhibition space, and he himself did not hesitate to expel a visitor who was drawing on one of the walls.[23] But it is not *Le Vide*'s sense of antiquated solemnity that greets the visitor to *The Humming Room*; rather it is an indisputable signal of authority, with an outcome made clear in Piper's installation drawing: surrounded by large signs in capital letters, the uniformed guard, hands crossed behind his back, blocks the room's entrance with his body. It's up to the viewer to demonstrate a willingness to conform to Piper's instructions before entering. Such a requirement echoes the many nonnegotiable situations in our daily lives in which we must take certain actions in order to gain access, from airport screening (taking off shoes, allowing ourselves to be patted down) to paying tolls. It might be a cliché but is nevertheless a fact that in modern times artists and authority do not play well together, and Piper is, of course, no exception. Her work regularly takes authority and its many abuses—as directed, for example, against gender and race—as one of its subjects.

Piper's recent work *Howdy #6* (page 310), realized for the first time at the Berlin Biennale, in 2016, meets the viewer very much as *The Humming Room* does, with a contradiction. It consists of a "no entry" symbol (a red circle with a white horizontal line) projected on a locked door, with the word "HOWDY"—the colloquial contraction for "How do you do?" that is particularly common in the western United States—appearing within the sign's white rectangle. The pictogram for barred access is thus turned into a framing device for the eruption of a contradiction. Visitors are simultaneously greeted—in a particularly welcoming way, even—and immediately forbidden to advance further. Piper heightened the irony by asking for the work to be installed on a door that cannot be opened by visitors, making the no-entry sign as pointless as the welcome. Of the first presentation of *Howdy #6*, Piper has recalled,

> The Berlin Biennale gave me my first opportunity to realize this piece. I had been doing studies of that particular sign—making drawings, taking photos—for a while, and thinking about the kinds of installations in which I would like to situate it. By that time, I was so far away from an attitude of respectful deference to institutional authority that nothing but demonstrated integrity and excellence could ever bring me back, and I certainly wasn't expecting *that* any time soon. Berlin Biennale 9 offered two perfect projection sites for this image—one on a door leading nowhere at the top of a very long stairwell, the other on a closed basement door at the bottom of a very long stairwell. They could not have been better. My preoccupation with that sign had a lot to do with what I was sensing in many countries in their reactions to the refugee crisis at that moment: an *official, administrative* ambivalence that combined compassion with fear, welcome with rejection, curiosity with distaste. Aside from the compassion part, I had sensed that same ambivalence in official, administrative American reactions to me when I lived there. And now I, too, was an immigrant, had fled from conflicts with authoritative American institutions that had exposed the malevolent underside of their benevolent exteriors.[24]

The Humming Room is not a forbidden space, but rather one that can be entered if the viewer agrees to submit to authority without any form of explanation or legitimization. Does the guard who stands in front of the room speak on behalf of the art space where the work is shown, the artist, the owner of the work, or all of them at once? How can he enforce his authority? Can he physically block a person from entering the room or evict an uncooperative viewer from the show? Or is he just an actor devoid of any real authority? The answers to these questions might not be of such importance, however; the success of the work seems to be predicated more on the sense of incredulity it instills in viewers. *The Humming Room*'s larger question is aimed at our natural obedience to apparently arbitrary forms of authority. The viewer's choice to play along or turn around is made even more significant by the especial benevolence of the instruction: to hum a tune while occupying the room, but its particular and contrasting resonance is due to its being located within a cultural institution and pointing to the underlying and often disguised authoritative nature of such institutions. From the security guards, who guide and control the viewers, to the art selected to be exhibited by the curators (which also guides and controls), a museum functions as a social space that generally abides by the same rules of the society of which it is the product. On the presence of security officers in museums, Piper has recalled,

> When I was growing up, through my parents I knew a lot of African-American artists who worked as museum guards; and also Sol [LeWitt] worked as a museum guard at one point. I can only speak to how museum guards affect my own experience of work in a museum. I'm always interested in them, and wonder what they do when they are not guarding other artists' artwork. I tend to project onto them the kind of lives and interests of people I have known who have been museum guards. I hope whoever guards *The Humming Room* at MoMA will get a kick out of making people hum a tune in order to get through the show.[25]

The Humming Room demonstrates very clearly the function of museums as social spaces, but it also opens the possibility for viewers to escape the constraints of institutional realities as well as the constraints of the self. Hummers are often unconscious of the fact that they are humming. If humming can fill a void of silence or block the sounds of the outside world, it may also, and perhaps more significantly, allow the individual to transcend the ego, like the chanting that is part of the practice of yoga—a practice well known to the artist. As Piper has explained, the interiority of humming carries a special resonance for her:

> A yoga class or *darshana* meeting usually ends with the chant of OM. You chant OM by taking in a long, deep breath, first filling your belly, then your diaphragm, then your lungs; then, as you open your mouth to form the

> vowel and gradually close it around the consonant, you very gradually expel the breath, starting in reverse order, first from the lungs, then from the diaphragm, then from the belly, while you draw out the consonant into a long *mmmmmmmmm*, until you have completely expelled all the breath you needed to hum the sound. This humming sound replicates a background vibration that is much lower than the human ear can register, and deeper than the human voice can make, but that can be accessed in deep states of meditation. That is why the OM has such a calming, grounding effect on the self at the end of a yoga class. But you can also find that hum in other spiritual traditions, e.g. Gregorian chant. The function is always the same, to anchor the individual ego in deeper levels of the self that transcends it.[26]

Over the duration of the act, the humming person is gradually taken away from everyday thoughts and somehow puts the conscious mind in check, and thus is able to connect more intensely or directly with another, often physical task being performed, such as sawing, eating—or encountering a work of art.

Allan Kaprow, the pioneer of performance art, who developed the notions of Environments and Happenings, focused a considerable amount of his work on the relationship between art and the everyday. Grounding his approach in the reading of Erving Goffman's *The Presentation of Self in Everyday Life*,[27] which postulates that ordinary routines of everyday life are similar to performances—although the performers are unaware of it—Kaprow explained,

> The performance of everyday routines, of course, is not really the same as acting a written script, since conscious intent is absent. There is a phenomenal and experiential difference. Being a performer (like being a lawyer) involves responsibility for what the word *performer* may mean and what being a performer may entail. Nor are everyday routines managed by a stage director, although within the theatrical metaphor parents, officials, teachers, guides, and bosses may be construed as equivalents. But again, these mentors would have to see themselves as directors of performance rather than instructors in social mores and professions outside the arts. What is interesting to art, though, is that everyday routines could be used as real offstage performances. An artist would then be engaged in performing a "performance."[28]

For many people, humming is an everyday routine. What Piper's *Humming Room* accomplishes with remarkable efficiency is to change the frame of perception around an absolutely otherwise mundane act. Visitors become performers as they enter the room: they—not the artist—turn what would otherwise be an everyday routine into a performance. Humming in itself, as the anthropologist Michael Taussig has explained, is similar to many everyday sounds, such as that of bees or traffic, belonging to the "sounds that fill the void, sounds that don't really count, background, we might say, stuff for the likes of John Cage who taunted the line demarcating sound from music."[29] He further notes that humming implies rhythm. We might say that humming is mostly a rhythm for lips that remain closed, as if incapable or unwilling to vocalize distinct sounds. It is, as noted above, a primarily self-absorbed action, often performed while doing particularly repetitive or long-lasting tasks. As a result humming, largely an introverted practice, allows a form of expression directed toward the self rather than the public, not unlike a prayer. It is a practice that isolates the individual, although in a manner, in both kind and degree, that is much different from some of Piper's older works, particularly *Untitled Performance at Max's Kansas City*. A humming person remains aware of and connected to the environment but at the same time mysterious to it. The tune being hummed is often difficult for proximate others to identify, and the action has the potential to bring out in them very different responses: perhaps it suggests a kind of benign distancing from the world; or a comforting thought, of family, of a grandmother knitting; or something as fraught as a repressed memory of exploitation, such as the songs hummed by slaves picking cotton under a harsh sun. But despite these responses, in the end, humming is all in the ear of the hummer. The psychiatrist Karen Hopenwasser has observed,

> Early in the film *12 Years a Slave*,[30] based upon the life of Solomon Northup, we see Northup's intense emotional struggle with his loss of freedom. Standing at a graveside with other slaves, we watch him listening but resisting participation in the song "Roll Jordan Roll." Slowly the song rises up from within him until we see him sing forcefully in unison with the others. At that moment we can appreciate the power of communal voices in building resilience and supporting survival. Elsewhere in the film we see the same impact of humming—fostering resilience and survival. The musical complexity of this film addresses the dialectics of slave songs as both resistance and "imagined reconciliation."[31]

This leads Hopenwasser to wonder what makes humans hum, if it is not to communicate:

> We hum when we feel well. We hum when we need to feel better. And we hum when the silence of helplessness would otherwise be lethal. The precursor of sorrow songs, in the various languages of enslaved Africans, evolved into the sorrow songs of slavery, the gospel, blues, the jazz of postbellum America and the freedom songs of the American Civil Rights Movement.[32]

Indeed, humming is not devoid of revolutionary or dissident capacities; it might obscure, for example, defiant lyrics from an overseer. You might hum because you could not or would not dare to sing aloud. As Piper has noted,

> It's potentially a very subversive weapon on its own, even without any lyrics. Imagine that you're sitting in a packed auditorium, forced to listen to a very pompous reigning authority deliver a stupid, witless, and self-aggrandizing lecture, and you start humming the tune of "Nobody Knows the Trouble I've Seen." Actually humming any tune at all under those circumstances could be much more

effective than shouting down the speaker, which is antidemocratic.[33]

The Humming Room's participants are directed to follow an instruction whose role seems not only to be weighed against the very arbitrariness of authority displayed to enforce it but also to liberate a sense of their own selves. Piper's work turns the idea of authority upside-down, achieving an almost laughable effect and, perhaps more important, inverting its very objective. Marcel Duchamp, an artist whose influence on the practices of first-generation Conceptual artists cannot be overstated, used such a strategy early in the twentieth century, but he lived in a very different time. For him authority was represented by science, a fairly newly invented discipline that radically changed the way human beings related to their environment. It was Duchamp who came up with the concept of "silly physics," upturning its logic and transforming its outcome.[34] And it might be no coincidence that Piper, when asked to describe *The Humming Room*, referred to it in a tongue-in-cheek manner, as an exercise in "silly authority."[35] She has further noted,

> *The Humming Room* offers a more distanced and compassionate standpoint on those situations of conflict and violence. Policemen are never just figures of authority or emblematic of violence. They are also individuals with families and friends and personal histories, and who often have been brutalized themselves by those in their environments. It is a very great shame that we need policemen at all to make us do what our conscience tells us to do. When policemen try to make us do what our conscience tells us not to do, just get out of their way and remember that at that moment, some of them probably hate their jobs and their lives, wish they didn't need the money, and are rabidly afraid of the victims they think they need to beat or kick or shoot in the back. They are living in a haze of fear of their own collaborative construction; they can't get out and you can't get in. Then you have to weigh the costs of resisting against the costs of hating yourself for betraying your values and becoming like them. It's never an easy choice.[36]

It is interesting that a work as immaterial as *The Humming Room*—as effortless in appearance as it is conceptually profound, as likely to generate laughter as anger, as well as being entirely dependent on the participation and willingness of visitors—has somehow become, over the planning of Piper's retrospective exhibition at MoMA, over multiple iterations of the floor plans and checklists, the crux of the show: the only work that compels visitors to understand that authority can only be truly understood when literally exercised. Its greatest achievement may be, however, that it is less a demonstration of the mechanisms of authority than their comic deconstruction. It is nothing else than the work's very instructions that undermine its authority.

And we, the curators of the exhibition, are ultimately the "silly authority" in charge of the project. Curators are invested with expertise, with control, but both are meaningless if not in service of artists and their work. We sometimes entertain the notion that a show can be "defining" for an artist, when to the contrary, some of the most influential artists of the twentieth century—such as Duchamp, Klein, and Broodthaers—have consistently worked against the very idea of definition, instead allowing, even encouraging, multiple interpretations of their work, allowing it to exist in an infinity of contexts. Piper is certainly one such artist. Instead of letting herself be defined by curatorial practices, she has proposed her own definition of the role of curators, dividing them into two categories, artistic curators and admin-curators:

> Artistic curators intuitively understand the authorial division of labor between artist and curator, and are skilled at mediating between artist and venue. They are transparent and forthright as to what they can and cannot offer. Our relationship is amicable and rational, whether or not we always agree. I always aim to protect the integrity of my work. But I usually defer to the curator's judgment about its installation and presentation. A healthy collaboration means clear communication, successful problem solving, and a final product we both can be proud of.
>
> Other curators have a more distanced relationship to their own creativity, and function primarily as institutional administrators. They aim to produce an exhibition that puts the artist, the work, and the installation in the service of an institutional, professional, or personal agenda. Institutional agendas might include strengthening the institution's profile in regional art, or competing for government funding. Professional agendas might include networking with peers in a specialized area, or winning promotion. Personal agendas might include promoting artists from one's own class background or diminishing the artist's professional independence. Admin-curators usually cannot state these agendas to the artist explicitly without damaging their relationship, and artists thwart them by insisting on the primacy of the work itself. The result is often poor communication, seemingly arbitrary or perfunctory institutional decisions, backhanded manipulation, and mistrust. Artistic collaboration and institutional mediation are harder with admin-curators. They do best dealing with dead artists.[37]

To select and arrange for display work that devolves, such as in Piper's case, a very specific kind of agency to the viewers entails a charged kind of responsibility, one that from the start we have thought to share with others. To plumb as thoroughly as possible the complex significations of Piper's work—the phenomenological structures, the ethical choices, the intimacy with which she urges change upon her viewers—we have published *Adrian Piper: A Reader* in addition to this catalogue, containing in-depth essays by art historians and philosophers. Together with the texts in the present volume, by the exhibition's curators and the artist herself, these essays cover Piper's most salient ideas: becoming an object, embodying social change, being and perceiving anomalies, and—one of her most pressing themes, treated elegantly and precisely in her own essay—how we approach art in our indexical present, in order to perceive ourselves without self-deception and be most open to what the artwork has to offer.

1. Adrian Piper, "On Wearing Three Hats," presentation at "Who Is She? Conversations with Multi-Talented Women," Third Annual Tillie K. Lubin Symposium, Rose Art Museum, Brandeis University, Waltham, Massachusetts, March 17, 1996; at Adrian Piper Research Archive Foundation Berlin (APRA) website, www.adrianpiper.com/docs/WebsiteNGBK3Hats.pdf.

2. "Do It," Independent Curators International website, www.curatorsintl.org/special-projects/do-it; and www.curatorsintl.org/special-projects/do-it/more.

3. Piper, interview with the author, Berlin, January 18–20, 2018.

4. Ibid.

5. Ibid.

6. Adrian Piper, "Food for the Spirit," *High Performance* 4, no. 1 (Spring 1981); reprinted in Piper, *Out of Order, Out of Sight*, vol. 1, *Selected Writings in Meta-Art, 1968–1992* (Cambridge, Mass.: MIT Press, 1996), p. 55.

7. Piper, "Untitled Performance for Max's Kansas City," 1981, in *Out of Order, Out of Sight*, vol. 1, p. 27; and John Perreault, "Only a Dummy," *Village Voice*, May 14, 1970, p. 16.

8. Vito Acconci, "Rubbing Piece," 1970, in Nick Kaye, ed., *Art into Theatre: Performance Interviews and Documents* (Amsterdam: Harwood Academic Press, 1996), p. 65.

9. Kaye, *Site-Specific Art: Performance, Place and Documentation* (London: Routledge, 2000), pp. 160–61. Acconci's quotes are from "Rubbing Piece" (see previous note).

10. Piper, "The Order of Celestial Laughter," 2017, APRA, www.adrianpiper.com/art/OCL_Credo.shtml.

11. Benjamin H. D. Buchloh, "First and Last: Two Books by Marcel Broodthaers," in Manuel J. Borja-Villel and Christophe Cherix, eds., *Marcel Broodthaers: A Retrospective* (New York: The Museum of Modern Art, 2016), pp. 40–49.

12. Broodthaers, "Dix mille francs de récompense: Une interview d'Irmeline Lebeer," in *Catalogue-Catalogus* (Brussels: Société des expositions du Palais des Beaux-Arts, 1974), pp. 64–68. Translated by Elizabeth Zuba, with Maria Gilissen. See also Borja-Villel and Cherix, "I Am Not a Filmmaker: Notes on a Retrospective," and Cathleen Chaffee, "Emblems of Authority," in *Marcel Broodthaers: A Retrospective*, pp. 16–21 and 248–51.

13. Piper, interview.

14. Among Piper's musical compositions are *Shiva DANCES, For God's Sake (for John Talbert)*, at APRA, www.adrianpiper.com/vs/shiva.shtml; and sound works such as *Construct Madrid* (2005).

15. Rosemary Mayer, "Performance & Experience," *Arts Magazine* 47 (December–January 1973): 34.

16. See Moira Roth, ed., *The Amazing Decade: Women and Performance Art in America, 1970–1980* (Los Angeles: Astroz Artz, 1983).

17. Piper and Dara Meyers-Kingsley, "MEDI(t)Ations: Adrian Piper's Videos, Installations, Performances, and Soundworks, 1968–1992," in Maurice Berger, ed., *Adrian Piper: A Retrospective* (Baltimore: University of Maryland Fine Arts Gallery, 1999), p. 178; and at APRA, www.adrianpiper.com/vs/sound_bach.shtml. The works Piper whistles to are Bach's Concerto in D minor for Three Harpsichords, BWV 1063; Concerto in A minor for Four Harpsichords, BWV 1065; Concerto in C major for Three Harpsichords, BWV 1064. The recording is *Bach: The Complete Concerti (Excepting the Brandenburgs)*, Mainz Chamber Orchestra, Günter Kehr, (conductor) and Martin Galling, Hedwig Bilgram, Franz Lehrndorfer, and Kurt Heinz Stolze (harpsichords), Turnabout/Vox, 1969.

18. Berger, "Styles of Radical Will: Adrian Piper and the Indexical Present," in *Adrian Piper: A Retrospective*, pp. 29–30.

19. Robert Storr, foreword to Piper, *Out of Order, Out of Sight*, vol. 1, p. xvii.

20. Jon Hendricks, *Fluxus Codex* (Detroit: The Gilbert and Lila Silverman Collection; New York: Harry N. Abrams, 1988), p. 474.

21. Piper, correspondence with the author, December 21, 2017.

22. Piper, interview.

23. See Kaira M. Cabañas, *The Myth of Nouveau Réalisme: Art and the Performative in Postwar France* (New Haven, Conn.: Yale University Press, 2013), pp. 48–61.

24. Piper, interview.

25. Ibid.

26. Ibid.

27. Erving Goffman, *The Presentation of Self in Everyday Life* (Garden City, N.Y.: Doubleday Anchor Books, 1959).

28. Allan Kaprow, "Participation Performance," *Artforum* 15, no. 7 (March 1977); reprinted in Kaprow, *Essays on the Blurring of Art and Life*, ed. Jeff Kelley (Berkeley: University of California Press, 1993), p. 187.

29. Michael Taussig, *The Corn Wolf* (Chicago: University of Chicago Press, 2015), p. 31.

30. The film *12 Years a Slave*, released in 2014, was directed by Steve McQueen, and based on *Twelve Years a Slave*, the 1853 slave narrative of Solomon Northup.

31. Karen Hopenwasser, "The Rhythm of Resilience: A Deep Ecology of Entangled Relationality," in Jill Salberg and Sue Grand, eds., *Wounds of History: Repair and Resilience in the Trans-Generational Transmission of Trauma* (London: Routledge, 2016), pp. 67 and 70.

32. Ibid.

33. Piper, interview.

34. See Walter Hopps, *The Dream Colony: A Life in Art*, ed. Deborah Treisman from interviews with Anne Doran (New York: Bloomsbury, 2017), p. 163.

35. Piper, conversation with the author, Berlin, March 1, 2017.

36. Piper, interview.

37. Piper, "Curators," in *Texte zur Kunst* 86 (June 2012): 142.

ADRIAN PIPER
UNITIES

DAVID PLATZKER

The Adrian Piper Research Archive Foundation Berlin (APRA) maintains copious volumes of the artist's earliest childhood drawings, produced in the early 1950s in her Washington Heights home and at New Lincoln School, which had campuses on Manhattan's Upper West and Upper East Sides.[1] At APRA, too, are notebooks from the 1960s documenting Piper's time at New York's School of Visual Arts (SVA), rooms of file cabinets containing writings and preparatory materials for individual works, and racks of videotapes and media works, in addition to storage for finished artworks, from her earliest to her most recent.

Spending time at APRA, studying Piper's work in depth, one comes to see consistent themes. Race, gender, and xenophobia are the topics most frequently noted by scholars and critics, but while this trinity of systems is indeed the subject of much of Piper's work between 1976 and 1996, it does not cover all of it. Another thread that winds and leads through her work from the mid-1960s to the present has been a rigorous commitment to and inquiry into the tenets and systems of Conceptual art.

Piper's artistic strategies, graphic sensibility, and root precepts of production are those of a first-generation Conceptual artist who came of age in the mid-1960s. In the opening of her richly detailed 1974 narrative "Talking to Myself: The Ongoing Autobiography of an Art Object," Piper concisely frames her organic shift from an illustrator with remarkable drafting skills to an artist whose vision and fertile ideas grounded her firmly in an emerging artistic movement:

> In my second year at Visual Arts I had a teacher, Joseph Raffaele, who insisted that we go to approximately fifteen galleries every two weeks, and write about what we had seen. . . . In that year I assimilated more, comprehended more, and produced more work than I had in all the previous years I had been working.
>
> Having this experience solved a problem which had brought me to an impasse in my work. . . . I had been totally committed to figurative art. But at the same time, I found myself interested in problems which had little to do with the *content* of particular work: problems which I later learned . . . to describe as e.g. illusionistic by non-perspectival space, colors versus form, the displacement of environmental space, etc. . . . Being exposed to contemporary art, e.g. Frank Stella, Carl Andre, Tony Smith, Don Judd, Kenneth Noland, etc. gave me the formal tools—hard-edge and color field painting, minimal sculpture—with which to treat these ideas.
>
> In addition, the work I saw demonstrated the possibility of posing entirely *new* problems as aesthetic concerns. I think the work of Sol LeWitt, especially his "46 Variations on Three Different Kinds of Cube" exhibit was the single most profound educational experience I had.[2] This, plus reading his "Notes on Conceptual Art" . . . did far more for my artistic development than the previous eleven years I had spent drawing nudes. From this point on, I felt freed, not only from the technical and formal constraints of figurative art, but also from my preconceptions about what art had to be.[3]

"Talking to Myself" introduces Piper's late-adolescent years as an artist, starting in 1966, in an era that for her—as well as for the whole of conceptualism—was a critical nexus in the emergence of an art that would break with the primacy of craft and the preciousness of execution and move toward one in which, as LeWitt asserted in "Paragraphs on Conceptual Art," in 1967, "the idea or concept is the most important aspect of the work."[4] In this declaration, LeWitt positioned himself, and a host of similarly engaged artists, as the progenitors of a cerebral art, one that eschewed using raw optical gratification as the principal method of determining the quality, and hence the inherent artistic and monetary value, of an artwork—an ethos that remains entirely present throughout Piper's work, from the mid-1960s to today.

For Piper this contrast first materialized in a mind-body disjuncture that she had addressed in 1965 and 1966, even before arriving at SVA, in a series of paintings and drawings whose titles are all preceded by the abbreviation LSD. In an interview with the artist and historian Matteo Guarnaccia, in 2003, Piper recalled her experiences with the drug, which she used six times over a period of six months, during her immersion in the 1960s counterculture. She relayed to Guarnaccia how it changed her optical, spiritual, and intellectual perceptions, influencing her and her art at the time:

> The paintings are very much about what it was like for me to go beyond the surfaces of things—to concentrate so intently on the fine detail and structure of a meditational object—on any object, really, any perceptual reality—that all of its surface sensory qualities, its conventional meanings and uses, its psychological associations and conceptual significance, all begin to move, breathe, vibrate, break up, and fall away. That's when you start to realize how much of "ordinary" reality is nothing more than a subjective mental construct. When the surfaces of perceptual reality start to hum and crack open to reveal what lies beyond them, that's where the deep insights live that are beyond words or concepts.[5]

She continued, "[None] of them [the LSD works] were done during psychedelic experiences, although they were influenced by what I learned during them." The majority of them are optically kaleidoscopic, corresponding to how the artist experienced the world while using the hallucinogen, although their subjects are indubitably not what she "saw"; rather, LSD acted as a tool for her understanding of alternative means of perception. Piper developed such learned experiences into a formal approach to systematizing otherwise indiscernible perspectives of the world in her art. At the same time she found nonchemical means of expanding her mind and body, by exploring transcendental realities through study of the Upanishads, the Bhagavad-Gita, and the Yoga Sutra, and intensive practices in meditation and yoga, both of which have remained lifelong passions.[6] Subsequent paintings such as *LSD Womb* (page 99), *LSD Bloodstream* (page 102), and *LSD Abstraction* (all 1965) feature hypnotic swirling patterns overlaying paisley-shaped and stained glass–like abstractions, a style also prevalent then in the brightly colored and high-contrast concert posters designed by the San Francisco–based graphic artists Alton Kelley, Rick Griffin, Wes Wilson, and Stanley Mouse, as well as Victor Moscoso, a former student of Josef Albers at Yale University.

This chapter in Piper's career was not limited to LSD-inspired abstraction; she often incorporated the human form in myriad ways as both compositional and graphic tools, using her own body in self-portraits such as *LSD Mirror Self-Portrait* (1965) **(page 95)**, *Negative Self-Portrait* (1966) **(page 97)**, and *LSD Self-Portrait from the Inside Out* (1966) **(page 97)**. In the first, drawn in graphite, Piper appears behind a piano stool in front of a mirror that we see only partly, suggested by its vertical sides and the curved lower edge of its frame. Her head, floating above the rendering of the stool, is the only visible part of her body. An unidentifiable draped object, perhaps a discarded sheet of paper, in the lower-right corner of the mirror adds another level of dimension to the image. A large, intricate paisley pattern, in shades of yellow, green, and ocher, swirls around Piper, partially covering the right side of her face; within the pattern one might see three small female heads almost entirely camouflaged by the swirls. The drawing has a surreal quality in the amorphous way that the picture plane is divided into five different depths presented by Piper's head, the stool, the unidentified object, the frame of the mirror, and the wispy, smoky colors that unify these strata. *Negative Self-Portrait*—an inked image of the nude artist sitting in a windowlike frame—as well as the painting for which it was a study, *LSD Self-Portrait from the Inside Out*, similarly employ multiple levels of dimensionality. Both are reversed like a photographic negative, with the presence of light turned to darkness.

Other works in the sequence include a portrait of her boyfriend, Steve Shomstein, painted in a stained-glass style, depicting him as he would have appeared to a viewer under the effects of the drug, as well as *LSD Self-Portrait with Tamiko* **(page 101)**, which includes her cat. As the series came to a close, in 1966, Piper completed a triptych of paintings called *Alice in Wonderland*, with its separate parts individually titled *Alice Down the Rabbit Hole*, *The Mad Hatter's Tea Party*, and *Alice and the Pack of Cards* **(figs. 1–3 and page 103)**. Their trippy narrative hews to that of Lewis Carroll's fantastical mid-nineteenth-century children's novel, *Alice's Adventures in Wonderland*, which was popular in the countercultural environment of the 1960s for its suggestions of mind expansion and enlightenment achieved through drug use, and which found its way into the mainstream when the psychedelic rock band Jefferson Airplane performed "White Rabbit" on the television show *The Smothers Brothers Comedy Hour*, in 1967.

Piper was not the only artist at SVA thinking about the dynamics of actualizing metaphysical conceptions into works of art. Her fellow students Joseph Kosuth and Christine Kozlov were also developing work that broke away from trying to approximate an idea or object on paper or canvas through the precision of rote draftsmanship. Mel Bochner, who was teaching art history at SVA at the time, was writing about and producing artwork that considered solipsism—"The theory, assumption, or belief: [a] That the self knows and can know nothing but its own modifications and states. [b] That the self is the only existent thing, or, inaccurately, that all reality is subjective"—as a means of realizing art objects that defined the intersection of the rationality of time and space and our limited capacity to recognize nonmaterial subjective concepts.[7] Piper would later delve far more deeply into solipsism in her work and writing. In "Moving from Solipsism to Self-Consciousness," written in September 1972 while studying philosophy at City College of New York, she concludes,

> The problem has become that of the balance between self and other within a single—my own—consciousness. Formerly the problem was that of solipsism, i.e. the balance between my own consciousness and a problematic external world. That seems to have resolved itself by the possibility of assimilating as much of that external world, as other, into my sense of myself. The more I assimilate, the more easily I am able to see myself as "an object in the world among others."[8]

This heady thinking would become increasingly apparent in Piper's subsequent works, in particular with her performative pieces, but this theoretical position was already beginning to form in Piper's earliest moments at SVA in the mid-1960s.

Closely following her LSD drawings and paintings was a set of thirty-five ink-and-pencil drawings titled *The Barbie Doll Drawings* (1967) **(pages 108–10)**, which deftly combine three-dimensional structures in space with episodic time frames.[9] The sequence, excised from one of Piper's many spiral-bound sketchbooks from the 1960s, is viscerally charged by its conflicting subjective and objective propositions. In precisely rendered fine lines, the drawings depict what appear to be awkwardly reassembled doll parts, sometimes with heads and body parts tied like balloons and occasionally floating over crevasses, accompanied by grotesque puppet heads and disembodied limbs. But it is entirely possible to recognize the carefully executed amalgams not simply as haphazard assemblages of doll parts, but as discrete, finely tuned compositional structures. This becomes more apparent toward the end of the series, when the disembodied parts begin to align intellectually and morph visually into what would be Piper's earliest Minimalist sculptures. And the series has an undeniable and overt sense of humor, if a rather grim one, although as in other of Piper's works, it is often obscured by the gravity of the immediate subject matter or the critical context.

The Barbie Doll Drawings were created at a moment of the artist's general shift from object to idea. The individual drawings in the sequence are both what they seem to be—works about gender—and what they seem not to be—pure, system-based Conceptual works, utilizing a fixed set of iconographic materials familiar to viewers permutated in combinations with no two results being wholly alike. A number of paintings, including *Self-Portrait at Age 5 with Doll* **(page 106)** and *Barbara Epstein with Doll* **(page 107)** (both 1966), incorporated actual dolls, which function as dimensional objects that project off the flat picture plane and out into space. These are precursors of works that express dimensionality, as is *Untitled Planes Painting* (1966) **(page 105)**, which achieved a similar effect by forwarding and recessing three male heads, this time painted on separate canvases in unaligned planes, such that the heads hover like faces in a crowd, each in its own physical universe.

The approach of producing a sequence of works anchored in a basic idea or set of parameters in a multitude of permutations remained a principal one for Piper. *Drawings about Paper and Writings about Words* **(pages 112–27)**, a sequence of more than fifty individual works, demonstrates her turn from objective representation toward permutations of color, materiality,

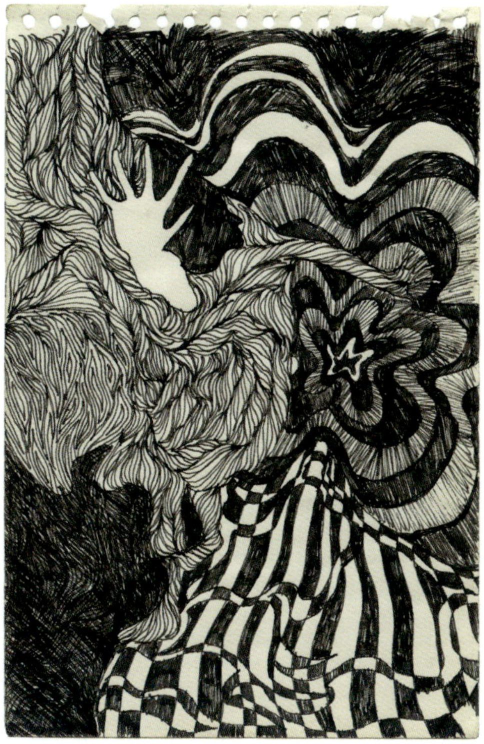

Fig. 1
LSD Alice sketch #1. 1966
8½ × 5½ in. (21.6 × 14 cm)
Rapidograph pen and ink on paper
Collection Adrian Piper Research Archive Foundation Berlin

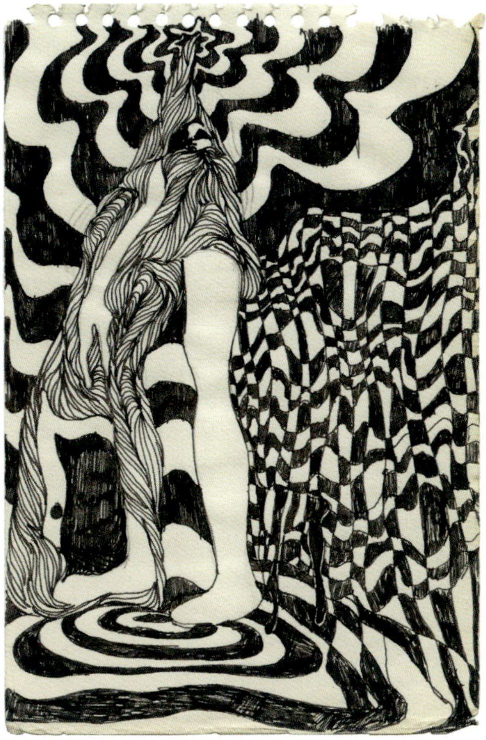

Fig. 2
LSD Alice sketch #2. 1966
8½ × 5½ in. (21.6 × 14 cm)
Rapidograph pen and ink on paper
Collection Adrian Piper Research Archive Foundation Berlin

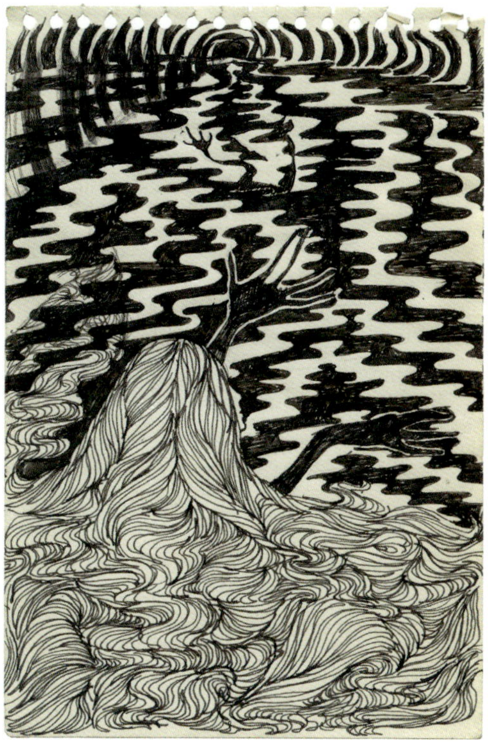

Fig. 3
LSD Alice sketch #3. 1966
8½ × 5½ in. (21.6 × 14 cm)
Rapidograph pen and ink on paper
Collection Adrian Piper Research Archive Foundation Berlin

surface, texture, and spatial relationships, all within the fixed area of a standard 8½ by 11–inch sheet of paper. The contrasts between *The Barbie Doll Drawings* and *Drawings about Paper and Writings about Words*—figuration versus abstraction, line drawing versus collage, shading, and contours—are formal distinctions; what remains absolutely consistent, however, is how riotously inventive both series are in exploring a system and the extent to which comprehension relies on a viewer's immediate recognition of its units, and Piper's play in developing nonrepeating structures using them. Similarly, the creation of a new element in a series relies on the logical reimagining of a preceding element, so that the result is an expanded object with qualities inherited from a predecessor—not unlike genetic code passed from generation to generation, acquiring new traits through the injection of new code, mutating through happenstance and age. Among the individual drawings in *Drawings about Paper and Writings about Words*, and even in a single sheet, it is immediately clear that Piper is exploring how three dimensions can be materialized from a standard two-dimensional space using only collage, perspectival techniques, and subtle coloring but eschewing other facilities for the representational rendering of objects, thus, in a way, producing *The Barbie Doll Drawings* but without dolls, floating heads, or geometric structures found in our observable world.

Conceptualism, Beyond the Confines of a Picture Plane

Piper's pursuit of ways to visually define conceptual space was not limited to works on paper. In 1967 and 1968 she began to produce paintings and sculptures that took this exploration further, starting with works such as *Untitled Planes Painting* and the wall- and floor-based sculptures *Double Recess* (page 129), *Protruded Rectangle Canvas*, and *Recessed Square* (page 128), all three from 1967. In contrast to the purity of Donald Judd's declaration that "a work needs only to be interesting," John McCracken's cool, fetishized execution, Carl Andre's unadorned materiality, and Robert Smithson's serial translations of mathematical and organic geometries into sculpture, Piper pursued an art that could express or actualize an ideal, something more infinite than what it is possible to manifest in a single, hermetically constrained art object.[10] *Nine-Part Floating Square* (1967) (page 131), like some of her earlier works, operates formally as a study of linkages between a work's physicality and its levels of not just physical but indeed conceptual depth. Objectively described, it comprises nine 18 by 18–inch (45.7 by 45.7–cm) canvases, each additionally divided by light pencil lines into nine 6 by 6–inch (15.2 by 15.2–cm) squares. A light gesso square of 36 by 36 inches (91.4 by 91.4 cm) is painted across the nine panels, not quite in the center but rather offset by six inches at the top and six inches at the right. The nine canvases are installed in three rows of three, separated by six inches, with a ruled grid penciled directly on the wall such that it precisely joins the penciled grids on the canvases.

As a study of the intersection of an ideal's recognition—the intellectualized ideal of joined elevations—with the realization of a three-dimensional artwork that demonstrates it, *Nine-Part Floating Square* manifests ideas Piper was working out in her early writing:

> I believe very strongly in the necessity of the physical realization of an idea: First, I am convinced that the final, concretized form of an idea is the true existence, in that it is then subject only to the physical laws of the deterioration of the material form and no longer the inevitable inconsistencies and fluctuations of the only-human artistic mind; second, if there exists any ultimately objective reality of an art at all (and I can't give any opinion as to whether there does or not), I'm sure it can exist only as a total additive vision in which everyone participates, and towards this end there must necessarily be a physical form that everyone can perceive and formulate a vision *of*.[11]

Piper thus formulated her exploration of dimensionality, using artistic tools to reason her way toward the fabrication of artistic objects. As the *Drawings about Paper, Writings about Words* works reveal in their similarities with and contrasts to *The Barbie Doll Drawings*, *Nine-Part Floating Square* shares and builds on what germinated in *Untitled Planes Painting*. Both sets of works conjure infrastructures that postulate a transparent analogue between defining space in a tactile manner and defining it against intellectual constructs.

Piper's interest in LeWitt's writing, which she first encountered in 1967, would seem to suggest that when she made *Nine-Part Floating Square* she was familiar with his wall drawings and temporal installations. But it wasn't until 1968 that LeWitt developed his instruction-based art, in *Wall Drawing 1: Drawing Series II 18 (A & B)*, placing Piper very much in the vanguard of such work. The relationship of LeWitt's writing to his actualized artwork inspired a host of artists, including Piper, who recognized his thinking—and vocabulary—as critical to the development of their skills of exposition and artistic output. In February 1968 Piper saw LeWitt's *46 Three-Part Variations on 3 Different Kinds of Cubes* at Dwan Gallery, in New York. The exhibition featured forty-six white-painted rectangular aluminum structures, each one built out of three stacked cubic units—different combinations of solid cubes, cubes with one side removed, or cubes with two parallel sides removed—following a logical progression such that no two structures were identical. The work's title, like those of Piper's previous works and ones that would follow, articulates the totality of the program that realizes and makes the work concrete. That is, the title of the object defines the object, and the object memorializes its title. Piper continued to develop her ideas about planned serial progressions throughout 1968, in works such as *Sixteen Permutations of a Planar Analysis of a Square* **(pages 136, 137)**, which paired a diagram showing all the possible permutations of the interior divisions of a square with a sculptural realization of one of those permutations, as well as *A Three-Dimensional Representation of Infinite Divisibility*, **(page 132)** with its floor-based sculptural companion, *Infinitely Divisible Floor Construction* **(page 133)**, each one a clearly constructed demonstration of a logical translation of geometric systems.

A wry sense of humor makes an occasional appearance in Piper's work, sometimes yielding a sliver of information about her personal life, although never straying from her systematic conceptualist mandate. *Meat into Meat* (1968) **(pages 142, 143)**, originally titled *Five Unrelated Time Pieces*, is a vivid merging of time-based art with Piper's growing political awareness and interpersonal relationships, staged as a private performance over three days, from October 11 to October 13.[12] Its narrative, recorded on a typewritten sheet of paper and in eight color snapshots, taken by Piper, concerns a pound of packaged ground beef shown on a dinning table at 3:15 p.m. on Friday; as four raw hamburger patties on a plate at 11:35 a.m. on Saturday; and frying in a pan on Saturday at 11:48 a.m.; followed by four images of David Rosner, her boyfriend at the time, wearing a white shirt with rolled-up sleeves and red tie while consuming the meat over a duration of six minutes.[13] In contrast to the many dry, frequently pseudoscientific conceptualist works being made at the time by male artists, *Meat into Meat* treats the female labor of preparing a meal for a boyfriend as a pointed, sinisterly comical slaying of time-based art: the parlaying of mundane activities—cooking and eating—into work that devours preconceptions about how art should formally manifest and palpably address its subject matter objectively. Piper would later describe the work with a flourish:

> I thought I was performing an abstract metaphysical investigation into the nature of space and time, but the subtext was my relationship with David. David was a good Marxist and a very committed political person and I was starting to get interested in feminism, going to my first consciousness-raising groups, doing yoga and this weirdo art, and being a vegetarian. Although David was always helping me do my work, there was always this running commentary about all this weirdo stuff and what did it mean and it was all silly to do it. So, in this piece in particular, I retaliated with my own running commentary about what it meant to be on the one hand a committed Marxist and on the other hand to be consuming enough meat to feed a small third-world country for a month.[14]

A set of color photocopies of the *Meat into Meat* photographs in the Adrian Piper Research Archive, in Berlin, is accompanied by a typewritten label that gives the work additional context:

> Found private confrontational perform-
> ance [see *Five Unrelated Time Pieces*]
> A. Piper, D. Rosner, 1 lb. hamburger.
> Topic: Marxism vs. vegetarianism

The orderly serial progression of *Meat into Meat* clearly fits in the same vein as Piper's prior systematic works: taking a singular idea and developing it in stages toward a conclusion, while allowing the internal permutations of the work to be exposed, step-by-step, from the conception—here, elements of interpersonal relationships and philosophical differences (as expressed by the obvious annoyance on Rosner's face and Piper's revealing of the flaws in his intellectual underpinnings). Piper later recognized *Meat into Meat* to be her first performance work, preceding those that would extend into the video works and meta-performances of the 1980s onward.[15]

Demonstrating Hypothesis

For the Hypothesis series, a body of work executed between 1968 and 1970, Piper relied on the same continuous temporal progression that was the foundation of *Meat into Meat*, using photography to document, preserve, and slice up time—all

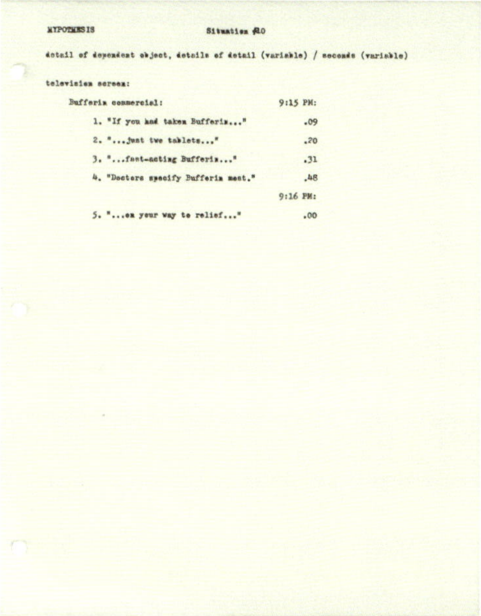

HYPOTHESIS Situation #10

detail of dependent object, details of detail (variable) / seconds (variable)

television screen:

Bufferin commercial: 9:15 PM:

1. "If you had taken Bufferin..." .09
2. "...just two tablets..." .20
3. "...fast-acting Bufferin..." .31
4. "Doctors specify Bufferin most." .48

9:16 PM:

5. "...on your way to relief..." .00

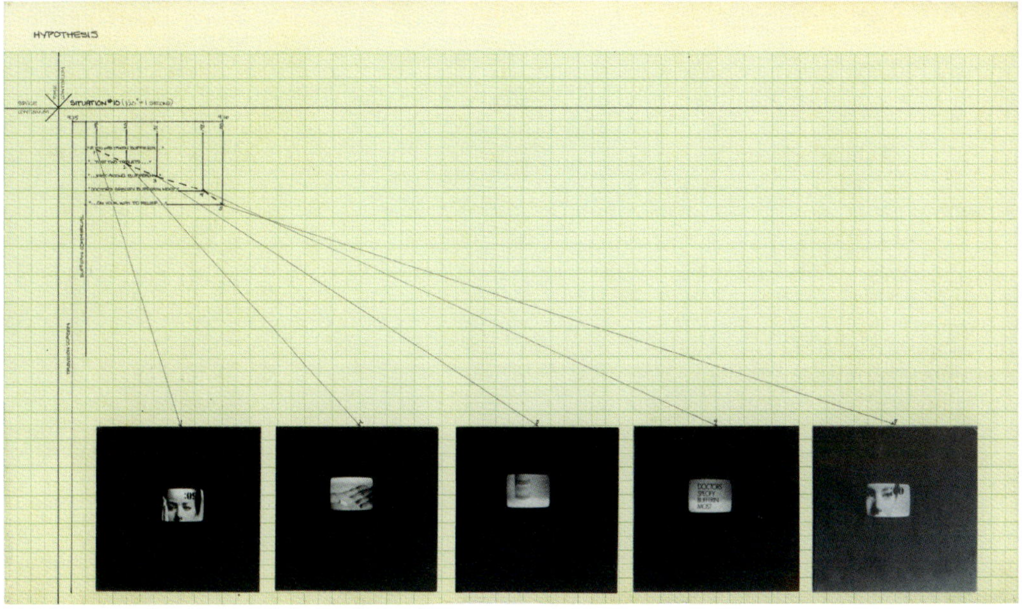

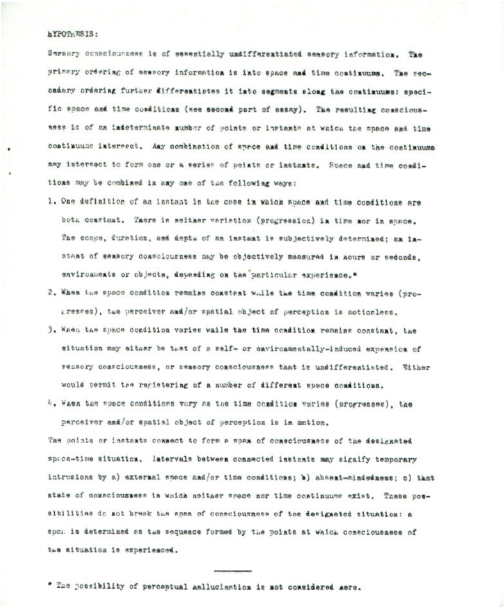

HYPOTHESIS:

Sensory consciousness is of essentially undifferentiated sensory information. The primary ordering of sensory information is into space and time continuums. The secondary ordering further differentiates it into segments along the continuums: specific space and time conditions (see second part of essay). The resulting consciousness is of an indeterminate number of points or instants at which the space and time continuums intersect. Any combination of space and time conditions on the continuums may intersect to form one or a series of points or instants. Space and time conditions may be combined in any one of the following ways:

1. One definition of an instant is the case in which space and time conditions are both constant. There is neither variation (progression) in time nor in space. The scope, duration, and depth of an instant is subjectively determined; an instant of sensory consciousness may be objectively measured in hours or seconds, environments or objects, depending on the particular experience.*
2. When the space condition remains constant while the time condition varies (progresses), the perceiver and/or spatial object of perception is motionless.
3. When the space condition varies while the time condition remains constant, the situation may either be that of a self- or environmentally-induced expansion of sensory consciousness, or sensory consciousness that is undifferentiated. Either would permit the registering of a number of different space conditions.
4. When the space conditions vary as the time condition varies (progresses), the perceiver and/or spatial object of perception is in motion.

The points or instants connect to form a span of consciousness of the designated space-time situation. Intervals between connected instants may signify temporary intrusions by a) external space and/or time conditions; b) absent-mindedness; c) that state of consciousness in which neither space nor time continuums exist. These possibilities do not break the span of consciousness of the designated situation: a span is determined as the sequence formed by the points at which consciousness of the situation is experienced.

* The possibility of perceptual hallucination is not considered here.

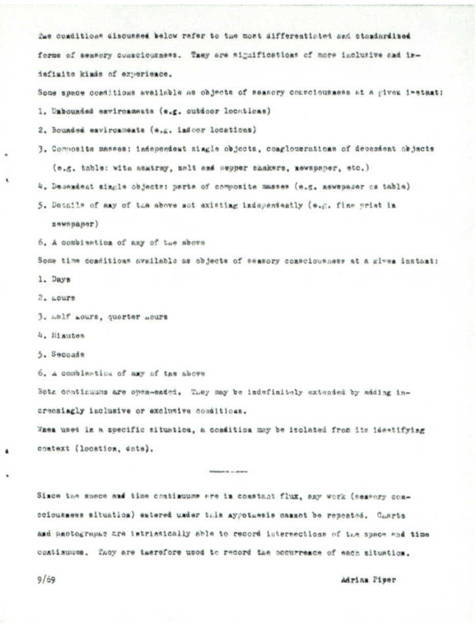

The conditions discussed below refer to the most differentiated and standardized forms of sensory consciousness. They are significations of more inclusive and indefinite kinds of experience.

Some space conditions available as objects of sensory consciousness at a given instant:

1. Unbounded environments (e.g. outdoor locations)
2. Bounded environments (e.g. indoor locations)
3. Composite masses: independent single objects, conglomerations of dependent objects (e.g. table: with ashtray, salt and pepper shakers, newspaper, etc.)
4. Dependent single objects: parts of composite masses (e.g. newspaper on table)
5. Details of any of the above not existing independently (e.g. fine print in newspaper)
6. A combination of any of the above

Some time conditions available as objects of sensory consciousness at a given instant:

1. Days
2. Hours
3. Half hours, quarter hours
4. Minutes
5. Seconds
6. A combination of any of the above

Both continuums are open-ended. They may be indefinitely extended by adding increasingly inclusive or exclusive conditions.

When used in a specific situation, a condition may be isolated from its identifying context (location, date).

Since the space and time continuums are in constant flux, any work (sensory consciousness situation) entered under this hypothesis cannot be repeated. Charts and photographs are intrinsically able to record intersections of the space and time continuums. They are therefore used to record the occurrence of each situation.

9/69 Adrian Piper

Fig. 4
Hypothesis: Situation #10. 1968–69
Typescript on mimeographed paper; gelatin silver prints and ink on graph paper; and two photolithograph pages
11 × 8½ in. (27.9 × 21.6 cm); 11 × 17³⁄₁₆ in. (27.9 × 43.6 cm); and each 11 × 8½ in. (27.9 × 21.6 cm)
Generali Foundation Collection—Permanent Loan to the Museum der Moderne Salzburg

actions inherent in a medium that captures an image in a fraction of a second.

Each work in the series is presented as three panels in simple frames, with one of the panels always containing a pair of text pages that lays out the series' fixed parameters. The remaining two panels contain a set of photographs mounted horizontally on a long piece of graph paper and a single typewritten index of the photographs, with descriptive text and time references. In these works Piper makes visible how a time continuum and space continuum can operate in simultaneity. The artist's subjectivity is also situated within this schema, albeit far more subtly. *Hypothesis Situation #10* (1968) **(fig. 4)**, as an exemplar of the series, surveys a one-minute-long television commercial for Bufferin pain medication, which Piper indexed with five black-and-white stills taken successively, the first at 9:15:09 p.m., and then the following four shot at random over the next fifty-one seconds. With the snapshots arranged and mounted sequentially along the bottom of the horizontal graph paper, Piper drew, in black ink, a single horizontal axis, labeling it "space continuum," and an intersecting perpendicular vertical axis for the "time continuum," a format she repeated in each *Hypothesis* work. In *Hypothesis Situation #10* an additional set of two vertical lines are labeled "television screen" and "Bufferin commercial," and a single horizontal line, scaling time as 1⁄20 of an inch per second, documents the moment that Piper pressed the camera's shutter. Along that line, descending from each of the five points marking the snapshots' times, are short lines that contain the advertisement's audio from those synchronic moments against Piper's diagrammatic charting and inlaid video stills:

> "If you had taken Bufferin . . ."
> " . . . just two tablets . . ."
> " . . . fast-acting Bufferin . . ."
> "Doctors specify Bufferin most."
> " . . . on your way to relief . . ."

Also descending from these five points are five diagonal rules that connect the time to the corresponding photographs: a woman, hand against her head, apparently suffering from a headache, at ":09," a hand holding a Bufferin tablet; a Bufferin bottle; the words "Doctors specify Bufferin most," and, in the final frame, the woman from the first image, now looking less aggrieved, at ":60," showing how quickly she has been relieved of her pain. The nineteen works in the Hypothesis series all involve Piper's authenticating her personal surroundings in this way, with the camera's lens, and by extension, verifying her own body "as equally a concrete physical object that could refer to itself as well as to other objects, and . . . finding the points of similarity and difference. . . . What I did was to document the contents of my consciousness at specific time intervals as the particular feature that distinguished me from other objects in the world."[16]

In the *Hypothesis* works Piper parses what would otherwise be inconsequential punctuations in time and memorializes them as frames in a single work: significant, but only appreciable as parts of something larger. If a single photographic snapshot were removed from its context, it would lose its structural relevance and become nothing more than a forgotten slice of time. By contrast, when set according to Piper's rules, as laid out in the text panel that accompanies each work in the series, the photographs reveal the unity and logic of the way she uses the camera to place herself in the position of an introspective observer: indexing the codifications of the world around her—be they cityscapes, her apartment, or images on a television screen—and essentially documenting her relationship to the physicality of the material world against the unceasing linearity of the passage of time. Piper noted the importance of the series, saying it was "the crucial link between the earlier conceptual work and the later, more political work I did having to do with race and gender objectification, otherness, identity, and xenophobia."[17]

The Hypothesis series can be thematically coupled with the singular portfolio *Here and Now* (1968) **(figs. 5, 6 and page 135)**, a set of sixty-four unbound sheets.[18] *Here and Now* merges the precept raised in *Nine-Part Floating Square*—a grid that lends substance to an abstraction more comprehensible through science and philosophy than art—with the temporal element of the Hypothesis series. What's new here is how time is linked to the grid without any associated reference points, either figurative or photographic: each moment is set in individual 1-inch squares within a grid of sixty-four, over the course of sixty-four mimeographed sheets. Piper devised an utterly simple—but by no means obvious—way to accentuate the paradox of the movement of time tied to a specific unchanging place, by having each page's single occupied square contain typewritten text defining its precise location. A text on the title page reads "not here," and, as Piper explained in "Xenophobia and the Indexical Present II: Lecture," of 1992, "The reason is because the text on the page does not refer to its own location, to its own position in space and time. It refers to the person who did the project, namely me, and to the time when it was done, namely November 1968."[19] On the first interior page, within the first square of the sixty-four-square grid, a text reads,

> HERE: the sq
> uare area in
> top row, righ
> t corner of
> page.

Variations on this text appear, page by page, square by square, from right to left on each line of the grid:

> HERE: the sq
> uare area i
> n 3rd row f
> rom top, 4th
> from right
> side.

This continues until the sixty-fourth square on the sixty-fourth page, which concludes,

> HERE: the sq
> uare area i
> n bottom ro
> w, left corn
> er of page.

Through this block-by-block narrative, *Here and Now* systemizes a temporal presence, as the reader moves laterally from page to page, at the same time quantifying the nonpresence—the dematerialization of the nonobject—of the artist, who has, in a previous place and time, used signifiers of language against a defined location in space. The stacked pages can be understood as a demonstration of time rendered against location at any point along a timeline, of any given moment being *here and now*.[21] *Seriation #1: Lecture* and *Seriation #2: Now*, two sound works from 1968, present aural complements to this idea, by substituting the sound of language for physical work. In the former, Piper used a rotary telephone to call for the time—an automated service that announced the time of day in ten-second intervals—and recorded twenty-nine minutes and seventeen seconds of the female voice reciting the hours and minutes; the effect of the work is a perceptual shift for the listener, who inhabits a time nonsynchronic with the recording. In the latter, Piper declaims the word "now," drawing it out in progressively shorter intervals, from a minute to a second, over the course of seventeen minutes and thirty-six seconds, in a further, and more ethereal, distillation of the concept.[20]

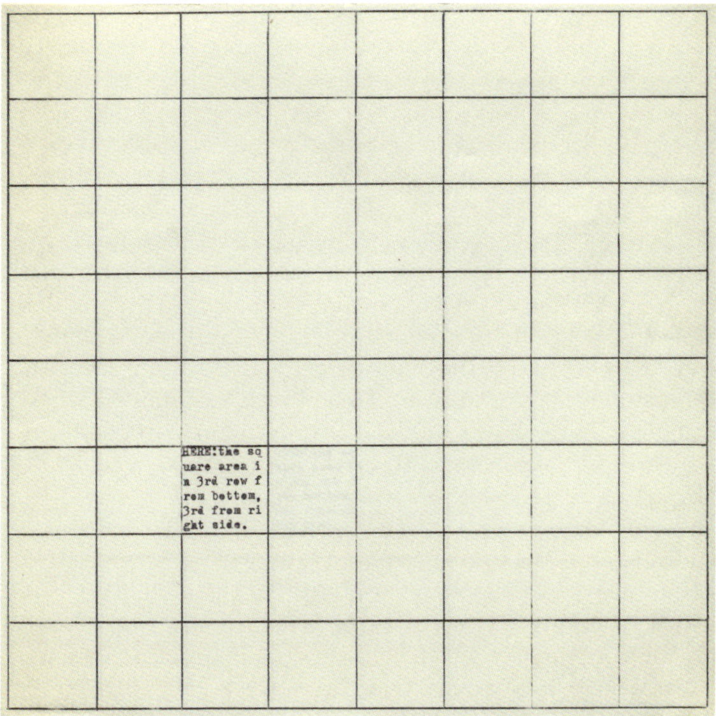

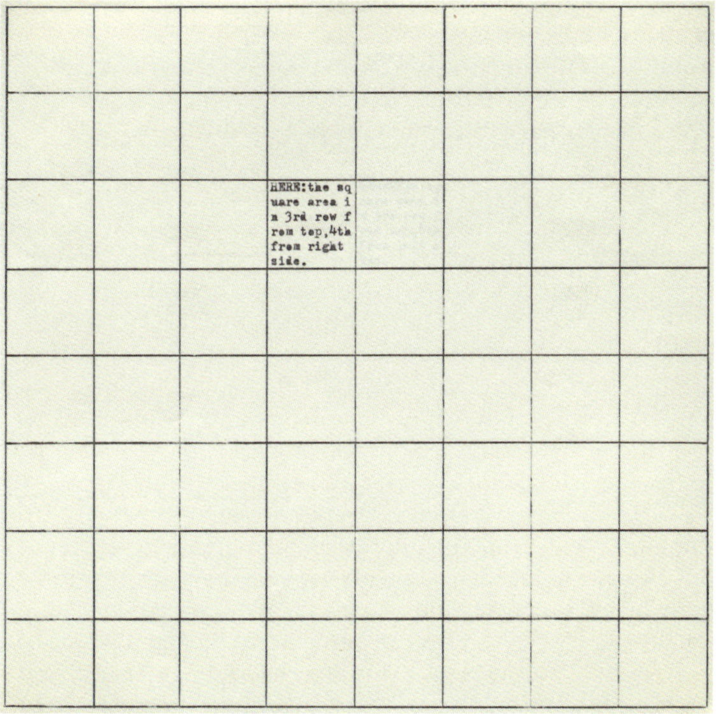

Fig 5, 6.
Here and Now. 1968
Cardboard portfolio with text on graph paper and text on mimeographed paper taped to box; and text on sixty-four loose sheets of mimeographed paper
Each sheet 9 × 9 in. (22.9 × 22.9 cm)
Collection Alan Cravitz and Shashi Caudill
Details:
page 43
page 20

Beyond Constraints

Throughout 1969 and after graduating from SVA that year, Piper sought new avenues and mediums for her ideas, two of which were artists' books and ephemeral works. These seem a natural extension of her new consideration of the location of time as a fourth dimension. The utility of inexpensive, easy-to-disseminate work was particularly well suited to page-by-page serial narrative constructions, and added a layer of transparency to the notion of "reading" art. Although many artists were producing books or projects for publication at that time (including John Baldessari, Robert Barry, Bochner, Stanley Brouwn, James Lee Byars, Hanne Darboven, Peter Downsbrough, Gilbert & George, Dan Graham, Kosuth, LeWitt, Lucy Lippard, Ed Ruscha, Smithson, Athena Tacha, and Lawrence Weiner), one of the medium's key figures was not an artist but the dealer Seth Siegelaub. Siegelaub, through the books he published, made the argument that the book format was the natural evolution of the dematerialized artwork and an appropriate conceptual alternative to physical gallery spaces—the artist's book wasn't just a book: it was an exhibition venue.

Piper's contact with Siegelaub came about not through publishing with him but by working as a receptionist and administrative assistant in his gallery, at 44 East Fifty-second Street, in New York, during the exhibition *January 5–31, 1969* (also known as the *January Show*) (fig. 7).[21] From that vantage point she frequently interacted with the artists in the exhibition—Barry, Douglas Huebler, Kosuth, and Weiner, most of whom she had previously known—and encountered a broad spectrum of visitors. Piper's role there was largely invisible, as the archetypal girl at the front desk, rather than that of an artistic peer making work that directly corresponded with, and even surpassed, that of the men being exhibited.[22]

Piper was never included in any of Siegelaub's exhibitions.[23] In fact, only a single woman, Kozlov, appeared in any of his conceptualist exhibitions, contributing a single page to the *March 1969* publication.[24] While working for him, however, Piper's first two publication projects were published in the fifth issue of *0 TO 9*, a journal begun by Vito Acconci and Bernadette Mayer in April 1967.[25] Her connection to the journal was through Rosemary Mayer, Piper's fellow student at SVA, Acconci's wife at the time, and the sister of Bernadette. *0 TO 9* was launched as a mimeographed and stapled edited selection of poems by, for the most part, emerging authors. By the fifth issue Acconci and Mayer had taken a more expansive editorial stance: to reflect the intersections of literature, theory, and text-based art, they invited visual artists—some of whom, such as LeWitt and Smithson, were contributors to Siegelaub's publications—to submit pageworks.[26] In addition to Piper's works, there were contributions from Richard Johnny John and Jerome Rothenberg, Smithson, John Perreault, Yvonne Rainer, Bernadette Mayer, Clark Coolidge, Acconci, Hannah Weiner, Les Levine, Eduardo Costa, Kenneth Koch, Philip Corner, Jack Anderson, Rosemary Mayer, and John Inslee.

One of Piper's pageworks, which she would later title *Untitled ("If you are a slow reader . . . ")* (page 157), is an expression of the intellectual meeting point of text composition, reader comprehension, and the passage of time.[27] Its first two sentences, each constituting a whole paragraph, declare how long it takes to read them: a slow reader will need approximately five seconds to read the first, quite simple sentence, of seventeen words, and a fast reader will need the same amount of time to read the second, more complex sentence, of thirty-nine words. The final sentence and paragraph of the work adds a mathematical problem to the question of how long it takes to be read. Beyond its droll humor, which is found in many of Piper's text-based works of that period, *Untitled ("If you are a slow reader . . . ")* pushes at time's boundaries, at the difference between the way it is fixed, like a clock or a metronome, and the way individuals operate within it and perceive its progression, in a similar manner to the *Hypothesis* works but with the mapping of sequential photographs swapped out for a block of text. In both, the structural components mark a system for testing the constraints of understanding the relationship between seeing information and experiencing it. The harmony of this work would not have been missed by those engaged in the temporal process of reading it in a literary journal.

0 TO 9's sixth and final issue, published in July 1969, was something of an extravaganza, with contributions by Jasper Johns, Rainer, Alan Sondheim, Lee Lozano, Lawrence Weiner, Bernar Venet, Barry, Graham, Corner, John Giorno, Huebler, Perreault, Smithson, Karen Pirups-Hvarre, Michael Heizer, Coolidge, Nels Richardson, Larry Fagin, Rosemary Mayer, Bern Porter, Hannah Weiner, and LeWitt, in addition to those of Acconci, Bernadette Mayer, and Piper, all of whom would soon be recognized as significant visual artists and poets of the era. Piper contributed two pieces to this issue, neither of which were announced by a title on the magazine's table of contents. *Street Works*, a supplement published as a coda to this final issue, contained documentation of artist-produced flyers, press releases, and handouts for a series of performances, organized by the artist Marjorie Strider and the poets Perreault and Hannah Weiner, that took place in Manhattan on March 15, 1969, April 18, 1969, and May 25, 1969. Each piece of ephemera in the volume represented the works of various artists and poets, but each date's performances bore the same Manhattan locations and hours. *Street Works II,* for example, took place

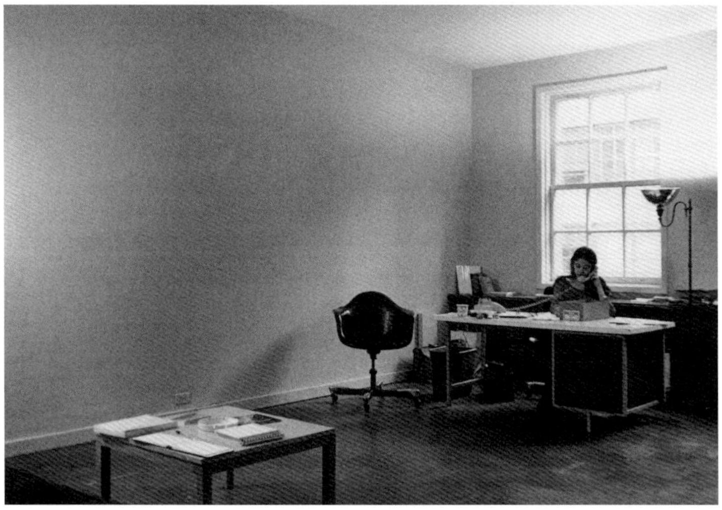

Fig. 7
Installation view of *January 5–31, 1969*, 44 East Fifty-second Street, New York, with Piper at the reception desk
Seth Siegelaub Papers. Gift of Seth Siegelaub and the Stichting Egress Foundation, Amsterdam, I.A.40. The Museum of Modern Art Archives, New York

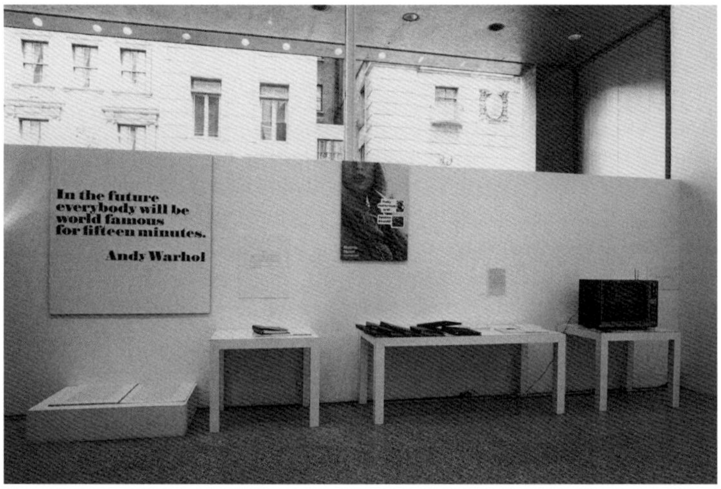

Fig. 8
Installation view of *Information*, The Museum of Modern Art, New York, July 2–September 20, 1970
Left to right: Andy Warhol, *IN THE FUTURE EVERYONE WILL BE WORLD FAMOUS FOR FIFTEEN MINUTES* (n.d.); Adrian Piper, *Context #7* (1970); and Carl Andre, *Seven Books of Poetry* (1969)
The Museum of Modern Art Archives, New York

on April 18, 1969, on the sidewalks of the city block defined by Sixth and Fifth Avenues from Thirteenth to Fourteenth Streets, during the one-hour span between 5 and 6 p.m. On that cool spring evening Piper presented *Untitled ("Street Works: Friday, April 18, 1969, 5–6 PM . . .")* (page 169)—three proposals for actions printed on a flyer that she distributed among the crowd, along with ephemera materials by many of the other participating artists.

One week prior to the announced time of the performance, Piper spent two hours traversing the area where the events would take place, "recording whatever occurred" on a portable tape deck, carrying on conversations with Richard Van Buren, Edwin Ruda, and Acconci; with Acconci some of the chatter takes on "interpersonal overtones I was completely unaware of at the time."[28] Returning to the same location the following week to perform in *Street Works II*, a one-hour series of events, Piper brought with her the same tape deck. Setting the speed to double, she played back the earlier recording while walking the same route, no doubt to an audience of confused passersby unable to garner much from its chipmunklike sounds mingling with the real-time street noises. The temporal displacement and confusion must have pleased Piper; it was very much the effect she was anticipating, as she herself noted in the recording, which she later issued as a nearly two-hour audio work, *Streetwork Streettracks I–II* (1969).[29] Thus one work is transformed into another, with the removal of something specific from one moment, the transfer and compression of that thing exactly one week later, and the later re-revealing of it as a stand-alone audio work, freed from the constrained conditions of live playback. This elasticity of time and place, a work transported to another time in another place, removes it from the performative structure it was crafted for, so that it becomes both performance relic and work to engage with in the present: the experience of an artist discussing a work that does not yet fully exist. It is, in effect, a work documenting its own creation.

These organized street works can also be understood as extensions of both the Pop art Happenings of the earlier 1960s and the street protests taking place in New York and throughout the country during the 1968 elections, the Civil Rights Movement, and the Vietnam War. Whereas the Happenings usually took place in galleries and performance spaces, the street works were unconfined by physically walled-in spaces. Enacted in open environments, comingled with the natural flow of pedestrians, these performances created unlimited possibilities for happenstance; with the sidewalk as the stage and the city as backdrop, the inhabitants of New York became active participants, willingly or not.

Piper, Rosemary Mayer, and the poet Aram Saroyan would be the only three artists and writers other than Acconci and Bernadette Mayer to publish their own books under the *0 TO 9* imprint. *Three Untitled Projects [for 0 to 9]: Some Areas in the New York Area* (1969), a set of three untitled books intended as independent works, expands Piper's inquiry into spatial relationships as fixed constructions defined by the limits of the human mind of *Here and Now*. The work was widely seen, thanks to Piper's singular distribution of the books. The set of three volumes, packed in a manila envelope, was sent by mail—as an independent mail-art exhibition—to 162 artists, collectors, critics, curators, dealers, friends, writers, and others.[30] The names and addresses of those being sent the books were indexed in two columns on both sides of a loose sheet of paper that was included in the envelope, with a red dot placed next to the recipient's name on the list in the packet that he or she received: each one thus was designated as a location of the exhibition.[31]

Each of these four elements—the three books and the index of names—demonstrates a distinct means of documenting and naming locations. The first book records the locations found at the intersections of horizontal and vertical creases on a standard Hagstrom map of New York's boroughs; the second book illustrates the area of a randomly chosen block of a map of Manhattan—the area between Second and Third Avenues bordered by East Forty-seventh and East Forty-eighth streets, identically marked in red ink in each copy—proportionally translated into increasingly smaller dimensions; the third book deconstructs four sheets of graph paper, using descending grid sizes and various measurements for the boxes on each of the four sheets (¼ inch, 1 pica, ⅛ inch, and ten squares to 1 inch, plus an equation to show how the fixed gridded scales could theoretically be extended to larger dimensions); and the sheet of the recipients' names and locations places the work in the here and now of the tangible world. The effect of the second book is not unlike that of Kees Boeke's *Cosmic View: The Universe in Forty Jumps*, which in forty "jumps" take a reader from a woman sitting in a chair with a baby in her arms to outer space, 2 billion light years away.[32] By putting the project directly in the hands of her influential intended recipients, Piper utilized one of the significant strengths of artists' books, which is to extend works of art to people—domestically and internationally—who might not otherwise see the work in a gallery setting.

In the remaining months of 1969 and through 1970, Piper's work was featured in some of the earliest and most important international exhibitions of Conceptual art, including *Language III*, at Dwan Gallery, New York; *557,087*, organized by Lucy Lippard, at the Seattle Art Museum Pavilion; *Konzeption/Conception: Dokumentation einer heutigen Kunstrichtung/Documentation of To-day's Art Tendency*, organized by Rolf Wedewer and Konrad Fischer, at Stadtisches Museum, Leverkusen, Germany; *955,000*, Lippard's expanded and updated version of her earlier exhibition, at Vancouver Art Gallery; *Art in the Mind*, organized by Athena Tacha Spear, at the Allen Memorial Art Museum, Oberlin College, Ohio; *Conceptual Art and Conceptual Aspects,* organized by Kosuth and Donald Karshan, at New York Cultural Center; and *Information*, Kynaston McShine's curatorial opus, at The Museum of Modern Art, New York. In all of these shows Piper would be one of only a handful of women, the only African American, and, with only two exceptions in the *Information* exhibition, the youngest artist in each of the exhibitions.[33]

Almost all of these shows were accompanied by catalogues that provided the artists with pages to be used as additional project space. Concurrent with *Number 7*, at Paula Cooper Gallery (May 18–June 15, 1969), and *Language III*, at Dwan Gallery (May 24–June 18, 1969), Piper independently produced *Untitled ("The area described by the periphery of this ad . . .")/ Area Relocation Series #2* (page 171), a newspaper-page project that appeared on the Galleries page of the May 29 issue of the *Village Voice*, alongside traditional advertisements for exhibitions at Leo Castelli, Paula Cooper, Judson, Howard Wise, and other galleries. Piper's artwork for the page—small, unadorned typewritten text held within the confines of a ruled rectangular box—read,

> The area described by
> the periphery of this
> ad has been relocated
> from Sheridan Square
> New York, N.Y.
> to (your address).
> —area relocation #2
> A. Piper

As an artwork hiding in plain sight, "the newspaper project" logically took Piper's concerns with relocations of space and applied them to a vastly larger venue, via the sheer scale of distribution of the *Village Voice*, whose weekly combined New York City, domestic, and international circulation of more than 130,000 copies constituted an audience vastly larger than a week's worth of regular gallery-goers or visitors to MoMA.[34] While Piper was not the first to deploy mass-market periodicals as an alternative space to show artwork—Dan Graham and Stephen Kaltenbach had been among the pioneers of artworks crafted for advertising space, in 1968—her work appeared only shortly after theirs and proved just as adept in occupying its new environment, outside the narrow confines of the art world's well-demarcated spaces and limited (predominantly white, middle-class) audience, to reach those who would not travel in any case to see physical exhibitions.[35]

Defining Context

With her *Context* works, Piper made a significant shift, from the model of art made under the sole authorship of an artist for passive consumption by an audience to one of works that not only invited audience participation but demanded it, as an external means of creation. In the *Context* works, the actions of others lent the art its content and material substance, without any filter on the part of the artist. The works were operating, in fact, as living objects. *Context #6* began its life as four pages in the *Art in the Mind* exhibition catalogue. The first page reads,

> I AM COLLECTING INFORMATION
>
> You are requested to
>
> 1) write, draw, or otherwise indicate any information suggested by the above statement on the following pages;
>
> 2) detach pages at perforation and mail to
>
> Adrian Piper
> 117 Hester Street
> New York, N.Y. 10002

The ensuing three leaves are labeled "context #6" at the top-left corner and have a line of faux perforations running down the left edge of each sheet. Thus, anyone willing to remove the pages from the publication would be directly collaborating with the artist to finish the piece, an action without which the work could not exist. In a vacuum, without such contingent participation, the work would not be activated, would not become an object responsive to its context.

Piper's contribution to the show perfectly mirrored Spear's original invitation to each participant:

> In the last couple of years a new kind of art—"idea" art—has developed alongside painting and sculpture, we feel that the limitations of an exhibition [of painting and sculpture] (in fact the limitations of a visual arts museum altogether) prevent us from showing to our students an important part of the present art scene. The work of a great number of good young artists is no longer exhibitable. Therefore, we have decided to have . . . an "imaginary" exhibition, *Art in the Mind*. A number of artists who are working in this new direction are being invited to send work which can adequately be described on typewriter size paper and xeroxed in any number of copies. The work could be grouped under such categories as these: conceptual art; language art; projects for street works; projects for ecological art; project for space art.[36]

In *Context #7*, for the *Information* show, Piper used a similar tactic, situating it as a dynamic, living, growing component of the exhibition. A text, mounted above a table where a three-ring binder filled with unprinted pages rested, read,

> You (the viewer) are requested to write, draw, or otherwise indicate any response suggested by this situation (this statement, the blank notebook and pen, the museum context, your immediate state of mind, etc.) in the pages of this notebook beneath this sign.
>
> The information entered in the notebook will not be altered or utilized in any way.

Set between an enlargement of Andy Warhol's infamous quote, published in the exhibition catalogue for his 1968 Moderna Museet show, "In the future everybody will be world famous for fifteen minutes" and a table holding Andre's *Seven Books of Poetry* (1969), *Context #7* changed throughout the exhibition's eighty-day run **(fig. 8)**.[37] As suggested by the title, it was the context that gave shape to the work, as visitors added their multiplicity of responses. The lethal war in Vietnam, the invasion of Cambodia, President Richard Nixon, MoMA, music, drugs, sexuality, *Information* itself—whatever was pertinent to viewers as they encountered this work among the others in the exhibition—all came in for comment on the binder's accumulating pages, ultimately filling 1,903 pages in seven binders with critical, funny, heartfelt, profane, sarcastic, silly, and politically piercing responses, thus completing Piper's artwork **(pages 176, 177)**. As an open and unfiltered system for the contributions of viewers, *Context #7*, as well as the other *Context* works, differed substantially from projects that entailed artists soliciting, editing, and compiling works by other artists, such as Bochner's *Working Drawings and Other Visible Things on Paper Not Necessarily Meant to Be Viewed as Art* (1966) **(fig. 9)**, also presented in plain black three-ring binders, or, indeed, the staple-bound volumes of *0 TO 9*.[38] As works whose times and locations were the perpetual indexical present of each viewer, the Context series unmistakably shared elements with Piper's preceding works; their substantial departure was the addition of active participation by viewers, each of whom recognizes their own present differently. The relaying of time and space, as reflected in Piper's introductory text, is a particularly lucid demonstration of this ideal.

The politically charged atmosphere of 1970s New York did not escape Piper's notice, but it was not only city and national politics that interested her; she was also involved with the Art Workers' Coalition (AWC), which attempted to turn the attention of artists, cultural workers, and art institutions to the exclusionary practices of the art world. At protests at the city's three major museums—MoMA, the Whitney Museum of American Art, and the Metropolitan Museum of Art—and an "opening hearing," held in the SVA auditorium on April 10, 1969, AWC members demanded the presence of people of color and women on boards of trustees, the ceding to artists of sacrosanct institutional control over the acquisition, display, and programming of art, and the elimination of paid admission. Every speech at the open hearing called for greater cooperation, responsibility, and transparency on the part of the museums.[39] This broadest possible framing of an all-inclusive community of artists and cultural institutions—MoMA in particular—would be sustained explicitly by these actions.

In this period of increasing discord, Piper withdrew her work from *Conceptual Art and Conceptual Aspects*, at the New York Cultural Center, in August of that year. Instead, she produced a statement, multiple drafts of which are contained in *Context #9*, to draw attention to the conditions beyond the limited, hermetic framework of the art world:

> The work originally intended for this space has been withdrawn. The decision to withdraw has been taken as a proactive measure against the increasingly pervasive conditions of fear. Rather than submit the work to the deadly and poisoning influence of these conditions, I submit its absence as evidence of the conditions other than those of peace, equality, truth, trust and freedom.

The Artist's Body in Public Spaces

In the spring of 1970 Piper made another paradigm shift, moving her practice off the static surface of sheets of paper and turning instead to performance, to identifying her body as a structural object among people, places, other objects, and the construct of time. The opportunity to actualize this shift was Hannah Weiner's invitation to participate, along with thirteen other artists, in *The Saturday Afternoon Show*, an offshoot of the *Street Works* projects, this time held indoors at Max's Kansas City, a popular art-world hangout, on May 2, 1970, between 2 and 3 p.m.[40] Amid a cacophony of simultaneous performative works, Piper enacted *Untitled Performance at Max's Kansas City* (pages 178, 179), a performance inspired conceptually by the *Hypothesis* works.[41]

In a sequence of photographs taken that day by Rosemary Mayer, we see Piper wearing a blindfold, a nose clip, wadded earplugs, a pair of long gloves over the long sleeves of

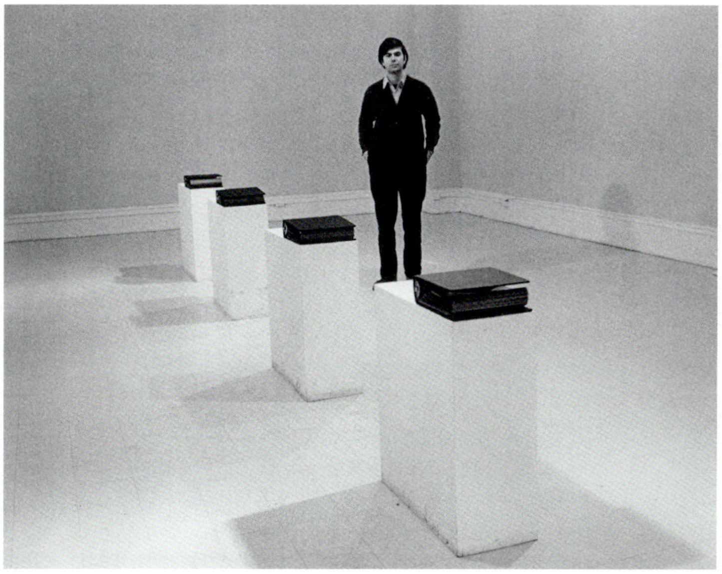

Fig. 9
Mel Bochner
Working Drawings and Other Visible Things on Paper Not Necessarily Meant to Be Viewed as Art. 1966
Four identical loose-leaf notebooks, each with one hundred Xeroxed copies of studio notes, working drawings, and diagrams collected and Xeroxed by the artist, displayed on four sculpture stands
Each notebook 11¾ × 11½ × 3⅛ in. (29.8 × 29.2 × 7.9 cm)
Installation view at *Working Drawings and Other Visible Things on Paper Not Necessarily Meant to Be Viewed as Art*, School of Visual Arts, New York, December 2–23, 1966
The Museum of Modern Art, New York. Gift of Dr. Kuo Yu-Shou (by exchange), Jill and Peter Kraus and Committee on Drawings Fund in honor of Connie Butler

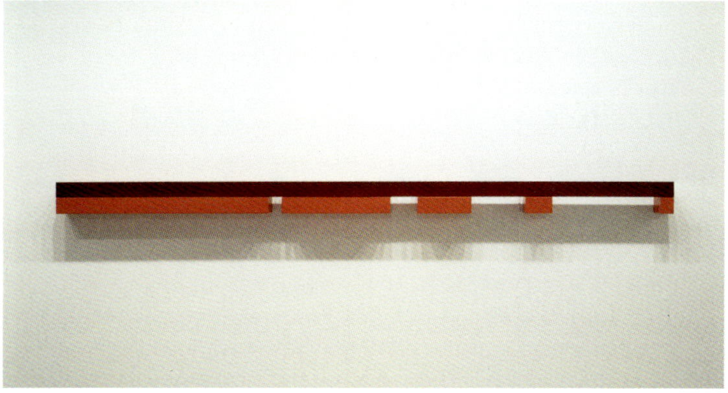

Fig. 10
Donald Judd
Untitled (Progression). 1965
Lacquer and enamel on aluminum
8¼ in. × 13 ft. 5in. × 8¼ in (20.9 × 408 × 20.9 cm)
The Ohio State University, Columbus. Courtesy Wexner Center for the Arts

a sweatshirt, and knee-high boots into which her pants are stuffed.[42] She circulates through the restaurant, passing groups of men and women sitting at tables and at the bar, who watch her and the photographer—who should be considered part of the action—with confused expressions. Piper advances blindly through the narrow confines of the bar and walks unguided into a service area, past two racks of glassware. Mayer, the embodiment of the camera, trails alongside Piper, capturing thin slices of time, measured in fractions of a second during the one-hour performance. In a remarkable juxtaposition, two of the photographs show, in the background, an equally lonely and awkwardly sited artwork, Judd's first Progression work (fig. 10), mounted on one of the restaurant's walls.[43]

Perreault wrote a lengthy account of the show in the *Village Voice*, taking note of both the successes and some of the amusing misfires:

> As far as I can report it, what happened was this. Vito Acconci, formerly Vito Hannibal Acconci, sat in a booth and rubbed his arm for one hour, causing a large red blotch to appear, which incidentally although photographed on the hour has not yet healed (see page 19). The image generated by this activity was not without overt references to masturbation, a practice [formerly] thought to lead to moronism. . . . Eduardo Costa, who was absent because of illness, arranged for the notorious Mr. T. and a friend to have dinner at Max's, thus continuing his interest in socially useful art works. (A practice more artists should be engaged in.) Ira Joel Haber played the same record over and over again on the juke box: "Let's Spend the Night Together" by the [Rolling] Stones, altering the environment in a non-visual but clearly perceptible (audible) way. Deborah Hay drank one glass of red wine in slow motion for an entire hour. Stephen Kaltenbach and Frank Owen tried to set up a string of very bright lights, but their collaboration became a piece about fuses and fuse boxes because the lights kept blowing out all the fuses. Abraham Lubelski had himself and his wife and his two children filmed while eating dinner. Scott Burton did not do the brilliant work he had originally planned. Hannah Weiner read aloud the official instructions to waitresses at Max's. Paul Pechter installed one of his permanent installations by discreetly drilling a hole in the floor and then plugging it up with a piece of lead. Adrian Piper plugged her ears and nose and shielded her eyes and wandered around the place for an hour, bumping into people, being bumped into, and creating a startling image. (I thought that a good piece would be not to tell her when three o'clock finally arrived. Ira Joel Haber announced that he had turned Adrian Piper into an illustration because at one point when she was stumbling around—quite beautifully—the sound to her sight, via juke box, was the Who's "Touch Me" from "Tommy.")[44]

Piper expressed to Mayer her frustrations with the event, which Mayer recorded in a postcard to her sister: "Adrian was blindfolded, nose & ear stoppered. But she wasn't happy bcs. she thought she didn't bump into enough people."[45] "I didn't like the idea that most everyone seemed to have been sitting down watching the performance instead of milling around at Max's as they usually do," Piper told the curator and art historian John Bowles. "I remember feeling a bit frustrated that I'd designed the piece for a bar but unbeknownst to me the bar had turned

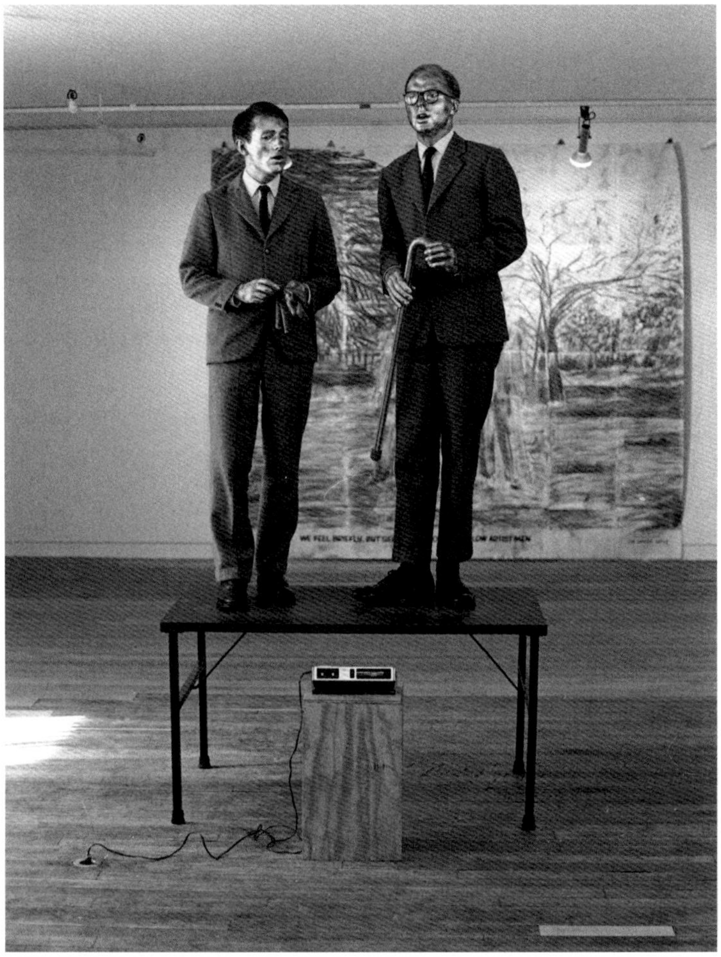

Fig. 11
Gilbert & George
The Singing Sculpture. 1969
Performance view at Sonnabend Gallery, New York, September 25–October 8, 1971

into a stage."[46] Because the performance took place on an early Saturday afternoon, in the lull between gallery hopping and that evening's openings and parties, the images of that day's performances reflect a lightly populated bar with viewers largely inattentive to the actions of *The Saturday Afternoon Show* happening around them.

A year before Gilbert & George would premiere *The Singing Sculpture* (fig. 11) in the United States, *Untitled Performance at Max's Kansas City* anticipated the concerns about objectification and the nature of self that the British artists would flatfootedly put forward.[47] Gilbert & George defined their unification as consisting of two people but a single artist, asking to be considered "living sculptures"—sculpture being, for them, the highest form of art. After her performance at Max's Kansas City, Piper defined a starting place for her *Catalysis* works with characteristic clarity: "I was thinking here more and more about myself as a three-dimensional object, and I was interested in exploring the difference between human objects, that is, objects that have subjectivity, and other kinds of objects that do not, other kinds of nonsentient objects."[48] Thus, she brokers a contrast between the Judd on the wall and the Piper within the walls of the restaurant—or indeed the Piper in the broader indices of the tangible world. *Untitled Performance at Max's Kansas City* can also be understood as a structured engagement with alienation from the artist's surroundings. This, in turn, suggests an external realization of an interior experience: removing herself from all points of contact with her surroundings, while simultaneously walling off everyone around her from seeing her as unique living being rather than an object to be observed.

The title of Piper's *Catalysis* works evokes the step in a scientific experiment when a chemical is added to a secondary body to bring about a complex physical reaction—the artist as the pinch of salt dropped in a pot of water on a stove to accelerate boiling: Piper, in these works, activating her body and personal space. In *Catalysis III* (August 1970) (page 180) she wore a hand-painted "WET PAINT" sign and clothing coated with sticky white paint to walk past throngs of shoppers on Fourteenth Street, provoking confused and chagrined stares from passersby, as seen in the photographs taken by Rosemary Mayer.[49] The next catalytic situation was *Catalysis IV* (1970) (page 181), for which she "dressed very conservatively, but stuffed a large red bath towel into the sides of my mouth until my cheeks bulged to about twice their normal size, letting the rest of it hang down my front, and riding the bus, subway, and Empire State Building elevator."[50] In five photographs by Mayer, we see women surrounding Piper on a bus, averting their gaze from her. In only one frame does a fellow passenger look directly at Piper, with a somber and disdainful glare.

Part of Piper's intent for the *Catalysis* works was to craft circumstances that would allow her to interact with the public without the public identifying the interaction as an artwork. If the patrons at Max's Kansas City encountering *The Saturday Afternoon Show* were aware that what was happening around them was art—too aware, perhaps, to react or even notice—then moving out into a public sphere, away from such a knowing and jaded audience, had the potential to catalyze a greater reaction. There is no photographic documentation of Piper's other *Catalysis* works, but they may have been even more provocative. Perreault has described performances in which Piper would "appear in various bookstores smeared with smelly grease . . . sit in libraries with a concealed tape recording of consistent burping. I'm sure any man with male chauvinist pig designs on her would be repulsed as soon as he came within striking distance."[51] On the sidewalk or in a bus, bookstore, department store, or library, Piper sought out reactive environments and situations in which passersby would not recognize that they had become active participants in these performances, while Piper witnessed the results like a scientist watching the bubbles in a test tube. In the *Catalysis* works Piper recognized, as she had with her projects for publications, the restrictions of the gallery exhibition and of the art world, populated as it was by people in the know. That closed world created an echo chamber that constrained the possibilities for artistic engagement and experimentation, limiting them to what might be presented within a conceptualized art-world context, compared with the boundless access, experiences, and opportunities offered by performing in public.

Beyond making art on the graph paper–like grid of New York City streets, in the *Catalysis* works Piper, as the catalyst, created the conditions inhabited by an outcast or social pariah, thus compelling viewers to deal with their fear of an individual utterly unlike themselves, whatever their own gender or race. But Piper was also pushing against different boundaries, something more like those found in Michael Fried's controversial essay "Art and Objecthood," which had appeared in the Summer 1967 issue of *Artforum*.[52] Fried argued that an individual's reaction to Minimalism—to works of sculpture in particular—could only be subjective, because the work offers no discernable narrative qualities: "The answer I want to propose is this: the literalist espousal of objecthood amounts to nothing other than a plea for a new genre of theatre; and theatre is now the negation of art. Literalist sensibility is theatrical because, to begin with, it is concerned with the actual circumstances in which the beholder encounters literalist work." In the *Catalysis* works Piper broke free of this quandary by activating the space around her, turning herself into the catalytic agent for the public to respond to, and superseding the dominance of Minimalist sculptural icons by inserting the human form as a theatrical object to be reconsidered.[53] Fried postulates that viewers must project substance onto anti-illusionist objects—that is, to clothe artworks in a skin to give them meaning; Piper, in the *Catalysis* works, inanimated herself, changing her outward appearance in order to guise herself as a contrary object, a disruptive element onto which spectators could cast interpretations.

Objecthood and Objectivity

Piper's exploration of other means of researching art and objecthood intensified in the summer of 1970. By herself, in her Hester Street loft, she was deeply engaged in a work of profound introspection that formed a diametric contrast with her very public *Catalysis* activities. In both *Concrete Infinity Documentation Piece* (1970) (pages 182–85) and *Food for the Spirit* (1971) (pages 186–93) she systematically deconstructed the study of her body as a material object, although she did so in ways that could not be actualized outside of these "private loft performances." The works are different in format and presentation, but for both of them Piper photographed herself in the same dark, static location, looking at herself head-on in a mirror while holding a Kodak Hawkeye Instamatic R4 camera. The camera was the performances' only witness, recording the artist from her knees to just above her head, in various states of dress, from fully clothed to nude. When she first presented these works, in the Spring 1981 issue of *High Performance*, she titled the essay "Food for the Spirit July 1971," but the four images published with it were drawn from *Concrete Infinity Documentation Piece*.[54] What separates the two performances is a year, the different bodies of texts associated with each work, the different performances that occasioned and are documented in each, the different visual qualities of the images, the string suspending her camera in the former work but not in the latter, and the artist's frame of mind as she produced each one.

In *Concrete Infinity Documentation Piece*, which began on June 1 and concluded on July 7, 1970, Piper recorded a series of neutral facts about her physical state over fifty-six sheets of graph paper. Each sheet that marks a day has a black-and-white photograph of the artist affixed to its top-right corner, a hand-written date above the image, and, in her neat handwriting, a single day's documentary details, composed according to style guidelines on a fifty-seventh sheet, which bears the heading "Object Maintenance":

> Write everything I do. Temp & weight on rising
> & going to bed. Picture once a day.
>
> No subject
> One verb/sentence
> No incoming information, environmental
> conditions, sensory input (saw, heard, smelled,
> touched, tasted)
>
> *Ate*: O.K. *Read*: O.K.
>
> Restrict content whenever possible.

By excluding all external conditions from her documentation, Piper recorded only objective truths. On June 1 she photographed herself wearing only underwear and a blank expression, and then proceeded to document what the object Adrian Piper had done that day, without subjectivity, thus divorcing her mind from her body:

> Got up at 6am. Weighed 99 lbs. Ate three teaspoons of soya lecithin. Drank a glass of orange juice mixed with rice polish, yeast, and bone meal. Swallowed a teaspoon of cod liver oil, and a teaspoon of wheat germ oil. Turned on radio to WNCN. Washed up. Swallowed one multiple vitamin, two B-complex and C vitamins, eight amino acid pills. Drank a glass of Te Kuanyin tea. Made bed. Shat. Brushed hair. Took picture. Got dressed. Listened to "Medical Week". Turned off radio. Wrote in diary. Crammed for Astronomy final. Turned on news. Peed. Drank a glass of Guo Jing tea with lemon. Brushed teeth. Crammed for astronomy final. Washed glass. Shat and peed. Crammed for Astronomy final. Retyped raw page. Peed. Weighed 98lbs. Crammed for astronomy final. Went down to grocery, collected mail, bought grapefruit juice, talked to Mrs. Brumer. Came back to upstairs. Opened mail. Drank a glass of rosehips tea. Called Dwan Gallery. Called Vito Acconci. Brushed teeth. Crammed for Astronomy final. Ate a bowl of cottage cheese mixed with soya granules. Washed bowl. Drank a glass of kelp and onion broth. Washed glass and spoon. Spoke to Vito Acconci on the phone. Crammed for Astronomy final. Peed and shat. Changed clothes. Called Dwan Gallery. Washed up. Called Vito Acconci. Turned on radio. Left house with "Context #8" piece. Met Vito Acconci on the subway. Went up to Dwan gallery. Spoke to superintendent. Spoke to freight elevator man. Went to coffee shop. Drank a glass of ice tea with lemon. Went to first stationary store. Went to second stationary store. Wrote three drafts of a note to Kay Epstein. Helped Vito Acconci draw instructions on his piece. Helped Vito Acconci wrap both pieces. Walked with Vito Acconci back to gallery building. Took subway downtown with Vito Acconci. Continued downtown to Grand St. station. Returned home. Took off clothes. Peed. Weighed 98 lbs. Turned off radio. Washed up. Ate two tablespoonfuls of wheatgerm. Drank seed papaya fruit water. Crammed for Astronomy final. Washed spoons, glass jar. Did exercises. Watched news. Peed. Drank seaweed and onion soup. Washed glass. Drank broccoli and parsley soup. Washed glass. Ate three teaspoons rice polish. Drank a glass of black lichee tea. Washed glass. Drank a glass of bouillon. Turned off TV. Brushed teeth. Watched sunset. Crammed for Astronomy final. Swallowed eight amino acid pills. Crammed for Astronomy final. Washed glass. Fixed light cord. Peed. Brushed teeth. Crammed for Astronomy final. Peed. Weighed 101 lbs. Drank a glass of Te Kuanyin Tea with lemon. Brushed hair. Crammed for Astronomy final. Took phone off hook. Crammed for Astronomy final. Washed glass. Sipped orange and grapefruit juice. Washed up. Brushed teeth. Peed. Weighed 100. Went to bed at 10:40. Body temperature: 91.5 F

When Piper made this stripped-down work, she was engrossed in her studies at the City College of New York, where she had been pursuing a degree in philosophy, with a minor in medieval and Renaissance musicology, since 1970.[55] The work's title makes clear that Piper was extending her *Concrete Infinity* works of 1968, including *Concrete Infinity 6-inch Square ["This square should be read as a whole . . ."]* (page 153) and *Concrete 8" Square ["The sides of this square measure 8" . . ."]* (page 152), which both used pure language to self-referentially build the typewritten form of the area defined by its own description, thus documenting itself "simultaneously to this abstract system."[56] Here she turned herself, a specific object, into part of a logical system in much the same way as in the *Concrete Infinity* works, with language and numerical measuring systems—by defining the contours of what an object *is* without providing the inner workings that take place behind the sheet of paper or the artist's internal monologue. This, too, draws on the dichotomy between two states of being, as in Plato's Allegory of the Cave: the idealized object is but a shadow made by the complex qualities that provide an actual object with material substance.

In the following year Piper's philosophical work and personal artistic investigations into the nature of selfhood accelerated dramatically. Encouraged by her best friend, Phillip Zohn, Piper embarked on what would become an ongoing obsessive professional study of Immanuel Kant's profound *Critique of Pure Reason*, the work that eventually led to her doctorate in philosophy, at Harvard University, in 1981.[57] It was this work, too, that in July 1971 led Piper back to the ideas she had explored in *Concrete Infinity Documentation Piece*, this time in an even more austere format. Throughout that hot month, she became deeply and intensely engaged in *Critique of Pure Reason*, losing herself in its complexities. She took breaks only for yoga or to leave her loft for groceries or meditative walks. She saw no friends during this time, and depended on juice and water alone for corporeal nourishment. As she slipped deeper into the book, Piper has recalled, "I thought I was losing my mind, in fact losing my sense of self completely."[58]

Food for the Spirit came into existence in this moment of crisis, in order to "anchor [herself] in the physical world."[59] Over the course of the summer, in the same place in her loft where she had taken the photographs for *Concrete Infinity Documentation Piece*, Piper photographed a sequence of fourteen black-and-white images showing herself, again, in various states of dress and undress. In each image, the bottom of the frame cuts across Piper's knees, and her head is set almost dead center, surrounded by shadowy details of the loft. A backlit window, with frosted safety glass and security bars, is clearly visible to the left of the artist in the first four images; in the rest of the sequence it fades in and out of the darkness, suggesting that the latter photographs were taken at night. In some of the better-lit images, we can make out a large metal bracket with a wire dangling from it, just to the right of the mirror at almost the same height as Piper's head. In only one image, the second in the sequence, which appears to be illuminated by a light near the ceiling and by daylight filtered through the window, is a fully packed bookshelf visible, reflected in the mirror behind Piper. In all of the images, as in *Concrete Infinity Documentation Piece*, Piper's face in the mirror is emotionless, and her camera, held with both hands, is positioned at her torso's midpoint. Throughout the sequence, the photographs become incrementally darker and denser, pulling the artist into their shadowy depths. Space, time, and seriality are the overriding thematic thread, materialized as sequential self-documentation by images, in *Food for the Spirit*, and in written record, in *Concrete Infinity Documentation Piece*.

Food for the Spirit's first public presentation, in 1987, included the photographs, a black three-ring binder with pages torn from Piper's edition of Norman Kemp Smith's 1929 translation of the *Critique of Pure Reason*, with her handwritten marginalia inscribed in ink, contained in plastic sleeves and 16 by 20–inch (40.6 by 50.8–cm) "photodocumentation for performance photograph," as well as commentary on the work that Piper had written and published in *High Performance*. A set of smaller photographs, perhaps printed at a drugstore, are interspersed among the pages of Kant and commentary in the binder.[60] (An audio tape, later recorded over and thus destroyed, was also part of the original work in which Piper recorded herself "repeating the passage in the *Critique* that was currently driving me to self-transcendence.")[61]

"I have always had a strong mystical streak," Piper wrote, in a text accompanying the work's first public exhibition, in 1987.[62] Of her physical self becoming a kind of apparition in her own mind, she said, she believed she may have been "abdicating my individual self on every level, becoming Kant's analysis of Transcendental Unity of Apperception in the Synthesis of Appearances according to the Rules Given by the Understanding for Reflective Self-Consciousness."[63] If in *Concrete Infinity Documentation Piece* Piper was focused on strictly describing herself as a resolutely impersonal object, lacking internal dialogue processing the thoughts behind her physical actions, in *Food for the Spirit* she turned her attention to the unity of her body and mind, with all that unity's inherent conflicts, which she sought to reconcile under the gaze of Kant.

Deepening Contexts

LeWitt lived a few floors below Piper, on Hester Street. He was twenty years and nine days older than Piper, but they were good friends, a relationship based on respect for each other's art, ideas, musical interests, and, no doubt, their fastidious Virgo personalities. In May 1969 Piper assisted with the execution of LeWitt's *Wall Drawing 11: A wall divided horizontally and vertically into four equal parts. Within each part, three of the four kinds of lines are superimposed.*, for Paula Cooper's *Number 7* exhibition, and two additional drawings on large, white-painted aluminum boxes at Dwan Gallery in September of the same year.[64]

Conceptual art was frequently chastised in the 1960s and '70s for what was perceived as a lack of humanistic interest, for the distillation of pure information into pseudoscience for misguided philosophical ends.[65] The removal of the self from the art object was understood not just as a dematerialization of the materiality of art but also as a negation of the artist's hand and the human qualities of pure beauty, form, and substance that had traditionally been expected of an artwork. Even some of the artists included under the rubric of Conceptual art—both at the time and retrospectively—were critical of it, such as Lee Lozano, who in the first of her private diaries jotted down,

> Kosuth's art it seems to me is more about words than it is about ideas. The words he picks have already been explored (e.g. "Abstract" (N.Y.C. Art), "Water," "Positive," "Negative" (science), or a quote directly from Warhol). The objects he hangs his words on are too close to paintings to be revolutionary. Aside from dumping the objects entirely, possibly the only interesting way he could go would be for him to find some brand new words, words that relate to the art of the *future*, or even to invent some words of his own.[66]

Kosuth did not hesitate to praise the work of Piper and others for their "development in a purer form of 'conceptual art,'" while at the same time he called out artists such as Baldessari and Bochner, whose work did not align with his own ideals.[67]

It would be myopic to say that the Conceptual artists sought to scrub their work of aesthetics and humanity, or to hew only to objective ideals of quality. The work of Piper, Acconci, Bas Jan Ader, Eleanor Antin, Hans Haacke, Huebler, Martha Rosler, and other first-generation conceptualists recognized the interconnections between artist, objecthood, and the ingrained social contract, and considered them elemental material conditions in their practices.[68]

In LeWitt's loft resided a sculptural object that resonated with his interest with the human body and systems. *Muybridge I*

(Schematic Representation) (1964), a long rectangular black-painted wooden box could be mistaken for a Minimalist work, but for a power cord that dangled from where it was mounted on the wall with ten evenly spaced small holes drilled in its front. When the work was switched on, the holes revealed ten illuminated interior spaces, each one independently flashing at random, one second on and a quarter second off, flickering like the shutter of a movie projector.[69] By putting an eye to each hole, a viewer could see that the work's stark exterior belied what was inside: ten black-and-white photographs of a nude woman against a black background, appearing to walk closer to the viewer (or to the photographer, Barbara Brown, who shot the images of an anonymous model) with each successive viewing hole, from a substantial distance away to close enough that the frame is filled by the area surrounding the model's belly button (fig. 12).[70]

As is noted in the work's title, LeWitt's piece is an homage to Eadweard Muybridge, the British photographer who, in the 1870s, used multiple cameras to document human and animal locomotion, including similar series showing men and women walking. LeWitt later wrote,

> The work of Eadweard Muybridge has had a great impact on my thinking. This piece was done after some years of thought and experimentation and was the source of much of the serial work. At this time there was a search for a more objective method of organization as a reaction against the idea that art was composed with great sensitivity by the artist throughout the production of the work. This reaction eventually led to a theory of art that offered the idea that the original conception (perhaps intuition) of the work of art was of primary importance; the work would be carried through without deviation. It proposed the notion of the artist as a thinker and originator of ideas rather than a craftsman.[71]

Muybridge I (Schematic Representation) was one of LeWitt's earliest pieces featuring modular, serial objects, a stepping-stone toward *46 Three-Part Variations on 3 Different Kinds of Cubes*.

Where LeWitt's work is open to subjective readings—a reconfiguration of Muybridge images for new audiences, a prurient peep show—*Food for the Spirit* was conceived not for an audience but for the artist herself, and can be understood objectively, as a work reflecting Piper as she was at a fixed moment in time and space. While in Muybridge's and LeWitt's works the movement of time is based on or communicated by the forward motion of models over a few seconds, for Piper's it is the variables of light that relay the passing of time.

What Do You Represent and How Do You Represent It?
From 1946 to 1961, periodicals such as *P.M.*, *Art News*, and others ran a comic strip by Ad Reinhardt called "How to Look" (fig. 13). In a panel that appears in many of its iterations, a simply drawn man, wearing a hat, points at a rectangular abstract painting. To the right of his head, representing either his thoughts or voice, a text reads, "Ha ha what does this represent?" Directly below this, we see that the painting has sprouted legs, a scowling face, narrowed eyes, a comically large nose, and an arm and finger pointing back at the man with enough force to throw him off balance, sending his hat flying off his head. Shocked, he falls backward, as the painting responds, "What do you represent?"[72]

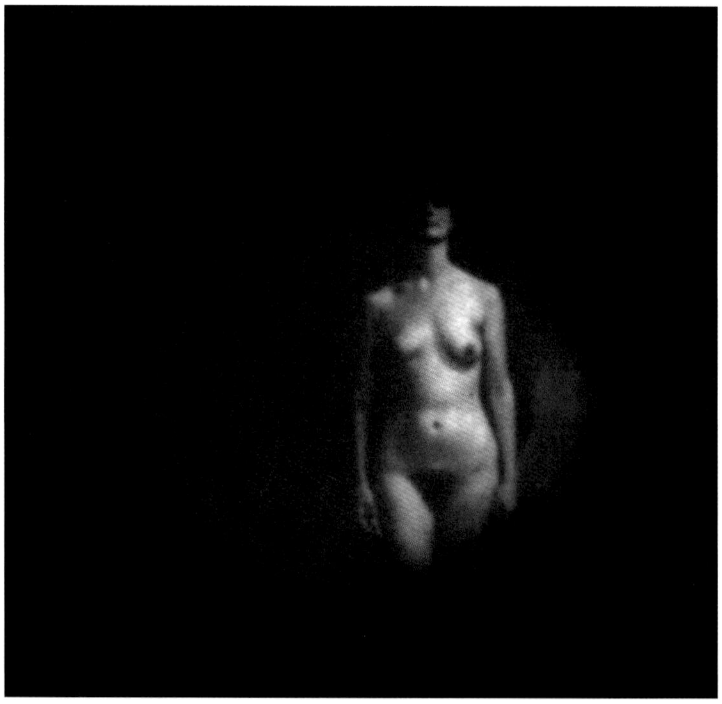

Fig. 12
Sol LeWitt
Muybridge I (Schematic Representation). 1964
Painted wood with ten compartments containing photographs by Barbara Brown and flashing lights
Each compartment 10⅝ in. × 8 ft. ¼ in. × 9-½ in. (26.9 × 244 × 24.1 cm)
LeWitt Collection, Chester, Connecticut
Detail: photograph by Barbara Brown as seen through drilled hole

From the LSD works, which transformed the possibility for transcendent experience into palpable, vivid drawings and paintings, to *Food for the Spirit*, which recognizes the image of the artist—not unlike Reinhardt's reactive painting—as a responsive object with a specific objective, the trajectory of Piper's work has been unwavering. Using systems, permutations within sequences, and rational, serial confrontations with the indexical present, Piper has incrementally and logically—and uniquely among her peers—advanced a holistic pattern of system-based art, intricately balancing, as she did with *The Barbie Doll Drawings*, what can be seen and knowingly categorized with the proposition that there also exists a plane that can only be understood through intuitive logic. *Meat into Meat* and the *Context* works deftly applied new gravity to this pattern by adding the agency of other parties, an element of controlled but ultimately unpredictable chance. With *Untitled Performance at Max's Kansas City* and then the *Catalysis* performances, Piper introduced herself as a specific object, to be considered rationally, as one would analyze a mathematical formula—as an integral, integrated, structural component in the artwork, rather than a person. Where *Concrete 8" Square ["The sides of this square measure 8" . . ."]* is comprehended through a set pattern of math and a vocabulary of definitional language, *Untitled Performance at Max's Kansas City* and the *Catalysis* works use photographic images to reflect the way time and space may be defined as durational units that can only exist within a fixed logical construct.

Concrete Infinity Documentation Piece and *Food for the Spirit* build from the same roots. In each, Piper materializes and forefronts herself, questioning the constraints of what can be ascertained through objective facts. From a more distant perspective, one pulled even farther from the vagaries and misinterpretations we bring to photographic images of people other than ourselves, she becomes an infinitely changeable variation on a cube, a catalyzing agent—an element of a larger system that comes into definition the farther back we step.

Like Reinhardt's angry painting, Piper's work inverts the role of the viewer from passive recipient to engaged participant. Using conceptualist tools as an extended arm and pointed finger, Piper tested the environment for the creation of work that went beyond the constraining conditions and traditional narratives of the art that had come before her, and in doing so she solidified a framework for the works that would follow.

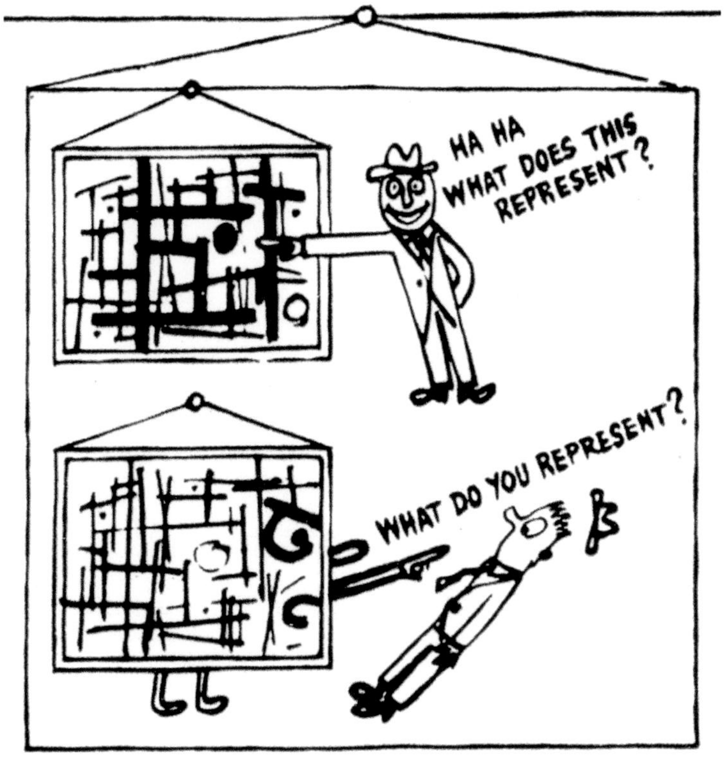

Fig. 13
Ad Reinhardt's comic "How to Look" (detail), published in *P.M.* magazine, May 12, 1946

1. When Adrian Piper first entered New Lincoln School, it was located at 31 West 110 Street. In 1956 the school's lower division relocated to 6 East 82 Street.

2. The exhibition *Sol LeWitt: 46 Three-Part Variations on 3 Different Kinds of Cubes* took place at Dwan Gallery, New York, February 3–28, 1968.

3. Piper, "Talking to Myself: The Autobiography of an Art Object," 1970–73, in Piper, *Out of Order, Out of Sight*, vol. 1, *Selected Writings in Meta-Art, 1968–1992* (Cambridge, Mass.: MIT Press, 1996), pp. 29–30.

4. LeWitt, "Paragraphs on Conceptual Art," *Artforum* 5, no. 10 (Summer 1967): 79–83. In a footnote to "My Art Education," an essay from 1968, Piper takes issue with some of LeWitt's precepts as expressed in his "Sentences on Conceptual Art": "Although I concur with him in thinking that the form chosen should not be governed by one's subjective tastes concerning 'what looks well,' I think also one's decision as to form merits a great deal of consideration as to that form which most clearly realizes the original idea." Piper, "My Art Education," 1968, in *Out of Order, Out of Sight*, vol. 1, p. 4n3. See also Piper, "Personal Chronology" on p. 315 of this volume.

5. Piper, in Matteo Guarnaccia, "Tele dal gusto acido all scoperta alla realtà," *Alias (Il manifesto)* 6, no. 14 (April 5, 2003): 4–5. English translation as "Interview with Adrian Piper," Adrian Piper Research Archive Foundation Berlin (APRA) website, adrianpiper.com/art/Over_the_Edge/interview.shtml.

6. Ibid.

7. See Mel Bochner, "Serial Art, Systems, Solipsism," *Arts Magazine* 41, no. 8 (Summer 1967): 39–43. The definition is from Webster's New International Dictionary of the English Language: Second Edition (Springfield, Mass.: G. & C. Merriam, 1937), p. 2,395. It concludes, "Kant used the term ethically, to denote pure self-seeking; but this usage is rare in English."

8. Piper, "Talking to Myself," p. 51.

9. It should be noted that the title of this work, *The Barbie Doll Drawings*, was not given by Piper but by one of her assistants, during cataloguing. This title misleads: the dolls depicted are not Barbie dolls but imagined dolls that do not at all resemble the Barbie line produced by Mattel. Piper did not title the drawings at the time of their execution.

10. Donald Judd, "Specific Objects," in William Chapin Seitz, ed., *Contemporary Sculpture: Arts Yearbook 8* (New York: Art Digest, 1965), pp. 74–82.

11. Piper, "A Defense of the 'Conceptual' Process in Art," 1967, in Piper, *Out of Order, Out of Sight*, vol. 2, *Selected Writings in Art Criticism, 1967–1992* (Cambridge, Mass.: MIT Press, 1996), pp. 3–4.

12. Piper, "Xenophobia and the Indexical Present II: Lecture," in Ine Gevers, ed., *Place Position Presentation Public* (Den Haag, the Netherlands: Jan van Eyck Akademie, 1993); reprinted, in a slightly different form, in *Out of Order, Out of Sight*, vol. 1, p. 261.

13. "Private performance" is a term specific to Piper, meaning a performance-based work staged in her apartment, without an audience. An expanded version of *Meat into Meat* includes a ninth image, of David, looking bloated, with a quart of milk in front of him and what appears to be a partially eaten bread roll or doughnut in his hand, glaring at the camera. See Maurice Berger, ed., *Adrian Piper: A Retrospective* (Baltimore: University of Maryland Fine Arts Gallery, 1999), p. 126.

14. Piper, "Xenophobia and the Indexical Present II," p. 261. Rosemary Mayer attended one of the consciousness-raising groups with Piper and documented it. See *Excerpts from the 1971 Journal of Rosemary Mayer*, ed. Marie Warsh (Brooklyn, N.Y.: Object Relations, 2016), p. 48.

15. Piper, "Xenophobia and the Indexical Present II," p. 261.

16. Piper, "About the Hypothesis Series," 1992, in *Out of Order, Out of Sight*, vol. 1, p. 19.

17. Ibid.

18. Piper has referred to *Here and Now* as a book, although as a block of unbound leaves housed in a folio box, it is more like a portfolio. Piper, "Xenophobia and the Indexical Present II," p. 259.

19. Ibid.

20. Berger, *Adrian Piper: A Retrospective*, p. 178.

21. Piper, "Personal Chronology," p. 315.

22. In 1970 Seth Siegelaub enlisted Lucy Lippard to organize a section of the catalogue for an exhibition that took place solely within the pages of *Studio International* magazine, and although Lippard did not include any women, David Antin, another curator of the project, drew in his wife, Eleanor Antin, as a contributor, and Hans Strelow's selection included Hanne Darboven. *Studio International* 180, no. 924 (July–August 1970).

23. "Seth could have made the decision alone about whether or not to include [me] in the *March 1969* show, rather than asking Barry, Huebler, Kosuth, and Weiner and accepting their No vote. But that's how he chose to structure his organization." Piper, conversation with the author, January 5, 2016.

24. Kozlov's contribution to *March 1969* appears after Kosuth's page and immediately before a blank page representing where LeWitt's contribution would have appeared, had he responded to Siegelaub's request.

25. The title *0 TO 9* was an homage to Jasper Johns's 0 through 9 series of drawings, prints, and paintings, which laid the numbers in that span on top of the other. One might envision the stacking of numbers as a metaphorical stacking of pages or ideas. See Bernadette Mayer, introduction to *0 TO 9: The Complete Magazine* (Brooklyn, N.Y.: Ugly Duckling Presse, 2006), pp. 13–14.

26. The fifth issue of *0 TO 9*, published in January 1969, opened, on page 3, with LeWitt's typewritten manifesto "Sentences on Conceptual Art," which proclaimed, in its first two lines, "1. Conceptual artists are mystics rather than rationalists. They leap to conclusions that logic cannot reach." It was reprinted in *Art–Language* 1, no. 1 (May 1969): 11–13. The manuscript is now in MoMA's collection.

27. *Untitled ("If you are a slow reader . . . ")* was eventually stored in a binder with eighteen other *Space-Time-Infinity* works to constitute *Nineteen Concrete Space-Time-Infinity Pieces*.

28. Piper, "Streetwork Streettracks I–II (1969; 01:43:28)," APRA, www.adrianpiper.com/vs/sound_streetwork.shtml.

29. Berger, *Adrian Piper: A Retrospective*, p. 178.

30. Piper, conversation with the author, October 20, 2017. A set of the three volumes was also sent to the School of Visual Arts, New York.

31. Many of the addressees were drawn from Siegelaub's address book. The list included the artists Acconci, Darboven, Dan Flavin, Eva Hesse, Huebler, Kosuth, Barry, LeWitt, Walter De Maria, Brice Marden, Bruce Nauman, Claes Oldenburg, Allen Ruppersberg, Smithson, and Lawrence Weiner—many of whom Siegelaub had invited to participate in the publication cum exhibition *March 1969*; the curators William Agee, Lawrence Alloway, James Butler, Kynaston McShine, Harald Szeemann; the dealers Leo Castelli, Paula Cooper, Virginia Dwan, and Konrad Fischer; the critics and writers Gregory Battcock, David Bourdon, Lippard, Annette Michelson, and Barbara Rose; and Siegelaub's collectors and business partners, in addition to Piper's family and friends. *Three Untitled Projects* was also included in *Number 7*, at Paula Cooper Gallery, New York.

32. Kees Boeke, *Cosmic View: The Universe in Forty Jumps* (Scranton, Penn.: John Day, 1957). *Cosmic View* was the basis of Charles and Ray Eames's nine-minute film *Powers of Ten and the Relative Size of Things in the Universe* (1977).

33. When *557,087* opened, Piper, at age twenty, was the youngest artist in the exhibition. She was also the youngest artist in *Konzeption/Conception*, *Art in the Mind*, and *Conceptual Art and Conceptual Aspects*. The only artists in *Information* who were younger than Piper were Milenko Matanović and David George Nez, members of the Slovenian collective Group OHO, both born in 1949.

34. For the *Village Voice*'s circulation numbers, see www.villagevoice.com/2005/10/18/1969/. Attendance at MoMA in fiscal years 1969 and 1970 were 910,852 and 1,011,315 individual visitors. See William S. Paley, "Report of the President," *The Museum of Modern Art Biennial Report, 1967–69*, p. 8; and "Report of the President," *The Museum of Modern Art Annual Report, 1969–70*, p. 4.

35. Graham's first project in an advertising space, *Figurative*, appeared in *Harper's Bazaar*, March 1968, p. 90. Between November 1968 and December 1969 Kaltenbach placed artworks as advertisements in twelve consecutive issues of *Artforum*.

36. Athena Tacha Spear's invitation to the artists was in part based on what she had read about them rather than on firsthand experience of their works. In a handwritten addition to her invitation to Strider, Spear wrote, "I know terribly little about your art aside from what [John] Perreault writes in [*Village*] *Voice*. Would you please send me a short biography and some extra information on (or samples of) your work, on top of what you submit to the show?" Spear, letter to Strider, February 6, 1970.

37. Andy Warhol et al., in *Andy Warhol* (Stockholm: Moderna Museet, 1968), n.p.

38. *Working Drawings and Other Visible Things on Paper Not Necessarily Meant to Be Viewed as Art* included contributions by Andre, Jo Baer, John Cage, Tom Clancy, Flavin, Milton Glaser, Dan Graham, Hesse, Alfred Jensen, Judd, Michael Kirby, William Kolakoski, Robert Lepper, LeWitt,

Robert Mangold, Robert Moskovitz, Smithson, Kenneth Snelson, and others.

39. See *A.W.C.: Open Hearing/An Open Public Hearing on the Subject: What Should Be the Program of the Art Workers Regarding Museum Reform and to Establish the Program of an Open Art Workers' Coalition,* and *A.W.C. Documents 1* (New York: Art Workers' Coalition, 1969).

40. The artists participating *in The Saturday Afternoon Show* were Acconci, Burton, Costa, Ira Joel Haber, Deborah Hay, Kaltenbach, Abe Lubelski, Frank Owen, Paul Pechter, Perreault, Piper, Brigid Polk, Strider, and Hannah Weiner. Max's Kansas City was located at 213 Park Avenue South.

41. Piper referred to the performance as *Untitled Catalysis for Max's Kansas City*, making it her first *Catalysis* work. Piper, "Xenophobia and the Indexical Present II," p. 262.

42. Rosemary Mayer's photographs constitute the documentation of *Untitled Performance at Max's Kansas City*, meaning that they are its residual evidence, standing in for the performative activity and becoming its lasting embodiment. *Untitled Performance at Max's Kansas City*, as with many of the Happenings and performances of the 1960s, exists today through photo documentation as discrete objects under the same, or similar, titles as the original live works.

43. Cat. no. 60, in Judd, Brydon Smith, Roberta Smith, and Flavin, *Donald Judd: A Catalogue of the Exhibition, 24 May–6 July, 1975; Catalogue Raisonné of Paintings, Objects, and Wood-Blocks, 1960–1974* (Ottawa: National Gallery of Canada, 1975), p. 125.

44. Perreault, "Only a Dummy," *Village Voice*, May 14, 1970, p. 16.

45. Rosemary Mayer, postcard to Bernadette Mayer, May 2, 1970. Bernadette Mayer Papers, Mandeville Special Collections Library, Geisel Library, University of California, San Diego. Quoted in John P. Bowles, *Adrian Piper: Race: Gender, and Embodiment* (Durham, N.C.: Duke University Press, 2011), pp. 135.

46. Piper, in Bowles, *Adrian Piper: Race: Gender, and Embodiment*, p. 135.

47. Gilbert & George, *The Singing Sculpture*, Sonnabend Gallery, New York, September 25–October 8, 1971.

48. Piper, "Xenophobia and the Indexical Present II," p. 262.

49. See Piper, "An Ongoing Essay," in Lippard, "Two Proposals: Lucy Lippard Presents the Ideas of Adrian Piper and Eleanor Antin," *Arts and Artist* 6, no. 12 (March 1972): 44–46.

50. Ibid, p. 45.

51. Perreault, "Women in the News," *Village Voice*, April 29, 1971, p. 31.

52. Michael Fried, "Art and Objecthood," *Artforum* 5, no. 10 (Summer 1967): 12–23. The same issue contained LeWitt's "Paragraphs on Conceptual Art" and Robert Morris's third installment of "Notes on Sculpture."

53. Piper, "Xenophobia and the Indexical Present II," p. 262.

54. Piper, "Food for the Spirit," *High Performance* 4, no. 1 (Spring 1981): 34–35; reprinted in *Out of Order, Out of Sight*, vol. 1, p. 55.

55. Piper graduated summa cum laude and Phi Beta Kappa from CCNY in 1974, with Research Honors in Philosophy, the Phi Beta Kappa Medal for the Best Honors Essay in the Social Sciences, the Ketchum Prize for Proficiency in the History of Philosophy, and the Sperling Prize for Excellence in Philosophy.

56. Piper, "Xenophobia and the Indexical Present II," p. 259.

57. Piper, "Flying," in Jane Farver, ed., *Adrian Piper: Reflections*, (New York: The Alternative Museum, 1987), p. 22. *Phillip Zohn Catalysis* (1972), a nearly ninety-minute audio work, featured Piper's end of a telephone conversation with Zohn about philosophy, her personal commitment to realizing her potential, and "finally [being] able to articulate some kind of truth about the world; and therefore about myself." Piper, "Phillip Zohn Catalysis," 1972/1989, in *Out of Order, Out of Sight*, vol. 1, p. 69.

58. Piper, "Food for the Spirit," p. 55.

59. Ibid.

60. Thomas Erben Gallery, which owns the original *Food for the Spirit*, produced editioned prints—made from copy negatives of the smaller photographs—in 1997, both as sets of fourteen and as individual images. Thomas Erben, conversation with the author, May 17, 2016. Also see the gallery's press release for *Adrian Piper: Food for the Spirit, July 1971*, December 11, 1997–January 31, 1998.

61. Piper, "Food for the Spirit," p. 55.

62. *Food for the Spirit* was first exhibited in *Adrian Piper: Reflections, 1967–1987*, The Alternative Museum, New York, April 18–May 30, 1987.

63. Piper, "Food for the Spirit," p. 55.

64. Susanna Singer, ed., *Sol LeWitt: Wall Drawings, 1968–1984* (Amsterdam: Stedelijk Museum, 1984), p. 164; and Alicia Legg, ed., *Sol LeWitt* (New York: The Museum of Modern Art, 1978), p. 179.

65. Piper has cited Rosalind Krauss's review of LeWitt's 1968 exhibition at Dwan Gallery (*Artforum*, vol. 6, no. 8 [April 1968], pp. 57–58) as an example of a misguided response to a conceptualist's work. Piper, conversation with Connie Butler and author, Berlin, August 30, 2015. For an example of withering pop-culture critique of American modernism, up through conceptualism—and of Lawrence Weiner in particular—see Tom Wolfe, *The Painted Word* (New York: Farrar, Straus & Giroux, 1975), pp. 103–9. See also Robert Hughes, "The Decline and Fall of the Avant-Garde," *Time*, December 18, 1972; reprinted in Gregory Battcock, ed., *Idea Art* (New York: E. P. Dutton, 1973), pp. 184–94.

66. Lee Lozano, May 9, 1968, entry in *Private Book 1, 1968–69* (New York: The Estate of Lee Lozano/Karma, 2016), n.p.

67. See Joseph Kosuth, "Art After Philosophy," *Studio International* 178, no. 915 (October 1969): 134–37; reprinted in Kosuth, *Art After Philosophy and After: Collected Writings, 1966–1990*, ed. Gabriele Guercio (Cambridge, Mass.: MIT Press, 1991), pp. 13–32. See also Kosuth, "An Answer to Criticisms," *Studio International* 179, no. 923 (June 1970): 245.

68. LeWitt did not eschew the idea of his works' social engagement; he spoke of his wall works as being analogous to musical scores, in which he, in providing instructions, was as "a composer who writes notes, and a pianist [whoever drafts the work on a wall] plays the notes . . . [leaving] ample room for both to make a statement of their own." LeWitt, *Art by Telephone*, vinyl LP record published as the catalogue for the exhibition of the same name at the Museum of Contemporary Art, Chicago, November 1–December 14, 1969.

69. Reinhard Bek, Partner, Bek & Frohnert LLC, Conservation of Contemporary Art, conversation with the author, August 18, 2017.

70. Barbara Brown, correspondence with the author, August 6, 2017. The author also thanks Sofia LeWitt and Janet Passehl, Curator, The LeWitt Collection, for their assistance in researching this work. LeWitt also developed *Schematic Drawing for Muybridge II* (1969; published 1970), an artist's book that mimicked the sculpture by placing the images sequentially on a single horizontal sheet that could be slid out of a paper folio sleeve to reveal the images one by one.

71. LeWitt, in Legg, ed., *Sol LeWitt*, p. 77.

72. Ad Reinhardt's art and writings were abundantly familiar to LeWitt and Piper. In a 2003 interview, LeWitt said, "Ad Reinhardt was an artist of ideas, and he was very influential. His writings were of great interest, as was his art. In fact, his example provided another direction: not Pop art and Fluxus but a more vital and productive way. His art really became the key to my thinking." LeWitt, in "Sol LeWitt to Saul Ostrow," *Bomb*, no. 85 (Fall 2003), www.bombmagazine.org/articles/sol-lewitt/. Piper had concentrated exposure to Reinhardt's work in 1969, when she typed an early version of Lippard's manuscript on Reinhardt that would become the basis for a 1980 monograph. Certain lines from Reinhardt's text "There Is Just One Painting," published in *Artforum*'s March 1966 issue, such as "There is just one art morality, just one art immorality, one art enemy, one art indignity, one art punishment, one art danger, one art conscience, one art guilt, one art virtue, one art reward," suggest that LeWitt's "Paragraphs" and "Sentences" were modeled formally, and intellectually, on Reinhardt's writing.

WAKE UP AND GET DOWN

ADRIAN PIPER'S DIRECT ADDRESS

CORNELIA BUTLER

I listened to Aretha's version of "Respect" until I had it completely memorized and could hear the entire song in my mind at will. Sometimes it "turned itself on" without my willing it. However, the piece was performed only at those times when I did will it. The piece consisted of my listening to the song in my mind and simultaneously dancing to it. I did a mixture of the Bugaloo, the Jerk, the Lindy, the Charleston, and the Twist, with a high degree of improvisation. I performed the piece while waiting on line at the bank, at a bus stop, and in the Public Library.
— Adrian Piper[1]

Aretha Franklin's anthem marked its fiftieth anniversary in 2017, a year of right-wing political revolution in the United States and around the world. The occasion of Adrian Piper's fifty-year retrospective exhibition lands in the United States at a moment when the national conversation about race, identity, immigration, and the golden rule are singularly and urgently unfolding in real time, embroiled in a cultural mood and climate of fear that is being fed from the top ranks of the government. What is striking when considering Piper's complex and uncompromising body of work over the course of her career is her devotion to a handful of ideas that remain as urgent and powerful now as they were in 1968, the year in which her work began to turn toward indexical public address. The strategies of directly addressing viewers in order to locate them in the here and now, rather than in the past or future, and employing a conceptual idiolect while also situating a deeply political and subjective response to the world are at the center of her practice and are essential to the ongoing impact, the contemporaneity, of her work. Piper has honed these strategies, in her art, writing, and life, for more than five decades.

Although Piper's practice is fundamentally conceptual, hers is a visual language, using appropriated photographs, text, installation, video, and performance. In this merging of the conceptual and visual, her work, deploying a realism appropriated from current social and political discourses, confronts viewers with directness and clarity that is startling among contemporary artists. Her imagined audience is a responsible viewer, one who, in a place of civil discourse, meets her and is willing to engage. Piper laid out the ideal effect of her work in the 1989 text "Xenophobia and the Indexical Present 1": "I want my work to contribute to the creation of a society in which racism and racial stereotyping no longer exist. In such a society, the prevailing attitude to cultural and ethnic others would be one not of tolerance but of acceptance."[2]

Not one to shy away from complicated and sometimes painful content, she goes on to articulate why this distinction, between tolerance and acceptance, is indeed important, a precise parsing of language that characterizes much of her practice as a writer and an artist. Her insistence on it speaks to an ethics of responsibility that underlies her work, a moral imperative that Piper moves from subject to viewer, as well as to a challenge she issues over and over again. Piper's voice as an artist and acute social critic has never been more relevant or more potent.

Invitation to Dance

Piper first danced to her internal Aretha Franklin in one of the *Catalysis* street performances in 1972. In 1975 she performed as the Mythic Being on the streets of Cambridge, Massachusetts, where she was living at the time. That same year at Artists Space in New York, she presented *Some Reflective Surfaces* **(fig. 1)**, a multilayered audience-oriented performance that included the song and featured a double-drag femme version of the artist's Mythic Being persona—with chalk-white pancake makeup, pencil mustache, starred beauty mark, and reflective sunglasses—and presented this performance again in 1976 at the Whitney Museum of American Art. So the male persona was activated in a number of different guises. In a text about *Aretha Franklin Catalysis* and *Some Reflective Surfaces*, Piper recalls being interested in popular "disco" dance figures as a form of ritualized sexual and political confrontation: "This type of dance was capable of expressing a whole spectrum of feelings people have about their own bodies—all the more eloquently because the rhythms of disco music (which I define to include . . . disco, funk, soul, Motown, salsa, and disco-jazz), while complex and densely textured, tend to be repetitive and to transform gradually, rather than being discontinuous and rhythmically simple like much rock music."[3]

In both performances of *Some Reflective Surfaces* the artist danced to "Respect" against a film, projected behind her, of her dancing to the same music on another occasion, with a group of fellow graduate students in the Harvard University philosophy department. The soundtrack also included a voiceover of Piper narrating an incident that took place during a period when, to support herself, she worked as a disco dancer in New York's Ginza and Entre Nous nightclubs (thanks to a fake cabaret license). She describes collaborating with two other dancers to choreograph a routine to perform together, rather than improvising individually, thus granting them a collective power: objectified for the pleasure of others, the dancers transformed themselves into empowered bodies.

Social dancing, dancing in public, as a subject for art was for Piper a natural extension of this labor and of her thinking about the political potential of disco and funk: "To succeed in dancing to disco music, and to perform the full spectrum of figures and gestures that are part of that, is to express one's sexuality, one's separateness, one's inner unity with one's own body; and in a sexually repressive, WASP-dominated culture, this is to express defiance."[4] Much the way Franklin turned Otis Redding's bluesy admonition, meant to coax a woman into sexy submission, into a feminist power ballad that has inspired people to dance and resist for fifty years, Piper's narrative transforms the conditions of dancing as sexy objects into the performances of powerful subjects. And she deploys this story, in her characteristically precise language, to get her audience moving.

In these works, her first foray into the political potential of dance, Piper's interpretation of "Respect," her dance stylings, and her monologue posit labor and self-fashioning at the core of artistic identity: what does it mean to put your body on the line as a medium of economic exchange? How does a (woman) artist perform her identity, and for whom? Must she perform an identity in order to have one? Although aware of the issues of power at stake for her personally, as a woman and an artist of acknowledged African descent, Piper incites nothing less than consideration of the most basic questions of gender and biological identity. Mixing and sorting the vernaculars of embedded

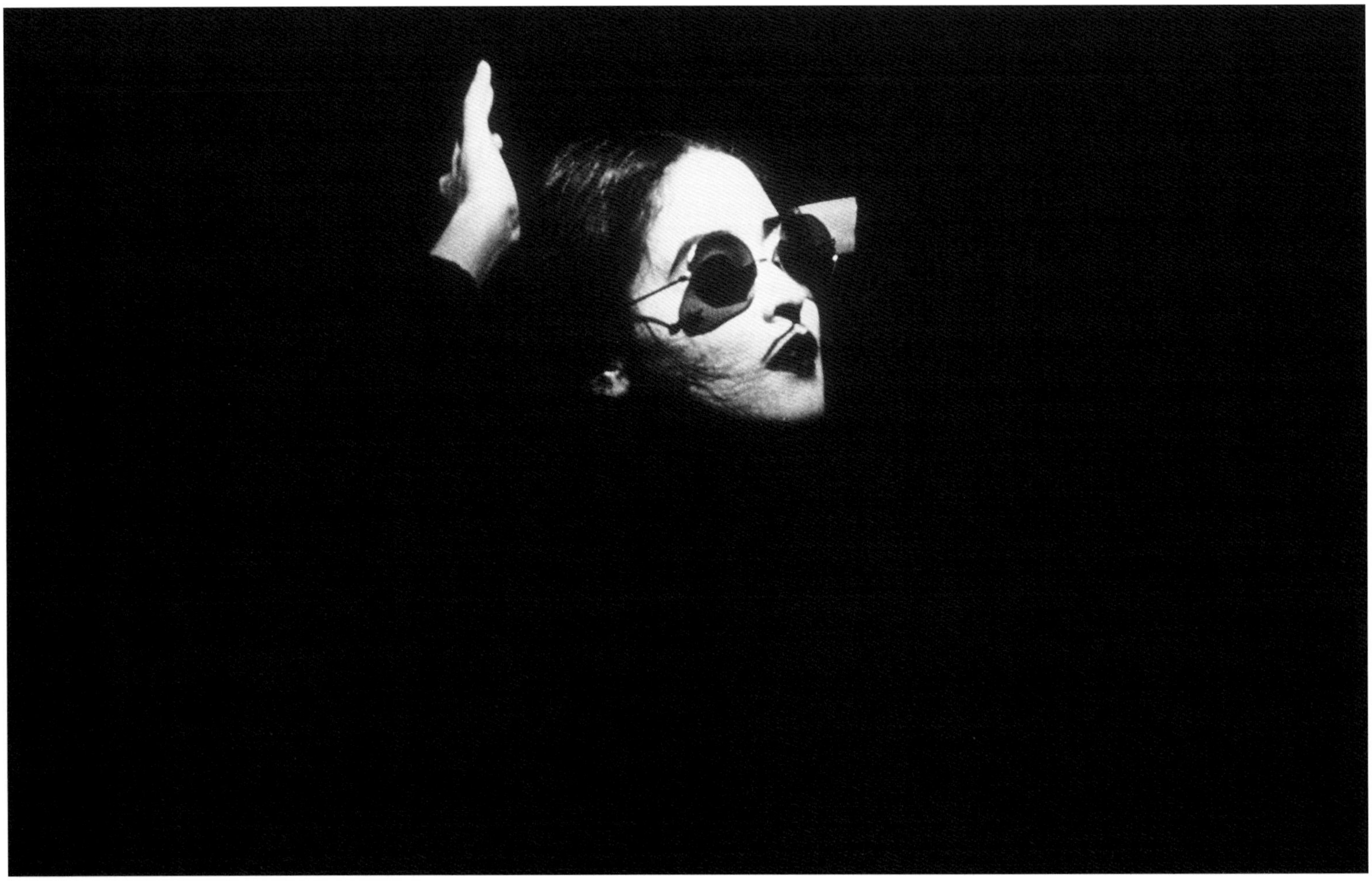

Fig. 1
Some Reflective Surfaces. 1975–76
Documentation of the audience-oriented performance at the Whitney Museum of American Art, New York, February 28, 1976. Two gelatin silver prints and 16mm film transferred to video (color, sound), 00:15:27
Prints 19½ × 15 in. (49.5 × 38.1 cm) and 15 × 19½ in. (38.1 × 49.5 cm)
Collection Adrian Piper Research Archive Foundation Berlin
Detail: print #2

racism, xenophobia, and sexism, Piper re-presents the images we have of ourselves, leading us to ask how we see difference, how we understand and name ourselves and one another. And, in the well-known words of Rodney King in the midst of the 1992 Los Angeles uprising, why can't we all just get along?[5]

Just as her personal political politics were manifest in her commitment to the Civil Rights Movement in the early 1960s, Piper's discovery, a decade later, of the collective power of dance put social engagement at the center of her practice. Using her body as a vehicle for disarming her public into direct engagement, Piper exploits its power—that of hers and of the viewer's—as a locus for meaning. Participation, one of the primary legacies of first-generation political Conceptual art, is a means of both democratizing the meaning of art and giving agency to its audience; and Piper's contribution to *Information*, organized by Kynaston McShine at The Museum of Modern Art in 1970, is another early work evidencing such an invitation, in the form of a set of empty notebooks in the gallery that viewers were encouraged to fill with whatever they liked (pages 176, 177).[6] The notebooks predated the visitor books now found in most art galleries, and in 1970 they advanced a much more earnest attempt at engagement. The solicitation of opinion and its subsequent expression, something not usually encouraged within the hallowed context of an institution, extends a political laying of claims, an invitation to conversation, an empowering of the audience in a way then unprecedented.

The genealogy of Piper's public engagement and indexical direct address extends back to her earliest conceptualist works, most explicitly in the text-based proposals of the *Concrete Space-Time-Infinity* pieces (1968–69). Reading, Piper shows, is a social act: the text is the vehicle for her voice, which activates the reader by heightening the self-awareness of mental activity. Many of her typewritten pageworks can be read as outer-directed assertions of fact, both personal and public. The *Concrete Space-Time-Infinity* works, among others, are objects that refer both to themselves and also, as Piper has said of the Hypothesis series (1968–70) (pages 144–47), "outward, to the world of abstract, symbolic meaning."[7] In the storage notebook entitled *Nineteen Concrete Space-Time-Infinity Pieces*, we find a statement by the artist about her work. Its title is *Untitled Statement ("My present work is involved . . . ")* (1968). This statement describes a transfer of action, through the act of reading, from the artist's conception of the work to the viewer's construction of its meaning:

> My present work is involved with the general nature of time and/or space. In any specific form, there is an infinite amount of information that can be conveyed about it, and an infinite number of permutations of it. These possibilities are obviously suggested only by the structure of the language used in dealing with or identifying its general character, and not through direct perception. One could continue to supply verbal information about it indefinitely. Therefore, it seems most logical to allow the physical boundaries of the specific form used to limit how much is stated about it. Another way of imposing limitations is to have the person to whom I'm giving the piece arbitrarily decide a) whether they want the piece to exist in time or space (thus deciding the nature of the medium used); b) the number of units of that medium they want the information carried to.[8]

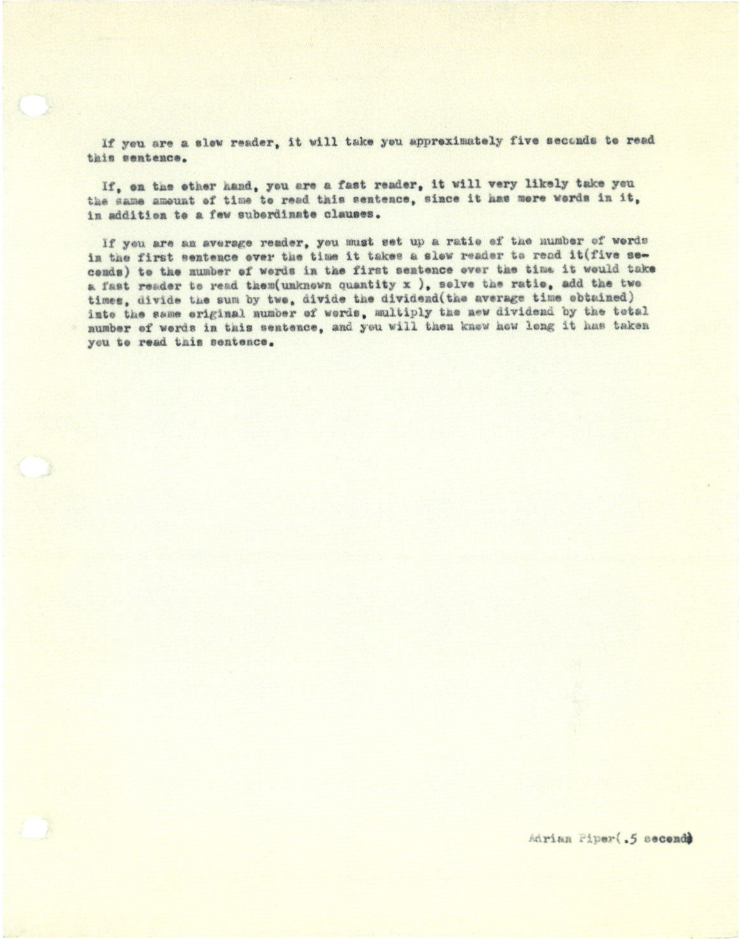

If you are a slew reader, it will take you approximately five seconds to read this sentence.

If, on the ether hand, you are a fast reader, it will very likely take you the same amount of time to read this sentence, since it has more words in it, in addition to a few subordinate clauses.

If you are an average reader, you must set up a ratie of the number of words in the first sentence ever the time it takes a slew reader to read it(five seconds) to the number of words in the first sentence ever the time it would take a fast reader to read them(unknown quantity x), selve the ratie, add the twe times, divide the sum by twe, divide the dividend(the average time obtained) inte the same original number of words, multiply the new dividend by the total number of words in this sentence, and you will then knew how long it has taken you to read this sentence.

Adrian Piper(.5 second)

Fig. 2
Nineteen Concrete Space-Time-Infinity Pieces. 1968–69
Notebook with fifteen pageworks. Ring binder with nineteen pages in plastic sleeves
Each page 11 × 8½ in. (27.9 × 21.6 cm); binder 11¹³⁄₁₆ × 10⁵⁄₁₆ × 1½ in. (26.8 × 30 × 3.9 cm)
Detail: *Untitled ("If you are a slow reader . . .")*. 1968
Typescript page
Generali Foundation Collection—Permanent Loan to the Museum der Moderne Salzburg

This statement refers to artworks Piper was producing during this period: single-page documents containing a performative potentiality—literally the possibility of movement of action or cognition from artist to viewer. These works form part of Conceptual art's history of interpersonal engagement. Some of Piper's texts are autological and take place in real time: "The time needed to read a line of print depends on the content and structure of the line" **(page 158)**, and "If you are a slow reader it will take you five seconds to read this sentence" **(fig. 2)**. The work presumes a reader, but its *punctum* lies in the indication, both modest and descriptive, of an action, the "maybe" of potential engagement and outcome. In the analog spirit of much early Conceptual art, the act of reading the text is intimate, but it is also conditional, based on the viewer's choice whether or not to do it. In spite of the work's ethical rigor and deadpan quality, there is also a sense of humor that has been largely eclipsed by the precision and seriousness of the voice. This humor is often clear in Piper's critical writing about her own work but also breaks through and, especially in recent works, reaches a level of transcendence and joy.

By 1969, in works such as those collected in the storage notebook entitled *Nine Abstract Space-Time-Infinity Pieces*, the performative potential has moved beyond the limited conceptual field of the page, from the internal and self-referential act of reading, to the viewer's immediate surroundings, external to the page. One of the nine pieces reads, "Proposal: to exhibit this piece whenever the opportunity presents itself" **(page 168)**. And in April 1969, as part of *Street Works*, Piper outlined various ways for nine participants to move around four designated blocks in Manhattan—running, walking, riding a bicycle—recording the view from the midpoint of each block with a Polaroid camera **(fig. 3)**. The participants would distribute the proposal—an open invitation to others to participate—on Fourteenth Street between Fifth and Sixth Avenues. Like her colleagues Vito Acconci and Robert Smithson, whose urban-mapping projects moved them out of the studio and into the public and even, in Smithson's case, into the frontiers of New Jersey and, later, the American West, Piper, through these projects, located her body and those of others in the public sphere.

The trope of the directive or administrative was common among first-generation Conceptual artists, an impulse that extended, in part, from those artists' desire to think about the nature and value of artistic labor. Piper's friend and mentor Sol LeWitt, as well as many other artists with whose work Piper's was shown, including Dan Graham, Lee Lozano, John Baldessari, and Mierle Ukeles, developed task-based strategies that adapted what the curator Helen Molesworth has called the "language and logic of work."[9] By contrast, Piper extended the conceptual framework of image and text by turning to aural methods of communication. In the *Seriation* sound works, of 1968, she signified the administrative with generic prerecorded voices. *Seriation #1: Lecture* features the blank recorded voice reached by dialing "Time" on the telephone—the "speaking clock" that intones "At the tone, the time will be 12:00"—delivering the time at ten-second intervals for a half-hour. The voice, extracted from its original context, has an almost forensic quality, foregrounding our rule-based, if arbitrary, relationship with the mechanized world and the

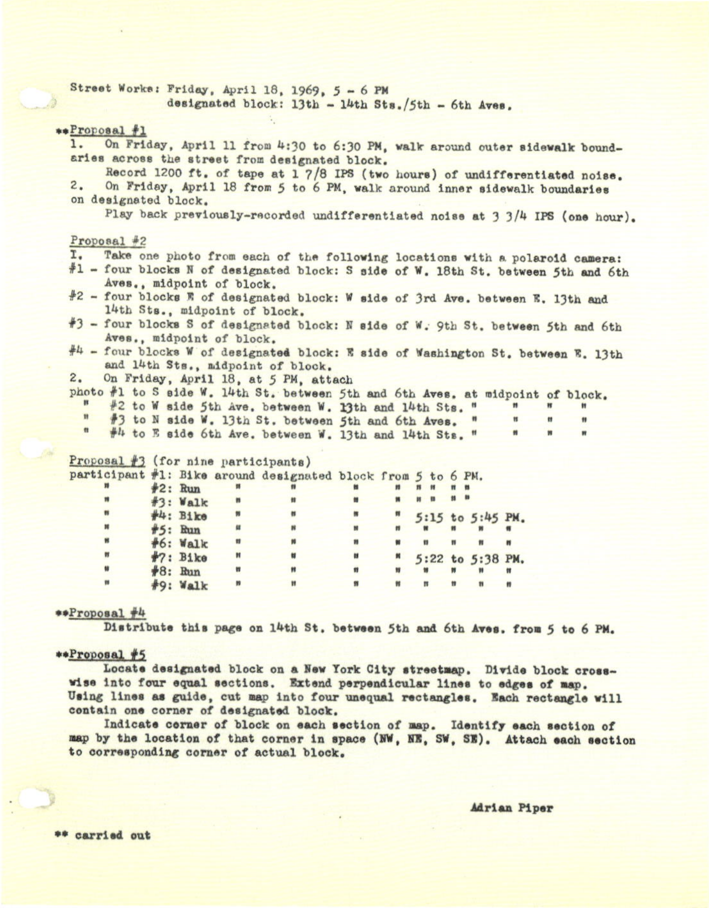

Street Works: Friday, April 18, 1969, 5 - 6 PM
designated block: 13th - 14th Sts./5th - 6th Aves.

**Proposal #1
1. On Friday, April 11 from 4:30 to 6:30 PM, walk around outer sidewalk boundaries across the street from designated block.
Record 1200 ft. of tape at 1 7/8 IPS (two hours) of undifferentiated noise.
2. On Friday, April 18 from 5 to 6 PM, walk around inner sidewalk boundaries on designated block.
Play back previously-recorded undifferentiated noise at 3 3/4 IPS (one hour).

Proposal #2
I. Take one photo from each of the following locations with a polaroid camera:
#1 - four blocks N of designated block: S side of W. 18th St. between 5th and 6th Aves., midpoint of block.
#2 - four blocks E of designated block: W side of 3rd Ave. between E. 13th and 14th Sts., midpoint of block.
#3 - four blocks S of designated block: N side of W. 9th St. between 5th and 6th Aves., midpoint of block.
#4 - four blocks W of designated block: E side of Washington St. between E. 13th and 14th Sts., midpoint of block.
2. On Friday, April 18, at 5 PM, attach
photo #1 to S side W. 14th St. between 5th and 6th Aves. at midpoint of block.
" #2 to W side 5th Ave. between W. 13th and 14th Sts. " " " "
" #3 to N side W. 13th St. between 5th and 6th Aves. " " " "
" #4 to E side 6th Ave. between W. 13th and 14th Sts. " " " "

Proposal #3 (for nine participants)
participant #1: Bike around designated block from 5 to 6 PM.
" #2: Run " " " " " " " "
" #3: Walk " " " " " " " "
" #4: Bike " " " " 5:15 to 5:45 PM.
" #5: Run " " " " " " " "
" #6: Walk " " " " " " " "
" #7: Bike " " " " 5:22 to 5:38 PM.
" #8: Run " " " " " " " "
" #9: Walk " " " " " " " "

**Proposal #4
Distribute this page on 14th St. between 5th and 6th Aves. from 5 to 6 PM.

**Proposal #5
Locate designated block on a New York City streetmap. Divide block crosswise into four equal sections. Extend perpendicular lines to edges of map. Using lines as guide, cut map into four unequal rectangles. Each rectangle will contain one corner of designated block.
Indicate corner of block on each section of map. Identify each section of map by the location of that corner in space (NW, NE, SW, SE). Attach each section to corresponding corner of actual block.

Adrian Piper

** carried out

Fig. 3
Nine Abstract Space-Time-Infinity Pieces. 1968–69
Notebook with eight pageworks. Ring binder with twenty-nine sheets in plastic sleeves
Each page 11 × 8½ in. (27.9 × 21.6 cm); binder 11¹³⁄₁₆ × 10⁹⁄₁₆ × 1½ in. (26.8 × 30 × 3.9 cm)
Detail: *Untitled ("Street Works: Friday, April 18, 1969, 5–6 PM . . .")*. 1969
Typescript page
Generali Foundation Collection—Permanent Loan to the Museum der Moderne Salzburg

measurement of time, which we thus experience indexically. *Seriation #1*, as Piper has said, is "directed towards giving a direct experience of the duration of the half hour."[10] The work also slyly suggests the absurdity of confirming our faith in an absolute such as time by listening to a recorded voice marking its passing—an idea that now seems quaint and nearly unimaginable as well (though the speaking telephonic clock is still available). The recorded voice here is the medium but is not itself the message: Piper is not enamored of technology as an end in itself, and her work has remained staunchly low-tech, deploying whatever is most expedient—in this case to elicit what she refers to in another work as "tools for listening."[11]

In *Seriation #2: Now*, the here and now is accentuated by the artist's intoning the word "now" between intervals of silence that diminish, according to a serial algorithmic function, from one minute to one second long, for a total of eighteen minutes. Piper has noted that some listeners have imparted a sexual meaning to the work, perhaps alluding to the slow crescendo of the "now." Although she denies this was her intent, the intervals between the artist's voice—the anticipation of its reappearance—do feel at least anxious, nearly excruciating. The systematic variation in intervals nevertheless prevents listeners from becoming accustomed to a pattern, lengthening their attention and testing the limits of what can be managed and comprehended; the elasticity of silence becomes a structural element through which meaning can be conveyed. This cadence of silence and speech is developed in other conversational works, such as *My Calling (Card) #1* and *#2* (1986–90) and *Cornered* (1988), which will be discussed later in this essay, and in which direct address is punctuated by meaningful pauses filled with the potential of individual and political transformation. *Seriation #2: Now*, like *Seriation #1*, can also be understood in terms of trust and endurance: the listener, by participating, has to have faith in the gesture and its execution—in the artist who disappears and reappears, punctuating the stretches of silence with moments of rupture. Such trust is experienced differently now, in our digital age, but it continues to be a way of constituting community, an approach that returns later in Piper's career. But in this work, the artist/listener relationship is intimate, extending across the silences and delay of the recorded conversation, and this intimacy, too, is a kind of trust, a kind of faith—like that of dialing out for a culturally agreed-upon signal of time.

Piper's references in the *Seriation* works range from the experimental compositions of John Cage to the automated worlds of Isaac Asimov's science fiction.[12] The year before, she had been listening to the composers Arnold Schoenberg, Karlheinz Stockhausen, and Cage, as well as to her contemporaries LaMonte Young, Terry Riley, and Steve Reich.[13] Reich, in his Minimalist compositions, also experimented with automated and found sound. Certainly Cage's *4'33"*, a symphony composed of a silence during which one or more instruments are not played for the duration of the work, also enlists the idea that bodies occupying a space together and sharing an absence, in this case the absence of sound, constitutes a social act. Cage's transference of the action of performance from musicians to audience is a profound gesture of faith. Cage, of course, also used silence and withdrawal, but Piper's particular and singular contribution lies in the attribution of meaning to those elements by situating the viewer's subjectivity at the center of them. Sound, like video, for many Conceptual artists provided a cheap, easy way to communicate more broadly, and these time-based mediums could also be marshaled toward an aesthetics of boredom and monotony, such as Piper's nascent consideration of what an audience would be able to endure.

Politics and Conceptual Art

Although it is common to ascribe political motivations to Conceptual works of the 1960s, Piper resists such claims for her early work. And, indeed, the typewritten pages and single-listener audio works, and the scope of activity they initiate, bespeak a certain insularity; they are modest in their reach, as though Piper sought not to change the world but to intervene one viewer/listener at a time. This one-on-one relationship with the viewer has continued throughout her career and into the present: a politics of engagement and transference of agency whose early roots are found in the *Catalysis* works and *Infiltration, 6/71*, an unrealized performance of 1971 **(figs. 4, 5)**. On two pages of typed text Piper proposes the parameters of a "Week-Long Population Catalysis Designed for the Town of New Haven and About 100 Participants," constituting interventions, or "alterations," to be carried out by participants at locations of business and leisure (bus station, post office, art galleries, museums, public library, movie house, restaurant), ranging from the humorous to the ridiculous and absurd. They seem meant to initiate some response by disrupting the banality of the day: "Cheeks smeared with vaseline and stuffed to bursting with cloth; small harmonica held between teeth or lips, sounded breath expelled"; "Chew large wads of bubble gum; blow large bubbles, allowing them to adhere to face, neck, clothes"; "Marinate clothes thoroughly in 1) Gallo wine, or 2) Cheap perfume, or 3) Sour milk." Piper extracts a high level of commitment from her participants, both deliberate viewers and unwitting passersby. *Infiltration*'s actions are exactly those that Piper had already executed in her solo *Catalysis* performances of 1970, some of which are documented in black-and-white photographs **(pages 180, 181)**. The *Catalysis* works of 1970–73 marked a significant shift in Piper's practice, as she distanced herself from making objects, interrogating that very process by deploying her body as an object. What appear to be Dada-like street actions—jarring and absurdist elements activated by the artist with the backdrop of an everyday place or situation—are in fact works executed *with* her body, as an alterable form, in close proximity to the body of the public. In 1971, thinking about how to use her body in order to get a response—as a kind of direct address—Piper wrote,

> I can no longer see discrete forms or objects in art as viable reflections or expressions of what seems to me to be going on in this society: They refer back to conditions of separateness, order, exclusivity, and the stability of easily accepted functional identities that no longer exist. . . . Making artificial and nonfunctional plastic alterations in my own bodily presence of the same kind as those I formerly made on inanimate or nonart materials. Here the art-making process and end product has the immediacy of being in the same time and space continuum as the viewer.[14]

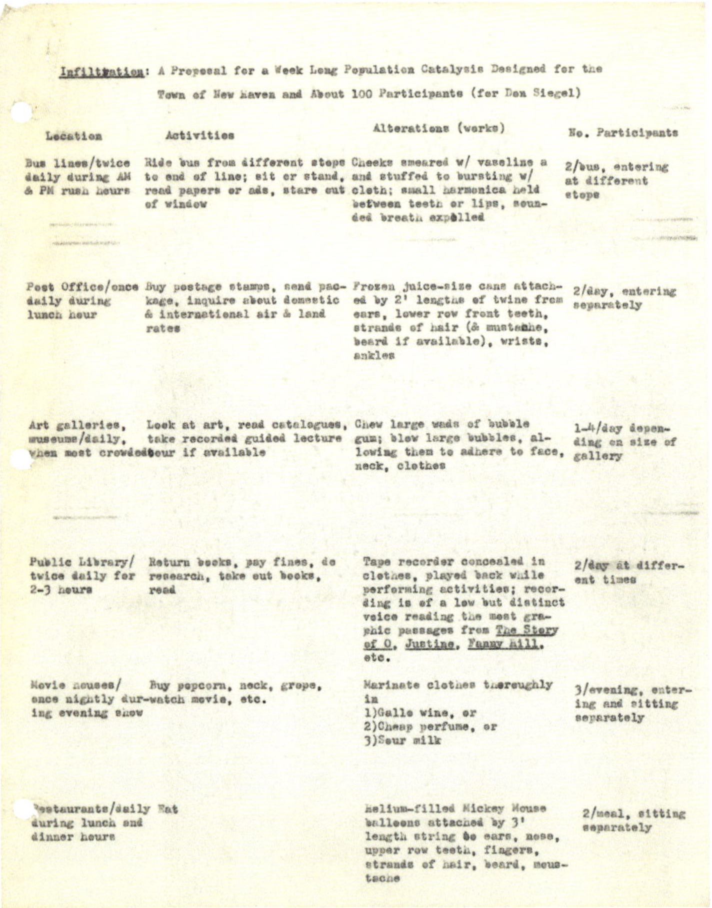

<u>Infiltration</u>: A Proposal for a Week Long Population Catalysis Designed for the Town of New Haven and About 100 Participants (for Don Siegel)

Location	Activities	Alterations (works)	No. Participants
Bus lines/twice daily during AM & PM rush hours	Ride bus from different stops to end of line; sit or stand, read papers or ads, stare out of window	Cheeks smeared w/ vaseline a and stuffed to bursting w/ cloth; small harmonica held between teeth or lips, sounded breath expelled	2/bus, entering at different stops
Post Office/once daily during lunch hour	Buy postage stamps, send package, inquire about domestic & international air & land rates	Frozen juice-size cans attached by 2' lengths of twine from ears, lower row front teeth, strands of hair (& mustache, beard if available), wrists, ankles	2/day, entering separately
Art galleries, museums/daily, when most crowded	Look at art, read catalogues, take recorded guided lecture tour if available	Chew large wads of bubble gum; blow large bubbles, allowing them to adhere to face, neck, clothes	1-4/day depending on size of gallery
Public Library/ twice daily for 2-3 hours	Return books, pay fines, do research, take out books, read	Tape recorder concealed in clothes, played back while performing activities; recording is of a low but distinct voice reading the most graphic passages from <u>The Story of O</u>, <u>Justine</u>, <u>Fanny Hill</u>, etc.	2/day at different times
Movie houses/ once nightly during evening show	Buy popcorn, neck, grope, watch movie, etc.	Marinate clothes thoroughly in 1)Gallo wine, or 2)Cheap perfume, or 3)Sour milk	3/evening, entering and sitting separately
Restaurants/daily during lunch and dinner hours	Eat	Helium-filled Mickey Mouse balloons attached by 3' length string to ears, nose, upper row teeth, fingers, strands of hair, beard, moustache	2/meal, sitting separately

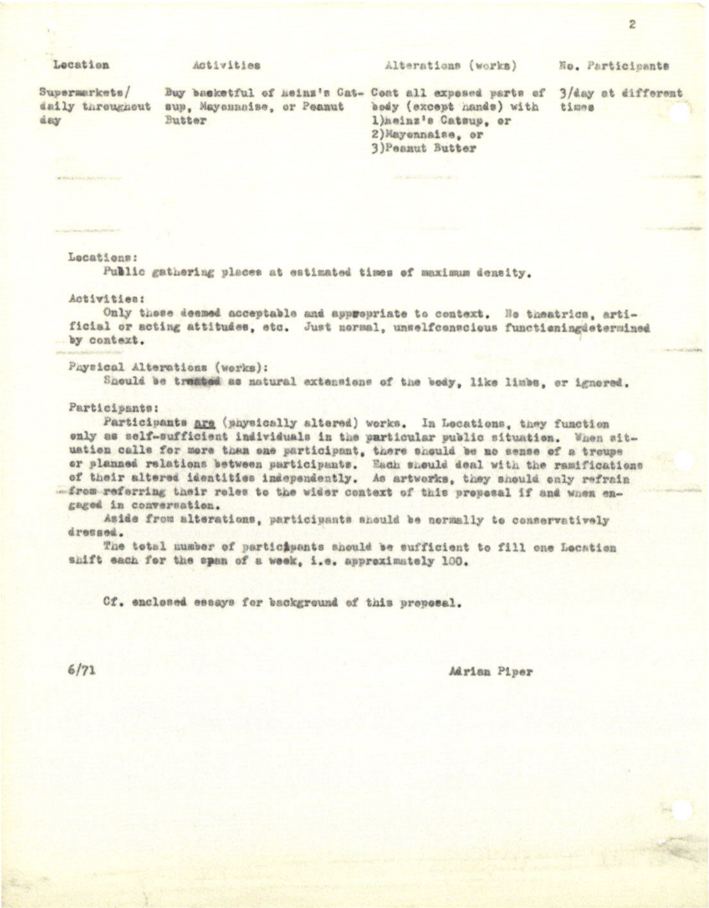

2

Location	Activities	Alterations (works)	No. Participants
Supermarkets/ daily throughout day	Buy basketful of Heinz's Catsup, Mayonnaise, or Peanut Butter	Coat all exposed parts of body (except hands) with 1)Heinz's Catsup, or 2)Mayonnaise, or 3)Peanut Butter	3/day at different times

Locations:
Public gathering places at estimated times of maximum density.

Activities:
Only those deemed acceptable and appropriate to context. No theatrics, artificial or acting attitudes, etc. Just normal, unselfconscious functioningdetermined by context.

Physical Alterations (works):
Should be treated as natural extensions of the body, like limbs, or ignored.

Participants:
Participants <u>are</u> (physically altered) works. In Locations, they function only as self-sufficient individuals in the particular public situation. When situation calls for more than one participant, there should be no sense of a troupe or planned relations between participants. Each should deal with the ramifications of their altered identities independently. As artworks, they should only refrain from referring their roles to the wider context of this proposal if and when engaged in conversation.

Aside from alterations, participants should be normally to conservatively dressed.

The total number of participants should be sufficient to fill one Location shift each for the span of a week, i.e. approximately 100.

Cf. enclosed essays for background of this proposal.

6/71 Adrian Piper

Figs. 4, 5
Infiltration, 6/71 (1971), from the notebook *Street Performance Proposals.* 1969–71
Carbon copies of two typescript pages on onionskin
Each 11 × 8½ in. (27.9 × 21.6 cm)
Generali Foundation Collection—Permanent Loan to the
Museum der Moderne Salzburg

Although Piper had actively participated in the politics of the Vietnam War and Civil Rights Movement before 1970, she had not consciously brought them into her art. When, in an interview in 1972, the critic and curator Lucy Lippard proposed that the *Catalysis* works were politically motivated, Piper clearly said that they were not.[15] Piper and Lippard, a leading curator and advocate of Conceptual art and one of Piper's significant interlocutors, were both active in the Art Workers' Coalition (AWC), which Piper joined in 1970; each was negotiating the relationship between their political and artistic lives. Lippard included Piper in *557,087*; *955,000*; and *c. 7,500*, three of her groundbreaking "numbers exhibitions" of Conceptual art, organized between 1969 and 1974; the exhibition names refer to the populations of the cities in which they took place (in this case, Seattle, Vancouver, and Valencia, California). The last of the three was the only exhibition comprising work by all women artists—Lippard's riposte to the commonly held notion that women did not make Conceptual art. Lippard's focus had turned toward feminism in 1970, when she began to ask how the very parameters and definition of Conceptual art might be opened up through the practices of artists such as Piper, who had introduced subjectivity and the social into the narrowly defined range of strategies and aesthetics.

In 1969, the year before the *Catalysis* works, Lippard invited Piper to participate in two exhibitions. The first, in May of that year, was *Number 7*, at Paula Cooper Gallery, organized in support of the AWC and framed as an exhibition not against the war but rather in favor of peace—with its austere Minimalist aesthetic intended as a salvo against the overt and conventionally figurative nature of the era's protest art.[16] LeWitt made his first wall drawing for this exhibition, and Piper has credited him with initially suggesting her work to Lippard.[17] The second exhibition, in November, was *Groups*, at the School of Visual Arts Gallery, in New York. Piper was the only woman artist in a group show of her peers, including Robert Barry, Jonathan Borofsky, Steve Gianakos, Douglas Huebler, and Alex Katz.[18] Each artist was asked to photograph a group or groups of people, known to the artist or not, every day for a week. Published later in *Studio International* magazine, with both the instructional text and each artist's results, *Groups* can be understood as an attempt to make an archive of the public through the photographic document. Piper's work, a set of seven Polaroid photographs of friends in her loft **(pages 174, 175)**, represents one of her earliest forays into photography. The texts that accompany them describe the materiality and content of the images in strictly formal and objectively measurable terms: the physical dimensions of the "object" (the snapshot itself), the tactile qualities of that object, and the estimated distribution and dimensions of the grayscale tones to be found on its surface. The fact that she chose to photograph friends in her loft, however, rather than strangers on the street, thus constructing a representation of social relationships, seems like a critical juncture in a previously solitary practice and marks an early moment of reckoning with her immediate public—her friends and interlocutors.[19]

Piper's break with strictly conceptual practice was not only about moving away from making objects; it was also about the world crashing in on this hermetically indexical practice. She later described the genesis of this break:

> In the spring of 1970 a number of events occurred that changed everything for me: (1) The invasion of Cambodia; (2) The Women's Movement; (3) Kent State and Jackson State; (4) The closing of CCNY, where I was in my first term as a philosophy major, during the student rebellion. . . . Mostly I did a lot of thinking about my position as an artist, a woman, and a black; and about the natural disadvantages of those attributes. . . . I see now that the crisis and solution was the result of the invasion by the "outside world" of my aesthetic isolation.[20]

Although Piper was one of the few women who moved easily within the boys' club of Conceptual art and her racial identity was not an issue because it was not visible, this moment of rupture—the beginning of undoing the reductive strictures of pure conceptual idiom—was a common refrain of resistance among women artists, a reaction to the exclusions of the advanced art of the late 1960s. Piper wouldn't turn to identity and race as subjects for her work until 1979, with the poignant *Political Self-Portrait* works **(pages 220–22)**, in which different snapshot images of Piper, altered by graphic interventions, are overlaid with first-person texts recounting episodes of sexist, racist, and class-discriminatory behavior she had experienced. The narrative voice is a measured one, distanced in time from the original incidents, so that the text becomes more universal, more accessible, if all the more poignant because the incidents are real. Her awareness of her racial identity, and of the ways in which it was consequential to others and therefore affected her, would begin to find expression in her writings in the late 1970s.

Inner World to Outer Public

In the *Catalysis* works Piper used her body as an object, moving outside the art world's spaces and audience to make more immediate contact with a public:

> It seems that since I've stopped using gallery space, and stopped announcing the pieces, I've stopped using art frameworks. There is very little that separates what I'm doing from quirky personal activity. Except I've been thinking a lot about the fact that I relate what I'm doing to people. . . . I subscribe to the idea that art reflects the society to a certain extent, and I feel as though a lot of the work I'm doing is being done because I am a paradigm of what the society is.[21]

Her move from solitary private performances, such as the *Catalysis* works, to works for which a reactive public was a key component pivoted on her coming to understand herself as a "self-conscious object."[22] Of greatest interest for the purposes of this text is Piper's fashioning of her various performance personae as she moved into the world as a self-conscious, self-realized object, and her exploitation of dance as a medium through which to do this. With her confidence, elastic articulation, and knowledge of dance as a discursive form with a history and practice, she has engaged with audiences in a visceral, physical way, as part of a larger project of transferring to and eventually embedding in them complex ideas about race and class.

To talk about personae is to talk about roles, and in various autobiographical texts, Piper has considered the many roles she has inhabited since her childhood. She returns to autobiography in order to reflect upon the ways in which her identity as an artist, a woman, and a person of acknowledged African descent was formed and has informed her work. Her most recent effort is *Escape to Berlin: A Travel Memoir*, published in 2018, which tracks the recent decades of her life, including her move from the United States to Berlin, in text interspersed with images by the artist; it is an autobiographical work as self-portrait. The various personae inventoried in her work and writings constitute a socially constructed self that includes musical prodigy, fashion model, street performer, discotheque dancer, analysand, artist, and yogi.[23] Autobiography as a form of writing exists outside Piper's artistic production, as a backdrop informed by a deep interest in popular forms of culture, and it is interspersed with references to music and dance, both of which were eventually integrated into the performance-lecture format that she invented to contain them.[24] "Kinds of Performing Objects I Have Been," one of her inventories of experience, of 1972, functions as an index for the Mythic Being, the persona in which Piper's ideas about objecthood and personhood were exteriorized in the form of an alter ego: a straight man who shares Piper's genetic history but whose experience of society and sexual politics is completely different. (In one iteration he gazes at the viewer, holding a cigarette to his lips, with a thought bubble declaring "I embody everything you most hate and fear." (page 207).) Piper considered her self-fashioning of the Mythic Being while fighting off a headache from the dual rigors of her modeling job and the birthing of a new persona. She should be in drag, but should he have a personal history? What does a "static emblem of alien confrontation" wear?[25] She found it exhausting to fully inhabit such a character—learning to walk in a masculine way, concealing her gender through the mantle of his bad taste and heterosexual swagger—and wondered if it would be the end of her art making.

The character of the Mythic Being would figure in various forms, in works in different mediums, from 1973 to 1976. He first appeared on the streets of New York; then in a series of ads in the pages of the *Village Voice* (pages 194–98); and later evolved into the transgender central protagonist in both versions of *Some Reflective Surfaces* and *It's Just Art* (1980) (pages 218, 219). In his first street performances, appearing in an afro wig, applied mustache, and oversized mirrored shades, the Mythic Being moved through the streets reciting various monologues, including a rant about his mother excerpted from Piper's journal—personal content turned into pithy, disjunctive commentary delivered with the seriousness of a conjuring, a mantra that allowed the character to move from Piper's apartment to the sidewalk, into public space, among an audience—from inner world to outer public. The journal texts also appeared in the *Village Voice* ads, in cartoonish thought bubbles crudely superimposed onto the photographs, creating a bizarre juxtaposition of diaristic musings with the almost ethereal presence of a shadowy male figure peering out from a crowded page of gallery ads. As if observing him as a conceptual and aesthetic problem, Piper said of the Mythic Being,

> 1. I would never dress that way if I were a man; nor would I ever be attracted to someone who dressed that way.
> 2. He is more than an outer shell, surprisingly. It takes more energy to sustain his attitudes, mannerisms, movements, etc., than I thought.
> 3. I find myself getting very involved in this mental framework. Chanting the mantra suspends me in a tightrope between two personalities.[26]

Suspended between the character's personality and the artist's intent, Piper channels the various mantras into direct address, speaking to her audience as a self-conscious object, pushing her subterranean thoughts out into public space. In the *Village Voice* works this address is achieved through the formal device of the thought bubble, which layers in the artist's voice—an interior voice, a narrative of subjectivity that dislodges the work from being only about Piper or her experience but rather negotiates something more abstract and therefore more generalized. The text of the bubbles, handwritten on a white background, underscores its origin in the intimate milieu of the journal entry, while also evoking the newspaper setting and, after the fact, giving the works an almost filmic quality. Here the Mythic Being's interior is somewhat comically out of context: prurient and slightly sleazy (as in a text that was censored by the editors of the *Village Voice*—"Don't feel particularly horny, but feel I should masturbate anyway just because I feel so good about doing it."—and replaced with a cryptic announcement that the ad intended for that space was available at the Jaap Rietmann bookstore in SoHo), but also poignant and specific to the concerns of a struggling artist in downtown New York ("I really wish I had a firmer grip on reality. Sometimes I think I have better ideas than anyone else around with the exception of Sol LeWitt and possibly Bob Smithson, whose ideas I really respect.") (fig. 6).[27]

In the complexly layered *It's Just Art*, which is organized around video documentation of a performance at Allen Memorial Art Museum, at Oberlin College, in 1980, a transgendered permutation of the Mythic Being (with thin mustache and Piper's own long, wavy hair), serenely regards the viewer from behind oversized sunglasses, while Piper, in voice-over, reads "The End of Cambodia?," an article by William Shawcross, published in the *New York Review of Books* in 1980, on the genocide in Cambodia carried out by the Khmer Rouge. As she reads, Rufus and Chaka Khan's disco ballad "Do You Love What You Feel?" plays at the same time.[28] The visual component of the work is similarly collaged: a montage of horrific news images of Cambodian refugees, the atrocities of the Khmer Rouge, and the American invasion. It is a disturbingly calm mash-up of violent images, coolly detached reportage, and the eerie, almost ethereal presence of the transgendered version of the Mythic Being, who stands in for our own dissociative response to the real consequences of war. The music is irresistible, and as we fall under the sway of its rhythms, we are drawn further into the parade of violence. Here the thought balloons function again as a mode of address, bringing the unspoken and the unconscious to the surface, making them impossible to ignore, and heightening "the self-conscious reaction of the actual viewing audience to the political information being disseminated."[29] Abstracted from his static position in the pages of the *Voice*, where he initially appeared in 1973–75, occupying the disconnected place between personal journal entries and overtly disturbing and uncomfortable social situations, the passive, femme Mythic Being of *It's Just Art* cynically turns the viewer into a voyeur of violence. The slippage between images, voiceover, and Piper's presence becomes a source of powerful tension.

Listening by Dancing

Piper's autobiographical texts speak to a life inflected by music and dance, including piano, violin, and ballet lessons, and her stint as a discotheque dancer. In 1980 she was listening to Patti Smith, The Police, and the Talking Heads; in 1981 she heard Ornette Coleman perform live. The strong presence of funk in *It's Just Art* turns African-American popular music into a key compositional and structural device. Piper recalls in her chronology that when she performed it in Seattle, in 1981, a member of the audience asked her why she was up on stage shaking her booty.[30]

Dance, with its particular balance of intimacy and abstraction, provides another mode of direct address in Piper's work, as both performance and conceptual framework:

> I was interested in further exploring the notion of dance as a medium of performer-audience confrontation in the specific context of the evasion of political responsibility. The use of physical movements and gestures in dance as a medium of communication is less explicit than speech and less intimate than physical displays of affection, sexuality, or aggression. At the same time it is more concrete than speech and more conventionalized—and therefore intersubjectively accessible—than physical displays of emotion.[31]

Funk Lessons, a collaborative performance staged seven times between 1983 and 1984, is among Piper's most iconic and most popular works (pages 230, 231). It is now widely shown as *Funk Lessons with Adrian Piper*, a film by Sam Samore of a performance at the University of California, Berkeley (1983), and has garnered a range of reactions, including being moved to tears.[32] The accessibility of the work, both live and in documentation—the music's compelling, mesmerizing rhythm and deeply American roots—is certainly part of the its longevity, but *Funk Lessons* is also a brilliant piece of institutional and social critique. Piper, in her disarming pedagogical persona, infiltrates the arena of social dance to deliver an embodied cultural education. The gold-embossed invitation mailed out as an advertisement for the performance offers "music appreciation" and "social dancing," and promises that the artist "[has] rhythm, will travel." The poster for a performance at New Langton Arts, San Francisco, featuring an image of Bootsy Collins, of Parliament-Funkadelic, decked out in full funk regalia, also advertised the performance as "a collaborative experiment in cross-cultural transfusion" (fig. 7).[33]

Piper's invitation to dance constitutes an optional social contract, an agreement entered into by the artist and any willing participants. Opting out is always a possibility, and part of the video's charm is watching the public, some reluctant, some eager to jump in, as they are drawn in by the irrepressible syncopation of funk rhythms and the artist's disarmingly approachable address. The artist's pedagogical voice in *Funk Lessons* would be the formal and conceptual center of Piper's direct-address works going forward; patient, professorial, and

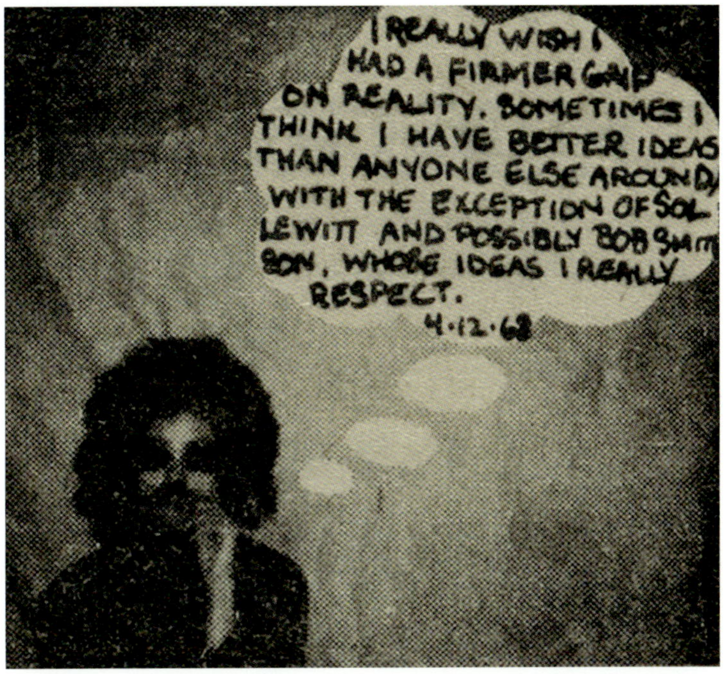

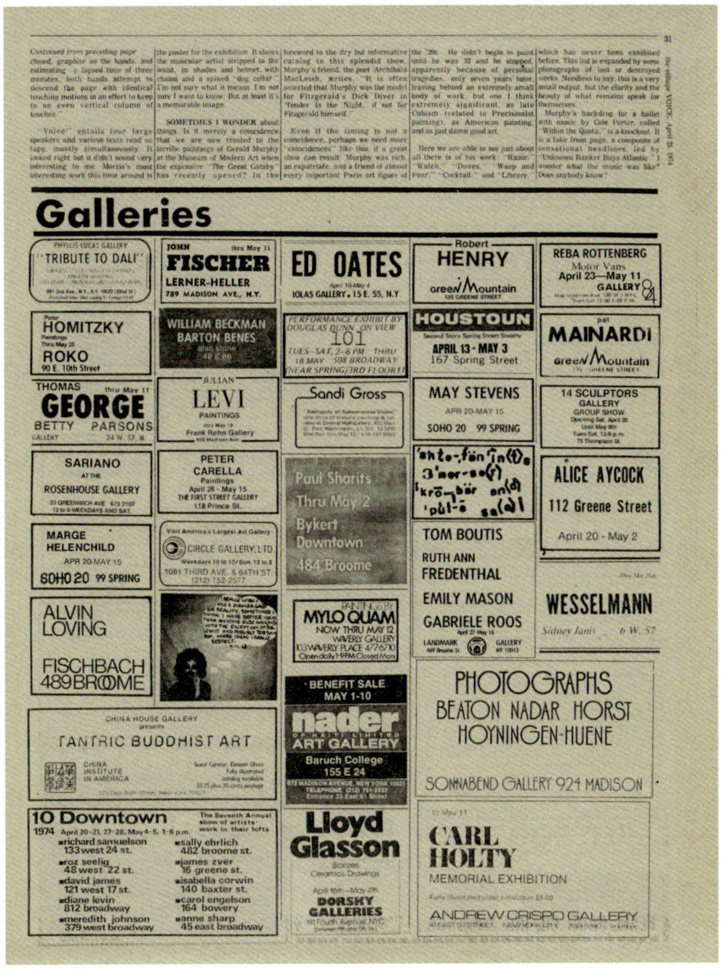

Fig. 6
The Mythic Being, Village Voice Ads. 1973–75
Advertisements appearing in the *Village Voice*. Seventeen newspaper pages
Each 17 × 14 in. (43.2 × 35.6 cm)
The Museum of Modern Art, New York. Purchased with funds provided by Donald L. Bryant, Jr., Agnes Gund, Marlene Hess and James D. Zirin, Marie-Josée and Henry R. Kravis, Donald B. Marron, The Edward John Noble Foundation, Katherine Farley and Jerry Speyer, and Committee on Drawings Funds in honor of Kathy Fuld. Details: *The Mythic Being, Cycle I: 4/12/68*. April 25, 1974

almost overly expositional, she is also funny and sly, withholding her own much more extensive experience with the subject. (That Piper is herself a great and exuberant dancer is revealed in later works.) But the goal of the performance is much less safe and more aspirational in its desire to destabilize received notions about cultural identity: as identified by the artist in the text "Notes on Funk," it is nothing less than to "restructure people's social identities, by making accessible to them a common medium of communication—funk music and dance—that has been largely inaccessible to white culture and has consequently exacerbated the xenophobic fear, hostility, and incomprehension that generally characterize the reaction of whites to black popular culture in this society."[34] Piper breaks down the cultural history and mechanics of funk in a way her audience can relate to, helping them move through any initial anxiety they may have, creating a situation in which the participants might be able to understand and confront their unacknowledged racist assumptions about African-American popular culture and its associations with class, rhythm, sexuality, and violence. None of this is made explicit or is overtly visible; nevertheless, the group ethos that forms as the artist and her participants dance together is powerful and moving to watch. There is, of course, no way to gauge social transformation. But in this, or indeed in any of Piper's work, the insistent clarity of her language and the trenchant and detailed cultural analysis make *Funk Lessons* one of the most affecting works of socially engaged art: it establishes a common ground, a meeting place for a vexed subject and a social space, at a time when such zones are rare indeed.

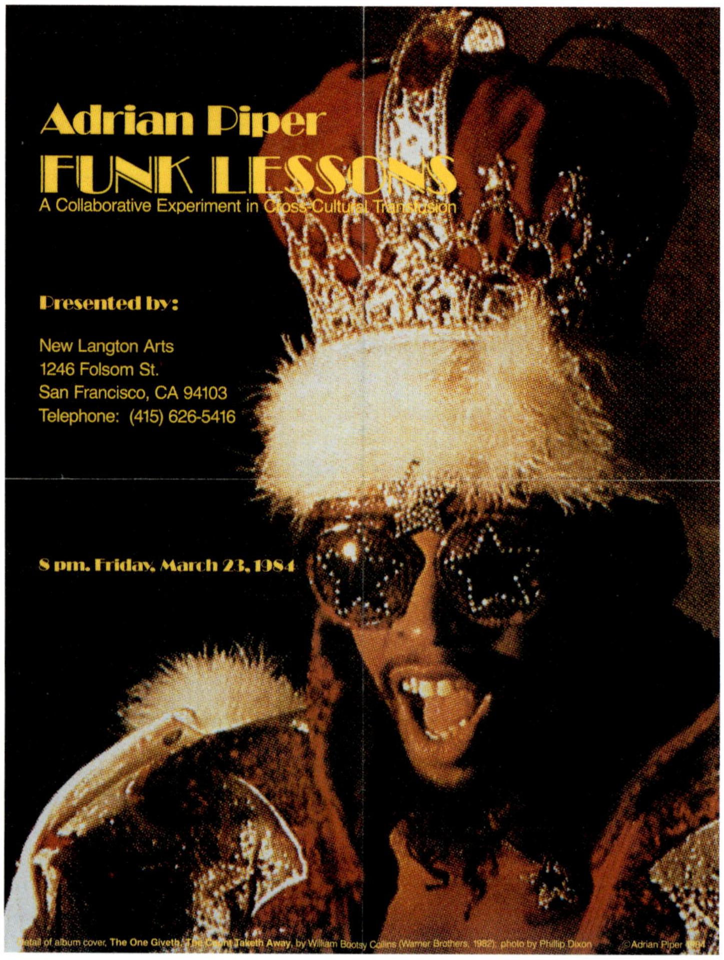

Fig. 7
Funk Lessons: A Collaborative Experiment in Cross-Cultural Transfusion. 1984
Photolithograph
24 × 18 in. (61 × 45.7 cm)
The Museum of Modern Art Library, New York

The success of *Funk Lessons* can be measured at least in part by the negative reactions it provoked. At the Minneapolis College of Art and Design, a poster advertising the event was defaced with vernacular language calling attention to the fact of Piper's racial identity—exposing the racist assumption that her identity is something she would actively try to hide.[35] This response, of course, goes right to the heart of the matter: what are the assumptions we make about one another? Piper's dancing public has reacted as well, with responses that range from reluctant and uptight to what Piper calls "an antidote to the syndrome of the Other: Fuck it. Let's boogie."[36] Indeed, she has framed the work as a developing language of communication:

> Funk constitutes a language of interpersonal communication and collective self-expression that has its origins in African tribal music and dance and is the result of the increasing interest of contemporary black musicians and the populace in those sources elicited by the Civil Rights Movement of the 1960s and early 1970s. . . . This medium of expression has been largely inaccessible to white culture, in part because of the different roles of social dance in white as opposed to black culture. . . . My immediate aim in staging the large-scale performance . . . was to enable everyone present to GET DOWN AND PARTY. TOGETHER.[37]

This is a radical idea: empowerment through collective experience and the embodiment of history and politics by those participating in it, toward the possibility of finding a place of greater cultural understanding and overcoming racial barriers. The consequences of transferring agency from artist to participant are subtle but potentially profound; what is transferred turns out to be the obligations and responsibilities of nothing less than enlightenment. What are the implications for an audience that internalizes a political and ethical question? Piper has written of using "the performance situation therapeutically, as a way of trying to come to terms with deeply internalized racist stereotypes by which we are all victimized in one way or another."[38] And all of this is brought about by Piper's particular form of experiential direct address; along with funk music, it becomes a medium of communication. No other artist in the early 1980s achieved such a deeply political and subversive collectivity.

Piper's relationship to funk, like Graham's to rock music, is an intervention in the history and reception of a popular art form.[39] But her activation of funk is as a physical medium, a dance form that simultaneously allows one-on-one contact and the building of something collective. Along with funk music it makes up a social glue that is able to contain the mixed responses to and anxieties about the cultural differences of her participating public. In *It's Just Art* this is carried out by the soul queen Chaka Kahn, but there is an underlying harshness in that work, in the slippage between the attraction of the music and the repulsion of the violent and disturbing images. Viewers drawn in by the music find themselves pushed out by the reality of their own lassitude.

Piper's meta-performances, participatory lectures based on the reprising and augmenting of already existing works, grew out of this lecture style—accessible, conversational, and encouraging direct dialogue among groups of people. They recall the teach-ins of the Vietnam era, both inspiring and practical, a way to proactively address the political issues of the 1960s in the consciousness-raising groups that became a structural part of the feminist political movement at the end of the decade. Piper was certainly familiar with these grass roots strategies through her work in the Civil Rights Movement, in consciousness-raising groups, in consciousness-raising groups with the Art Worker's Coalition, and as an organizer herself, of a consciousness-raising group in 1971.[40] The first such performance, *Funk Lessons Meta-Performance*, in 1987, was both pedagogical and participatory; the culminating meta-performance, *Shiva Dances with the Art Institute of Chicago*, in 2004, was part lecture, part instruction, and part social dance—one of the most powerful works of participatory art of the last fifty years. This work, which provides the thematic origin of this essay, is reconsidered later on.

Decide Who You Are

Piper kept some distance from the contentious culture wars of the 1990s, but her works from that decade uniquely mark the era's discourses of race and xenophobia, through her own experiences of blackness, whiteness, and otherness. Indeed, her work so precisely reflects the questions of justice and equity achieving wider attention now, in 2018, that it feels prescient. Her discourse of resistance began with the "*reactive guerrilla performances* . . . intervention in order to prevent co-optation" of *My Calling (Card) #1* and *#2* (page 246).[41] These performances borrowed the form of the professional business card, that predigital mode of social networking. Each card is printed in a slightly different way. The first, given to people making racist remarks (or tacitly agreeing with them) in Piper's presence, is on light- or medium-brown paper; the second, given to men making unwanted advances in bars and discos, is on white card stock and appears more like a standard business card.[42] The text on both cards is written in the first person, and both are very firm and polite. Both performances in effect turn the tables on race- and gender-based assumptions with a transaction, one initiated by a racist comment or unwanted come-on and completed with the taking of a card and the internalizing, or not, of the information it contains.

In both cases, the direct address of the cards creates an intimate confrontation. The one entailed by *My Calling (Card) #1* is somewhat more complex, because the card gives the recipient new information: that Piper is black. As the offender absorbs the text on the card, the transaction is certainly likely to activate change, whether through defensiveness, retreat, or (perhaps) apology. Like the *Catalysis* performances, the calling-card encounters were personal actions executed with unsuspecting participants; as in those performances, an exchange is initiated, a social turn is launched. *My Calling (Card) #1* and *#2* are regularly shown in galleries, but such display is only secondary to their functioning within the world of human social relations—although, indeed, they retain their remarkable power even in exhibition settings: Piper recedes as the responsibility for respectful interaction is turned back onto the viewer left holding the proverbial card. The hegemony of the accepted art-viewing environment cannot remain intact in the presence of such works.

Piper's participatory modes became more pointed in the 1990s, and at the same time more ambitious in their invitation, raising the conceptual and political stakes. The familiar architecture of the voting booth in *Vote/Emote* (1990) feels quaint and oddly optimistic, in its nod to privacy and choice—belying, of course, the history of voter exclusion and suppression. The title, too, is somewhat provocative, suggesting that we vote with something more (or less) than our rational minds, a binary frequently found at the ethical center of Piper's work. Each of four booths contains a backlit image of protesters of visibly African descent and a notebook in which viewers are instructed to list "fears of what we might know about you," "fears of how we might treat you," "fears of what we might think of you," and "fears of what we might do with your accumulations." This intimate space—a putative space of neutrality and privacy—allows viewers to receive these direct instructions, which challenge them to confess and reflect on their most privately held notions about identity and character, in a way perhaps less immediately destabilizing than direct conversation. Among these provocations, the question of what might be done with our accumulations is intriguing. Bodies and their residue, the remains of a life, come up in several of Piper's works from around that time, including *The Big Four Oh* (1988) (page 249) and *What Will Become of Me* (1985–ongoing) (pages 234, 235). "Accumulations" may refer to the things that evidence a life. But it may also refer to accumulations of people—to the power of collective protest and representation, in the contexts of both political protest and political art.[43] In *Vote/Emote* Piper again exploits the pull between the anonymous and the personal, between private and public ethics, challenging viewers to put themselves on the line, to choose.

The environment of *Cornered* (page 248) recalls the formal and orderly qualities of a classroom: a video monitor positioned in a gallery corner, isolated from the viewer by an overturned wood table and faced by a triangular array of chairs. On the wall behind the monitor, on either side of it, are copies of Piper's father's two birth certificates, one identifying him as "white," the other as "octoroon." In the video Piper calmly and insistently interrogates her viewers about their racial presumptions. Her congenial, professorial delivery and prim appearance, in plain blue sweater and white pearls, are decidedly at odds with the confrontational face-off set up by the installation: artist and viewer are both cornered, divided by the table positioned as a barricade, as if in self-defense. "I'm black," Piper says in the video. "Now let's deal with this social fact and the fact of my stating it together." In *Passing beyond Passing*, a video of 2004, she notes the varied reactions of *Cornered*'s viewers, who sort themselves into various identities depending on their reactions to the work; many of them, she observes, presume themselves to be white.[44]

Cornered, Piper has said, faces "the illusion of otherness, the illusion that each of us is defined not just by our individual uniqueness but by our racial uniqueness. . . . In *Cornered* I try to undercut this ideology [of uniqueness] by exploding the myth of racial separation."[45] Viewer and artist occupy the space together, but here it is the artist who speaks, in a relationship that is contingent upon the silence of the audience, and the fears and actions that this silence mitigates. *Cornered* remains within Minimalism's formal lexicon and is visually anchored to the architecture of the gallery, a connection made overt in one of the volumes of Piper's writings, which places an image of *Out of the Corner*, Piper's 1990 update of the work, just below one showing LeWitt's *46 Three-Part Variations on 3 Different Kinds of Cubes* (1967) (figs. 8, 9).[46] In both *Cornered* and *Out of the Corner*, the chairs extend out into the viewing space, inviting viewers to sit and engage in an act of conscious listening. The tension in these works lies precisely in the problem of listening versus hearing, in whether or not viewers take the opportunity for reflection, and this is what moves it into the participatory sphere that Piper's work continues to occupy.[47]

In "The Triple Negation of Colored Women Artists," an essay from 1990, Piper looks at the way in which artwork by CWAs (her acronym) is only ever discussed in light of the artists' identities, resulting in the "Eurocentric art world's negation of CWAs along three dimensions: as coloreds, as women, and as artists."[48] She was responding to another essay, the artist Howardena Pindell's "Art World Racism: A Documentation," of 1989, which, by amassing art-world statistics, tracked the exclusion of African-American artists from mainstream art institutions. Piper was already cautious about the art-world embrace of multiculturalism, the redress and inclusion on the part of museums intended to respond to decades, even centuries, of exclusion, and her text could be a primer on the early years of the culture wars:

> I am encouraged by this recent development, but I am also suspicious of its long-term significance. It coincides too neatly with an interest in difference and otherness in other fields such as comparative literature, history, and anthropology, *in which the main subject of investigation is the person, not the artifact*. . . . The object of preoccupation defined by these issues is not the artifact but rather its producer as "other."[49]

In the present, no curator or historian can claim to be unaware of the artistic triple bind faced by women of color, but in 1990 the notion of turning that very disadvantage into a space of empowerment was a radical proposal. *What It's Like, What It Is #3* (1991) (pages 258, 259), created for the exhibition *Dislocations*, organized by Robert Storr at MoMA, makes plain this formula for erasure and negation inside the context of the museum. Storr commissioned projects that critiqued the history of and absences from institutions such as MoMA, and the exhibition as a whole would later be understood as a harbinger of the contentious decade to come. Projects were dispersed in several locations throughout the building, including the galleries dedicated to painting and sculpture. Works by Piper, Chris Burden, and David Hammons were installed on the third floor, and work by Bruce Nauman in the basement, spaces frequently used for contemporary exhibitions. (That *What It's Like, What It Is #3* would be reinstalled thirty years later, for her retrospective, in MoMA's atrium, where Barnett Newman's obelisk had been placed for the opening of the Museum's new Yoshio Taniguchi building, in 2004, functions as a different kind of pointed institutional critique.)[50]

What It's Like, What It Is #3 is a white cube—almost blindingly white—containing a single square column with video monitors installed on each of its sides, toward the top, with stadium-style seating around it. Viewers seated in this antiseptic environment find themselves faced with a talking head—an African-American man—denying stereotypes about his identity and blackness in a seemingly unending list, in the same flat pedagogical voice used by Piper in *Cornered*: "I'm not pushy. I'm not sneaky. I'm not lazy. I'm not noisy. I'm not vulgar. I'm not rowdy. I'm not horny. I'm not scary. I'm not shiftless. I'm not crazy. I'm not servile. I'm not stupid. I'm not dirty. I'm not smelly. I'm not childish. I'm not evil."[51] These derogatory epithets seem to trap the speaker—a black man held within the constraints of the hegemonic institution, the white cube standing in for museum architecture but also specifically recalling LeWitt's early serial plane sculptures. The work implicates the viewer as well, who must contend with the blame implied in the man's insistent denial of these common racist assumptions. A narrow strip of mirror surrounds the inside perimeter of the work, infinitely reflecting and repeating the talking head, and forcing the (overwhelmingly white) viewers to watch themselves being directly addressed, both as a group and one to one, effectively and firmly riveting them to their seats.[52] The highly structured inverted pyramid of *What It's Like, What It Is #3* expands upon the shape and simple theatricality of *Cornered*: a single voice, speaking plainly, in a highly orchestrated environment, delivering uncomfortable truths.

Whom does Piper engage with this work? No viewer can remain passive: each becomes a participant faced with ethical choices about what to ignore and what to take away. The receptive viewer is reminded that racial identity is as much of a construction as the white cube—a now-formulaic understanding of identity that Piper's proposals move beyond. The assumed neutrality of the institution is a similar product of cultural conditioning, received by one generation after another—

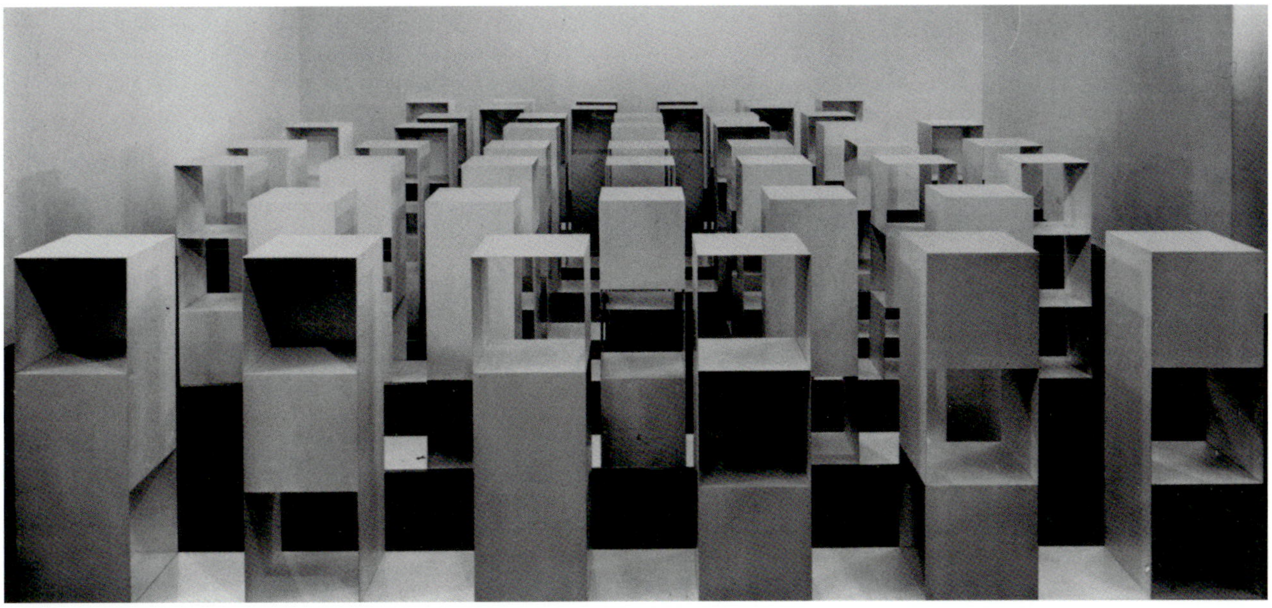

Fig. 8
Sol LeWitt
46 Three-Part Variations on 3 Different Kinds of Cubes. 1967
Enamel on forty-six aluminum structures
Each 45 × 15 × 15 in. (114 × 38 × 38 cm)
Installation view in *46 Three-Part Variations on 3 Different Kinds of Cubes*, Dwan Gallery, New York, February 3–28, 1968

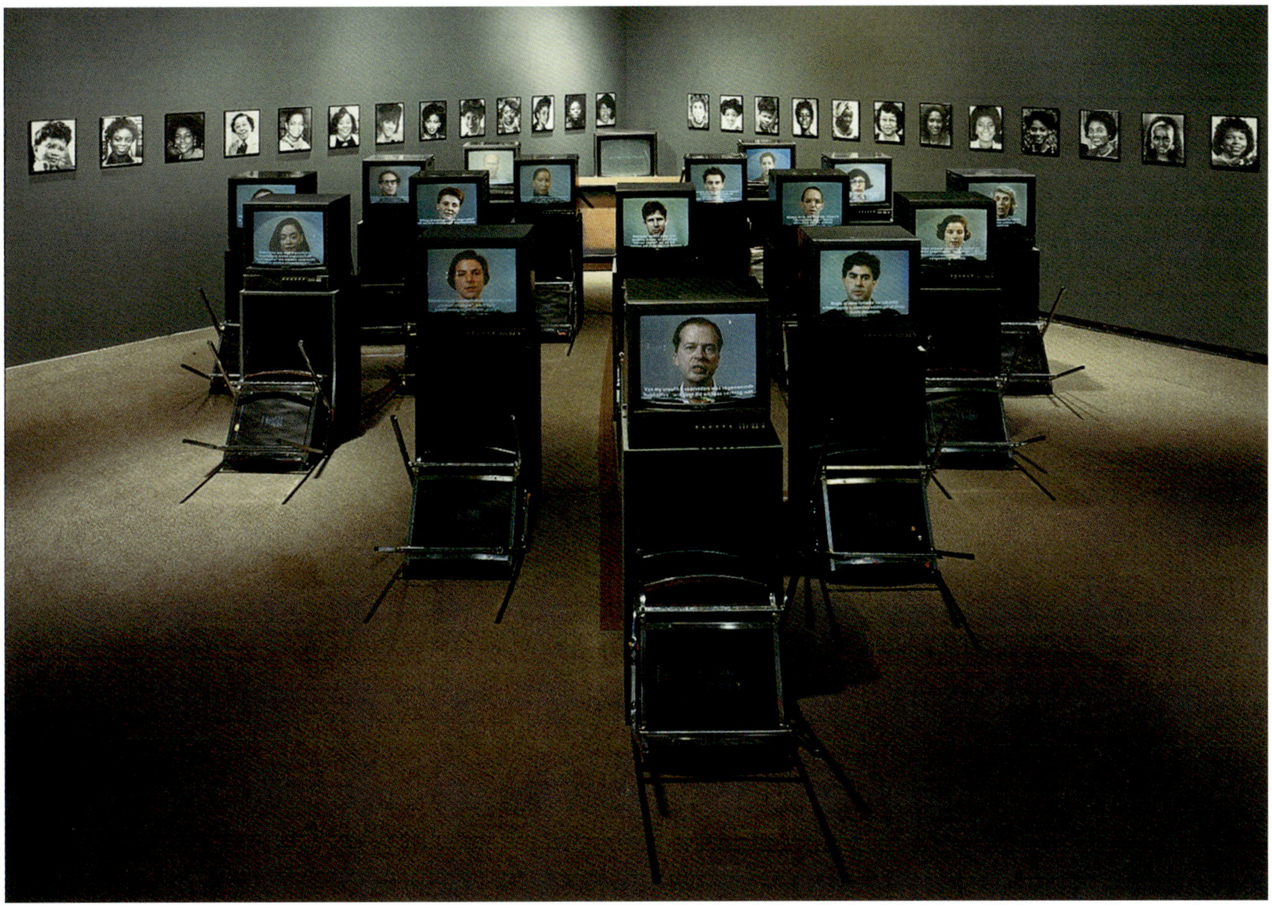

Fig. 9
Out of the Corner. 1990
Video installation. Video (color, sound), 00:26:00, with seventeen monitors, sixteen pedestals, table, seventeen chairs, and sixty-four gelatin silver prints
Dimensions variable
Whitney Museum of American Art, New York

in fact, a myth. And while this may now seem trite, it is a postmodern legacy that remains difficult for many people to accept, as evidenced by the enormous backlash against immigrants and people of color heightened by the election to the U.S. presidency, in 2016, of Donald Trump, who himself rehearses, with his vocal minority, the most primitively racist ideas.

Among the many early-1990s interventions into museum institutions, by a generation of artists acting out against the received binaries that dictated how race and class were understood, the critique in Piper's work remains the most pointed and most uncompromising, in part because it insists on interpersonal human confrontation, rather than formulaic abstraction, to activate a shift in consciousness. It is startling, now, with nearly thirty years of hindsight, to realize how trenchant these works were at the time and how urgent they still are. As the football star Colin Kaepernick continues to be punished for refusing to stand during the National Anthem—kneeling, instead, to highlight cultural indifference and racial divisiveness—it is as critical as it ever was to dispel assumptions about African-American masculinity.

In his essay for the *Dislocations* catalogue, Storr considers Piper's relationship to abstraction, noting that it is retrospective, as she gave it up when she shifted from a purely conceptual practice in pursuit of something rooted in the real. He quotes from her text "Flying," of 1987:

> Abstraction is flying. Abstracting is ascending to higher and higher levels of conceptual generalization; soaring back and forth, reflectively circling around above the specificity and immediacy of things and events in space and time.... Abstraction is also flight.... Abstraction is freedom from the socially prescribed and consensually accepted.... Abstraction is a solitary journey through the conceptual universe, with no anchors, no cues, no signposts, no maps.[53]

Piper's movement away from abstraction evolved into direct address to viewers, into locating us in the political and social here and now. Her turn to the subjects of racism and xenophobia—a response to the experience, as Piper has described it, of other people's need to assign her a racial category, in essence to directly address her and "tell me who and what [they] thought I was"— was a turn toward a realism that specifically borrows images and text from the real world, as a means of opening a conversation.[54]

In 1991 Anita Hill, a young African-American lawyer, testified to being sexually harassed by Clarence Thomas, the African-American nominee to the Supreme Court of the United States. The televised confirmation hearings and the accompanying media commentary were riveting and deeply disturbing, as Hill was turned from victim into a racist and sexist caricature of a scheming female—an infuriating pivot that for many women was indelible and formative.[55] It was a moment that repositioned national discussion about race based on the power dynamic between the powerful male Supreme Court nominee and the lone female protagonist simply speaking the truth. In Piper's Decide Who You Are series, made the same year, Hill is both concrete image and symbol of a lone but startlingly frank voice, of an unassailable form of speech (pages 260–67). She appears in nineteen of the twenty works, in a photograph showing her as an eight-year-old child, a visual and ethical anchor for the work and the symbolic center of the series.

Each work consists of framed magazine and newspaper photographs set between two panels whose images remain the same: Hill on the right and, on the left, a drawing by Piper of a small soapstone Chinese sculpture, inherited from her uncle, of the Three Wise Monkeys (see no evil, hear no evil, speak no evil). The media images vary, but they can be read as a constellation of victims and perpetrators of various kinds of violence and class and racial conflict—police brutality, murder, hunting, as well as the kind of white-collar crime whose damage reaches down into the poorest families. *Decide Who You Are #19: Torch Song Alert* **(fig. 10)** groups an image of police officers in riot helmets next to an overturned car with, above it, close-up images of Clark Clifford, Charles Keating, and the former U.S. President George H. W. Bush, all of them powerful men who have remained unscathed by their various crimes.[56] The image of Anita Hill is overlaid with text, assembled by Piper from comments by and conversations with her colleagues, listing dismissive and defensive rejoinders to protests against race or gender discrimination. Such speech, the *Decide* works suggest, also inflicts violence. In Hill's case this violence was both explicit and implicit; the sexist and racist responses to her claims allowed the public to instrumentalize her body and privacy, opening them to discussion and judgment.

In the left-hand panels of the *Decide* works, overprinted on the image of the three monkeys, are Piper's personal writing.[57] These texts, including that text printed on every iteration of the Hill image, were published in 1992, by Paula Cooper Gallery, with additional condensed texts that amplify the problems of the misread and misrepresented body. The compilation of defensive excuses, threats, and rationalizations that overlays Hill's image, single spaced and all uppercased, pile up relentlessly, assaulting viewers directly and adamantly insisting that we take a side, that we choose a voice with which to align and to consider why we have done so. How do we decide who we are? The threshold of ethics, the moment when a viewer must make a choice or consciously opt out, forms the structural logic of many of Piper's works from the 1990s to the present. And the ethical choice is always clear. The Decide Who You Are series concedes nothing. The gauge of complicity it proposes is uncompromising; silence, it suggests, whether Hill's or our own, is not an option.

The Decide texts are deserving of a separate study of their own, on the complex marshaling of different voices to express acerbic, darkly ironic political satire ("How to Handle Black People: A Beginner's Manual," "Field Work") as well as brutal violence ("Hardball," "Parasite," "Skinned Alive"). These voices accumulate into an anthology of positions on power. One of the texts, which reappears in *Self-Portrait 2000* (2001), beginning "HEY, GOD!," curses an uncaring god, rattles our cage with alliteration and profanity, and grapples directly with a world without moral order—a world that seems to have abandoned reason.[58] It is as true and resonant now as it was in 1992. In *Please, God*, a work from 1990, the appeal takes a very different tone, tempered by the possibility of innocence, in a looped video of scrolling text that asks for protection from the treatment that young African-American girls will likely endure, set against footage of nine-year-old girls dancing as Billie

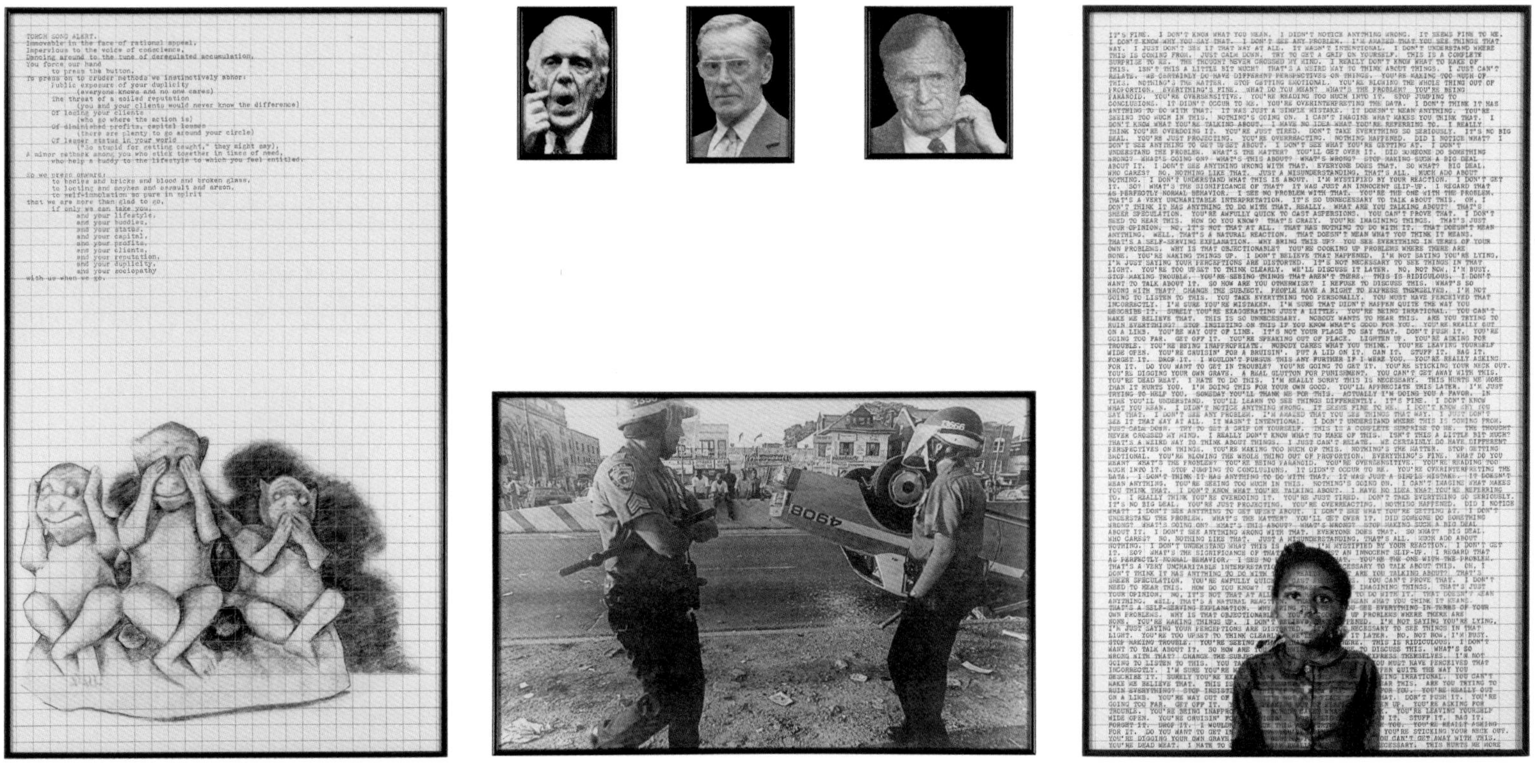

Fig. 10
Decide Who You Are #19: Torch Song Alert. 1992
Screenprinted images and text printed on six sheets of paper, mounted on foam core
72 × 42 in. (182.8 × 106.7 cm); 14 × 8½ in. (35.6 × 21.6 cm); 14½ × 9¾ in.
(36.8 × 24.8 cm); 14 × 13¼ in. (35.6 × 33.7 cm); 34¼ × 52 in. (87 × 132.1 cm);
and 72 × 42 in. (182.8 × 106.7 cm)
Solomon R. Guggenheim Museum, New York. Purchased with funds contributed by
the International Director's Council and the Photography Council

Holliday sings "God Bless the Child."[59] Piper's works on race operate both from a position of pessimism while also offering the possibility of hope. They insist on the present as an ethical compass, and are a reminder of where we have been.

Love, Peace, and Soul[60]

The philosopher Diarmuid Costello, writing about Piper's meta-performances, has argued that the multiple roles of philosopher, artist, and practitioner of yoga necessitate a multivalent practice that is itself a model of artistic self-fashioning.[61] The artist's public identity can be conceived as a performative part of her practice that is deeply informed by the Kantian idea of an identity always in formation.[62]

Shortly before she left the United States for good, in 2005, Piper was invited to the Art Institute of Chicago to present *Shiva Dances with the Art Institute of Chicago*, as part of a lecture series on hip-hop and global culture, which now exists as the meta-performance video of the same title (fig. 11). Piper projected the Color Wheel Series of digital images (pages 272, 273), with music and light effects, as the backdrop to a lecture performance. Piper has described this series in terms of the intersection of the color wheel—a Western construction, used for the display of the Pantone Matching System for the standardization and control of color—with Shiva, the Hindu god of yoga and dance.[63] Shiva, manifesting in the Color Wheel Series as Lord Nataraja, dances away evil and "destroys all names and forms," an apt and beautiful metaphor for the kind of social event proposed by Piper's dance-based works: literally going beyond language and joining bodies in movement to transcend social boundaries and norms.[64] Piper's disposition of colors—assigning them to the three Acting Heads in each image, using more than a thousand of them to represent the concealment of layers of identity, harnessing the idea of white as "the miscegenation of all colors," designating a specific set of works for each event in which they are shown—provides an almost infinite number of configurations.[65] When shown as individual works, the effect is different from that of being components of a meta-performance, but the potential of dance to break down the layers of illusion that stand between us and reality remains.

Shiva Dances with the Art Institute of Chicago was a performance event that combined a lecture and demonstration on funk music and dance, followed by a selection of film clips, at the end of which the audience spontaneously begins to dance along with her, the most stirring part of the work. The event concludes with a conversation between the artist and her audience about the meaning of the preceding experiences. In the first section, Piper breaks down funk as a dance form in a movement-based call and response, in which she suggests that her participants try out some dance elements, first nodding their heads, then standing and bouncing. These movements, she says, constitute tools for listening, as the body becomes a vehicle for a multisensory experience facilitating "cross cultural contact."[66] To watch the members of her audience—some of whom appear to be listening to the music and, perhaps, trying out these dance moves for the first time—is powerful. (Some audience members may have been familiar with Piper's work, but it's likely that many were there for the hip-hop, thus accessing Piper's conceptual practice through the more immediately accessible lens of current popular culture.)

A key part of the pedagogical portion of the lecture is a quick lesson in cultural history, which Piper accomplishes through a series of excerpts. First she shows the original *Funk Lessons* video, which historically grounds her subject, and as she is in that earlier work, Piper is disarming, friendly, and succinct. This is followed by clips from five Hollywood films that appropriate the device of teaching social dancing in order to overcome cultural and racial differences. These clips, in which hip-hop and funk function as critical protagonists, include *Honey* (2003), in which the combination of dance moves and basketball moves leads to a choreographed reconciliation; *Bringing Down the House* (2003), in which Queen Latifah loosens up a tightly wound Steve Martin; and a fantastically absurd scene from *Head of State* (2003), in which Chris Rock gets a room full of upper-middle-class white people to get down. The last clip in the series comes from the 2002 British film *The Guru*, in which an Indian dance teacher comes to New York City to find his fortune. His mishaps as a foreigner, both ironic and earnest, in white upper-middle-class culture lead to a hilarious, and joyful, cultural mash-up that brings people together across class and racial lines through dance. In all these films, it seems, uptight white people need people of color to show them how to relax. Dance is the social glue that brings together seemingly irreconcilable groups; with a lesson in pop-cultural history and a live demonstration, Piper posits dance as a defense against and a corrective for racism.

The lecture-demonstration's participatory aspect expands unexpectedly when an African-American woman breaks free of the gently moving, passively listening audience and climbs onto the stage to dance with Piper. She is immediately followed by more people, who seem jubilant, if a little surprised to find themselves there. The soundtrack at this point is a hypnotic section from *Shiva DANCES, for God's Sake (for John Talbert)* (2002), a sound work by Piper, which combines her voice with piano, Hindu chanting, and electronic stylings. We are urged, on the cover of the CD of the work, to "Wake Up and Get Down," to a melodic warm-up followed by ten minutes of "serious, funky, get-down-and-party, multilayered r&b rhythms. . . . Great for high-energy yoga, Dancekinetics, raves, world music dance parties."[67]

Dance as celebration is at the center of *Adrian Moves to Berlin* (page 304), a video created in 2007, two years after Piper had permanently left the United States. In Berlin's Alexanderplatz, the urban meeting point of the former East and West Germanys, she dances to the Euro beats of Berlin house music from the early 2000s. Here we finally see, in a looped, long-format video, what a skilled and graceful dancer she is. Her joyful singular figure occupies the vast public space—one that is strangely without scale in the peculiar manner of many of the city's public spaces after the fall of the Berlin Wall and the subsequent two decades of reconstruction. Piper has called this open-ended dance an improvisational "endurance task performance," and it is also, indeed, a rumination on artistic labor.[68] The construction workers who wander in and out of the video's background are, like Adrian, part of a process—Germany's reunification—bigger than themselves. The delight evident in the action and the location in which it takes place suggest that Piper's spirits have been lifted at the prospect of living and working in a country where two sides of a cultural

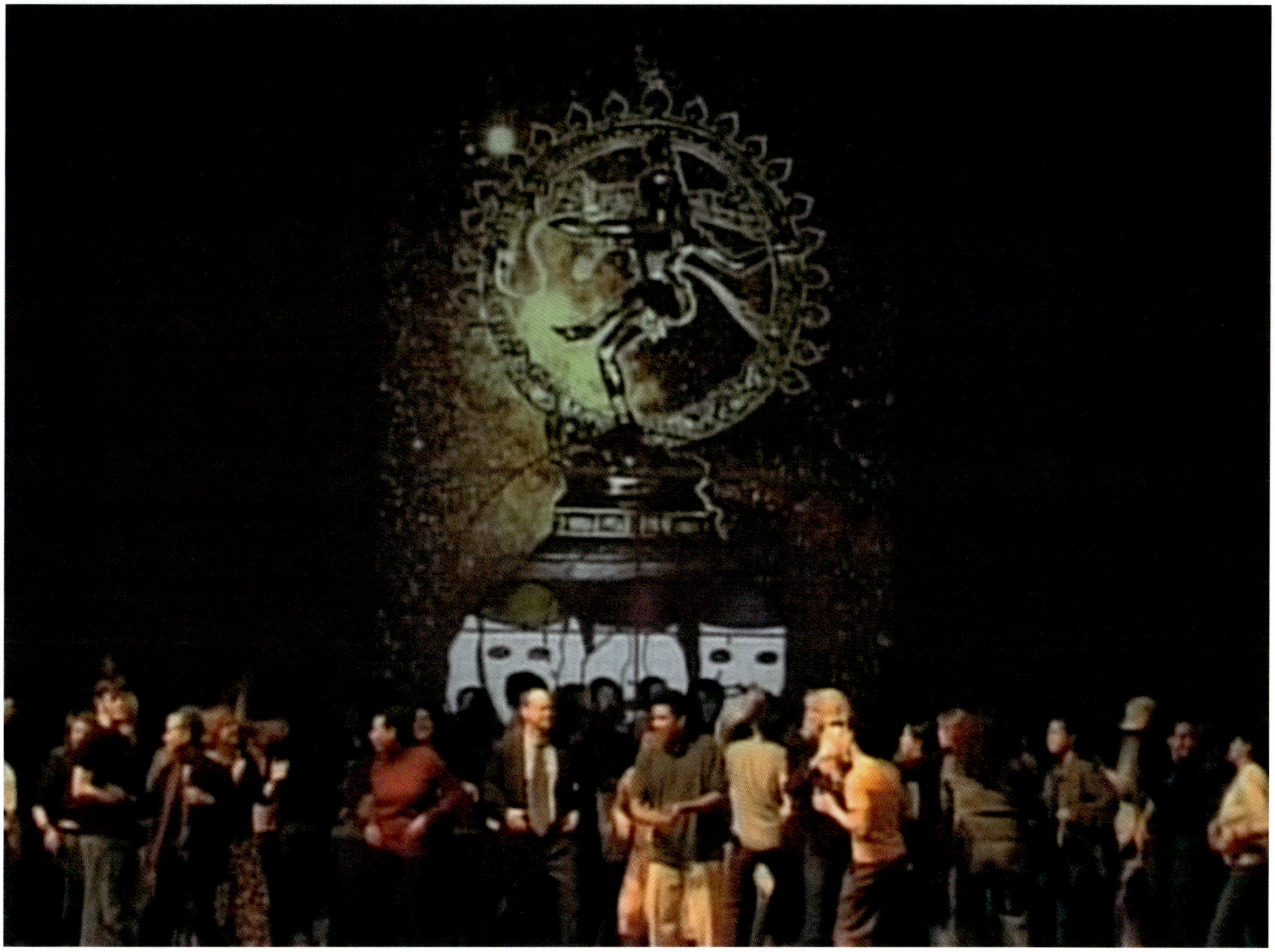

Fig. 11
Shiva Dances with the Art Institute of Chicago. 2004
Documentation of the participatory performance-lecture. Video (color, sound), 01:43:18
Collection Adrian Piper Research Archive Foundation Berlin
Detail: video still at 00:51:52

divide can be bridged through the hard (and always imperfect) work of individual citizens. The next chapter of her artistic and philosophical production, in this new environment, seems to open with new life and vigor, and a renewed sense of the possibilities of a social practice such as hers.

Imagining a Future

In September of 2012, in *Thwarted Projects, Dashed Hopes, A Moment of Embarrassment* (page 306), Piper announced that she was retiring from being black. The work, in the form of a document posted on her website, politely suggests the option of, in the future, calling her The Artist Formerly Known as African American, an echo of how the multitalented artist Prince was famously referred to, from 1993 to 2000, a period in which he adopted an unpronounceable glyph for his name, as "the Artist Formerly Known as Prince." While Prince's reinvention was the product of frustration with his record label, Piper's provocative conceptual gesture is not entirely dissimilar in its audacity. The tone of its last line is ironic—"Please join me in celebrating this exciting new adventure in pointless administrative precision and futile institutional control!"— but the work is very much an aspirational and concrete challenge to the authority of institutionalized identity formation. *Thwarted Projects, Dashed Hopes, A Moment of Embarrassment* intervenes in the language of identity and identity politics, which is too reductive and inadequate to contain any one person's biological heritage and various social identifications, and, as well, ignores the systematic and institutional discrimination that is the result.

The latter disjuncture echoes the way in which the term "post-black" was originally conceived by the curator Thelma Golden and the artist Glenn Ligon, as a contradiction, to describe artists who do not want to be limited to a racial category but whose work is, Golden has said, "steeped . . . in redefining complex notions of blackness."[69] We may well be, as Piper tells us in *Cornered*, beyond absolutes of racial identity, but the world is not beyond racism. Piper's chutzpah in calling out this idea both models it—in a way similar to its introduction, in her professorial voice, in *Cornered*—and attempts to put it to rest. Piper's withdrawal came just as a new round of culture wars was ignited in the United States, as activists—and media attention—returned to the issue of ongoing police violence against African-American men, reaching a crescendo not seen since the 1960s. By releasing *Thwarted Projects* on her website, Piper made canny use of digital media as a disembodied forum, open sourced and accessible—a form that anticipates the current rage for the genealogy websites that connect people with their family ancestries. *Thwarted Projects* has also been reproduced in print and for exhibition, positioning and circulating its declaration as a kind of manifesto to be activated depending on the context.[70]

Local attention to race-based violence coalesced in 2013 with the foundation of the national organization Black Lives Matter, which was formed in response to the acquittal of George Zimmerman in the shooting death of Trayvon Martin, an unarmed teenager. Piper intended *Imagine [Trayvon Martin]* (2013) (fig. 12), a printed poster, to be distributed gratis from the APRA Foundation Berlin website and by the galleries where it was shown. The poster shows a ghosted image of the young boy with crosshairs superimposed over his face and, along the bottom of the image, the simple, first-person admonition to "Imagine what it was like to be me." Martin gazes levelly at the viewer even as he disappears from view; his words remain, suggesting an empathic moment of reckoning and also recalling John Lennon's emblematic anthem, written in 1971, at the height of the Vietnam War, which exhorts us to dream of a world without categories or restrictions. *Imagine [Trayvon Martin]* asks us to think about and honor a little boy, an identity snuffed out in an epidemic of violence that seems to know no end.

In "On Wearing Three Hats," an essay of 1996, Piper considers her varied practices as an artist, a philosopher, and a yoga practitioner.[71] The three hats—a riff, in effect, on the feminist trope of the constantly multitasking woman—can be taken as a model for artistic self-fashioning, a way of rooting one's practice in the world. This has implications for current art production, such as social practice, a discipline that developed in the early 2000s through works by Tania Bruguera, Suzanne Lacey, and others, and through writings by the art historians Claire Bishop and Shannon Jackson.[72] In social-practice works these artists often intentionally take up roles that fall outside of traditional studio practice, in order to reach audiences and open conversations beyond the confines and politics of the object-driven art economy. In her most recent work, Piper brings her conceptual and participatory strategies to questions of ethics, in which truth exists as something that matters. *The Probable Trust Registry: The Rules of the Game #1–3* (2013) (pages 308, 309), her most monumental participatory work to date, is a social contract, a work fundamentally about trust—

> the foundation of a society in which human transactions of all kinds are conducted in a successful, peaceful, and orderly manner. This is a society in which each individual can rely on the others to abide by the same rules, and therefore one in which justified expectations can be fulfilled. It offers to each person the possibility of means to efficiently pursue and achieve her or his personal goals, within a community in which each supports this aspiration in the others.[73]

Viewers are invited to sign a contract that commits them to three statements: "I will always be too expensive to buy. I will always mean what I say. I will always do what I say I am going to do." These are simple ideas, but they bear profound ethical and political implications, amounting to an invitation to form a community based on honor and trust.

Through her art and her philosophical work, Piper addresses an expanded public. Her yoga practice, to the degree that it has been incorporated directly into her artwork and moved beyond a solitary practice (which she also maintains), becomes a vehicle for a radically reconfigured "we," an abstraction of the audience she both engages and releases. This longtime pursuit of transcendence has yielded a work on the ethics of humor: *The Order of Celestial Laughter*, released at her website in 2017, is defined by its Credo and is made up of individuals who can laugh at themselves. The work is described as a group performance with no spatiotemporal dimensions. Membership is secret and by invitation only.[74]

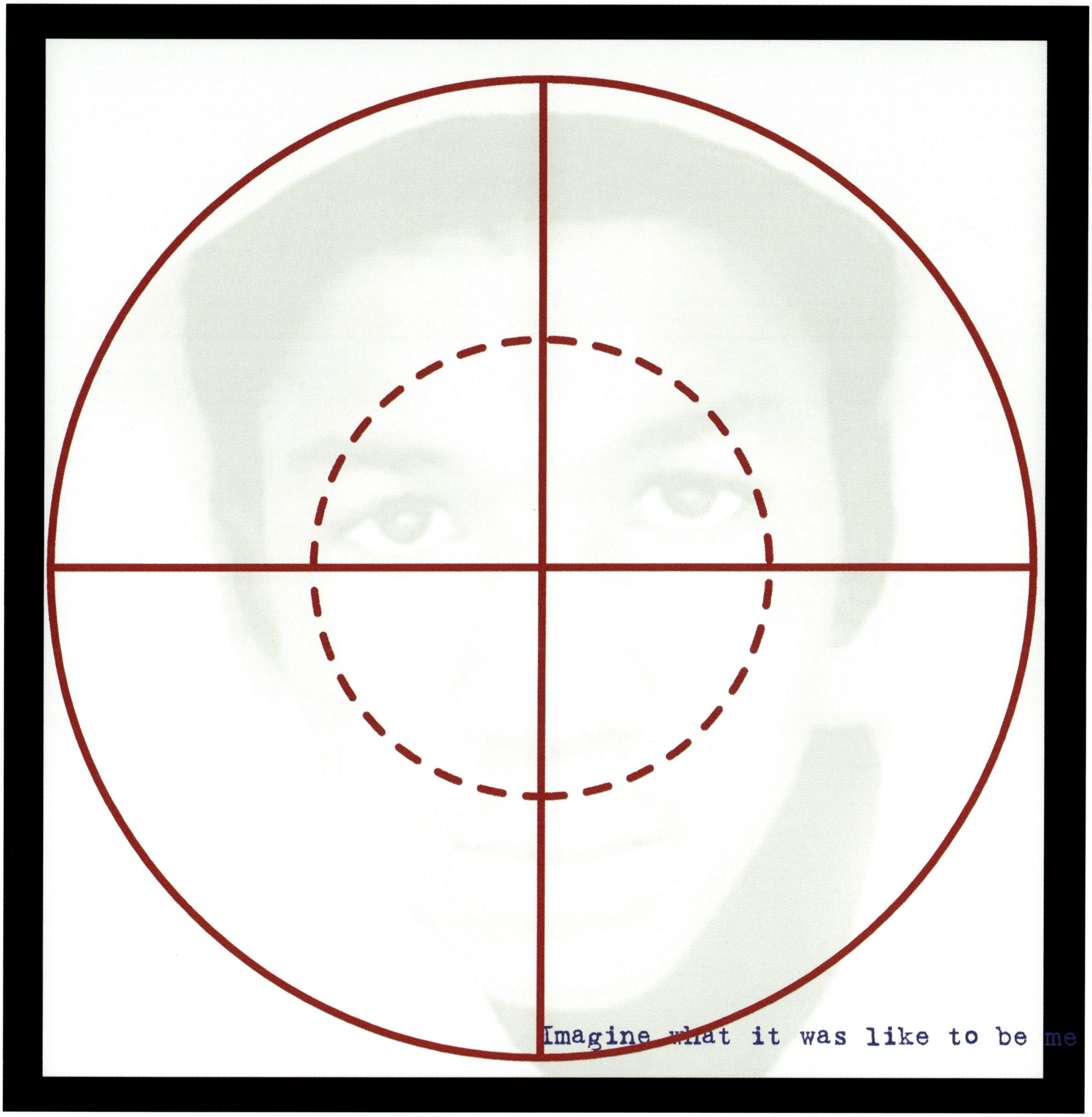

Fig. 12
Imagine [Trayvon Martin]. 2013
Photolithograph
10 7/16 × 10 3/4 in. (26.5 × 27.3 cm)
Collection Adrian Piper Research Archive Foundation Berlin

1. Adrian Piper, "Moving from Solipsism to Self-Consciousness," September 1972, in "Talking to Myself: The Ongoing Autobiography of an Art Object," 1970–73, in Piper, *Out of Order, Out of Sight*, vol. 1, *Selected Writings in Meta-Art, 1968–1992* (Cambridge, Mass.: MIT Press, 1996), p. 48.

2. Piper, "Xenophobia and the Indexical Present 1: Essay," 1989, in Mark O'Brien, ed., *Reimaging America: The Arts of Social Change* (Philadelphia: New Society Press, 1990); reprinted in *Out of Order, Out of Sight*, vol. 1, p. 245.

3. Piper, "Some Reflective Surfaces I," 1975, in *Out of Order, Out of Sight*, vol. 1, p. 151.

4. Ibid.

5. Rodney King is the subject of Piper's "Black Box/White Box" (1992).

6. See Julia Bryan Wilson, *Art Workers: Radical Practice in the Vietnam War Era* (Berkeley: University of California Press, 2009), p. 199.

7. Piper, "About the Hypothesis Series," 1992, in *Out of Order, Out of Sight*, vol. 1, p. 19.

8. Piper, draft of a letter to Terry Atkinson, 1968. Piper taped a carbon copy of the draft onto a sheet of bond paper and stored it in the *Nineteen Concrete Space-Time-Infinity* notebook, to give viewers of the following works an overview of what they would be seeing. See Piper, "Letter to Terry Atkinson," 1969, in *Out of Order, Out of Sight*, vol. 1, p. 15.

9. See Helen Molesworth, "Work Ethic," in Molesworth, ed., *Work Ethic* (Baltimore: The Baltimore Museum of Art; University Park: The Pennsylvania State University Press, 2004), pp. 25–51, 42. Benjamin Buchloh coined the term "Conceptual art" in "Conceptual Art, 1962–1969: From the Aesthetic of Administration of the Critique of Institutions," *October* 55 (Winter 1990): 128.

10. See Piper's page-work *Taped Lecture on Seriation (given November 7, 1968)* (1968) on page 156 of this volume. A sample of the sound work is at APRA, www.adrianpiper.com/vs/sound_seriation1.shtml.

11. Piper, *Shiva Dances with the Art Institute of Chicago* (2004). Piper mentions "tools for listening" in the video.

12. Piper, in conversation with the author, Berlin, Spring 2017.

13. Piper, "Personal Chronology," p. 315 in this volume.

14. Piper, "Talking to Myself," p. 42.

15. Lippard, "Catalysis: An Interview with Adrian Piper," *The Drama Review: TDR* 16, no. 1 (March 1972): 77–78.

16. See Wilson, "Lucy Lippard's Feminist Labor," *Art Workers: Radical Practice in the Vietnam War Era*, pp. 146–48. See also Cornelia Butler, "Women–Concept–Art: Lucy Lippard's Numbers Shows," in *From Conceptualism to Feminism: Lucy Lippard's Numbers Shows, 1969–74* (London: Afterall Books, 2012), pp. 16–69.

17. Piper, correspondence with the author, spring 2014.

18. Although Lippard invited SVA students to participate in the exhibition, and a few women did, Piper is the only woman artist who appears in the published version. See Lippard, "Groups," *Studio International* 179, no. 920 (March 1970): pp. 93–99.

19. The texts that accompany the *Groups* photographs speak in an even more deadpan, scientifically objective voice than that of *Concrete Infinity Documentation Piece* (1970). Both were influenced by Alain Robbe-Grillet's descriptive voice in his novels. Piper, correspondence with the author, January 18, 2018. See also Piper, "Personal Chronology," p. 315.

20. Piper, "Talking to Myself," pp. 30–31.

21. Piper, in Lippard, "Catalysis," p. 78

22. Piper, "Kinds of Performing Objects I Have Been: Notes for Rosemary Mayer's 'Performance and Experience,'" 1972, in *Out of Order, Out of Sight*, vol. 1, pp. 89–90.

23. Ibid., p. 89.

24. Piper, "Personal Chronology."

25. Piper, "Notes on the Mythic Being I–III," 1976, in *Out of Order, Out of Sight*, vol. 1, p. 138.

26. Piper, "Preparatory Notes for *The Mythic Being*," 1973–74, in *Out of Order, Out of Sight*, p. 104.

27. Ibid., p. 110.

28. William Shawcross, "The End of Cambodia?" *New York Review of Books*, January 24, 1980. See the excellent account of *It's Just Art* in an essay by Begum Yasar and Aliza Svarts, in Yasar, ed., *Adrian Piper* (New York: Levy Gorvy, 2017).

29. Piper, "It's Just Art," *High Performance* 4, no. 1 (Spring 1981); reprinted in *Out of Order, Out of Sight*, vol. 1, p. 178.

30. Piper, "Personal Chronology," p. 316.

31. Piper, "It's Just Art," p. 177.

32. See Piper and Dara Meyers-Kingsley, "MEDI(t)Ations: Adrian Piper's Videos, Performances, and Soundworks, 1968–92," in Maurice Berger, ed., *Adrian Piper: A Retrospective* (Baltimore: University of Maryland Fine Arts Gallery, 1999), p. 175.

33. Piper has recalled visiting Bootsy Collins's manager and watching videos of live performance tapes of his band Parliament-Funkadelic. Piper, "Personal Chronology," p. 317. In 1984 she made a sound work, *Assorted Anti-Post-Modernist Artifacts*, using Collins's music.

34. Piper, "Notes on Funk I–IV," 1983–85, in *Out of Order, Out of Sight*, vol. 1, p. 198.

35. Ibid., p. 207.

36. Ibid., p. 208.

37. Ibid., p. 195.

38. Ibid., p. 203.

39. Dan Graham's documentary montage *Rock My Religion* (1984) charts the subterranean relationship of rock 'n' roll to organized religion and American Christian revivalist rituals.

40. Piper, "Personal Chronology," p. 315.

41. Piper, "My Calling (Cards) #1 and #2," 1990, in *Out of Order, Out of Sight*, vol. 1, p. 219.

42. The original version of *My Calling (Card) #1*, with Piper's name at the bottom, is medium brown in color; the second version with no name is light brown, but with "© Angry Art" on the back.

43. Recently the notions of occupying or "holding space" have been applied to a kind of activism that involves bodies taking up space in public, and to its symbolic potential. Witness the images of the millions of people who marched in protest following the 2017 inauguration of U.S. President Donald Trump, contrasted with those of the sparsely attended official event. The Occupy Wall Street protest began in 2011 to highlight income inequality and the failure of financial institutions to act for the good of the public, but it quickly spread to become a more generalized international movement, comprising such activities as Occupy Museums (including The Museum of Modern Art) to call attention to the disparities in representation and inclusion. The history of collective and collaborative practices as counteractions against institutions of all kinds spans the twentieth century. See, for example, Claire Bishop, *Artificial Hells: Participatory Art and the Politics of Spectatorship* (New York: Verso, 2012).

44. *Passing beyond Passing* combines documentation of *Cornered*, along with a lecture, discussion, and clips of Hollywood films in which passing for white is part of the plot.

45. Piper, in Berger, "The Critique of Pure Racism: An Interview with Adrian Piper," in *Adrian Piper: A Retrospective*, pp. 77–78.

46. Figs. 17 and 18, in "The Logic of Modernism," 1992, in Piper, *Out of Order, Out of Sight*, vol. 2, *Selected Writings in Art Criticism, 1967–1992* (Cambridge, Mass.: MIT Press, 1996), p. 208.

47. Piper, "Goodbye to Easy Listening," in *Adrian Piper: PRETEND* (New York: John Weber Gallery, 1990); reprinted in *Out of Order, Out of Sight*, vol. 2, pp. 175–78.

48. Piper, "The Triple Negation of Colored Women Artists," in *Next Generation: Southern Black Aesthetic* (Chapel Hill: University of North Carolina Press, 1990); reprinted in *Out of Order, Out of Sight*, vol. 2, pp. 161–73.

49. Ibid., p. 164.

50. MoMA's programming of the atrium in the Yoshio Taniguchi building is worth a thorough look but is beyond the scope of this essay. In recent years there have been several exhibitions and programs that have addressed the hierarchies and politics that are embedded in the space and architecture of the Museum, most notably the re-creation of Sanja Iveković's *Lady Rosa of Luxembourg* (2001), a pregnant woman atop an obelisk, in *Sanja Iveković: Sweet Violence*, in 2011–12. These also include the ongoing use of the atrium for performance that dismantles and critiques the history of modern dance, and Pipilotti Rist's *Pour Your Body Out (7354 Cubic Meters)*, in 2008–09, which turned the space into a womblike public chamber for contemplation. The idea to install *What It's Like, What It Is #3* in MoMA's Marron Atrium came from the Museum's director, Glenn Lowry.

51. See Robert Storr, *Dislocations* (New York: The Museum of Modern Art, 1991), pp. 24–26.

52. Most of the evidence that museum attendance in the early 1990s was overwhelmingly white is largely anecdotal, but the Mellon Foundation and the American Association of Art Museum Directors have recently published a first-ever study of diversity in museums which has received widespread attention in the field. See Peggy Levitt, "Museums Must Attract Diverse Visitors or Risk Irrelevance," *The Atlantic*, November 9, 2015. See also J. Mark Davidson Schuster, *Research Division Report #23: The Audience for American Art Museums* (Washington, D.C.: National Endowment for the Arts; Santa Ana, Calif: Seven Locks Press, 1992), pp. 6, 8, 12, 24, 39.

53. Piper, "Flying," in Jane Farver, ed., *Adrian Piper: Reflections, 1967–1987* (New York: The Alternative Museum, 1987), p. 20; quoted in Storr, *Dislocations*, p. 26.

54. Piper, "Passing for White, Passing for Black," *Transition* 58 (1992); reprinted in *Out of Order, Out of Sight*, vol. 1, p. 282. See also Piper, "Lip Service with a Smile, in *Escape to Berlin; A Travel Memoir* (Berlin: APRA Foundation Berlin, 2018), pp. 135–65.

55. Anita Hill's remarkable memoir *Speaking Truth to Power*, published in 1997, reintroduced the Quaker phrase in its title into the mainstream lexicon. Hill's astonishing testimony galvanized a new generation of feminist activism that has most recently surfaced in the #MeToo movement, launched in response to widespread allegations of sexual harassment in the entertainment and media industries and in politics. That many people speaking up about sexual abuse in 2017 were unaware that the original Me Too campaign was in fact started a decade ago by Tarana Burke—an African-American woman—to support victims of sexual assault has demonstrated one of the ways in which women of color are often confined to the sidelines in conversations about contemporary feminist issues. Hill has become a respected spokesperson for the movement and is leading a task force on sexual harassment in the workplace.

56. The financier Charles Keating was convicted of racketeering and fraud in the savings & loan crisis of the late 1980s; Clark Clifford, a former U.S. secretary of defense, was charged with fraud, conspiracy, and taking bribes in the collapse of the Bank of Credit and Commerce International but was not indicted due to his failing health.

57. Piper, "IT'S FINE," xvii, 8/2/91, in *Decide Who You Are* (New York: Paula Cooper Gallery, 1992), n.p.

58. Piper, "HEY, GOD!" xxxv, 6/7/92, in ibid.

59. The question of the troubled future for African-American children, boys in particular, continues to be a charged subject for artists and writers; it is the subject of Ta-Nehisi Coates's *Between the World and Me* (2015), an essay, addressed to Coates's teenage son, about the realities of growing up black and middle class. Coates reflects on his upbringing, in the 1980s in Baltimore, and is pessimistic about what has changed since then, and about overcoming systemic racism and white supremacy in the United States. Conversely Arthur Jafa's film anthem *Love Is the Message* (2016), set to the powerful gospel-inspired music of Chance the Rapper, suggests the possibility of redemption and hope, despite the ongoing violence being done to black bodies and black culture. Jafa's film, in my opinion, would not be possible without Piper's work of the 1990s, which remains as contemporary as ever.

60. Don Cornelius, the creator of *Soul Train*, the epic American dance show, signed off each episode with these three words.

61. See Diarmuid Costello, "Xenophobia, Stereotypes, and Empirical Acculturation: Neo-Kantianism in Adrian Piper's Performance-based Conceptual Art," in *Adrian Piper: A Reader* (New York: The Museum of Modern Art, 2018), pp. 167–72. See also Piper, "On Wearing Three Hats," presentation at " Who Is She? Conversations with Multi-Talented Women," Third Annual Tillie K. Lubin Symposium, Rose Art Museum, Brandeis University, March 17, 1996; and at APRA, www.adrianpiper.com/docs/WebsiteNGBK3Hats.pdf.

62. Simon Leung, conversation with the author, fall 2016. Leung cites Piper's influence on his practice, including the idea of identity always in formation.

63. Piper, "The Color Wheel Series," 2004, APRA, www.adrianpiper.com/art/docs/2004TheColorWheelSeries.pdf, p. 3. Another manifestation of the series appears in print. Piper, in John P. Bowles et al., "Blinded by the White: Art and History at the Limits of Whiteness," *Art Journal* 60, no. 4 (Winter 2001): 38–67. Here the images appear as an artist's project that respond to the subject of the magazine's issue on whiteness. The texts and artists' projects of that issue are among the few examples, within the art context, of an explicit discussion of whiteness. Among those texts, Piper's is unique is arguing that whiteness as a racial concept is a self-serving fiction. See also Piper, "Whiteless," *Art Journal* 60, no. 4 (2001): 62–67.

64. Swami Sivananda, *Lord Siva and His Worship* (Tehri Garhwal, India: Divine Life Society, 1996), pp. 62–63. Quoted in Piper, "The Color Wheel Series," p. 3.

65. Piper, "The Color Wheel Series," p. 2.

66. Piper, "Shiva Dances with the Art Institute of Chicago," APRA, www.adrianpiper.com/vs/video_sd.shtml.

67. Piper, "Shiva DANCES, for God's Sake," APRA, www.adrianpiper.com/vs/shiva.shtml

68. Piper, "Adrian Moves to Berlin," APRA, www.adrianpiper.com/vs/video_am.shtml.

69. The idea of "post-black" became the theoretical foundation of *Freestyle*, an exhibition organized by Golden at The Studio Museum in Harlem in 2001. Golden, introduction to Golden, ed., *Freestyle* (New York: The Studio Museum in Harlem, 2001). Debate about the term continues into the present.

70. Several years after making *Thwarted Projects, Dashed Hopes, A Moment of Embarrassment*, Piper undertook extensive genealogical research into her family ancestry, and found many of these websites to be reliable sources of useful information.

71. Piper, "On Wearing Three Hats."

72. See, for example, Shannon Jackson, *Social Works: Performing Art, Supporting Publics* (New York: Routledge, 2011); and Bishop, *Artificial Hells*. It is worth noting that neither of these important scholars has yet have incorporated Piper into their arguments about participatory art.

73. Exhibition brochure, *Adrian Piper: The Probable Trust Registry; The Rules of the Game #1–3*, Hamburger Bahnhof- Museum fur Gegenwart, Berlin, February 24–September 3, 2017.

74. Piper, "The Order of Celestial Laughter," 2017, at APRA, www.adrianpiper.com/art/OCL_Credo.shtml.

THE REAL THING STRANGE[1]

ADRIAN PIPER

I would like to thank the British Society of Aesthetics for inviting me to deliver the Empson Lecture at Cambridge University. It is a very great honor. And thanks to all of you for coming to hear this talk. It is a wonderful opportunity to think about my work in a new way, and I promise not to abuse it by descending into a paroxysm of self-indulgent blather about that work!

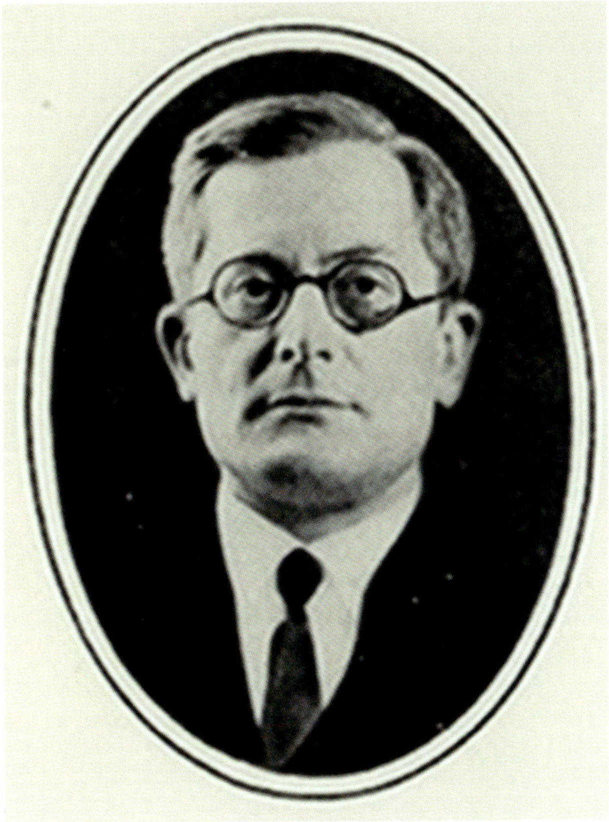

Instead I would like to lay the groundwork for my later conclusions with a few words about William Empson, the renowned poet and critic who both founded and later dissented from the New Criticism movement in Anglo-American literature. In 1925 Empson won an undergraduate mathematics scholarship to Cambridge. He distinguished himself in both mathematics and English. As he didn't have the benefit of an APRA Foundation Berlin Multi-Disciplinary Fellowship to encourage the development of both talents (find out more at adrianpiper.com), he ultimately chose English as his major. At the age of twenty-three, he self-published his first collection of poems, followed by his best-known work of literary criticism, *Seven Types of Ambiguity*, when he was twenty-four. Both works were groundbreaking in the clarity, precision, and analytic detachment of their language. For the second, Empson was nominated for a fellowship at Magdalene College.

Shortly thereafter, however, condoms were discovered in his dormitory room, where he was purportedly caught in the act with a lady friend. For this university offense of sexual misconduct, and despite his excellent academic record, Cambridge stripped him of his scholarship, kicked him out of the university and banished him from the city. He moved to Bloomsbury and in 1930 departed to Tokyo to teach. He published his second groundbreaking book of poems and his second, equally revolutionary work of criticism, *Some Versions of the Pastoral*, in 1935. In 1937 he was kicked out of Japan for making a pass at a cabdriver, and moved on to a teaching position at Peking University—only to be driven out by the Japanese invasion. So instead he traveled in China for two years, itinerantly teaching English poetry entirely from memory. During World War II he was back in London, working alongside George Orwell and T. S. Eliot at the BBC and broadcasting to the Far East. After the war, he returned again to Peking University, where he taught for five years, until increasingly onerous Maoist restrictions on teaching and freedom of expression drove him back to England.

1. The Empson Lecture 2013, delivered to the British Society of Aesthetics Annual Conference, Cambridge University, September 21, 2013. I would particularly like to thank Caroline Auty and Maarten Steenhagen for providing administrative and technical support, and Diarmuid Costello and Jason Gaiger for moral and scholarly support.

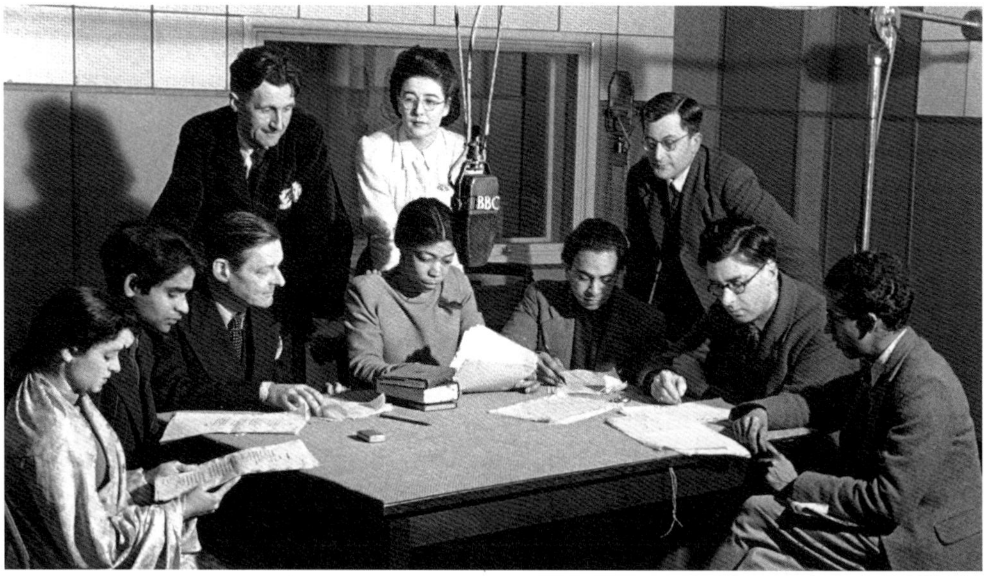

Empson accepted a professorship in the English department at the University of Sheffield in 1953 and remained there as its chair until his retirement, in 1972. With honorary doctorates from the Universities of East Anglia in 1968, Bristol in 1971, and Sheffield in 1974, Cambridge University joined the general acclaim with an honorary doctorate in 1977, roughly fifty years after it had expelled him.

He was knighted by Queen Elizabeth two years later and, with his usual impeccable timing, saluted his friend Orwell one last time by dying in 1984. His serious and long-standing interest in Buddhist philosophy and meditation helped him to navigate the vicissitudes of his life with a mix of equanimity and satirical humor. The *New York Times* describes his prose as "[combining] wisdom with shock value, snappy insults with long-honed insights."[2] I really like this guy.

So I am truly delighted to be following in Empson's footsteps, at least as regards moving around and getting kicked out of places. But I am also going to try to emulate Empson in some other ways as well. The title of my talk is taken from Empson's poem of the 1940s, "Let It Go," and I shall follow his wise counsel at many points. I will be responding to the very generous request to address in this lecture the relationship between my art work and my philosophy work. I am happy to rise to this challenge, even though I am not publicly discussing my art work at this time. This long-standing policy is fully consistent with the substance of Empson's poem. He says,

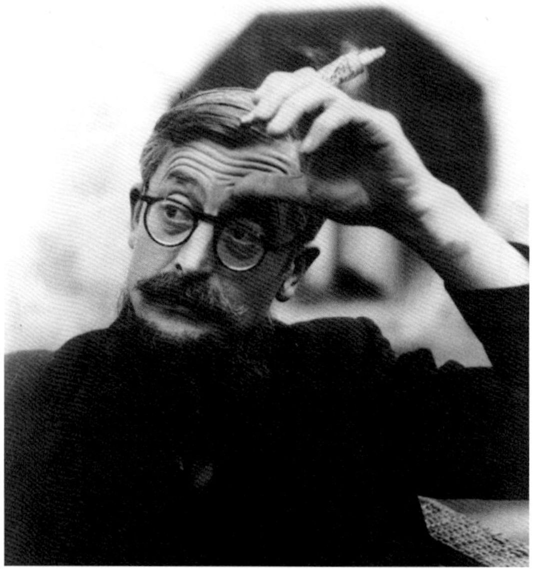

2. Stephen Burt, "Adventures in Ambiguity," *New York Times*, September 10, 2006.

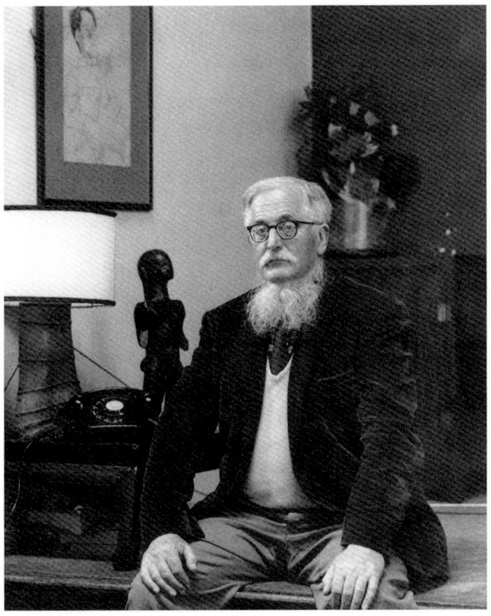

It is this deep blankness is the real thing
strange.
The more things happen to you the more
you can't
Tell or remember even what they were.

The contradictions cover such a range.
The talk would talk and go so far aslant.
You don't want madhouse and the whole
thing there.[3]

When asked what this poem was about, Empson is said to have replied that it was about deciding not to write poetry anymore. I don't think this is what the poem is about, and I don't believe Empson thought it was, either. I think he said that in order to get rid of someone who was too lazy to do the work of finding out what the poem was about for himself, by reading it closely, thinking about it deeply, and giving it his own meaning. I think Empson meant to suggest that questions like that one *made* him want to stop writing poetry. Happily, he changed his mind and went on to write a great deal more.

It is not difficult to understand why he answered as he did. After having communicated and expressed himself in the poem, the question of what the poem was about then called on him to explain at the meta-level what he had already communicated and expressed in the poem. This was tantamount to denying that the poem had expressed and communicated successfully in the first place. Empson's poem calls our attention to something—this deep blankness—that is ordinarily obfuscated by the compulsion to tell and remember and talk up. So the request to talk up the poem itself could hardly have been welcome. By using poetic discourse in a way that reveals rather than obscures or tries to pin down the real thing strange, the poem becomes a plea on behalf of the real, and on behalf of the strange. Thus Empson's answer protected "this deep blankness . . . the real thing strange" from precisely the kind of discussion in which "the talk would talk and go so far aslant" that the work itself would disappear from view.

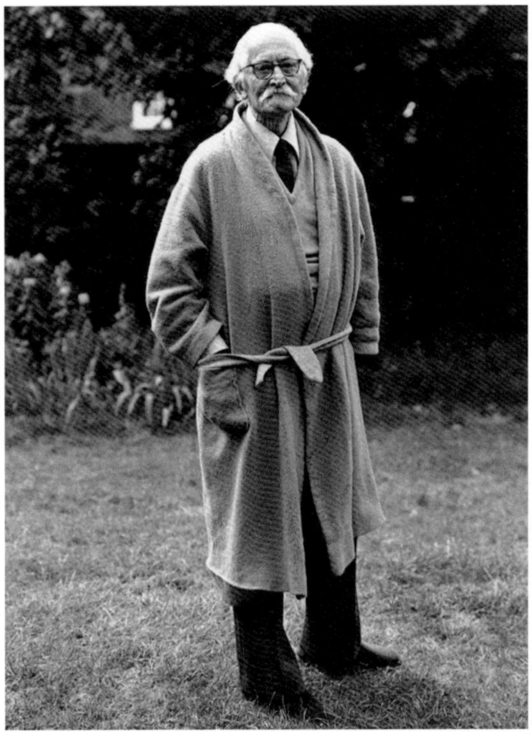

3. William Empson, "Let It Go," 1949, in *The Complete Poems*, ed. John Haffenden (London: Penguin, 2001).

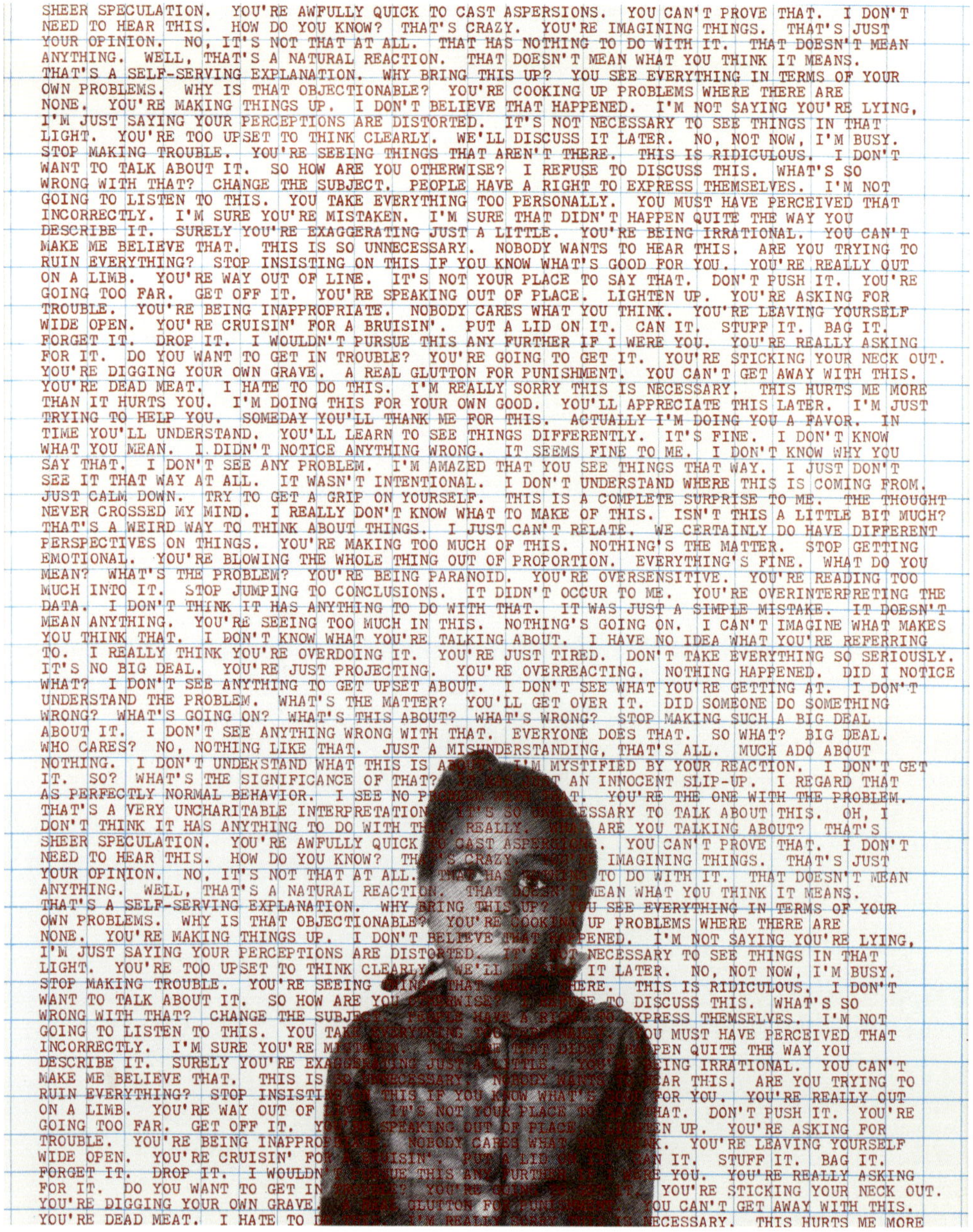

My decision not to talk **IT'S FINE.** about my own work is one way of **I DON'T KNOW WHAT YOU MEAN.** sheltering the **I DIDN'T NOTICE ANYTHING WRONG.** real thing strange **IT SEEMS FINE TO ME.** from talk that talks **I DON'T KNOW** and goes so far aslant **WHY YOU SAY THAT.** that it obscures **I DON'T SEE ANY PROBLEM.** the real thing strange from view, **I'M AMAZED** behind a scrim **THAT YOU SEE THINGS THAT WAY.** of formulaic platitudes **I JUST DON'T SEE IT THAT WAY AT ALL.** whose primary function **IT WASN'T INTENTIONAL.** is to sedate and suffocate **I DON'T UNDERSTAND WHERE THIS IS COMING FROM.** the cognitive struggle **JUST CALM DOWN.** that every artwork demands **TRY TO GET A GRIP ON YOURSELF.** of its serious viewers.
THIS IS A COMPLETE SURPRISE TO ME. Instead I want to focus **THE THOUGHT NEVER**

CROSSED MY MIND. on that struggle itself, I REALLY DON'T KNOW the struggle between WHAT TO MAKE OF THIS. "this deep blankness . . . ISN'T THIS A LITTLE BIT MUCH? the real thing strange," THAT'S A WEIRD WAY TO THINK ABOUT THINGS. and the talk that talks I JUST CAN'T RELATE. and goes very far aslant WE CERTAINLY DO HAVE DIFFERENT PERSPECTIVES ON THINGS. indeed. This is a different sort of road YOU'RE MAKING TOO MUCH OF THIS. into the relationship NOTHING'S THE MATTER. between my artwork STOP GETTING EMOTIONAL. and my philosophy work, YOU'RE BLOWING THE WHOLE THING OUT OF PROPORTION. one that avoids the madhouse EVERYTHING'S FINE. and the whole thing there, WHAT DO YOU MEAN? by subjecting the madhouse itself WHAT'S THE PROBLEM? to extended scrutiny. YOU'RE BEING PARANOID. YOU'RE OVERSENSITIVE. YOU'RE READING TOO MUCH INTO IT.[4]

Here is one such work that I am not going to talk about, but which nevertheless might serve as a fitting expression of that very resolve.

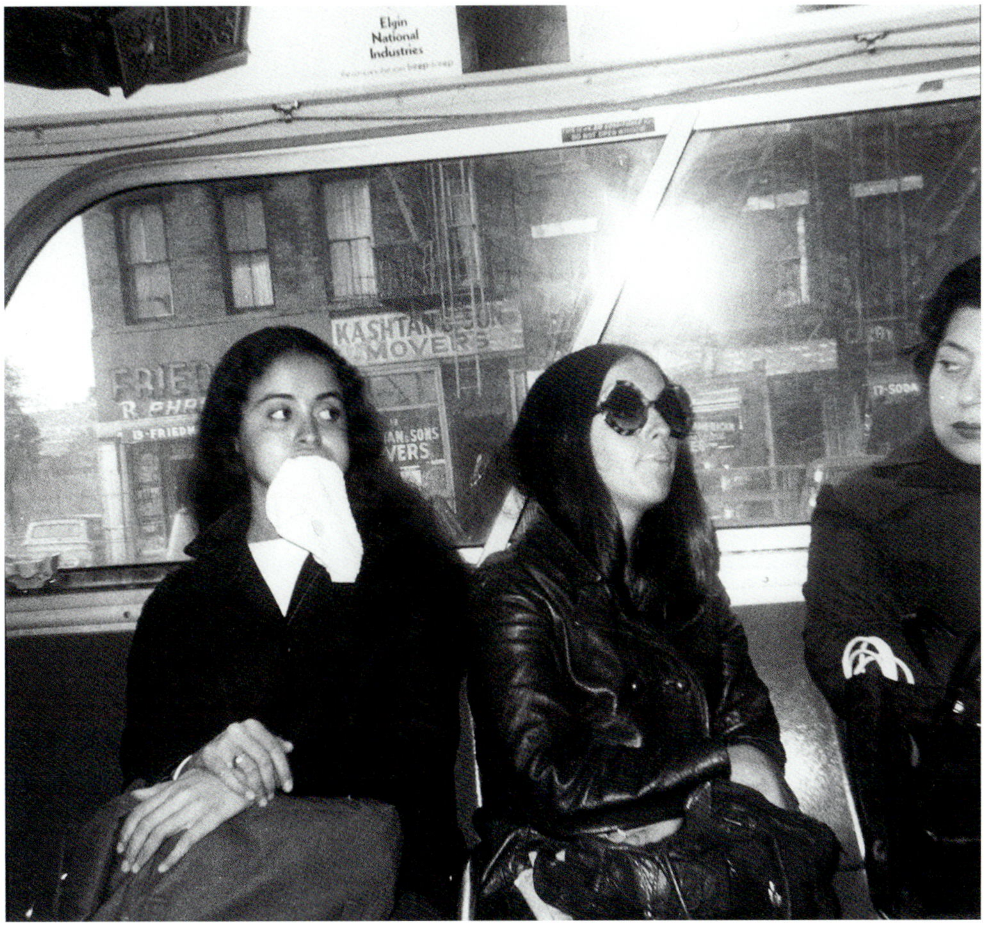

Instead I want to anchor the relationship between my art work and my philosophy work in the text from which my two-volume philosophical work, *Rationality and the Structure of the Self*, takes its inspiration, namely Immanuel Kant's *Critique of Pure Reason*. My interest in Kantian themes predates my first encounter with Kant. In 1969 I was an art student. I had written an essay about the artwork I exhibited in

4. Adrian Piper, recording of text from right-hand panel of *Decide Who You Are* (1992), at www.adrianpiper.com/vs/sound_decide.shtml.

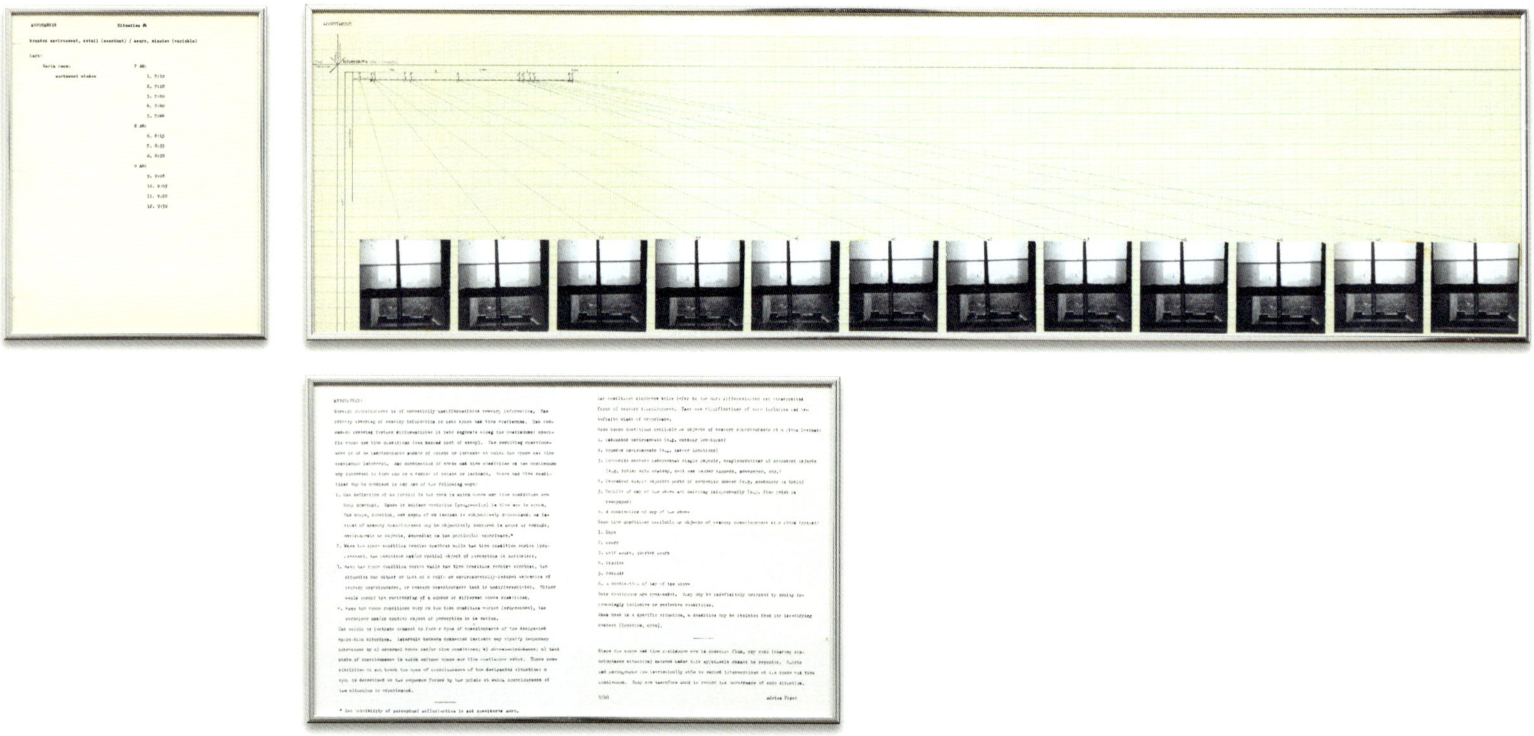

Joseph Kosuth's *Conceptual Art and Conceptual Aspects* show at the New York Cultural Center, on the subject of space and time as forms of perception. A philosophy-student friend who read it insisted that I read Kant's *Critique of Pure Reason*, particularly the Transcendental Aesthetic. I have been held captive by the first *Critique* ever since—in art as well as in philosophy.

My captivity to Kant is easy to detect in the second volume of *Rationality and the Structure of the Self*. In the first part of the book, I develop in detail the comprehensive Kantian model of rationality that I claim both structures our thinking and motivates our behavior. In the second part, I try to show how real-life deviations from this model tend to systematically confirm its reliability. But my focus in that work is on the substantive model, and how it must be elaborated in order to accommodate those deviations. Here I want to take a closer look at the deviations themselves—the conceptual, theoretical, and aesthetic anomalies that elicit from the self the cognitive rescue operations I describe there. My account of conceptual and theoretical anomaly is of course indebted to Thomas Kuhn's discussion of anomaly in science. But my appreciation of Kuhn's analysis was schooled by my prior encounter with Kant's more detailed treatment in the *Critique of Pure Reason*.

So I am going to turn now to Kant's conjectures about the possibility of unsynthesized intuitions. I shall want to establish that Kant is committed to the existence of unsynthesized intuitions, and then to draw some conclusions about their significance, both for my work and for yours. So you can see that there are some concealed premises here, and that the argument rests on a shameless appeal to Kant's authority! But maybe that will be all right. I hope also to emulate Empson's exemplary practice as a literary critic, of reading an author's text closely and extracting insights from detailed analysis of particular words, phrases, and sentences.

5. Recently a related discussion has developed, both in Kant scholarship and in contemporary philosophy of mind, as to the existence and nature of so-called nonconceptual content. The remarks that follow do not attempt to engage that discussion, because my reaction to it is an instinctively artistic one: of skepticism as to whether such an issue can be settled through conceptual analysis. Kant's account, by contrast, takes for granted the existence of what he would call "unsynthesized intuitions," takes for granted that they have a certain nature, and asks how they influence and relate to higher-order cognitive activity. This question strikes me, as an artist, as a more promising candidate for conceptual analysis.

So let's look at passage (A). Here Kant is considering whether we can intuit objects without comprehending what it is we are intuiting—or, to use his vocabulary, whether they can appear to us in intuition without satisfying the criteria of synthetic unity required by the understanding.[5] I have divided the text into indicative and subjunctive clauses, so that we can distinguish clearly between the places in which Kant is making factual assertions and the places in which he is entertaining counterfactual possibilities. He says,

Passage (A)	
Indicative	**Subjunctive**
(1) [the] categories of the understanding do not represent to us the conditions under which objects are given in intuition at all.	
(2) So objects can certainly [*allerdings*] appear to us,	
(3) without necessarily having to relate to functions of the understanding,	
(4) and therefore without the understanding *a priori* containing their conditions. . . .	
(5) For without functions of the understanding, appearances can certainly [*allerdings*] be given in intuition. . . .	
(6) For that objects of sensible intuition must accord with the formal conditions of sensibility lying *a priori* in the mind is clear,	(7) because otherwise they would not be objects for us.
(8) But that they furthermore must accord with the conditions that the understanding needs for the synthetic unity of thought is a conclusion that is not so easy to see.	(9) For appearances could be at best [*allenfalls*] so constituted,
	(10) that the understanding would not find them in accordance with the conditions of its unity at all.
	(11) And everything would lay in such confusion
	(12) that, for example, in the series of appearances nothing would present itself that would provide a rule of synthesis,
	(13) and therefore would correspond to the concept of cause and effect.
	(14) So this concept would be completely empty, void, and without meaning.
	(15) Appearances would nevertheless present objects to our intuition,
(16) for intuition by no means needs the functions of thought.	
	(*KrV*, A 89.20/B 122.05–A 91.03/B 123.17)[6]

The Kant mavens present today will notice that my translation of this passage diverges from the standard ones at certain points. Although I do break up several of Kant's run-on sentences, comparison with the German original will show that my translation is otherwise as literal as possible.

In the indicative-mood clauses, Kant's remarks are based on facts that he takes himself to have established in the Transcendental Aesthetic. At A 19 he defined intuition as that manner or means by which we are in "unmediated relation" to objects. He nowhere specifies in greater detail in what our unmediated relation to objects consists. Instead he argued in the Transcendental Aesthetic that intuition is what locates our representations in space and time. So in Kant's view, spatiotemporal location is the *result* of being in unmediated relation to objects, not a *precondition* of it. This implies that this unmediated relation itself, whatever it is, cannot itself be a spatiotemporal one. And at B 67–69 Kant made explicit the implication that this thesis applies to *all* empirical representations: in locating representations in space and time, we thereby

6. (1) Die Kategorien des Verstandes dagegen stellen uns gar nicht die Bedingungen vor, unter denen Gegenstände in der Anschauung gegeben werden, (2) mithin können uns allerdings Gegenstände erscheinen, (3) ohne daß sie sich notwendig auf Funktionen des Verstands beziehen müssen, (4) und dieser also die Bedingungen derselben a priori enthielte. . . . (5) denn ohne Funktionen des Verstandes können allerdings Erscheinungen in der Anschauung gegeben werden. . . . (6) Denn daß Gegenstände der sinnlichen Anschauung den im Gemüt a priori liegenden formalen Bedingungen der Sinnlichkeit gemäß sein müssen, ist daraus klar, (7) weil sie sonst nicht Gegenstände für uns locate not only other things but also ourselves as empirical subjects in space and time. Here in passage (A), in clauses (A.2) through (A.4), he now adds that this procedure by which we intuit all such things as spatiotemporal bears no *necessary* relation to the procedure by which we make sense of them. If there is a relation between what we intuit and what we understand, it must be a contingent one.

Kant then asserts in clause (A.5), and repeats in clause (A.16), that we can definitely intuit objects independently of any higher cognitive functions for conceptualizing them. Such higher functions constitute a separate procedure that organizes spatiotemporal objects into mutual relation, by sorting them into groups according to their most fundamental properties—or, as Kant would put it, by subsuming them under the categories of the understanding. Kant is asserting in clauses (A.2) through (A.5) and (A.16) that intuition is not only conceptually independent of understanding; it is also functionally independent. In Kant's view in passage (A), we definitely can intuit objects whether or not we comprehend them. Despite the heavy weather that Robert Paul Wolff and others make of passage (A), Kant's meaning in these clauses seems to me to be quite clear. Whether it is consistent with what he says elsewhere is a separate matter. Kant's claims here raise prima facie problems for the interpretation of the Transcendental Deduction in both A and B editions that I am going to ignore for purposes of this discussion.

In the subjunctive-mood clauses, Kant then entertains the counterfactual possibility that we might not be able to understand any of the many things to which we directly and immediately relate. It could happen that even the best-constituted appearances might be incomprehensible to us as unified objects. Kant presses this point particularly in clauses (A.9) to (A.10). Call this the *worst-case scenario*. In the worst-case scenario, not even the most constitutionally sound among our spatiotemporal intuitions would satisfy the conceptual requirements that enable us to make sense of them—for example, by fitting them into a causal network, or by consistently ascribing properties to them in terms of which we can identify them repeatedly over time as enduring objects.

Kant elaborates the worst-case scenario in clauses (A.11) through (A.14): a confusing series of appearances is intuited and spatiotemporally positioned but offers nothing to which the concepts of substance or causality might correctly apply. Such appearances are still situated in time, and they still have spatial location. And we still represent them; here see not only clauses (A.2) and (A.15), but also Kant's definition of intuition at B 132 as "that representation that can be given prior to all thought."[7] However, we do not represent them *as* unified objects; and there is no unified self *to whom* we represent them. For, as Kant tells us in the Subjective Deduction in the A edition, a subject is unified if and only if what appears to it is similarly unified as an object (A 108).[8]

sein würden; (8) daß sie aber auch überdem [*sic*] den Bedingungen, deren der Verstand zur synthetischen Einsicht des Denkens bedarf, gemäß sein müssen, davon ist die Schlußfolge nicht so leicht einzusehen. (9) Denn es könnten wohl allenfalls Erscheinungen so beschaffen sein, (10) daß der Verstand sie den Bedingungen seiner Einheit gar nicht gemäß fände, (11) und alles so in Verwirrung läge, (12) daß z.B. in der Reihenfolge der Erscheinung sich nichts darböte, was eine Regel der Synthesis an die Hand gäbe, (13) und also dem Begriffe der Ursache und Wirkung entspräche, (14) so daß dieser Begriff also ganz leer, nichtig und ohne Bedeutung wäre. (15) Erscheinungen

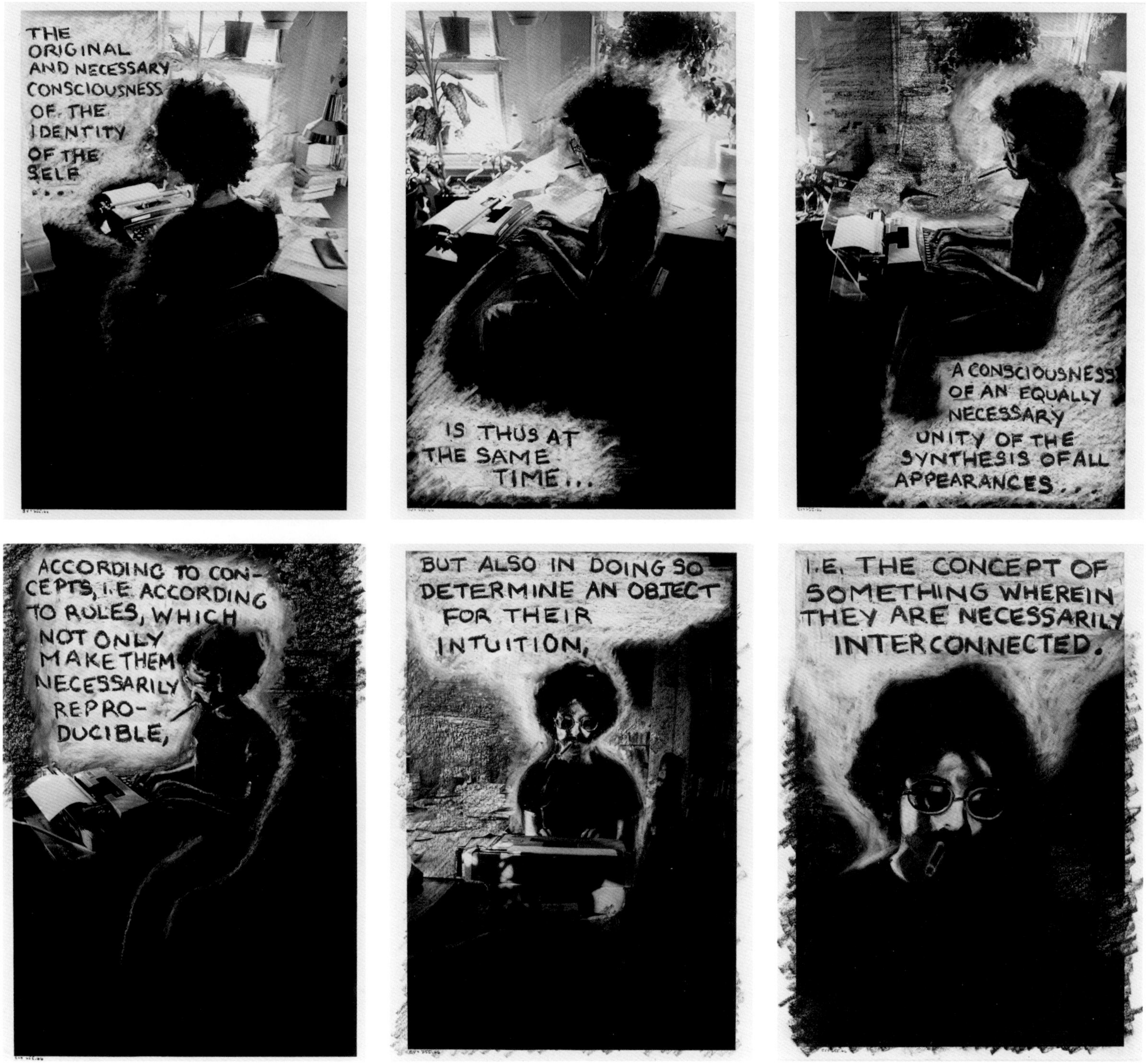

würden nichtsdestoweniger unserer Anschauung Gegenstände darbieten, (16) denn die Anschauung bedarf der Funktionen des Denkens auf keine Weise (*KrV*, A 89.20/ B 122.05–A 91.03/ B 123.17) Immanuel Kant, *Kritik der reinen Vernunft*, 1781 and 1787 Herausg. Raymund Schmidt (Hamburg: Felix Meiner Verlag, 1976). Henceforth references to this work are paginated in the text according to the standard A/B pagination. All translations by the author.

7. Diejenige Vorstellung, die vor allem Denken gegeben sein kann, heißt *Anschauung*. *KrV*, B 132.04–05.

8. Also ist das ursprüngliche und notwendige Bewußtsein der Identität seiner selbst zugleich ein Bewußtsein einer ebenso notwendigen Einheit der Synthesis aller Erscheinungen nach Begriffen, d. i. nach Regeln, die sie nicht allein notwendig reproduzibel machen, sondern dadurch auch ihrer Anschauung einen Gegenstand bestimmen,

And he adds in the B Deduction that "the empirical consciousness that accompanies different representations is in itself diverse and without relation to the identity of the subject" (B 133).[9] So to be temporarily incapable of comprehending any of these different representations conceptually is also to lack the unified self that is supposed to do the comprehending. In the worst-case scenario I actually would, as Kant claims, "have as many-colored and diverse a self as I have representations of which I am conscious to myself" (B 134).[10]

However, the worst-case scenario is even worse than that. Kant reaches his conclusion, in both the A and the B Deductions, after having analyzed only *one* synthesizing procedure, not two. He has nowhere suggested that there is a first procedure of conceptual organization that unifies the subject and a second one that unifies the object. Rather, there is only *one* such procedure for systematizing the connections among representations. This single procedure differentiates subject from object, and unifies each. The functions of judgment that enable us consistently to ascribe properties to objects and subsume particulars under concepts are *numerically identical* to the functions that organize the subject into an internally coherent psychological entity. As he says in passage (B),

> (B) [It] is clear that, as we have to do only with the manifold of our representations, and that X (the object) that corresponds to them is nothing to us because it is supposed to be something different from all our representations, *the unity that the object makes necessary could be nothing other than the formal unity of consciousness in the synthesis of the manifold of representations* (*KrV*, A 105.03–09; italics mine).[11]

So for Kant, the unity of the subject and the unity of the object are interdependent in this very strong sense. But we have just seen that according to Kant, the unmediated relation between these strongly interdependent entities cannot itself be a spatiotemporal one, because it is this very relation that engenders the spatiotemporal one. It would seem, then, that this relation is unmediated in a very strong sense indeed: at the precognitive level, there is no *spatiotemporal* distance, distinction or differentiation between subject and object at all. Here we enter the metaphysically spooky noumenal realm of things in themselves, about which knowledge is in principle impossible and speculation futile.

But the worst-case scenario has unacceptable implications even if we avoid any such speculation. For it implies that there is no way for subjects and objects even to arise. There is no impersonal synthetic cognitive activity that might, from this state, generate discrete, sentient entities that bear spatiotemporal relationships to other such entities. Thus in the worst-case scenario, unsynthesized intuitions foreclose empirical experience of any kind—of self, of action, of objects, of world—altogether. Under these circumstances, mental representations permanently remain in a presorted, undifferentiated state, a "buzzing, blooming confusion," to use William James's words. They are like a flurry of postcards that are being continually sent out from some indefinite and unspecified departure point, without any identifiable destination at which they are to be received and sorted. They are intentional, but have neither motive nor purpose.

Now Kant reassures us, in both the A and B Deductions, that we do not need to worry about the worst-case scenario. For in fact it turns out that even appearances must be synthesized, at least at an elementary level, in order for them to be unified as appearances (A 98–99). And the very same functions of judgment that unify perceptual data into appearances are those which also unify appearances into objects (A 105).

d.i. den Begriff von etwas, darin sie notwendig zusammenhängen. *KrV*, A 108.08–15.

9. Denn das empirische Bewußtsein, welches verschiedene Vorstellungen begleitet, ist an sich zerstreut und ohne Beziehung auf die Identität des Subjekts. *KrV*, B 133.07–09).

10. . . . denn sonst würde ich ein so vielfarbiges verschiedenes Selbst haben, als ich Vorstellungen habe, deren ich mir bewußt bin. *KrV*, B 134.08–10.

11. Es ist aber klar, daß, da wir es nur mit dem Mannigfaltigen unserer Vorstellungen zu tun haben, und jenes X, was ihnen korrespondiert (der Gegenstand), weil er etwas von allen

An unsynthesized appearance is one that, after all, has been organized at least at the elementary perceptual level of what Kant calls *ap*prehension (A 99). It remains unsynthesized in the sense that it has not been further sorted and organized at the higher, more complex levels of conceptual and rational *com*prehension (A 103). Unsynthesized appearances are the ones that, on the one hand, do achieve the status of discrete presences, but for which, on the other, it is an open question whether or not they achieve the higher cognitive status of comprehensible objects. Kant's aim in the A Deduction is to explain how, at least in the normal case, apprehension and comprehension function in tandem to engender the empirical world of objects, events, and states of affairs with which we are familiar. In order for this empirical world to exist for us, these appearances can and must satisfy the requirements of comprehensibility that the understanding imposes (B 138).

So Kant's claim is that *if* we are to experience appearances as objects, we must be able to understand them conceptually. However, I find no evidence, either in passage (A) or elsewhere in the *Critique*, of a blanket claim that *every* appearance by definition must be similarly comprehensible. We can think of such a blanket claim as descriptive of what we might provisionally call the *best-case scenario*, in which all of the representations we intuit, including our representations of ourselves, are organized by the categories of the understanding into comprehensible objects of thought. In the best-case scenario, to intuit something is not merely to call the cognitive functions of understanding into operation; it is thereby to secure a conceptual identity and place for each and every thing we intuit.

However, the best-case scenario is in fact not all that good. For that scenario implies that we can in principle comprehend everything we can intuit, i.e., that there is no distinction between the objects that empirically appear to us and the objects we understand. This just seems wrong, and perhaps most obviously wrong in the case of trying to understand works of contemporary art. As viewers we are continually presented with, and moreover expect to be presented with, many things, conditions,

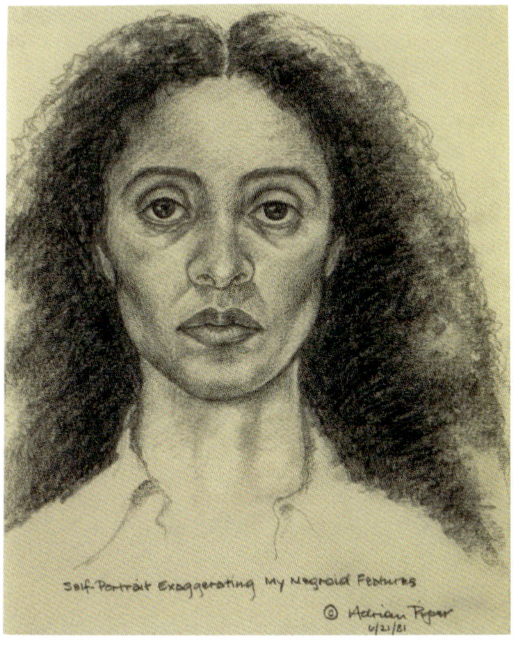

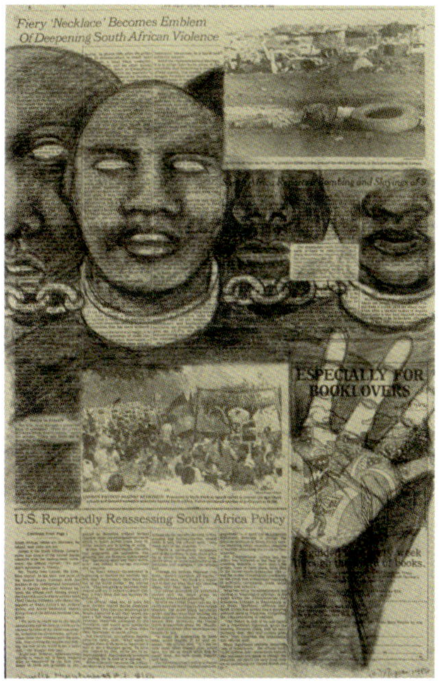

unsern Vorstellungen Unterschiedenes sein soll, für uns nichts ist, die Einheit, welche der Gegenstand notwendig macht, nichts anderes sein könne, als die formale Einheit des Bewußtseins in der Synthesis des Mannigfaltigen der Vorstellungen. *KrV*, A 105.03–09.

and states of affairs that we do not understand, and therefore can barely register in awareness on a first viewing.

But of course our failures of comprehension are hardly limited to these cases. Nor are they necessarily conditioned by a simple lack of information, education, or sophistication. Sometimes they are conditioned by the limitations of our cognitive capacities themselves—by their limited receptivity, flexibility, scope, depth, strength, or responsiveness. The empirical world just is a lot bigger and more complex than we are, and our creative capacities are a lot more complex and unpredictable than we may think they are. Our curiosity about the unfamiliar is not infinite, and may all too quickly shade into panic or revulsion. A serious commitment to empirical realism

What exactly is the aesthetic content of this work?

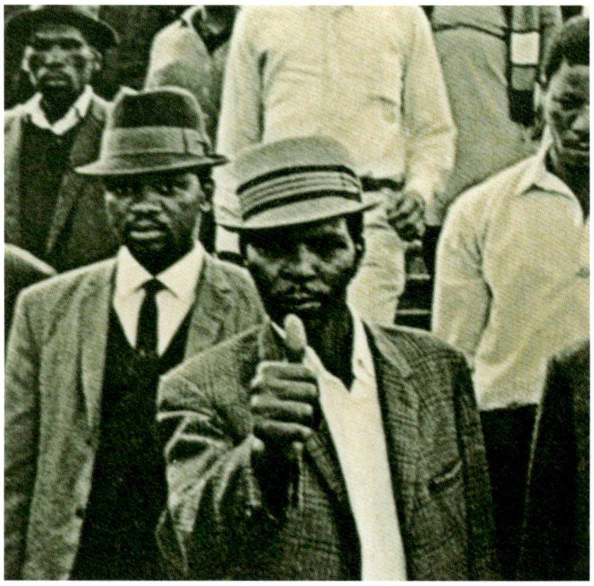

requires our acknowledgment of a natural, social, and cultural world that transcends our ability to make sense of it—and, therefore, our acknowledgment of the infinite possible series of given appearances that, in Kant's analysis of reason, perpetually challenges our higher-level theories to do so. So Kant's empirical realism needs the distinction between those appearances that are conceptually synthesized by the understanding and those that are not, in order to block the naive subjectivism that wrongly infers from Kant's account that we each somehow "construct our own worlds" in any primitively solipsistic sense.

The distinction between synthesized and unsynthesized intuitions is not the same as that between phenomena and noumena. Rather, it is a distinction *within* the phenomena, between those appearances that we recognize as unified objects and those we merely intuit as spatiotemporally located presences. It is a distinction between two kinds of empirical entity that alerts us to the existence of an empirical world, including an empirical self, that lies beyond the mind's ability to grasp it. As a matter of principle, Kant cannot tell us in what this larger empirical world consists, any more than he can tell us in what the noumenal world consists. Nor can he say specifically *what it is* that empirically appears to us in a form that is thus unsuitable to our powers of comprehension. We can only infer from Kant's analysis of those powers what it is not.

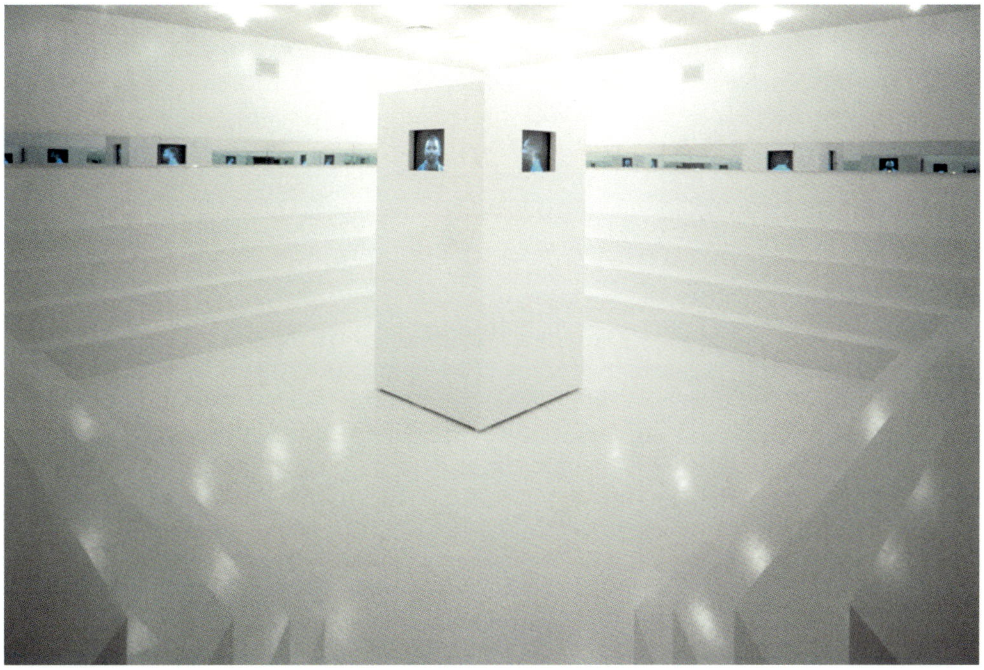

Hence of appearances that do not satisfy the requirements of synthetic unity, Kant says in passage (C) that

Passage (C)	*Passage (A)*
(1) it would be possible for appearances to crowd in upon the soul,	(11) And everything would lay in such confusion (15) Appearances would nevertheless present objects to our intuition,
(2) and yet to be such as would never allow of experience.	(7) because otherwise they would not be objects for us. (10) that the understanding would not find them in accordance with the conditions of its unity at all.
(3) Since connection in accordance with universal and necessary laws would be lacking,	(12) that, for example, in the series of appearances nothing would present itself that would provide a rule of synthesis, (13) and therefore would correspond to the concept of cause and effect.
(4) all relation of knowledge to objects would fall away.	(14) So this concept would be completely empty, void, and without meaning.
(5) The appearances might, indeed, constitute intuition without thought, but not knowledge;	(2) So objects can certainly [*allerdings*] appear to us, (3) without necessarily having to relate to functions of the understanding, (5) For without functions of the understanding, appearances can certainly [*allerdings*] be given in intuition. (16) for intuition by no means needs the functions of thought.
(6) and consequently would be for us as good as nothing.	
(*KrV* A 111.03–07)[12]	(*KrV*, A 89.20/B 122.05–A 91.03/B 123.17)

As we can see in the table, Kant in passage (C) is reprising and concluding the argument he offered in passage (A). Clause (C.1) recapitulates clauses (A.11) and (A.15), on the possibility of intuiting unsorted and unrecognizable presences. (C.2) condenses (A.7)'s and (A.10)'s denial that we could consciously experience such presences. (C.3) reprises (A.12) to (A.13) on the irregularity, unpredictability, and disconnectedness of such presences. (C.4) elaborates (A.14)'s inference to the state of cognitive vacuity that would result. And (C.5) summarily acknowledges in the subjunctive mood the same

12. Einheit der Synthesis nach empirischen Begriffen würde ganz zufällig sein und, gründeten diese sich nicht auf einen transzendentalen Grund der Einheit, (1) so würde es möglich sein, daß ein Gewühle von Erscheinungen unsere Seele anfüllte, (2) ohne daß doch daraus jemals Erfahrung werden könnte. (4) Alsdann fiele aber auch all Beziehung der Erkenntnis auf Gegenstände weg, (3) weil ihr die Verknüpfung nach allgemeinen und notwendigen Gesetzen mangelte, (5) mithin würde sie zwar gedankenlose Anschauung, aber niemals Erkenntnis, (6) also für uns soviel als gar nichts sein. *KrV* A 111.03–07.

point Kant has already asserted in indicative-mood clauses (A.2), (A.3), (A.5), and (A.16), that intuition is conceptually and functionally independent of understanding. Finally, clause (C.6) drives this now expanded argument to its conclusion: that even if unsynthesized intuitions might indeed exist, they nevertheless "would be for us as good as nothing." To this he later adds that they "would be nothing to me" (B 132)[13] and "would not belong to any experience, therefore would be without an object, and nothing but a blind play of representations, that is, less even than a dream" (A 112).[14]

I suggested earlier that the systematic relation between intuition and understanding must be a contingent one for Kant. We have also seen that this relation is contingent on the presupposition of unified experience: *if* we as coherent subjects are to have a coherent experience of whatever it is we intuit, that intuition itself must be cognitively coherent. But this does not entail that intuitions that violate this presupposition by definition do not exist. What we see from a comparison of passages (A) and (C) is that Kant means to acknowledge the possibility of unsynthesized intuitions on the one hand, yet to deny their cognitive significance on the other: yes, they might exist, he admits, but where they do, they are cognitively unimportant. I think Kant was wrong about this, and I shall shortly try to explain why.

In the *actual-case scenario*, then, some intuitions are synthetically unified, whereas others are not. The actual-case scenario is that in which Kant's description of the worst-case scenario in clauses (A.10) to (A.15) and (C.1) to (C.5) holds only for a limited class of intuitions. As we have already seen, unsynthesized intuitions are those collections of representations that are unified into appearances by the elementary operation of *ap*prehension, but not further unified and classified into recognizable objects by the advanced operations of *com*prehension. Although we have sorted these representations into discrete presences that are situated in space and exist in time, we have not succeeded in applying to them the higher-order functions of the understanding that enable us to recognize them as part of the world of objects, events, and states of affairs with which we are familiar.

So Kant's use of the term "object" in passage (A) to refer to these presences is erroneous and premature. From now on, in order to refer to unsynthesized intuitions, I am going to replace Kant's talk of "objects" in passage (A) with Empson's striking term "things," in order to express the perspectival and noncommittal stance of the subject for whom unsynthesized intuitions do *not necessarily* ever achieve unified objecthood. The first stanza of Empson's poem rightly suggests that whether or not such a thing can or ever does achieve the status of a recognizable object must remain a moot question.

I have also already indicated my fondness for Empson's observation that "it is this deep blankness is the real thing strange." This first line of the poem contains at least two senses of the term "real": a comparative sense and an absolute sense. First, it surveys and evaluates the unlimited range of strange things that happen to one. There is, on the one side, the overwhelming and seemingly endless avalanche of strange things and happenings that multiply and mutate unpredictably. We can see even from my brief introductory narrative of Empson's life that it was an ongoing proliferation of "things [and events] strange" from very early on. Virtually *nothing* in his life turned out as he had probably expected. Empson's account of the cognitive effect of such a proliferation is exactly right:

> The more things happen to you the more you can't
> Tell or remember even what they were.

13. Das: Ich denke, muß alle meine Vorstellungen begleiten können; denn sonst würde etwas in mir vorgestellt werden, was gar nicht gedacht werden könnte, welches ebensoviel heißt, als die Vorstellung würde entweder unmöglich, oder wenigstens für mich nichts sein. *KrV*, B 131.16, B 132.01–04.

14. Diese würden aber alsdann auch zu keiner Erfahrung gehören, folglich ohne Objekt, und nichts als ein blindes Spiel der Vorstellungen, d. i. weniger, als ein Traum sein. *KrV*, A 112.10–13.

If the confrontation with one such thing suspends mental functioning for a long moment, repeated confrontation with a succession of such things suspends it for a succession of long moments. That succession of moments is lost not only to the possibility of concept subsumption, i.e., identification; it is thereby also lost to the possibility of concept retention and recall. The momentary inability to consistently ascribe a predicate to the thing equally forecloses the possibility of locating

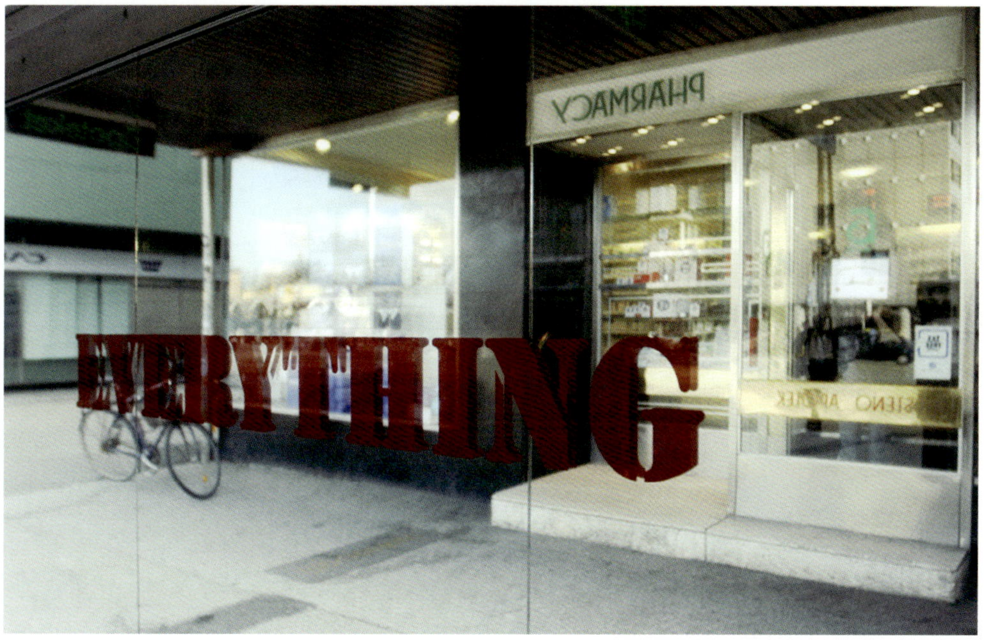

it under the concept that predicate denotes, and therefore of searching for the particular that instantiates that concept in order call it up at a later point. "You can't tell or remember even what things were," because the things themselves stubbornly and repeatedly defy your ability to tell what they are. "The contradictions cover such a range" because whether the predicate or its negation applies to the thing changes from moment to moment. As ineffable presences, anomalous things of all kinds deepen that deep blankness even more, and fill it with their strangeness.

On the other side, there is the culmination of that process of increasing speechlessness in response to those strange things and happenings: "this deep blankness" that is *really* strange. Yes, a seemingly unending proliferation of strange things that happen to one overtaxes one's ability to capture them in concepts, words, or memory. But the *real* thing strange is the deep blankness that results from that moment, when the mind is so saturated with unfamiliarity that cognitive functioning is suspended altogether.

I submit that the "deep blankness" Empson describes in this opening line of "Let It Go" refers to the same state that Kant describes in clauses (A.14) and (C.4), in which an anomalous presence appears in our vicinity: we intuit it, but it fails to behave in accordance with our conventional expectations of cause and effect—producing in us a state of conceptual nullity, a cessation of cognitive functioning, as Kant says, "completely empty, void, and without meaning." The difference between Kant's and Empson's approach is that Kant regards this state of cognitive suspension negatively. For him, it is a moment of confusion and vacancy, mental stasis, a harbinger of the

Everything
will be
taken
away

progressive intellectual deterioration and dementia that marred the last decade of his life. So he discounts and belittles it even in theory.

By contrast, Empson's sensitivity to his own creative process as a poet, together with his deep engagement with Buddhist philosophy and meditation, lead him to regard this state with interest and respect: as a conceptual silence, a moment of stillness and repose, an alert but wordless mindfulness brought forth by the presence of the unfamiliar, relative to which "the talk that talks" and goes "so far aslant" is an object of ridicule and revulsion. Empson's poem identifies "this deep blankness" as itself "the real thing strange"—stranger than all of the multiplicity of strange things that "happen to you," overwhelming your ability to "tell or remember even what they were." It is this moment of profound incomprehension, of speechless, ineffable cognitive shutdown, more powerful than the unending avalanche of events that assault the outer limits of the mind's ability to process them, that itself commands his fascination—just the opposite of Kant's dismissive attitude.

But as is true for Kant, Empson's "deep blankness" achieves its depth only through the intuitive presences it reveals—and can reveal only when the mind is quiet, shocked into silence by what is so unfamiliar that none of the words or concepts in one's cache are adequate to capture it. Here we arrive at the second meaning of the word "real" in Empson's poem: its allusion to an absolute empirical reality that disturbs our awareness even as it defies our futile attempts to capture it in thought. In the second volume of *Rationality and the Structure of the Self*, my analyses of conceptual, theoretical, and aesthetic anomaly stipulate that the relationship between what Empson calls "the real thing strange" and "this deep blankness" is one of cause and effect: that it is the anomaly that causes the cognitive paralysis. But my account does not violate Empson's insight that it is the deep blankness, the moment of temporarily arrested cognitive functioning, that itself affords us access to the hidden reality of the strange and unfamiliar things that engender it. The things may cause the blankness, but it is the blankness that reveals the things—the unfamiliar phenomena, the experiential anomalies that temporarily suspend the ongoing functions of conceptualization, and that we therefore fail to cognitively recognize at all.

The things that provoke these reactions are the real things that are given to us and affect us without commanding our conscious comprehension. In Kant's characterization of the worst-case scenario in passages (A) and (C), unsynthesized intuitions comprise spatiotemporally located things, states, and occurrences that transform arbitrarily. They go in and out of our purview unpredictably, without any discernible

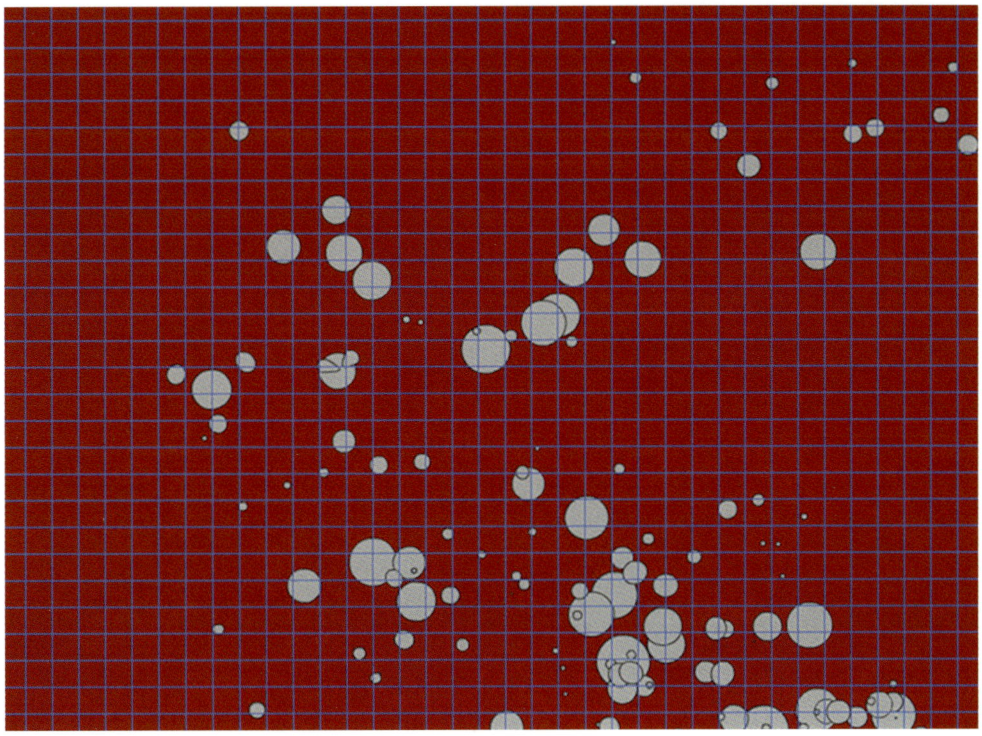

systematic connection to other such things, states, and occurrences that are undergoing their own metamorphoses. These metamorphoses themselves are so fleeting and unstable that they make impossible a consistent ascription of properties to particular objects, and therefore a consistent identification and differentiation of such objects in terms of their properties. For the usual mechanisms by which we make sense of objects—seeking out their causal connections with other familiar objects and events, ascribing to them some of the same properties by which we identify other objects and events, situating them in familiar contexts through their properties and relations—are brought to a standstill. The failure of these organizing mechanisms releases into the mind a flood of things and presences and events with which it has no resources to cope. Unsynthesized intuitions inherently constitute a state of confusion and disorganization that the subject is perceiving, and therefore a condition of psychological confusion and disorganization in the subject herself.

Unsynthesized intuitions may be either third-personal or first-personal, depending on whether we locate them spatially as outside us or as inside us. In the third-personal case, we are passive spectators to those things and happenings that are located outside us, where arbitrarily given visual, tactile, and auditory occurrences, sense-data, forms, and ideas are in direct and intimate proximity to us, filling our awareness and indeed temporarily capsizing it. And in the first-personal case, we are also passive instruments of those unsynthesized intuitions that are located *in*side us, where other sorts of visual, tactile, and auditory occurrences, sense-data, forms, and ideas are also in direct and intimate proximity to us; where mental events, thoughts, images, impulses, and premonitions are given in an arbitrary and shifting temporal sequence that disrupts, paralyzes, or fragments purposeful action. We are passive in both the third-personal and the first-personal cases because of the disruption of intentional agency both conditions effect.

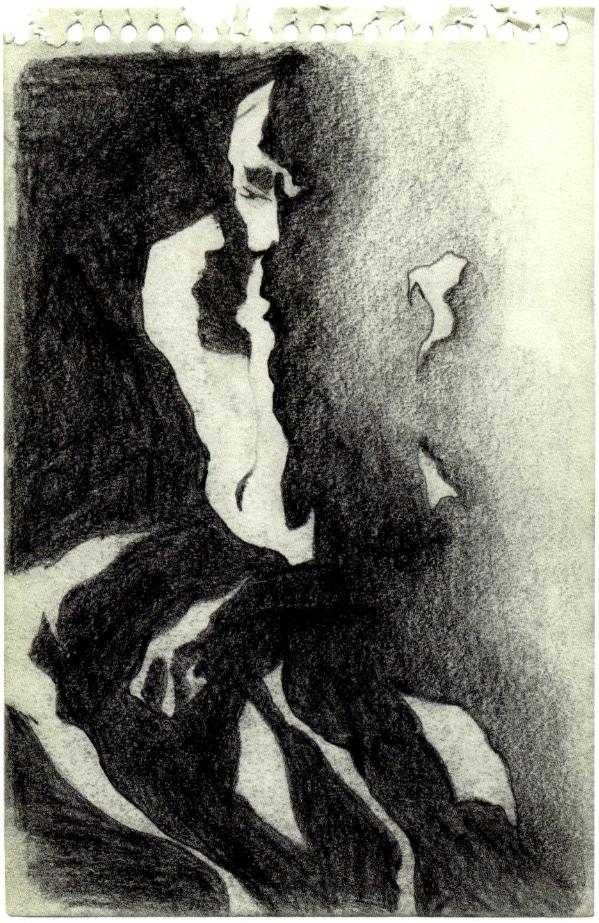

Let's take the third-personal case first. Earlier I mentioned Kant's conclusion at A 108 that the subject is coherently unified if and only if the object is similarly coherently unified by a set of concepts that meaningfully and consistently organize experience. I also noted in discussing passage (B) Kant's stipulation of a single synthetic procedure that differentiates subject from object, and unifies each. The implication for his account of third-personal unsynthesized intuition is clear, and terrifying: these unsynthesized presences do not merely "crowd in upon the soul," as Kant describes. They threaten to overtake and decompose the soul back into the unsorted mass of representations with which it began; to obliterate the distinction between subject and object; and to dissolve the subject as an independent psychological entity into the very things that he fails to understand. With that loss of differentiation go observational distance, spatiotemporal and social orientation, perspective, self-definition, detachment, and objectivity as well. Indeed everything that enables one to distinguish oneself psychologically as an identifiable agent is, for that moment or succession of moments, lost, dissolved into the object.

But the first-personal case is no different, because, as we have just seen, the very presence of unsynthesized intuitions, wherever they come from, undermines the distinction between these two standpoints. Things and presences and happenings and states that well up or appear or burst forth or compel goal-directed activity that seems paradoxically without discernible purpose are no less threatening to the psychological integrity and boundaries of the self when they possess one than they are when they confront one. In both cases, then, unsynthesized intuitions loosen our grip on our subjectivity and our agency, because the unstable spatiotemporality of these things and happenings and states render our discreteness and self-differentiation as subjects equally unstable. So our confrontation with these things is nameless and disorienting, regardless of whether we are viewing them or producing them out of ourselves.

Now this talk was supposed to be about the relation between my art work and my philosophy work, and perhaps you are wondering what all that I've said so far has to do with it. The answer is that I have been showing you what that relation is. I have been doing the philosophical work, and bringing to bear some of the philosophical work I have already done, on the project of directing you to that place in the mind where my art work lives and where *you* have to live and be comfortable, if you want to meet any contemporary artwork, including mine, on its own territory. And I have been showing you just a few of the real things strange you will find if you explore that territory. This is the territory that stretches beyond the reach of conceptualization and convention, beyond the reach of favored tags such as art vs. non-art and good art vs. bad art and art vs. craft and art vs. nature—and therefore far beyond Kant's third *Critique* conception of the free play of the cognitive faculties in a universally communicable judgment of taste.[15] For this territory extends further into the deep regions of the mind than the limitations of judgment, language, intellect, or self can comfortably contain.

To be at home in this place means to be comfortable with unsynthesized intuitions: with unfamiliar things and happenings and states and presences that confound and silence the mind and decompose the ego. This is the place you are called on to visit if you want to get acquainted with a contemporary work of art at the intuitive level I have been discussing. Empson rightly locates the "madhouse" not *here*, in the direct and unmediated, indexical, and intuitive relation to the thing, but rather "in the *whole* thing *there*," in the conceptually unified but mediated relation, where "the contradictions cover such a range," and where "the talk would talk and go so far aslant." The madhouse he rejects is not unsynthesized intuition, but rather the premature attempt to verbalize it.

Cultivating a direct and unmediated relation to unsynthesized intuition on its own terms is not a sufficient condition for finally understanding it. But it is a necessary condition. It is necessary to seek out that anomalous presence beyond the edge of awareness that defies integration into conscious experience. And it is necessary

15. Kant, *Kritk der Urteilskraft*, 1790, ed. Karl Vorländer. (Hamburg: Felix Meiner Verlag, 1974), I.9.

to become comfortable with the bewildered state of wordless confusion, anxiety, and conceptual and conative disorientation it effects. This is the state of vigilant alertness that maximizes receptivity to whatever the real thing strange has to offer.

Of course it is also open to you to skip that part, and proceed directly to a different project, of trying to capture the thing intellectually, by relying on wall labels and museum tours and reviews and other people's comments and discussions and analyses—indeed, analyses of precisely the sort to which I have just subjected Empson's poem—in order to classify the work under its proper conceptual headings. In these cases, higher-level cognition is little more than a vacuous wheel-spinning operation, without connection to the road beneath the wheels. But this also is not enough for understanding, as Kant reminds us in passage (D):

> (D) Without sensibility no object would be given to us, and without understanding none would be thought. Thoughts without content are empty, intuitions without concepts are blind. It is therefore just as necessary to make the concepts of the object sensible (that is, to add to them the object in intuition), as to make the intuitions of the object comprehensible (that is, to bring them under concepts). . . . Only through their union can knowledge arise (*KrV*, A 51.16–32, B 75.17–B 76.01).[16]

So Kant's point, and Empson's point, and mine, is that no talk that talks can substitute for direct, unguarded, and sustained exposure to the intuitive presence of the artwork on terms that cannot be talked at all. Once you have ventured that far, you can let those wall labels go.

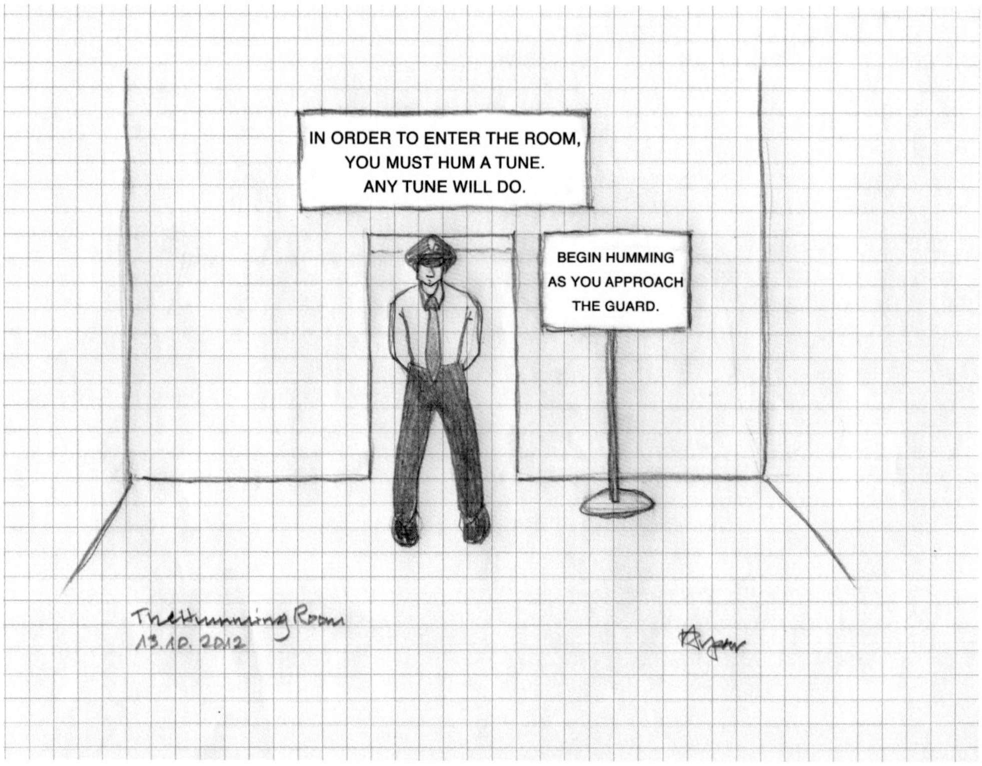

Thanks.

16. Ohne Sinnlichkeit würde uns kein Gegenstand gegeben, und ohne Verstand keiner gedacht werden. Gedanken ohne Inhalt sind leer, Anschauungen ohne Begriffe sind blind. Daher ist es ebenso notwendig, seine Begriffe sinnlich zu machen (d.i. ihnen den Gegenstand in der Anschauung beizufügen), als seine Anschauungen sich verständlich zu machen (d.i. sie unter Begriffe zu bringen). . . . Nur daraus, daß sie sich vereinigen, kann Erkenntnis entspringen (*KrV*, A 51.16–32, B 75.17–B 76.01.

Page 73: William Empson, 1930s

Page 74 (top): T. S. Eliot (third from left), George Orwell (fourth from left), William Empson (third from right), and others, 1942

Page 74 (bottom): William Empson, 1950s

Page 75 (top): William Empson, 1965

Page 75 (bottom): William Empson, 1980s

Page 76: Adrian Piper. *Decide Who You Are: Right-Hand (Constant) Panel*. 1992. Screenprinted image and text on paper, mounted on foam core, 72 × 42 in. (182.8 × 106.7 cm). Various public and private collections

Pages 76, 77: Adrian Piper. *Decide Who You Are: Right-Hand (Constant) Panel Text*. 1992. Audio loop, 00:52:24, and duo performance, duration variable. Collection Adrian Piper Research Archive Foundation Berlin

Page 77: Adrian Piper. *Catalysis IV*. 1970. Documentation of the performance. Five gelatin silver prints, each 16 × 16 in. (40.6 × 40.6 cm). Photograph by Rosemary Mayer. Generali Foundation Collection—Permanent Loan to the Museum der Moderne Salzburg. Detail: photograph #2

Page 78: Adrian Piper. *Hypothesis: Situation #4*. 1968–69. Typescript page on mimeographed paper; gelatin silver prints and ink on graph paper; and two photolithograph pages, 11 × 8½ in. (27.9 × 21.6 cm); $10\tfrac{15}{16}$ × 40⅝ in. (27.8 × 103.2 cm); and each 11 × 8½ in. (27.9 × 21.6 cm). Collection Adrian Piper Research Archive Foundation Berlin

Page 81: Adrian Piper. *The Mythic Being: A 108*. 1975. Oil crayon on six gelatin silver prints, each 25½ × 17¾ in. (64.7 × 45 cm). Collection Candace King Weir

Page 83 (left): Adrian Piper. *Self-Portrait Exaggerating My Negroid Features*. 1981. Pencil on paper, 10 × 8 in. (25.4 × 20.3 cm). The Eileen Harris Norton Collection

Page 83 (right): Adrian Piper. *Vanilla Nightmares #7*. 1986. Charcoal on newspaper, 23⅞ × 13¾ in. (60.6 × 34.9 cm). Weatherspoon Art Museum, Greensboro, North Carolina. Museum purchase with funds from the Benefactors Fund

Page 84: Adrian Piper. *Aspects of the Liberal Dilemma*. 1978. Mixed-medium installation. Black-and-white photograph framed under Plexiglas, audio, and lighting, photograph 18 × 18 in. (45.7 × 45.7 cm); installation dimensions variable. University of California, Berkeley Art Museum and Pacific Film Archive. Gift of the Peter Norton Family Foundation. Detail: photograph

Page 85: Adrian Piper. *What It's Like, What It Is #3*. 1991. Video installation. Video (color, sound), constructed wood environment, four monitors, mirrors, and lighting, dimensions variable. Installation view in *Dislocations*, The Museum of Modern Art, New York, October 20, 1991–January 7, 1992. The Museum of Modern Art, New York. Acquired in part through the generosity of Lonti Ebers, Marie-Josée and Henry Kravis, Candace King Weir, and Lévy Gorvy Gallery, and with support from The Modern Women's Fund

Page 87: Adrian Piper. *Everything #8*. 2006. Mixed-medium installation for KBH Kunsthal, Copenhagen. Vitrine with glass, mirrors, and stenciled text on pedestal, 46 in. × 6 ft. 4 ¾ in. × $32\tfrac{11}{16}$ in. (117 × 200 × 83 cm). Collection Adrian Piper Research Archive Foundation Berlin

Page 88: Adrian Piper. *Everything #1*. 2003. Printed text on paper, 11 × 8⅕ in. (27.9 × 21.6 cm). Collection Adrian Piper Research Archive Foundation Berlin

Page 89: Adrian Piper. *The Spurious Life-Death Distinction (Part II of The Pac-Man Trilogy)*. 2006. Animated video (color, sound), 00:45:00. Collection Adrian Piper Research Archive Foundation Berlin. Detail: video still at 00:05:36

Page 90: Adrian Piper. *Shattered Thinker*. 1967. Pencil on paper, 8 ½ × 5 ½ in. (21.6 cm × 14 cm). Private collection, U.S.A.

Page 92: Adrian Piper. *The Humming Room*. 2012. Exhibition instruction. Pencil on graph paper with digital additions, 8½ × 11 in. (21.6 × 27.9 cm). Collection Adrian Piper Research Archive Foundation Berlin

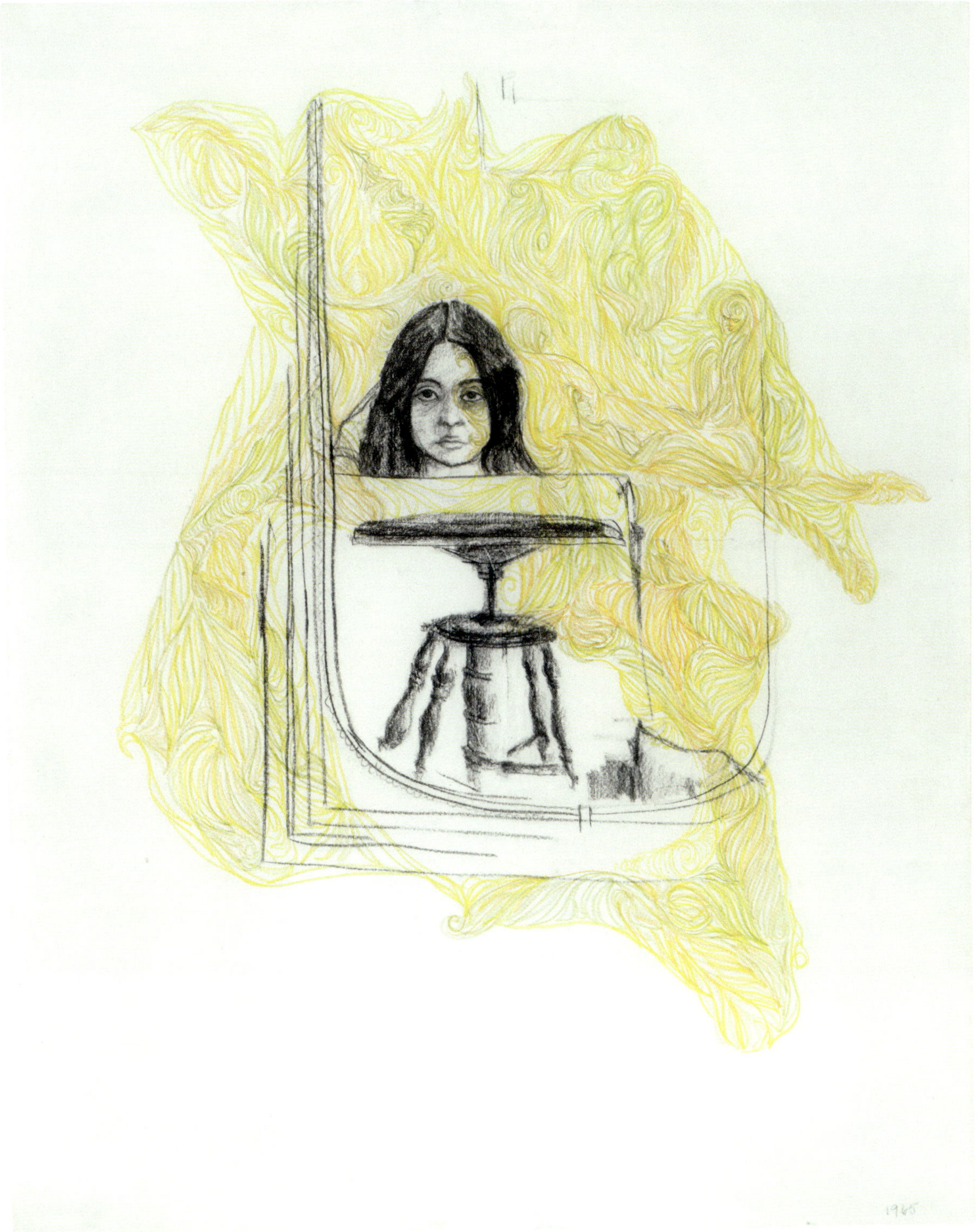

LSD Mirror Self-Portrait. 1965
Charcoal and colored pencil on paper
22½ × 17¼ in. (57.2 × 43.8 cm)
Collection Liz and Eric Lefkofsky

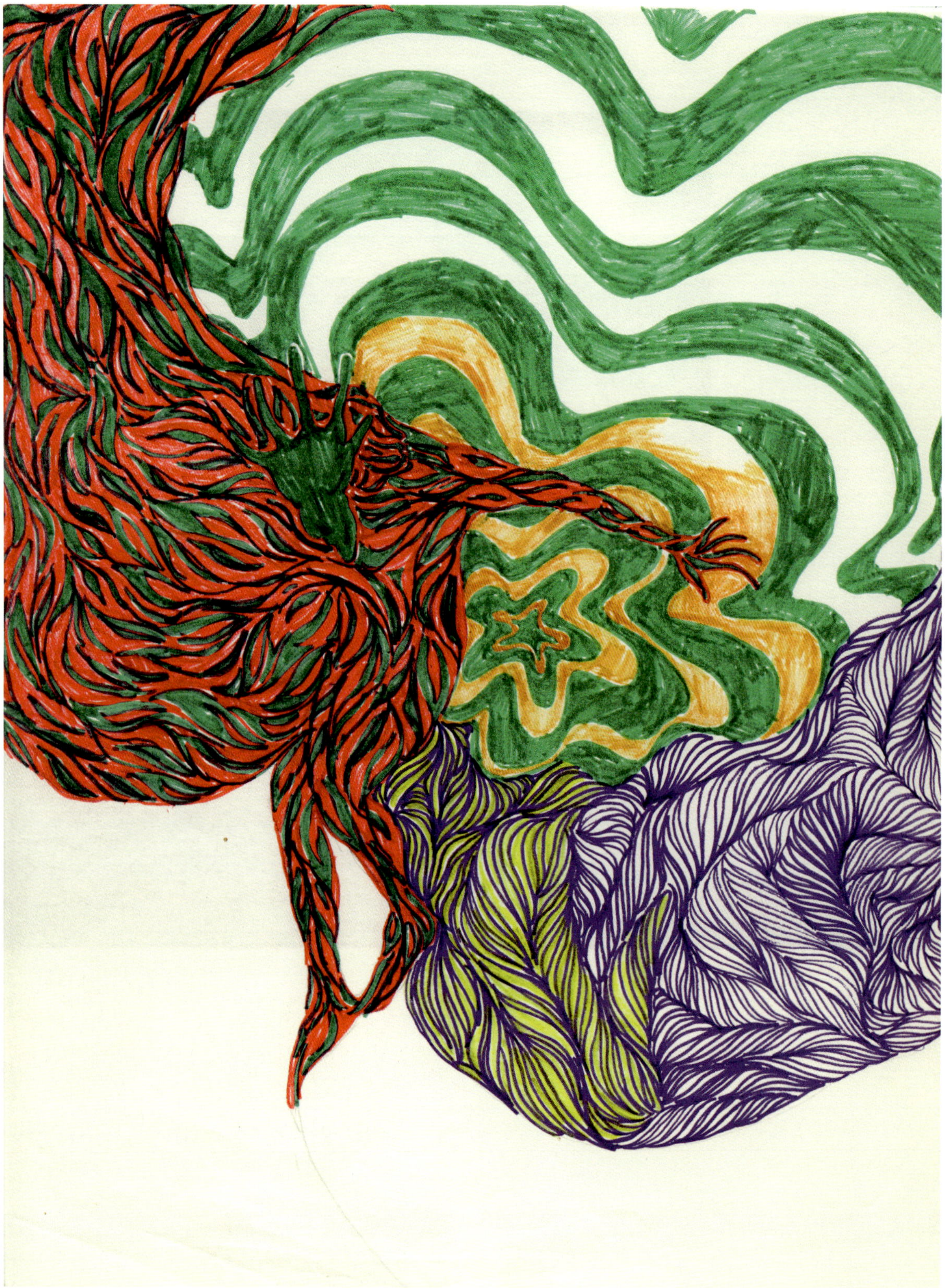

LSD Alice [Study for Alice Down the Rabbit Hole]. 1965
Felt-tip pen, ballpoint pen, and pencil on paper
11¹³⁄₁₆ × 9 in. (30 × 22.8 cm)
Collection Adrian Piper Research Archive Foundation Berlin

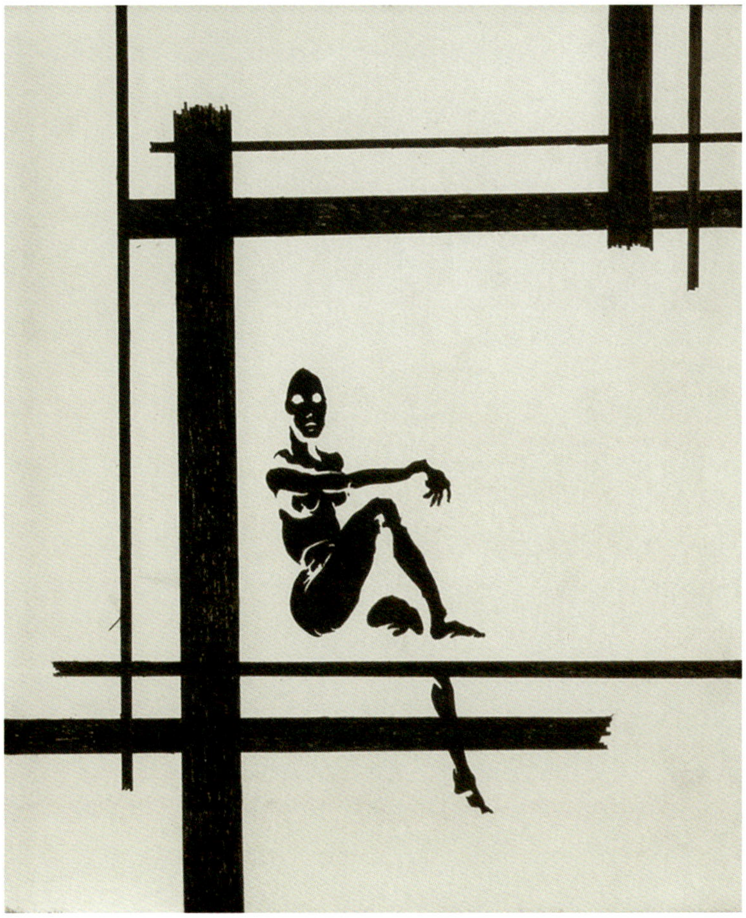

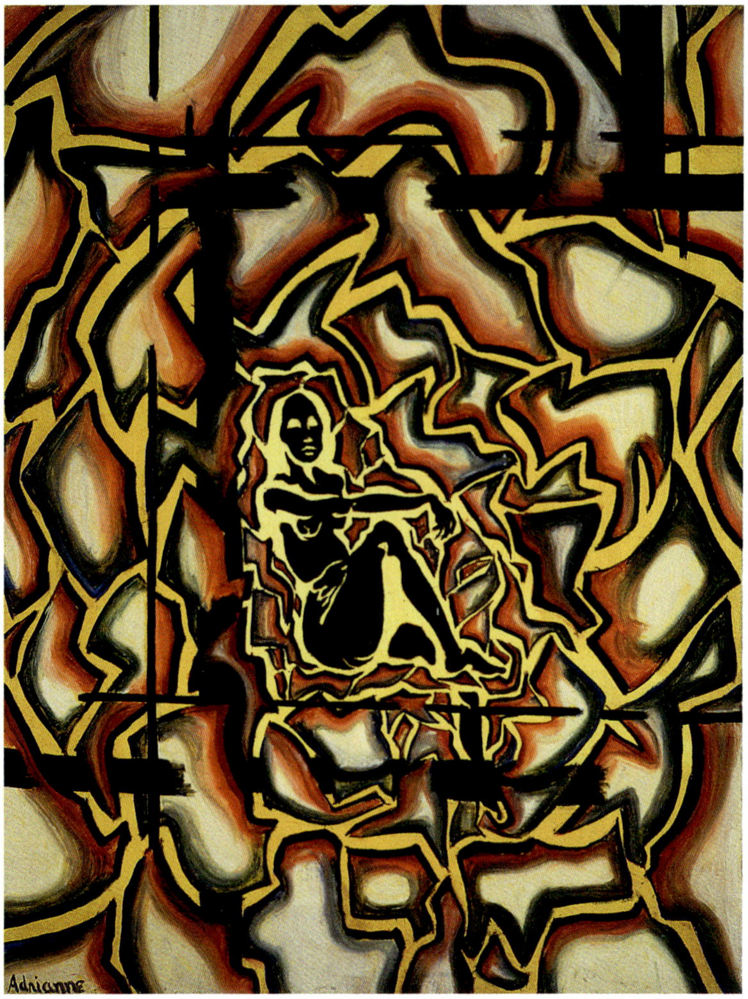

Negative Self-Portrait. 1966
Felt-tip pen on paper
$17\frac{11}{16} \times 14\frac{3}{4}$ in. (45 × 37.5 cm)
Emi Fontana Collection

LSD Self-Portrait from the Inside Out. 1966
Acrylic on canvas
40 × 30 in. (101.6 × 76.2 cm)
Emi Fontana Collection

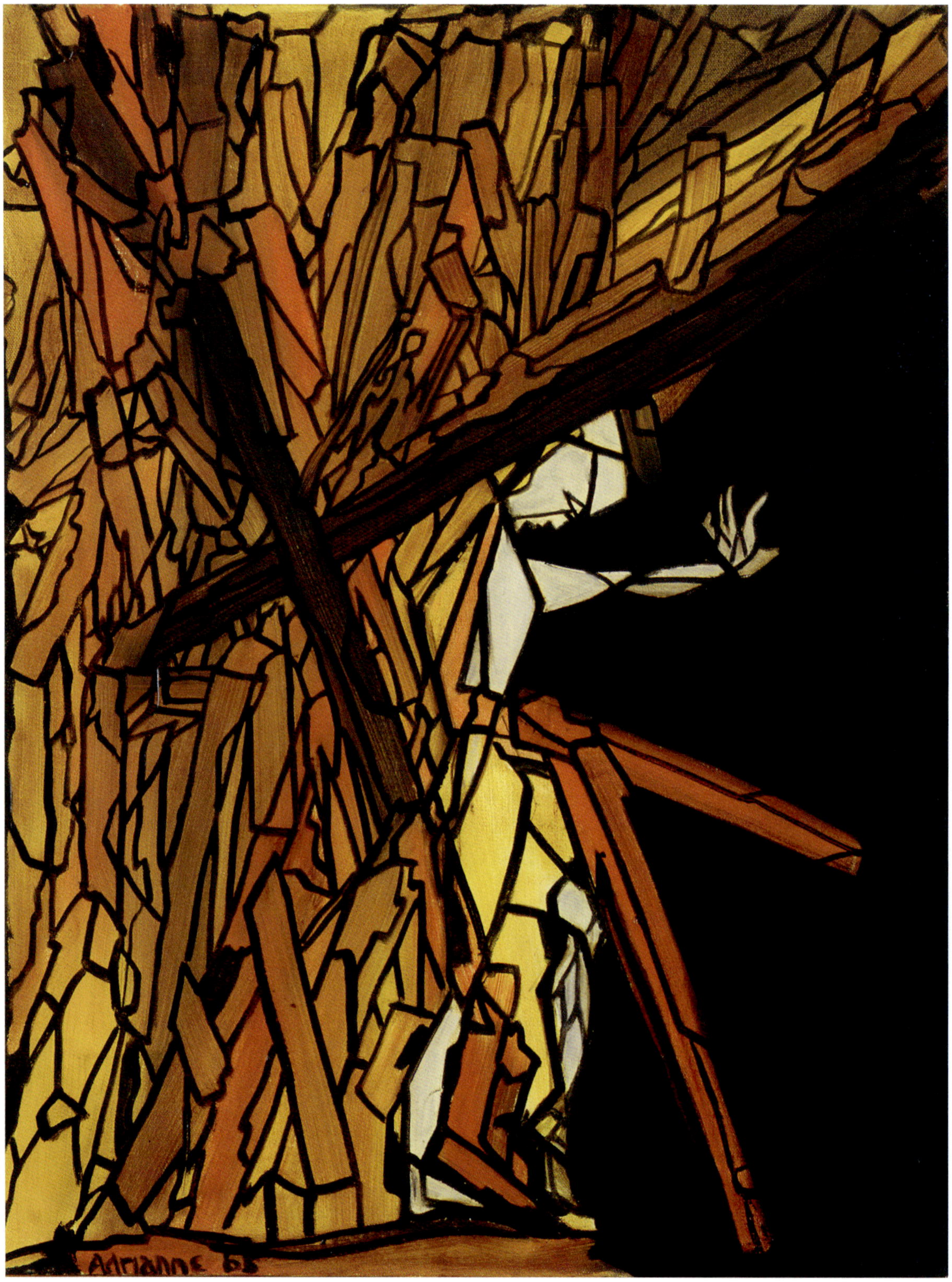

Over the Edge. 1965
Oil on canvas
24⅝ × 18⁹⁄₁₆ in. (62.6 × 47.2 cm)
Collection Adrian Piper Research Archive Foundation Berlin

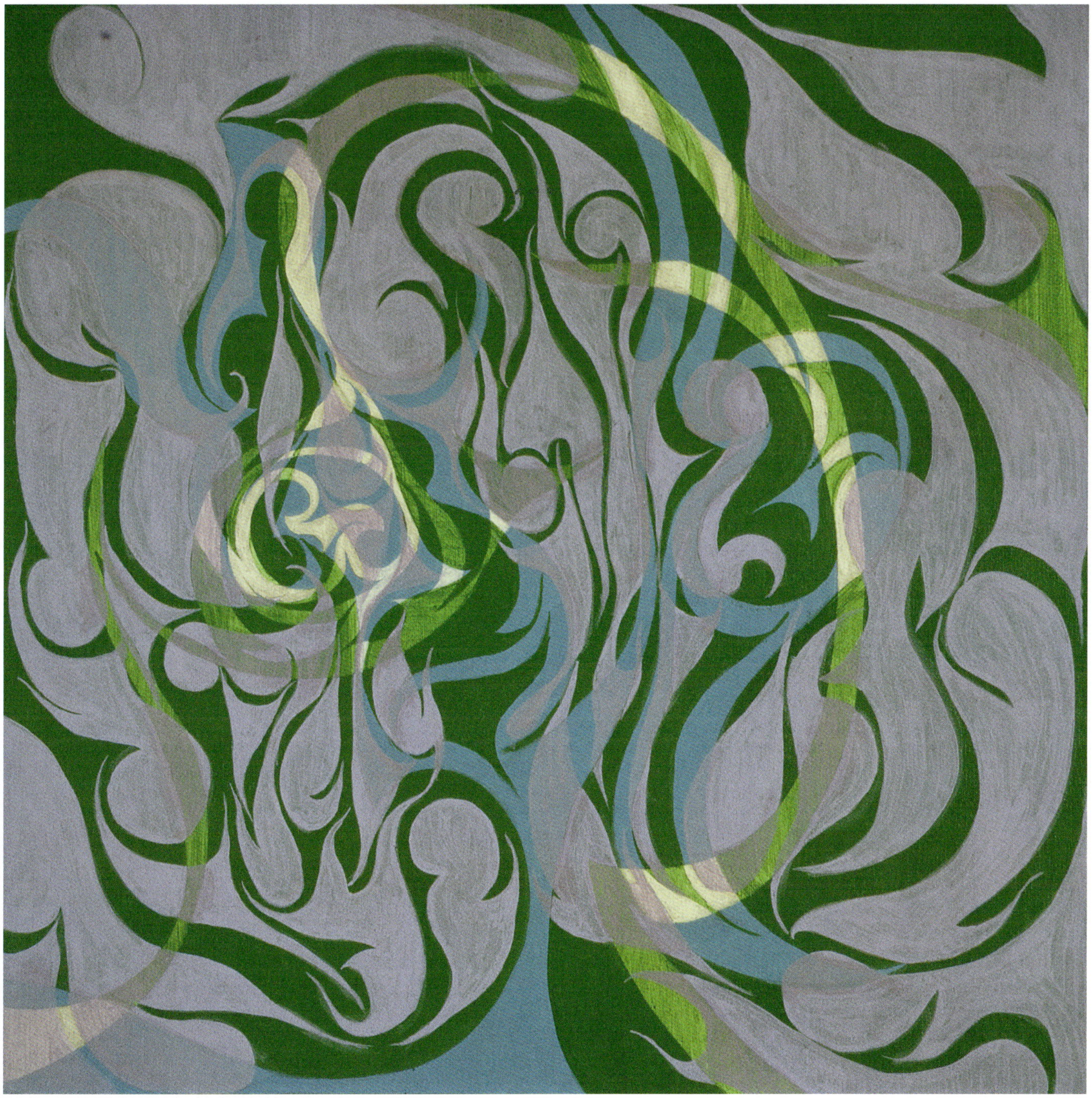

LSD Womb. 1965
Acrylic on canvas
26 × 26 in. (66 × 66 cm)
Emi Fontana Collection

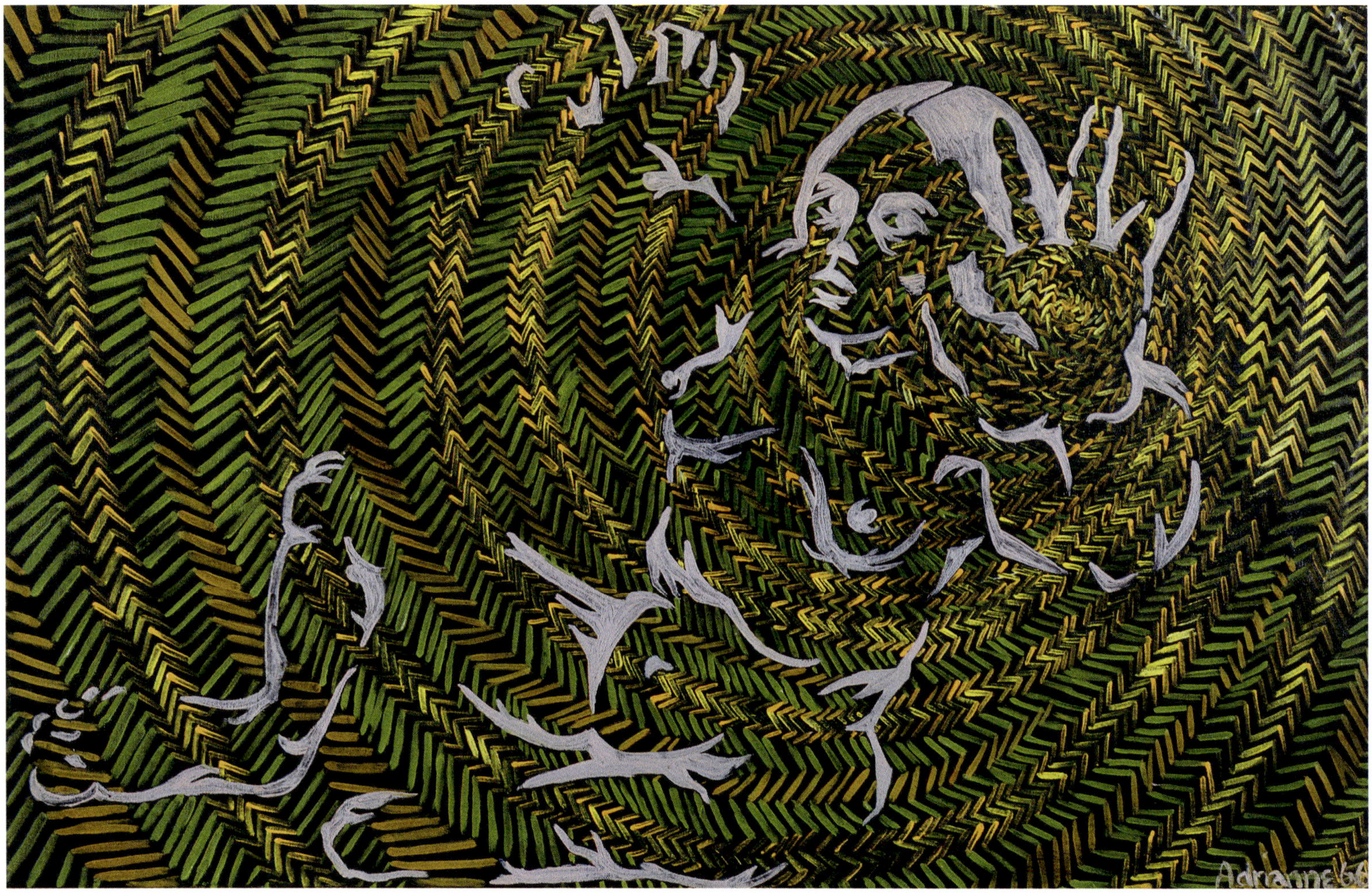

LSD Void. 1966
Acrylic on canvas
26 × 40 in. (66 × 101.6 cm)
Emi Fontana Collection

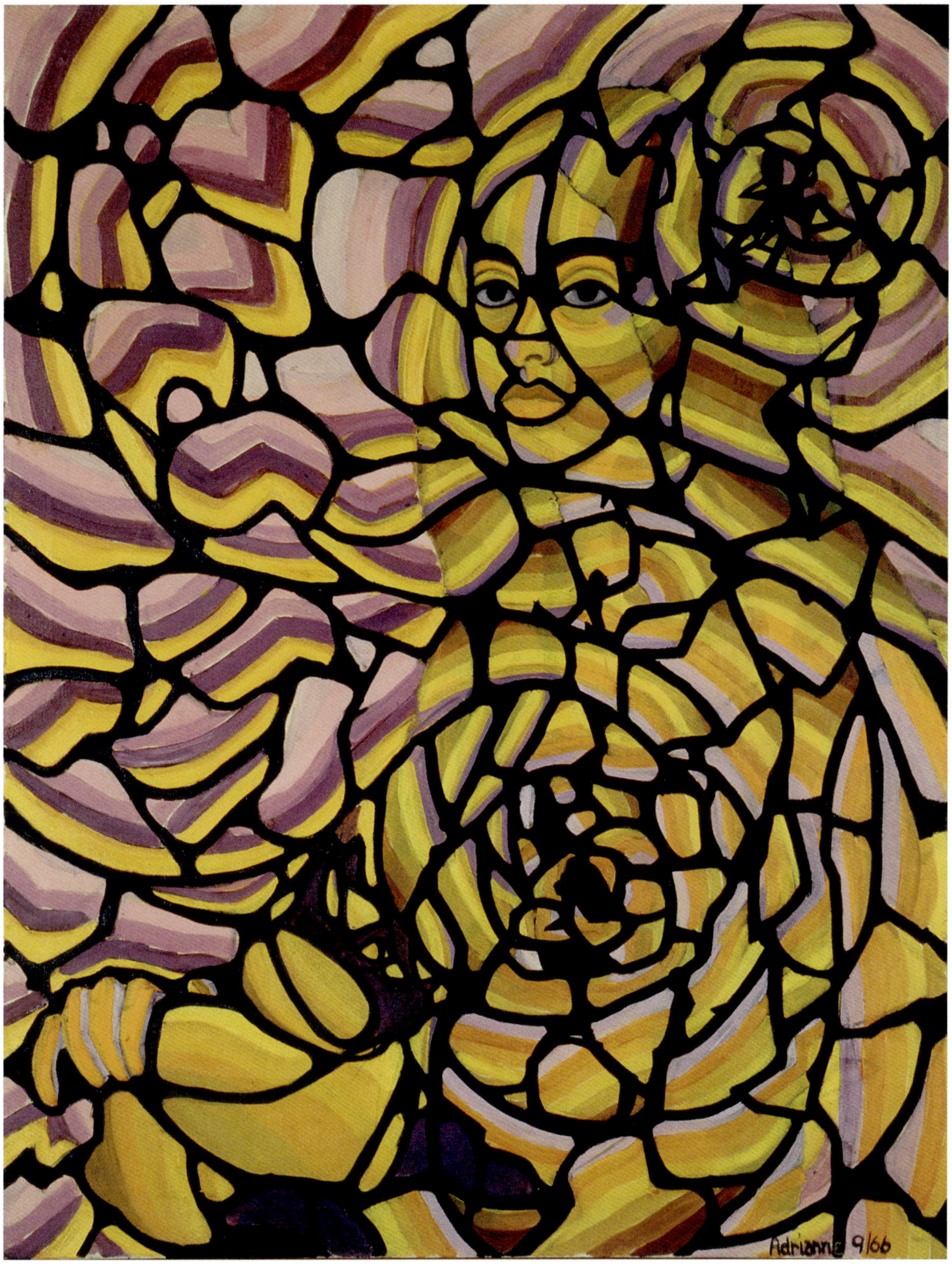

LSD Self-Portrait with Tamiko. 1966
Acrylic on canvas
40 9/16 × 30 5/16 in. (103 × 77 cm)
Private collection

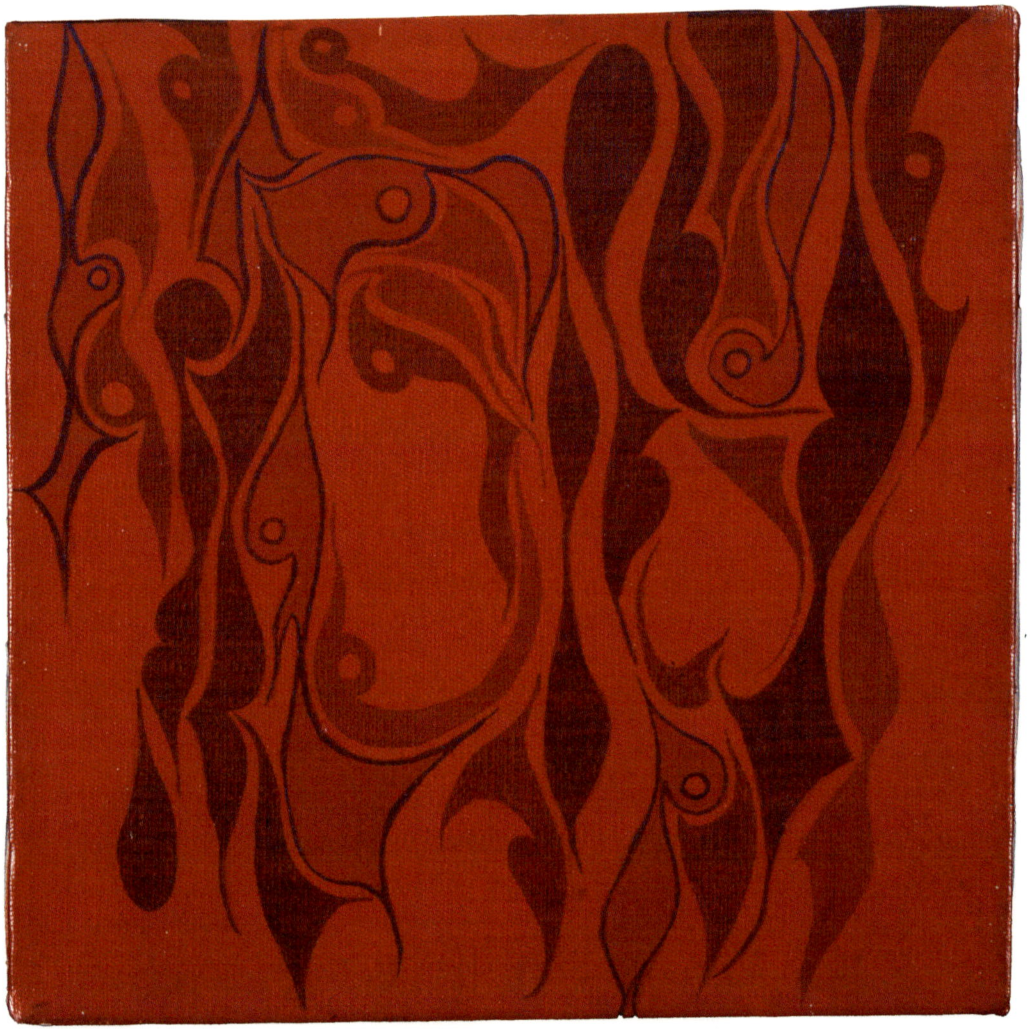

LSD Bloodstream. 1965
Acrylic on canvas
12 × 12 in. (30.5 × 30.5 cm)
Collection Simona & Francesco Fantinelli

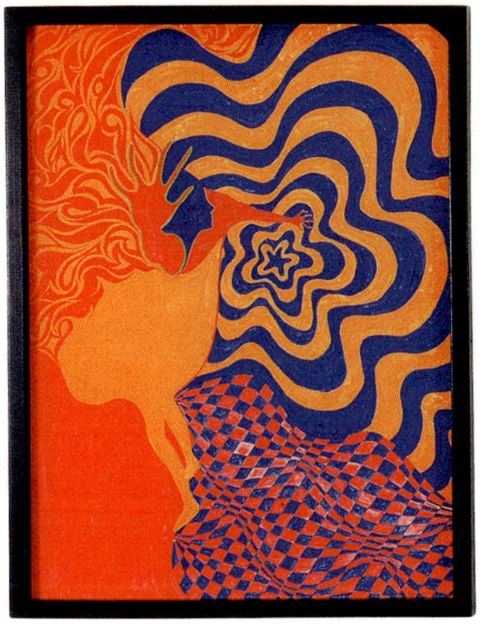

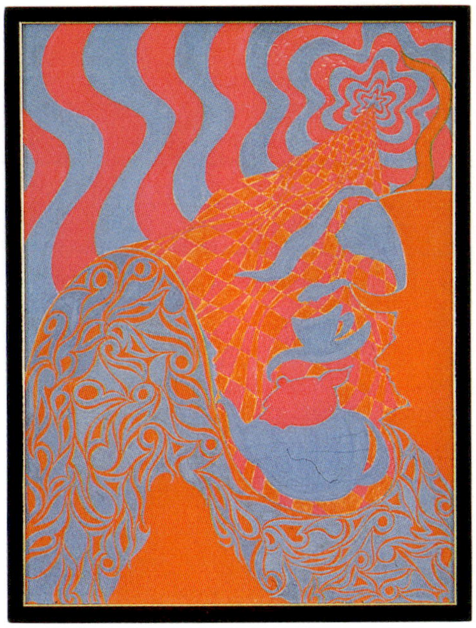

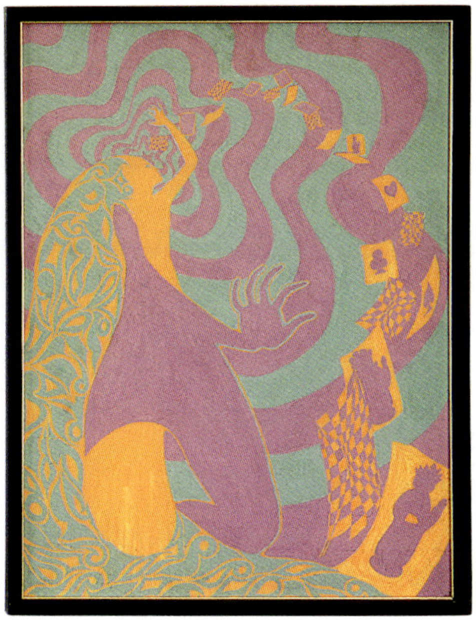

Alice in Wonderland: Alice and the Pack of Cards. 1966
Tempera on canvas board
24 × 18 in. (61 × 45.7 cm)
Collection Konrad Baumgartner, Milan

Alice in Wonderland: The Mad Hatter's Tea Party. 1966
Tempera on canvas board
24 × 18 in. (61 × 45.7 cm)
Collection Konrad Baumgartner, Milan

Alice in Wonderland: Alice Down the Rabbit Hole. 1966
Tempera on canvas board
24 × 18 in. (61 × 45.7 cm)
Collection Konrad Baumgartner, Milan

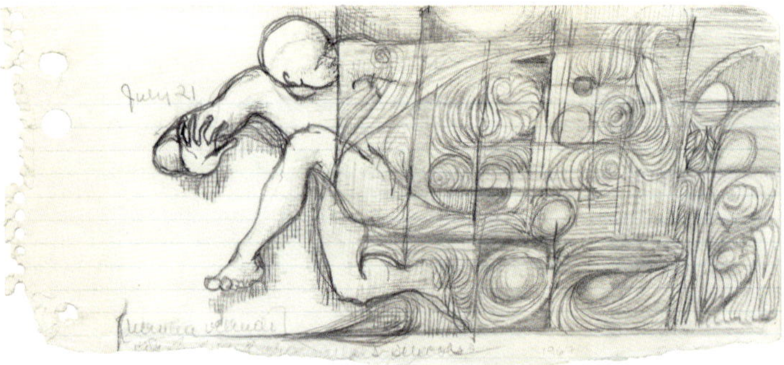

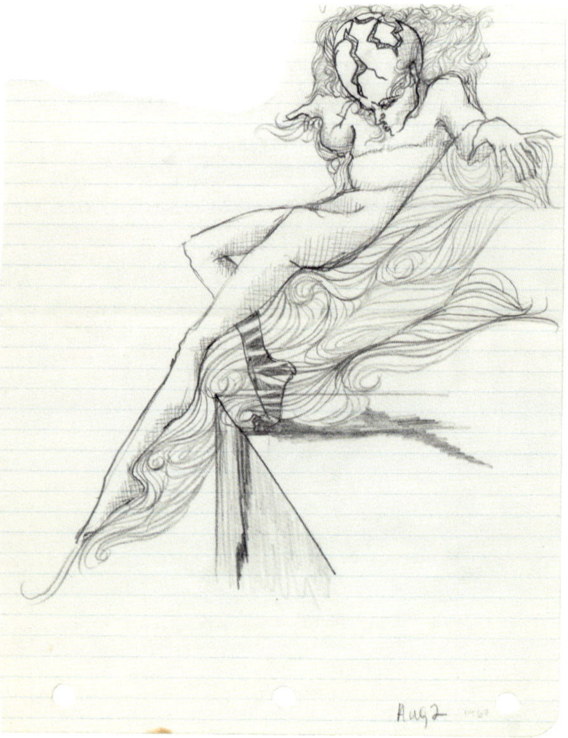

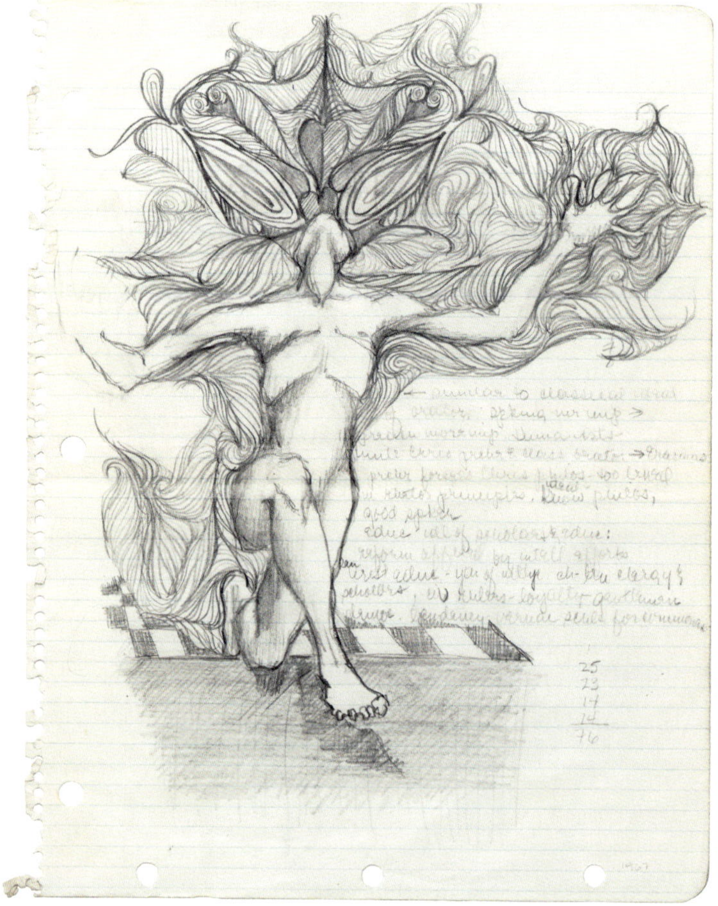

Over the Edge 1 (Study). 1967
Pencil on notebook paper
4⅛ × 8½ in. (10.4 × 21.6 cm)
Collection Adrian Piper Research Archive Foundation Berlin

Over the Edge 2 (Study). 1967
Pencil on notebook paper
9 × 6¹⁵⁄₁₆ in. (22.8 × 17.6 cm)
Collection Adrian Piper Research Archive Foundation Berlin

Over the Edge 3 (Study). 1967
Pencil on notebook paper
11 × 8⁷⁄₁₆ in. (27.9 × 21.4 cm)
Collection Adrian Piper Research Archive Foundation Berlin

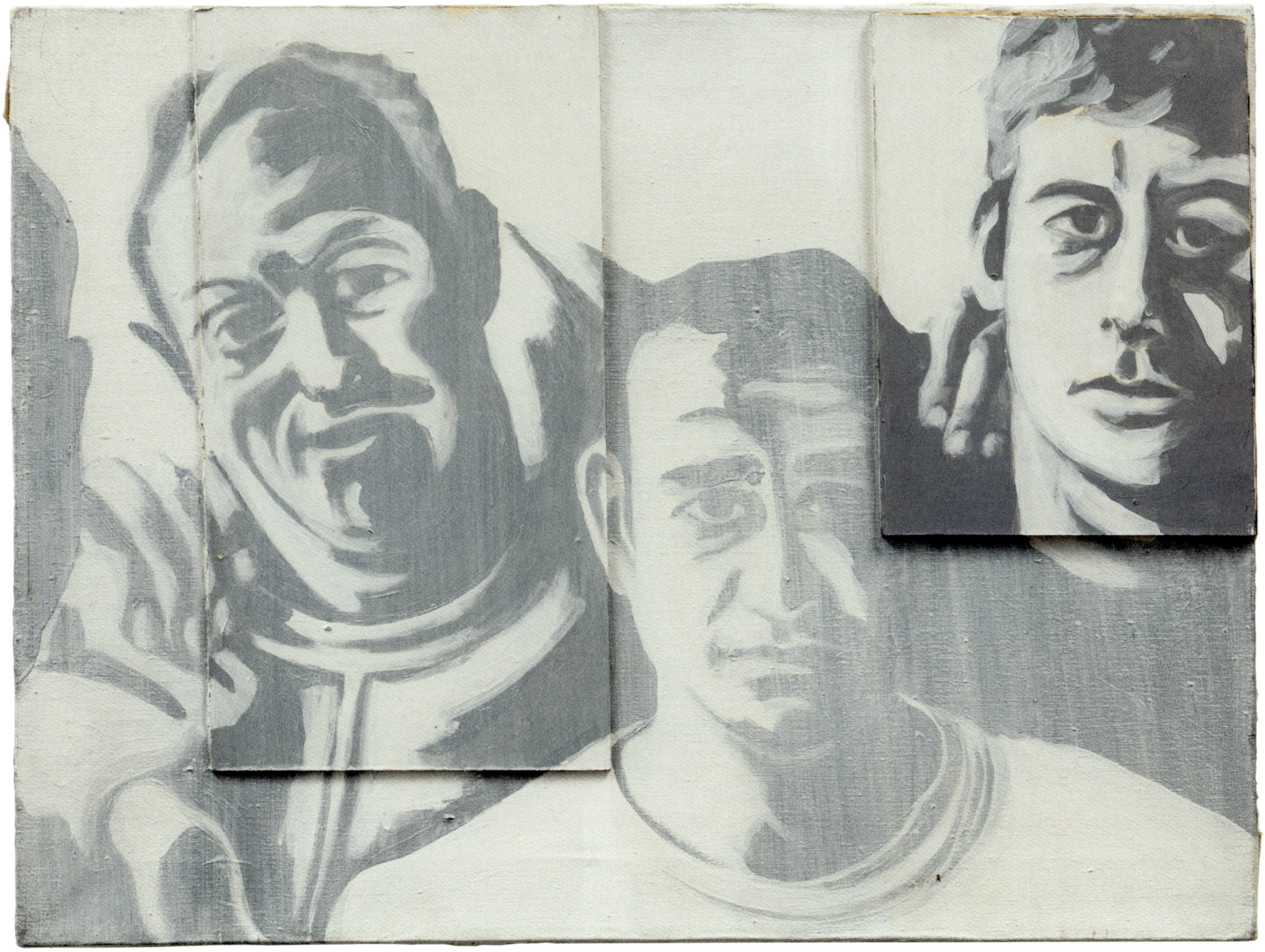

Untitled Planes Painting. 1966
Acrylic on wood, mounted on acrylic on canvas
18 × 24 in. (45.7 × 61 cm)
Collection Adrian Piper Research Archive Foundation Berlin

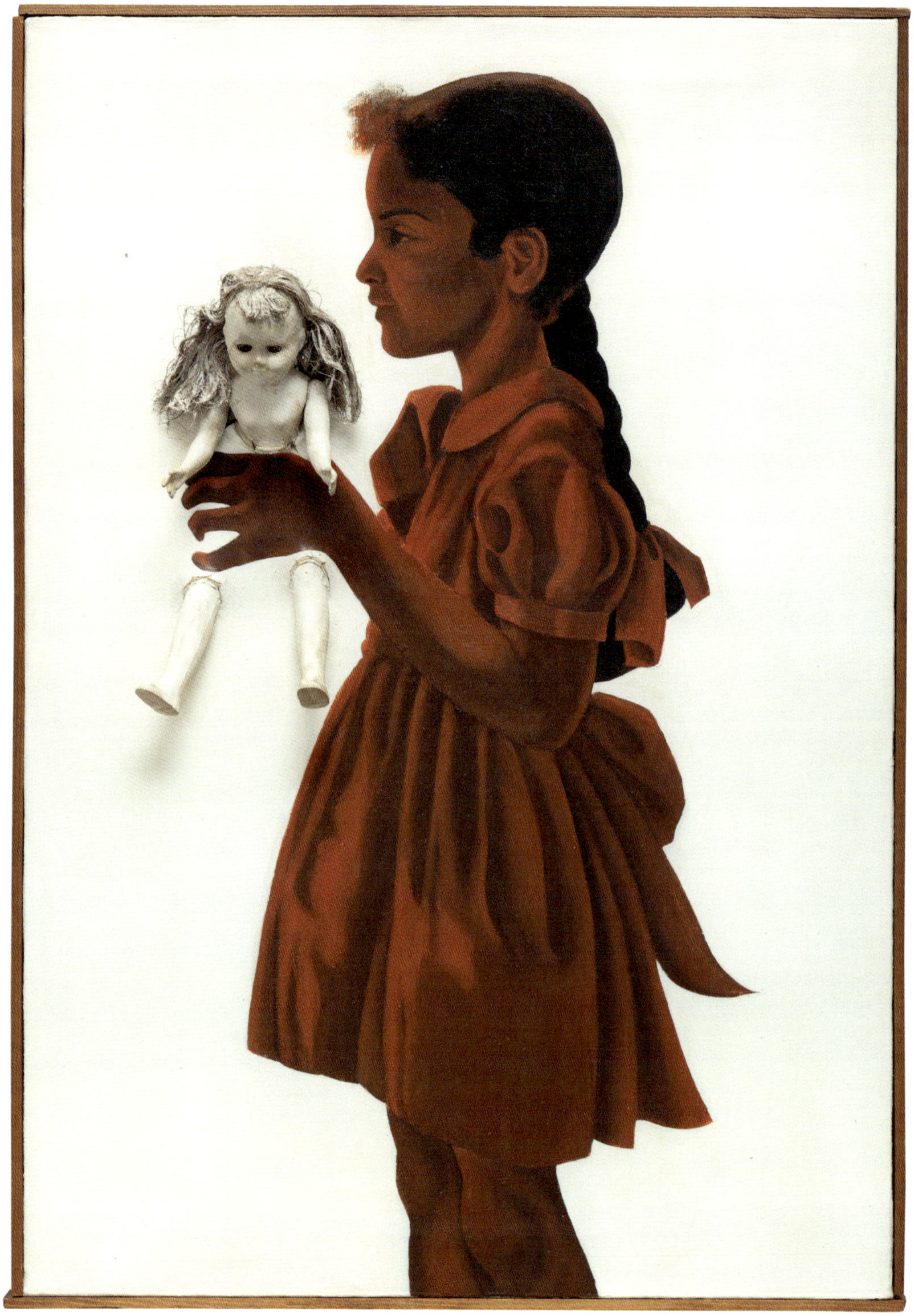

Self-Portrait at Age 5 with Doll. 1966
Oil on canvas with doll
29¾ × 19¾ in. (75.5 × 50.2 cm)
Collection Adrian Piper Research Archive Foundation Berlin

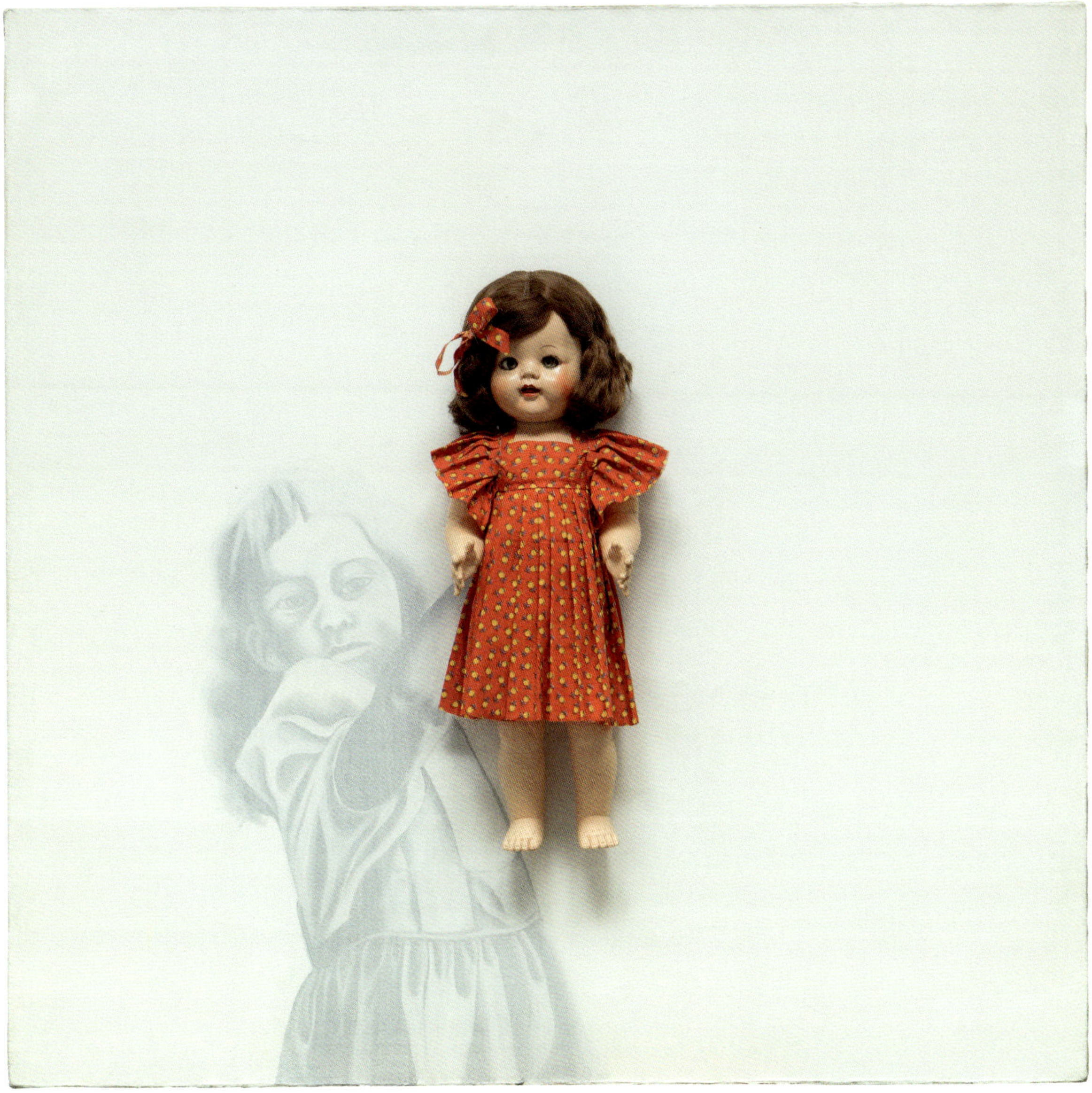

Barbara Epstein and Doll. 1966
Acrylic on canvas with doll
41⅝ × 41 in. (105.7 × 104.2 cm)
Collection Adrian Piper Research Archive Foundation Berlin

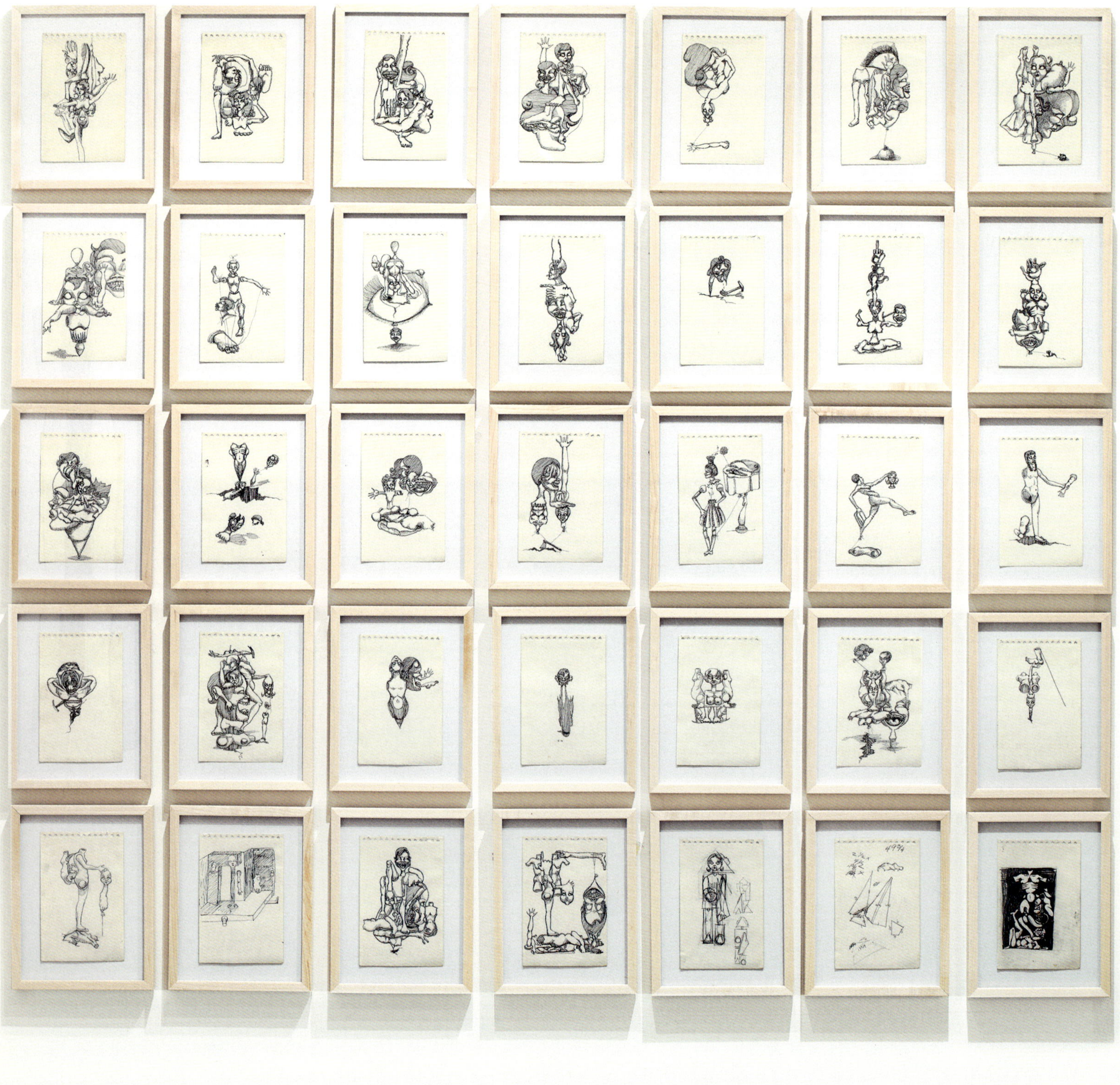

The Barbie Doll Drawings. 1967
Rapidograph pen, ink, and/or pencil on thirty-five sheets of notebook paper
Each 8½ × 5½ in. (21.6 × 14 cm)
The Museum of Modern Art, New York. Acquired through the generosity of Catie and Donald Marron, The Friends of Education of The Museum of Modern Art, Carol and Morton Rapp, Richard S. Zeisler Bequest (by exchange), Committee on Drawings and Prints Fund, Riva Castleman Endowment Fund, John B. Turner Fund, and Monroe Wheeler Fund

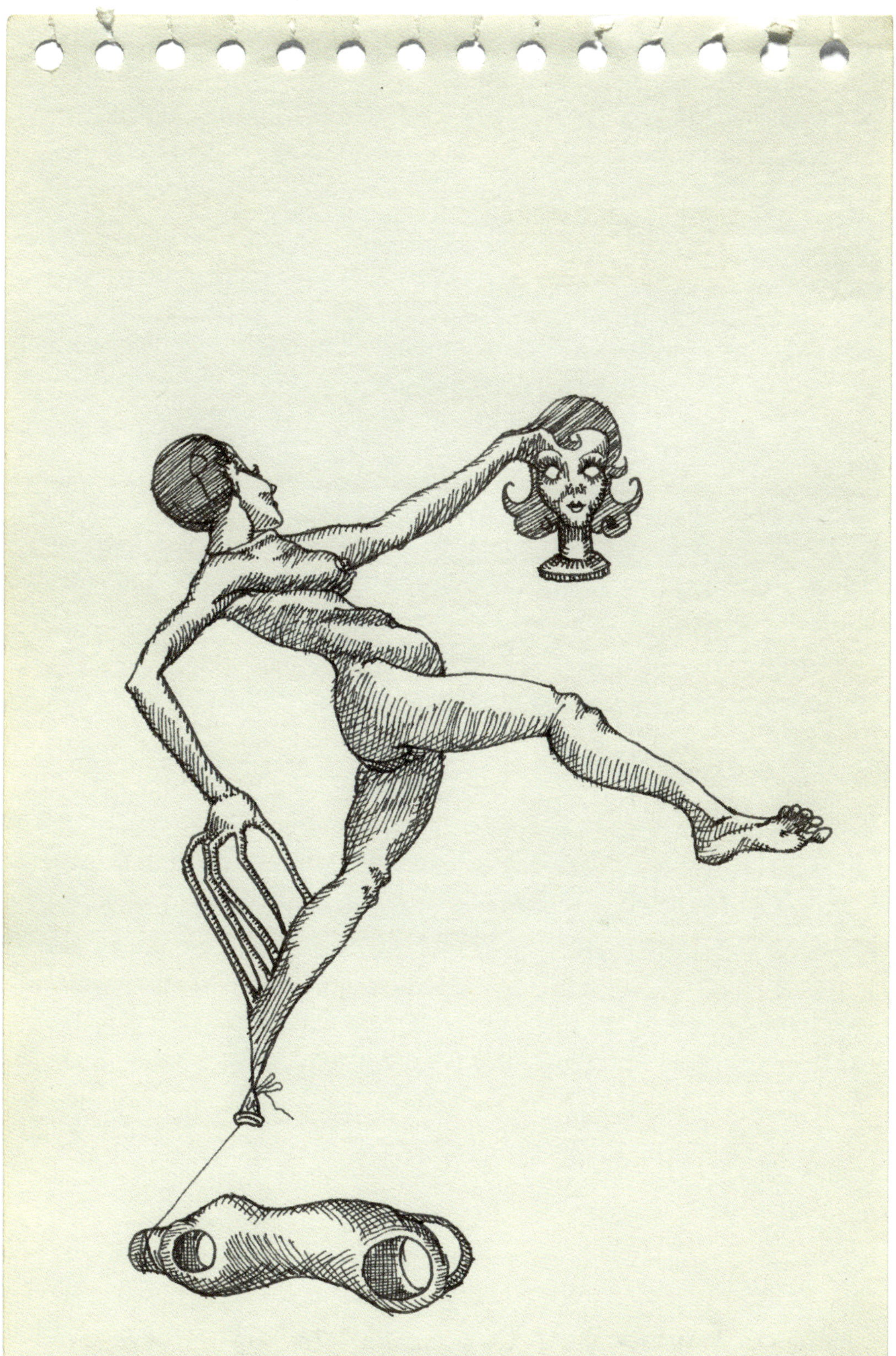

Detail:
Barbie Doll Drawing #20

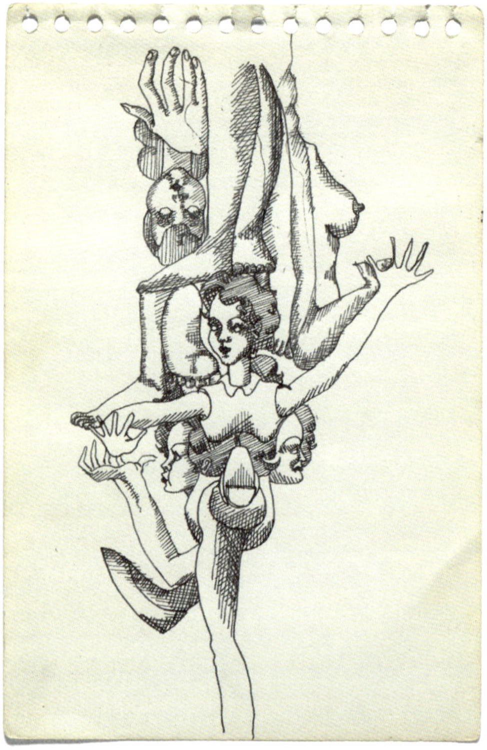

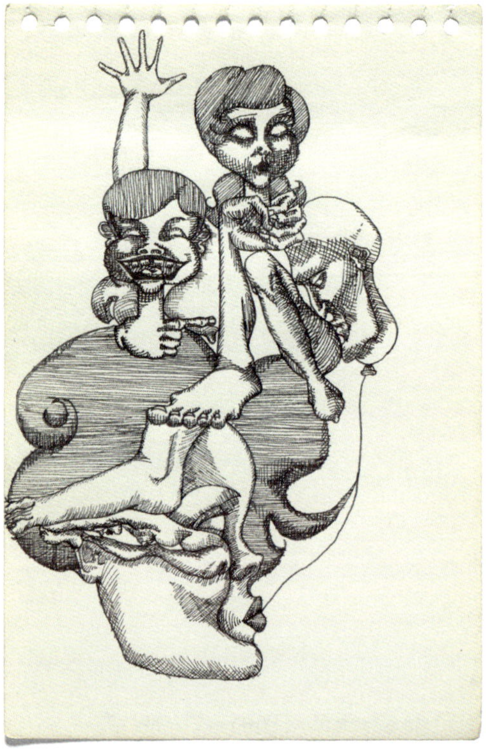

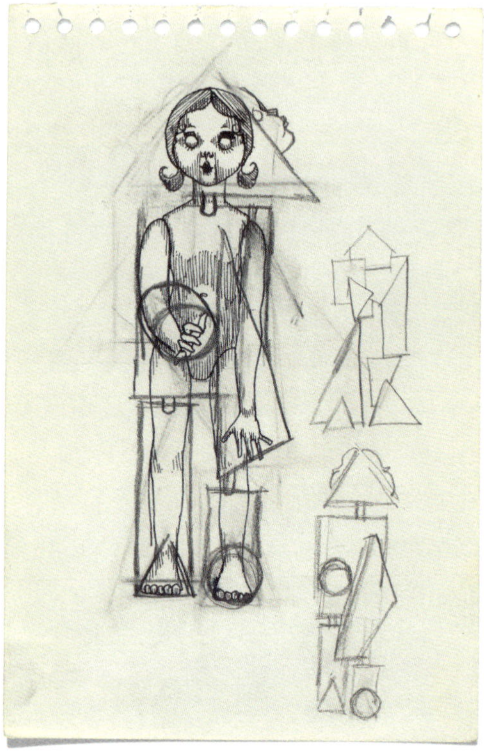

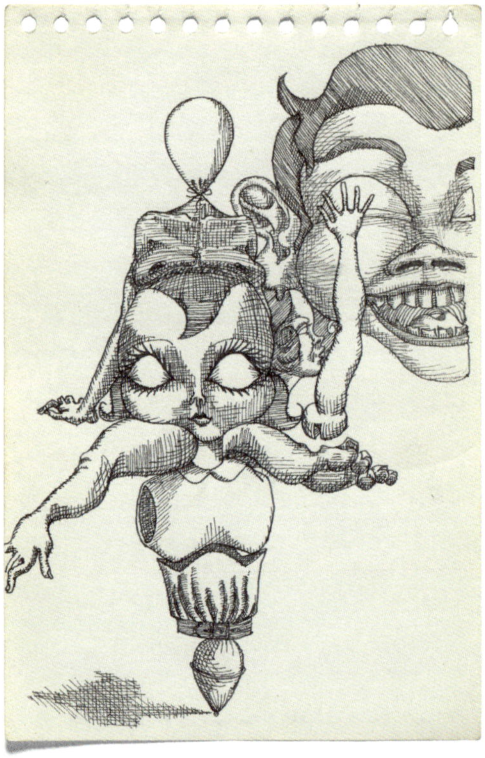

The Barbie Doll Drawings. 1967 (see page 108)
Details:
Barbie Doll Drawing #1
Barbie Doll Drawing #33

Barbie Doll Drawing #4
Barbie Doll Drawing #8

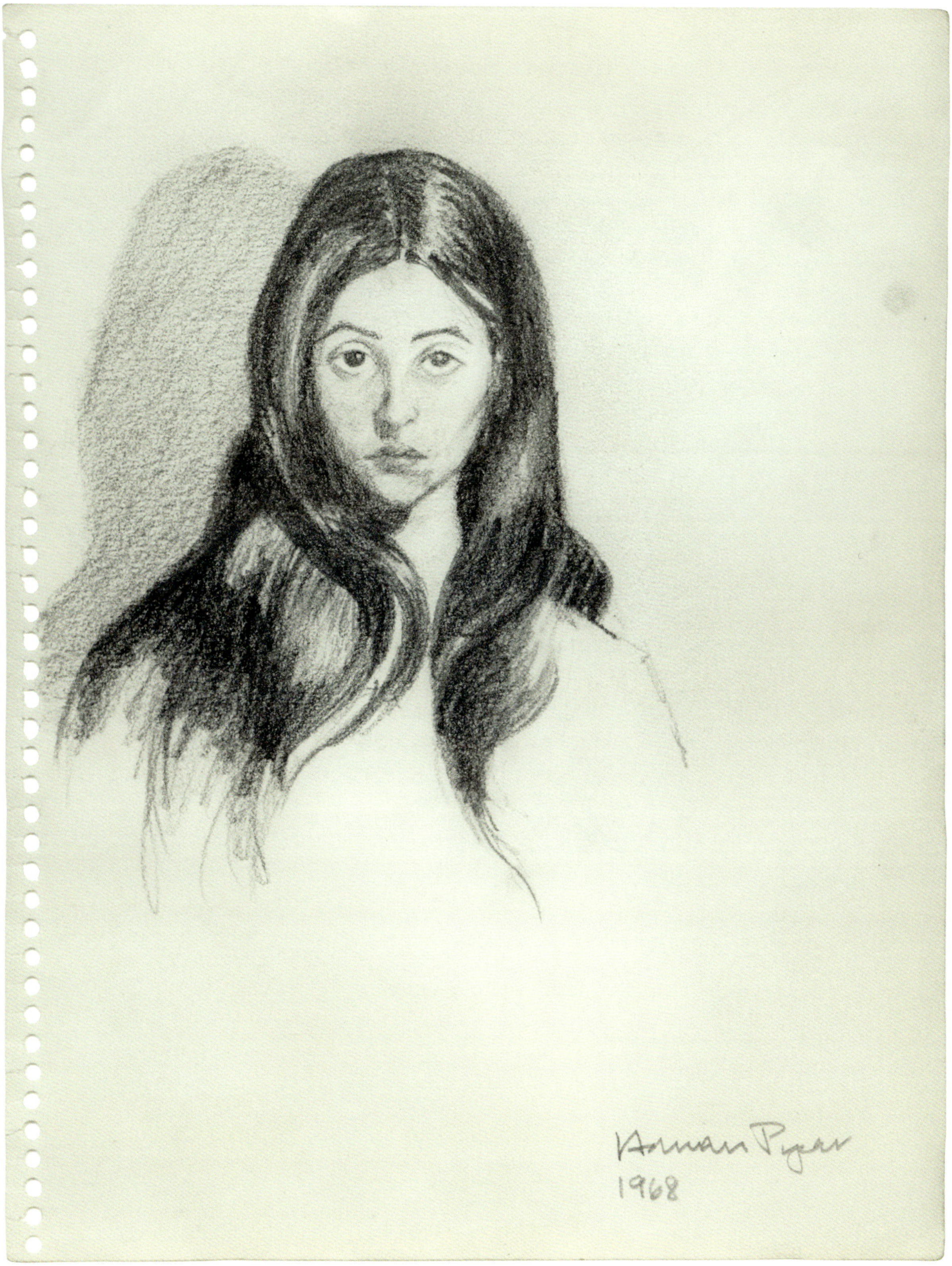

Untitled Self-Portrait. 1967 (later signed "1968")
Pencil and charcoal on paper
11 × 8½ in. (27.9 × 21.6 cm)
Collection Sands and Robin Murray-Wassink, WASSINIQUE INC., Amsterdam

Drawings about Paper and Writings about Words #1. 1967
Pencil on notebook paper
11 × 8½ in. (27.9 × 21.6 cm)
Collection Adrian Piper Research Archive Foundation Berlin

Drawings about Paper and Writings about Words #5. 1967
Pencil and charcoal on notebook paper
11 × 8½ in. (27.9 × 21.6 cm)
Collection Louise Fishman

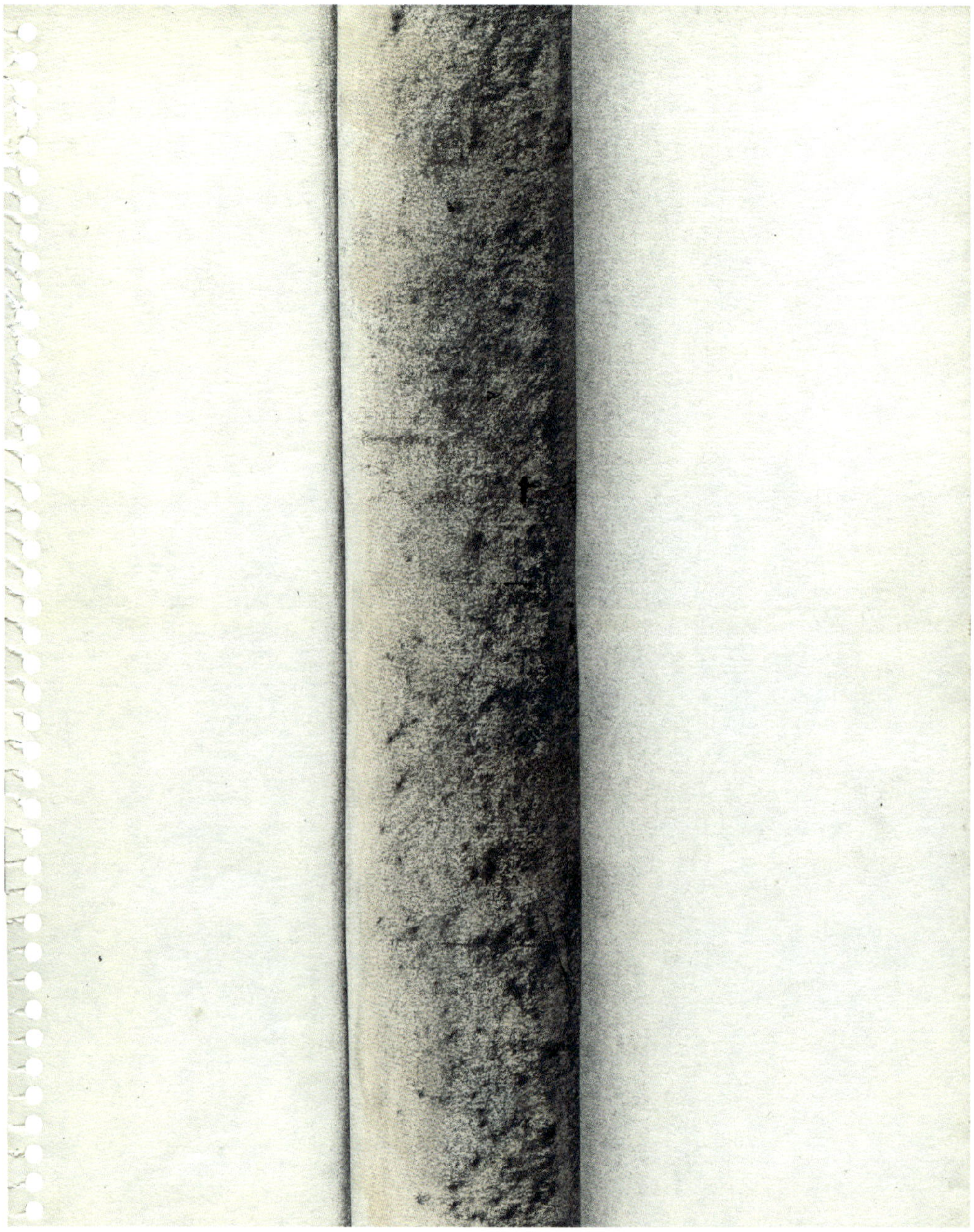

Drawings about Paper and Writings about Words #6. 1967
Cut-and-pasted paper, pencil, charcoal, and pastel on notebook paper
11 × 8½ in. (27.9 × 21.6 cm)
Collection Adrian Piper Research Archive Foundation Berlin

Drawings about Paper and Writings about Words #8. 1967
Cut-and-pasted paper and pencil on notebook paper
11 × 8½ in. (27.9 × 21.6 cm)
Collection Adrian Piper Research Archive Foundation Berlin

Drawings about Paper and Writings about Words #11. 1967
Cut-and-pasted paper and pencil on notebook paper
11 × 8½ in. (27.9 × 21.6 cm)
Collection Adrian Piper Research Archive Foundation Berlin

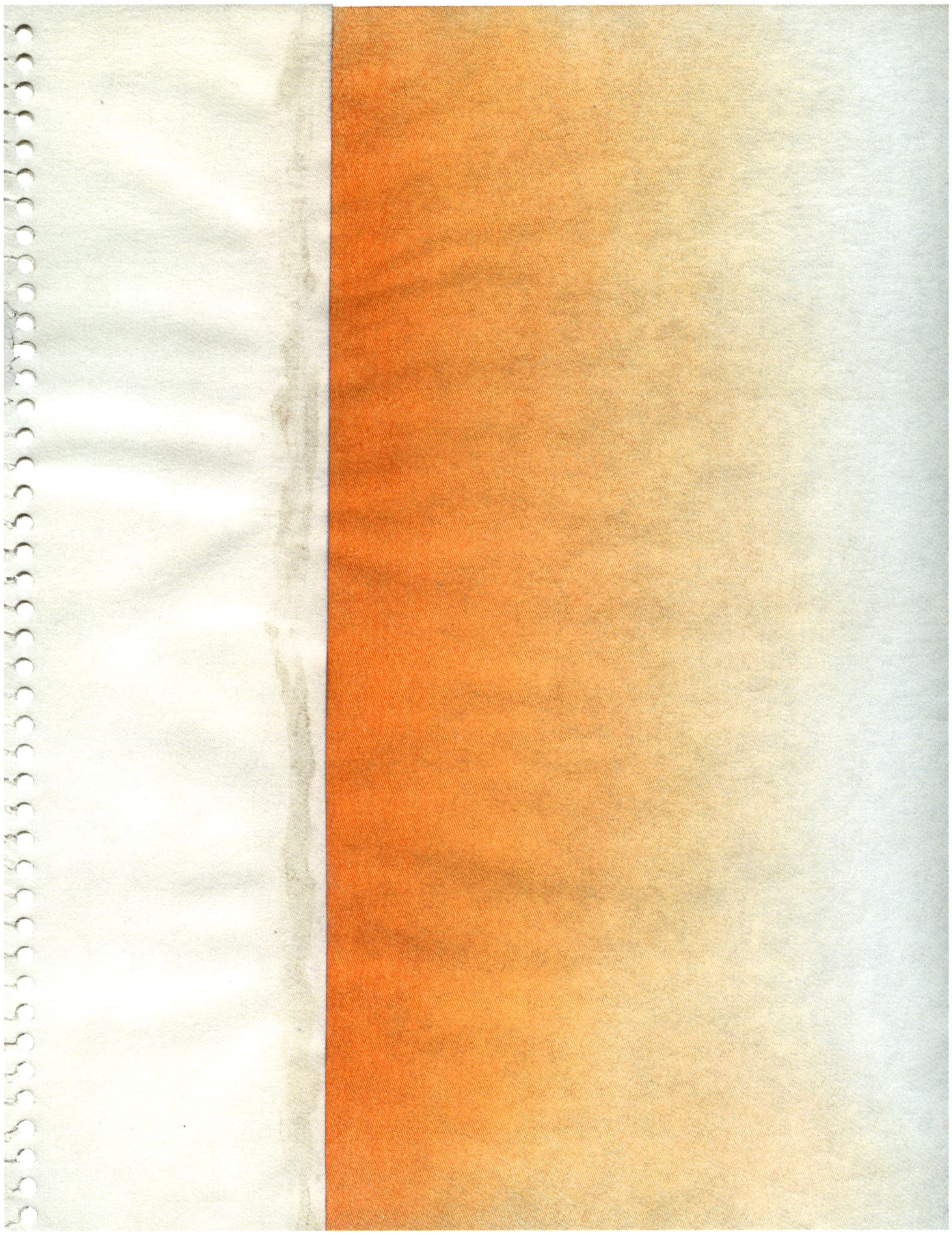

Drawings about Paper and Writings about Words #16. 1967
Cut-and-pasted paper and pastel on notebook paper
11 × 8½ in. (27.9 × 21.6 cm)
Collection Adrian Piper Research Archive Foundation Berlin

Drawings about Paper and Writings about Words #17. 1967
Cut-and-pasted paper and pencil on notebook paper
11 × 8½ in. (27.9 × 21.6 cm)
Collection Gregory R. Miller and Michael Wiener

Drawings about Paper and Writings about Words #24. 1967
Felt-tip pen on graph paper
11 × 8½ in. (27.9 × 21.6 cm)
Collection Adrian Piper Research Archive Foundation Berlin

Drawings about Paper and Writings about Words #25. 1967
Gouache on graph paper
11 × 8½ in. (27.9 × 21.6 cm)
Collection Adrian Piper Research Archive Foundation Berlin

Drawings about Paper and Writings about Words #27. 1967
Gouache on graph paper
11 × 8½ in. (27.9 × 21.6 cm)
Collection Gregory R. Miller and Michael Wiener

Drawings about Paper and Writings about Words #33. 1967
Pencil on notebook paper
11 × 8½ in. (27.9 × 21.6 cm)
Collection Adrian Piper Research Archive Foundation Berlin

Drawings about Paper and Writings about Words #46. 1967
Cut-and-pasted paper bag, charcoal, and pencil on notebook paper
11 × 8½ in. (27.9 × 21.6 cm)
The Museum of Modern Art, New York. The Judith Rothschild Foundation Contemporary Drawings Collection Gift (purchase, and gift, in part, of The Eileen and Michael Cohen Collection)

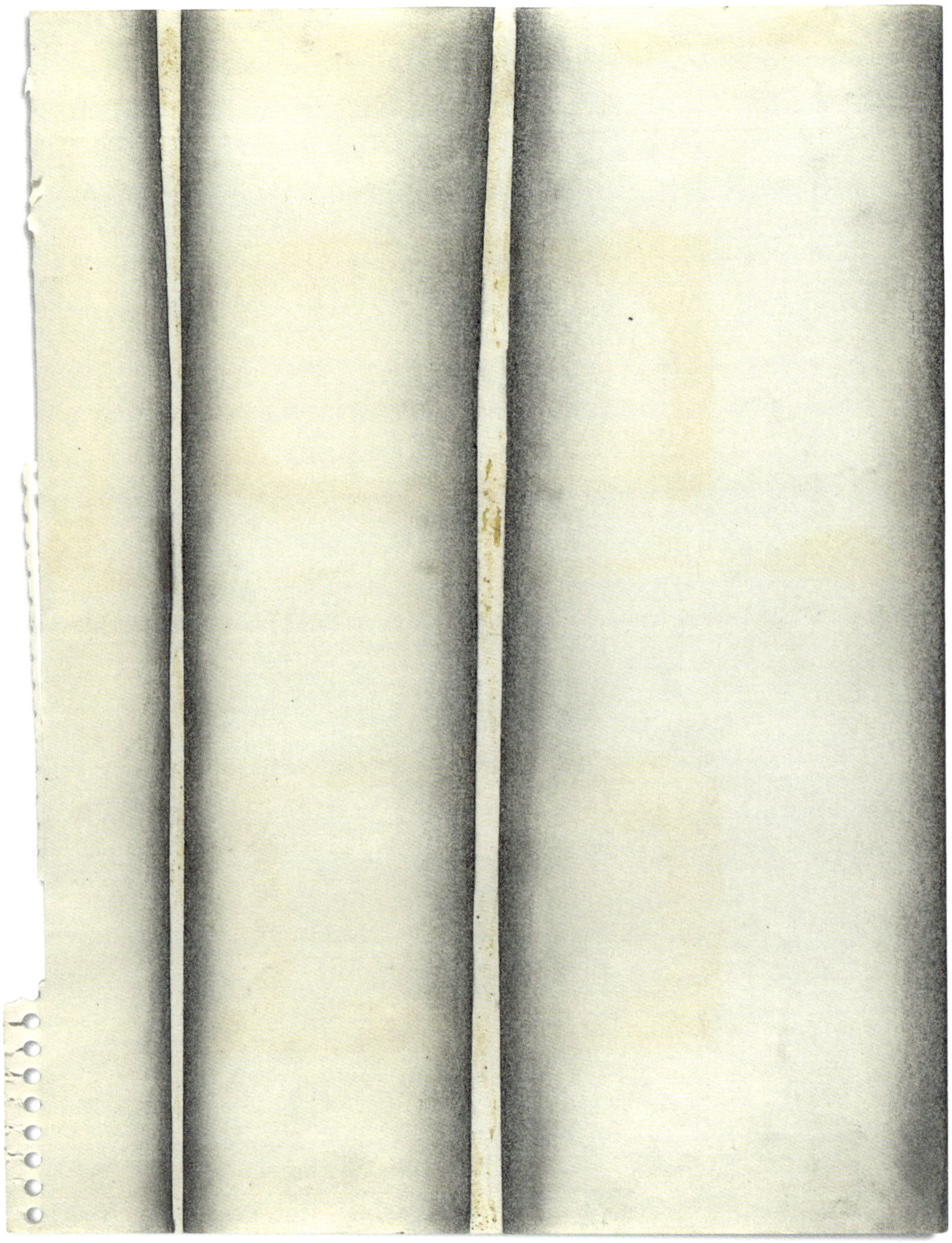

Drawings about Paper and Writings about Words #47. 1967
Pencil and charcoal on notebook paper
11 × 8½ in. (27.9 × 21.6 cm)
The Museum of Modern Art, New York. The Judith Rothschild Foundation Contemporary Drawings Collection Gift (purchase, and gift, in part, of The Eileen and Michael Cohen Collection)

Drawings about Paper and Writings about Words #49. 1967
Pastel on notebook paper
11 × 8½ in. (27.9 × 21.6 cm)
Collection Adrian Piper Research Archive Foundation Berlin

Drawings about Paper and Writings about Words #48. 1967
Pencil on notebook paper in plastic sleeve with crayon
11 × 8½ in. (27.9 × 21.6 cm)
The Museum of of Modern Art, New York. The Judith Rothschild Foundation Contemporary Drawings Collection Gift (purchase, and gift, in part, of The Eileen and Michael Cohen Collection)

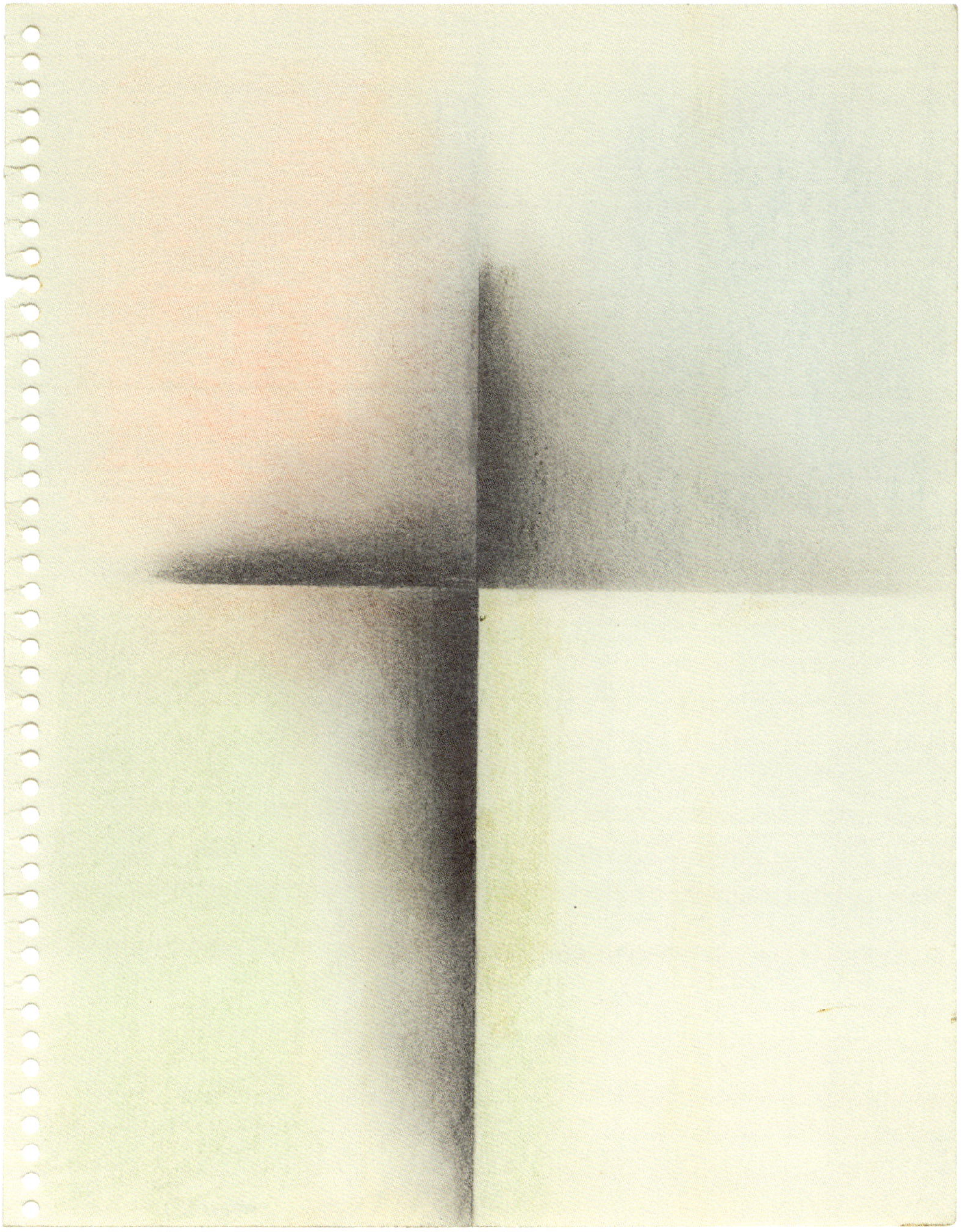

Drawings about Paper and Writings about Words #51. 1967
Pencil and pastel on notebook paper
11 × 8½ in. (27.9 × 21.6 cm)
Collection Adrian Piper Research Archive Foundation Berlin

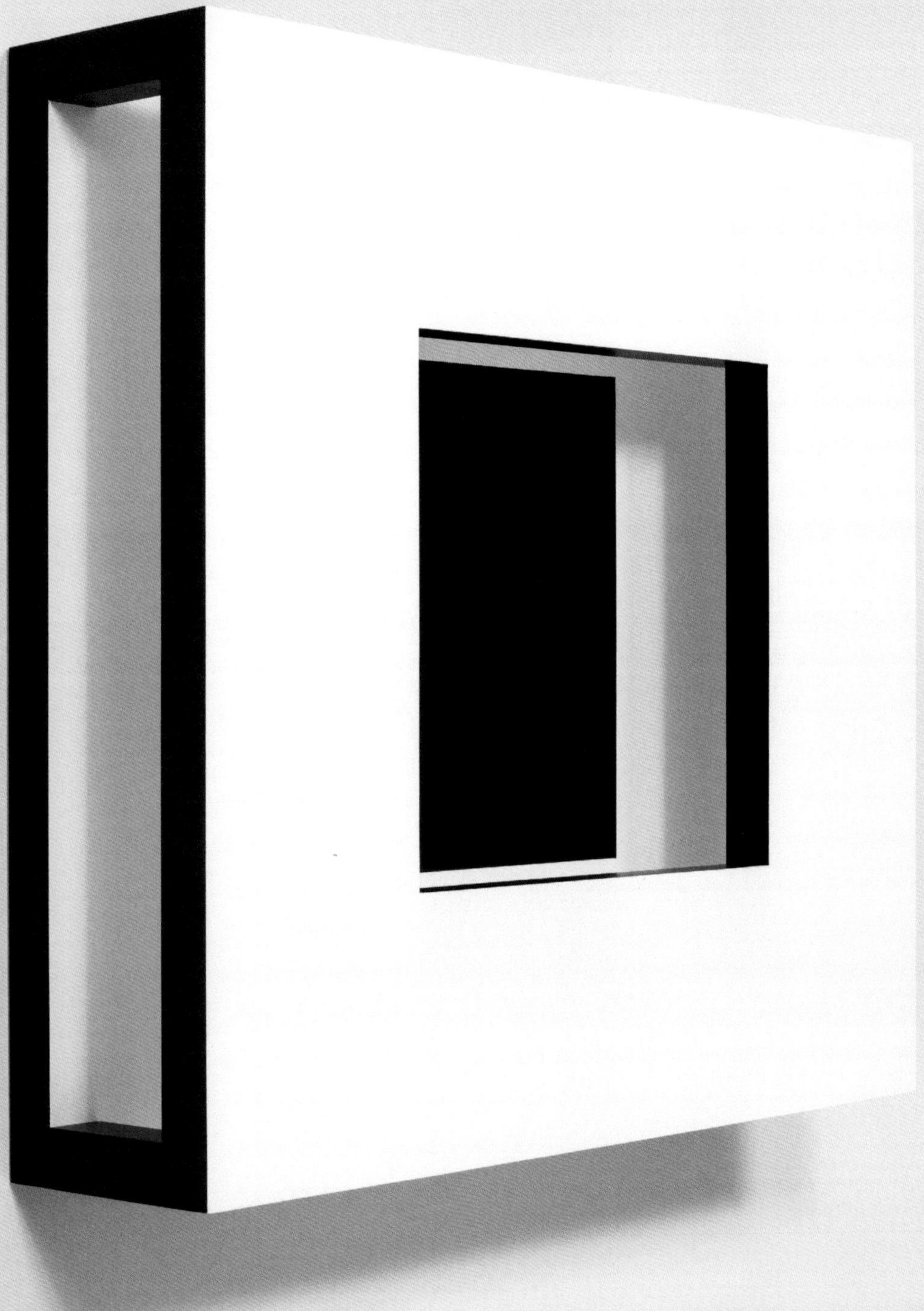

Recessed Square. 1967
Masonite on wood frame (refabricated 2017)
36 × 36 × 9 in. (91.4 × 91.4 × 22.9 cm)
Collection Adrian Piper Research Archive Foundation Berlin

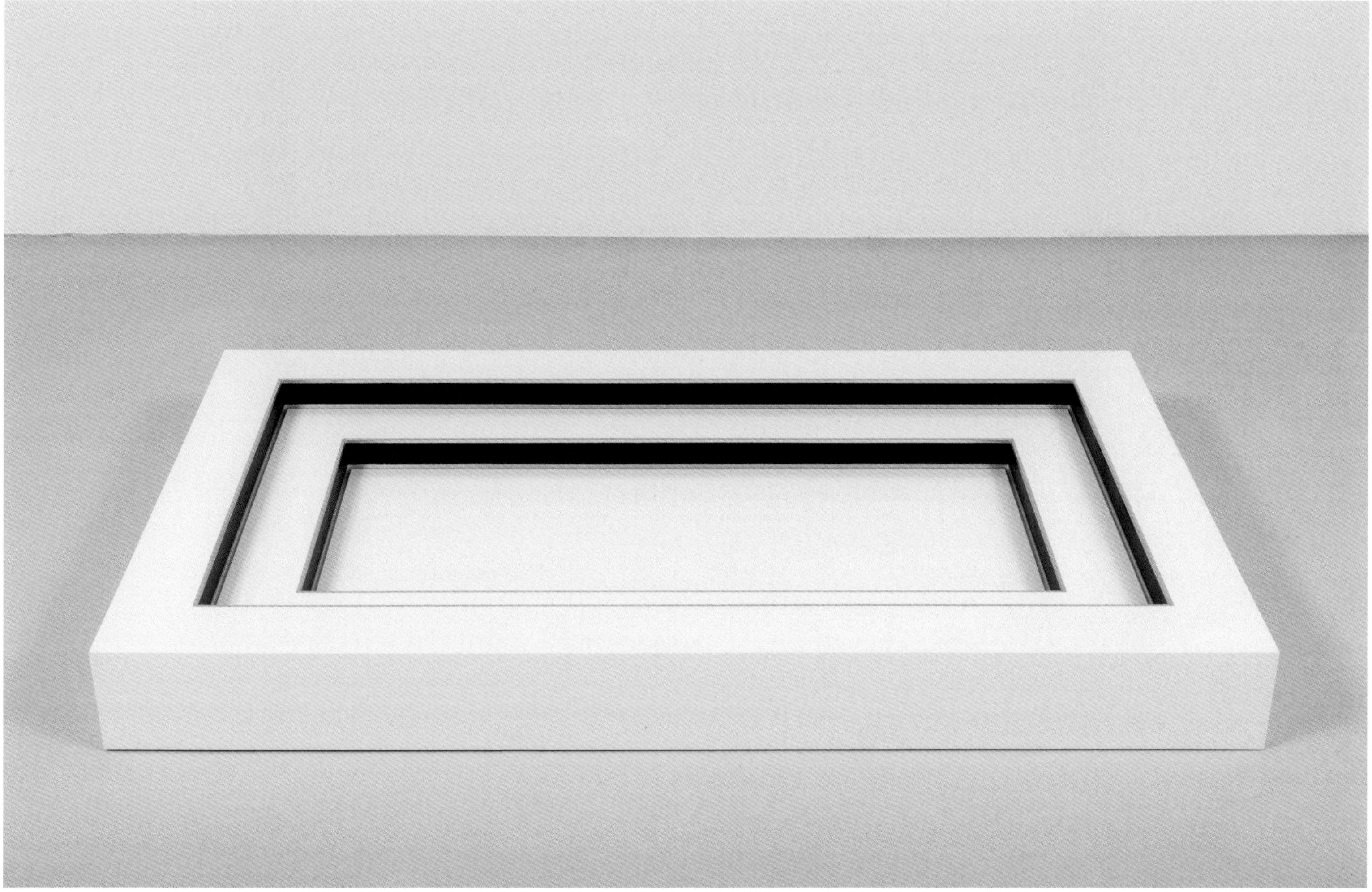

Double Recess. 1967
Masonite, wood frame, gesso, paint, and metallic paint (refabricated 2017)
36 × 60 × 6 in. (91.4 × 152.4 × 15.2 cm)
Collection Adrian Piper Research Archive Foundation Berlin

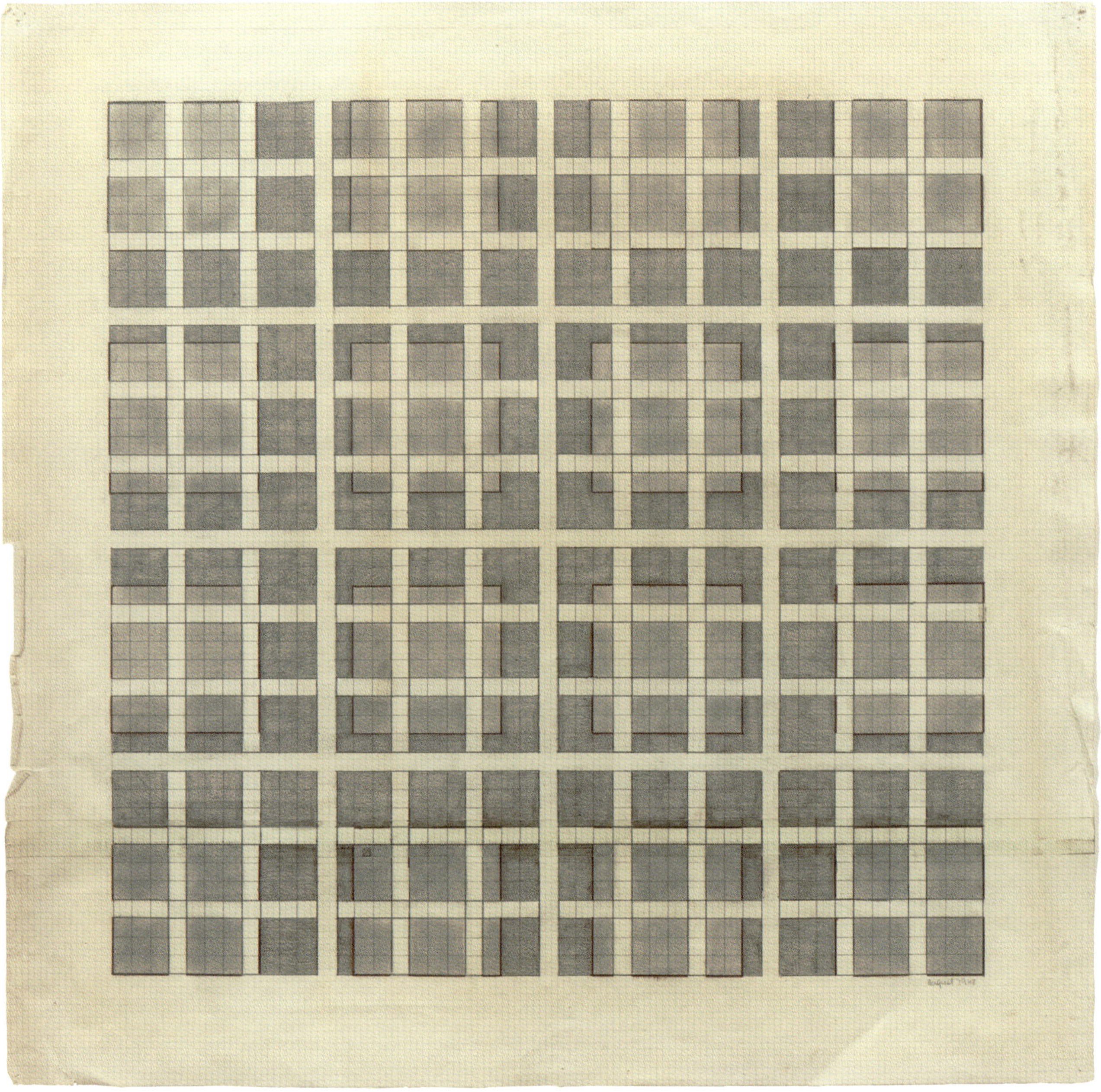

Sixteen Permutations of a Nine-Part Floating Square. 1968
Pencil on graph paper and tape
22 × 22 in. (55.9 × 55.9 cm)
Collection Gregory R. Miller and Michael Wiener

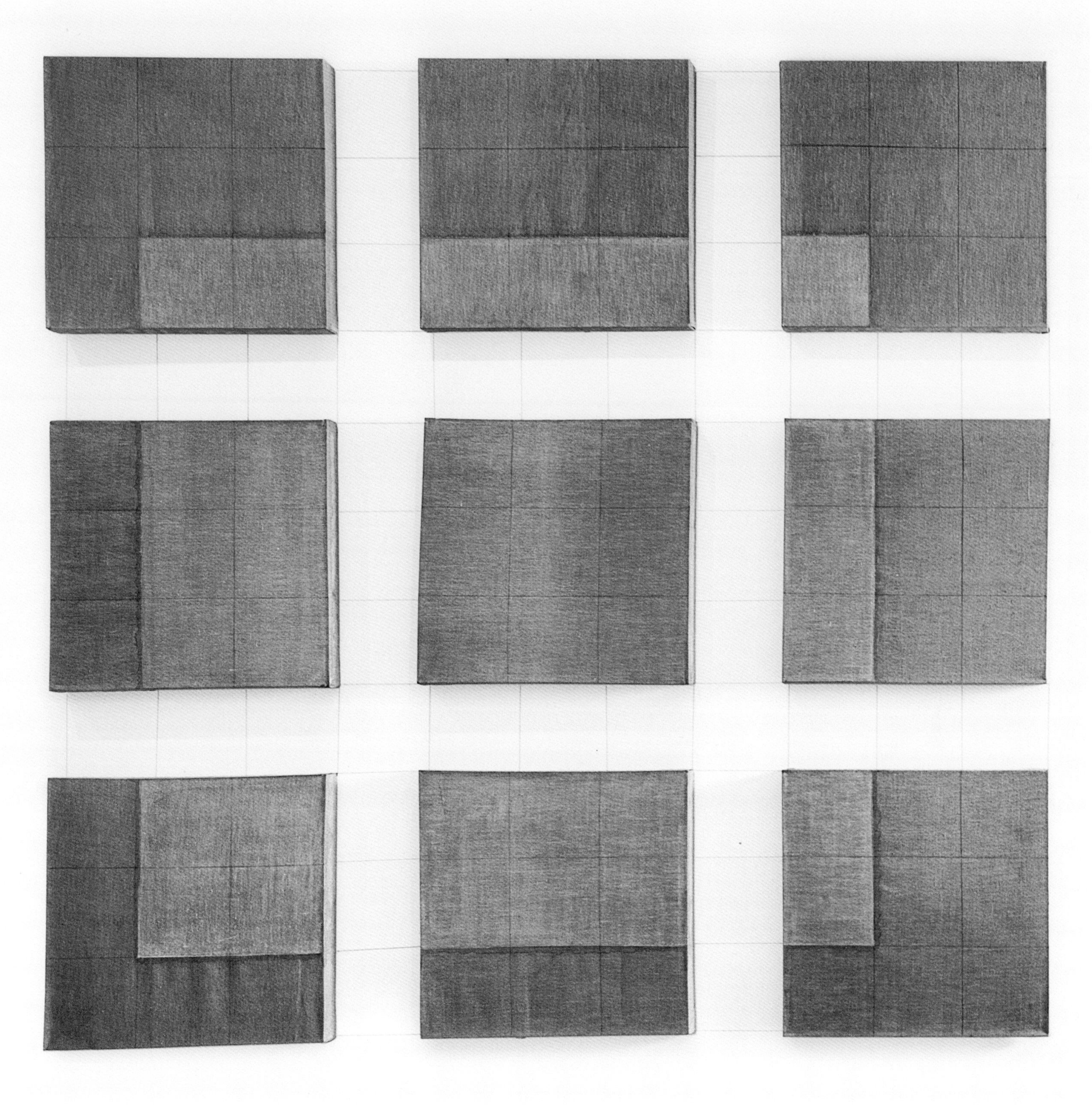

Nine-Part Floating Square. 1967
Pencil and gesso on nine canvases, with pencil on wall
Each canvas 24½ × 24½ in. (62.2 × 62.2 cm); overall 66 × 66 in. (167.6 × 167.6 cm)
Collection Gregory R. Miller and Michael Wiener

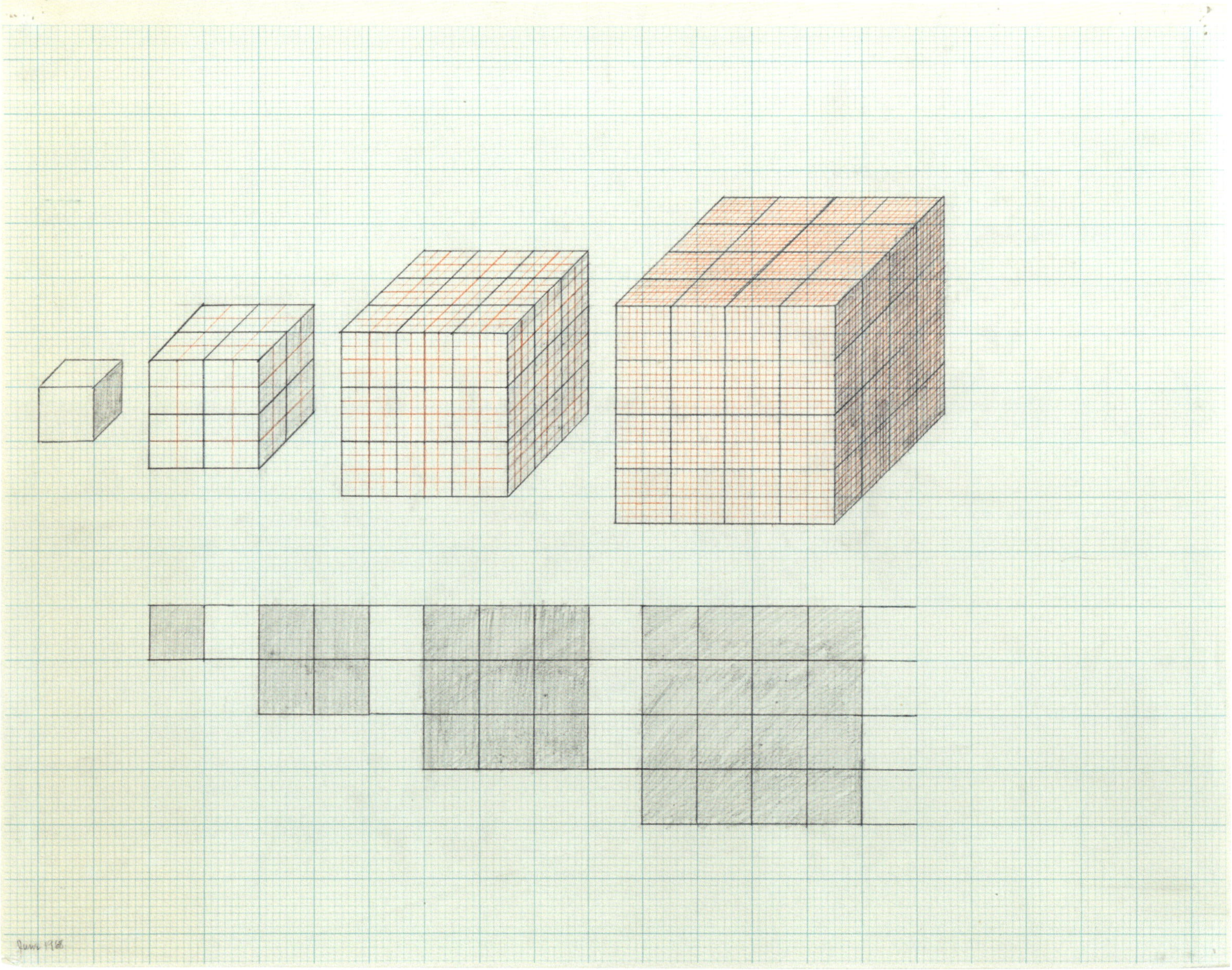

A Three-Dimensional Representation of Infinite Divisibility. 1968
Pencil and colored pencil on graph paper
17½ × 22¼ in. (44.4 × 56.5 cm)
Collection Adrian Piper Research Archive Foundation Berlin

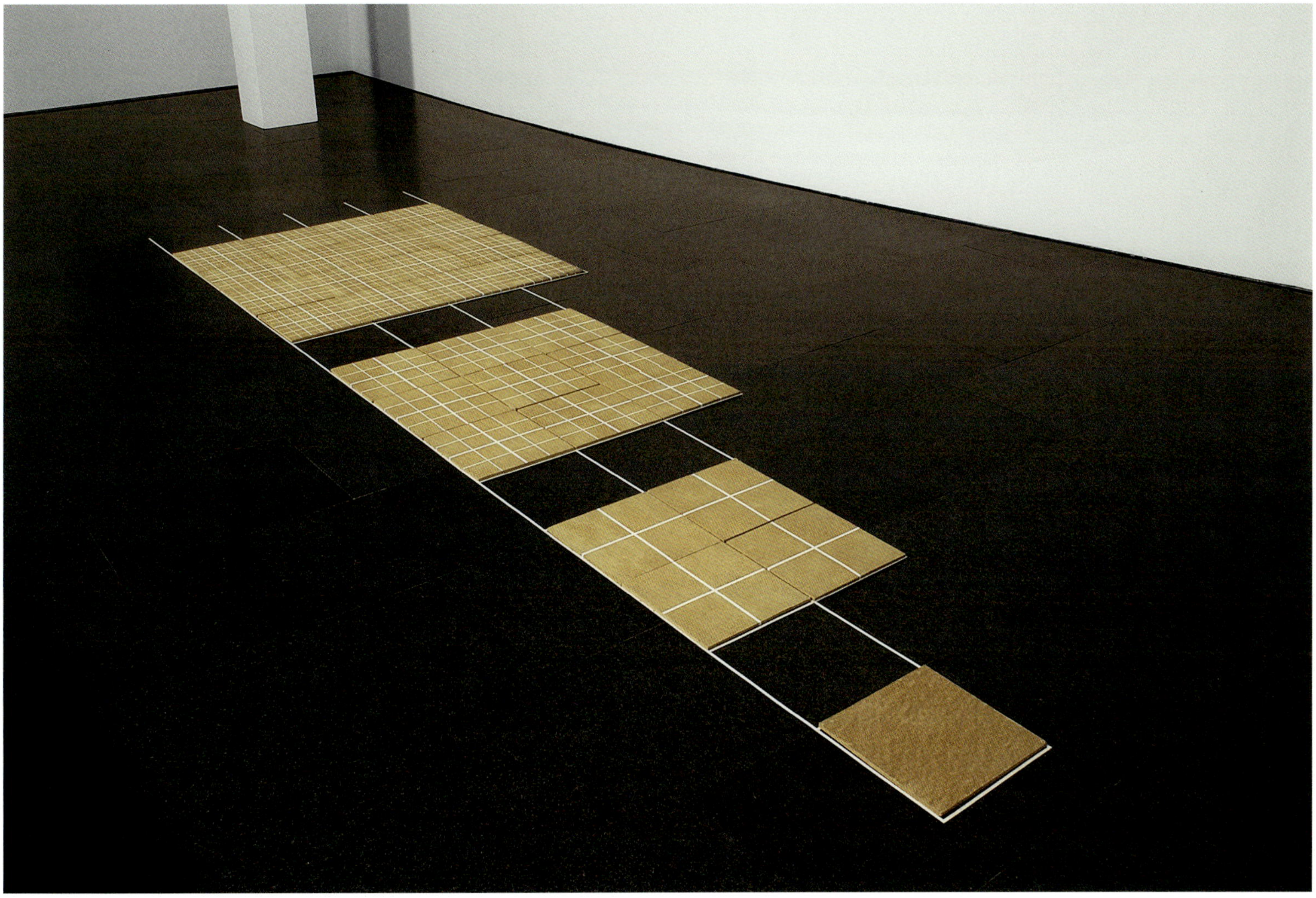

Infinitely Divisible Floor Construction. 1968
Mixed-medium installation. Tape and particle board (refabricated 2002)
47¼ in. × 13 ft. 9⅜ in. (120 x 420 cm)
Collection Adrian Piper Research Archive Foundation Berlin

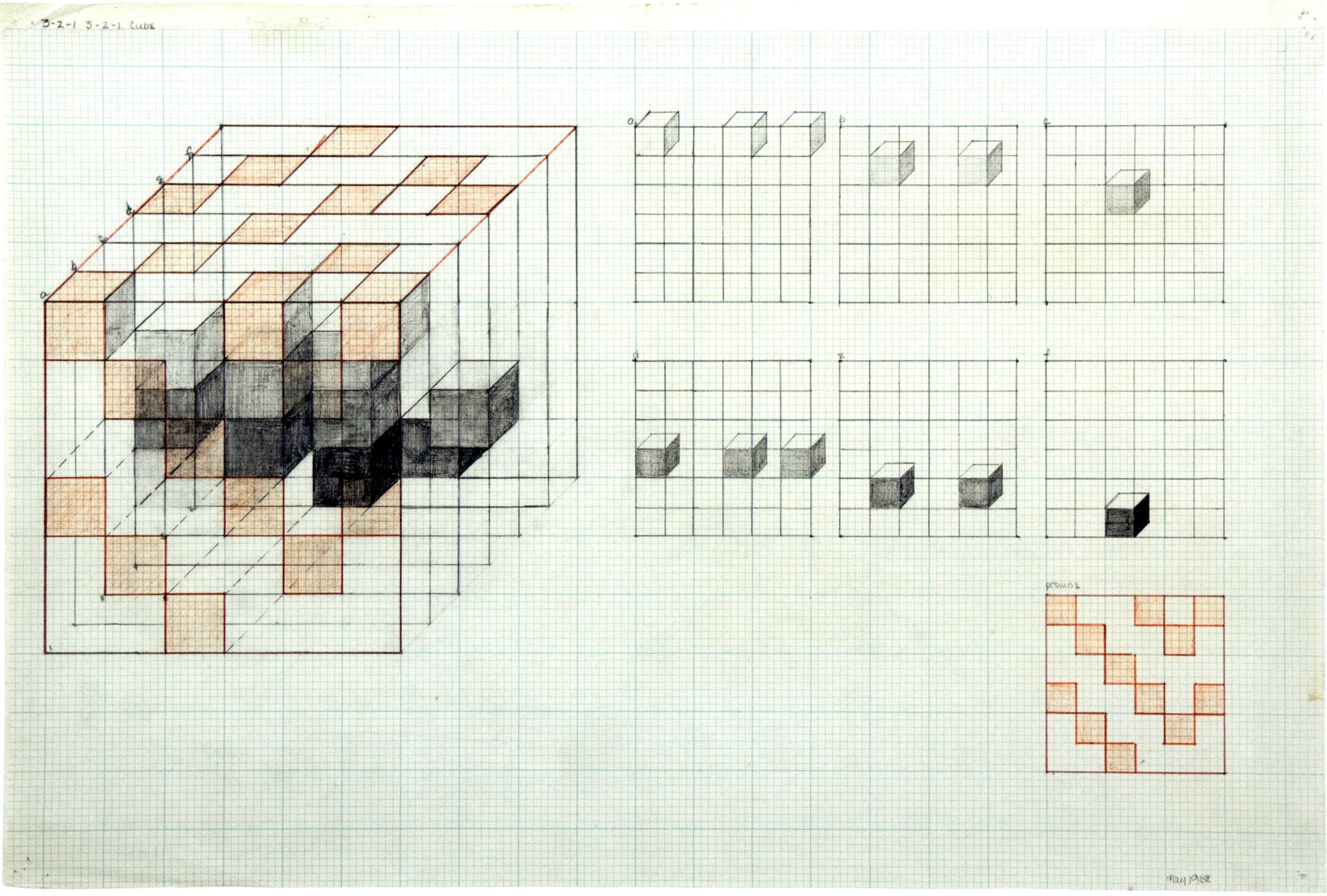

3-2-1 Cube 3-2-1 Cube (Permutations on a Suspended Cube). 1968
Colored ink, colored pencil, and pencil on graph paper
15 × 22¼ in. (38.1 × 56.5 cm)
Collection Adrian Piper Research Archive Foundation Berlin

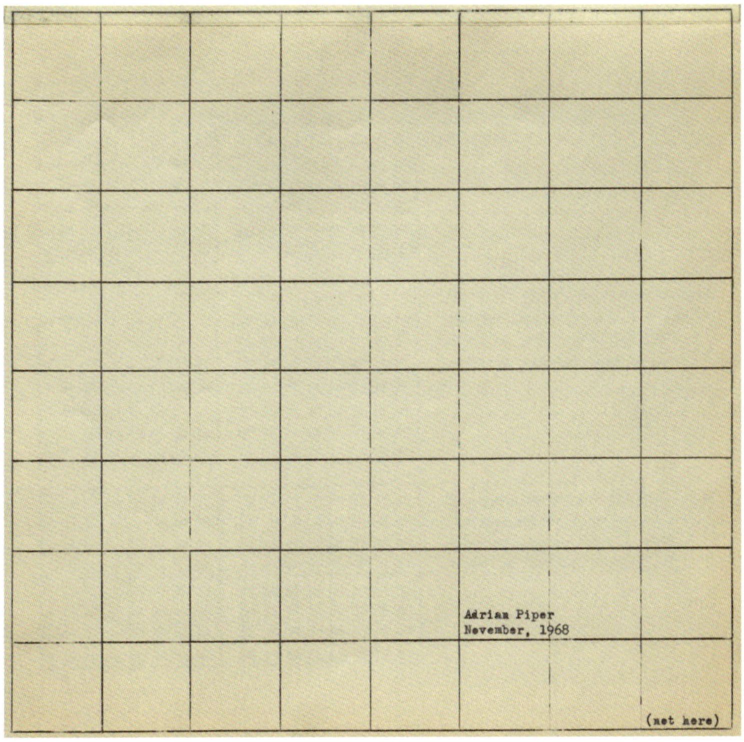

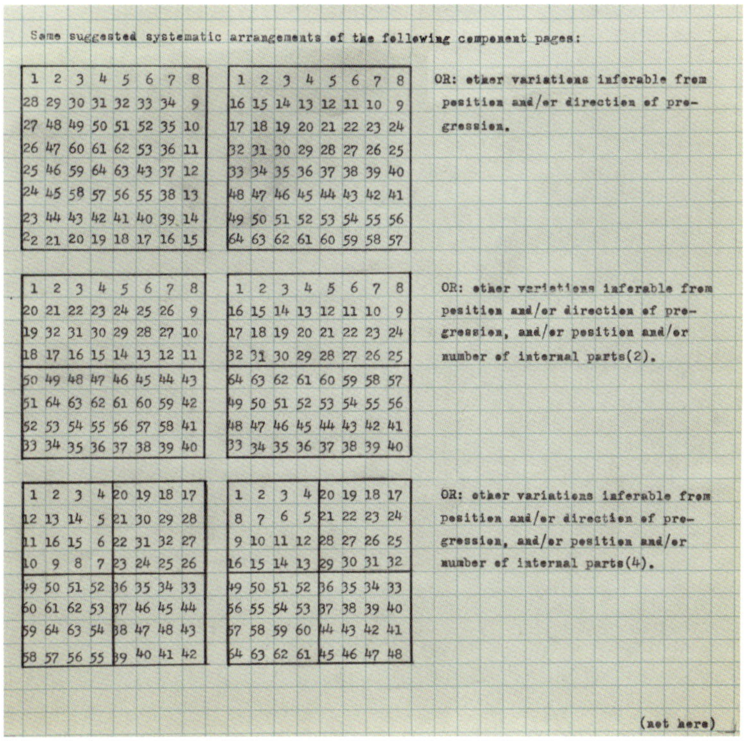

Some suggested systematic arrangements of the following component pages:

1	2	3	4	5	6	7	8
28	29	30	31	32	33	34	9
27	48	49	50	51	52	35	10
26	47	60	61	62	53	36	11
25	46	59	64	63	43	37	12
24	45	58	57	56	55	38	13
23	44	43	42	41	40	39	14
22	21	20	19	18	17	16	15

1	2	3	4	5	6	7	8
16	15	14	13	12	11	10	9
17	18	19	20	21	22	23	24
32	31	30	29	28	27	26	25
33	34	35	36	37	38	39	40
48	47	46	45	44	43	42	41
49	50	51	52	53	54	55	56
64	63	62	61	60	59	58	57

OR: other variations inferable from position and/or direction of progression.

1	2	3	4	5	6	7	8
20	21	22	23	24	25	26	9
19	32	31	30	29	28	27	10
18	17	16	15	14	13	12	11
50	49	48	47	46	45	44	43
51	64	63	62	61	60	59	42
52	53	54	55	56	57	58	41
33	34	35	36	37	38	39	40

1	2	3	4	5	6	7	8
16	15	14	13	12	11	10	9
17	18	19	20	21	22	23	24
32	31	30	29	28	27	26	25
64	63	62	61	60	59	58	57
49	50	51	52	53	54	55	56
48	47	46	45	44	43	42	41
33	34	35	36	37	38	39	40

OR: other variations inferable from position and/or direction of progression, and/or position and/or number of internal parts(2).

1	2	3	4	20	19	18	17
12	13	14	5	21	30	29	28
11	16	15	6	22	31	32	27
10	9	8	7	23	24	25	26
49	50	51	52	36	35	34	33
60	61	62	53	37	46	45	44
59	64	63	54	38	47	48	43
58	57	56	55	39	40	41	42

1	2	3	4	20	19	18	17
8	7	6	5	21	22	23	24
9	10	11	12	28	27	26	25
16	15	14	13	29	30	31	32
49	50	51	52	36	35	34	33
56	55	54	53	37	38	39	40
57	58	59	60	44	43	42	41
64	63	62	61	45	46	47	48

OR: other variations inferable from position and/or direction of progression, and/or position and/or number of internal parts(4).

(not here)

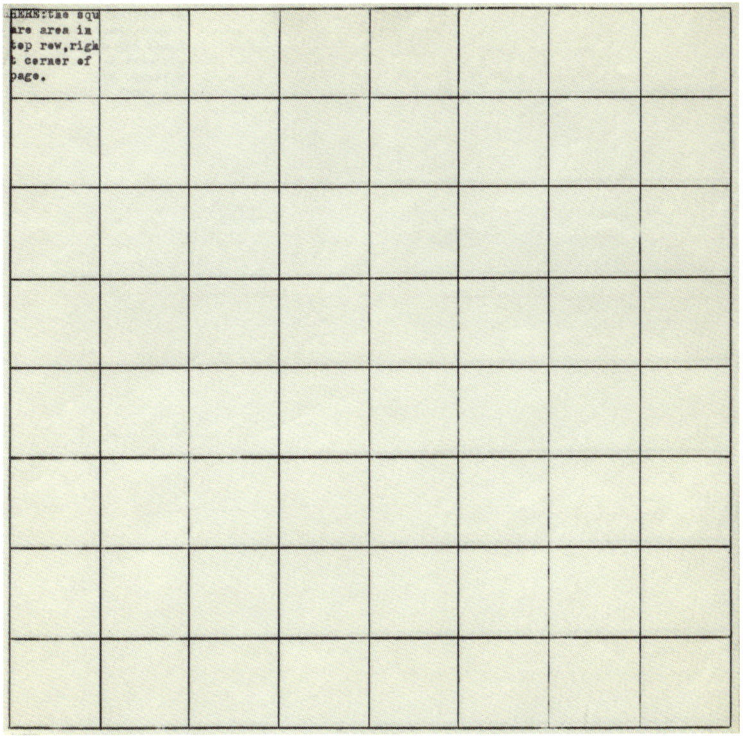

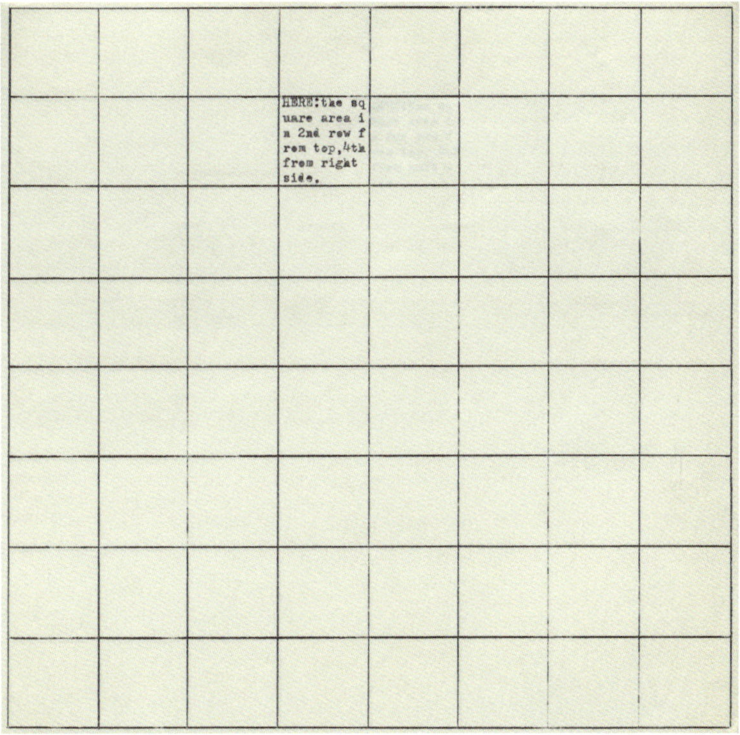

Here and Now. 1968
Cardboard portfolio with text on graph paper and text on mimeographed paper taped to box; and text on sixty-four loose sheets of mimeographed paper
Each sheet 9 × 9 in. (22.9 × 22.9 cm)
Collection Alan Cravitz and Shashi Caudill
Details:
frontispiece
page 1

systems page
page 12

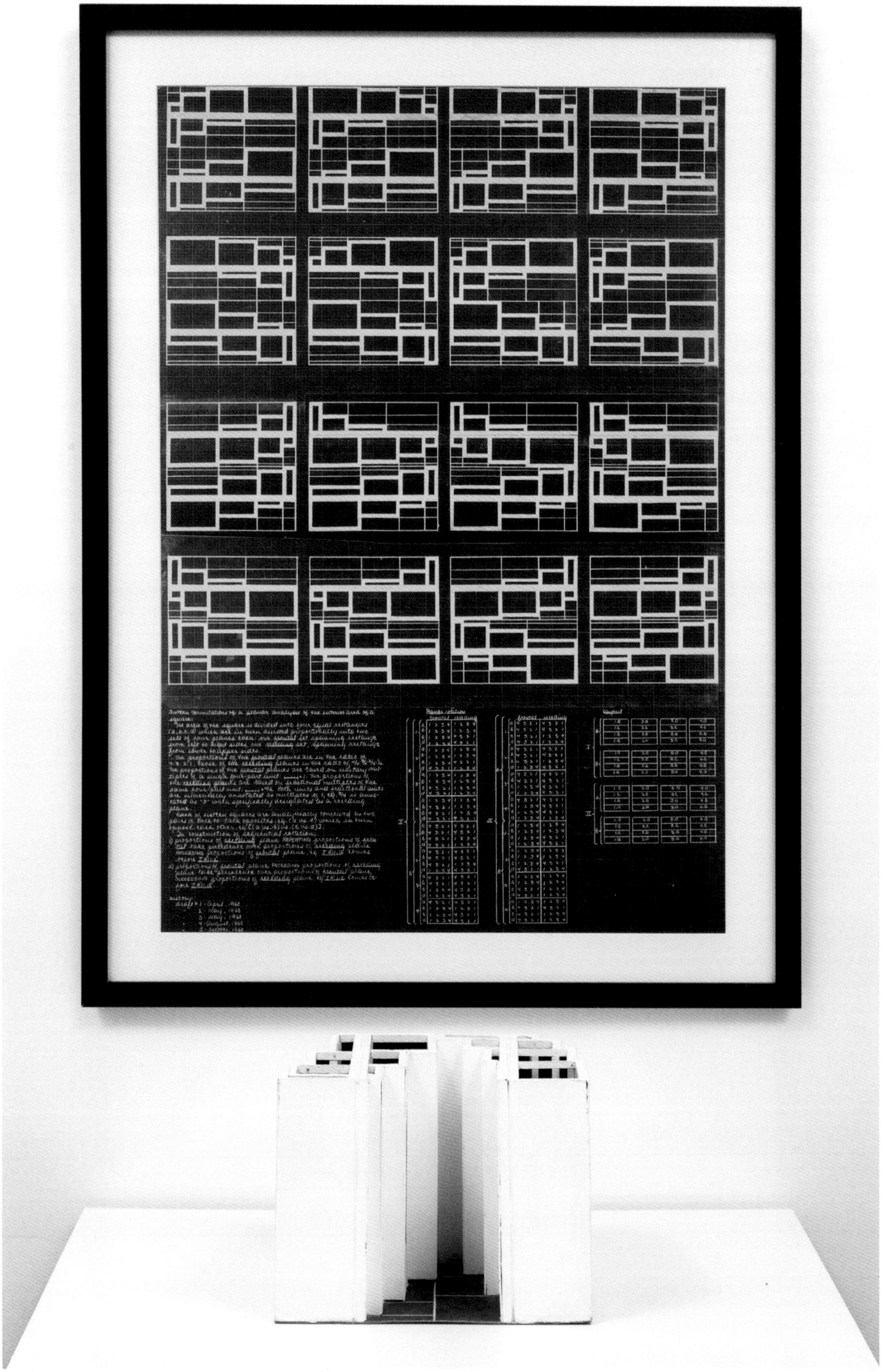

Sixteen Permutations of a Planar Analysis of a Square. 1968
Mixed-medium installation. Photostat and wood model
Photostat 32⅞ × 21⅞ in. (83.5 × 55.5 cm); model 10⅝ × 10⅜ × 8⅛ in. (27 × 26.4 × 20.6 cm)
Collection Adrian Piper Research Archive Foundation Berlin

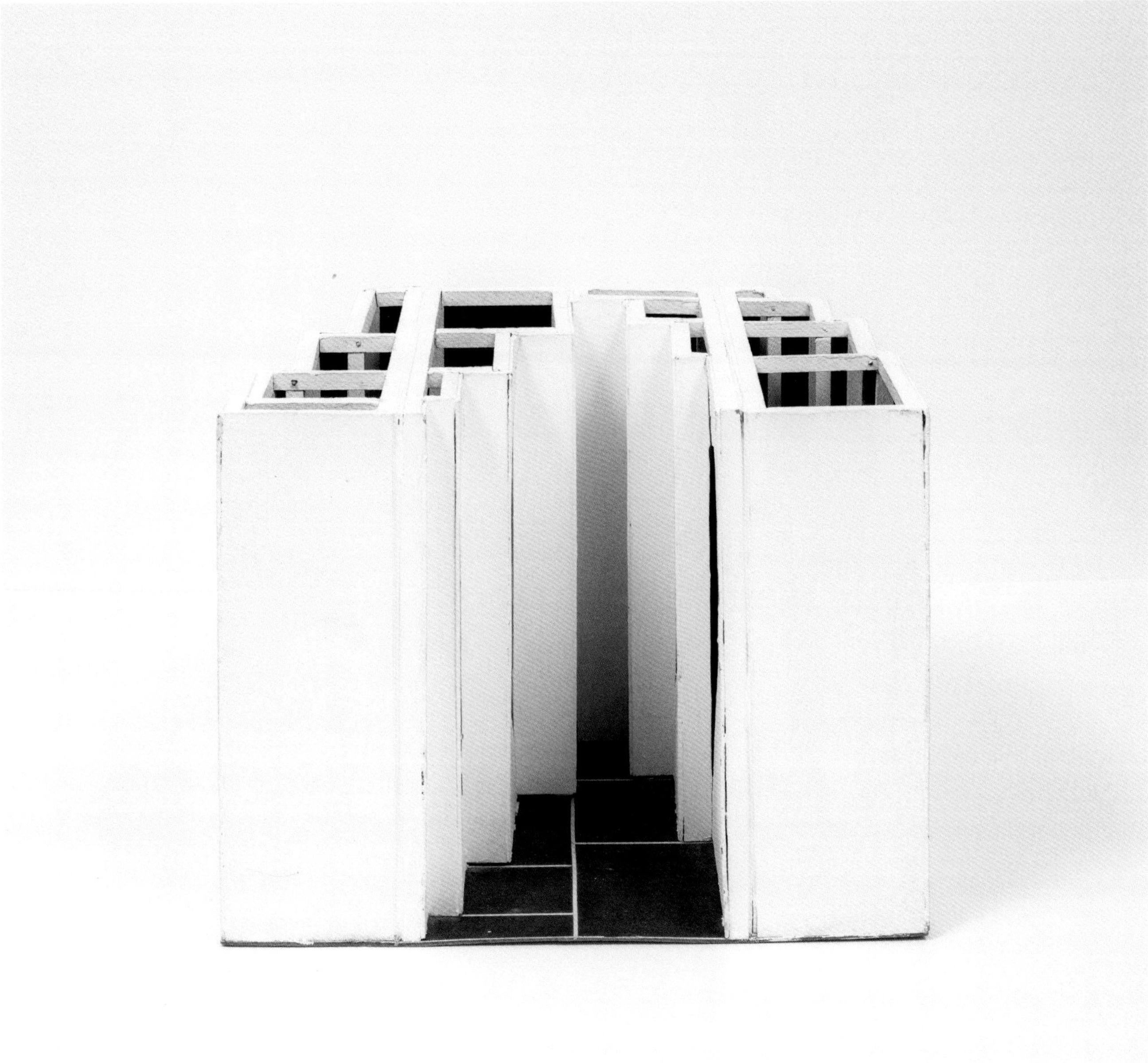

Detail: scale model

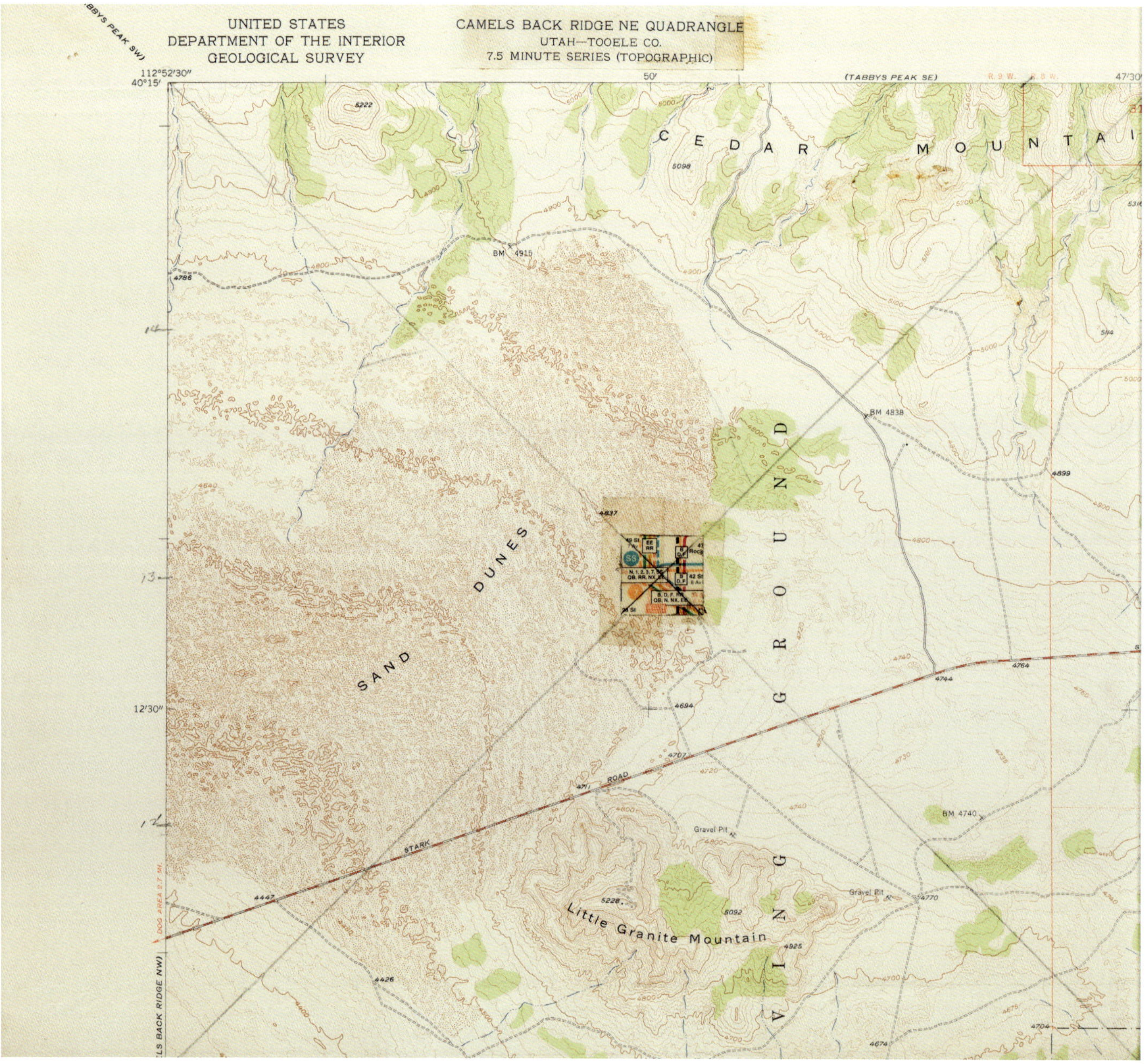

Utah-Manhattan Transfer. 1968
Pencil and ballpoint pen on cut-and-pasted maps, mounted on two pieces of foam core
First panel 13¼ × 14³⁄₁₆ in. (33.7 × 36 cm); second panel 12 × 12 in. (30.5 × 30.5 cm)
Collection Adrian Piper Research Archive Foundation Berlin

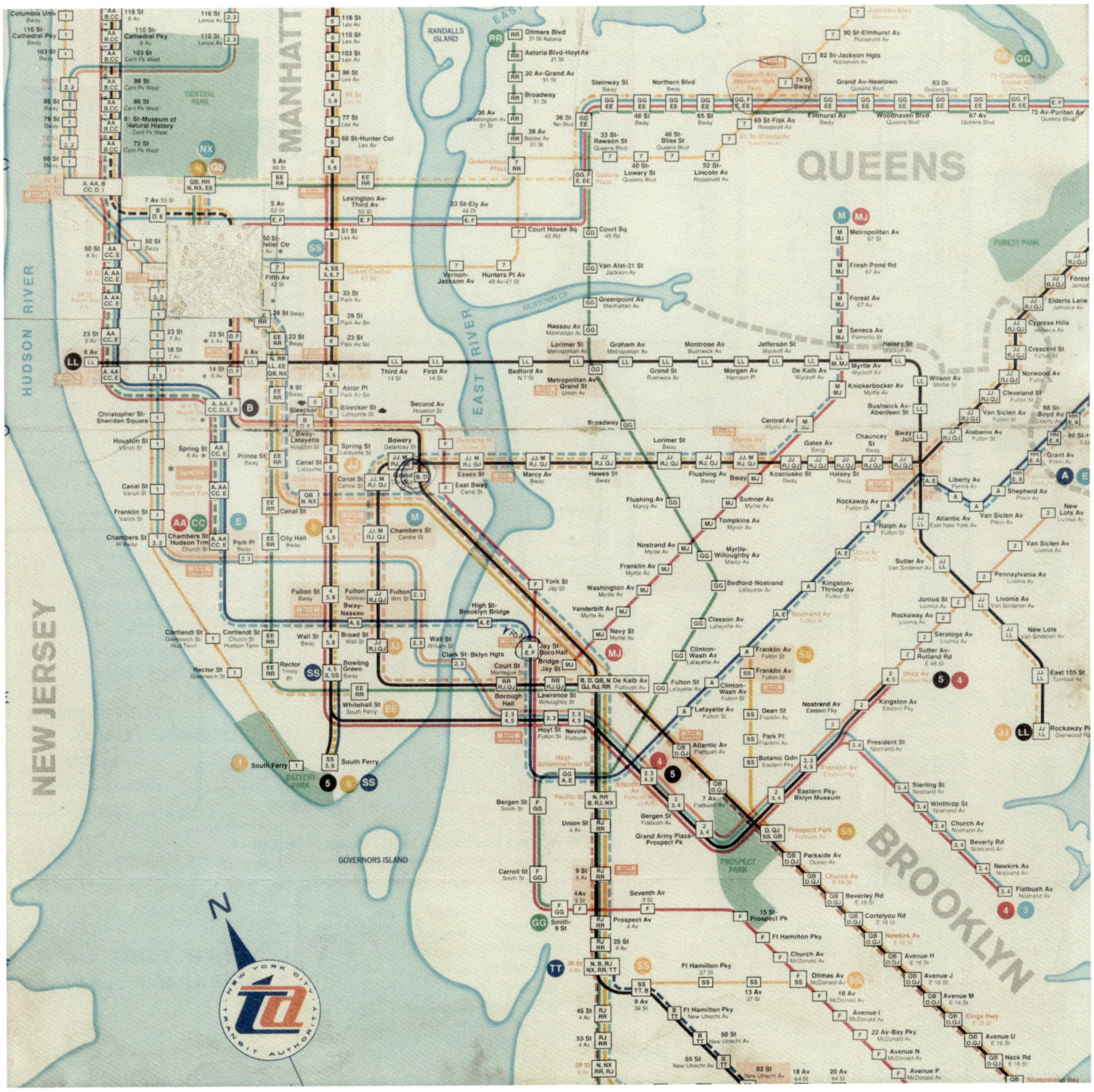
MANHATT
QUEENS
BROOKLYN
NEW JERSEY
HUDSON RIVER
EAST RIVER
RANDALLS ISLAND
CENTRAL PARK
FOREST PARK
PROSPECT PARK
GOVERNORS ISLAND
NEWTOWN CR
N
NEW YORK CITY TRANSIT AUTHORITY

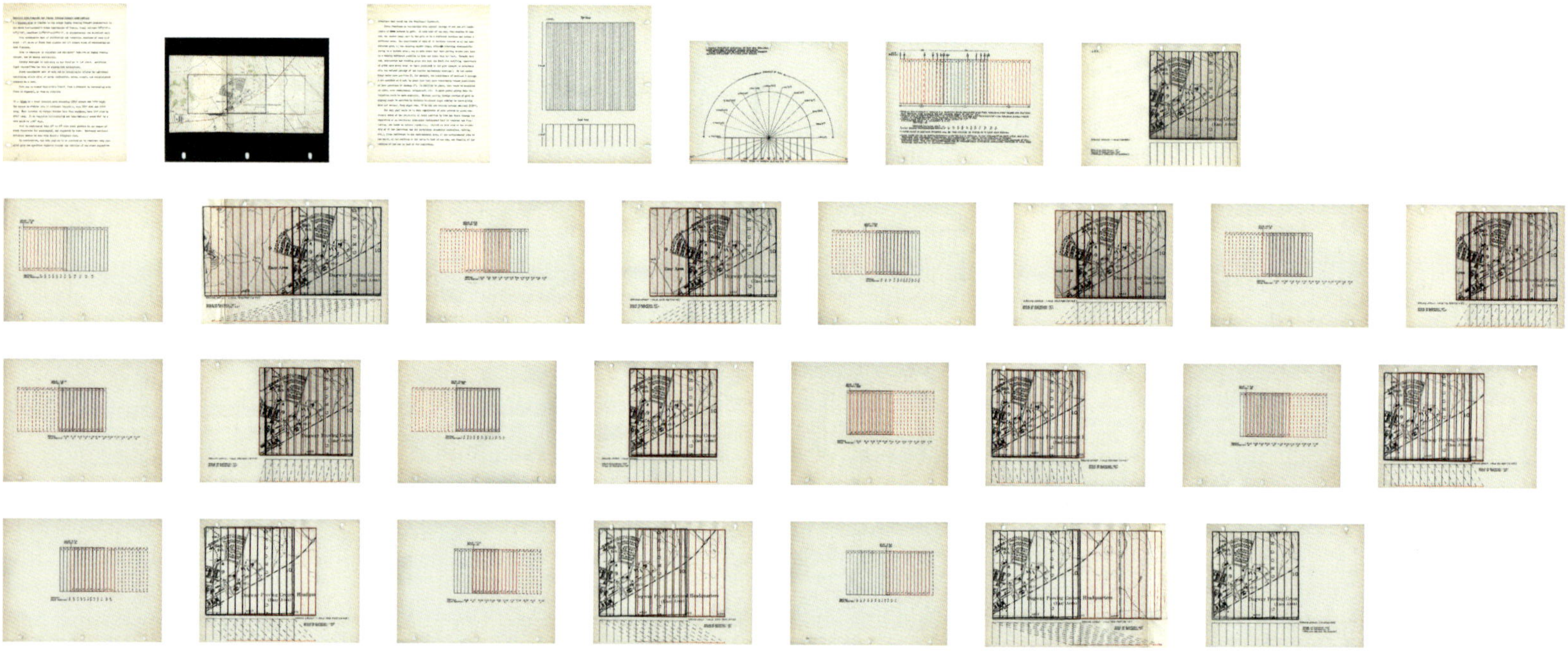

Parallel Grid Proposal for Dugway Proving Grounds Headquarters. 1968
Two typescript pages; ink and colored ink on fourteen sheets of paper; architectural tape on acetate over ink on thirteen photostats; and ink on cut-and-pasted map, mounted on colored paper
Twenty-five sheets each 8½ × 11 in. (21.6 × 27.9 cm); two sheets each 8½ × 12¹¹⁄₁₆ in. (21.6 × 32.2 cm); and three sheets each 11 × 8½ in. (27.9 × 21.6 cm)
Collection Beth Rudin DeWoody

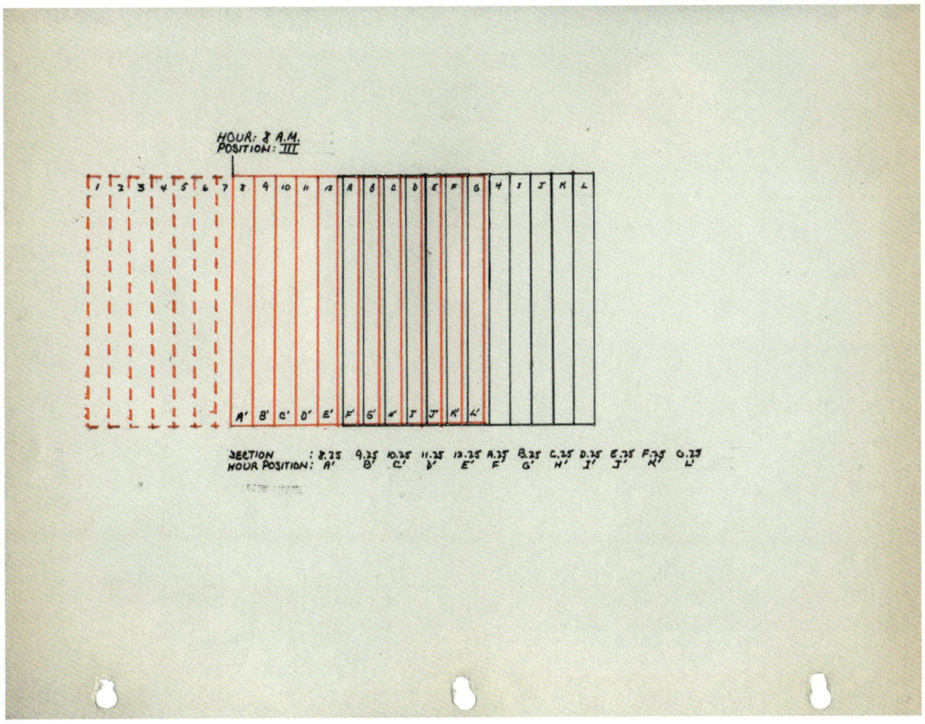

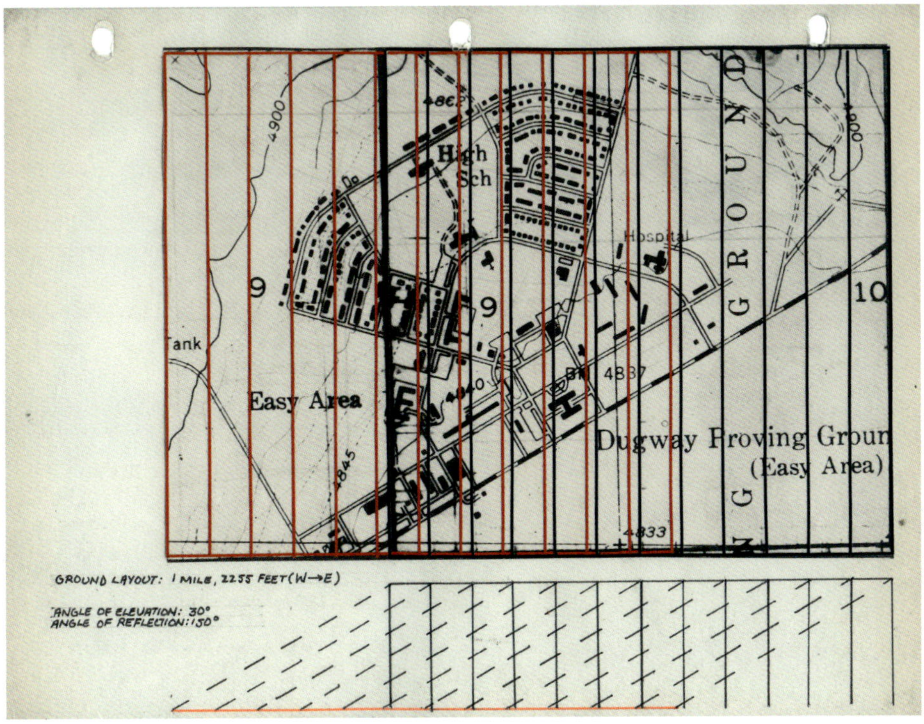

Details:
Parallel Grid Proposal for Dugway Proving Grounds Headquarters #10
Parallel Grid Proposal for Dugway Proving Grounds Headquarters #11

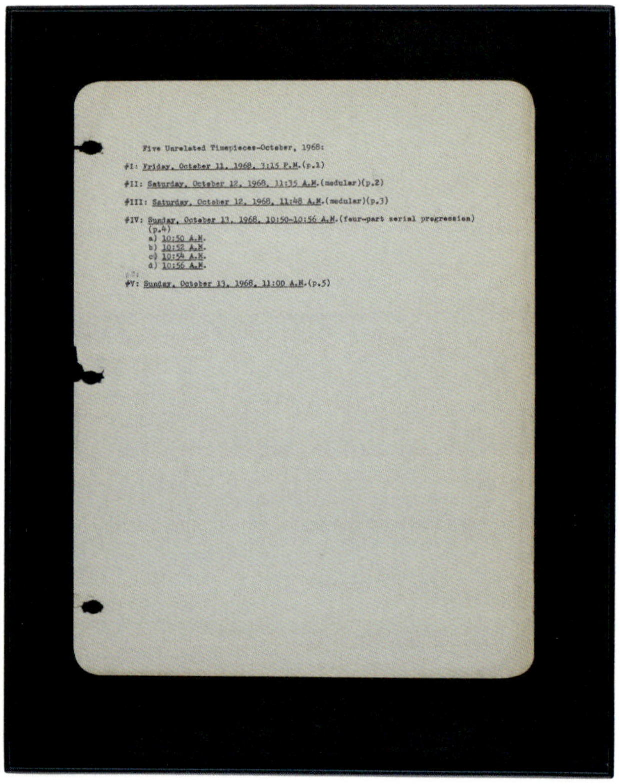

Five Unrelated Timepieces-October, 1968:

#I: Friday, October 11, 1968, 3:15 P.M.(p.1)

#II: Saturday, October 12, 1968, 11:35 A.M.(modular)(p.2)

#III: Saturday, October 12, 1968, 11:48 A.M.(modular)(p.3)

#IV: Sunday, October 13, 1968, 10:50-10:56 A.M.(four-part serial progression)
(p.4)
a) 10:50 A.M.
b) 10:52 A.M.
c) 10:54 A.M.
d) 10:56 A.M.

#V: Sunday, October 13, 1968, 11:00 A.M.(p.5)

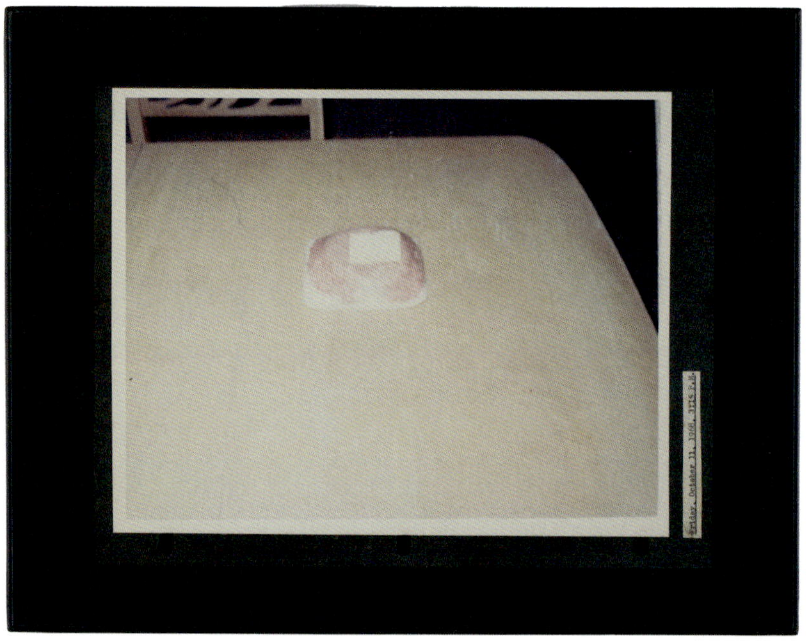

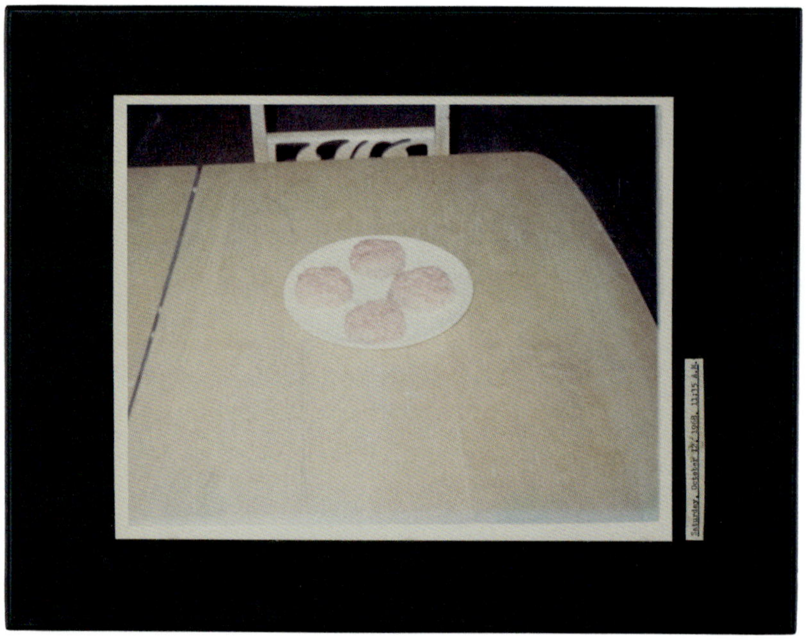

Five Unrelated Time Pieces (Meat into Meat). 1968
Notebook with typescript page, eight photographs, and text mounted on colored paper
Each page 9½ × 11½ in. (24.1 × 29.2 cm) or 11½ × 9½ in. (29.2 × 24.1 cm)
Collection Paul & Karen McCarthy

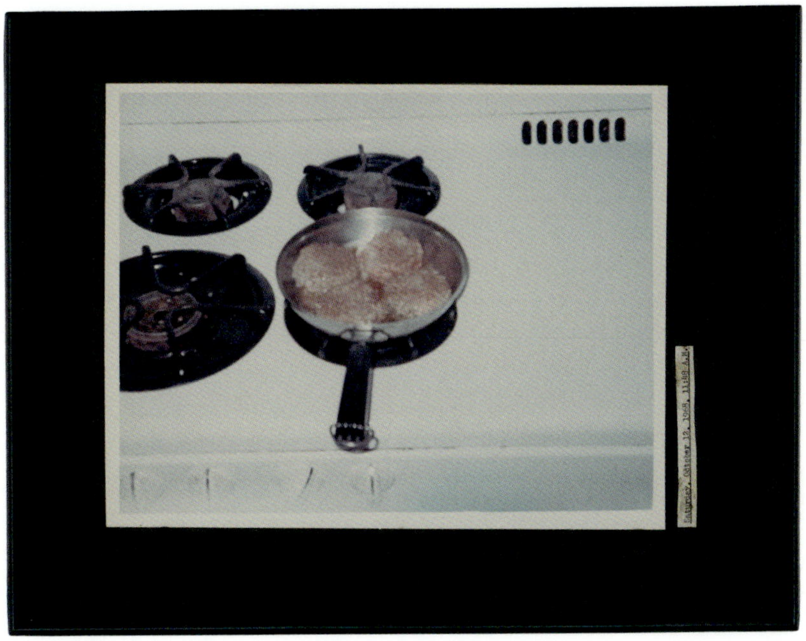
Saturday, October 12, 1968, 11:49 A.M.

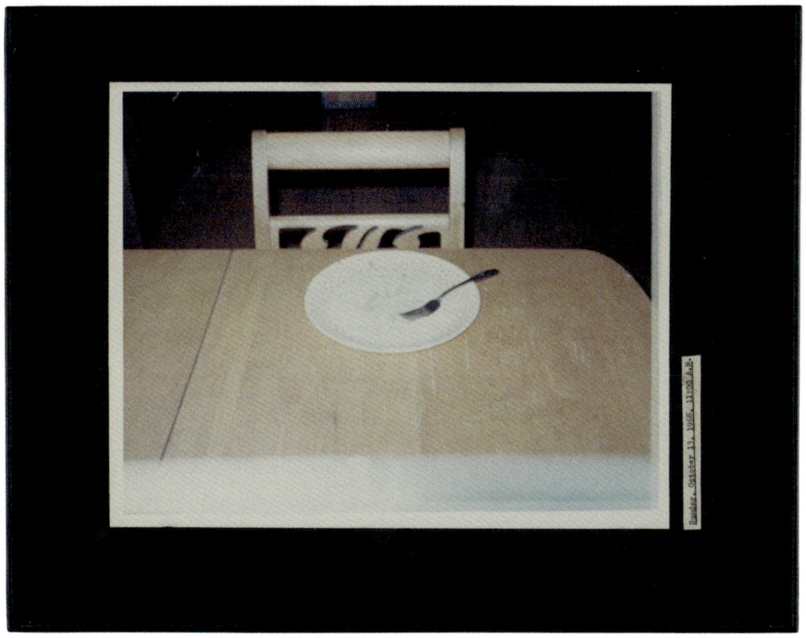
Sunday, October 13, 1968, 11:00 A.M.

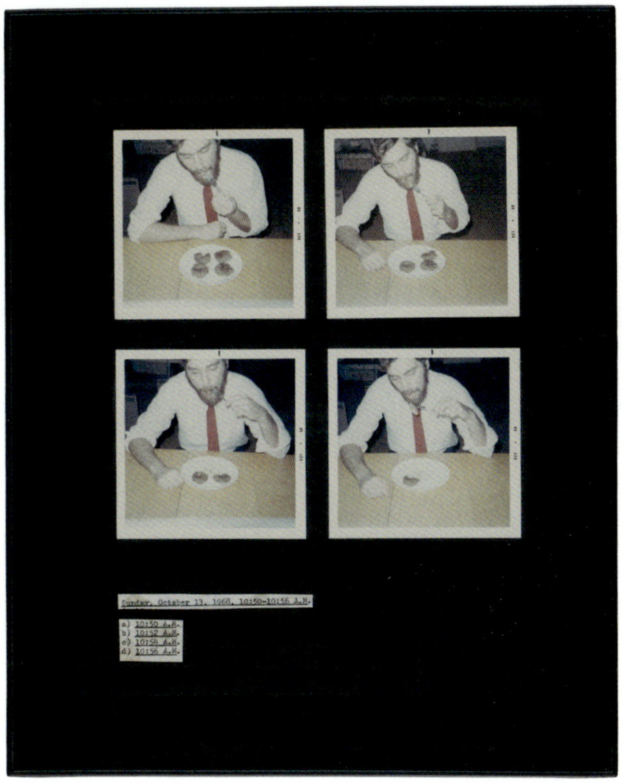
Sunday, October 13, 1968, 10:50–10:56 A.M.
a) 10:50 A.M.
b) 10:52 A.M.
c) 10:54 A.M.
d) 10:56 A.M.

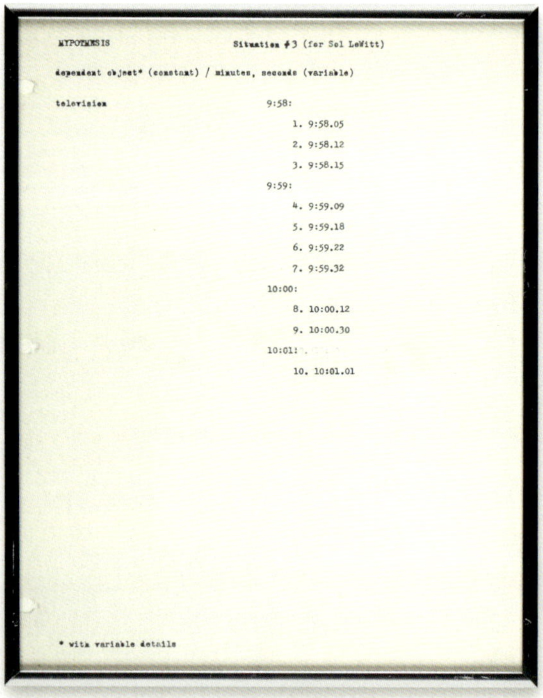

HYPOTHESIS — Situation #3 (for Sol LeWitt)

dependent object* (constant) / minutes, seconds (variable)

television

9:58:

1. 9:58.05
2. 9:58.12
3. 9:58.15

9:59:

4. 9:59.09
5. 9:59.18
6. 9:59.22
7. 9:59.32

10:00:

8. 10:00.12
9. 10:00.30

10:01:

10. 10:01.01

* with variable details

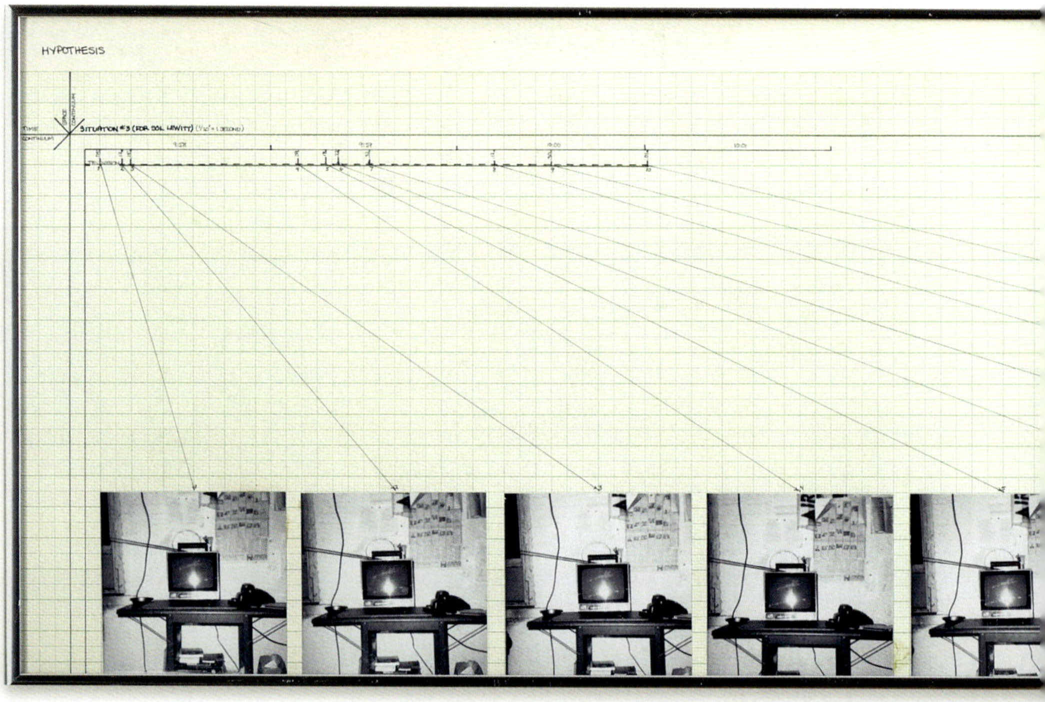

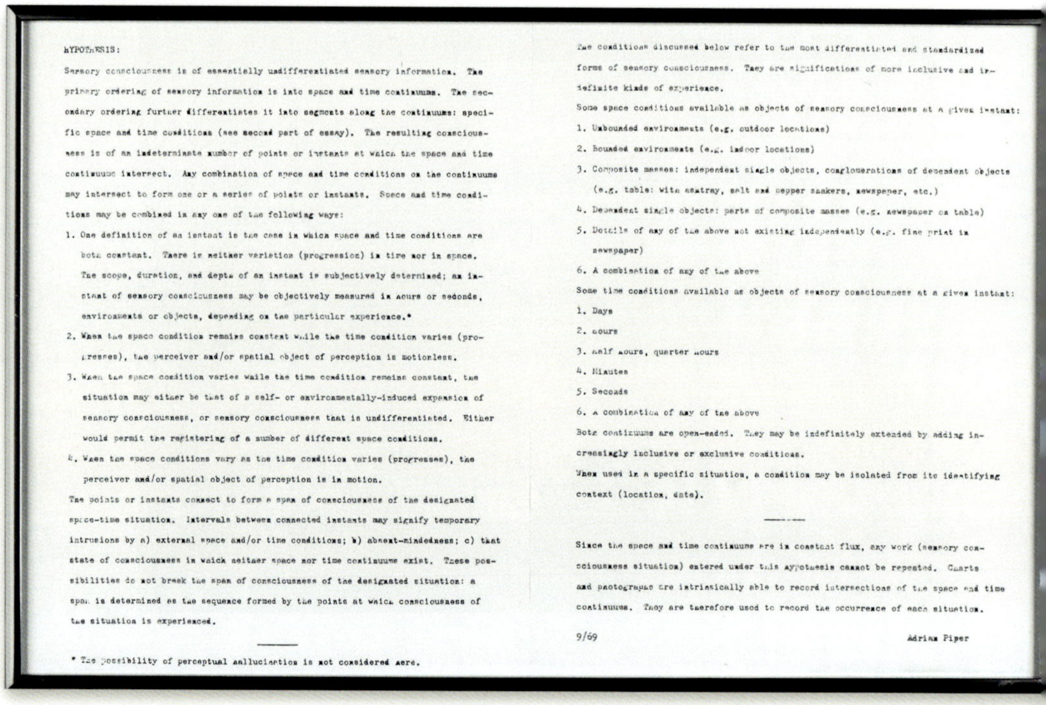

HYPOTHESIS:

Sensory consciousness is of essentially undifferentiated sensory information. The primary ordering of sensory information is into space and time continuums. The secondary ordering further differentiates it into segments along the continuums: specific space and time conditions (see second part of essay). The resulting consciousness is of an indeterminate number of points or instants at which the space and time continuums intersect. Any combination of space and time conditions on the continuums may intersect to form one or a series of points or instants. Space and time conditions may be combined in any one of the following ways:

1. One definition of an instant is the case in which space and time conditions are both constant. There is neither variation (progression) in time nor in space. The scope, duration, and depth of an instant is subjectively determined; an instant of sensory consciousness may be objectively measured in hours or seconds, environments or objects, depending on the particular experience.*
2. When the space condition remains constant while the time condition varies (progresses), the perceiver and/or spatial object of perception is motionless.
3. When the space condition varies while the time condition remains constant, the situation may either be that of a self- or environmentally-induced expansion of sensory consciousness, or sensory consciousness that is undifferentiated. Either would permit the registering of a number of different space conditions.
4. When the space conditions vary as the time condition varies (progresses), the perceiver and/or spatial object of perception is in motion.

The points or instants connect to form a span of consciousness of the designated space-time situation. Intervals between connected instants may signify temporary intrusions by a) external space and/or time conditions; b) absent-mindedness; c) that state of consciousness in which neither space nor time continuums exist. These possibilities do not break the span of consciousness of the designated situation: a span is determined as the sequence formed by the points at which consciousness of the situation is experienced.

---

* The possibility of perceptual hallucination is not considered here.

The conditions discussed below refer to the most differentiated and standardized forms of sensory consciousness. They are significations of more inclusive and indefinite kinds of experience.

Some space conditions available as objects of sensory consciousness at a given instant:

1. Unbounded environments (e.g. outdoor locations)
2. Bounded environments (e.g. indoor locations)
3. Composite masses: independent single objects, conglomerations of dependent objects (e.g. table: with ashtray, salt and pepper shakers, newspaper, etc.)
4. Dependent single objects: parts of composite masses (e.g. newspaper on table)
5. Details of any of the above not existing independently (e.g. fine print in newspaper)
6. A combination of any of the above

Some time conditions available as objects of sensory consciousness at a given instant:

1. Days
2. Hours
3. Half hours, quarter hours
4. Minutes
5. Seconds
6. A combination of any of the above

Both continuums are open-ended. They may be indefinitely extended by adding increasingly inclusive or exclusive conditions.

When used in a specific situation, a condition may be isolated from its identifying context (location, date).

Since the space and time continuums are in constant flux, any work (sensory consciousness situation) entered under this hypothesis cannot be repeated. Charts and photographs are intrinsically able to record intersections of the space and time continuums. They are therefore used to record the occurrence of each situation.

9/69 Adrian Piper

Hypothesis: Situation #3 (for Sol LeWitt). 1968–69
Typescript on mimeographed paper; gelatin silver prints and ink on graph paper; and two photolithograph pages
11 × 8½ in. (27.9 × 21.6 cm); 11 × 33⅞ in. (27.9 × 86 cm); and each 11 × 8½ in. (27.9 × 21.6 cm)
Collection Adrian Piper Research Archive Foundation Berlin

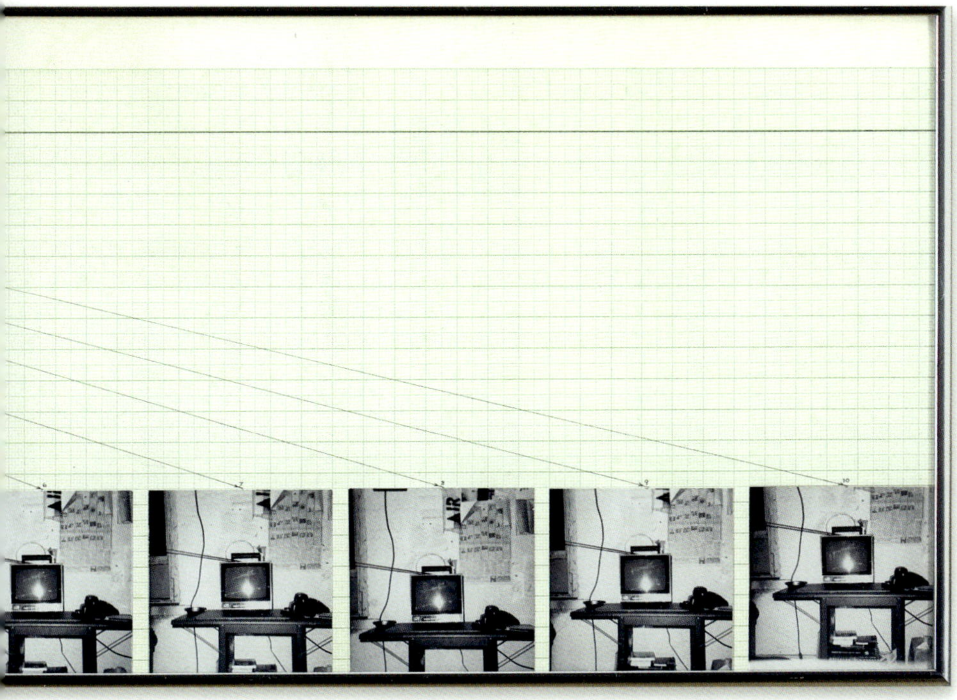

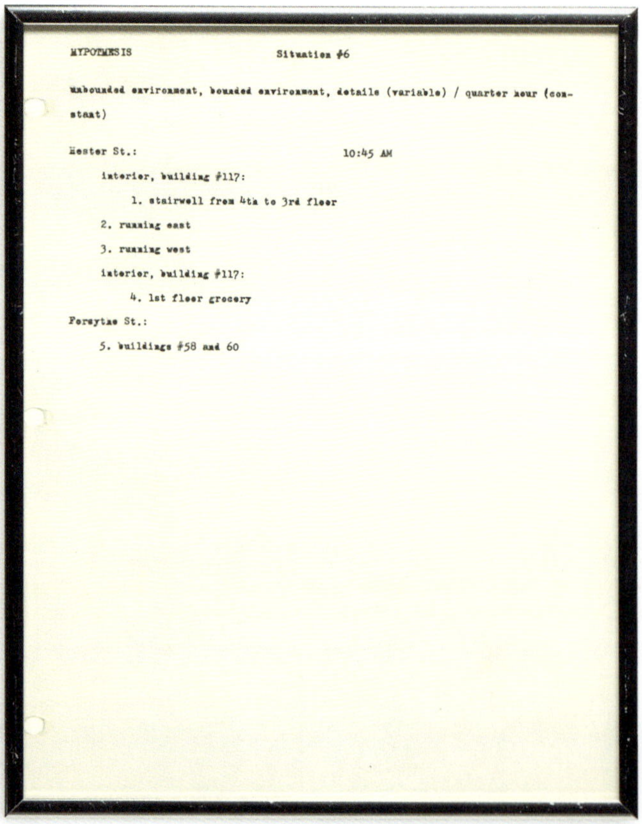

HYPOTHESIS Situation #6

unbounded environment, bounded environment, details (variable) / quarter hour (constant)

Hester St.: 10:45 AM

interior, building #117:

1. stairwell from 4th to 3rd floor

2. running east

3. running west

interior, building #117:

4. 1st floor grocery

Forsythe St.:

5. buildings #58 and 60

Hypothesis: Situation #6. 1968–69
Typescript on mimeographed paper; gelatin silver prints and ink on graph paper; and two photolithograph pages
11 × 8½ in. (27.9 × 21.6 cm); 11 × 18 in. (27.9 × 45.4 cm); and each 11 × 8½ in. (27.9 × 21.6 cm)
Walker Art Center, Minneapolis. T. B. Walker Acquisition Fund

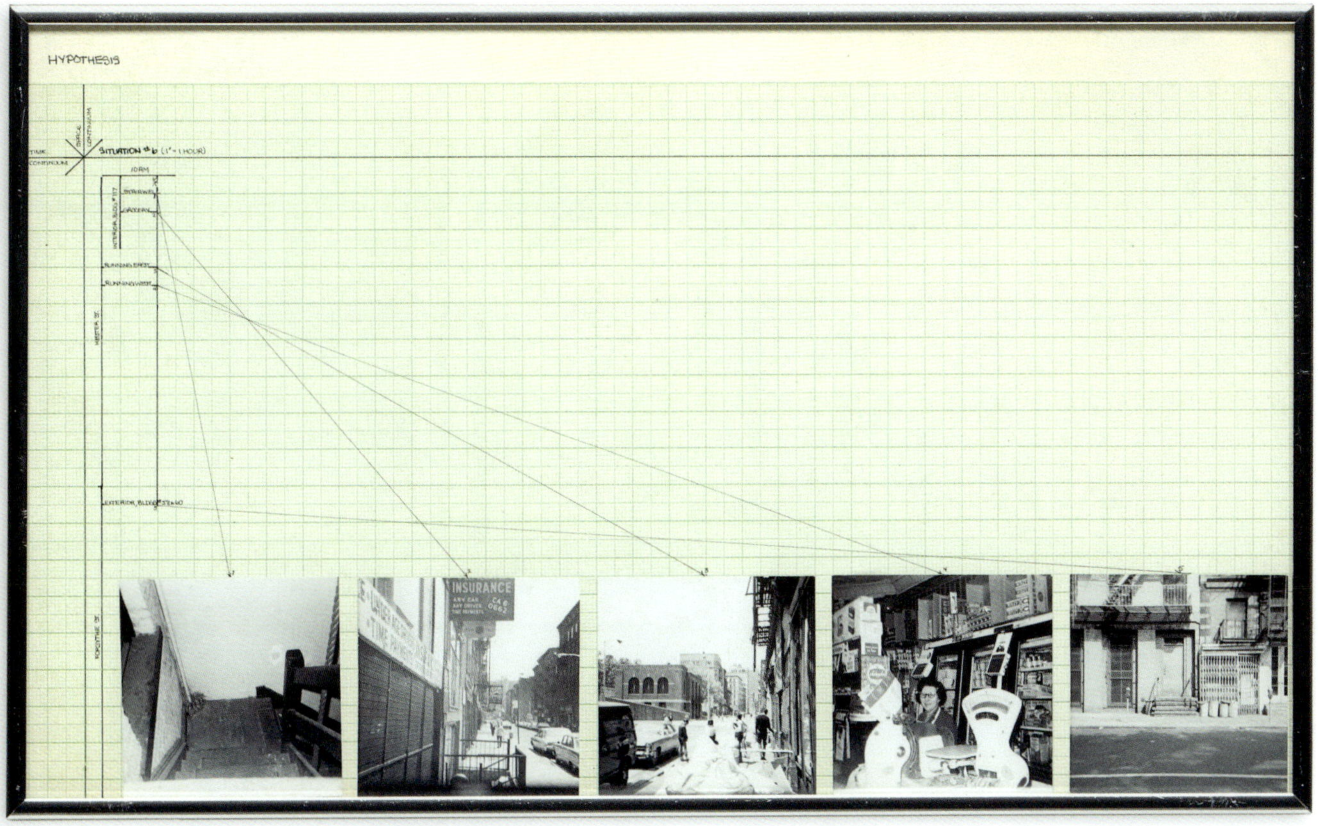

HYPOTHESIS:

Sensory consciousness is of essentially undifferentiated sensory information. The primary ordering of sensory information is into space and time continuums. The secondary ordering further differentiates it into segments along the continuums: specific space and time conditions (see second part of essay). The resulting consciousness is of an indeterminate number of points or instants at which the space and time continuums intersect. Any combination of space and time conditions on the continuums may intersect to form one or a series of points or instants. Space and time conditions may be combined in any one of the following ways:

1. One definition of an instant is the case in which space and time conditions are both constant. There is neither variation (progression) in time nor in space. The scope, duration, and depth of an instant is subjectively determined; an instant of sensory consciousness may be objectively measured in hours or seconds, environments or objects, depending on the particular experience.*
2. When the space condition remains constant while the time condition varies (progresses), the perceiver and/or spatial object of perception is motionless.
3. When the space condition varies while the time condition remains constant, the situation may either be that of a self- or environmentally-induced expansion of sensory consciousness, or sensory consciousness that is undifferentiated. Either would permit the registering of a number of different space conditions.
4. When the space conditions vary as the time condition varies (progresses), the perceiver and/or spatial object of perception is in motion.

The points or instants connect to form a span of consciousness of the designated space-time situation. Intervals between connected instants may signify temporary intrusions by a) external space and/or time conditions; b) absent-mindedness; c) that state of consciousness in which neither space nor time continuums exist. These possibilities do not break the span of consciousness of the designated situation: a span is determined as the sequence formed by the points at which consciousness of the situation is experienced.

---

* The possibility of perceptual hallucination is not considered here.

The conditions discussed below refer to the most differentiated and standardized forms of sensory consciousness. They are significations of more inclusive and indefinite kinds of experience.

Some space conditions available as objects of sensory consciousness at a given instant:

1. Unbounded environments (e.g. outdoor locations)
2. Bounded environments (e.g. indoor locations)
3. Composite masses: independent single objects, conglomerations of dependent objects (e.g. table: with ashtray, salt and pepper shakers, newspaper, etc.)
4. Dependent single objects: parts of composite masses (e.g. newspaper on table)
5. Details of any of the above not existing independently (e.g. fine print in newspaper)
6. A combination of any of the above

Some time conditions available as objects of sensory consciousness at a given instant:

1. Days
2. Hours
3. Half hours, quarter hours
4. Minutes
5. Seconds
6. A combination of any of the above

Both continuums are open-ended. They may be indefinitely extended by adding increasingly inclusive or exclusive conditions.

When used in a specific situation, a condition may be isolated from its identifying context (location, date).

Since the space and time continuums are in constant flux, any work (sensory consciousness situation) entered under this hypothesis cannot be repeated. Charts and photographs are intrinsically able to record intersections of the space and time continuums. They are therefore used to record the occurrence of each situation.

9/69 Adrian Piper

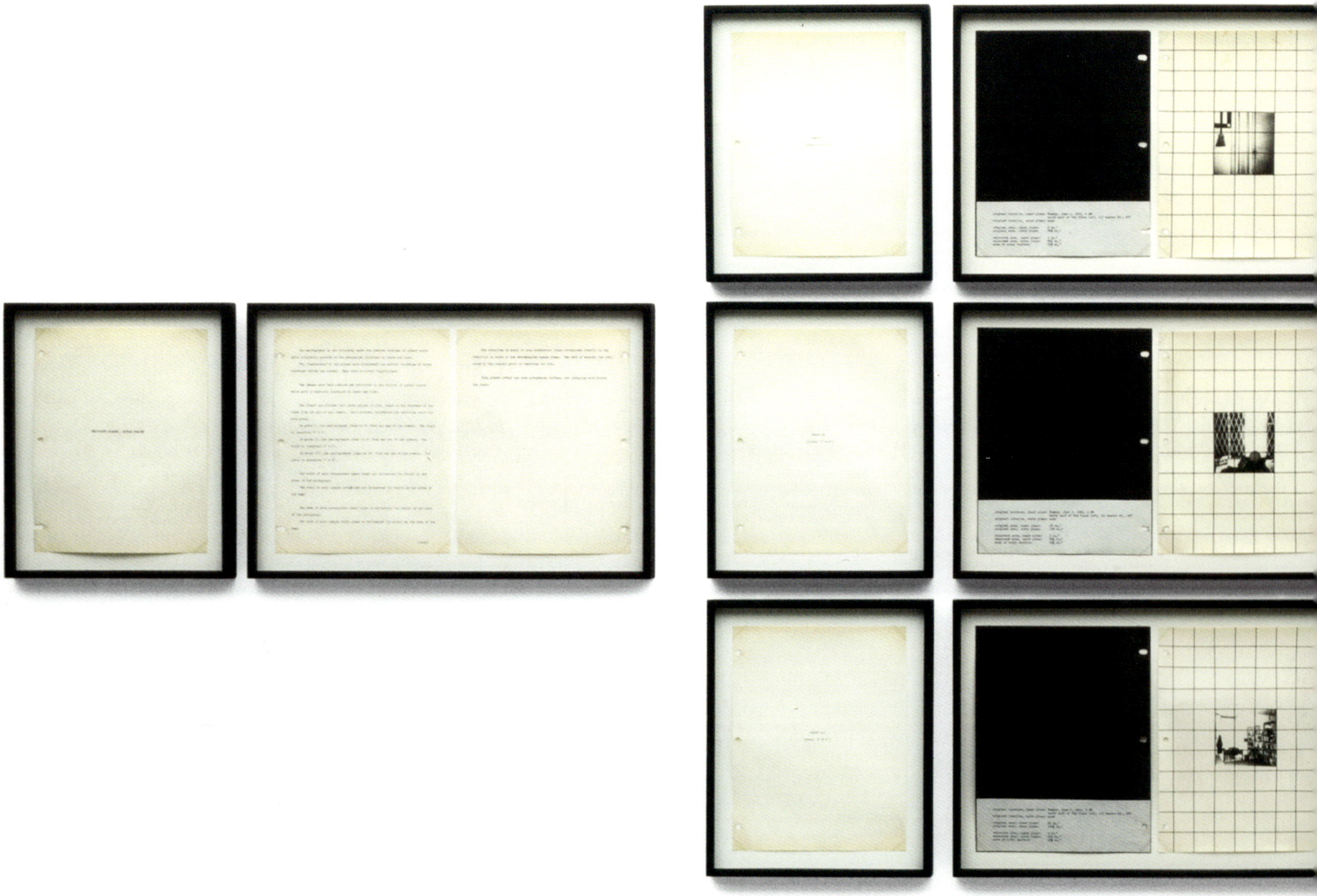

Relocated Planes I: Indoor Series, 6/69. 1969
Notebook with six typescript pages; ballpoint pen on four typescript pages; twelve photostats of architectural tape on acetate over photograph on paper; and cut-and-pasted text on twelve sheets of colored paper
Each page approx. 11 × 8½ in. (27.9 × 21.6 cm)
Generali Foundation Collection—Permanent Loan to the Museum der Moderne Salzburg

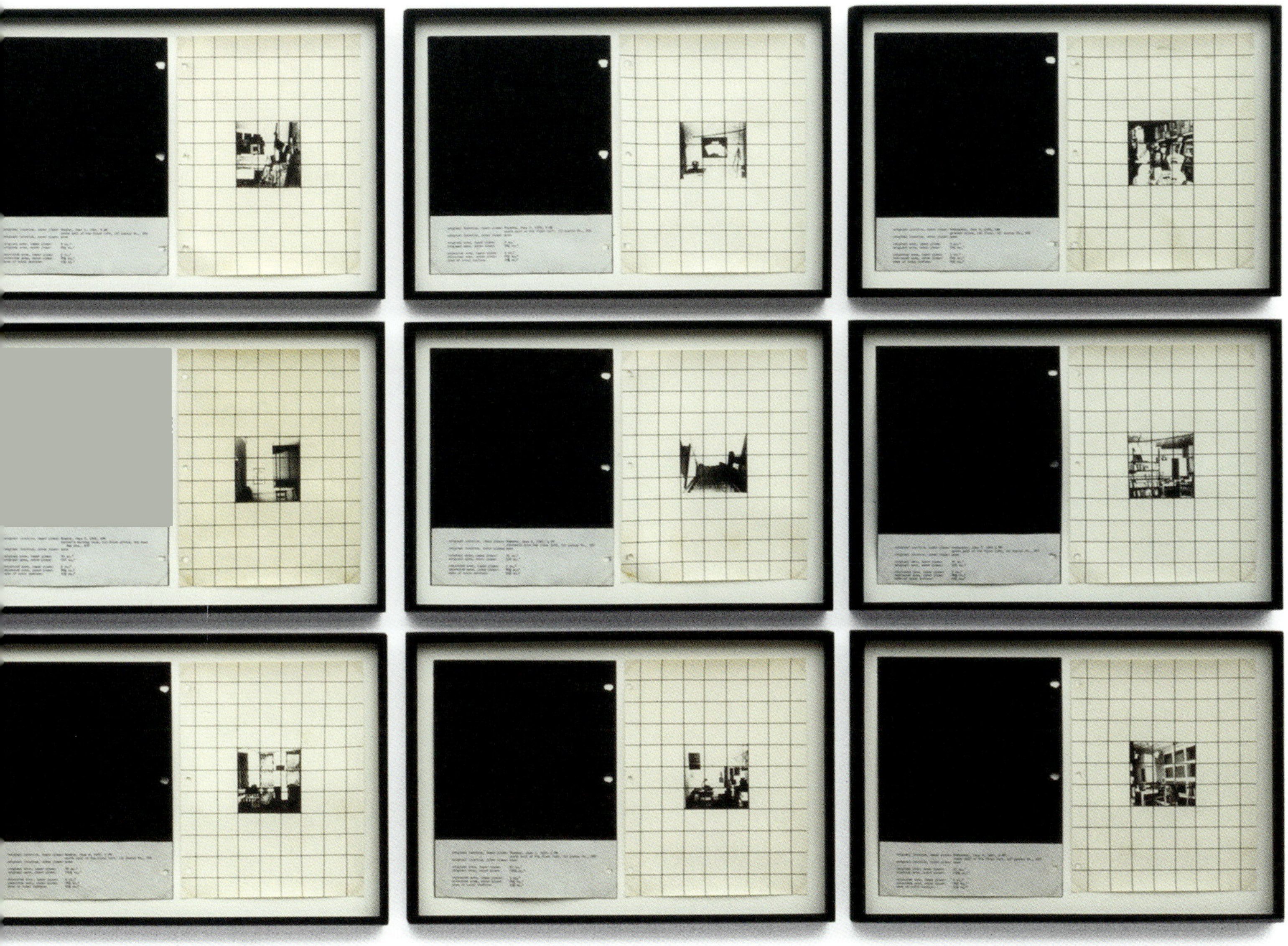

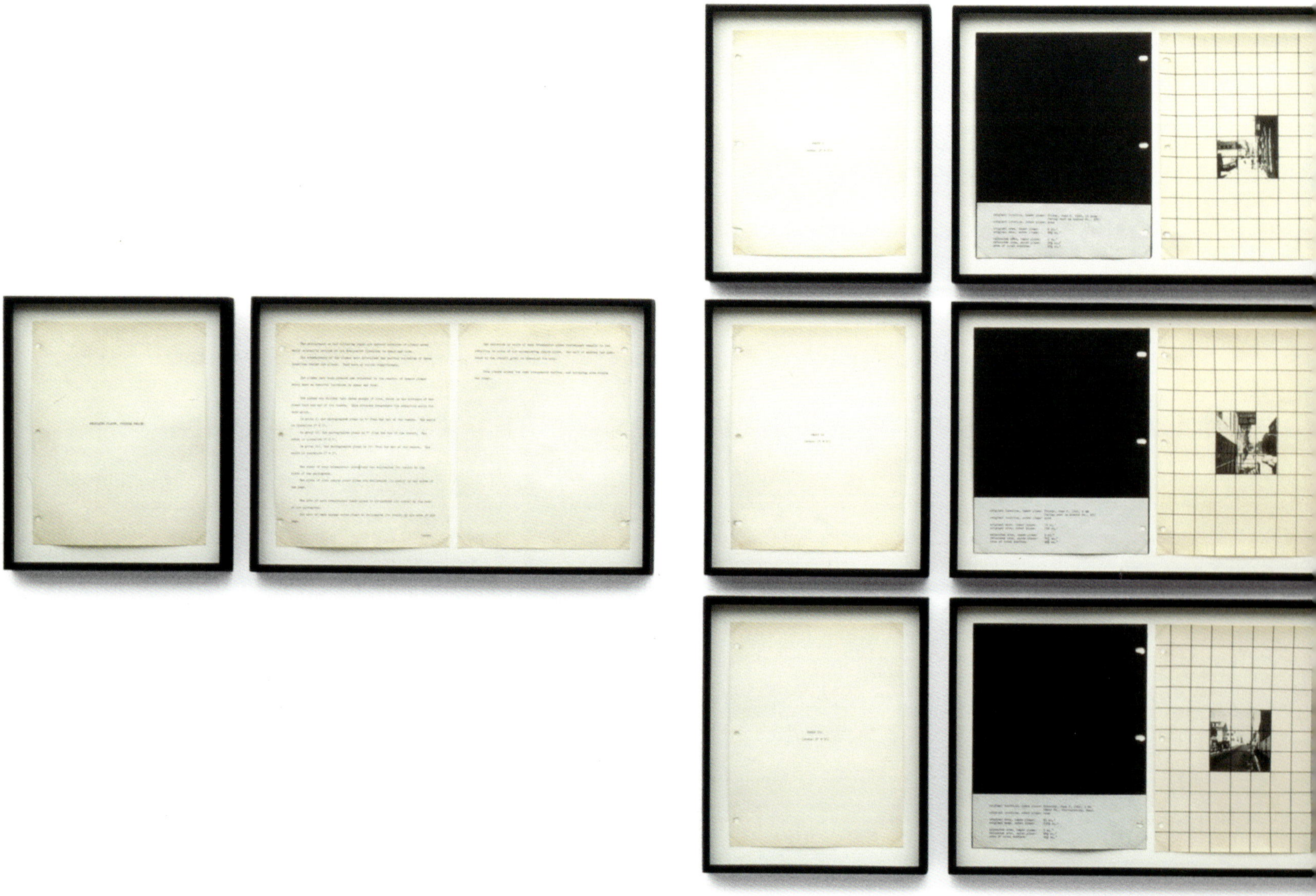

Relocated Planes II: Outdoor Series
Notebook with six typescript pages; ballpoint pen on four typescript pages; twelve photostats of architectural tape on acetate over photograph on paper; and cut-and-pasted text on twelve sheets of colored paper
Each page approx. 11 × 8½ in. (27.9 × 21.6 cm)
Generali Foundation Collection—Permanent Loan to the Museum der Moderne Salzburg

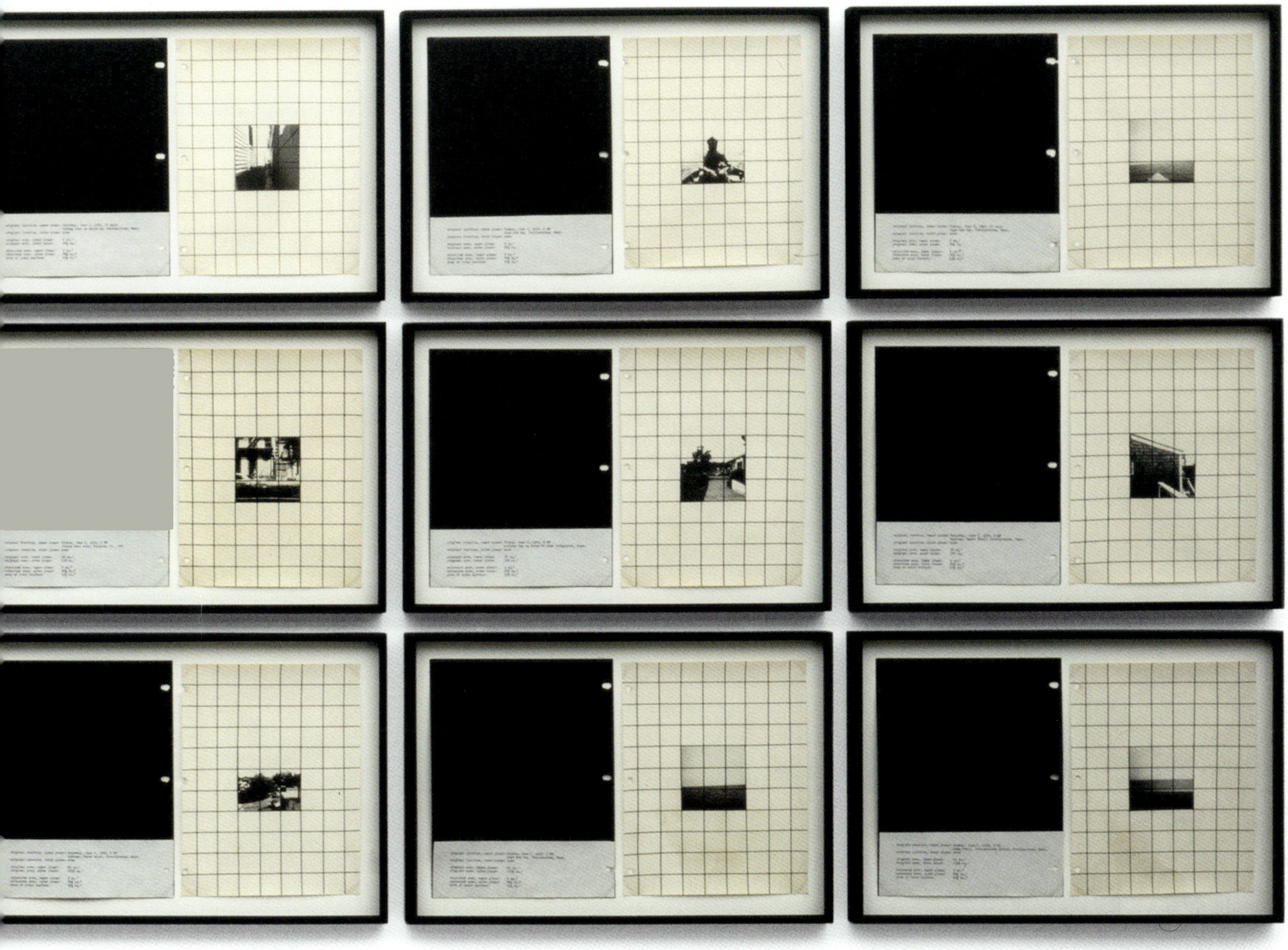

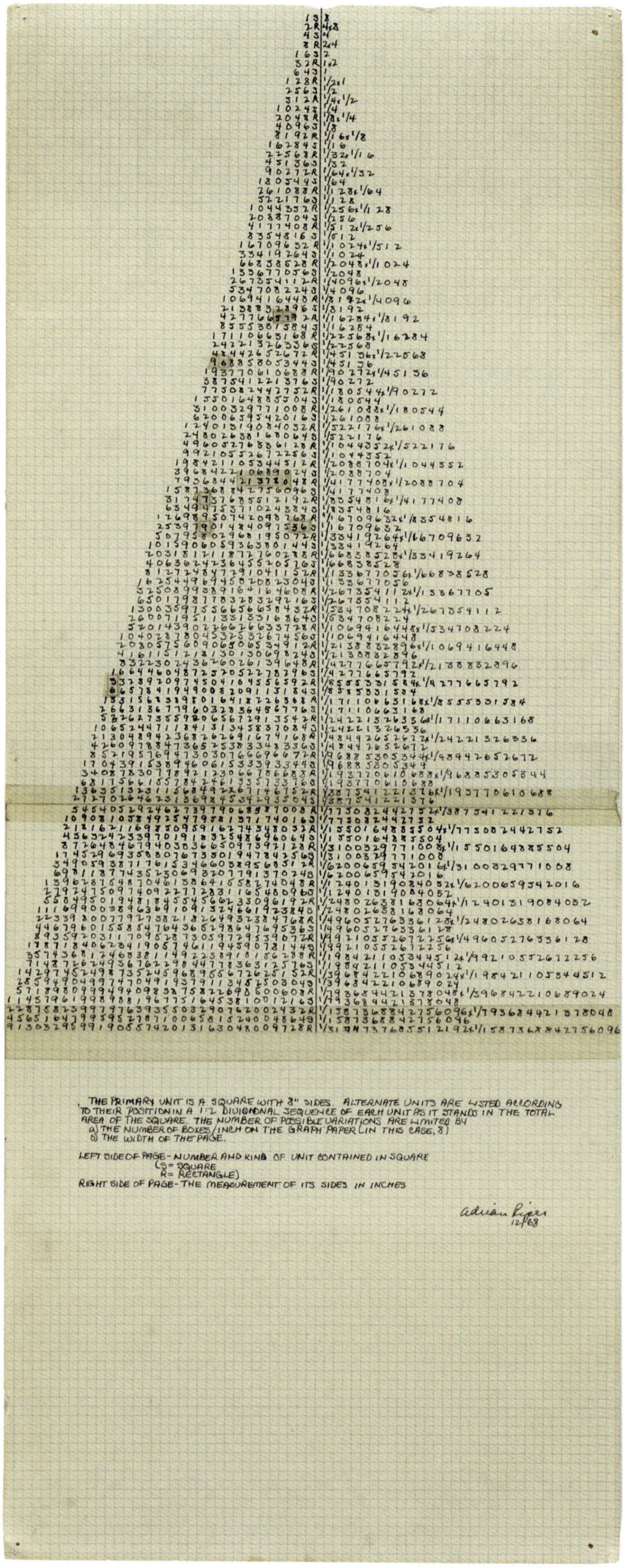

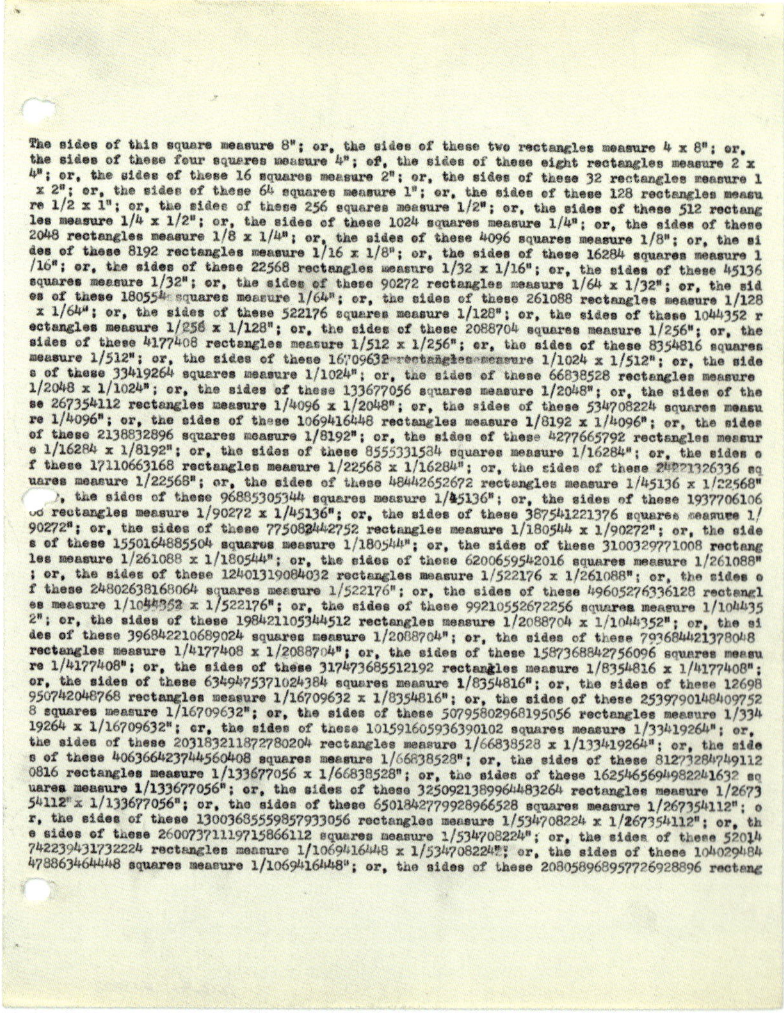
The sides of this square measure 8"; or, the sides of these two rectangles measure 4 x 8"; or,
the sides of these four squares measure 4"; of, the sides of these eight rectangles measure 2 x
4"; or, the sides of these 16 squares measure 2"; or, the sides of these 32 rectangles measure 1
x 2"; or, the sides of these 64 squares measure 1"; or, the sides of these 128 rectangles measu
re 1/2 x 1"; or, the sides of these 256 squares measure 1/2"; or, the sides of these 512 rectang
les measure 1/4 x 1/2"; or, the sides of these 1024 squares measure 1/4"; or, the sides of these
2048 rectangles measure 1/8 x 1/4"; or, the sides of these 4096 squares measure 1/8"; or, the si
des of these 8192 rectangles measure 1/16 x 1/8"; or, the sides of these 16284 squares measure 1
/16"; or, the sides of these 22568 rectangles measure 1/32 x 1/16"; or, the sides of these 45136
squares measure 1/32"; or, the sides of these 90272 rectangles measure 1/64 x 1/32"; or, the sid
es of these 180554 squares measure 1/64"; or, the sides of these 261088 rectangles measure 1/128
x 1/64"; or, the sides of these 522176 squares measure 1/128"; or, the sides of these 1044352 r
ectangles measure 1/256 x 1/128"; or, the sides of these 2088704 squares measure 1/256"; or, the
sides of these 4177408 rectangles measure 1/512 x 1/256"; or, the sides of these 8354816 squares
measure 1/512"; or, the sides of these 16709632 rectangles measure 1/1024 x 1/512"; or, the side
s of these 33419264 squares measure 1/1024"; or, the sides of these 66838528 rectangles measure
1/2048 x 1/1024"; or, the sides of these 133677056 squares measure 1/2048"; or, the sides of the
se 267354112 rectangles measure 1/4096 x 1/2048"; or, the sides of these 534708224 squares measu
re 1/4096"; or, the sides of these 1069416448 rectangles measure 1/8192 x 1/4096"; or, the sides
of these 2138832896 squares measure 1/8192"; or, the sides of these 4277665792 rectangles measur
e 1/16284 x 1/8192"; or, the sides of these 8555331584 squares measure 1/16284"; or, the sides o
f these 17110663168 rectangles measure 1/22568 x 1/16284"; or, the sides of these 24221326336 sq
uares measure 1/22568"; or, the sides of these 48442652672 rectangles measure 1/45136 x 1/22568"
[illegible], the sides of these 96885305344 squares measure 1/45136"; or, the sides of these 1937706106
06 rectangles measure 1/90272 x 1/45136"; or, the sides of these 387541221376 squares measure 1/
90272"; or, the sides of these 775082442752 rectangles measure 1/180544 x 1/90272"; or, the side
s of these 1550164885504 squares measure 1/180544"; or, the sides of these 3100329771008 rectang
les measure 1/261088 x 1/180544"; or, the sides of these 6200659542016 squares measure 1/261088"
; or, the sides of these 12401319084032 rectangles measure 1/522176 x 1/261088"; or, the sides o
f these 24802638168064 squares measure 1/522176"; or, the sides of these 49605276336128 rectangl
es measure 1/1044352 x 1/522176"; or, the sides of these 99210552672256 squares measure 1/104435
2"; or, the sides of these 198421105344512 rectangles measure 1/2088704 x 1/1044352"; or, the si
des of these 396842210689024 squares measure 1/2088704"; or, the sides of these 793684421378048
rectangles measure 1/4177408 x 1/2088704"; or, the sides of these 1587368842756096 squares measu
re 1/4177408"; or, the sides of these 3174736855121 92 rectangles measure 1/8354816 x 1/4177408";
or, the sides of these 6349475371024384 squares measure 1/8354816"; or, the sides of these 12698
950742048768 rectangles measure 1/16709632 x 1/8354816"; or, the sides of these 25397901484 09752
8 squares measure 1/16709632"; or, the sides of these 50795802968195056 rectangles measure 1/334
19264 x 1/16709632"; or, the sides of these 101591605936390102 squares measure 1/33419264"; or,
the sides of these 203183211872780204 rectangles measure 1/66838528 x 1/133419264"; or, the side
s of these 406366423744560408 squares measure 1/66838528"; or, the sides of these 81273284749112
0816 rectangles measure 1/133677056 x 1/66838528"; or, the sides of these 1625465694982241632 sq
uares measure 1/133677056"; or, the sides of these 3250921389964483264 rectangles measure 1/2673
54112" x 1/133677056"; or, the sides of these 6501842779928966528 squares measure 1/267354112"; o
r, the sides of these 13003685559857933056 rectangles measure 1/534708224 x 1/267354112"; or, th
e sides of these 26007371119715866112 squares measure 1/534708224"; or, the sides of these 52014
742239431732224 rectangles measure 1/1069416448 x 1/534708224"; or, the sides of these 104029484
478863464448 squares measure 1/1069416448"; or, the sides of these 208058968957726928896 rectang

Concrete 8" Square ["The sides of this square measure 8" . . ."]. 1968
Ink and tape on graph paper, mounted on foam core; and typescript page
21½ × 8½ in. (54.6 × 21.6 cm) and 11 × 8½ in. (27.9 × 21.6 cm)
The Museum of Modern Art, New York. Gift of Gilbert B. and Lila Silverman Instruction Drawing Collection, Detroit

This square should be read as a whole; or, these two vertical rectangles
should be read from left to right or right to left; or, these two horizo
ntal rectangles should be read from top to bottom or bottom to top; or,
these four squares should be read from upper left to upper right to lowe
r right to lower left or upper left to upper right to lower left to lowe
r right or upper left to lower left to lower right to upper right or upp
er left to lower left to lower right to upper right or upper left to low
er right to lower left to upper right or upper left to lower right to up
per right to lower left or upper right to lower right to lower left to u
pper left or upper right to lower right to upper left to lower left or u
pper right to upper left to lower left to lower right or upper right to
upper left to lower right to lower left or upper right to lower left to
upper left to lower right or upper right to lower left to lower right to
to upper left or lower right to lower left to upper left to upper right
or lower right to lower left to upper right to upper left or lower right
to upper right to upper left to lower left or lower right to upper right
to lower left to upper left or lower right to upper left to upper right
to lower left or lower right to upper left to lower left to upper right
or lower left to upper left to upper right to lower right or lower left
to upper left to lower right to upper right or lower left to lower right
to upper right to upper left or lower left to lower right to upper left
to upper right or lower left to upper right to lower right to upper left
or lower left to upper right to upper left to lower right; or, these eig
ht horizontal rectangles should be read from top left to top right to up
per middle right to lower middle right to bottom right to bottom left to
to lower middle left to upper middle left or top left to top right to up
per middle left to upper middle right to lower middle left to lower midd
le right to bottom left to bottom right or top left to upper middle left
to lower middle left to bottom left to bottom right to lower middle righ
t to upper middle right to top right or top left to upper middle left to
upper middle left to bottom left to top right to upper middle right to l
ower middle right to bottom right or top left to upper middle right to l
ower middle left to bottom right to bottom left to lower middle right to
upper middle left to top right or top right to upper middle right to low
er middle right to bottom right to bottom left to lower middle left to u
pper middle left to top left or top right to top left to upper middle ri
ght to upper middle left to lower middle right to lower middle left to b

Concrete Infinity 6-inch Square ["This square should be read as a whole . . ."]. 1968
Typescript page in square mat
Page 11 × 8½ in. (27.9 × 21.6 cm)
Collection Alan Cravitz and Shashi Caudill

ADRIAN PIPER

two recent works:
1) (212) PL 1-2345
2) (212) PL 1-6789

October

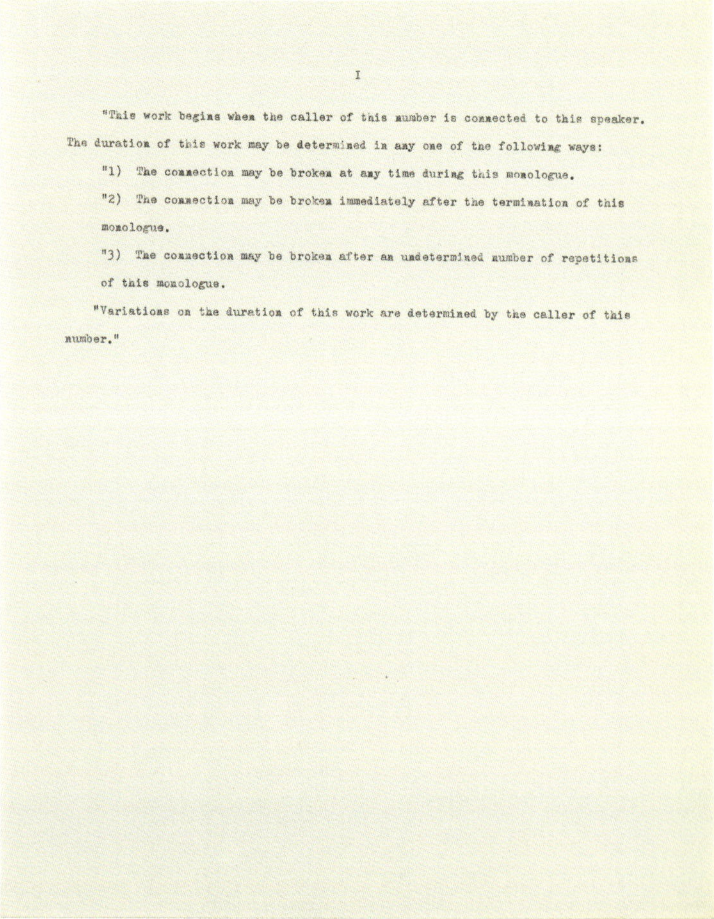

I

"This work begins when the caller of this number is connected to this speaker. The duration of this work may be determined in any one of the following ways:

"1) The connection may be broken at any time during this monologue.

"2) The connection may be broken immediately after the termination of this monologue.

"3) The connection may be broken after an undetermined number of repetitions of this monologue.

"Variations on the duration of this work are determined by the caller of this number."

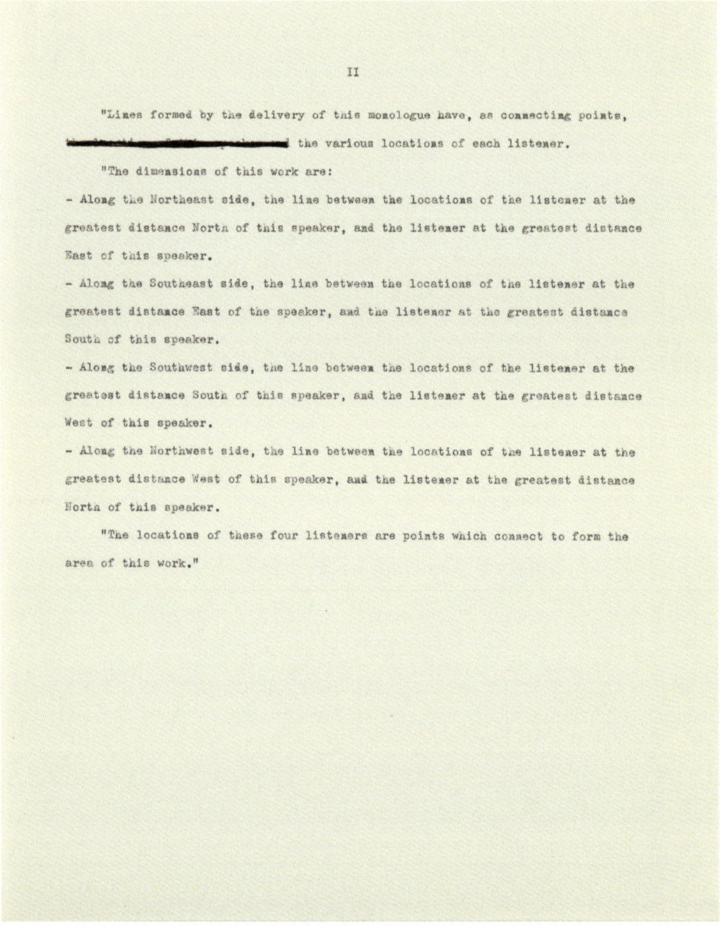

II

"Lines formed by the delivery of this monologue have, as connecting points, [redacted] the various locations of each listener.

"The dimensions of this work are:

- Along the Northeast side, the line between the locations of the listener at the greatest distance North of this speaker, and the listener at the greatest distance East of this speaker.
- Along the Southeast side, the line between the locations of the listener at the greatest distance East of the speaker, and the listener at the greatest distance South of this speaker.
- Along the Southwest side, the line between the locations of the listener at the greatest distance South of this speaker, and the listener at the greatest distance West of this speaker.
- Along the Northwest side, the line between the locations of the listener at the greatest distance West of this speaker, and the listener at the greatest distance North of this speaker.

"The locations of these four listeners are points which connect to form the area of this work."

Two Recent Works. 1968
Three typescript pages
Each 11 × 8½ in. (27.9 × 21.6 cm)
Collection Adrian Piper Research Archive Foundation Berlin

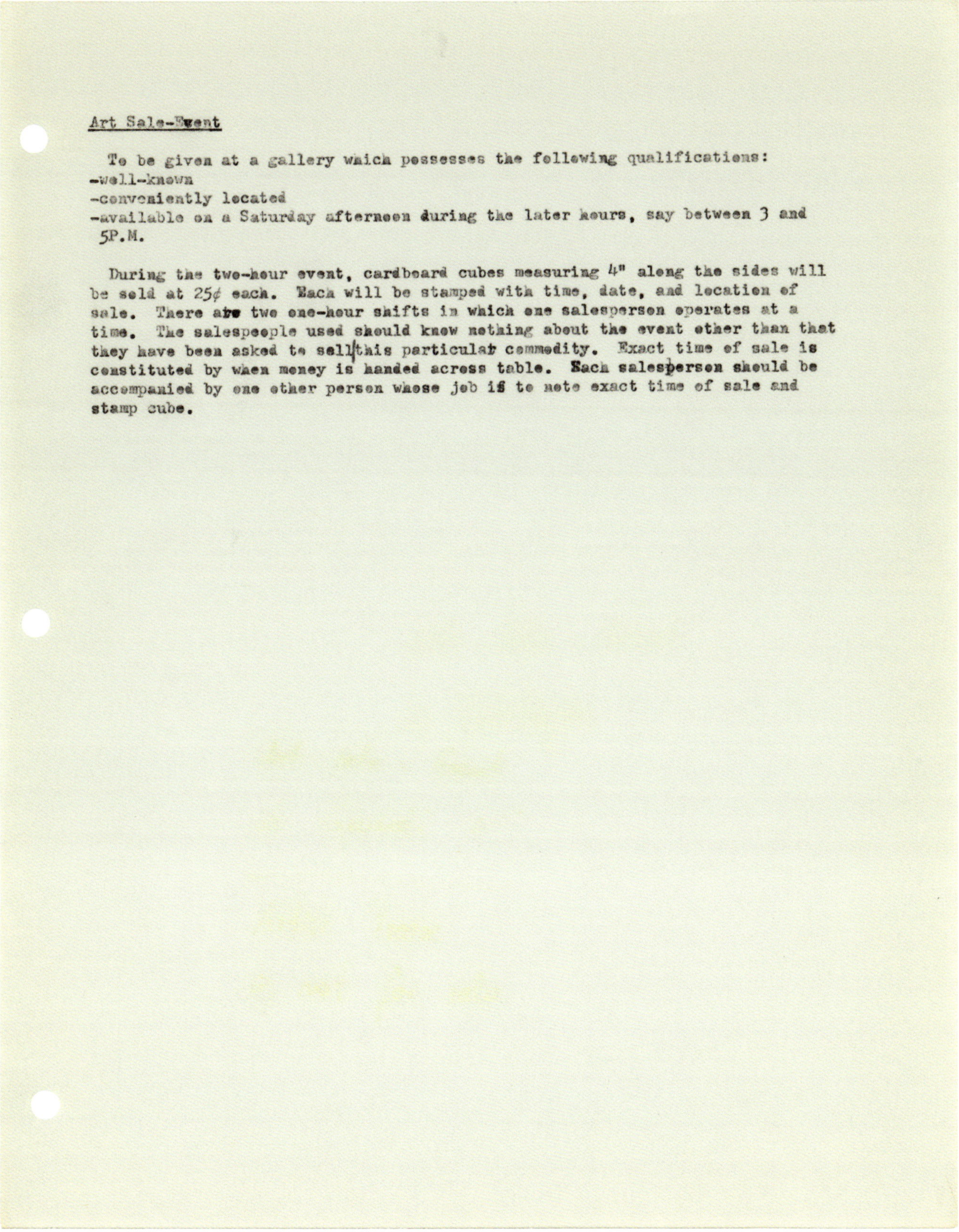

Art Sale-Event

To be given at a gallery which possesses the following qualifications:
-well-known
-conveniently located
-available on a Saturday afternoon during the later hours, say between 3 and 5P.M.

During the two-hour event, cardboard cubes measuring 4" along the sides will be sold at 25¢ each. Each will be stamped with time, date, and location of sale. There are two one-hour shifts in which one salesperson operates at a time. The salespeople used should know nothing about the event other than that they have been asked to sell this particular commodity. Exact time of sale is constituted by when money is handed across table. Each salesperson should be accompanied by one other person whose job is to note exact time of sale and stamp cube.

Art-Sale Event. 1968
Typescript page
11 × 8½ in. (27.9 × 21.6 cm)
Collection Adrian Piper Research Archive Foundation Berlin

<u>Taped Lecture on Seriation</u>(given November 7, 1968)

A recorded half hour of the daylight savings time announcement available on the telephone. Announcement is interrupted by disconnection at two-minute intervals. Number therefore has to be continually redialed. This operation takes approximately ten seconds to perform—the same length of time needed to make a single announcement, and is recorded as part of lecture. The half hour recorded should coincide with the time of presentation.

seriation:"...the analysis of any action into serial components..."
—George Kubler, <u>The Shape of Time</u>
(series:"a number of similar things or persons arranged in a row or coming after one another."—<u>Webster's New World Dictionary</u>)

The choice of the time announcement was directed towards giving a direct experience of the duration of the half hour. The continuity of the announcement throughout the half hour unifies it as an action performed in time. The primary unit of seriation is ten seconds:the announcements are given at ten second intervals, describe ten seconds of time, and are interrupted by ten seconds of dialing. The half hour is further subdivided by the interruption of the continuity of the announcements by the disconnection. The secondary serial components, then, are alternately two minutes, ten seconds, two minutes, ten seconds, etc.

Nineteen Concrete Space-Time-Infinity Pieces. 1968–69
Notebook with fifteen pageworks. Ring binder with nineteen typescript pages in plastic sleeves
Each page 11 × 8½ in. (27.9× 21.6 cm); binder 11¹³⁄₁₆ × 10⁹⁄₁₆ × 1½ in. (30 × 26.8 × 3.9 cm)
Generali Foundation Collection—Permanent Loan to the Museum der Moderne Salzburg

Taped Lecture on Seriation (given November 7, 1968) (1968), in *Nineteen Concrete Space-Time-Infinity Pieces*. Typescript page

If you are a slow reader, it will take you approximately five seconds to read this sentence.

If, on the other hand, you are a fast reader, it will very likely take you the same amount of time to read this sentence, since it has more words in it, in addition to a few subordinate clauses.

If you are an average reader, you must set up a ratio of the number of words in the first sentence over the time it takes a slow reader to read it(five seconds) to the number of words in the first sentence over the time it would take a fast reader to read them(unknown quantity x), solve the ratio, add the two times, divide the sum by two, divide the dividend(the average time obtained) into the same original number of words, multiply the new dividend by the total number of words in this sentence, and you will then know how long it has taken you to read this sentence.

Adrian Piper(.5 seconds)

Untitled ("If you are a slow reader . . .") (1968), in *Nineteen Concrete Space-Time-Infinity Pieces*. Typescript page

<u>The time needed to read a line of print depends on the content & structure of the line</u>

1)monotonous monotonous monotonous monotonous monotonous monotonous monotonous
2)linear Read morr qu iklythanThese inn w hich th ereare sOMe iRRregu l aRitise

3)<u>lines</u>:in which there're more--NECESSITIES(?)--for "punctuation", take MUCH longer!
4)somelineshavenopunctuationatallandtakeevenlongerifoneistoproperlyunderstandthem

5)When you,,reading this, are personally addressed, I'll bet you read pretty slowly
6)as compared to the time given to a line which doesn't address anyone in particular.

7)Concerning specific instances in which supermultisyllables are quasiutilized
8)they do not read as fast as when words of one sound are used, or sound as smooth.

---

enil eht fo erutcurts & tnetnoc eht no sdneped tnirp fo enil a daer ot dedeen emit ehT

Untitled ("The time needed to read a line . . .") (1968), in *Nineteen Concrete Space-Time-Infinity Pieces*. Typescript page

The piece stands in a rat
io of 1:3 to its designat
ed space and is situated
to the right center of it
it is further characteriz
ed by the continuity of i
ts internal parts of whic
h there are 75 these part
s being divisable into a
number of distinct catego
ries which are internally
distributed throughout th
e total area of the piece
in order to supplement th
basically logical structu
re of it as cognizance of
this structure is vital.

Untitled ("This piece stands in a ratio of 1:3 . . .") (1968), in *Nineteen Concrete Space-Time-Infinity Pieces*. Typescript page

ttom surface area of this white, rectangular object is $8\frac{1}{2}$" x 11". Directly above it is a second
ngle of the same color and dimensions. Directly above the second is a third rectangle of the sam
olor and dimensions. Directly above the third is a fourth rectangle of the same color and dimensio
ns. Directly above the fourth is a fifth rectangle of the same color and dimensions. Directly above
the fifth is a sixth rectangle of the same color and dimensions. Directly above the sixth is a sevent
h rectangle of the same color and dimensions. Directly above the seventh is an eighth rectangle of th
e color and dimensions. Directly above the eighth is a ninth rectangle of the same color and dim
ensions. Directly above the ninth is a tenth rectangle of the same color and dimensions. Directly ab
ove the tenth is an eleventh rectangle of the same color and dimensions. Directly above the eleventh
is a twelfth rectangle of the same color and dimensions. Directly above the twelfth is a thirteenth r
ectangle of the same color and dimensions. Directly above the thirteenth is a fourteenth rectangle of
the same color and dimensions. Directly above the fourteenth is a fifteenth rectangle of the same col
or and dimensions. Directly above the fifteenth is a sixteenth rectangle of the same color and dimens
ions. Directly above the sixteenth is a seventeenth rectangle of the same color and dimensions. Dire
ctly above the seventeenth is an eighteenth rectangle of the same color and dimensions. Directly abov
e the eighteenth is a nineteenth rectangle of the same color and dimensions. Directly above the ninet
eenth is a twentieth rectangle of the same color and dimensions. Directly above the twentieth is a tw
enty-first rectangle of the same color and dimensions. Directly above the twenty-first is a twenty-se
cond rectangle of the same color and dimensions. Directly above the twenty-second is a twenty-third r
ectangle of the same color and dimensions. Directly above the twenty-third is a twenty-fourth rectang
le of the same color and dimensions. Directly above the twenty-fourth is a twenty-fifth rectangle of
the same color and dimensions. Directly above the twenty-fifth is a twenty-sixth rectangle of the sam
e color and dimensions. Directly above the twenty-sixth is a twenty-seventh rectangle of the same col
or and dimensions. Directly above the twenty-seventh is a twenty-eighth rectangle of the same color a
nd dimensions. Directly above the twenty-eighth is a twenty-ninth rectangle of the same color and dim
ensions. Directly above the twenty-ninth is a thirtieth rectangle of the same color and dimensions.
Directly above the thirtieth is a thirty-first rectangle of the same color and dimensions. Directly a
bove the thirty-first is a thirty-second rectangle of the same color and dimensions. Directly above t
he thirty-second is a thirty-third rectangle of the same color and dimensions. Directly above the thi
rty-third is a thirty-fourth rectangle of the same color and dimensions. Directly above the thirty-fo
urth is a thirty-fifth rectangle of the same color and dimensions. Directly above the thirty-fifth is
a thirty-sixth rectangle of the same color and dimensions. Directly above the thirty-sixth is a thirt
y- th rectangle of the same color and dimensions. Directly above the thirty-seventh is a thirty-
eighth rectangle of the same color and dimensions. Directly above the thirty-eighth is a thirty-ninth
rectangle of the same color and dimensions. Directly above the thirty-ninth is a fortieth rectangle o
f the same color and dimensions. Directly above the fortieth is a forty-first rectangle of the same c
olor and dimensions. Directly above the forty-first is a forty-second rectangle of the same color and
dimensions. Directly above the forty-second is a forty-third rectangle of the same color and dimensio
ns. Directly above the forty-third is a forty-fourth rectangle of the same color and dimensions. Di
rectly above the forty-fourth is a forty-fifth rectangle of the same color and dimensions. Directly
above the forty-fifth is a forty-sixth rectangle of the same color and dimenstion. Directly above th
e forty-sixth is a forty-seventh rectangle of the same color and dimensions. Directly above the fort
y-seventh is a forty-eighth rectangle of the same color and dimensions. Directly above the forty-eig
hth is a forty-ninth rectangle of the same color and dimensions. Directly above the forty-ninth is a
fiftieth rectangle of the same color and dimensions. Directly above the fiftieth is a fifty-first re
ctangle of the same color and dimensions. Directly above the fifty-first is a fifty-second rectangle
of the same color and dimensions. Directly above the fifty-second is a fifty-third rectangle of the
same color and dimensions. Directly above the fifty-third is a fifty-fourth rectangle of the same co
lor and dimensions. Directly above the fifty-fourth is a fifty-fifth rectangle of the same color and
dimensions. Directly above the fifty-fifth is a fifty-sixth rectangle of the same color and dimensio
ns. Directly above the fifty-sixth is a fifty-seventh rectangle of the same color and dimensions. D
irectly above the fifty-seventh is a fifty-eighth rectangle of the same color and dimensions. Direct
ly above the fifty-eighth is a fifty-ninth rectangle of the same color and dimensions. Directly abov
e the fifty-ninth is a sixtieth rectangle of the same color and dimensions. Directly above the sixti
eth is a sixty-first rectangle of the same color and dimensions. Directly above the sixty-first is a
sixty-second rectangle of the same color and dimensions. Directly above the sixty-second is a sixty-t
hird rectangle of the same color and dimensions. Directly above the sixty-third is a sixty-fourth re
ct of the same color and dimensions. Directly above the sixty-fourth is a sixty-fifth rectangle
of the same color and dimensions. Directly above the sixty-fifth is a sixty-sixth rectangle of the s
ame color and dimensions. Directly above the sixty-sixth is a sixth-seventh rectangle of the same co
lor and dimensions. Directly above the sixty-seventh is a sixty-eighth rectangle of the same color a
nd dimensions. Directly above the sixty-eighth is a sixty-ninth rectangle of the same color and dime
nsions. Directly above the sixty-ninth is a seventieth rectangle of the same color and dimensions.
Directly above the seventieth is a seventy-first rectangle of the same color and dimensions. Directl
ya above the seventy-first is a seventy-second rectangle of the same color and dimensions. Directly

Untitled ("The bottom surface area . . .") (1968), in *Nineteen Concrete Space-Time-Infinity Pieces*. Recto of *Untitled ("The upper surface area . . .")*. Typescript page

The upper surface area of this white, rectangular object is 8½" x 11". Directly beneath it is a seco
nd rectangle of the same color and dimensions. Directly beneath the second is a third rectangle of t
he same color and dimensions. Directly beneath the third is a fourth rectangle of the same color and
dimensions. Directly beneath the fourth is a fifth rectangle of the same color and dimensions. Dire
ctly beneath the fifth is a sixth rectangle of the same color and dimensions. Directly beneath the s
ixth is a seventh rectangle of the same color and dimensions. Directly beneath the seventh is an eig
hth rectangle of the same color and dimensions. Directly beneath the eighth is a ninth rectan[illegible]f
the same color and dimensions. Directly beneath the ninth is a tenth rectangle of the same co[illegible]nd
dimensions. Directly beneath the tenth is an eleventh rectangle of the same color and dimensions. D
irectly beneath the eleventh is a twelfth rectangle of the same color and dimensions. Directly benea
th the twelfth is a thirteenth rectangle of the same color and dimensions. Directly beneath the thir
teenth is a fourteenth rectangle of the same color and dimensions. Directly beneath the fourteenth i
s a fifteenth rectangle of the same color and dimensions. Directly beneath the fifteenth is a sixtee
nth rectangle of the same color and dimensions. Directly beneath the sixteenth is a seventeenth rect
angle of the same color and dimensions. Directly beneath the seventeenth is an eighteenth rectangle
of the same color and dimensions. Directly beneath the eighteenth is a ninteenth rectangle of the sa
me color and dimensions. Directly beneath the ninteenth is a twentieth rectangle of the same color a
nd dimensions. Directly beneath the twentieth is a twenty-first rectangle of the same color and dime
nsions. Directly beneath the twenty-first is a twenty-second rectangle of the same color and dimensi
ons. Directly beneath the twenty-second is a twenty-third rectangle of the same color and dimensions
. Directly beneath the twenty-third is a twenty-fourth rectangle of the same color and dimensions.
Directly beneath the twenty-fourth is a twenty-fifth rectangle of the same color and dimensions. Di
rectly beneath the twenty-fifth is a twenty-sixth rectangle of the same color and dimensions. Direct
ly beneath the twenty-sixth is a twenty-seventh rectangle of the same color and dimensions. Directly
beneath the twenty-seventh is a twenty-eighth rectangle of the same color and dimensions. Directly b
eneath the twenty-eighth is a twenty-ninth rectangle of the same color and dimensions. Directly bene
ath the twenty-ninth is a thirtieth rectangle of the same color and dimensions. Directly beneath the
thirtieth is a thirty-first rectangle of the same color and dimensions. Directly beneath the thirty-
first is a thirty-second rectangle of the same color and dimensions. Directly beneath the thirty-sec
ond is a thirty-third rectangle of the same color and dimensions. Directly beneath the thirty-third
is a thirty-fourth rectangle of the same color and dimensions. Directly beneath the thirty-fourth is
a thirty-fifth rectangle of the same color and dimensions. Directly beneath the thirty-fifth is a th
irty-sixth rectangle of the same color and dimensions. Directly beneath the thirty-sixth is a[illegible]y
-seventh rectangle of the same color and dimensions. Directly beneath the thirty-seventh is a thirty
-eighth rectangle of the same color and dimensions. Directly beneath the thirty-eighth is a thirty-n
inth rectangle of the same color and dimensions. Directly beneath the thirty-ninth is a fourtieth re
ctangle of the same color and dimensions. Directly beneath the fortieth is a forty-first rectangle o
f the same color and dimensions. Directly beneath the forty-first is a forty-second rectangle of the
same color and dimensions. Directly beneath the forty-second is a forty-third rectangle of the same
color and dimensions. Directly beneath the forty-third is a forty-fourth rectangle of the same color
and dimensions. Directly beneath the forty-fourth is a forty-fifth rectangle of the same color and d
imensions. Directly beneath the forty-fifth is a forty-sixth rectangle of the same color and dimensi
ons. Directly beneath the forty-sixth is a forty-seventh rectangle of the same color and dimensions.
Directly beneath the forty-seventh is a forty-eighth rectangle of the same color and dimensions. D
irectly beneath the forty-eighth is a forty-ninth rectangle of the same color and dimensions. Direct
ly beneath the forty-ninth is a fiftieth rectangle of the same color and dimensions. Directly beneat
h the fiftieth is a fifty-first rectangle of the same color and dimensions. Directly beneath the fif
ty-first is a fifty-second rectangle of the same color and dimensions. Directly beneath the fifty-se
cond is a fifty-third rectangle of the same color and dimensions. Directly beneath the fifty-third i
s a fifty-fourth rectangle of the same color and dimensions. Directly beneath the fifty-fourth is a
fifty-fifth rectangle of the same color and dimensions. Directly beneath the fifty-fifth is a fifty-
sixth rectangle of the same color and dimensions. Directly beneath the fifty-sixth is a fifty-sevent
h rectangle of the same color and dimensions. Directly beneath the fifty-seventh is a fifty-eighth r
ectangle of the same color and dimensions. Directly beneath the fifty-eighth is a fifty-ninth rectan
gle of the same color and dimensions. Directly beneath the fifty-ninth is a sixtieth rectangle of the
same color and dimensions. Directly beneath the sixtieth is a sixty-first rectangle of the same color
and dimensions. Directly beneath the sixty-first is a sixty-second rectangle of the same color and di
mensions. Directly beneath the sixty-second is a sixty-third rectangle of the same color and d[illegible]io
ns. Directly beneath the sixty-third is a sixty-fourth rectangle of the same color and dimensions. D
irectly beneath the sixty-fourth is a sixty-fifth rectangle of the same color and dimensions. Direct
ly beneath the sixty-fifth is a sixty-sixth rectangle of the same color and dimensions. Directly ben
eath the sixty-sixth is a sixty-seventh rectangle of the same color and dimensions. Directly beneath
the sixty-seventh is a sixty-eighth rectangle of the same color and dimensions. Directly beneath the
sixty-eighth is a sixty-ninth rectan gle of the same color and dimensions. Directly beneath the
y-ninth is a seventieth rectangle of the same color and dimensions. Directly beneath the seven'

Untitled ("The upper surface area . . .") (1968), in *Nineteen Concrete Space-Time-Infinity Pieces*. Verso of *Untitled ("The bottom surface area . . .")*. Typescript page

<u>Seriation #2(Now)</u> (November 11, 1968)

A taped 20-minute segment divided into 5-minute intervals.

In the first 5-minute interval, the word "NOW" is repeated once every minute.
" " second " " " " " " " " " ½-minute.
" " third " " " " " " " " " ¼-minute.
" " fourth " " " " " " " continuously.

The word "NOW" takes approximately 1.5 seconds to say.

Each 5-minute interval is accompanied by a slide which is flashed on during the 1.5 seconds when the word "NOW" is being said. The slides contain the following information:

#1-

(here)
NOW:1.5 seconds / not-NOW:58.5 seconds

#2-

(here)
NOW:1.5 seconds / not-NOW:28.5 seconds

#3-

(here)
NOW:1.5 seconds / not-NOW:13.5 seconds

#4-

(here)
NOW:1.5 seconds / not-NOW:negligible

Seriation #2 (Now) (November 11, 1968) (1968), in *Nineteen Concrete Space-Time-Infinity Pieces.* Typescript page

Text of a piece for Larry Wiener 1/14/69

medium:tape recording (length 600' @ 7½ IPS)

units: 1

"The length of this single recorded section is approximately 15 minutes.
Or, the length of these 2 recorded sections are approximately 7 minutes, 30
seconds each. Or, the length of these 4 recorded sections are approximately
3 minutes, 45 seconds each. Or, the length of these 8 recorded sections are
approximately 1 minute, 52.5 seconds each. Or, the length of these 16 recor-
ded sections are approximately 56.25 seconds each. Or, the length of these
32 recorded sections are approximately 28.125 seconds each. Or, the length
of these 64 recorded sections are approximately 14.0625 seconds each. Or,
the length of these 128 recorded sections are approximately 7.03125 seconds
each. Or, the length of these 256 recorded sections are approximately 3.51-
5625 seconds each. Or, the length of these 512 recorded sections are approximate-
ly 1.2578125 seconds each. Or, the length of these 1,024 recorded sections
are approximately .62890625 seconds each. Or, the length of these 2,048 re-
corded sections are approximately .314453125 seconds each. Or, the length
of these 4,096 recorded sections are approximately .1572265625 seconds each.
Or, the length of these 8,192 recorded sections are approximately .07861378-
125 seconds each. Or, the length of these 16,384 recorded sections are approx-
imately .0196534453125 seconds each. Or, the length of these 75,536 recorded
sections are approximately .00982672265625 seconds each. Or, the length of
these 151,072 recorded sections are approximately .004913361328125 seconds
each. Or, the length of these 302,144 recorded sections are approximately
.0024566806640625 seconds each. Or, the length of these 604,288 recorded
sections are approximately .00122834033203125 seconds each. Or, the length
of these 1,208,576 recorded sections are approximately .000614170166015625
seconds each. Or, the length of these 2,417,152 recorded sections are approx-
imately .0003070850830078125 seconds each. Or, the length of these 4,834,304
recorded sections are approximately .00015354254150390625 seconds each. Or,
the length of these 9,668,608 recorded sections are approximately .00007677-
1270751953125 seconds each. Or, the length of these 19,337,216 recorded sec-
tions are approximately .0000383856353759765625 seconds each. Or, the length
of these 38,674,432 recorded sections are approximately .000019192817687988-
28125 seconds each. Or, the length of these 77,348,864 recorded sections
are approximately .00000958640834399414 0625 seconds each. Or, the length
of these 154,697,728 recorded sections are approximately .00000479320417199-
70703125 seconds each. Or, the length of these 319,395,456 recorded sections
are approximately . 000002396602085998535 10625 seconds each. Or, the length
of these 638,790,912 recorded sections are approximately .00000119830104299-
6727553125 seconds each. Or, the length of these 1,277,581,824 recorded sec-
tions are approximately . 000000599150521998363 7765625 seconds each. Or,
the length of these 2,555,163,648 recorded sections are approximately .000-
00029957526099928637765625 seconds each. Or, the length of these 5,110,327,
296 recorded sections are approximately .0000001497876304996431998906 25 sec-
onds each. Or, the length of these 10,220,654,492 recorded sections are approx-
imately .000000074893815249821599940 3125 seconds each. Or, the length of these
20,441,309,184 recorded sections are approximately .000000037446907 6249107-
9997015625 seconds each. Or, the length of these 40,882,618,368 recorded
sections are approximately .0000000187234538124503999850 78125 seconds each.
Or, these 81,765,236,736 recorded sections are approximately .00000000 9361-
72690622519999753 90625 seconds each. Or, these 163,530,473,472 recorded sec-
-tions are approximately .00000000468586340311259999876953125 seconds each.
Or, the length of these 327,060,946,944 recorded sections are approximately
.000000002342931701536299999384265625 seconds each. Or, the length of these
654,121,893,888 recorded sections are approximately .000000001171465850768-
1499996921328125 seconds each. Or, the length of these 130,824,387,776 re-
corded sections are approximately .0000000006857329253840749998460664 0625
seconds each. Or, the length of these 2,616,487,575,552 recorded sections
are approximately .00000000034286646269304759993804430 4136 seconds each. Or,
the length of these 5,232,975,151,104 recorded sections are approximately
.0000000001714332313460137499640166015625 seconds each. Or, the length of
these 10,465,950,302,208 recorded sections are approximately .00000000085-
716616789006875983008400 78136 seconds each. Or, the length of these 20,931,
900,604,416 recorded sections are approximately .0000000000428583068390034 3-
799100415039 5625 seconds each. Or, the length of these 41,863,801,203,832
recorded sections are approximately .0000000000214296539695017189955020756-
978125 seconds each. Or, the length of these 83,727,602,417,664 recorded sec-
tions are approximately .00000000001071487698475085949775103784890625 seconds
each. Or, etc."

(Progression continues for total duration of tape)

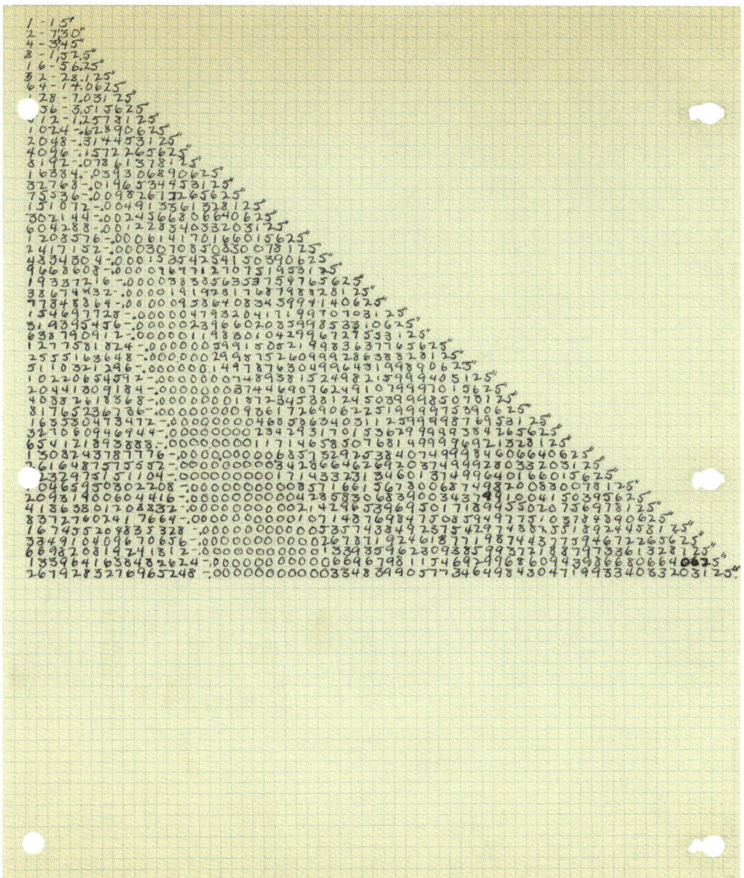

Text of a Piece for Larry Wiener, 1/14/69 (1969), in *Nineteen Concrete Space-Time-Infinity Pieces*.
Three typescript pages; and ballpoint pen on graph paper (Note: This work was made for the artist Lawrence Weiner.)

Maps schematizing different elements existing in Manhattan were selected for use. Specifically chosen were:

1. a street map
2. a bus routes map
3. a subway routes map
4. a zip code area map

On each map, all areas representing various types of systematic obstructions in above-ground three dimensional space were cancelled, i.e.

1. On the street map, all blocks were cancelled (map #1).
2. On the bus routes map, all streets functioning as bus routes were cancelled (map #2).
3. On the subway routes map, all streets with subway stations plus a one street radius of those streets were cancelled. Subway routes per se were not cancelled because they do not function in above-ground three dimensional space (map #3).
4. On the zip code area map, all interzone areas were cancelled (map #4).

All schematic symbols of systematic spatial obstruction in the form of building elevations, traffic, pedestrians, or postal activity were in this way eliminated. Other obstructions are random and/or unpredictable, and were therefore ignored.

The alteration of the maps culminate to represent the area of Manhattan as it actually is: a two dimensional geometric plane. In this context, the remaining streets shown on this plane represent unobstructed geometric line segments which exist wholly in the surface of the plane (map #5).

The length of each segment is determined according to the street map scale: 5/8" = 3000'.

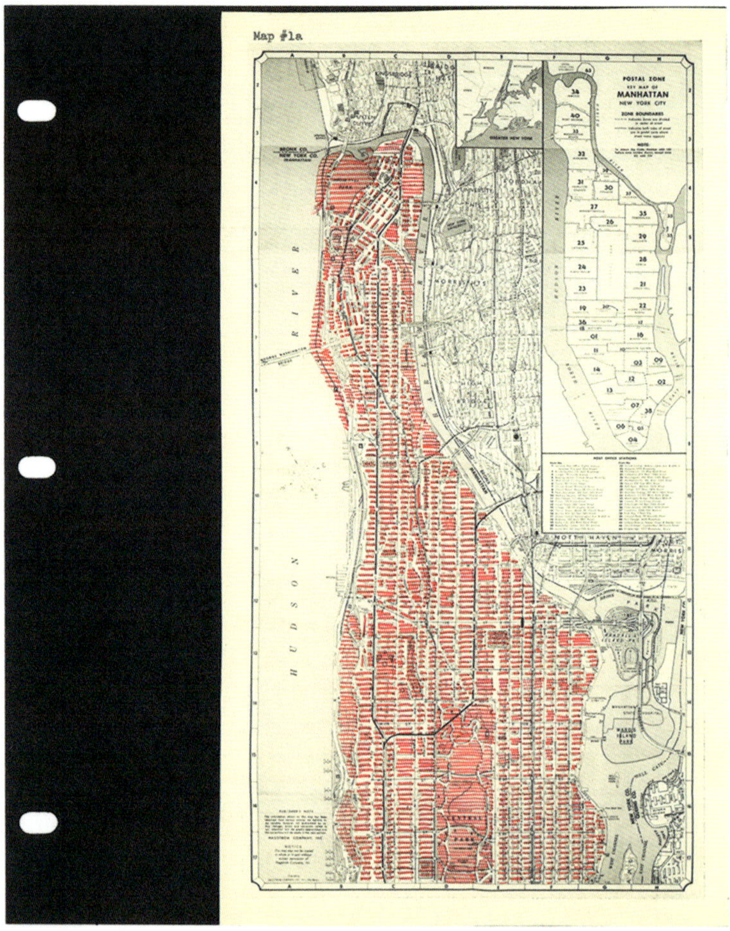

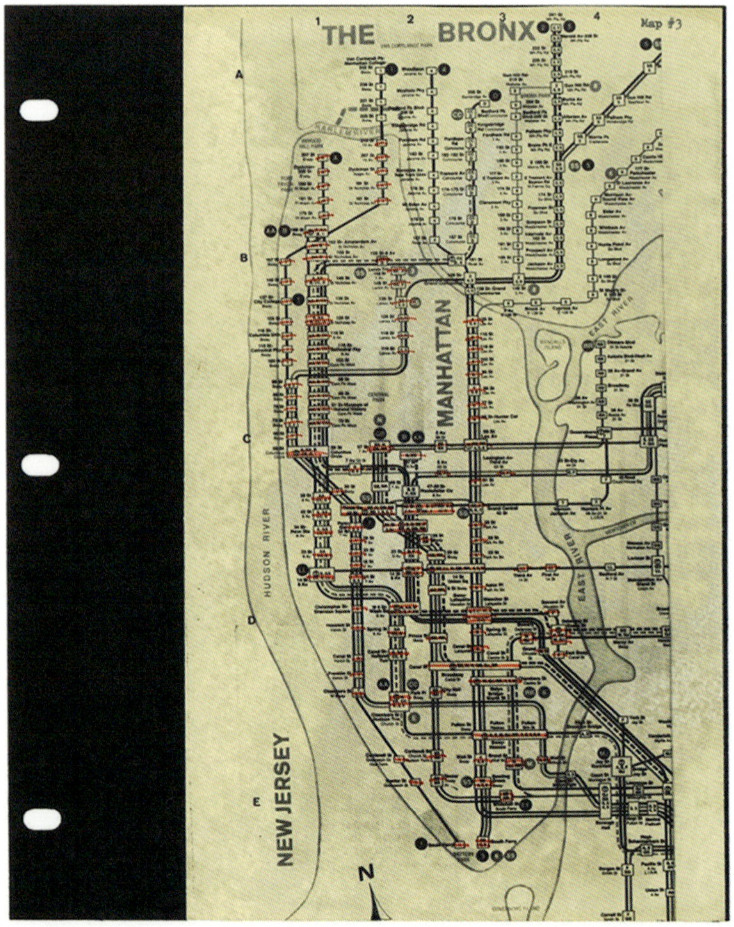

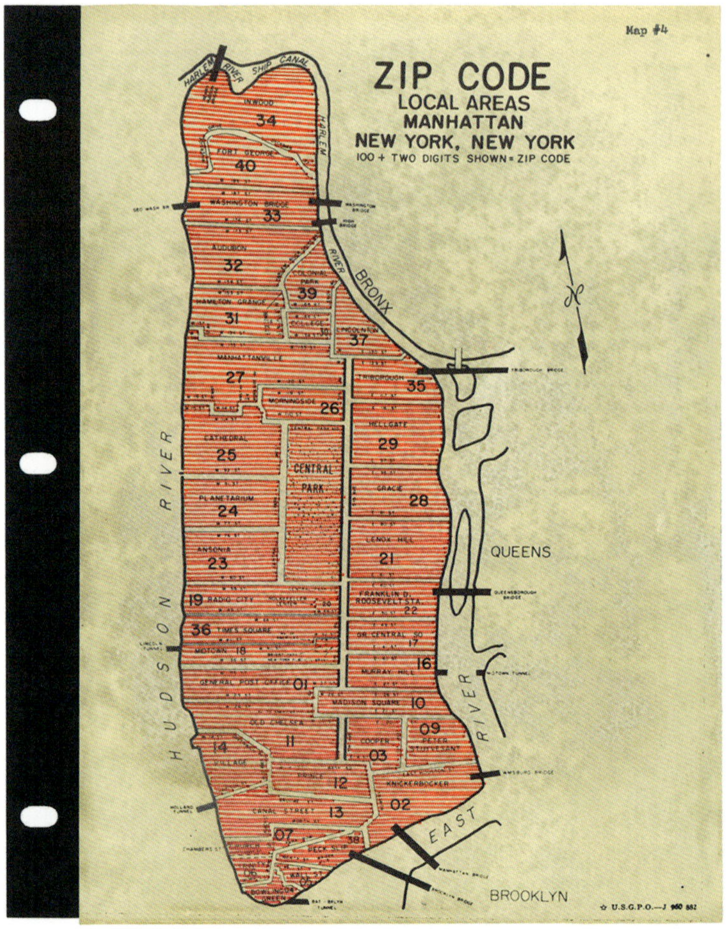

Nine Abstract Space-Time-Infinity Pieces. 1968–69
Notebook with eight pageworks. Ring binder with twenty-nine sheets in plastic sleeves
Each page 11 × 8½ in. (27.9 × 21.6 cm); binder 11$^{13}/_{16}$ × 10$^{9}/_{16}$ × 1½ in. (30 × 26.8 × 3.9 cm)
Generali Foundation Collection—Permanent Loan to the Museum der Moderne Salzburg

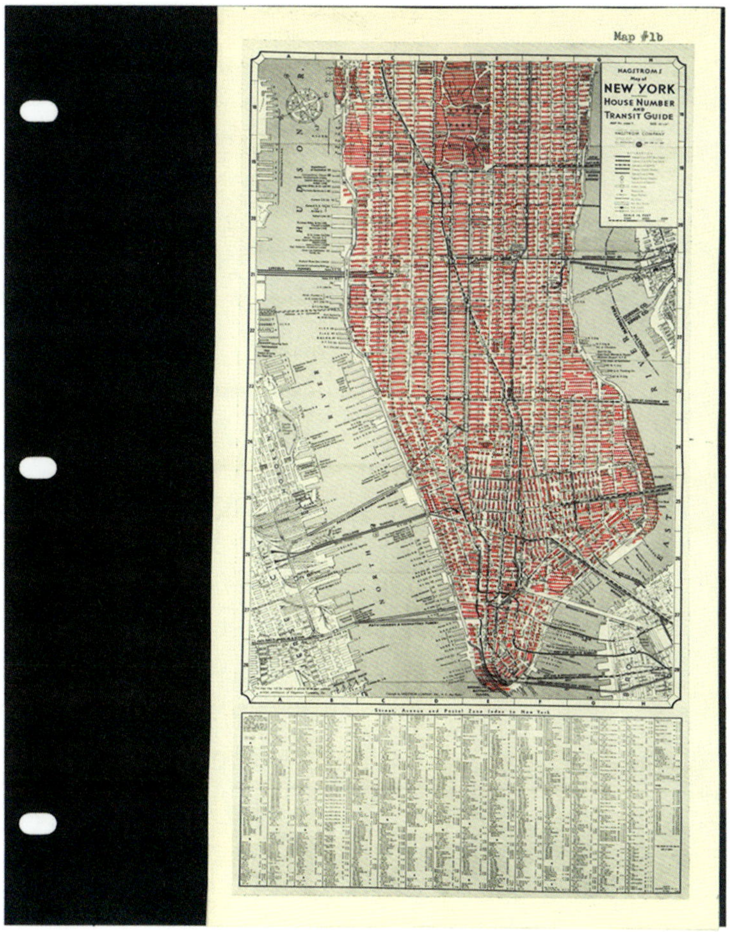

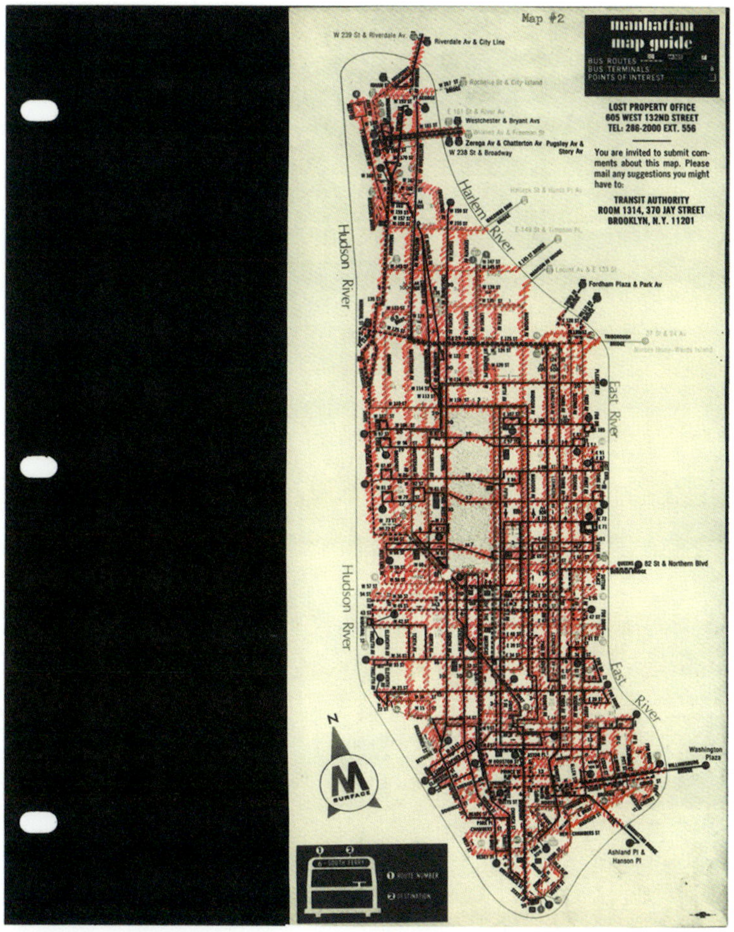

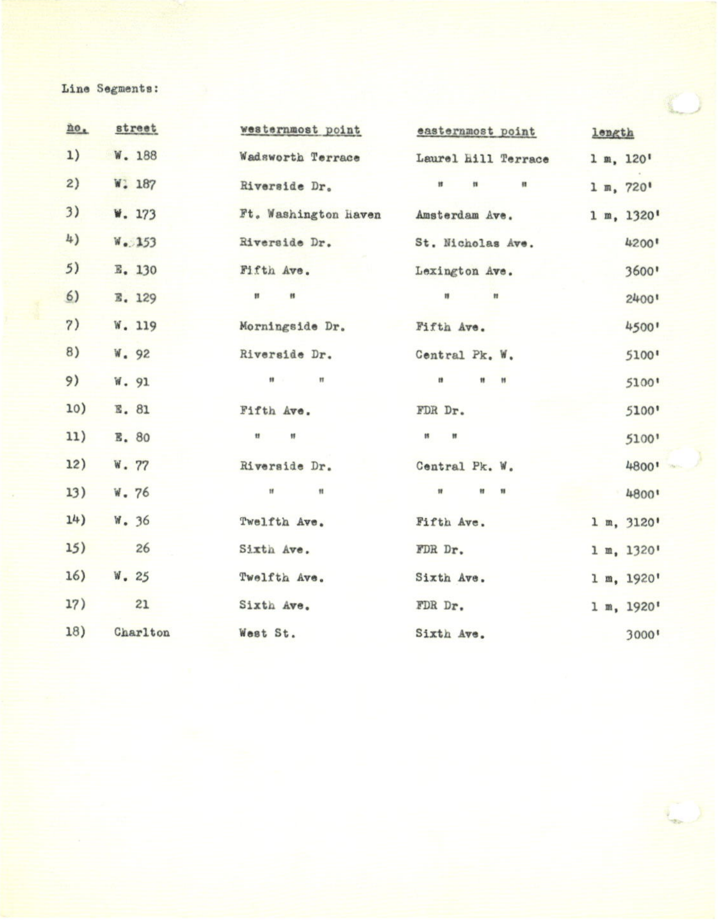

Line Segments:

no.	street	westernmost point	easternmost point	length
1)	W. 188	Wadsworth Terrace	Laurel Hill Terrace	1 m, 120'
2)	W. 187	Riverside Dr.	" " "	1 m, 720'
3)	W. 173	Ft. Washington Haven	Amsterdam Ave.	1 m, 1320'
4)	W. 153	Riverside Dr.	St. Nicholas Ave.	4200'
5)	E. 130	Fifth Ave.	Lexington Ave.	3600'
6)	E. 129	" "	" "	2400'
7)	W. 119	Morningside Dr.	Fifth Ave.	4500'
8)	W. 92	Riverside Dr.	Central Pk. W.	5100'
9)	W. 91	" "	" " "	5100'
10)	E. 81	Fifth Ave.	FDR Dr.	5100'
11)	E. 80	" "	" "	5100'
12)	W. 77	Riverside Dr.	Central Pk. W.	4800'
13)	W. 76	" "	" " "	4800'
14)	W. 36	Twelfth Ave.	Fifth Ave.	1 m, 3120'
15)	26	Sixth Ave.	FDR Dr.	1 m, 1320'
16)	W. 25	Twelfth Ave.	Sixth Ave.	1 m, 1920'
17)	21	Sixth Ave.	FDR Dr.	1 m, 1920'
18)	Charlton	West St.	Sixth Ave.	3000'

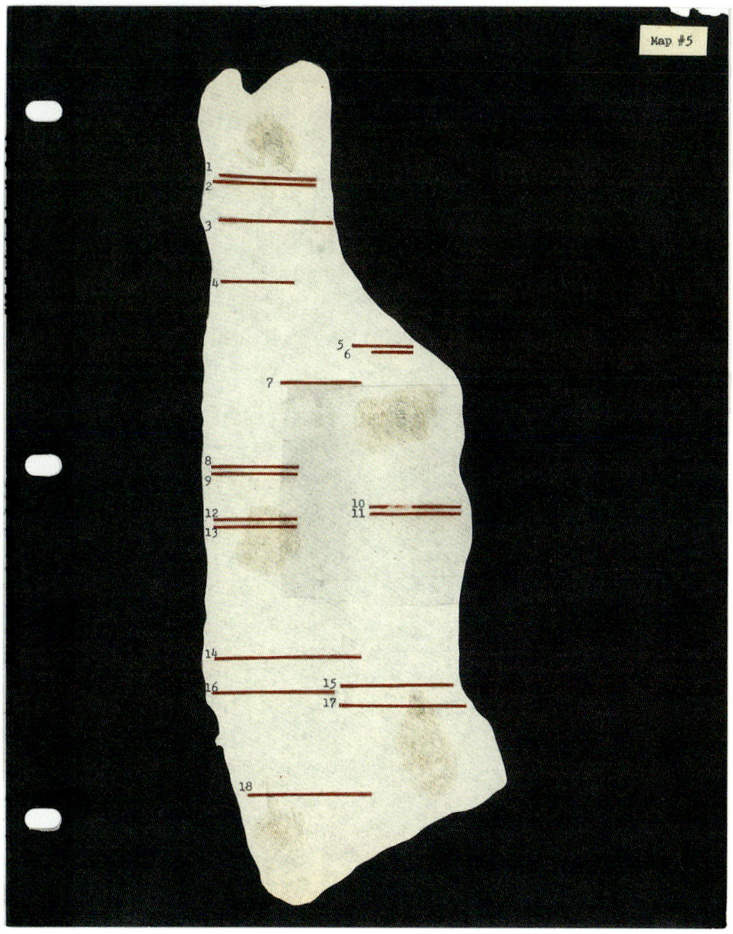

Untitled ("Maps schematizing different elements . . ."), 1–5/1969 (1969), in *Nine Abstract Space-Time-Infinity Pieces.*
Colored felt-tip pen on six maps mounted on colored paper; and two typescript pages

The top side of the following page represents a void space of undefined dimensions.

Over it is centered an area measuring 3 2/5 x 4 2/5 miles.

The top side of the preceding page represents a void space of undefined dimensions.

Over it is centered an area measuring 2 1/8 x 2 3/4 inches.

Untitled ("The top side of the following page . . .") and *Untitled ("The top side of the preceding* page . . .") (1969), in *Nine Abstract Space-Time-Infinity Pieces*. Two typescript pages

First page following: A 390 sq. mile area partially defining its surrounding void space.
Second page following: Underlying corrective

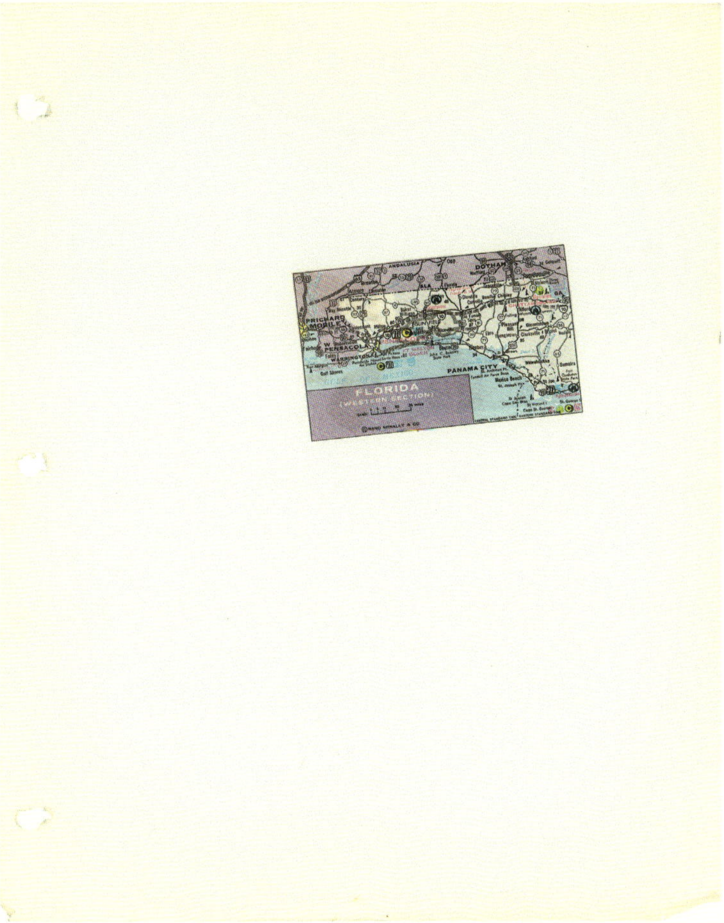

Untitled ("First page following . . .") (1969), in *Nine Abstract Space-Time-Infinity Pieces.*
Typescript page; and cut-and-pasted paper on onionskin paper over graph paper with text (graph paper not reproduced)

Proposal: to exhibit this piece whenever the opportunity presents itself.

Adrian Piper
February 10, 1969

Untitled ("Proposal: to exhibit this piece . . ."), (February 10, 1969) (1969), in *Nine Abstract Space-Time-Infinity Pieces*. Typescript page

Street Works: Friday, April 18, 1969, 5 - 6 PM
designated block: 13th - 14th Sts./5th - 6th Aves.

**Proposal #1
1. On Friday, April 11 from 4:30 to 6:30 PM, walk around outer sidewalk boundaries across the street from designated block.
Record 1200 ft. of tape at 1 7/8 IPS (two hours) of undifferentiated noise.
2. On Friday, April 18 from 5 to 6 PM, walk around inner sidewalk boundaries on designated block.
Play back previously-recorded undifferentiated noise at 3 3/4 IPS (one hour).

Proposal #2
I. Take one photo from each of the following locations with a polaroid camera:
#1 - four blocks N of designated block: S side of W. 18th St. between 5th and 6th Aves., midpoint of block.
#2 - four blocks E of designated block: W side of 3rd Ave. between E. 13th and 14th Sts., midpoint of block.
#3 - four blocks S of designated block: N side of W. 9th St. between 5th and 6th Aves., midpoint of block.
#4 - four blocks W of designated block: E side of Washington St. between E. 13th and 14th Sts., midpoint of block.
2. On Friday, April 18, at 5 PM, attach
photo #1 to S side W. 14th St. between 5th and 6th Aves. at midpoint of block.
" #2 to W side 5th Ave. between W. 13th and 14th Sts. " " " "
" #3 to N side W. 13th St. between 5th and 6th Aves. " " " "
" #4 to E side 6th Ave. between W. 13th and 14th Sts. " " " "

Proposal #3 (for nine participants)
participant #1: Bike around designated block from 5 to 6 PM.
" #2: Run " " " " " " " "
" #3: Walk " " " " " " " "
" #4: Bike " " " " 5:15 to 5:45 PM.
" #5: Run " " " " " " " "
" #6: Walk " " " " " " " "
" #7: Bike " " " " 5:22 to 5:38 PM.
" #8: Run " " " " " " " "
" #9: Walk " " " " " " " "

**Proposal #4
Distribute this page on 14th St. between 5th and 6th Aves. from 5 to 6 PM.

**Proposal #5
Locate designated block on a New York City streetmap. Divide block crosswise into four equal sections. Extend perpendicular lines to edges of map. Using lines as guide, cut map into four unequal rectangles. Each rectangle will contain one corner of designated block.
Indicate corner of block on each section of map. Identify each section of map by the location of that corner in space (NW, NE, SW, SE). Attach each section to corresponding corner of actual block.

Adrian Piper

** carried out

Untitled ("Street Works: Friday, April 18, 1969, 5-6 PM . . .") (1969), in *Nine Abstract Space-Time-Infinity Pieces*. Typescript page

<u>0 to 9</u>

	zero	4	////
/	one	3	///
//	two	3	///
///	three	5	/////
////	four	4	////
/////	five	4	////
//////	six	3	///
///////	seven	5	/////
////////	eight	5	/////
/////////	nine	4	////

0 to 9 (for Vito Acconci) (1969), in *Nineteen Concrete Space-Time-Infinity Pieces*. Typescript page

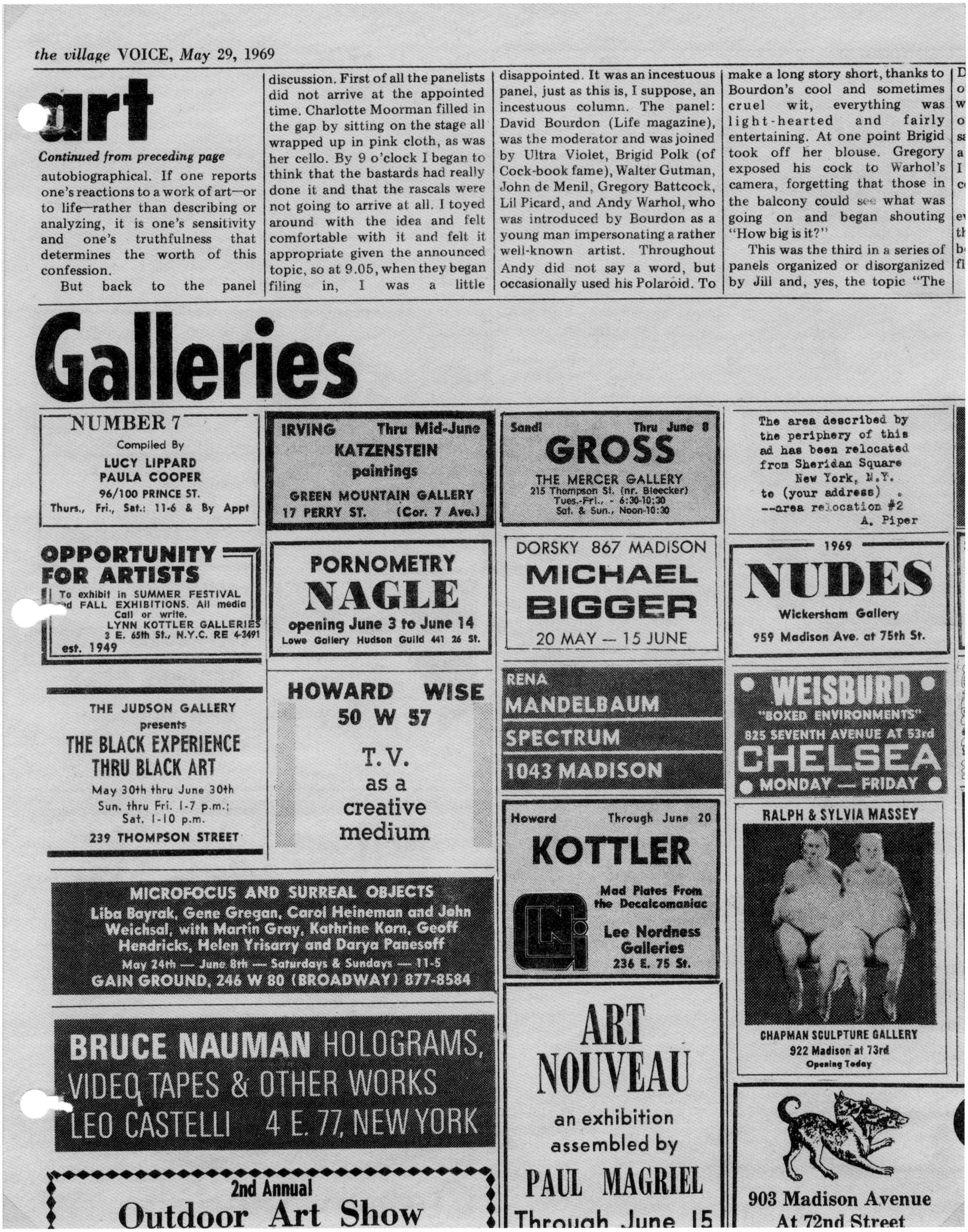

the village VOICE, *May* 29, 1969

art

Continued from preceding page

autobiographical. If one reports one's reactions to a work of art—or to life—rather than describing or analyzing, it is one's sensitivity and one's truthfulness that determines the worth of this confession.

But back to the panel discussion. First of all the panelists did not arrive at the appointed time. Charlotte Moorman filled in the gap by sitting on the stage all wrapped up in pink cloth, as was her cello. By 9 o'clock I began to think that the bastards had really done it and that the rascals were not going to arrive at all. I toyed around with the idea and felt comfortable with it and felt it appropriate given the announced topic, so at 9.05, when they began filing in, I was a little disappointed. It was an incestuous panel, just as this is, I suppose, an incestuous column. The panel: David Bourdon (Life magazine), was the moderator and was joined by Ultra Violet, Brigid Polk (of Cock-book fame), Walter Gutman, John de Menil, Gregory Battcock, Lil Picard, and Andy Warhol, who was introduced by Bourdon as a young man impersonating a rather well-known artist. Throughout Andy did not say a word, but occasionally used his Polaroid. To make a long story short, thanks to Bourdon's cool and sometimes cruel wit, everything was light-hearted and fairly entertaining. At one point Brigid took off her blouse. Gregory exposed his cock to Warhol's camera, forgetting that those in the balcony could see what was going on and began shouting "How big is it?"

This was the third in a series of panels organized or disorganized by Jill and, yes, the topic "The

Galleries

The area described by
the periphery of this
ad has been relocated
from Sheridan Square
New York, N.Y.
to (your address) .
--area relocation #2
A. Piper

Untitled ("The area described by the periphery of this ad . . .")/Area Relocation Series #2. 1969
Advertisement appearing in the *Village Voice*, May 29, 1969. Newspaper page
Approx. 10¹⁵⁄₁₆ × 8⅝ in. (27.8 × 21.9 cm)
Collection Adrian Piper Research Archive Foundation Berlin

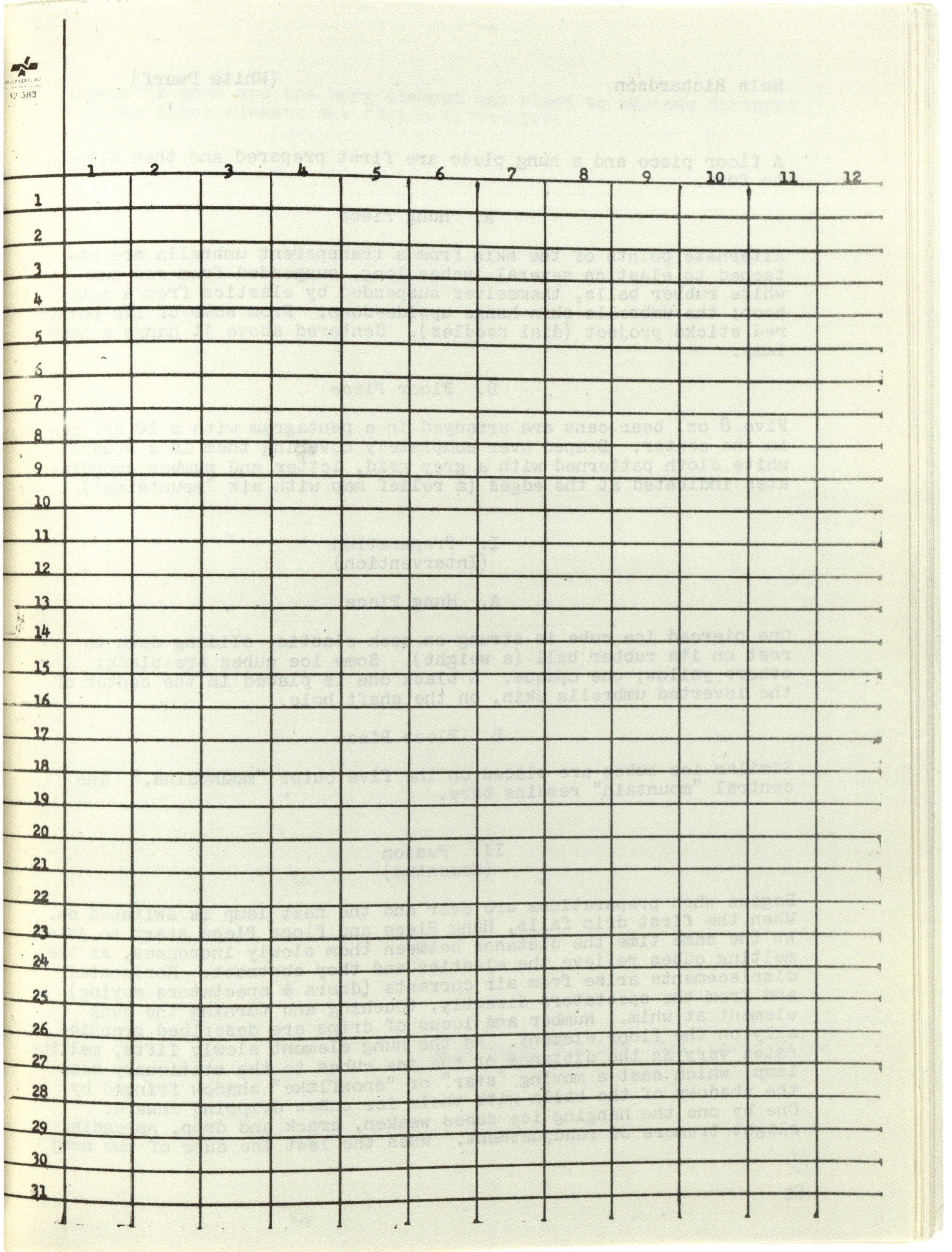

Untitled work in *0 TO 9* magazine, no. 6 (July 1969), p. 81
Edited by Bernadette Mayer and Vito Acconci
The Museum of Modern Art Library, New York

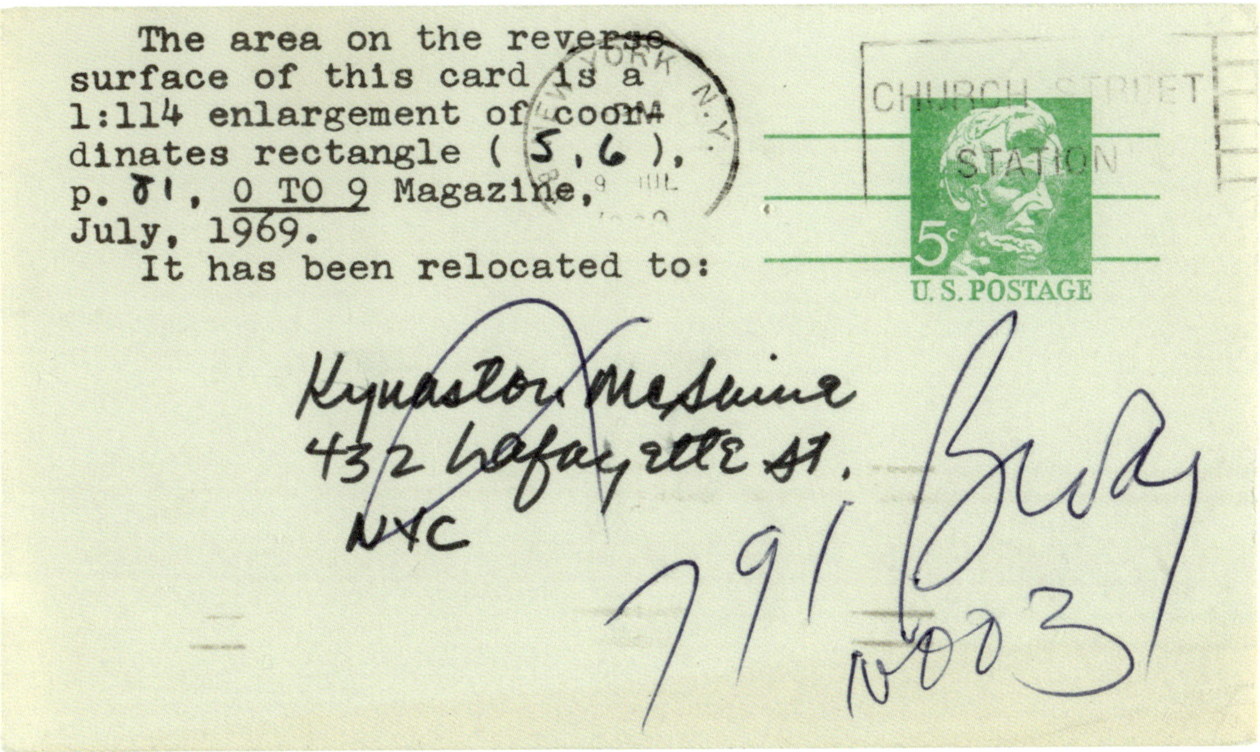

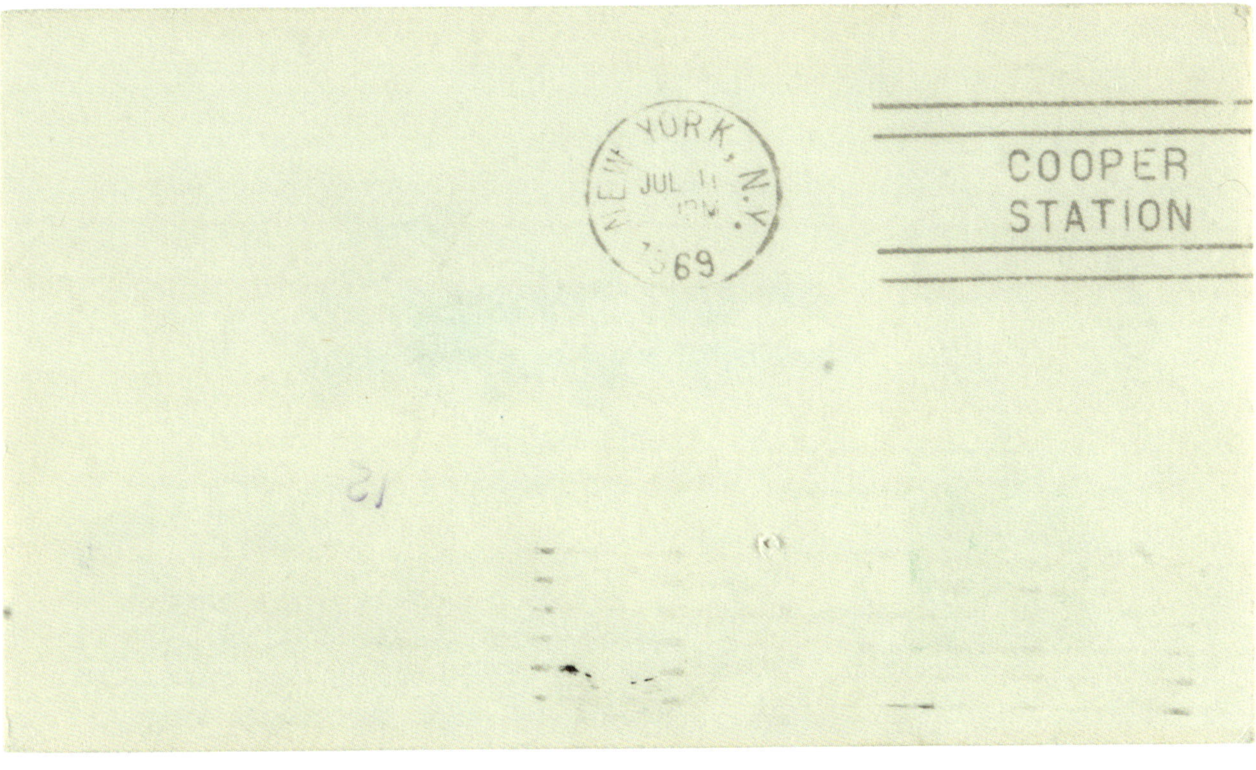

Untitled postcard from Adrian Piper to Kynaston McShine (recto and verso). July 1969
Felt-tip pen on photolithograph
3½ × 5 in. (8.9 × 12.7 cm)
The Museum of Modern Art Archives, New York

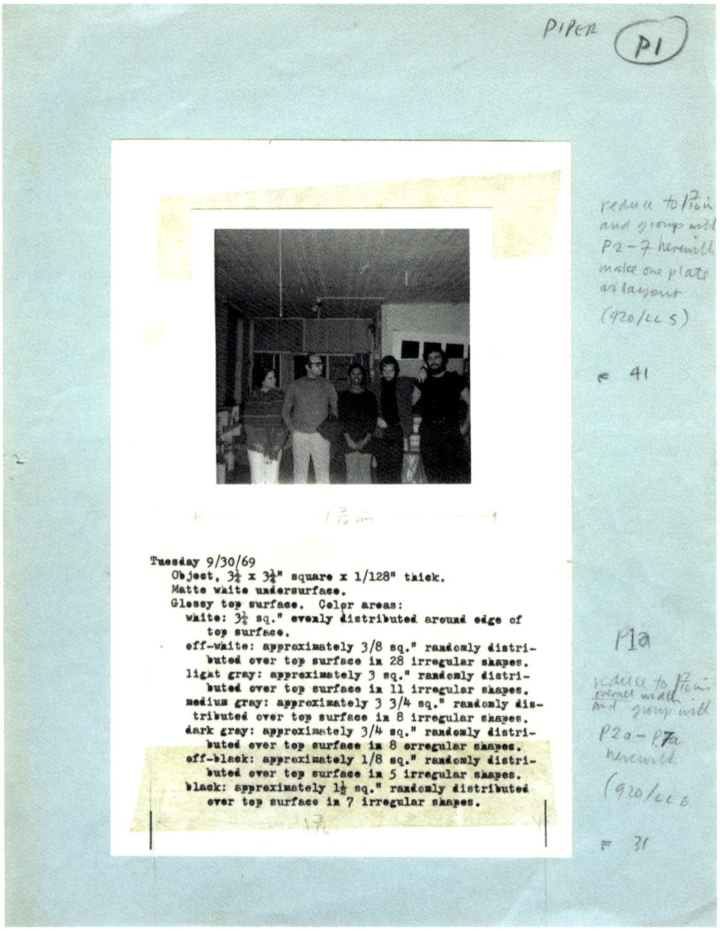

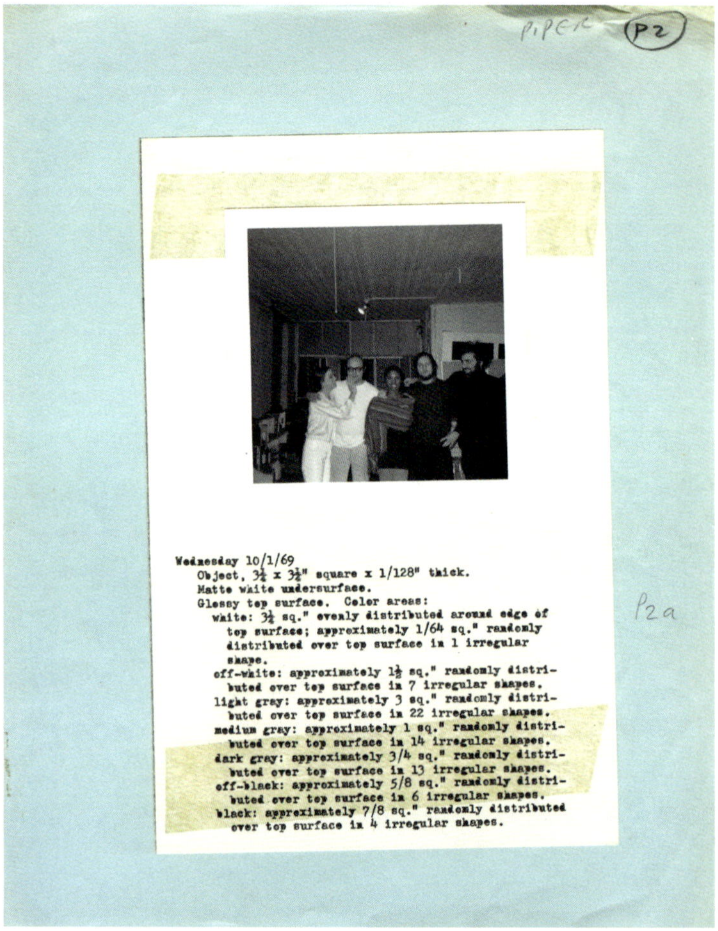

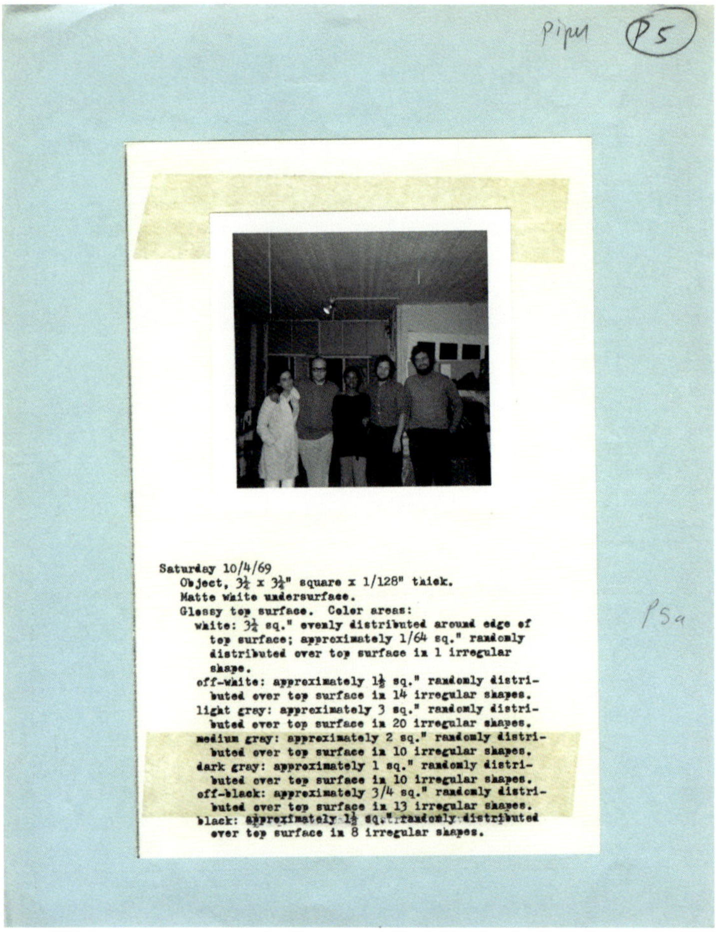

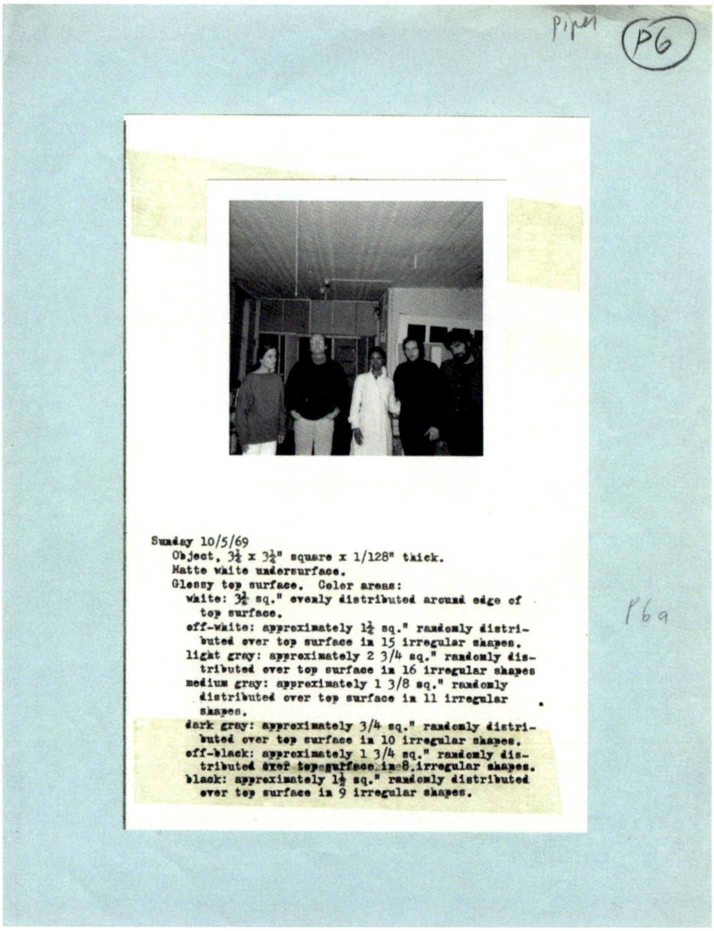

Untitled: Groups. 1969
Seven black-and-white photographs and texts with pencil on colored paper
11 × 8½ in. (27.9 × 21.6 cm)
Collection Adrian Piper Research Archive Foundation Berlin

Piper P3

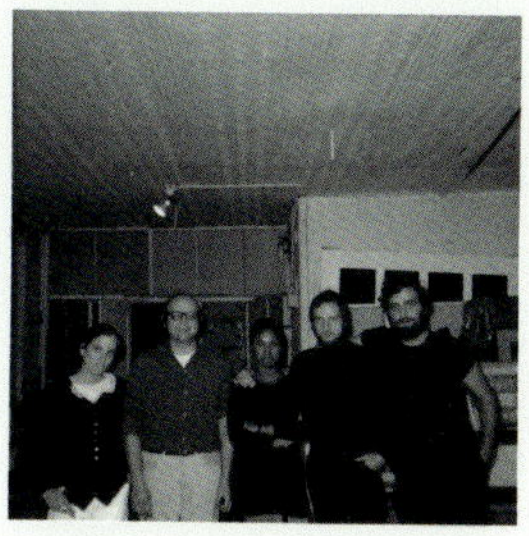

Thursday 10/2/69
Object, $3\frac{1}{4}$ x $3\frac{1}{4}$" square x 1/128" thick.
Matte white undersurface.
Glossy top surface. Color areas:
white: $3\frac{1}{4}$ sq." evenly distributed around edge of top surface; approximately 1/64 sq." randomly distributed over top surface in 1 irregular shape.
off-white: approximately 3/8 sq." randomly distributed over top surface in 15 irregular shapes.
light gray: approximately 3 sq." randomly distributed over top surface in 23 irregular shapes.
medium gray: approximately $\frac{1}{2}$ sq." randomly distributed over top surface in 5 irregular shapes.
dark gray: approximately 2 sq." randomly distributed over top surface in 12 irregular shapes.
off-black: approximately $\frac{1}{4}$ sq." randomly distributed over top surface in 5 irregular shapes.
black: approximately 3 sq." randomly distributed over top surface in 6 irregular shapes.

P3a

Piper P4

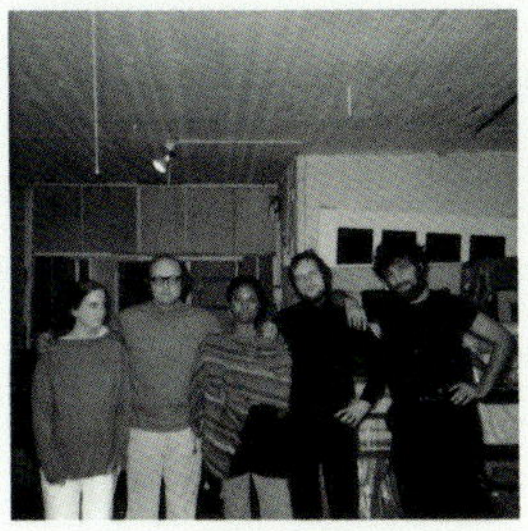

Friday 10/3/69
Object, $3\frac{1}{4}$ x $3\frac{1}{4}$" square x 1/128" thick.
Matte white undersurface.
Glossy top surface. Color areas:
white: $3\frac{1}{4}$ sq." evenly distributed around edge of top surface; approximately 1/64 sq." randomly distributed over top surface in 1 irregular shape.
off-white: approximately 3/4 sq." randomly distributed over top surface in 12 irregular shapes.
light gray: approximately $2\frac{1}{2}$ sq." randomly distributed over top surface in 12 irregular shapes.
medium gray: approximately $2\frac{1}{4}$ sq." randomly distributed over top surface in 8 irregular shapes.
dark gray: approximately $1\frac{1}{2}$ sq." randomly distributed over top surface in 8 irregular shapes.
off-black: approximately $\frac{1}{2}$ sq." randomly distributed over top surface in 9 irregular shapes.
black: approximately $2\frac{1}{2}$ sq." randomly distributed over top surface in 7 irregular shapes.

P4a

Piper P7

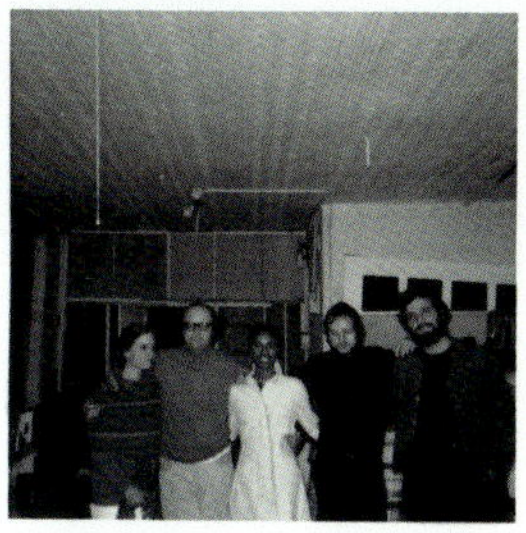

Monday 10/6/69
Object, $3\frac{1}{4}$ x $3\frac{1}{4}$" square x 1/128" thick.
Matte white undersurface.
Glossy top surface. Color areas:
white: $3\frac{1}{4}$ sq." evenly distributed around edge of top surface.
off-white: approximately $1\frac{1}{4}$ sq." randomly distributed over top surface in 16 irregular shapes.
light gray: approximately 3 3/4 sq." randomly distributed over top surface in 10 irregular shapes.
medium gray: approximately 2 sq." randomly distributed over top surface in 11 irregular shapes.
dark gray: approximately 3/4 sq." randomly distributed over top surface in 8 irregular shapes.
off-black: approximately 1 sq." randomly distributed over top surface in 9 irregular shapes.
black: approximately 1 sq." randomly distributed over top surface in 12 irregular shapes.

P7a

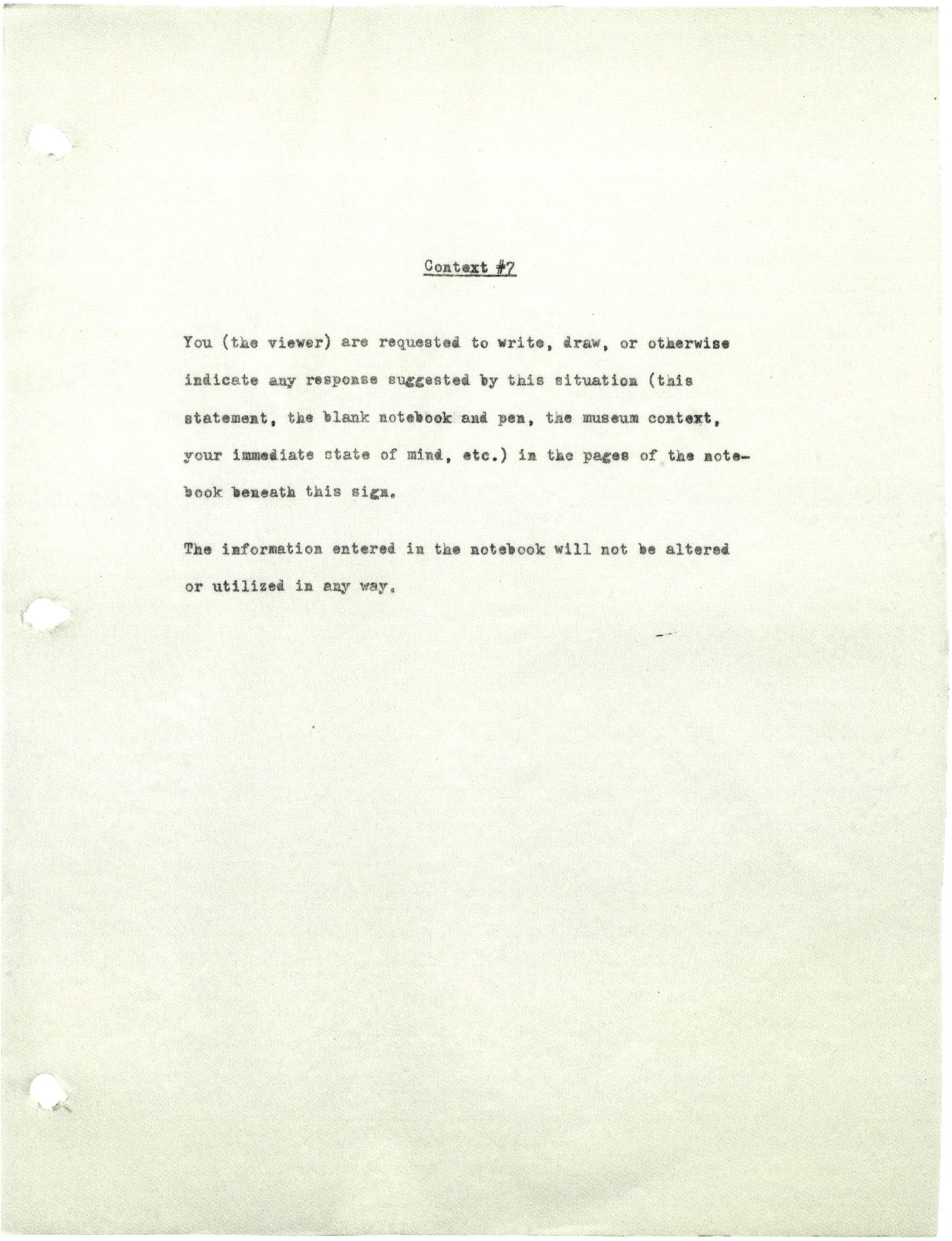

Context #7

You (the viewer) are requested to write, draw, or otherwise indicate any response suggested by this situation (this statement, the blank notebook and pen, the museum context, your immediate state of mind, etc.) in the pages of the notebook beneath this sign.

The information entered in the notebook will not be altered or utilized in any way.

Context #7. 1970
Seven ring binders with typescript page and ink, pencil, crayon, postage stamps, photographs, and sugar package on paper
Each binder 11¾ × 11 × 3 in. (29.8 × 27.9 × 7.6 cm)
Walker Art Center, Minneapolis. T. B. Walker Acquisition Fund
Detail: frontispiece

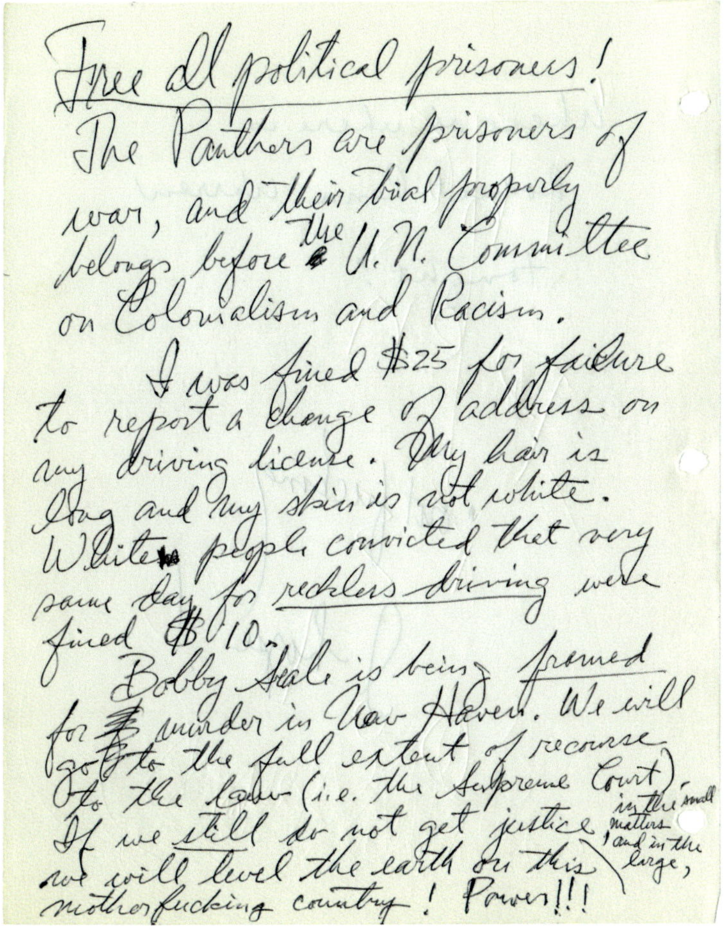

Free all political prisoners!
The Panthers are prisoners of war, and their trial properly belongs before the U.N. Committee on Colonialism and Racism.

I was fined $25 for failure to report a change of address on my driving license. My hair is long and my skin is not white. White people convicted that very same day for reckless driving were fined $10.

Bobby Seale is being framed for murder in New Haven. We will go to the full extent of recourse to the law (i.e. the Supreme Court). If we still do not get justice, in the small matters and in the large, we will level the earth on this motherfucking country! Power!!!

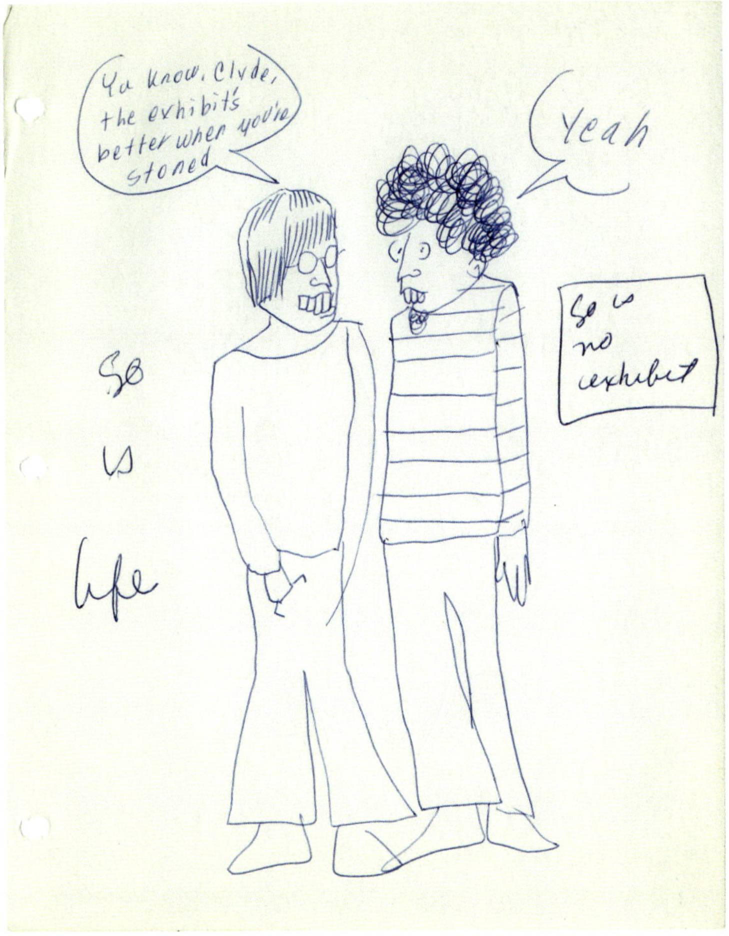

Details:
Untitled ("Free all political prisoners! . . .")
Untitled ("You know, Clyde . . .")

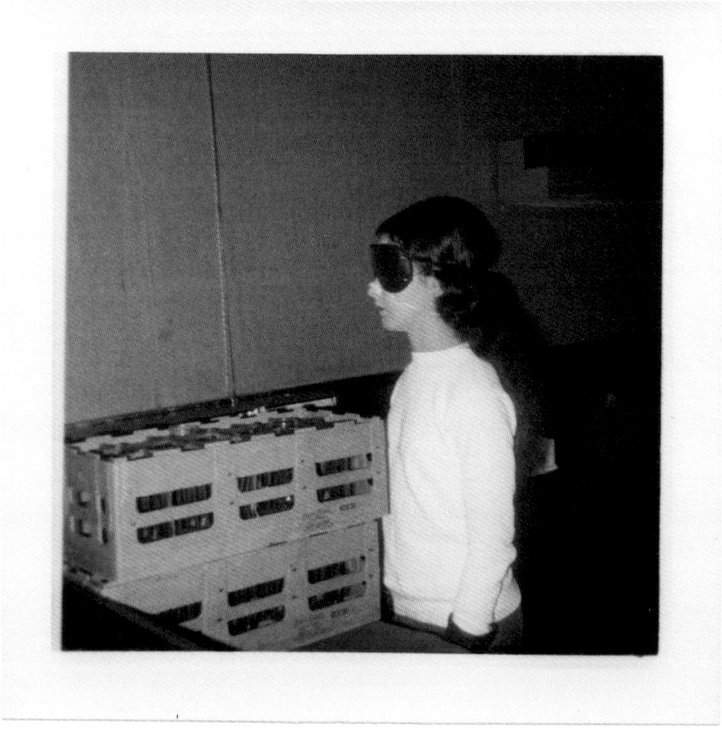

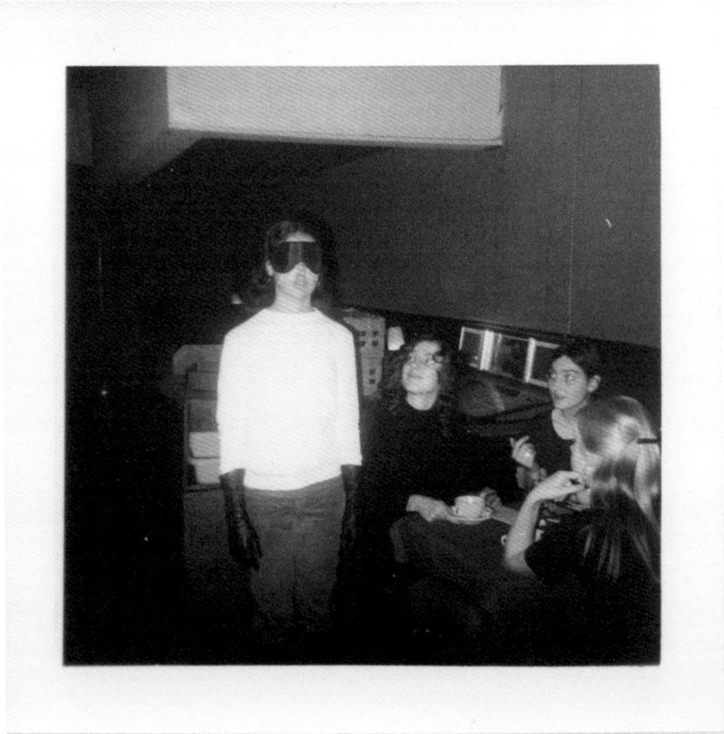

Untitled Performance at Max's Kansas City. 1970
Documentation of the performance. Four gelatin silver prints
Each 3⁹⁄₁₆ × 3⁹⁄₁₆ in. (9 × 9 cm)
Photographs by Rosemary Mayer
Collection Adrian Piper Research Archive Foundation Berlin

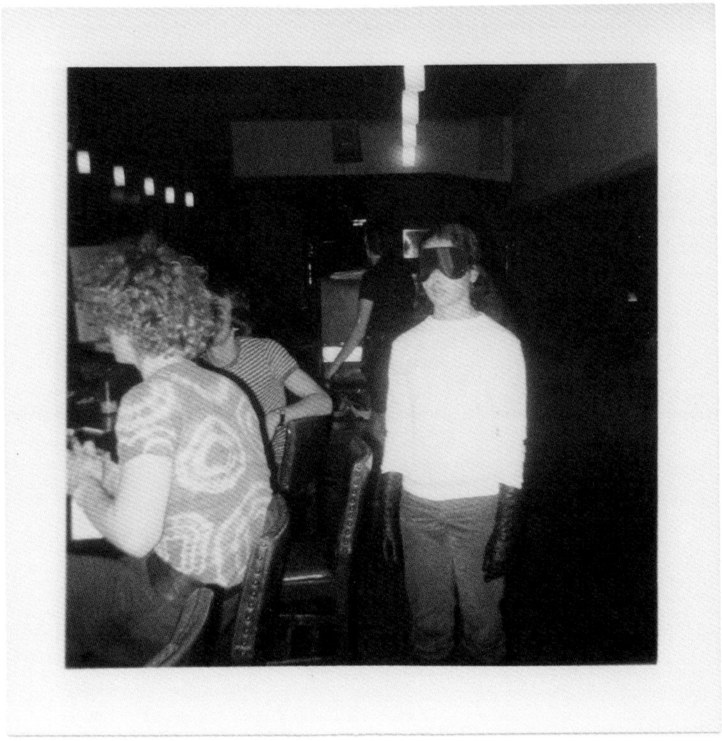

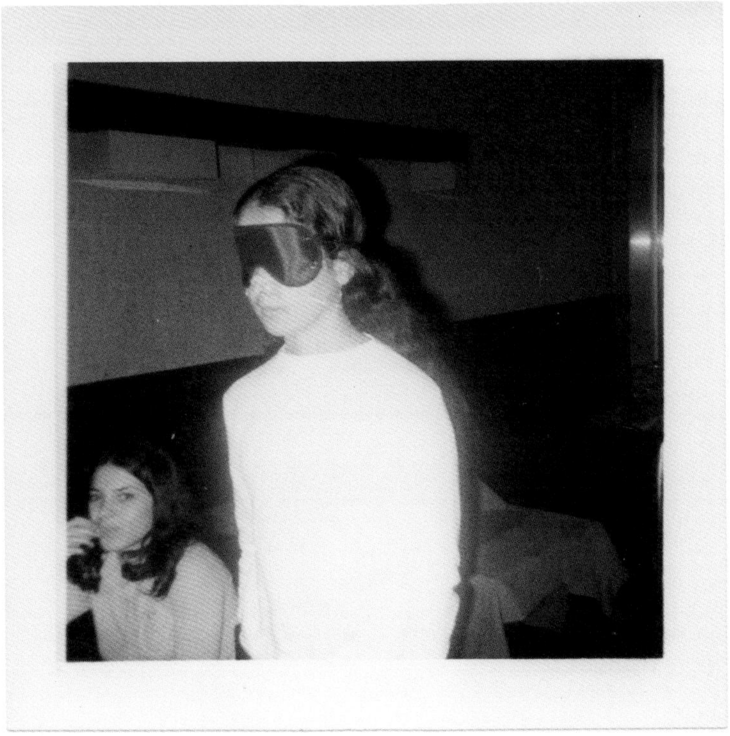

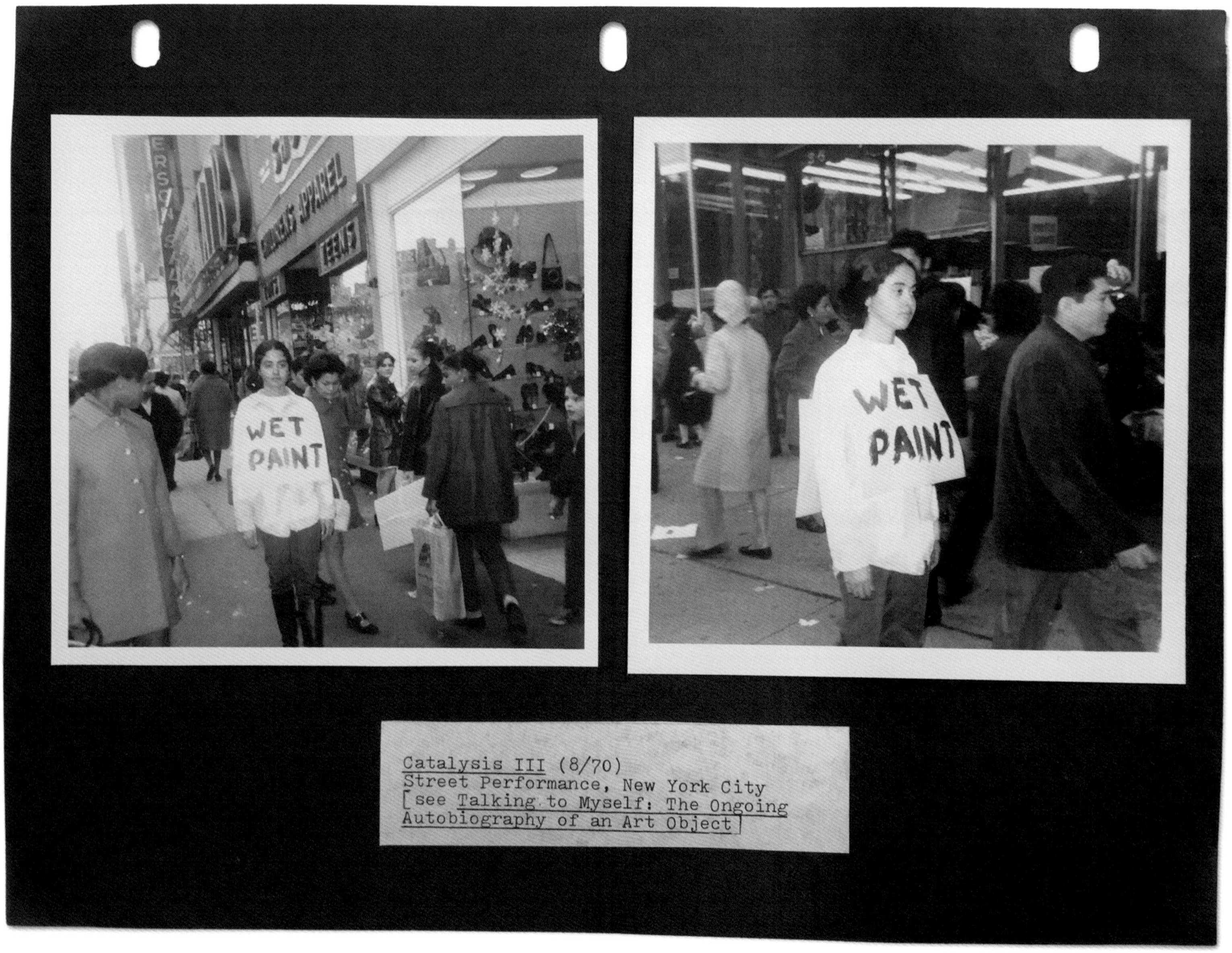

Catalysis III. 1970
Documentation of the performance.
Two gelatin silver prints and text mounted on colored paper
Overall 8½ × 11 in. (21.6 × 27.9 cm)
Photographs by Rosemary Mayer
Collection Thomas Erben, New York

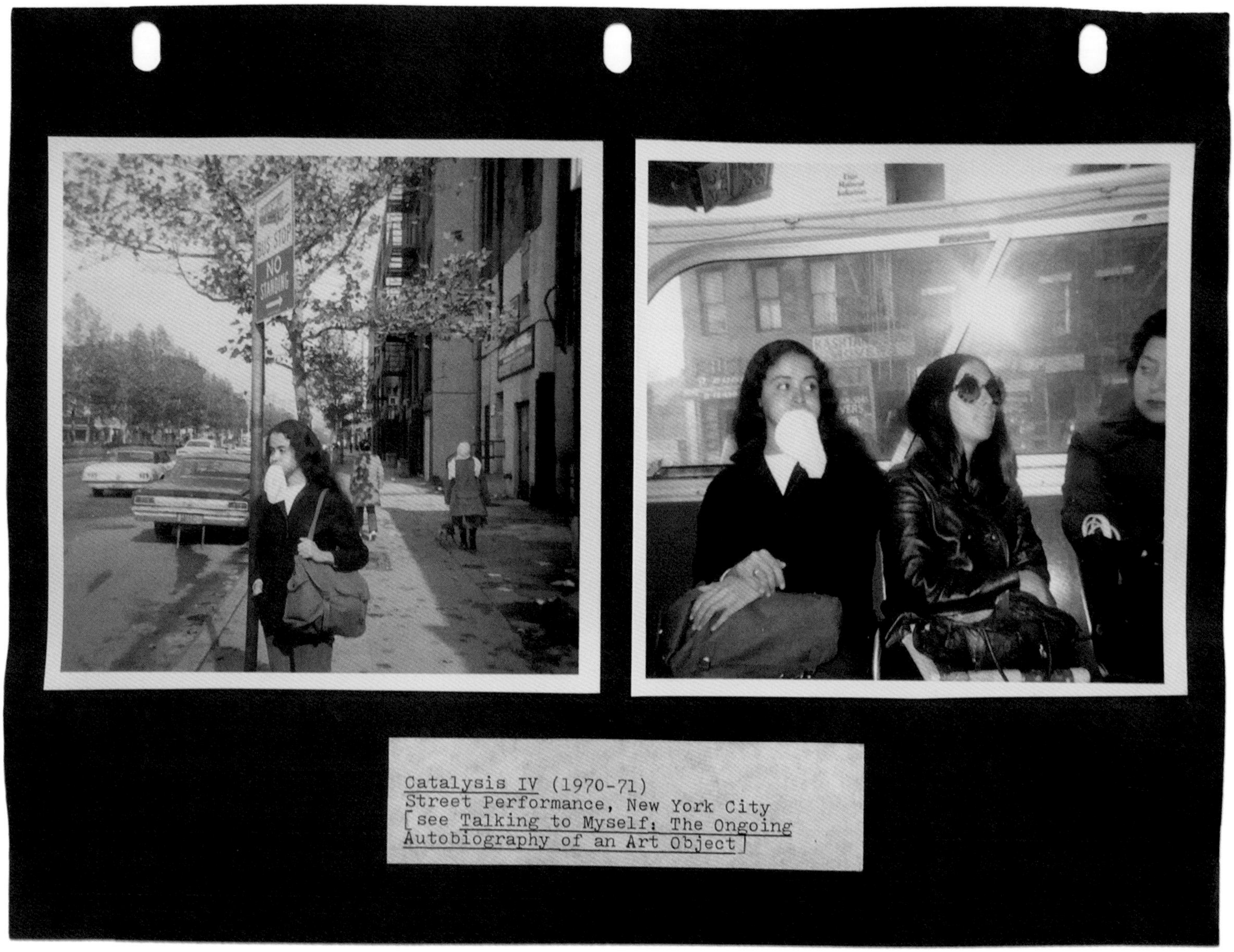

Catalysis IV. 1970
Documentation of the performance.
Two gelatin silver prints and text mounted on colored paper
Overall 8½ × 11 in. (21.6 × 27.9 cm)
Photographs by Rosemary Mayer
Collection Thomas Erben, New York

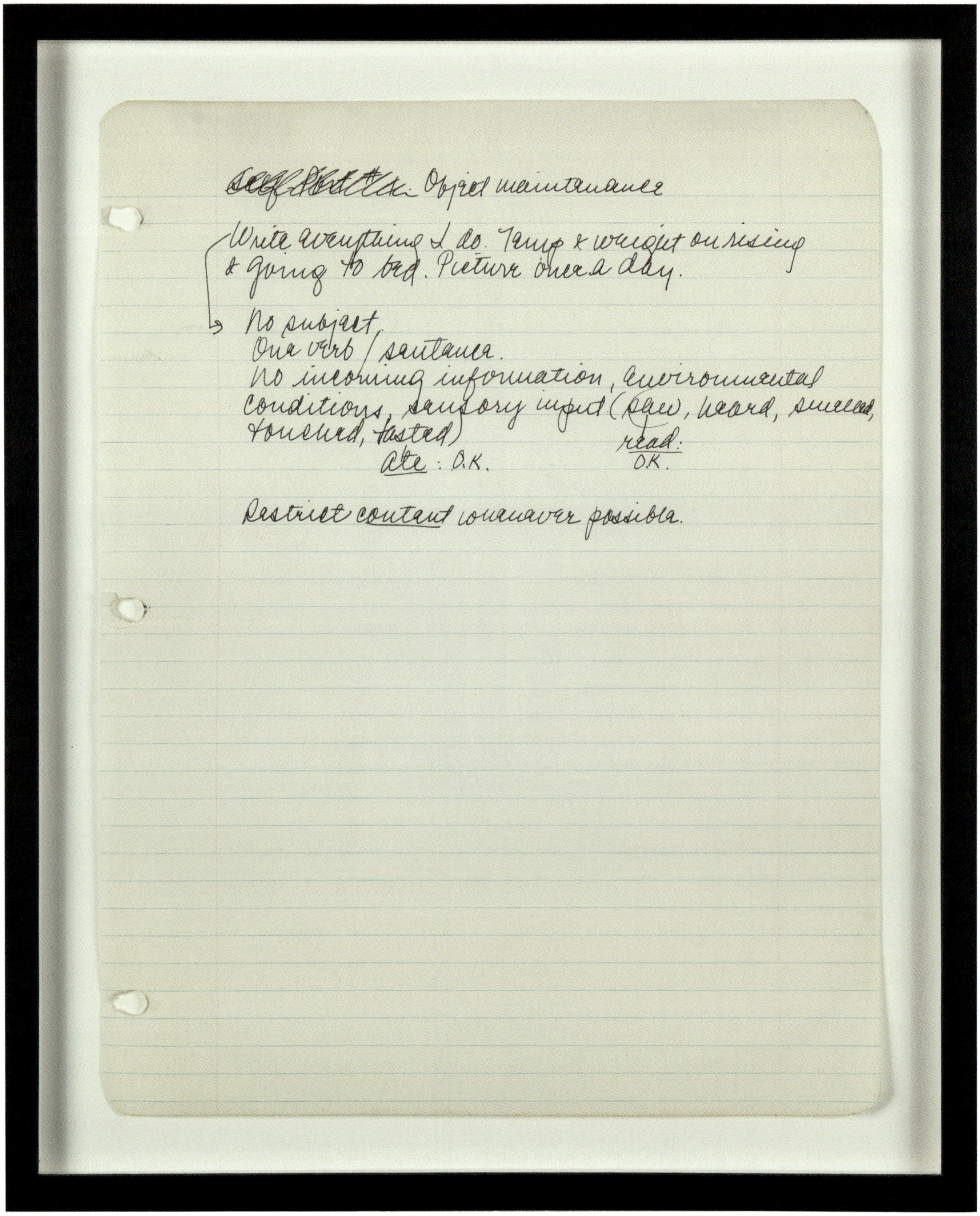

~~Self Portrait~~ Object maintenance

Write everything I do. Temp & weight on rising & going to bed. Picture once a day.

No subject.
One verb / sentence.
No incoming information, environmental conditions, sensory input (saw, heard, smelled, touched, tasted)

ate: O.K.   read: O.K.

Restrict content whenever possible.

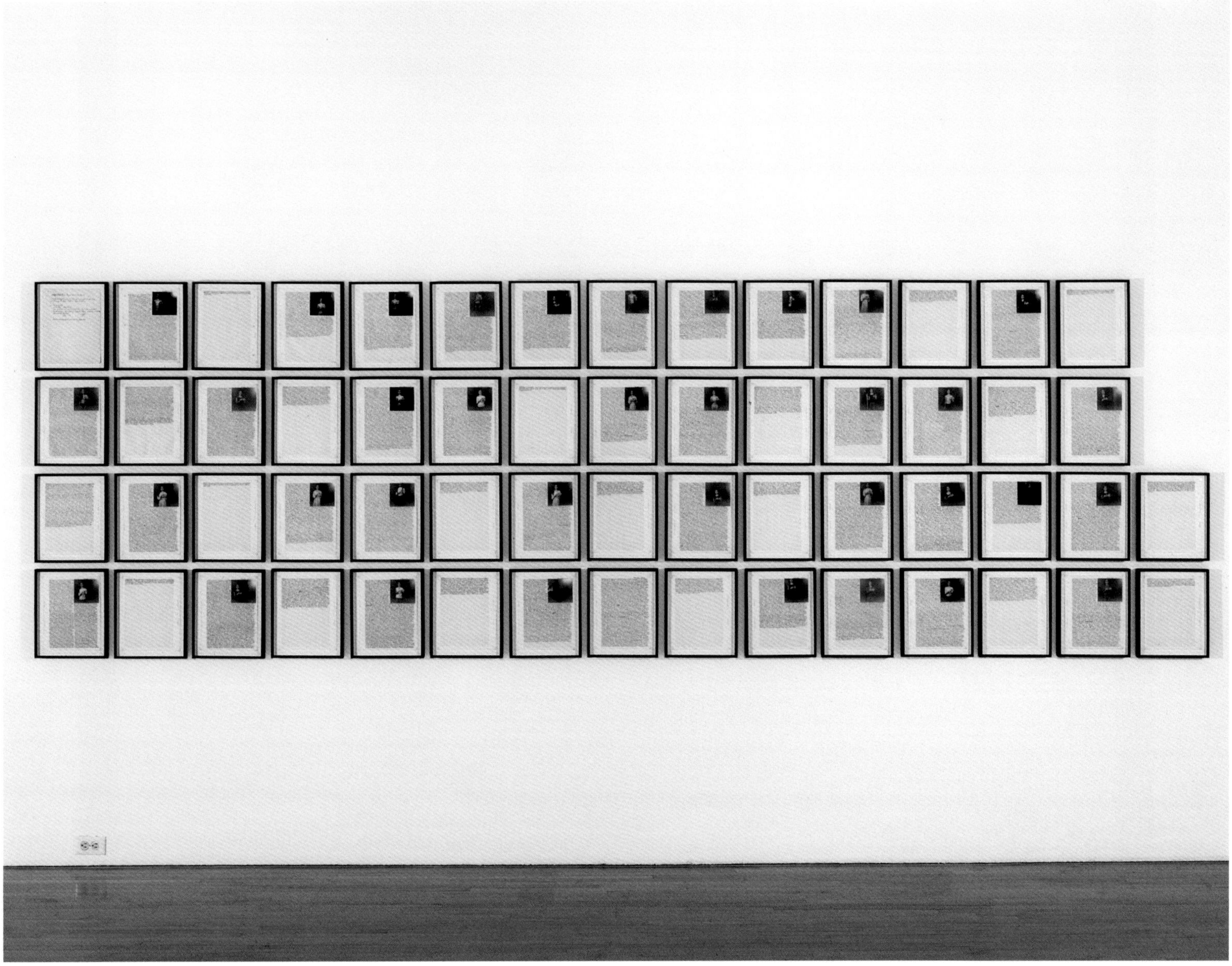

Concrete Infinity Documentation Piece. 1970
Handwritten text on notebook paper; and black-and-white photographs and handwritten text on fifty-six sheets of graph paper
Each sheet 10¾ × 8½ in. (27.3 × 21.6 cm)
The Museum of Contemporary Art, Los Angeles. Purchased with funds provided by the Drawings Committee
Detail (left): *Untitled ("Object maintenance")*

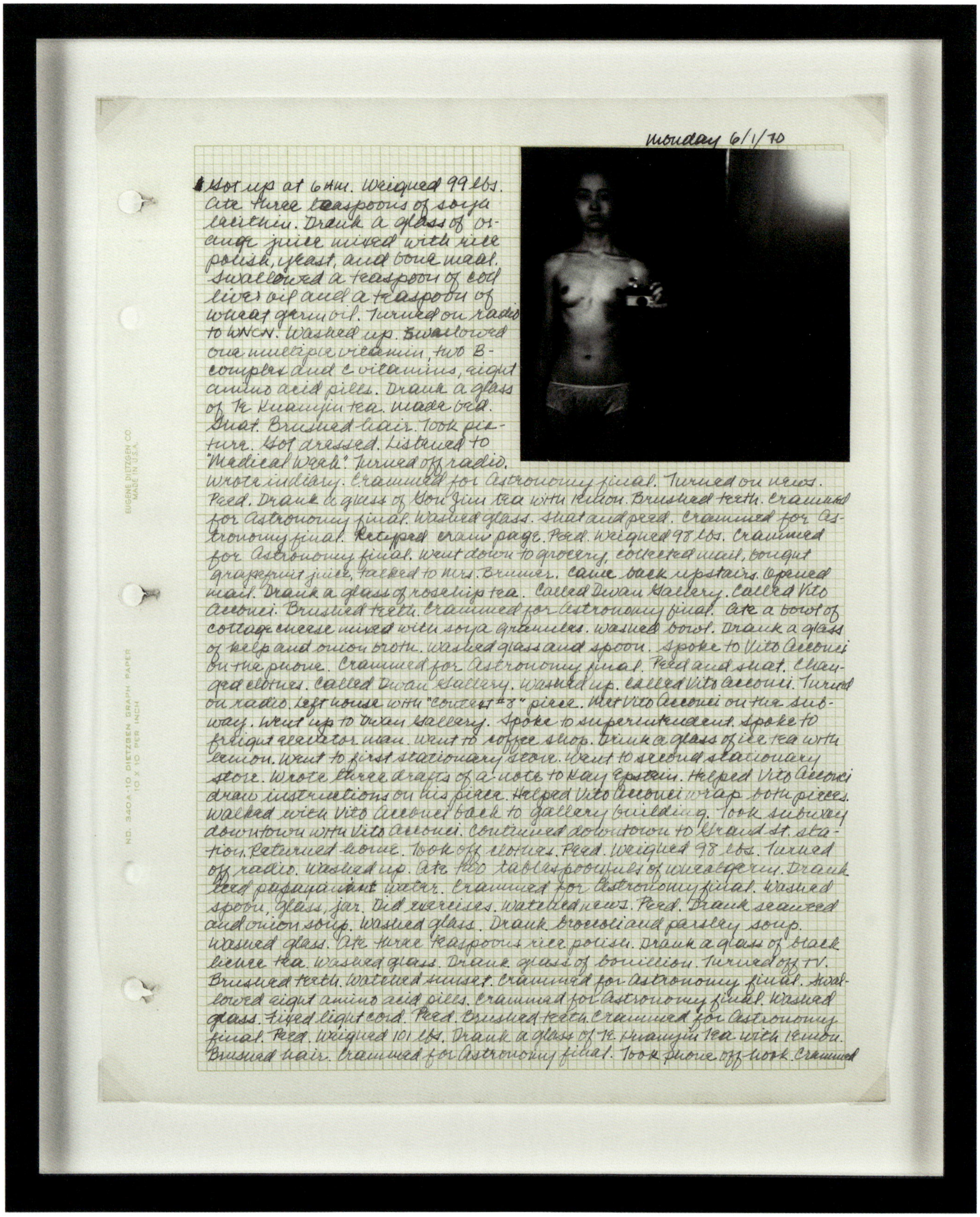

Monday 6/1/70

Got up at 6 AM. Weighed 99 lbs. Ate three teaspoons of soya lecithin. Drank a glass of orange juice mixed with rice polish, yeast, and bone meal. Swallowed a teaspoon of cod liver oil and a teaspoon of wheat germ oil. Turned on radio to WNCN. Washed up. Swallowed one multiple vitamin, two B-complex and C vitamins, eight amino acid pills. Drank a glass of Te Kuanyin tea. Made bed. Shat. Brushed hair. Took picture. Got dressed. Listened to "Medical Week." Turned off radio. Wrote in diary. Crammed for Astronomy final. Turned on news. Peed. Drank a glass of Hon Jim tea with lemon. Brushed teeth. Crammed for Astronomy final. Washed glass. Shat and peed. Crammed for Astronomy final. Retyped exam page. Peed. Weighed 98 lbs. Crammed for Astronomy final. Went down to grocery, collected mail, bought grapefruit juice, talked to Mrs. Brunner. Came back upstairs. Opened mail. Drank a glass of rosehip tea. Called Dwan Gallery. Called Vito Acconci. Brushed teeth. Crammed for Astronomy final. Ate a bowl of cottage cheese mixed with soya granules. Washed bowl. Drank a glass of kelp and onion broth. Washed glass and spoon. Spoke to Vito Acconci on the phone. Crammed for Astronomy final. Peed and shat. Changed clothes. Called Dwan Gallery. Washed up. Called Vito Acconci. Turned on radio. Left house with "Context #8" piece. Met Vito Acconci on the subway. Went up to Dwan Gallery. Spoke to superintendent. Spoke to freight elevator man. Went to coffee shop. Drank a glass of ice tea with lemon. Went to first stationary store. Went to second stationary store. Wrote three drafts of a note to Kay Epstein. Helped Vito Acconci draw instructions on his piece. Helped Vito Acconci wrap both pieces. Walked with Vito Acconci back to gallery building. Took subway downtown with Vito Acconci. Continued downtown to Grand St. station. Returned home. Took off clothes. Peed. Weighed 98 lbs. Turned off radio. Washed up. Ate two tablespoonfuls of wheatgerm. Drank iced papaya mint water. Crammed for Astronomy final. Washed spoon, glass, jar. Did exercises. Watched news. Peed. Drank seaweed and onion soup. Washed glass. Drank broccoli and parsley soup. Washed glass. Ate three teaspoons rice polish. Drank a glass of black licorice tea. Washed glass. Drank glass of bouillion. Turned off TV. Brushed teeth. Watched sunset. Crammed for Astronomy final. Swallowed eight amino acid pills. Crammed for Astronomy final. Washed glass. Fixed light cord. Peed. Brushed teeth. Crammed for Astronomy final. Peed. Weighed 101 lbs. Drank a glass of Te Kuanyin tea with lemon. Brushed hair. Crammed for Astronomy final. Took phone off hook. Crammed

EUGENE DIETZGEN CO. MADE IN U.S.A.

NO. 340A-10 DIETZGEN GRAPH PAPER 10 X 10 PER INCH

Concrete Infinity Documentation Piece. 1970 (see page 183)
Details: *Untitled ("Monday 6/1/70"), first page* and *Untitled ("Monday 6/1/70"), second page*

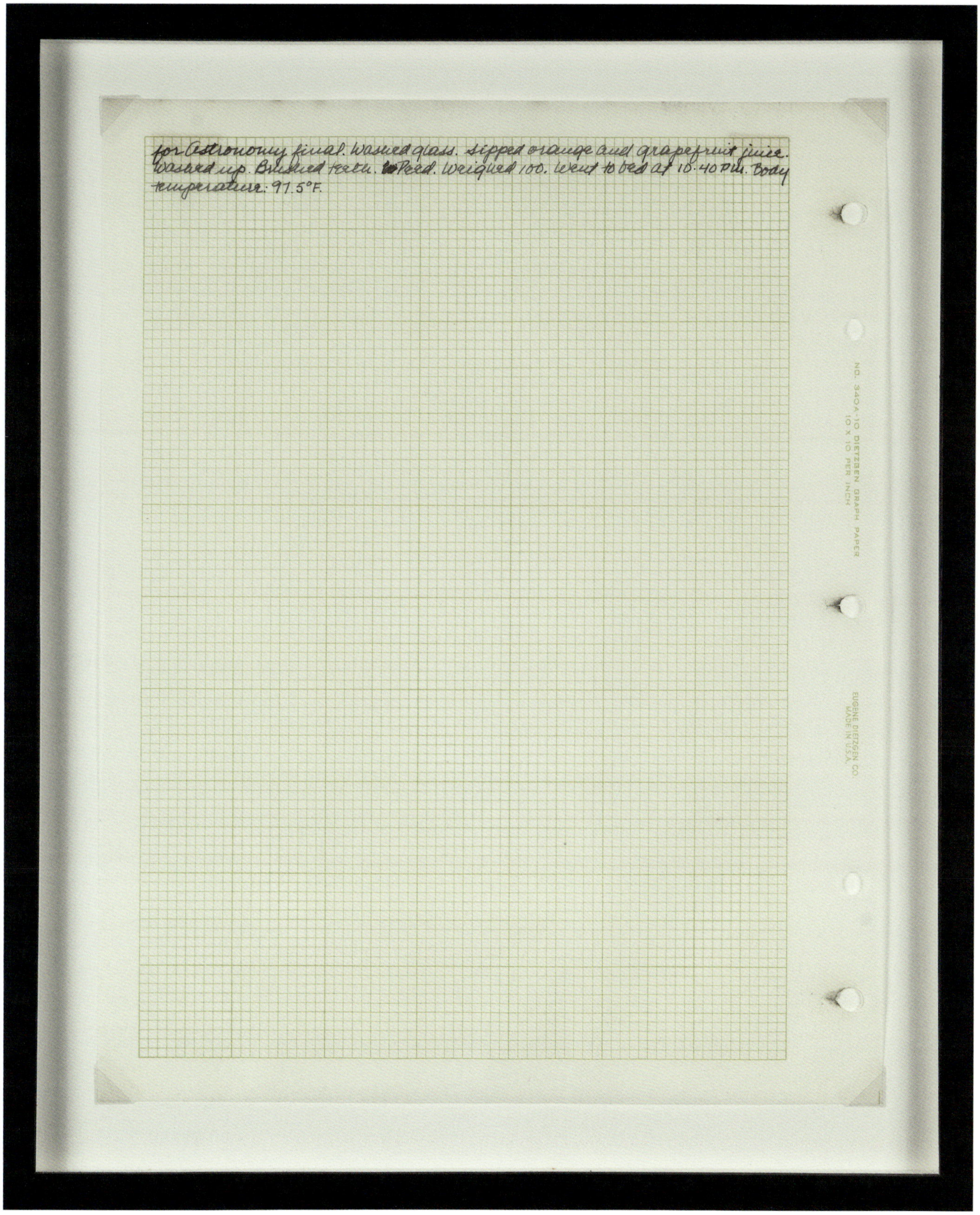
for Astronomy final. Washed glass. Sipped orange and grapefruit juice.
Washed up. Brushed teeth. Peed. Weighed 100. Went to bed at 10:40 P.M. Body
temperature: 97.5°F.
NO. 340A-10 DIETZGEN GRAPH PAPER
10 X 10 PER INCH
EUGENE DIETZGEN CO.
MADE IN U.S.A.

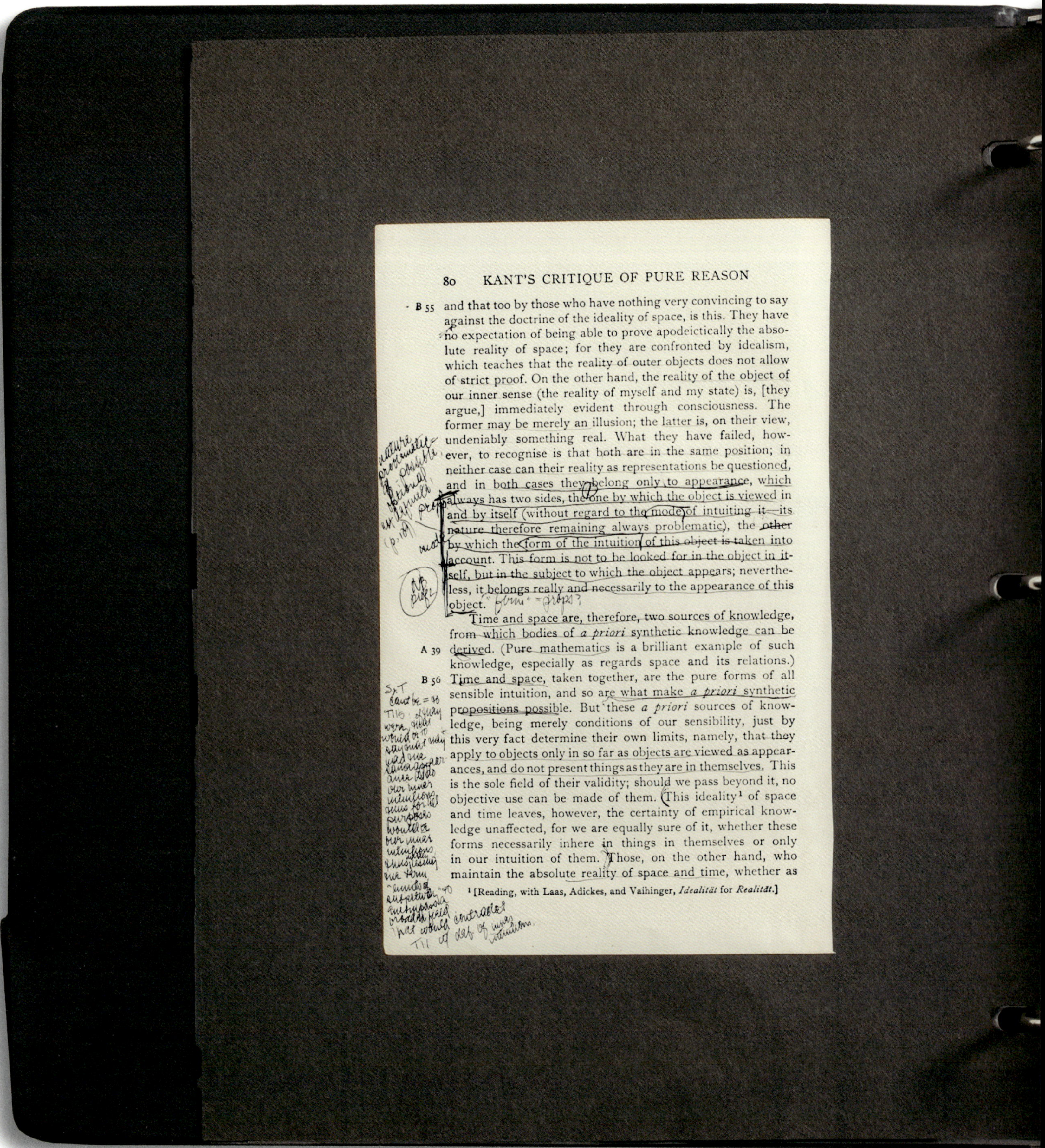

80 KANT'S CRITIQUE OF PURE REASON

B 55 and that too by those who have nothing very convincing to say against the doctrine of the ideality of space, is this. They have no expectation of being able to prove apodeictically the absolute reality of space; for they are confronted by idealism, which teaches that the reality of outer objects does not allow of strict proof. On the other hand, the reality of the object of our inner sense (the reality of myself and my state) is, [they argue,] immediately evident through consciousness. The former may be merely an illusion; the latter is, on their view, undeniably something real. What they have failed, however, to recognise is that both are in the same position; in neither case can their reality as representations be questioned, and in both cases they belong only to appearance, which always has two sides, the one by which the object is viewed in and by itself (without regard to the mode of intuiting it—its nature therefore remaining always problematic), the other by which the form of the intuition of this object is taken into account. This form is not to be looked for in the object in itself, but in the subject to which the object appears; nevertheless, it belongs really and necessarily to the appearance of this object.

Time and space are, therefore, two sources of knowledge, from which bodies of *a priori* synthetic knowledge can be
A 39 derived. (Pure mathematics is a brilliant example of such knowledge, especially as regards space and its relations.)
B 56 Time and space, taken together, are the pure forms of all sensible intuition, and so are what make *a priori* synthetic propositions possible. But these *a priori* sources of knowledge, being merely conditions of our sensibility, just by this very fact determine their own limits, namely, that they apply to objects only in so far as objects are viewed as appearances, and do not present things as they are in themselves. This is the sole field of their validity; should we pass beyond it, no objective use can be made of them. This ideality[1] of space and time leaves, however, the certainty of empirical knowledge unaffected, for we are equally sure of it, whether these forms necessarily inhere in things in themselves or only in our intuition of them. Those, on the other hand, who maintain the absolute reality of space and time, whether as

[1] [Reading, with Laas, Adickes, and Vaihinger, *Idealität* for *Realität*.]

Food for the Spirit. 1971
Ring binder with fourteen gelatin silver prints and forty-four annotated pages torn from a paperback edition of Immanuel Kant's *Critique of Pure Reason*, mounted on colored paper, in plastic sleeves
Binder 11½ × 10 × 1½ in. (29.2 × 25.4 × 3.8 cm)
Collection Thomas Erben, New York
Detail: pages 4 and 5

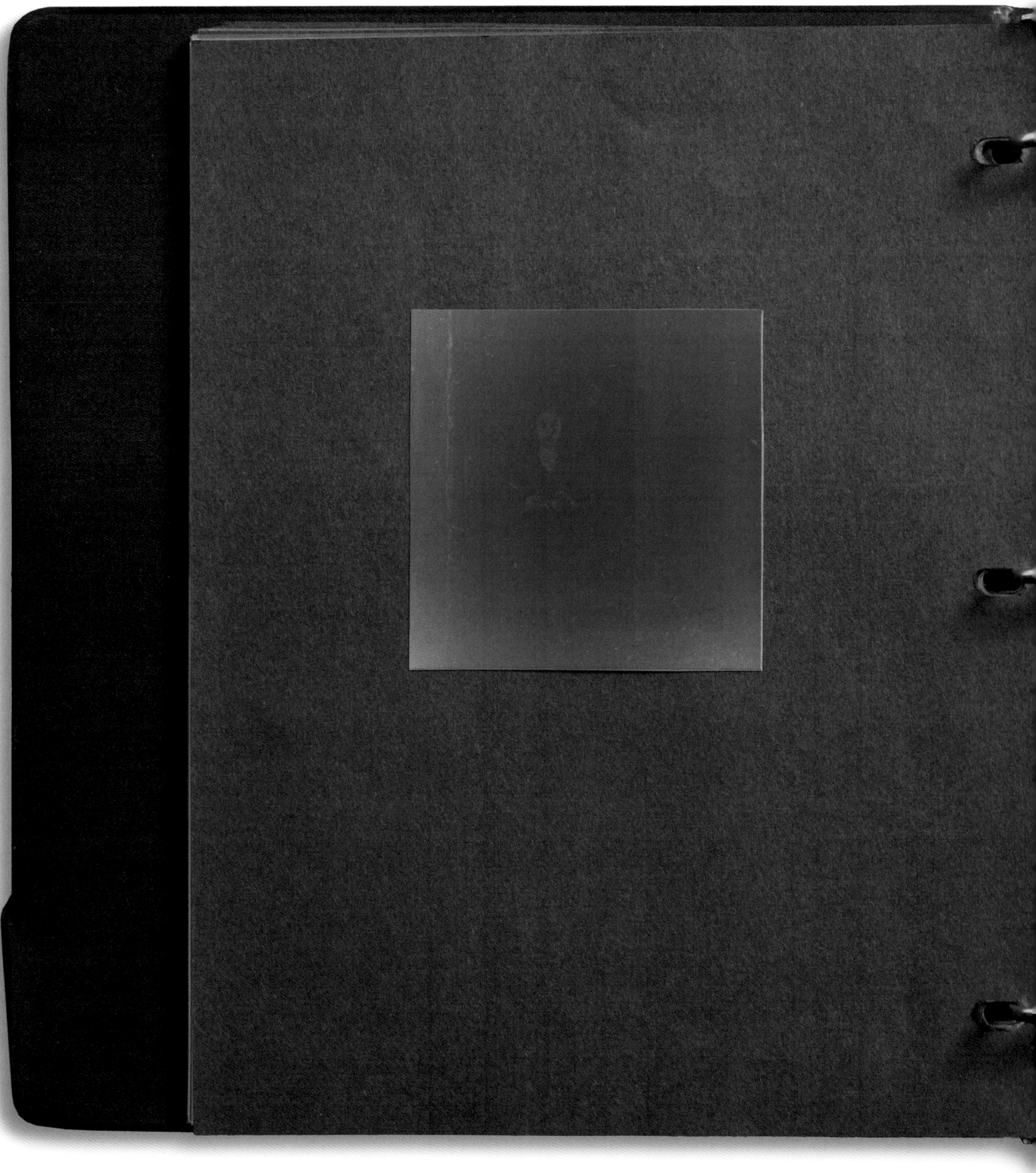

Food for the Spirit. 1971 (see page 186)
Detail: pages 24 and 25

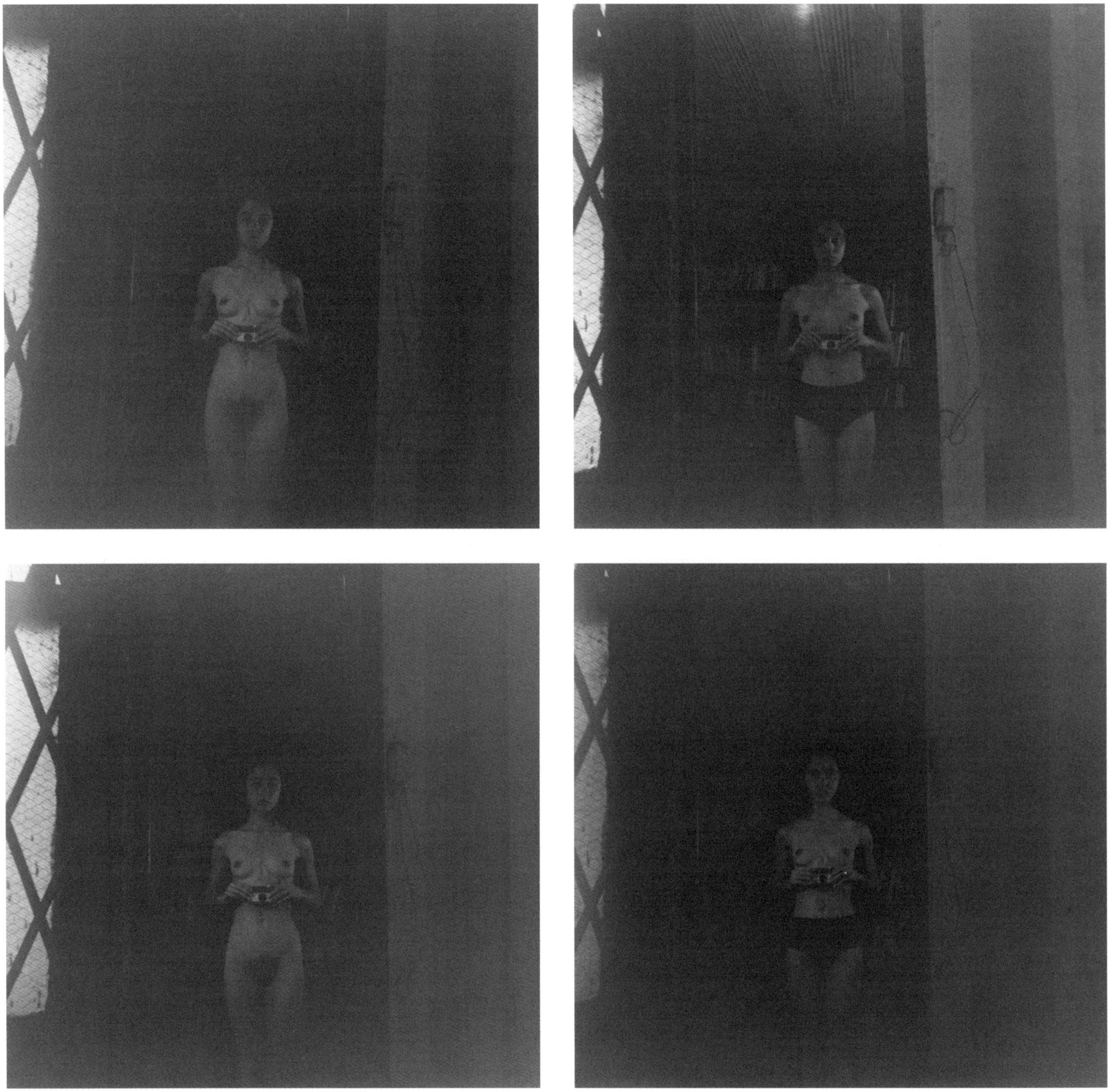

Food for the Spirit. 1971
Fourteen gelatin silver prints (reprinted 1997)
Each $14\frac{9}{16} \times 14\frac{13}{16}$ in. (37 × 37.7 cm)
The Museum of Modern Art, New York. The Family of Man Fund

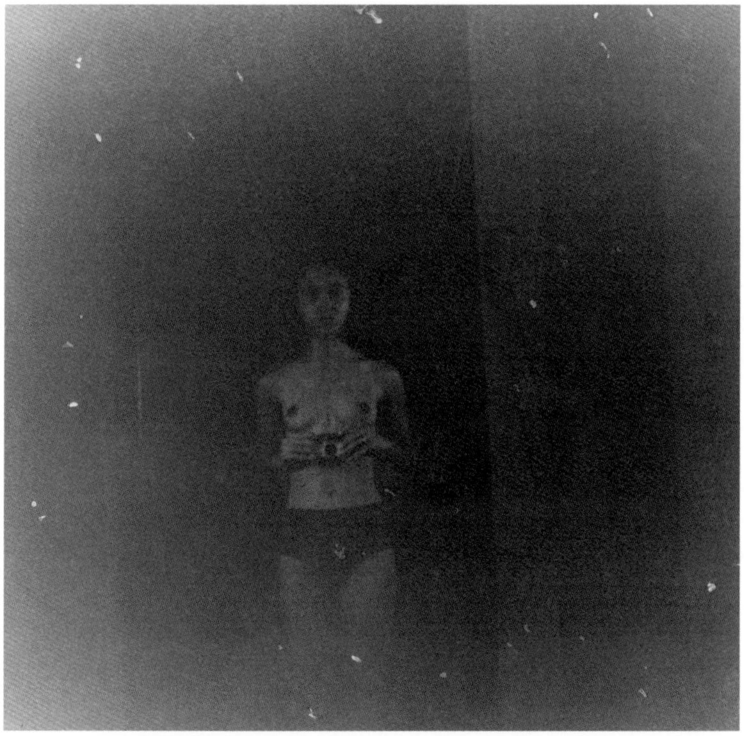

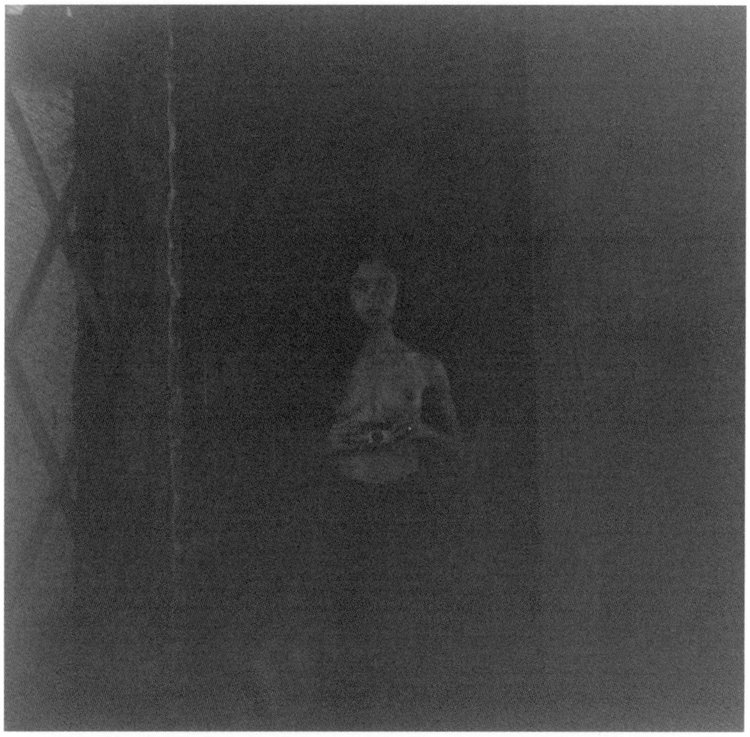

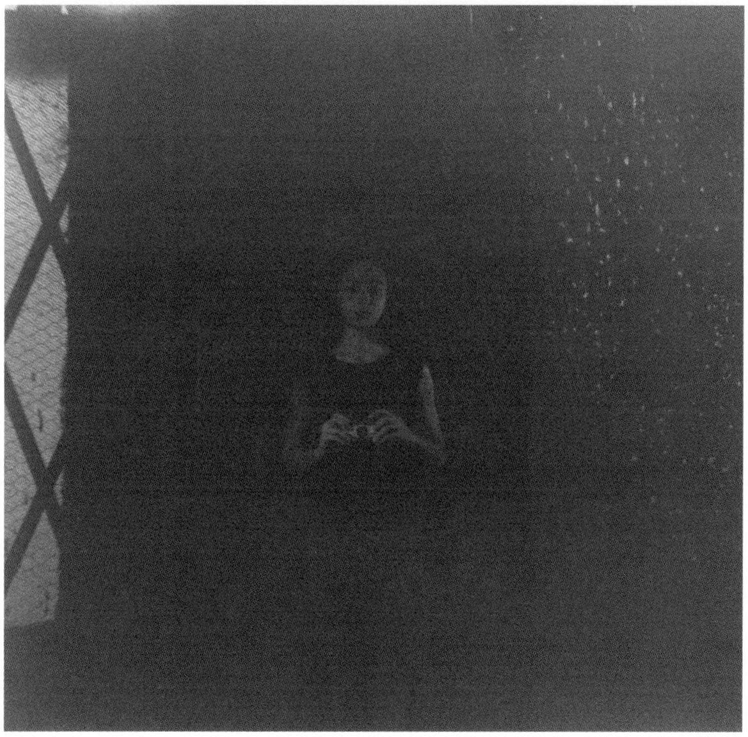

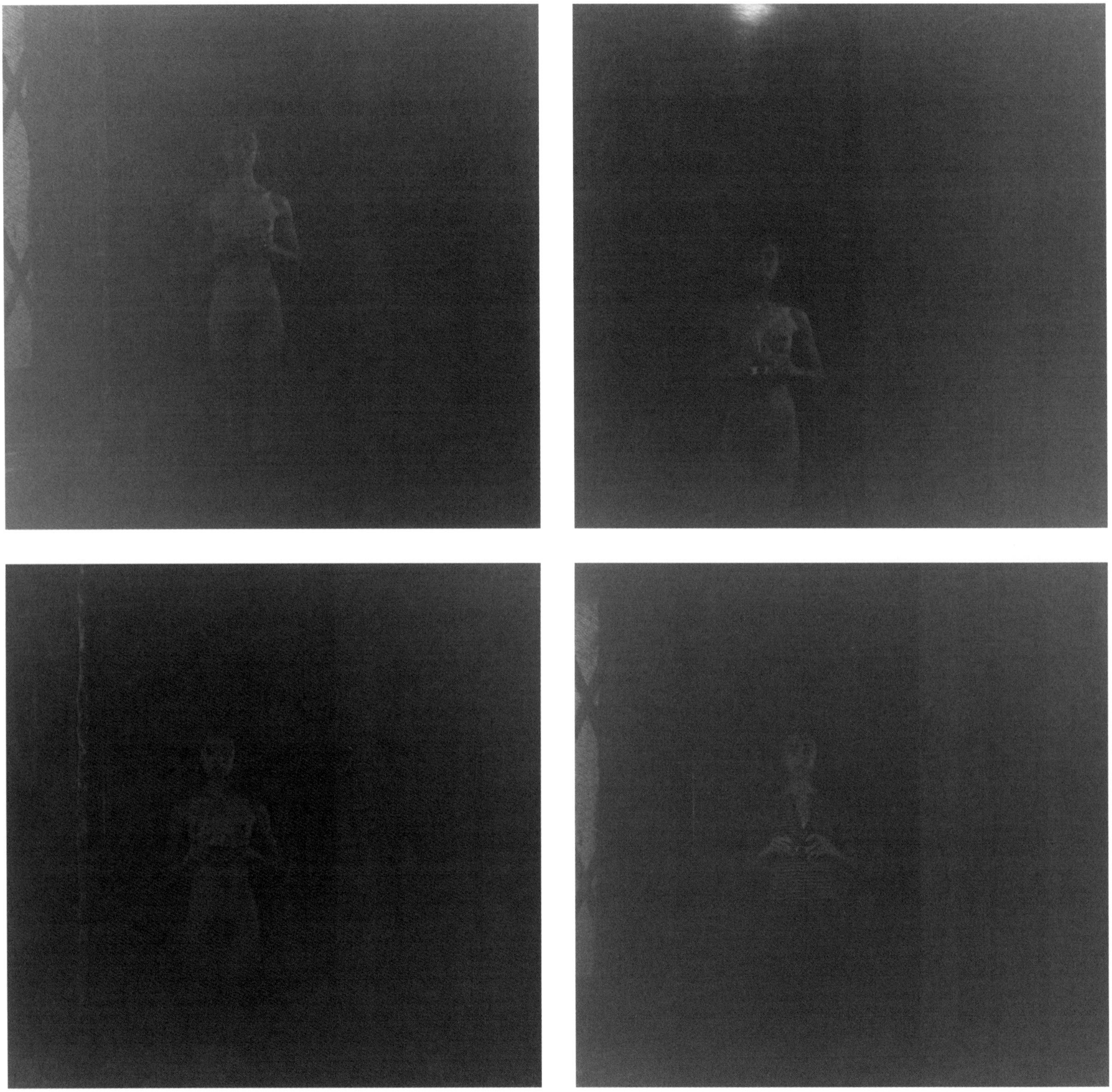

Food for the Spirit. 1971 (see page 190)

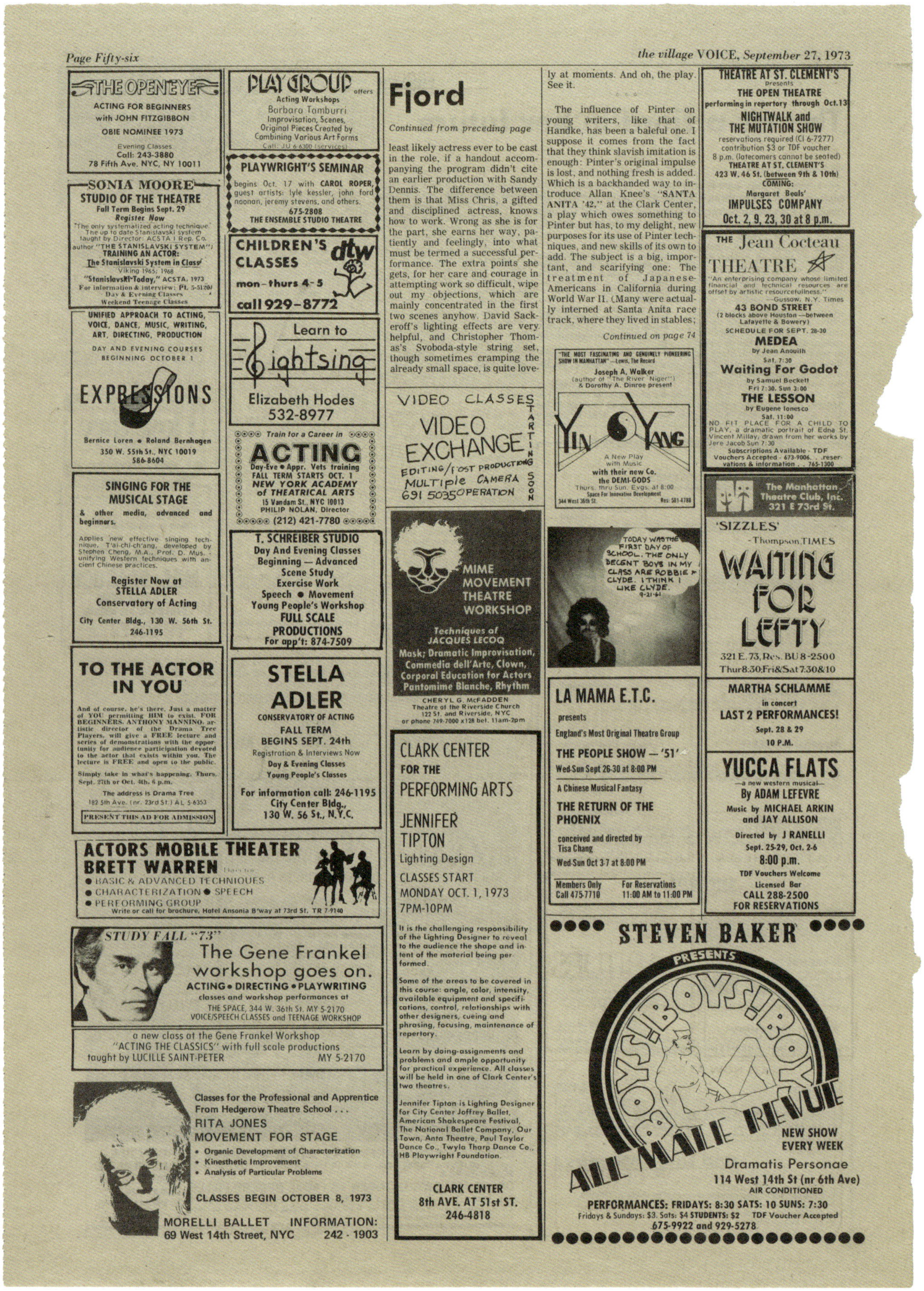

Page Fifty-six

the village VOICE, September 27, 1973

THE OPENEYE
ACTING FOR BEGINNERS
with JOHN FITZGIBBON
OBIE NOMINEE 1973
Evening Classes
Call: 243-3880
78 Fifth Ave. NYC, NY 10011

SONIA MOORE
STUDIO OF THE THEATRE
Fall Term Begins Sept. 29
Register Now
"The only systematized acting technique." The up to date Stanislavski system taught by Director: ACSTA I Rep. Co. author "THE STANISLAVSKI SYSTEM"; TRAINING AN ACTOR: The Stanislavski System in Class
Viking 1965; 1968
"Stanislavski Today," ACSTA, 1973
For information & interview: PL 5-5120
Day & Evening Classes
Weekend Teenage Classes

UNIFIED APPROACH TO ACTING, VOICE, DANCE, MUSIC, WRITING, ART, DIRECTING, PRODUCTION
DAY AND EVENING COURSES BEGINNING OCTOBER 1
EXPRESSIONS
Bernice Loren • Roland Bernhagen
350 W. 55th St., NYC 10019
586-8604

SINGING FOR THE MUSICAL STAGE
& other media, advanced and beginners.
Applies new effective singing technique, T'ai-chi-ch'ang, developed by Stephen Cheng, M.A., Prof. D. Mus. - unifying Western techniques with ancient Chinese practices.
Register Now at
STELLA ADLER
Conservatory of Acting
City Center Bldg., 130 W. 56th St.
246-1195

TO THE ACTOR IN YOU
And of course, he's there. Just a matter of YOU permitting HIM to exist. FOR BEGINNERS. ANTHONY MANNINO, artistic director of the Drama Tree Players, will give a FREE lecture and series of demonstrations with the opportunity for audience participation devoted to the actor that exists within you. The lecture is FREE and open to the public.
Simply take in what's happening. Thurs. Sept. 27th or Oct. 4th, 6 p.m.
The address is Drama Tree
182 5th Ave. (nr. 23rd St.) AL 5-6353
PRESENT THIS AD FOR ADMISSION

PLAYGROUP offers
Acting Workshops
Barbara Tamburri
Improvisation, Scenes, Original Pieces Created by Combining Various Art Forms
Call: JU 6-6300 (services)

PLAYWRIGHT'S SEMINAR
begins Oct. 17 with CAROL ROPER, guest artists: lyle kessler, john ford noonan, jeremy stevens, and others.
675-2808
THE ENSEMBLE STUDIO THEATRE

CHILDREN'S CLASSES
dtw
mon-thurs 4-5
call 929-8772

Learn to Sightsing
Elizabeth Hodes
532-8977

Train for a Career in
ACTING
Day-Eve • Appr. Vets training
FALL TERM STARTS OCT. 1
NEW YORK ACADEMY of THEATRICAL ARTS
15 Vandam St., NYC 10013
PHILIP NOLAN, Director
(212) 421-7780

T. SCHREIBER STUDIO
Day And Evening Classes
Beginning — Advanced
Scene Study
Exercise Work
Speech • Movement
Young People's Workshop
FULL SCALE PRODUCTIONS
For app't: 874-7509

STELLA ADLER
CONSERVATORY OF ACTING
FALL TERM
BEGINS SEPT. 24th
Registration & Interviews Now
Day & Evening Classes
Young People's Classes
For information call: 246-1195
City Center Bldg., 130 W. 56 St., N.Y.C.

Fjord

Continued from preceding page

least likely actress ever to be cast in the role, if a handout accompanying the program didn't cite an earlier production with Sandy Dennis. The difference between them is that Miss Chris, a gifted and disciplined actress, knows how to work. Wrong as she is for the part, she earns her way, patiently and feelingly, into what must be termed a successful performance. The extra points she gets, for her care and courage in attempting work so difficult, wipe out my objections, which are mainly concentrated in the first two scenes anyhow. David Sackeroff's lighting effects are very helpful, and Christopher Thomas's Svoboda-style string set, though sometimes cramping the already small space, is quite lovely at moments. And oh, the play. See it.

* * *

The influence of Pinter on young writers, like that of Handke, has been a baleful one. I suppose it comes from the fact that they think slavish imitation is enough: Pinter's original impulse is lost, and nothing fresh is added. Which is a backhanded way to introduce Allan Knee's "SANTA ANITA '42," at the Clark Center, a play which owes something to Pinter but has, to my delight, new purposes for its use of Pinter techniques, and new skills of its own to add. The subject is a big, important, and scarifying one: The treatment of Japanese-Americans in California during World War II. (Many were actually interned at Santa Anita race track, where they lived in stables;

Continued on page 74

VIDEO CLASSES STARTING SOON
VIDEO EXCHANGE
EDITING/POST PRODUCTION
MULTIPLE CAMERA OPERATION
691 5035

MIME MOVEMENT THEATRE WORKSHOP
Techniques of JACQUES LECOQ
Mask; Dramatic Improvisation, Commedia dell'Arte, Clown, Corporal Education for Actors Pantomime Blanche, Rhythm
CHERYL G. McFADDEN
Theatre of the Riverside Church
122 St. and Riverside, NYC
or phone 749-7000 x128 bet. 11am-2pm

CLARK CENTER FOR THE PERFORMING ARTS
JENNIFER TIPTON
Lighting Design
CLASSES START MONDAY OCT. 1, 1973
7PM-10PM
It is the challenging responsibility of the Lighting Designer to reveal to the audience the shape and intent of the material being performed.
Some of the areas to be covered in this course: angle, color, intensity, available equipment and specifications, control, relationships with other designers, cueing and phrasing, focusing, maintenance of repertory.
Learn by doing-assignments and problems and ample opportunity for practical experience. All classes will be held in one of Clark Center's two theatres.
Jennifer Tipton is Lighting Designer for City Center Joffrey Ballet, American Shakespeare Festival, The National Ballet Company, Our Town, Anta Theatre, Paul Taylor Dance Co., Twyla Tharp Dance Co., HB Playwright Foundation.
CLARK CENTER
8th AVE. AT 51st ST.
246-4818

"THE MOST FASCINATING AND GENUINELY PIONEERING SHOW IN MANHATTAN" —Lewis, The Record
Joseph A. Walker (author of "The River Niger") & Dorothy A. Dinroe present
YIN YANG
A New Play with Music
with their new Co. the DEMI-GODS
Thurs. thru Sun. Evgs. at 8:00
Space For Innovative Development
344 West 36th St. Res: 581-4788

TODAY WAS THE FIRST DAY OF SCHOOL. THE ONLY DECENT BOYS IN MY CLASS ARE ROBBIE & CLYDE. I THINK I LIKE CLYDE.
9-21-61

LA MAMA E.T.C.
presents
England's Most Original Theatre Group
THE PEOPLE SHOW — '51'
Wed-Sun Sept 26-30 at 8:00 PM
A Chinese Musical Fantasy
THE RETURN OF THE PHOENIX
conceived and directed by Tisa Chang
Wed-Sun Oct 3-7 at 8:00 PM
Members Only Call 475-7710
For Reservations 11:00 AM to 11:00 PM

THEATRE AT ST. CLEMENT'S
presents
THE OPEN THEATRE
performing in repertory through Oct. 13
NIGHTWALK and THE MUTATION SHOW
reservations required (CI 6-7277)
contribution $3 or TDF voucher
8 p.m. (latecomers cannot be seated)
THEATRE AT ST. CLEMENT'S
423 W. 46 St. (between 9th & 10th)
COMING:
Margaret Beals'
IMPULSES COMPANY
Oct. 2, 9, 23, 30 at 8 p.m.

THE Jean Cocteau THEATRE
"An enterprising company whose limited financial and technical resources are offset by artistic resourcefulness."
—Gussow, N.Y. Times
43 BOND STREET
(2 blocks above Houston—between Lafayette & Bowery)
SCHEDULE FOR SEPT. 28-30
MEDEA
by Jean Anouilh
Sat. 7:30
Waiting For Godot
by Samuel Beckett
Fri 7:30, Sun 3:00
THE LESSON
by Eugene Ionesco
Sat. 11:00
NO FIT PLACE FOR A CHILD TO PLAY, a dramatic portrait of Edna St. Vincent Millay, drawn from her works by Jere Jacob Sun 7:30
Subscriptions Available - TDF Vouchers Accepted - 673-9006. . .reservations & information . . 765-1300

The Manhattan Theatre Club, Inc.
321 E 73rd St.
'SIZZLES' -Thompson, TIMES
WAITING FOR LEFTY
321 E. 73, Res. BU 8-2500
Thur 8:30; Fri & Sat 7:30 & 10

MARTHA SCHLAMME
in concert
LAST 2 PERFORMANCES!
Sept. 28 & 29
10 P.M.

YUCCA FLATS
—a new western musical—
By ADAM LEFEVRE
Music by MICHAEL ARKIN and JAY ALLISON
Directed by J RANELLI
Sept. 25-29, Oct. 2-6
8:00 p.m.
TDF Vouchers Welcome
Licensed Bar
CALL 288-2500
FOR RESERVATIONS

ACTORS MOBILE THEATER
BRETT WARREN
• BASIC & ADVANCED TECHNIQUES
• CHARACTERIZATION • SPEECH
• PERFORMING GROUP
Write or call for brochure, Hotel Ansonia B'way at 73rd St. TR 7-9140

STUDY FALL "73"
The Gene Frankel workshop goes on.
ACTING • DIRECTING • PLAYWRITING
classes and workshop performances at
THE SPACE, 344 W. 36th St. MY 5-2170
VOICE/SPEECH CLASSES and TEENAGE WORKSHOP

a new class at the Gene Frankel Workshop
"ACTING THE CLASSICS" with full scale productions
taught by LUCILLE SAINT-PETER MY 5-2170

Classes for the Professional and Apprentice From Hedgerow Theatre School . . .
RITA JONES
MOVEMENT FOR STAGE
• Organic Development of Characterization
• Kinesthetic Improvement
• Analysis of Particular Problems
CLASSES BEGIN OCTOBER 8, 1973
MORELLI BALLET INFORMATION:
69 West 14th Street, NYC 242 - 1903

STEVEN BAKER
PRESENTS
BOYS! BOYS! BOYS!
ALL MALE REVUE
NEW SHOW EVERY WEEK
Dramatis Personae
114 West 14th St (nr 6th Ave)
AIR CONDITIONED
PERFORMANCES: FRIDAYS: 8:30 SATS: 10 SUNS: 7:30
Fridays & Sundays: $3. Sats: $4 STUDENTS: $2 TDF Voucher Accepted
675-9922 and 929-5278

The Mythic Being, Village Voice Ads. 1973–75
Advertisements appearing in the *Village Voice*. Seventeen newspaper pages
Each 17 × 14 in. (43.2 × 35.6 cm)
The Museum of Modern Art, New York. Purchased with funds provided by Donald L. Bryant, Jr., Agnes Gund, Marlene Hess and James D. Zirin, Marie-Josée and Henry R. Kravis, Donald B. Marron, The Edward John Noble Foundation, Katherine Farley and Jerry Speyer, and Committee on Drawings Funds in honor of Kathy Fuld
Detail: *The Mythic Being, Cycle I: 9/21/61*. September 27, 1973

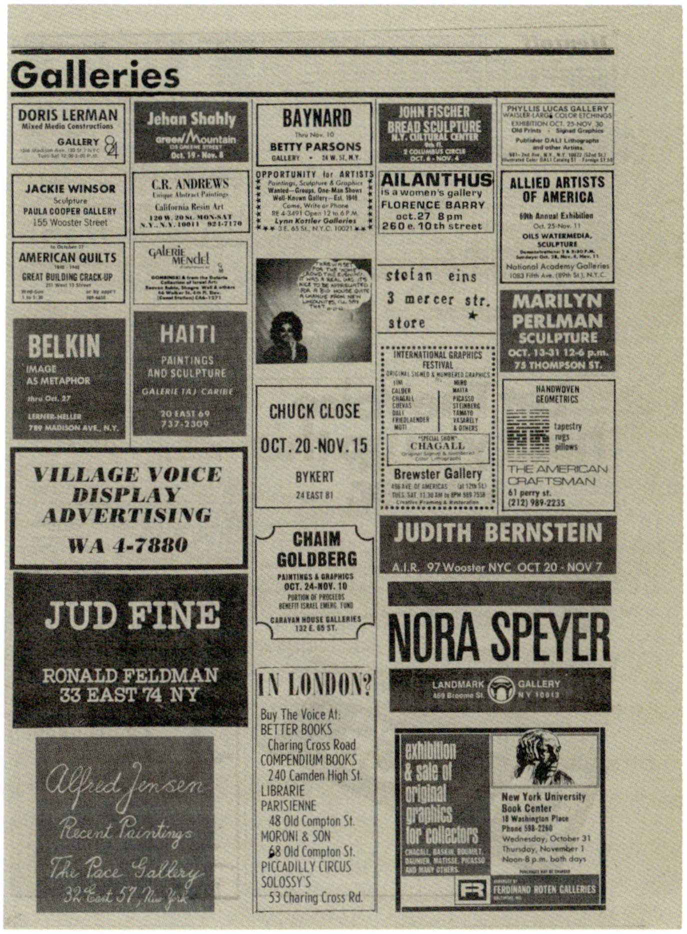

Galleries

DORIS LERMAN
Mixed Media Constructions

Jehan Shahly
green Mountain
Oct. 19 - Nov. 8

BAYNARD
BETTY PARSONS

JOHN FISCHER
BREAD SCULPTURE

PHYLLIS LUCAS GALLERY

JACKIE WINSOR
Sculpture
PAULA COOPER GALLERY
155 Wooster Street

C.R. ANDREWS
California Resin Art

AILANTHUS
is a women's gallery
FLORENCE BARRY
oct.27 8pm
260 e. 10th street

ALLIED ARTISTS OF AMERICA

AMERICAN QUILTS
GREAT BUILDING CRACK UP

stefan eins
3 mercer str.
store

MARILYN PERLMAN
SCULPTURE
OCT. 13-31
75 THOMPSON ST.

BELKIN
IMAGE AS METAPHOR

HAITI
PAINTINGS AND SCULPTURE
GALERIE TAJ CARIBE

INTERNATIONAL GRAPHICS FESTIVAL

CHUCK CLOSE
OCT. 20-NOV. 15
BYKERT
24 EAST 81

HANDWOVEN GEOMETRICS

Brewster Gallery

THE AMERICAN CRAFTSMAN
61 perry st.
(212) 989-2235

VILLAGE VOICE
DISPLAY
ADVERTISING
WA 4-7880

CHAIM GOLDBERG

JUDITH BERNSTEIN
A.I.R. 97 Wooster NYC OCT 20 - NOV 7

JUD FINE
RONALD FELDMAN
33 EAST 74 NY

NORA SPEYER
LANDMARK GALLERY

IN LONDON?
Buy The Voice At:
BETTER BOOKS
Charing Cross Road
COMPENDIUM BOOKS
240 Camden High St.
LIBRARIE PARISIENNE
48 Old Compton St.
MORONI & SON
68 Old Compton St.
PICCADILLY CIRCUS
SOLOSSY'S
53 Charing Cross Rd.

exhibition & sale of original graphics for collectors
New York University Book Center
FERDINAND ROTEN GALLERIES

Alfred Jensen
Recent Paintings
The Pace Gallery
32 East 57, New York

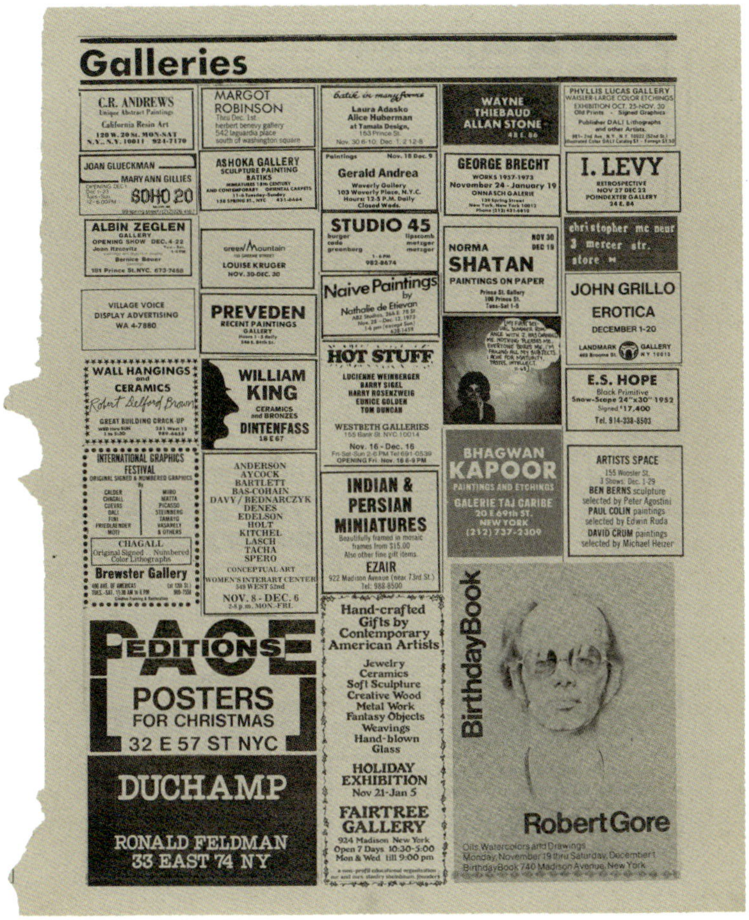

Galleries

C.R. ANDREWS
California Resin Art

MARGOT ROBINSON

WAYNE THIEBAUD
ALLAN STONE

PHYLLIS LUCAS GALLERY

JOAN GLUECKMAN
MARYANN GILLIES
SOHO 20

ASHOKA GALLERY

Gerald Andrea

GEORGE BRECHT

I. LEVY

ALBIN ZEGLEN

STUDIO 45

NORMA SHATAN
PAINTINGS ON PAPER

christopher mc neur
3 mercer str.
store

JOHN GRILLO
EROTICA

VILLAGE VOICE
DISPLAY ADVERTISING
WA 4-7880

Naive Paintings

PREVEDEN

HOT STUFF

E.S. HOPE

WALL HANGINGS and CERAMICS

WILLIAM KING
DINTENFASS

BHAGWAN KAPOOR
PAINTINGS AND ETCHINGS
GALERIE TAJ CARIBE

ARTISTS SPACE

INTERNATIONAL GRAPHICS FESTIVAL

INDIAN & PERSIAN MINIATURES
EZAIR

Brewster Gallery

NOV. 8 - DEC. 6

Hand-crafted Gifts by Contemporary American Artists
HOLIDAY EXHIBITION
FAIRTREE GALLERY

PACE EDITIONS
POSTERS
FOR CHRISTMAS
32 E 57 ST NYC

DUCHAMP
RONALD FELDMAN
33 EAST 74 NY

BirthdayBook
Robert Gore

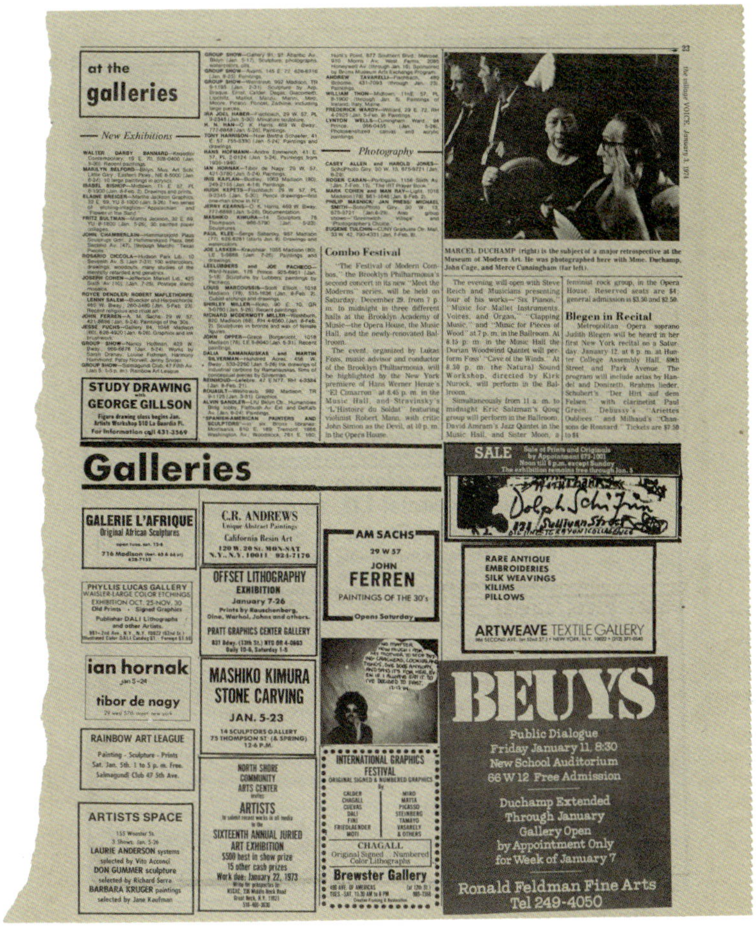

at the galleries

Photography

STUDY DRAWING
GEORGE GILLSON

Combo Festival

Blegen in Recital

Galleries

GALERIE L'AFRIQUE
Original African Sculptures

C.R. ANDREWS
California Resin Art

AM SACHS
JOHN FERREN
PAINTINGS OF THE 30's

PHYLLIS LUCAS GALLERY

OFFSET LITHOGRAPHY EXHIBITION

RARE ANTIQUE
EMBROIDERIES
SILK WEAVINGS
KILIMS
PILLOWS

ARTWEAVE TEXTILE GALLERY

ian hornak
tibor de nagy

MASHIKO KIMURA
STONE CARVING
JAN. 5-23

RAINBOW ART LEAGUE

BEUYS
Public Dialogue
Friday January 11, 8:30
New School Auditorium
66 W 12 Free Admission
Duchamp Extended
Through January
Gallery Open
by Appointment Only
for Week of January 7
Ronald Feldman Fine Arts
Tel 249-4050

ARTISTS SPACE

ARTISTS
SIXTEENTH ANNUAL JURIED ART EXHIBITION

INTERNATIONAL GRAPHICS FESTIVAL

Brewster Gallery

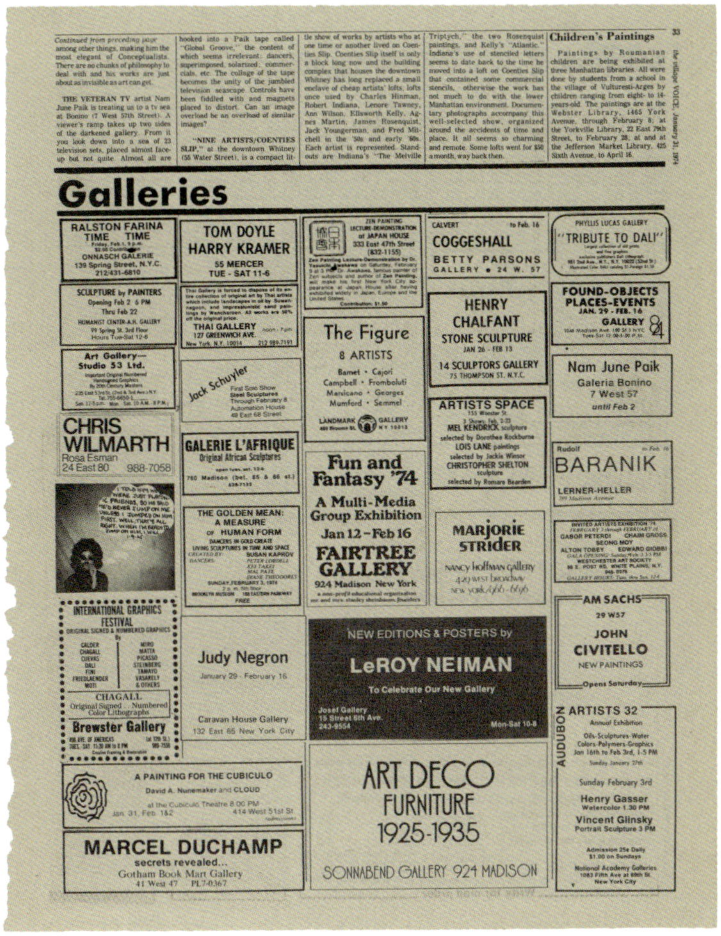

Children's Paintings

Galleries

RALSTON FARINA
TIME TIME
ONNASCH GALERIE

TOM DOYLE
HARRY KRAMER

COGGESHALL
BETTY PARSONS

"TRIBUTE TO DALI"

SCULPTURE by PAINTERS

THAI GALLERY

HENRY CHALFANT
STONE SCULPTURE

FOUND-OBJECTS
PLACES-EVENTS

The Figure
8 ARTISTS

Nam June Paik
Galeria Bonino
7 West 57

CHRIS WILMARTH
Rosa Esman

Jack Schuyler

ARTISTS SPACE

BARANIK

GALERIE L'AFRIQUE
Original African Sculptures

Fun and Fantasy '74
A Multi-Media Group Exhibition
Jan 12-Feb 16
FAIRTREE GALLERY
924 Madison New York

THE GOLDEN MEAN:
A MEASURE OF HUMAN FORM

MARJORIE STRIDER

AM SACHS
JOHN CIVITELLO
NEW PAINTINGS

INTERNATIONAL GRAPHICS FESTIVAL

Judy Negron

NEW EDITIONS & POSTERS by
LeROY NEIMAN

ARTISTS 32
AUDUBON

Brewster Gallery

A PAINTING FOR THE CUBICULO

ART DECO
FURNITURE
1925-1935
SONNABEND GALLERY 924 MADISON

MARCEL DUCHAMP
secrets revealed...
Gotham Book Mart Gallery

Details:

The Mythic Being, Cycle I: 10/27/62. October 25, 1973
The Mythic Being, Cycle I: 12/12/64. January 3, 1974

The Mythic Being, Cycle I: 11/63. November 29, 1973
The Mythic Being, Cycle I: 1/9/65. January 31, 1974

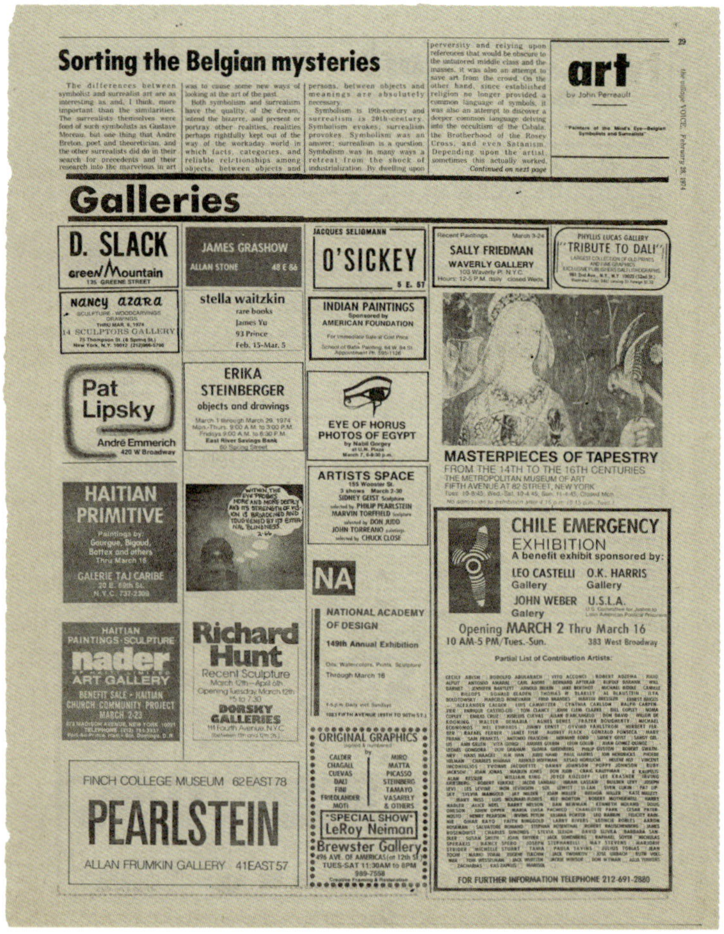

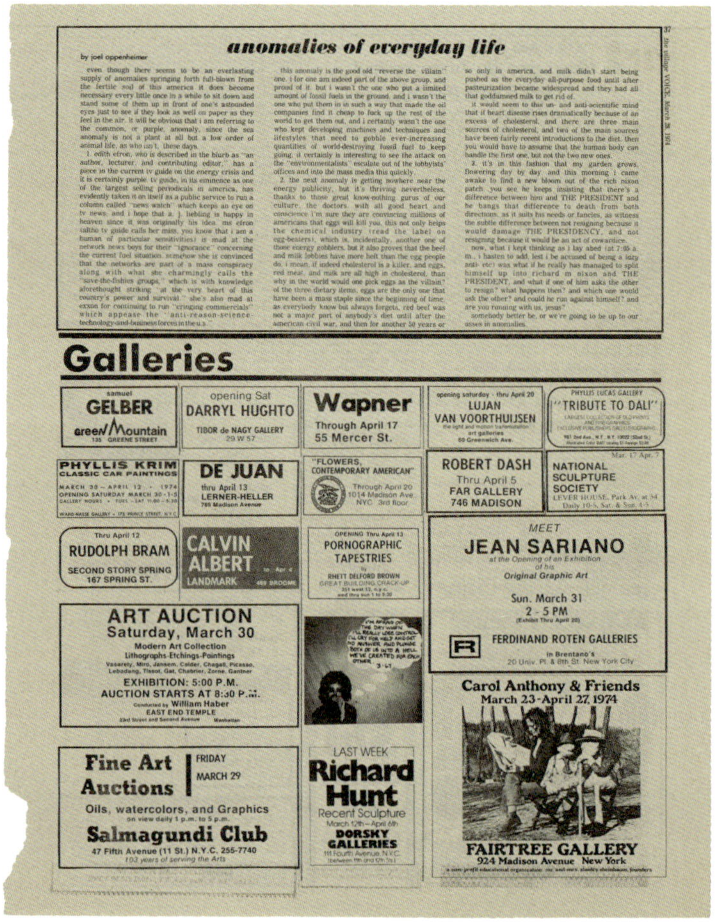

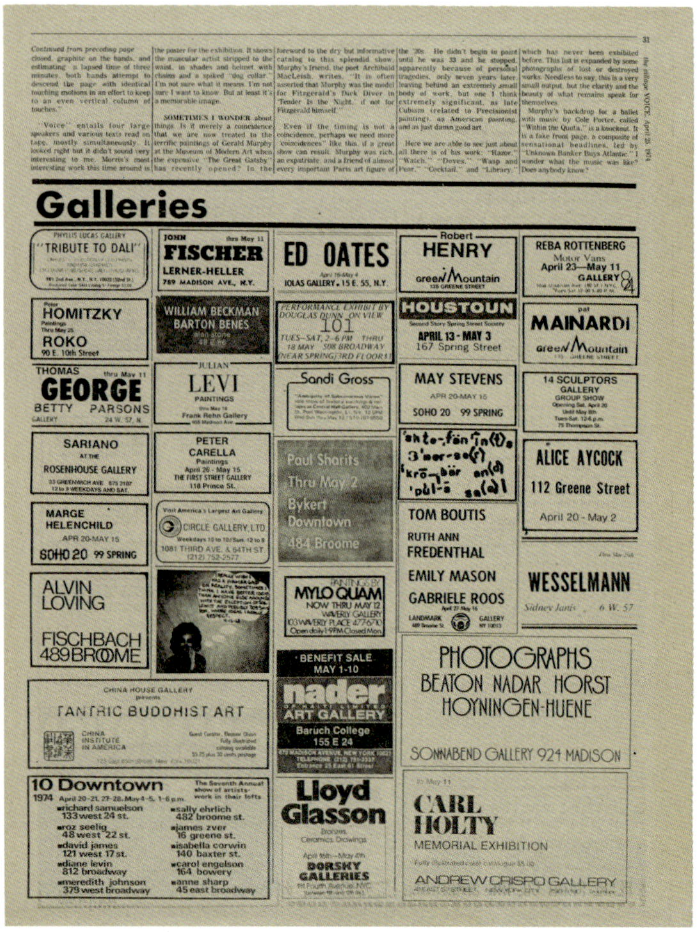

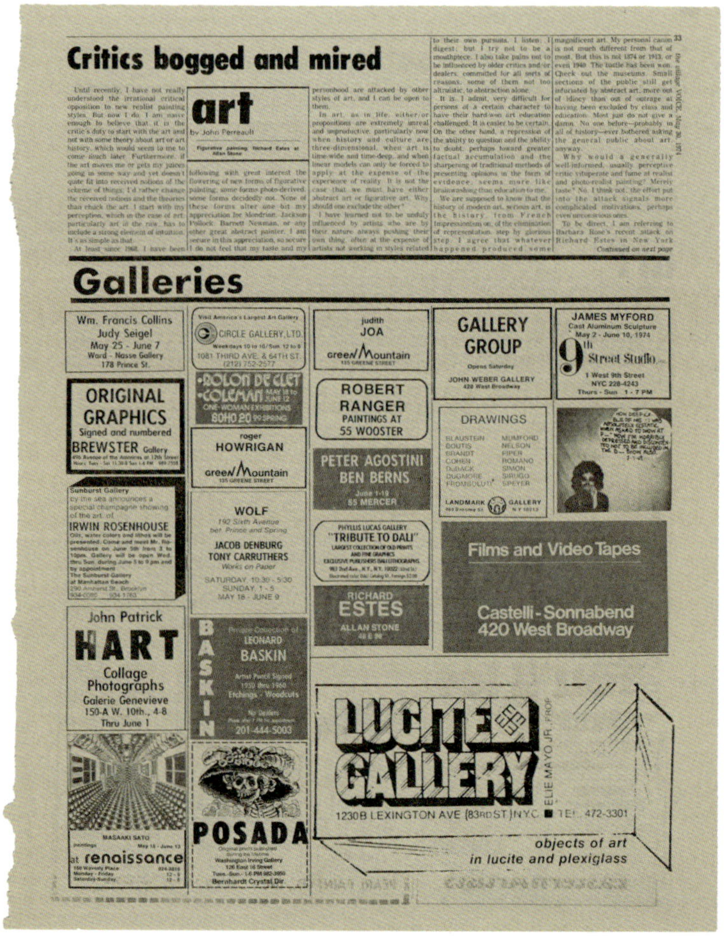

The Mythic Being, Village Voice Ads. 1973–75 (see page 194)
Details:
The Mythic Being, Cycle I: 2/66. February 28, 1974
The Mythic Being, Cycle I: 4/12/68. April 25, 1974
The Mythic Being, Cycle I: 3/67. March 28, 1974
The Mythic Being, Cycle I: 5/7/69. May 30, 1974

31 the village VOICE, July 25, 1974

Culture Shock

by Annette Kuhn

IN THE HEYDAY of old master buying at the turn of the century and into the '30s, no painting bought was considered complete without a portfolio of expertises—dog-eared photos, their backs covered with illegible scrawls by unknown European museum officials or prolific but not necessarily profound scholars. One could decipher phrases like "bellisima figura," "el dibujo," "das Meister's Hand," and perhaps the artistic signature of the certifying authority. These expertises rarely meant anything to anyone except the buyer, who was as impressed with European culture as his wife and daughter were with European aristocracy.

So a great many paintings with a great many expertises attesting to the hand of a famous master float around. Indeed, you can still buy one from certain scholars and impoverished museum officials. But it means nothing to almost anyone except the totally naive collector.

So where do you, the owner of a painting with a great name attached to it, go for verification? You can persuade some museums to give you a verbal discourse on your painting. You can go to Parke-Bernet and get a written appraisal of worth, but no great scholarly examination. Or you can go to the International Foundation for Art Research. Give them all the information you have on your painting and they will issue a report either confirming what you already know, or telling you the bad news—the work is nowhere near as good as you thought it was. The examination costs $150 plus expenses per object, the fee covering a technical analysis where needed, a provenance check, and, the hardest test of all, a submittal to the appropriate connoisseurs—such people as Louis Goldenberg, president of Wildenstein, Harry Bober, medievalist at NYU's Institute of Fine Arts, John Rewald, 19th century specialist at City University, Bernard Bothmer, classicist at the Brooklyn Museum, and many other impressive people of the academic, museum, and gallery world here and abroad.

This sleuthing in the murky field of art must be fun for the advisers. They get to handle art, discuss it, *and* ultimately cover themselves—because the resulting report is issued in the name of the foundation, not the individual specialist. Art Research is non-profit, and its services are available to anyone who has a serious piece of art. So if you are courageous and can stand bad news about your masterpiece, get in touch with International Foundation for Art Research, 654 Madison Avenue, New York City 10021.

WHAT DO WARHOL, Motherwell, Lichtenstein, Steinberg, Kelly, Hayter, Masson, Lieberman, Oldenburg, Stella, Rauschenberg, and Johns have in common? You guessed it. They all love Meyer Schapiro. Meyer Schapiro, mind, is one of the four or five greatest art historians ever. He is a semanticist, political activist, social historian. He can talk and draw and teach, and out of two apples construct a whole universe. Some people think he is a magician. His friends have made him a portfolio of prints, which will be on view at the Metropolitan Museum of Art in October. The museum is located somewhere between Columbia University, where Meyer Schapiro teaches, and the rest of the world, which is his study.

IN ALL THE FLAPS Nixon has raised, he has never gotten a rise out of the cultural establishment. He never invited great artists to the White House as Kennedy did. He never turned down portraits of himself as Johnson did. Yet he is generous with the arts.

When Nixon became President in 1968, appropriations for the National Endowment for the Arts, started in 1966, were around $7.5 million per year. By 1972 they were some $29.7 million, and they are now running $60.7 million. This is a most amazing and civilized jump—from $7 to $60 million—and attributable in great part to the blinkers-on, straight-arrow determination of Nancy Hanks, an ex-Rockefeller staffer, and, for the Nixon years, chairman of the NEA.

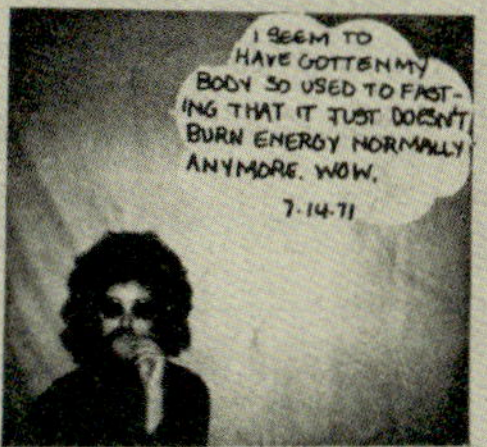

Detail:
The Mythic Being, Cycle I: 7/14/71. July 25, 1974

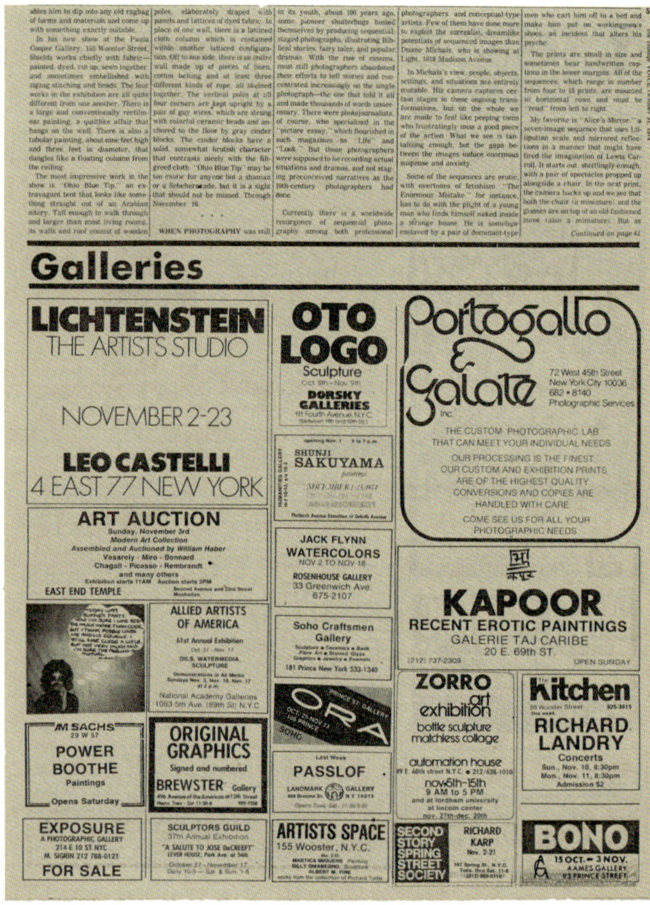

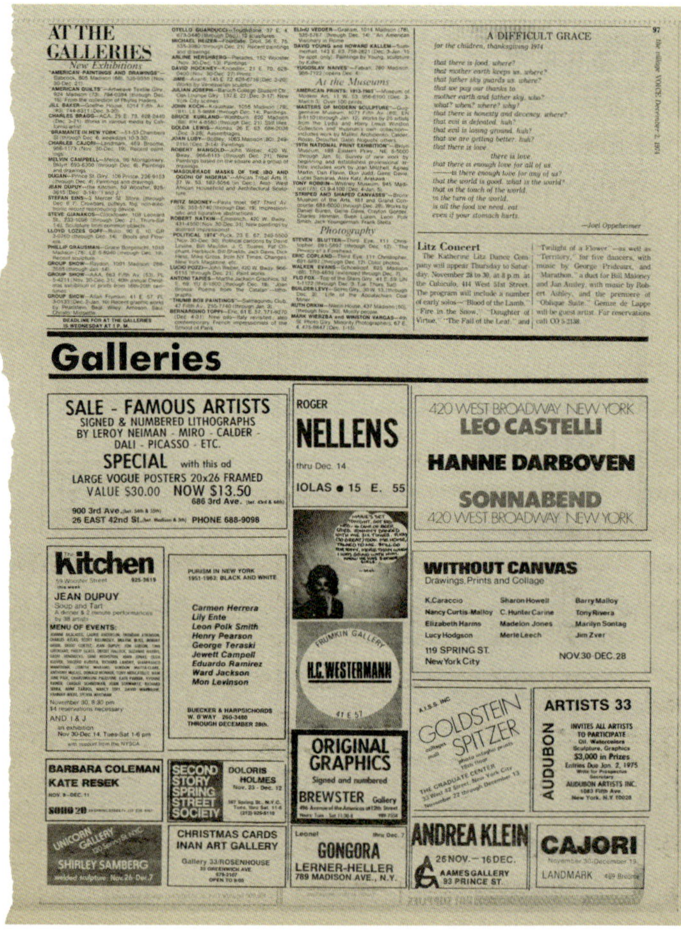

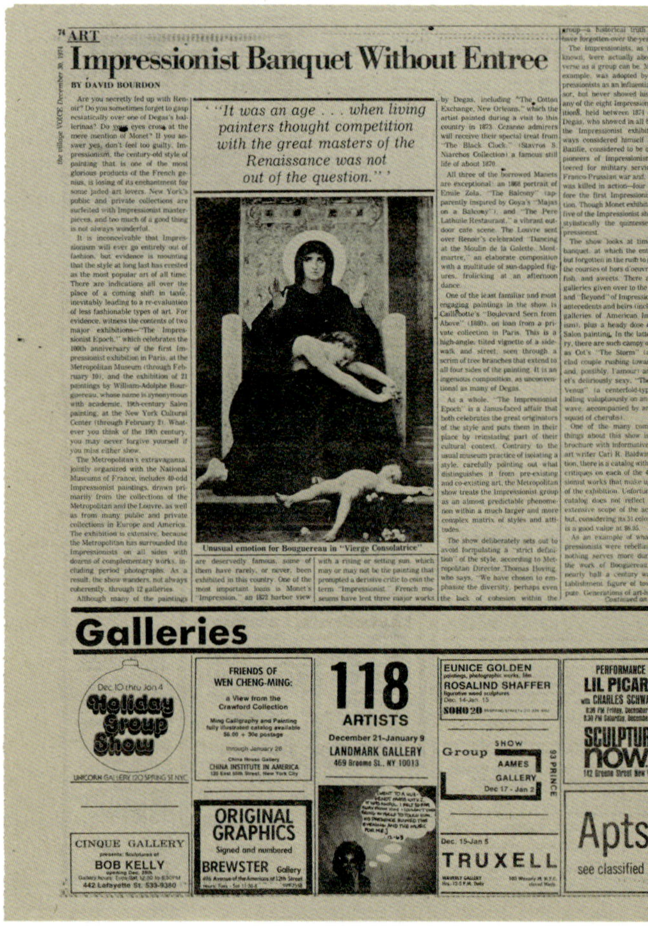

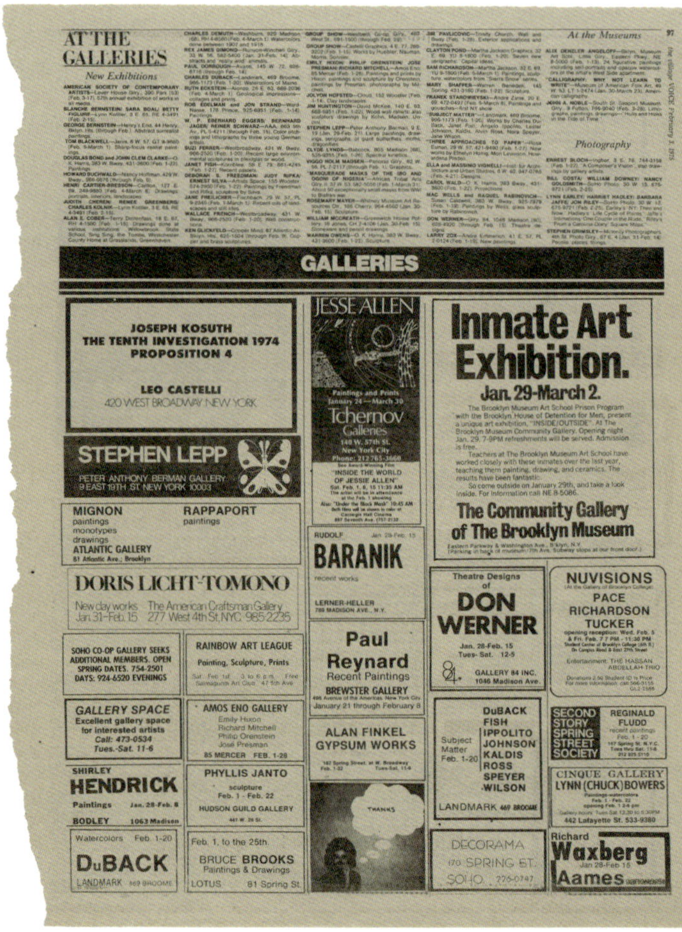

The Mythic Being, Village Voice Ads. 1973–74 (see page 194)
Details:
The Mythic Being, Cycle II: 10/13/61. October 31, 1974
The Mythic Being, Cycle II: 12/63. December 30, 1974
The Mythic Being, Cycle II: 11/24/62. December 2, 1974
The Mythic Being, Cycle II: Thanks. February 3, 1975

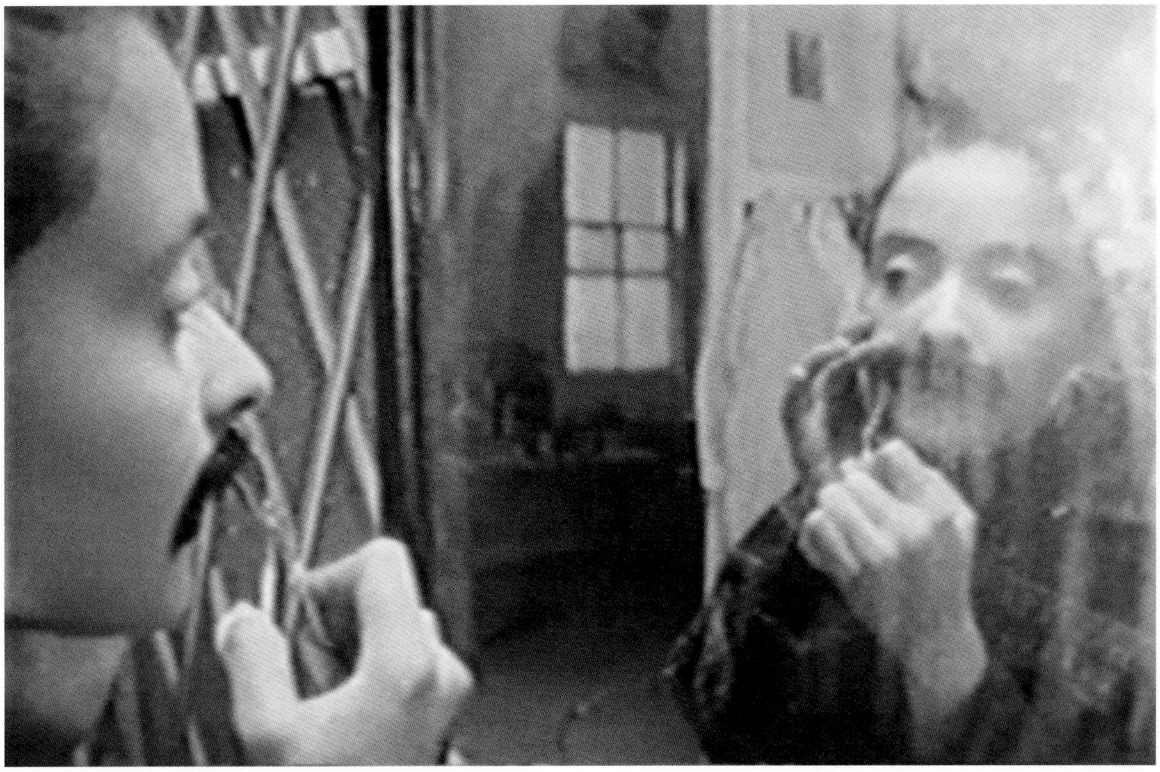

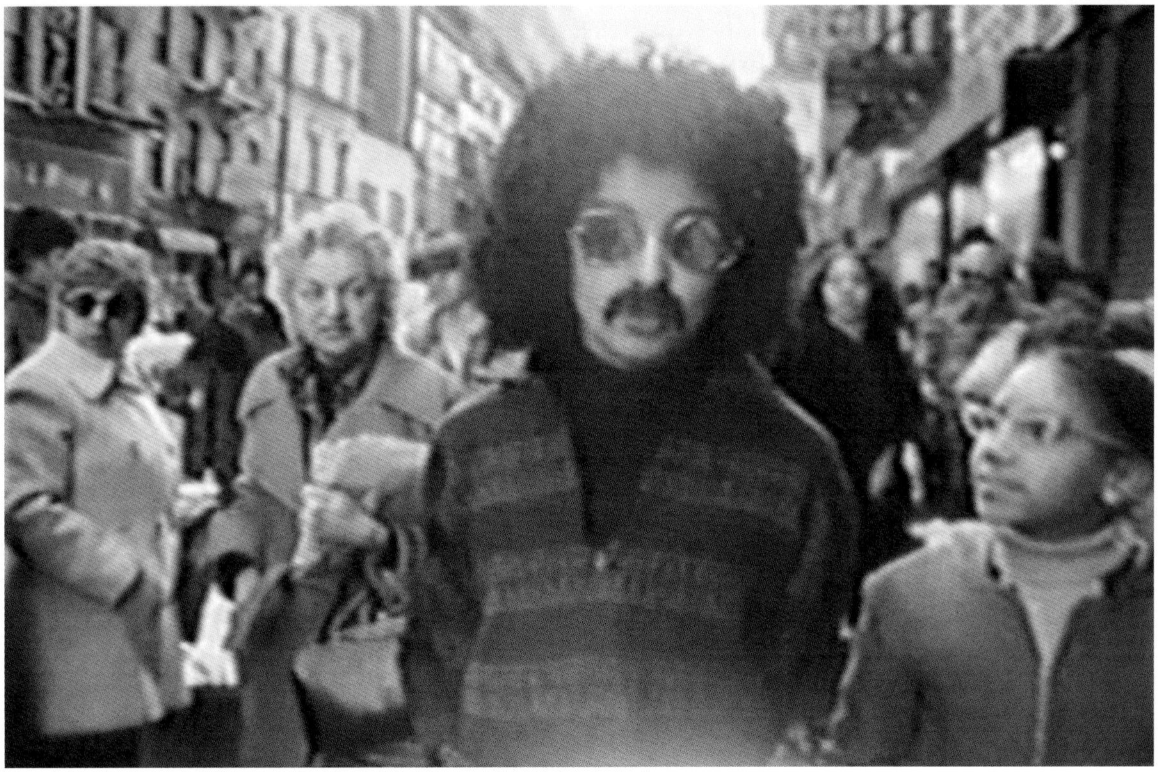

The Mythic Being. 1973
Video excerpted from *Other Than Art's Sake* (1973), by Peter Kennedy. 16mm film transferred to video (black and white, sound), 00:08:00
Collection Adrian Piper Research Archive Foundation Berlin
Details:
video still at 00:03:53
video still at 00:06:20

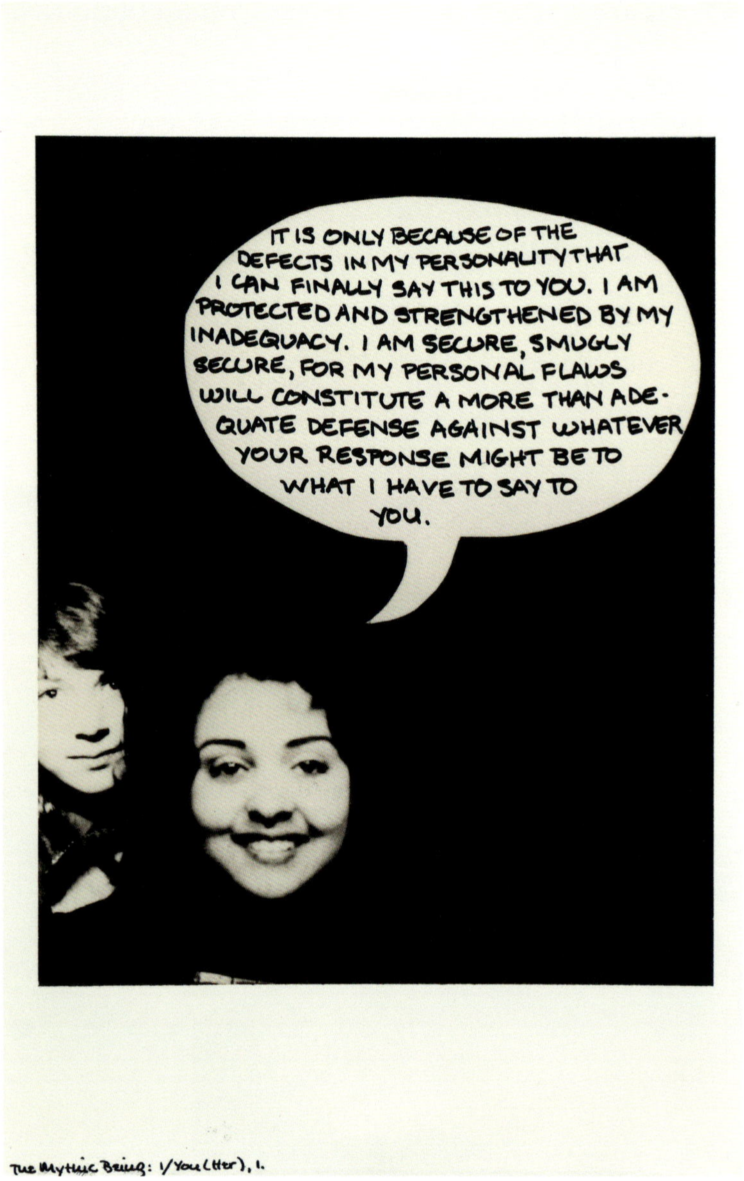

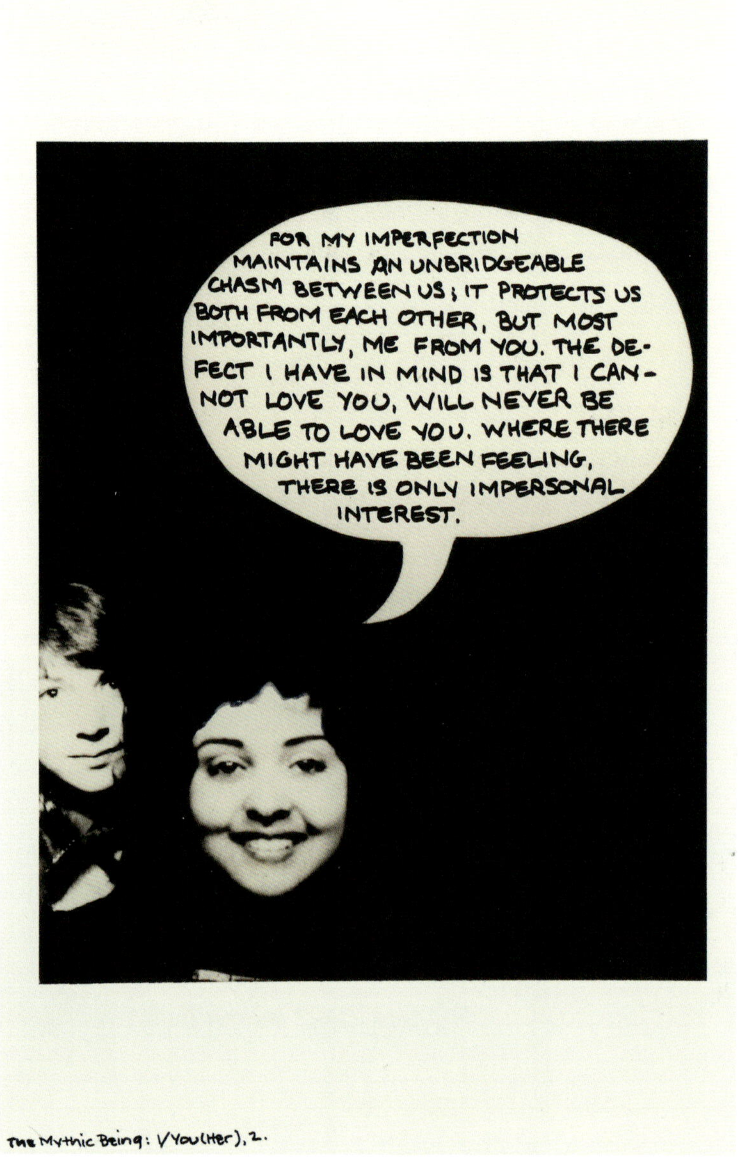

The Mythic Being: I/You (Her). 1974
Gouache, tempera, and cut-and-pasted paper labels on ten black-and-white enlarged photographs
Each 8 × 5 in. (20.3 cm × 12.7 cm)
Walker Art Center, Minneapolis. T. B. Walker Acquisition Fund

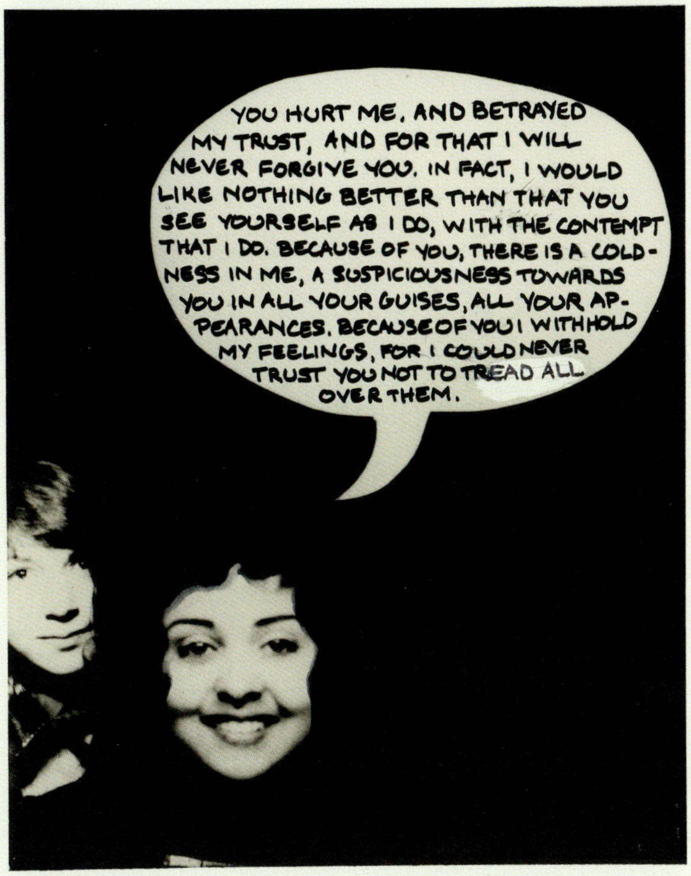

The Mythic Being: I/You (Her), 3.

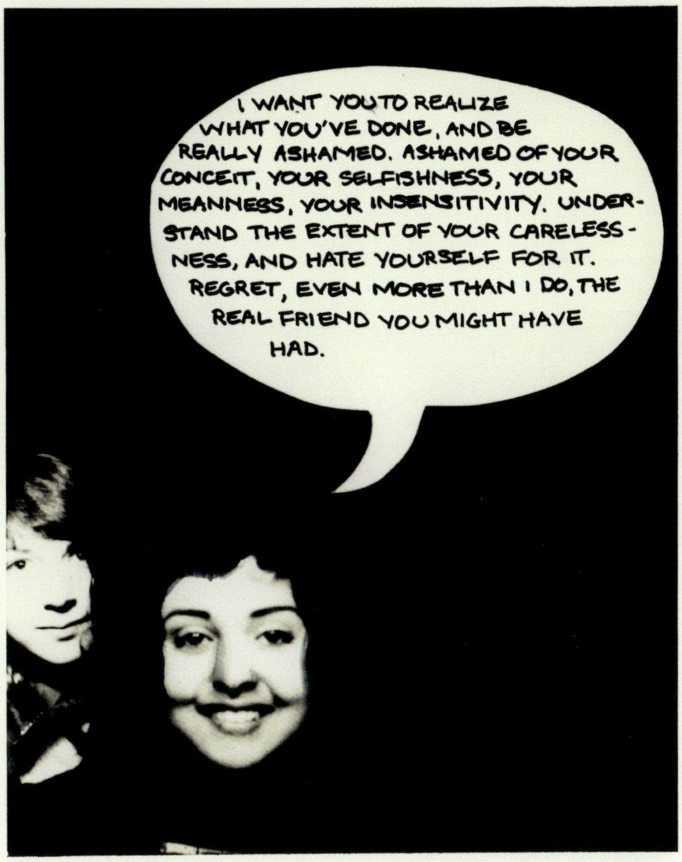

The Mythic Being: I/You (Her), 4.

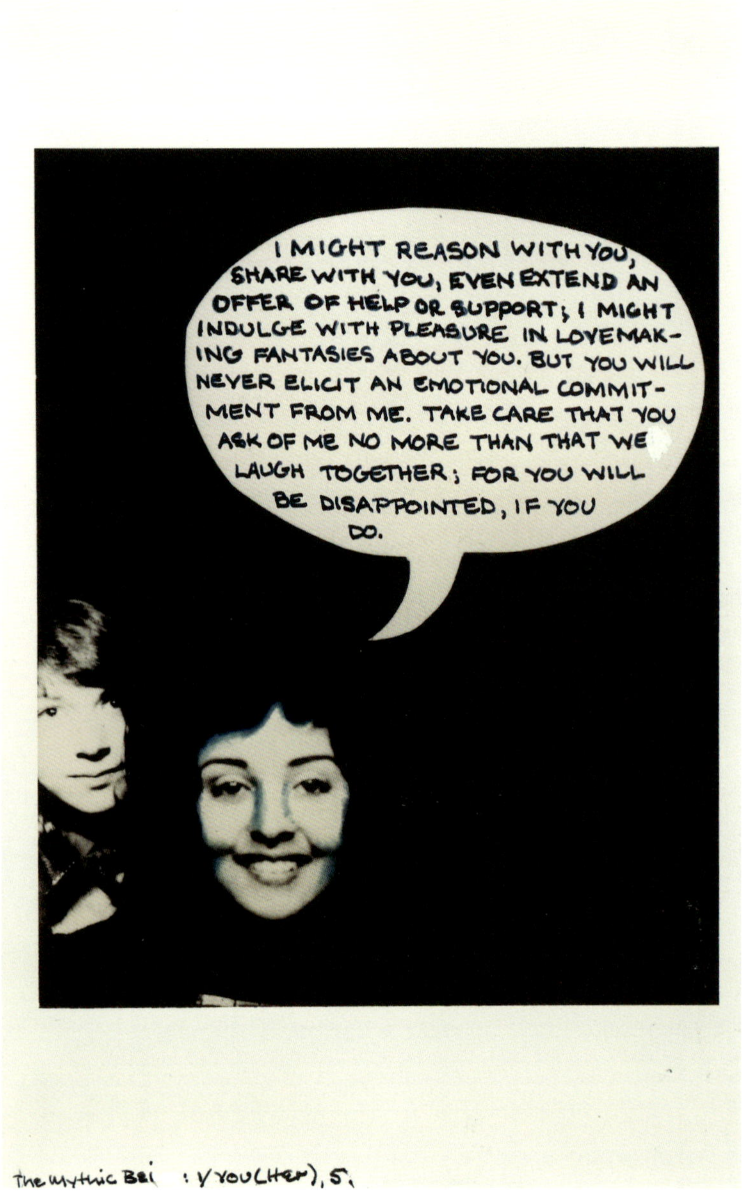

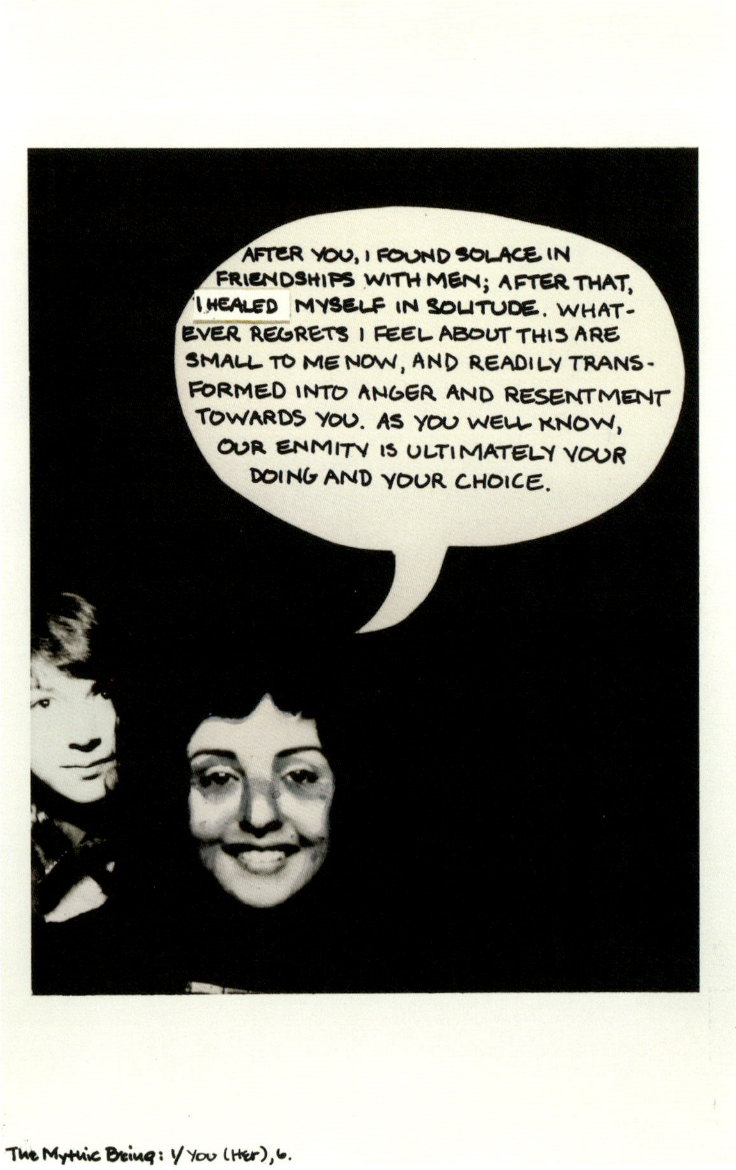

The Mythic Being: I/You (Her). 1974 (see page 200)

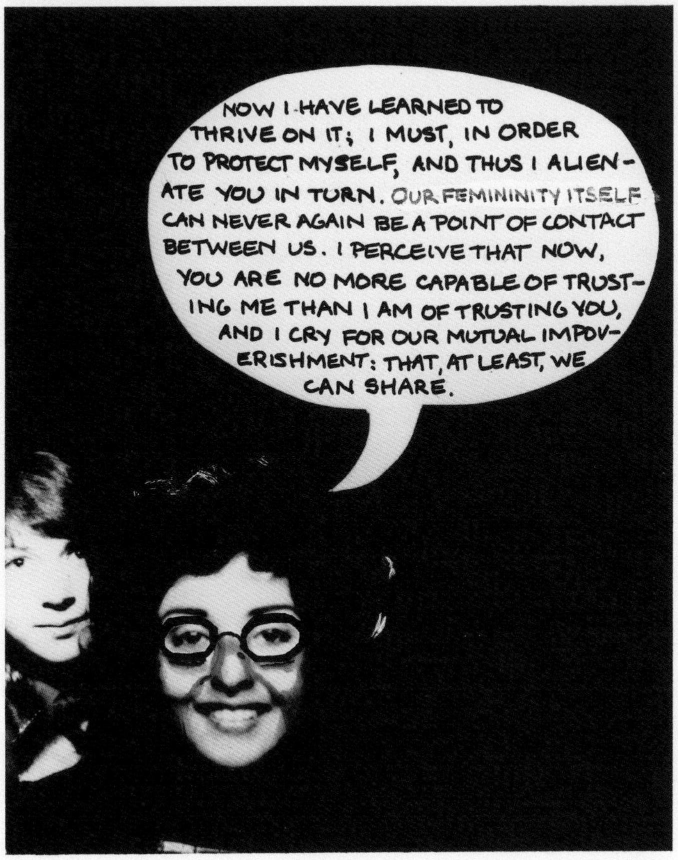

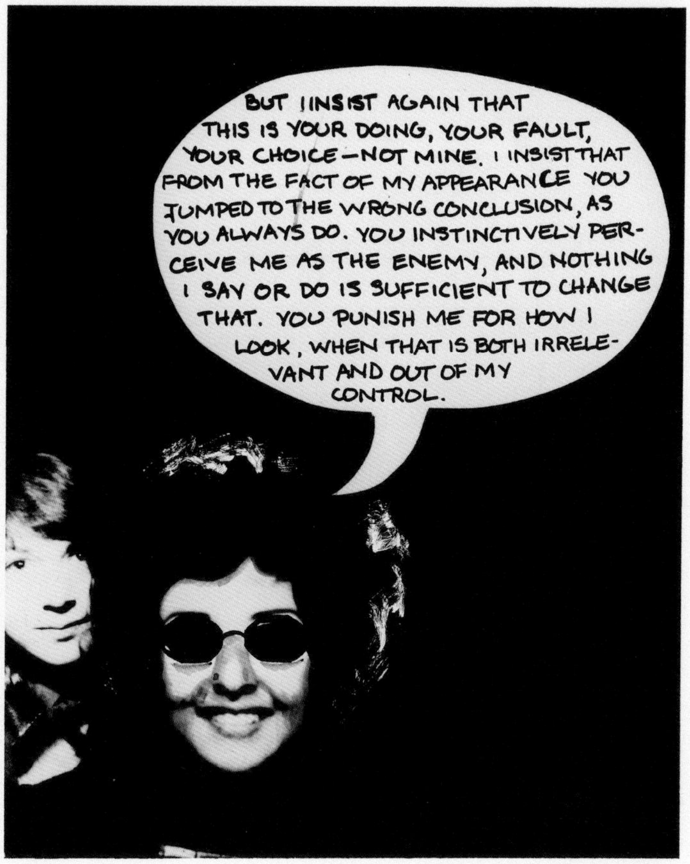

The Mythic Being: I/You (Her), 8.

The Mythic Bei : I/You (Her), 7.

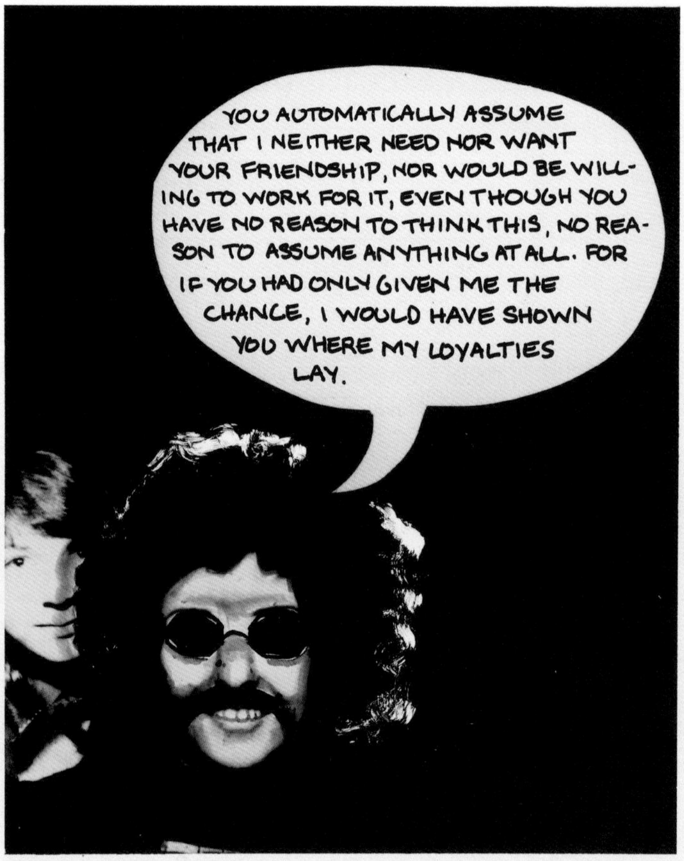

The Mythic Being: I/You (Her), 9.

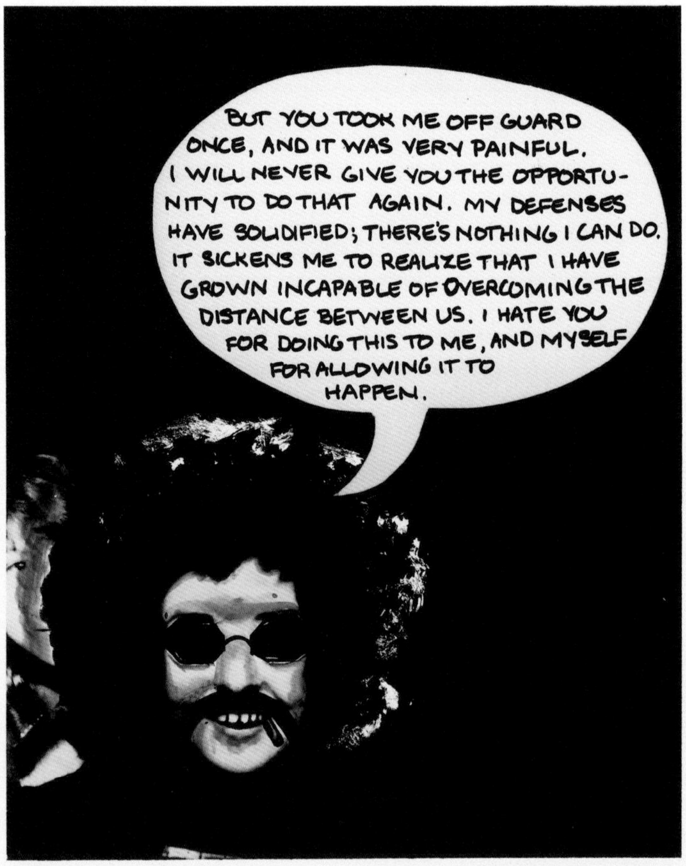

The Mythic Being: I/You (Her), 10.

The Mythic Being: I/You (Her). 1974 (see page 200)

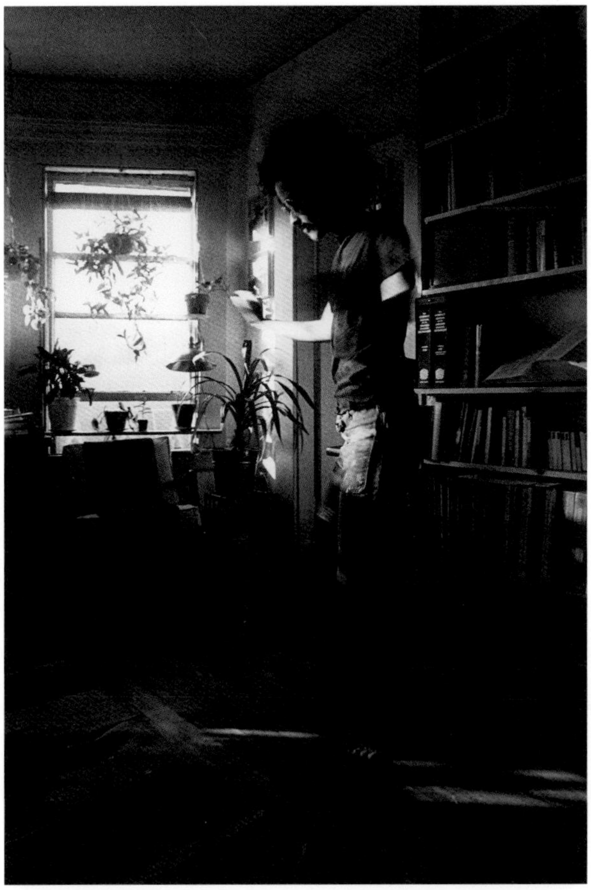

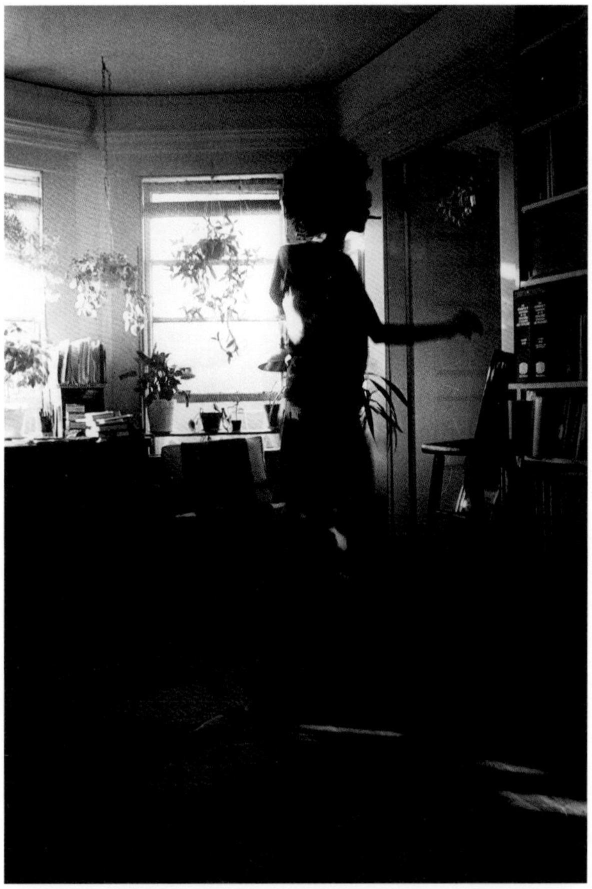

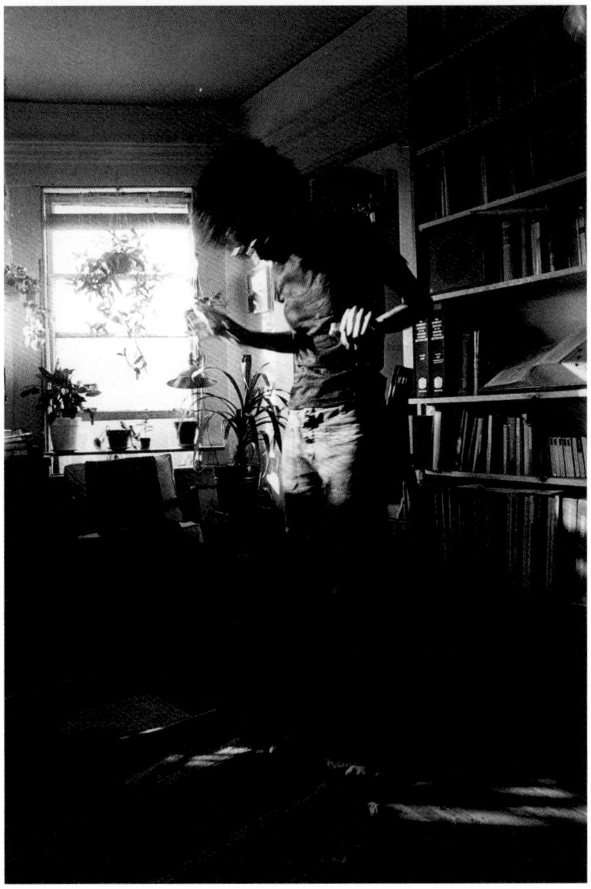

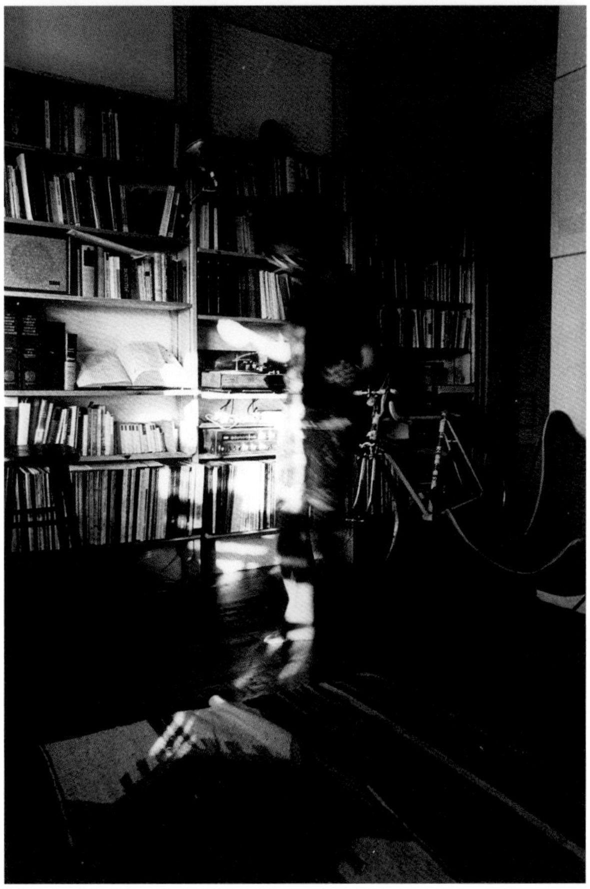

The Mythic Being: Dancing. 1974
Fourteen gelatin silver prints
Each 10 × 8 in. (25.4 × 20.3 cm)
Collection Adrian Piper Research Archive Foundation Berlin
Details:
photograph #1
photograph #11

photograph #4
photograph #8

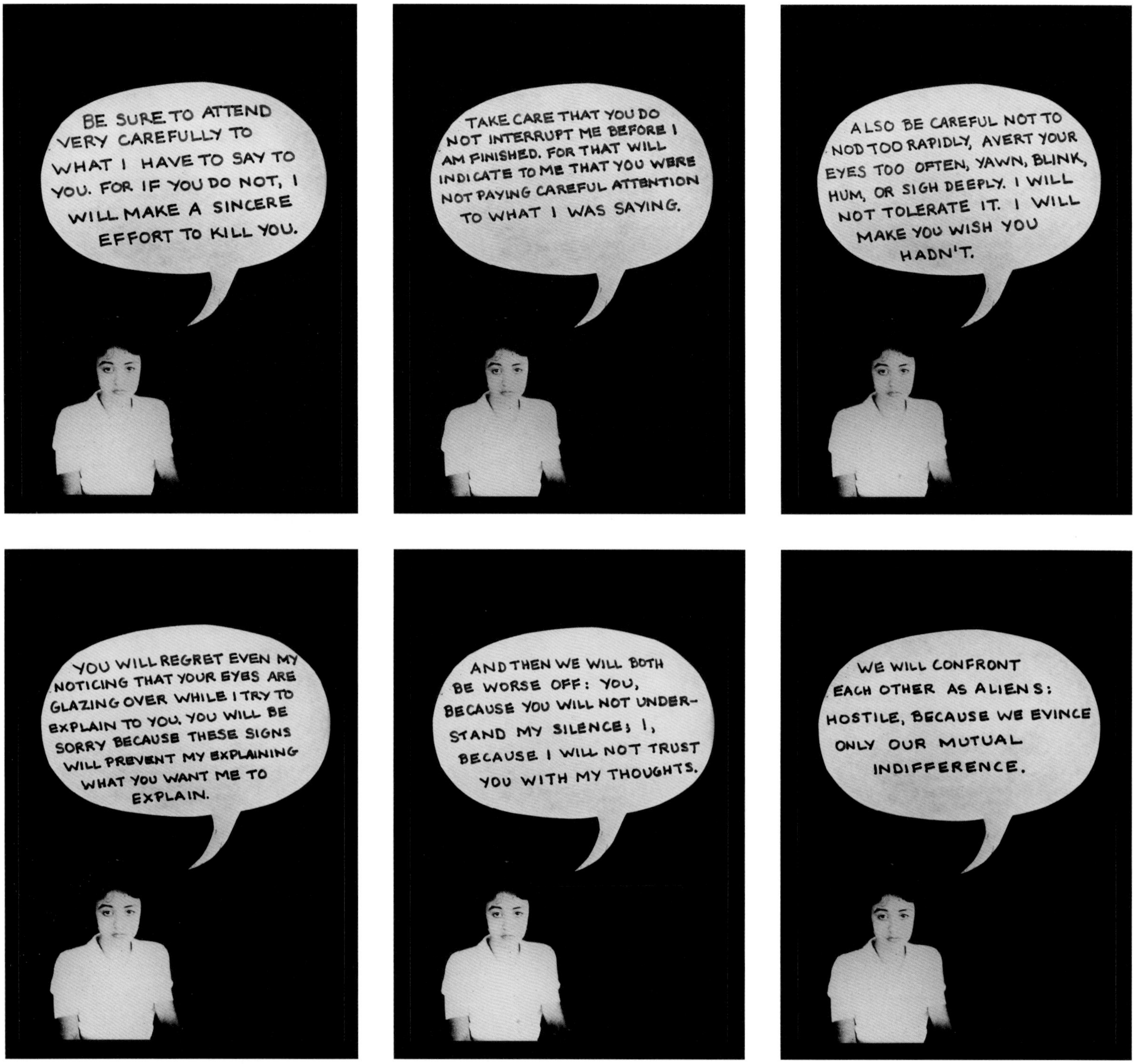

I/You/(Us). 1975
Photostats mounted on six pieces of foam core
Each 17 × 14 in. (43.2 × 35.5 cm)
Institut d'Art Contemporain, Rhône-Alpes

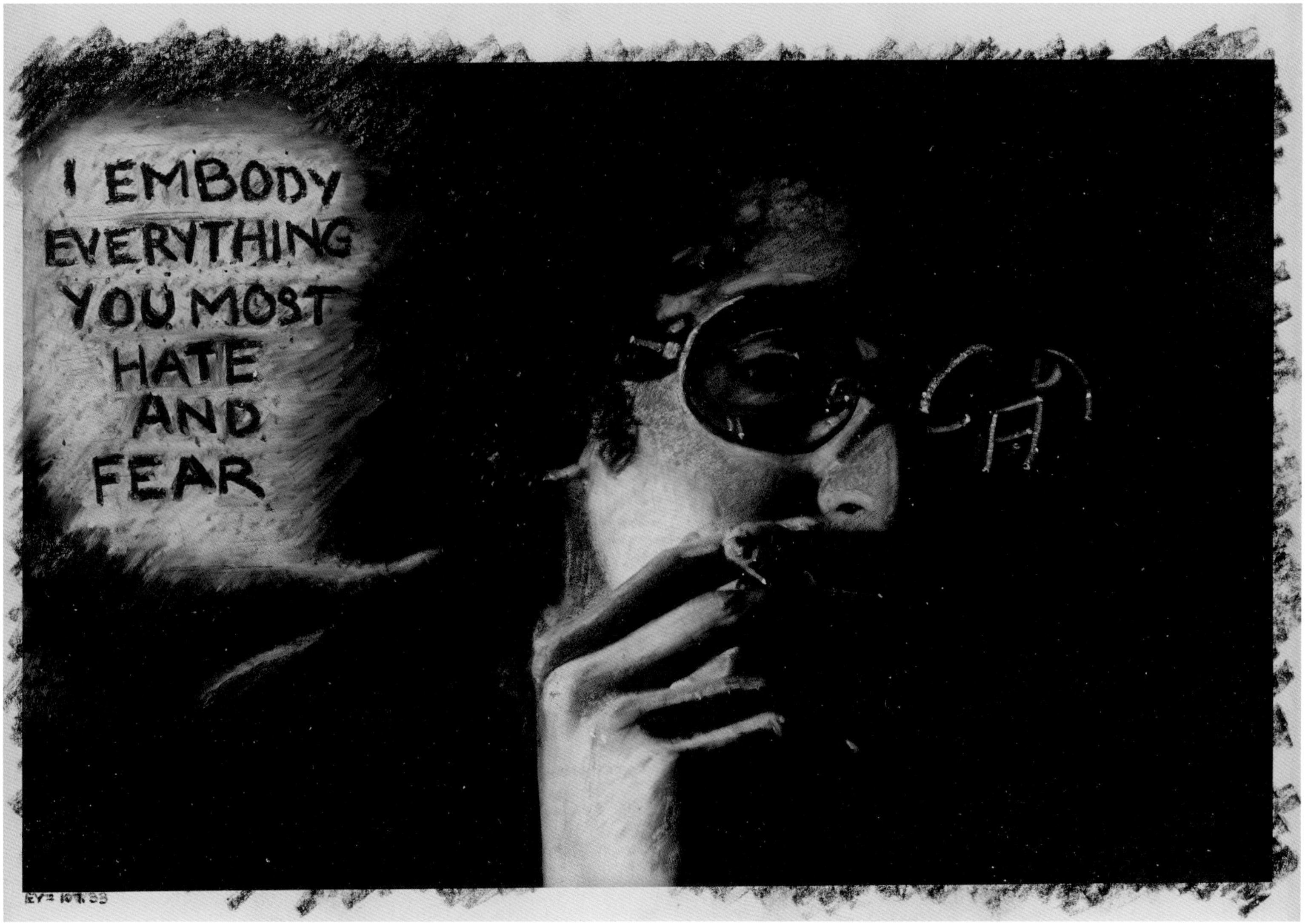

The Mythic Being: I Embody Everything You Most Hate and Fear. 1975
Oil crayon on gelatin silver print
8 × 10 in. (20.3 × 25.4 cm)
Collection Thomas Erben, New York

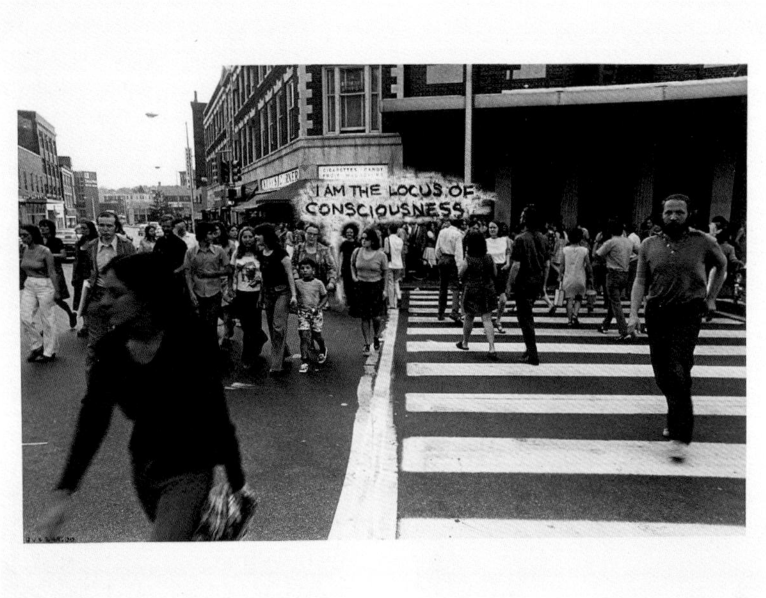

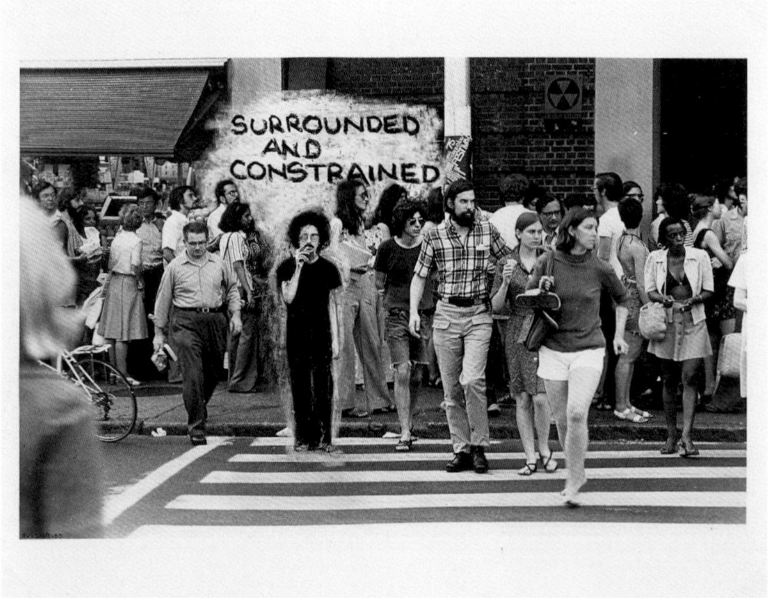

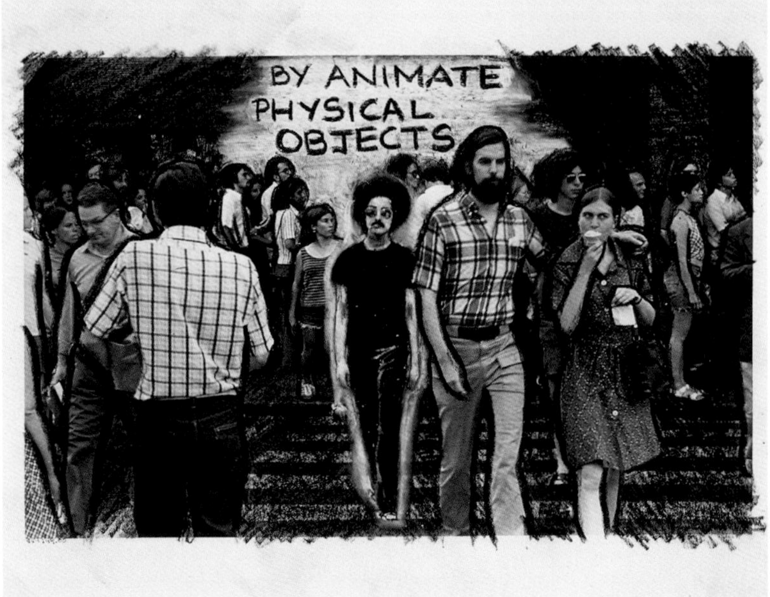

The Mythic Being: I Am the Locus #1–5. 1975
Oil crayon on five gelatin silver prints
Each 8 × 10 in. (20.3 × 25.4 cm)
Smart Museum of Art, The University of Chicago. Purchase, gift of Carl Rungius, by exchange

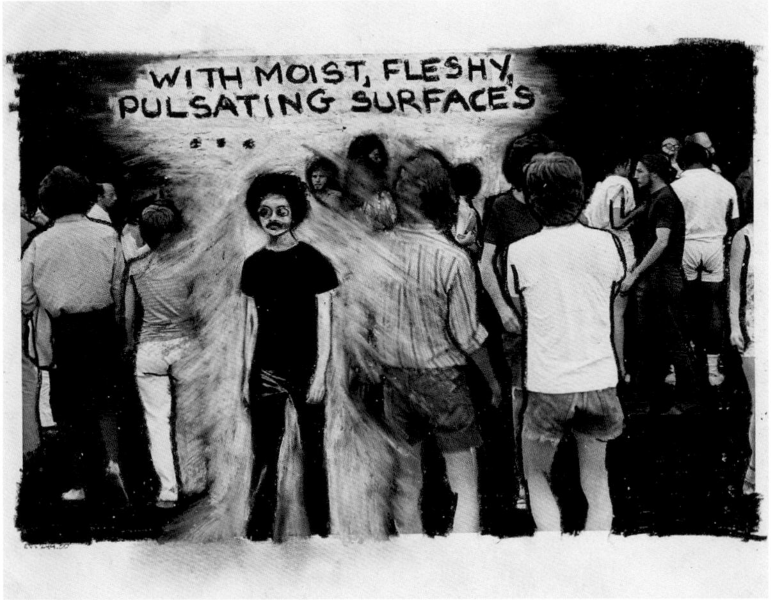
WITH MOIST, FLESHY, PULSATING SURFACES

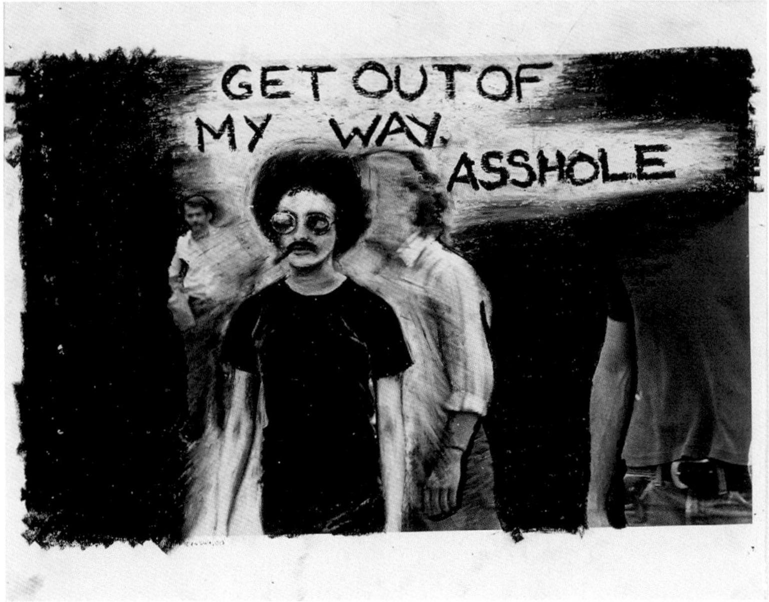
GET OUT OF MY WAY, ASSHOLE

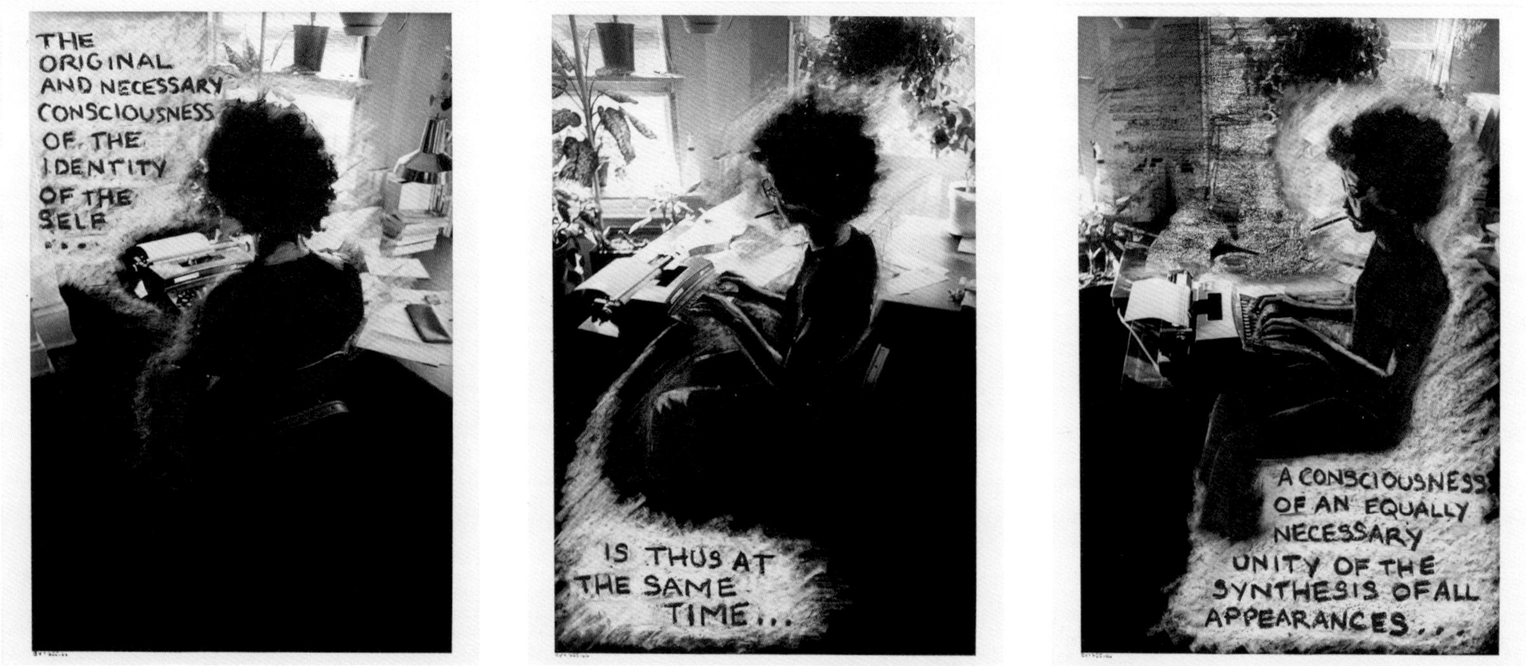

The Mythic Being: A 108. 1975
Oil crayon on six gelatin silver prints
Each 25½ × 17¾ in. (64.7 × 45 cm)
Collection Candace King Weir

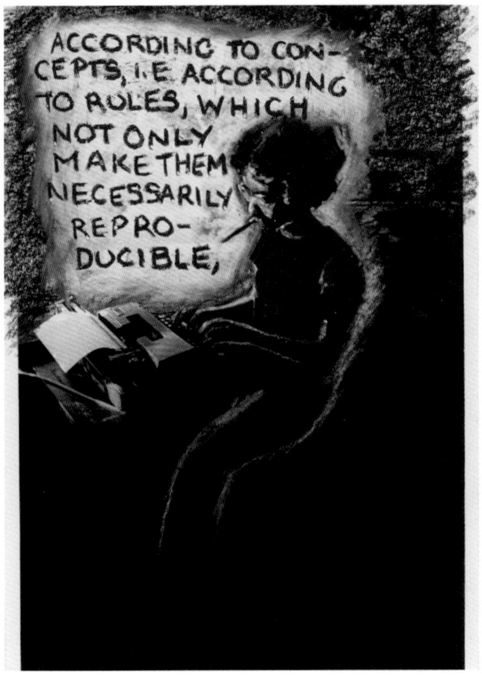
ACCORDING TO CON-
CEPTS, I.E. ACCORDING
TO RULES, WHICH
NOT ONLY
MAKE THEM
NECESSARILY
REPRO-
DUCIBLE,

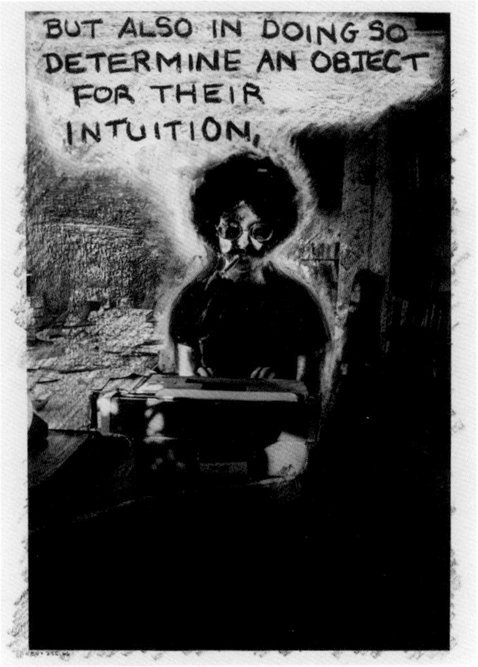
BUT ALSO IN DOING SO
DETERMINE AN OBJECT
FOR THEIR
INTUITION,

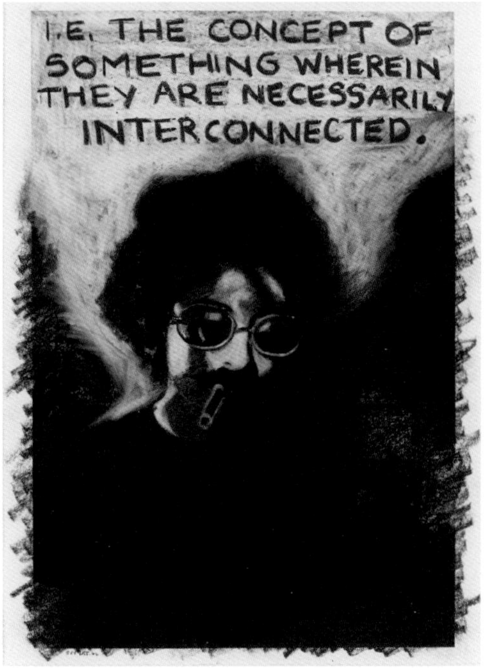
I.E. THE CONCEPT OF
SOMETHING WHEREIN
THEY ARE NECESSARILY
INTERCONNECTED.

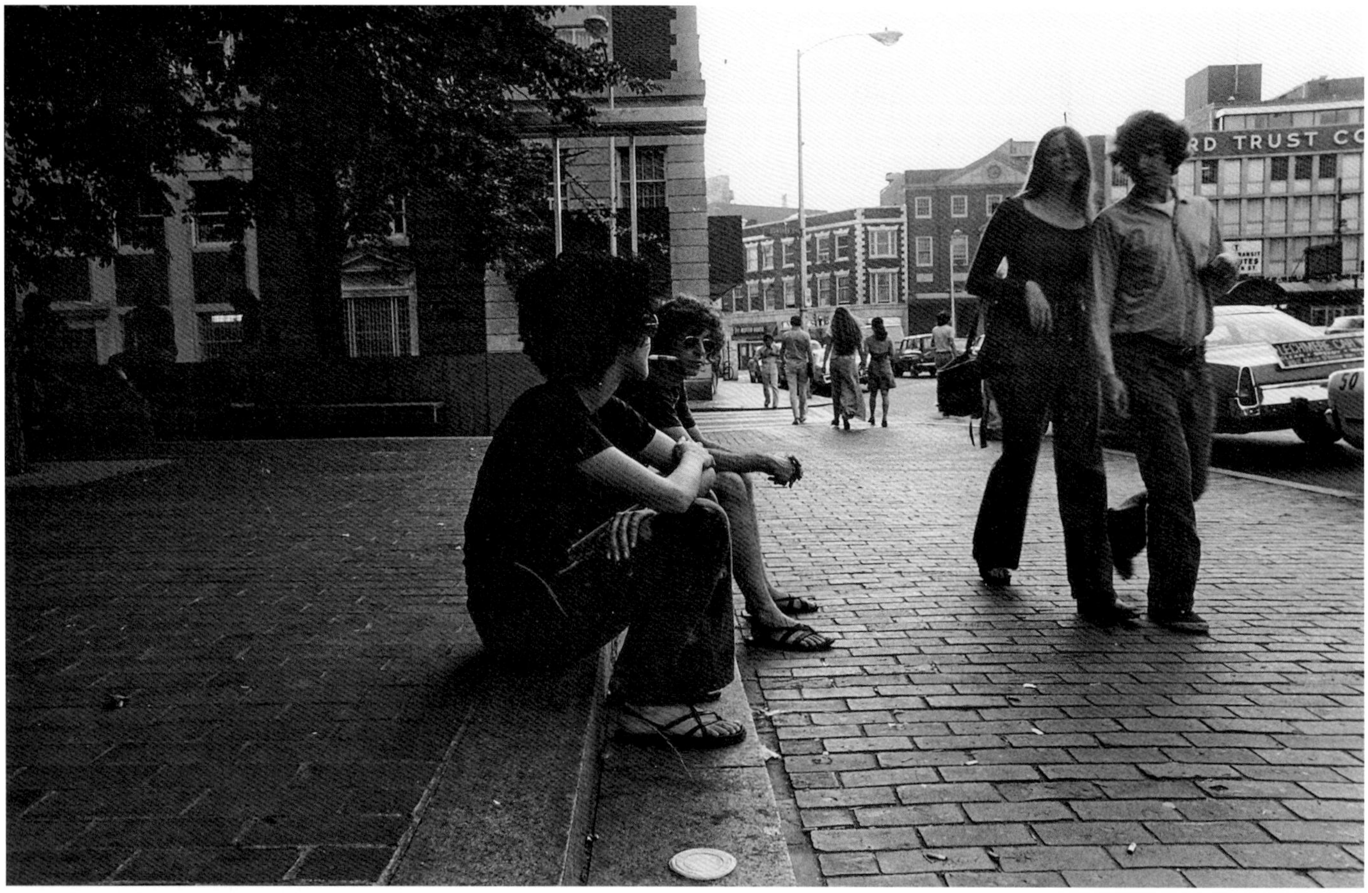

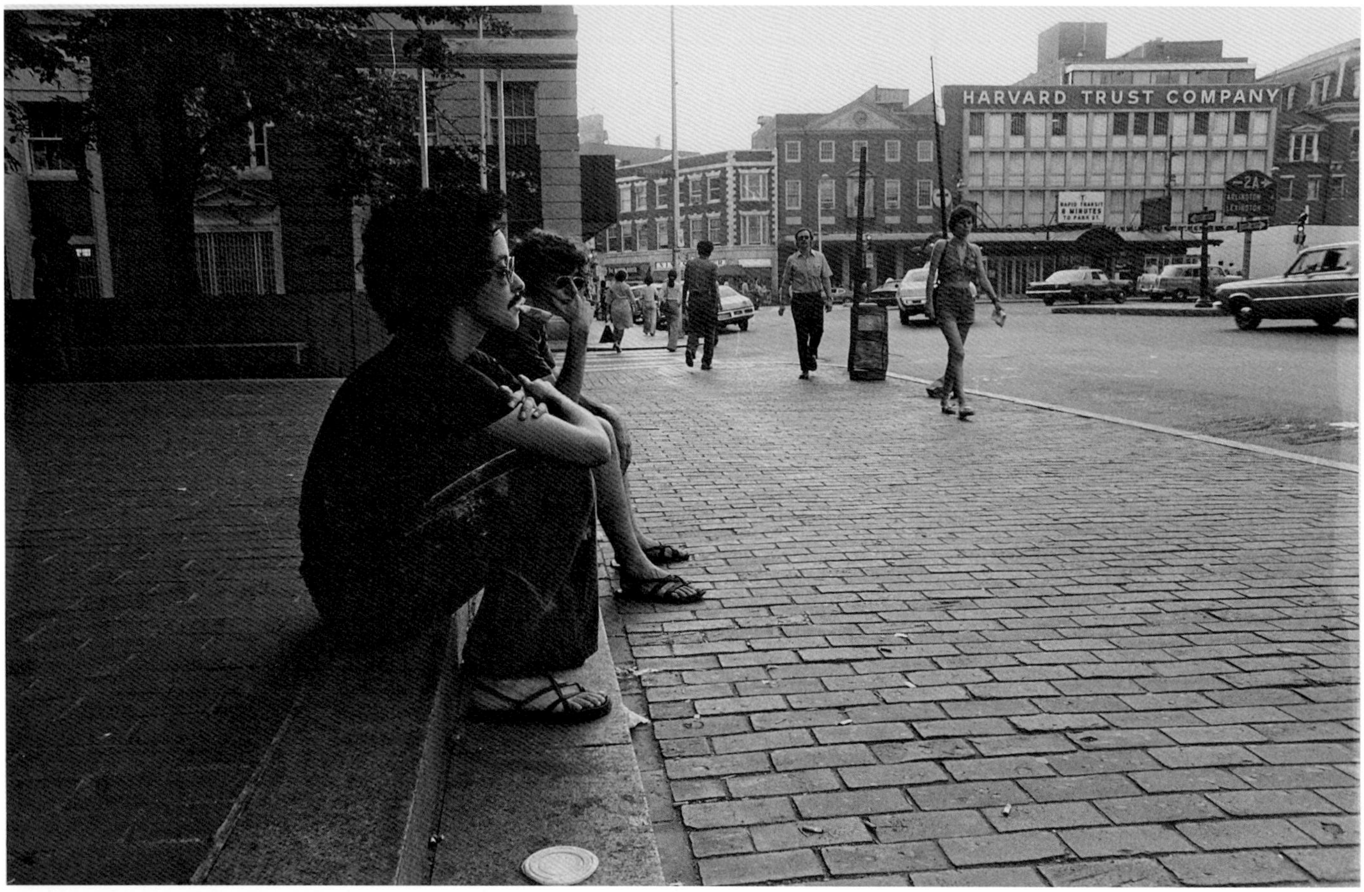

The Mythic Being: Cruising White Women. 1975
Documentation of the performance. Three gelatin silver prints
Each 8 × 10 in. (20.3 × 25.4 cm)
The Eileen Harris Norton Collection

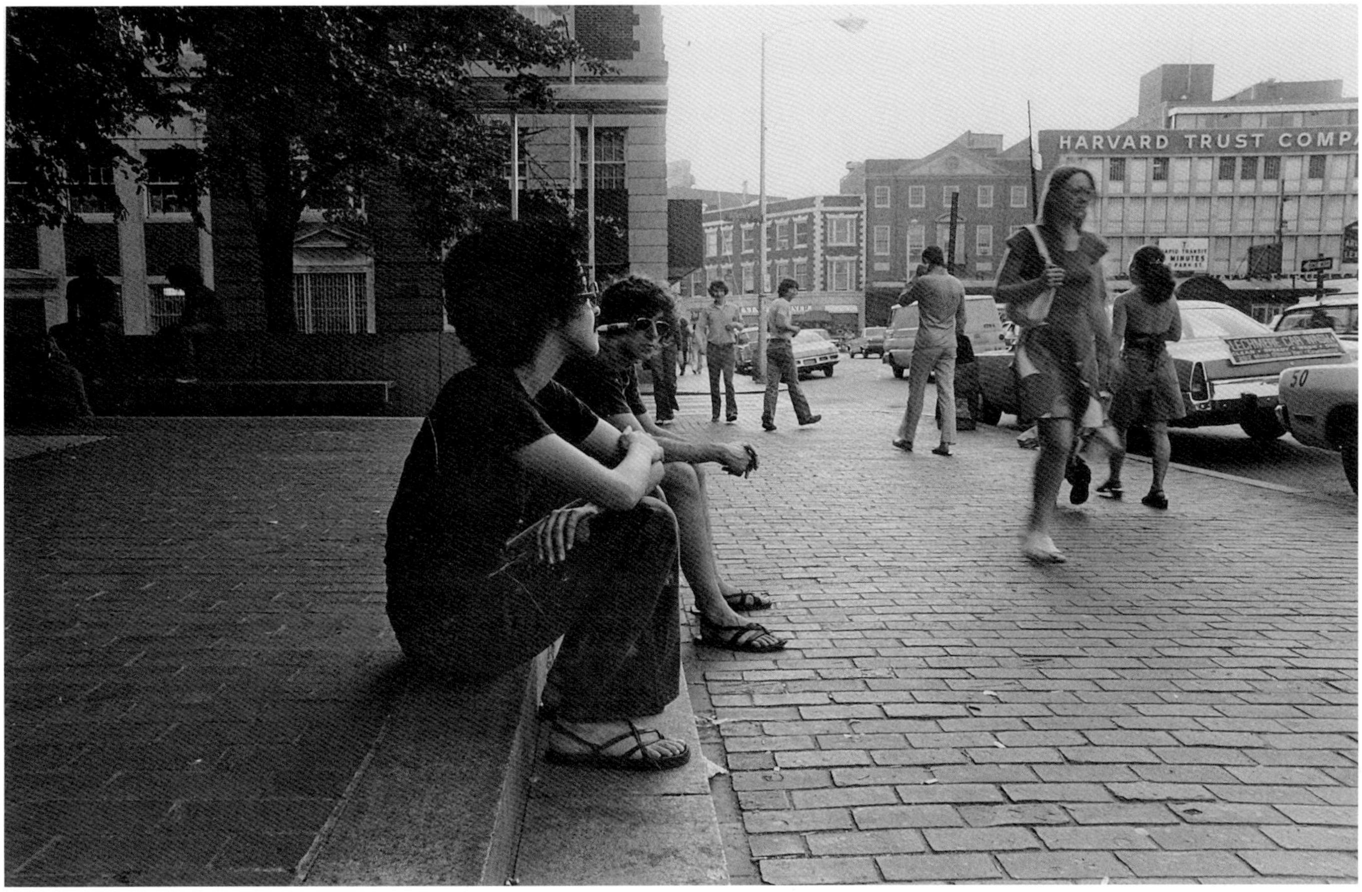
HARVARD TRUST COMPA

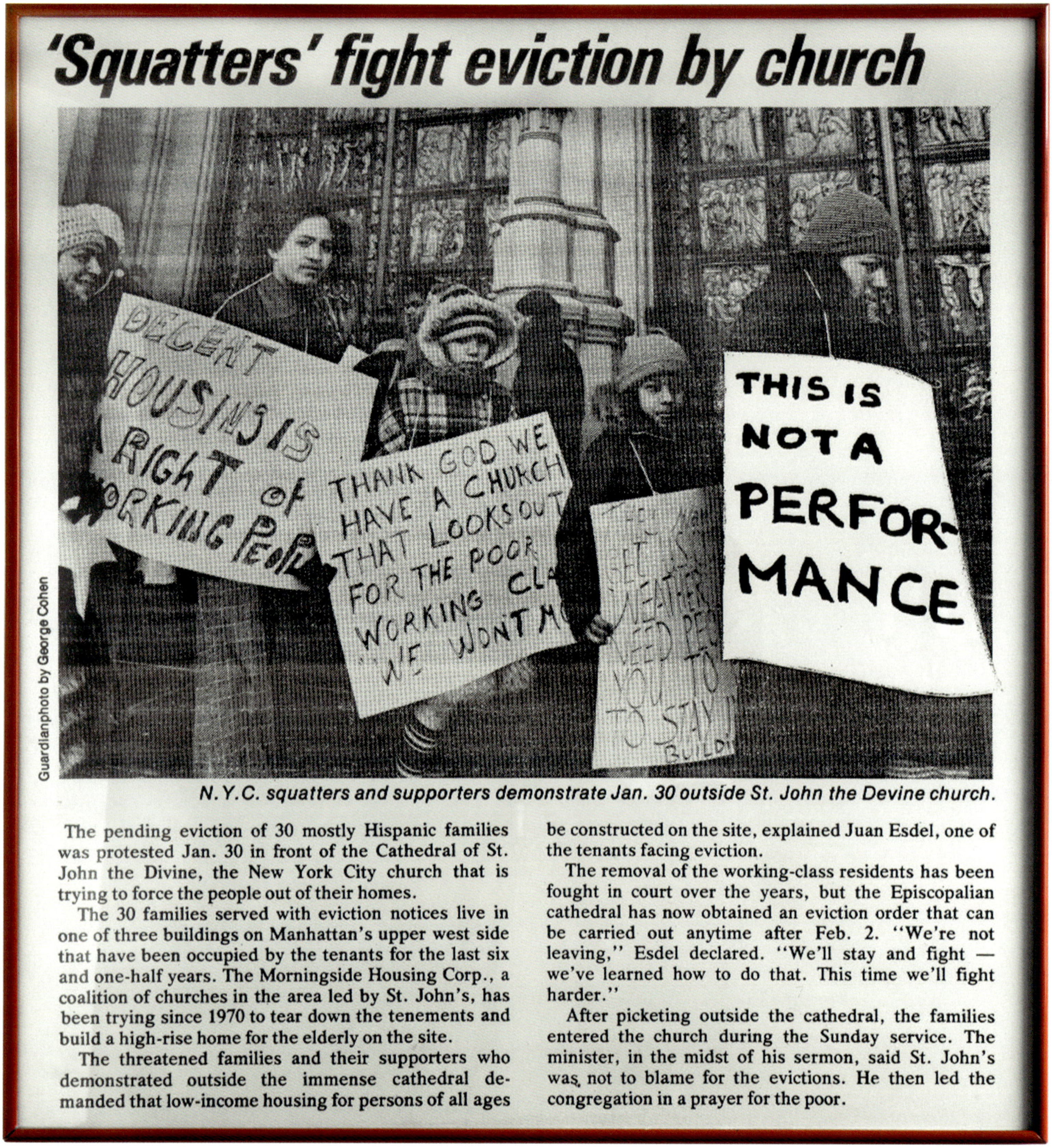
'Squatters' fight eviction by church

N.Y.C. squatters and supporters demonstrate Jan. 30 outside St. John the Devine church.

The pending eviction of 30 mostly Hispanic families was protested Jan. 30 in front of the Cathedral of St. John the Divine, the New York City church that is trying to force the people out of their homes.

The 30 families served with eviction notices live in one of three buildings on Manhattan's upper west side that have been occupied by the tenants for the last six and one-half years. The Morningside Housing Corp., a coalition of churches in the area led by St. John's, has been trying since 1970 to tear down the tenements and build a high-rise home for the elderly on the site.

The threatened families and their supporters who demonstrated outside the immense cathedral demanded that low-income housing for persons of all ages be constructed on the site, explained Juan Esdel, one of the tenants facing eviction.

The removal of the working-class residents has been fought in court over the years, but the Episcopalian cathedral has now obtained an eviction order that can be carried out anytime after Feb. 2. "We're not leaving," Esdel declared. "We'll stay and fight — we've learned how to do that. This time we'll fight harder."

After picketing outside the cathedral, the families entered the church during the Sunday service. The minister, in the midst of his sermon, said St. John's was not to blame for the evictions. He then led the congregation in a prayer for the poor.

This Is Not the Documentation of a Performance. 1976
Ink on screenprint of newspaper article
49 × 45 in. (124.5 × 114.3 cm)
Collection Lonti Ebers, New York

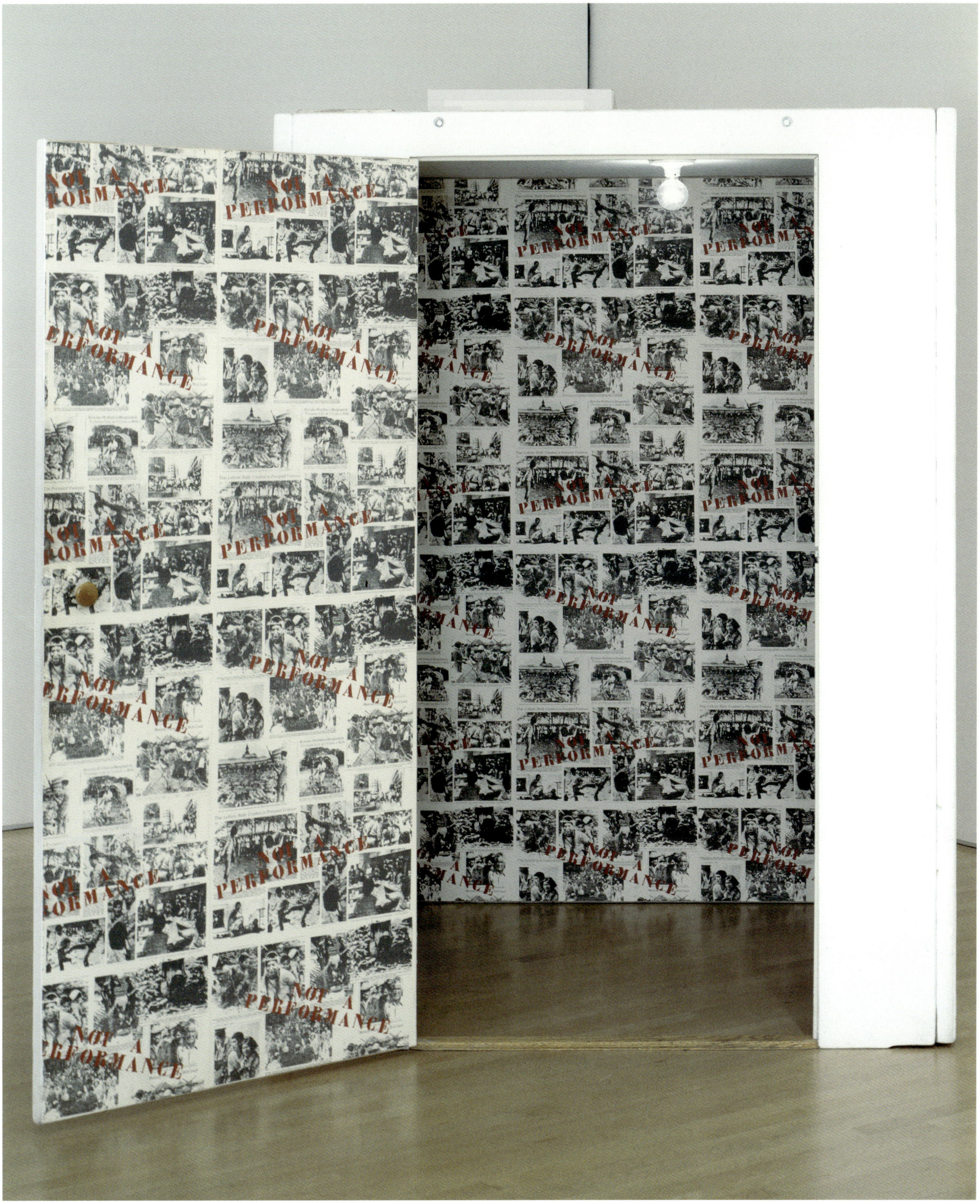

Art for the Art World Surface Pattern. 1976
Mixed-medium installation. Constructed wood environment, custom-printed wallpaper, stenciled text, audio, and naked light bulb
7 ft. × 60 in. × 60 in. (213.4 × 152.4 × 152.4 cm)
San Francisco Museum of Modern Art. Purchase through a gift of Shawn and Brook Byers

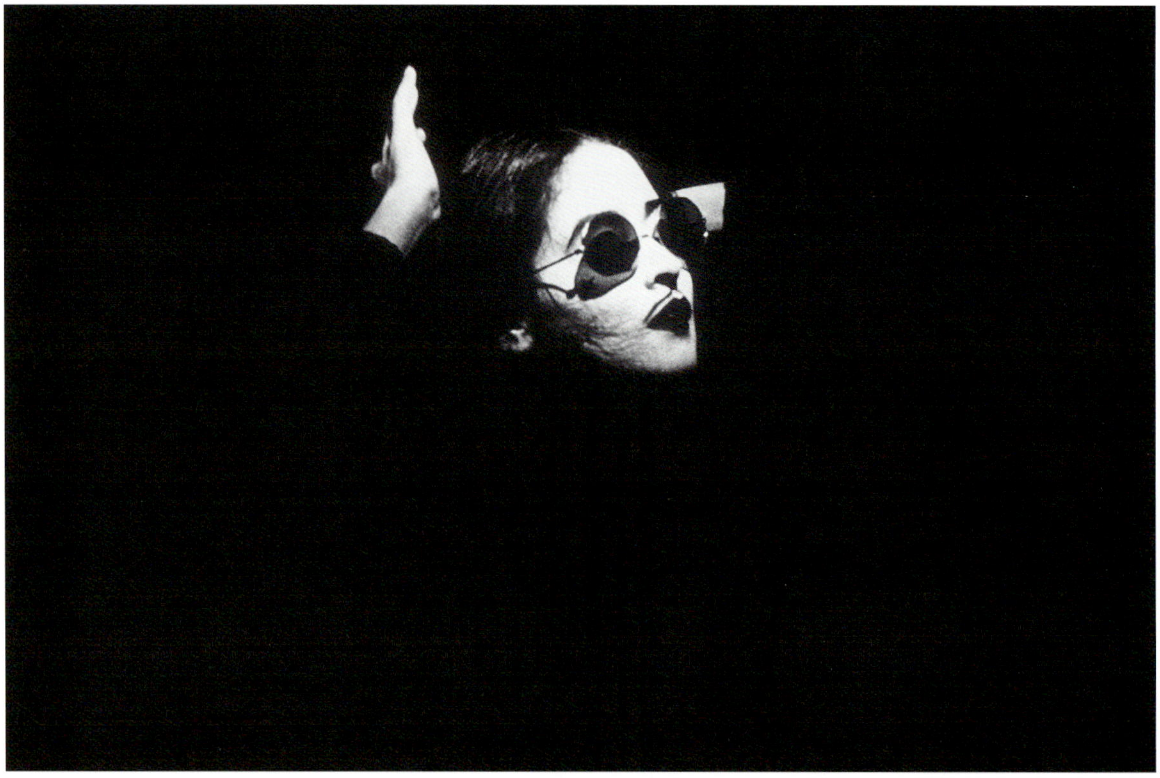

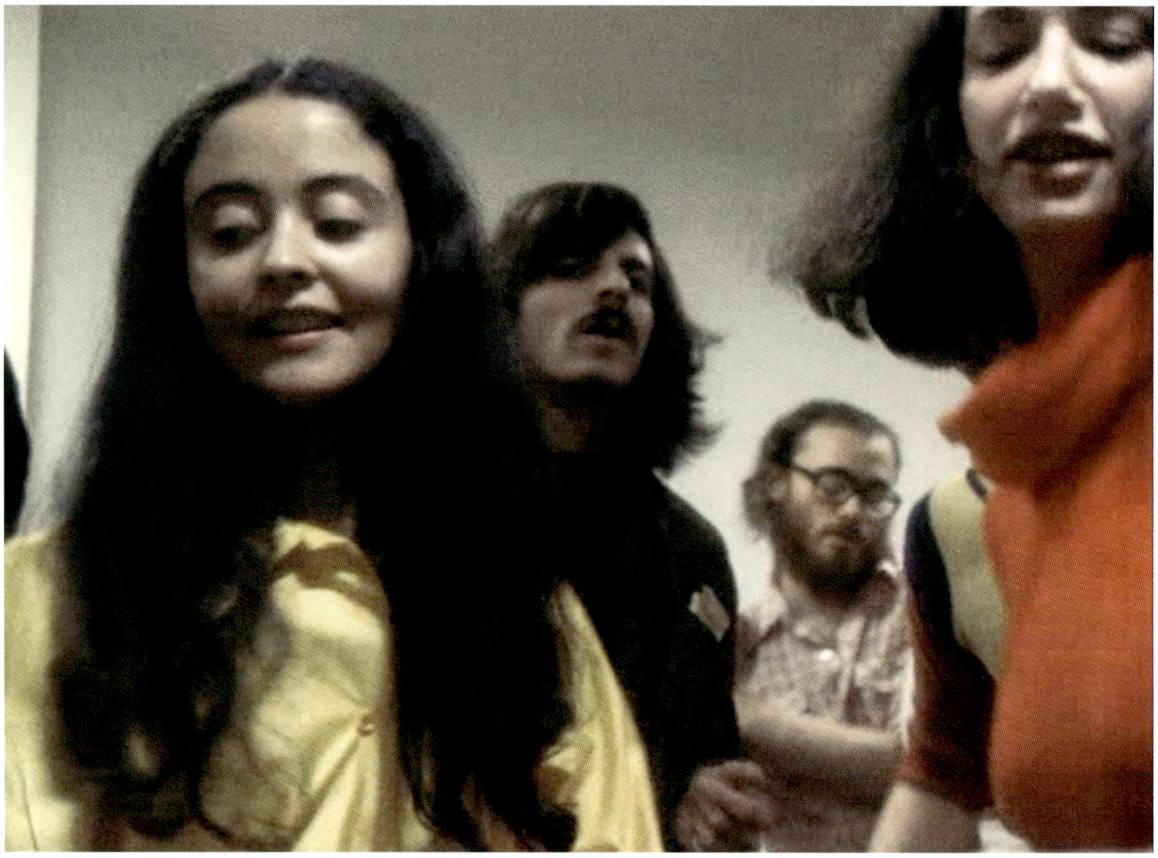

Some Reflective Surfaces. 1975–76
Documentation of the audience-oriented performance at the Whitney Museum of American Art, New York, February 28, 1976.
Two gelatin silver prints and 16mm film transferred to video (color, sound), 00:15:27
Prints 19½ × 15 in. (49.5 × 38.1 cm) and 15 × 19½ in. (38.1 × 49.5 cm)
Collection Adrian Piper Research Archive Foundation Berlin
Details:
print #2
video still at 00:00:52

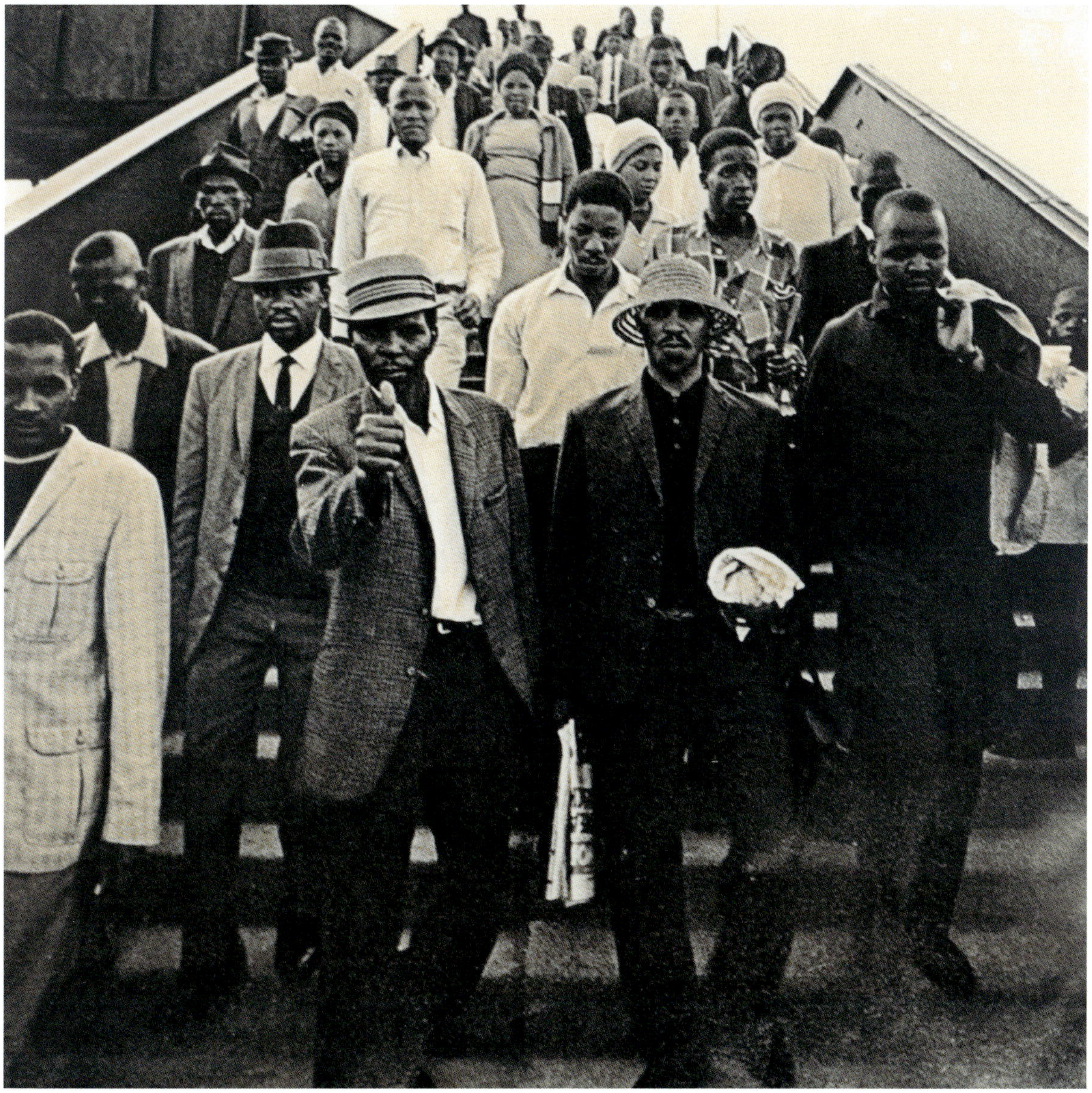

Aspects of the Liberal Dilemma. 1978
Mixed-medium installation. Black-and-white photograph framed under Plexiglas, audio, and lighting
Photograph 18 × 18 in. (45.7 × 45.7 cm); installation dimensions variable
University of California, Berkeley Art Museum and Pacific Film Archive. Gift of the Peter Norton Family Foundation
Detail: photograph

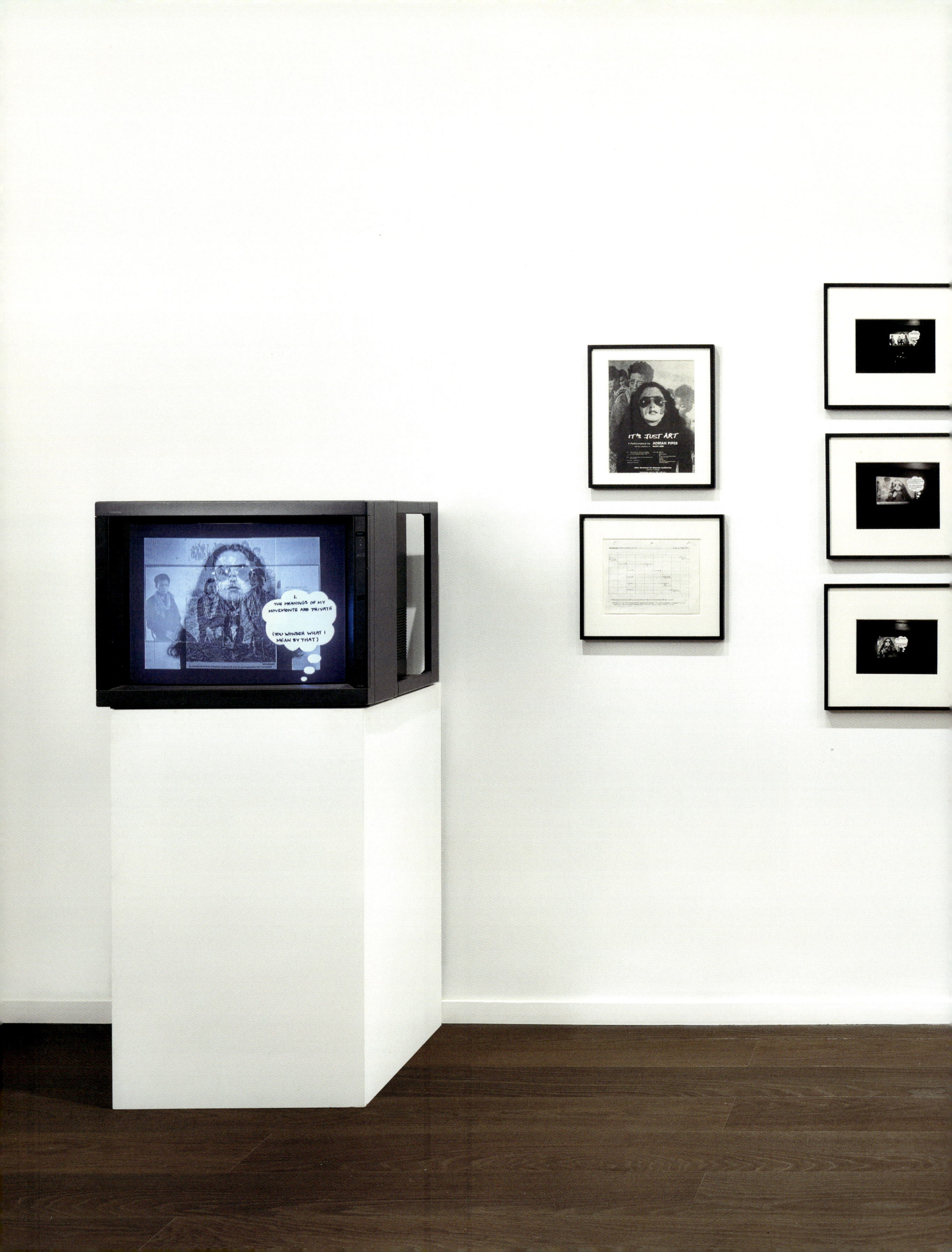
I.
THE MEANINGS OF MY MOVEMENTS ARE PRIVATE
(YOU WONDER WHAT I MEAN BY THAT)
IT'S JUST ART
A Performance by ADRIAN PIPER

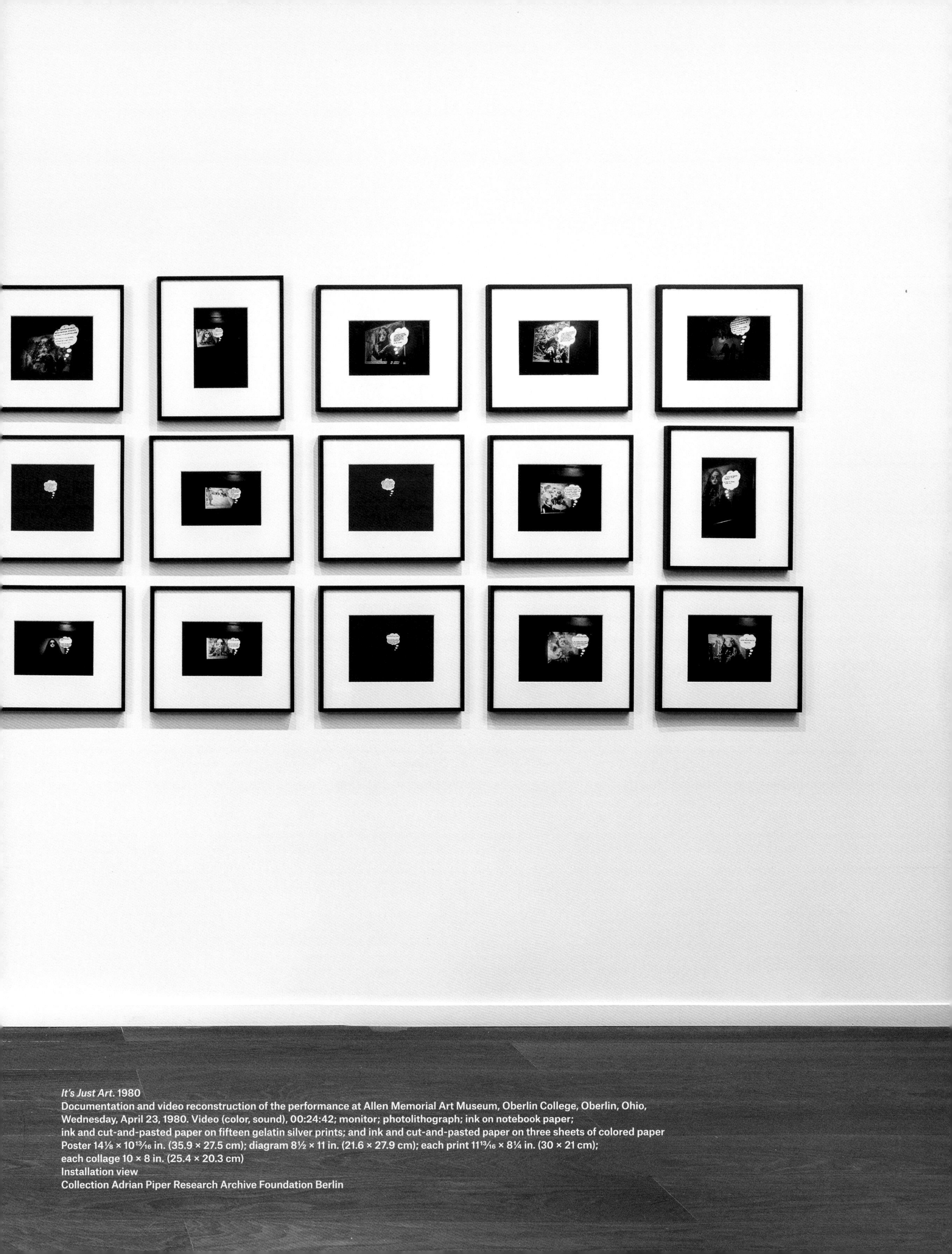

It's Just Art. 1980
Documentation and video reconstruction of the performance at Allen Memorial Art Museum, Oberlin College, Oberlin, Ohio, Wednesday, April 23, 1980. Video (color, sound), 00:24:42; monitor; photolithograph; ink on notebook paper; ink and cut-and-pasted paper on fifteen gelatin silver prints; and ink and cut-and-pasted paper on three sheets of colored paper
Poster 14⅛ × 10¹³⁄₁₆ in. (35.9 × 27.5 cm); diagram 8½ × 11 in. (21.6 × 27.9 cm); each print 11¹³⁄₁₆ × 8¼ in. (30 × 21 cm); each collage 10 × 8 in. (25.4 × 20.3 cm)
Installation view
Collection Adrian Piper Research Archive Foundation Berlin

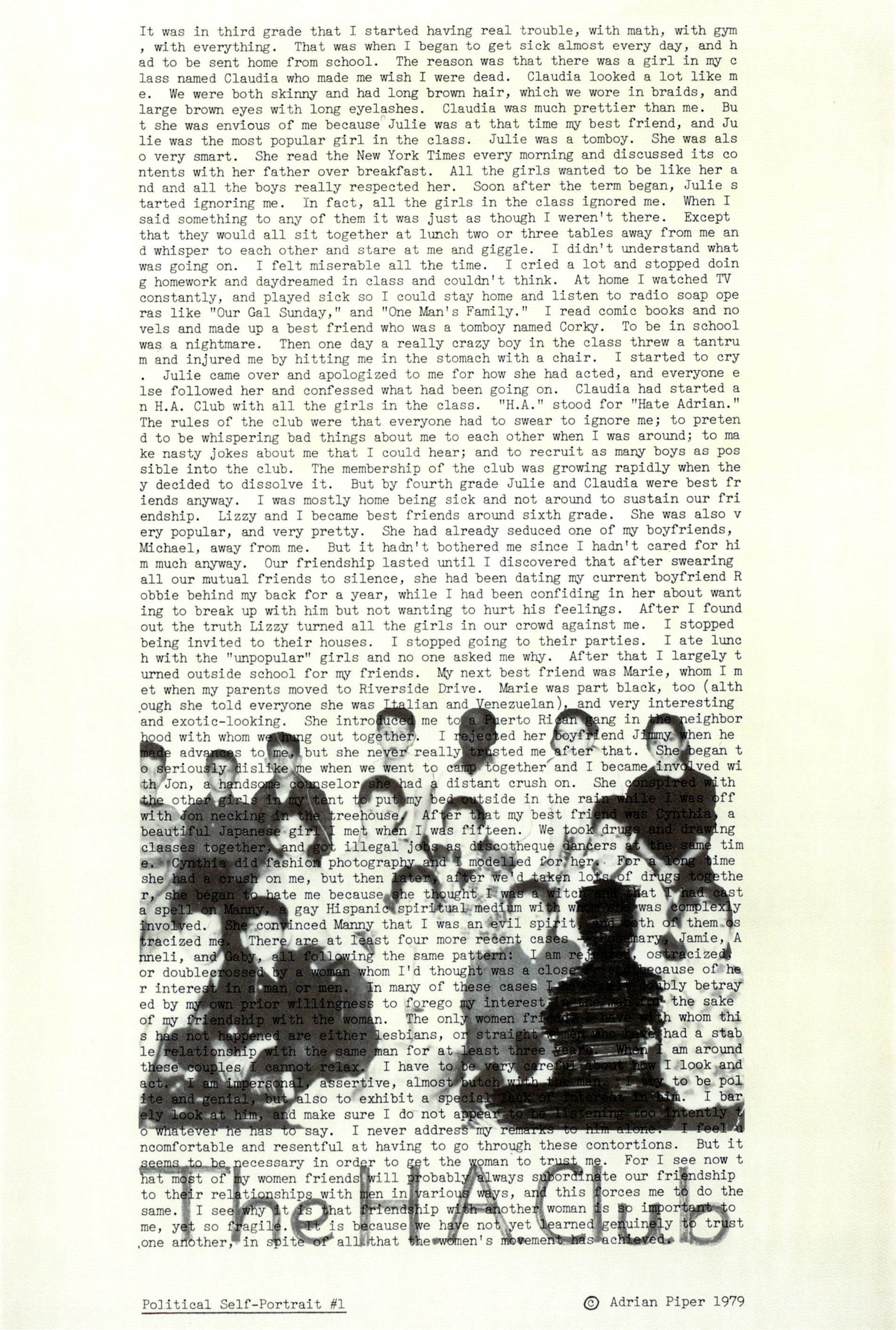

It was in third grade that I started having real trouble, with math, with gym
, with everything. That was when I began to get sick almost every day, and h
ad to be sent home from school. The reason was that there was a girl in my c
lass named Claudia who made me wish I were dead. Claudia looked a lot like m
e. We were both skinny and had long brown hair, which we wore in braids, and
large brown eyes with long eyelashes. Claudia was much prettier than me. Bu
t she was envious of me because Julie was at that time my best friend, and Ju
lie was the most popular girl in the class. Julie was a tomboy. She was als
o very smart. She read the New York Times every morning and discussed its co
ntents with her father over breakfast. All the girls wanted to be like her a
nd and all the boys really respected her. Soon after the term began, Julie s
tarted ignoring me. In fact, all the girls in the class ignored me. When I
said something to any of them it was just as though I weren't there. Except
that they would all sit together at lunch two or three tables away from me an
d whisper to each other and stare at me and giggle. I didn't understand what
was going on. I felt miserable all the time. I cried a lot and stopped doin
g homework and daydreamed in class and couldn't think. At home I watched TV
constantly, and played sick so I could stay home and listen to radio soap ope
ras like "Our Gal Sunday," and "One Man's Family." I read comic books and no
vels and made up a best friend who was a tomboy named Corky. To be in school
was a nightmare. Then one day a really crazy boy in the class threw a tantru
m and injured me by hitting me in the stomach with a chair. I started to cry
. Julie came over and apologized to me for how she had acted, and everyone e
lse followed her and confessed what had been going on. Claudia had started a
n H.A. Club with all the girls in the class. "H.A." stood for "Hate Adrian."
The rules of the club were that everyone had to swear to ignore me; to preten
d to be whispering bad things about me to each other when I was around; to ma
ke nasty jokes about me that I could hear; and to recruit as many boys as pos
sible into the club. The membership of the club was growing rapidly when the
y decided to dissolve it. But by fourth grade Julie and Claudia were best fr
iends anyway. I was mostly home being sick and not around to sustain our fri
endship. Lizzy and I became best friends around sixth grade. She was also v
ery popular, and very pretty. She had already seduced one of my boyfriends,
Michael, away from me. But it hadn't bothered me since I hadn't cared for hi
m much anyway. Our friendship lasted until I discovered that after swearing
all our mutual friends to silence, she had been dating my current boyfriend R
obbie behind my back for a year, while I had been confiding in her about want
ing to break up with him but not wanting to hurt his feelings. After I found
out the truth Lizzy turned all the girls in our crowd against me. I stopped
being invited to their houses. I stopped going to their parties. I ate lunc
h with the "unpopular" girls and no one asked me why. After that I largely t
urned outside school for my friends. My next best friend was Marie, whom I m
et when my parents moved to Riverside Drive. Marie was part black, too (alth
ough she told everyone she was Italian and Venezuelan), and very interesting
and exotic-looking. She introduced me to a Puerto Rican gang in the neighbor
hood with whom we hung out together. I rejected her boyfriend Jimmy when he
made advances to me, but she never really trusted me after that. She began t
o seriously dislike me when we went to camp together and I became involved wi
th Jon, a handsome counselor she had a distant crush on. She conspired with
the other girls in my tent to put my bed outside in the rain while I was off
with Jon necking in the treehouse. After that my best friend was Cynthia, a
beautiful Japanese girl I met when I was fifteen. We took drugs and drawing
classes together, and got illegal jobs as discotheque dancers at the same tim
e. Cynthia did fashion photography and I modelled for her. For a long time
she had a crush on me, but then later, after we'd taken lots of drugs togethe
r, she began to hate me because she thought I was a witch and that I had cast
a spell on Manny, a gay Hispanic spiritual medium with whom she was complexly
involved. She convinced Manny that I was an evil spirit, and both of them os
tracized me. There are at least four more recent cases — Rosemary, Jamie, A
nneli, and Gaby, all following the same pattern: I am rejected, ostracized,
or doublecrossed by a woman whom I'd thought was a close [illegible] because of he
r interest in a man or men. In many of these cases I [illegible]ubly betray
ed by my own prior willingness to forego my interest [illegible] the sake
of my friendship with the woman. The only women fri[illegible]th whom thi
s has not happened are either lesbians, or straight [illegible] had a stab
le relationship with the same man for at least three [illegible]. When I am around
these couples I cannot relax. I have to be very care[illegible] I look and
act. I am impersonal, assertive, almost butch with [illegible] to be pol
ite and genial, but also to exhibit a special [illegible]. I bar
ely look at him, and make sure I do not appear [illegible] intently t
o whatever he has to say. I never address my [illegible]. I feel u
ncomfortable and resentful at having to go through these contortions. But it
seems to be necessary in order to get the woman to trust me. For I see now t
hat most of my women friends will probably always subordinate our friendship
to their relationships with men in various ways, and this forces me to do the
same. I see why it is that friendship with another woman is so important to
me, yet so fragile. It is because we have not yet learned genuinely to trust
one another, in spite of all that the women's movement has achieved.

Political Self-Portrait #1

© Adrian Piper 1979

***Political Self-Portrait #1 (Sex)*. 1979**
Photostat
29⅝ × 19⅝ in. (75.3 × 49.9 cm)
Collection Margaret and Daniel S. Loeb

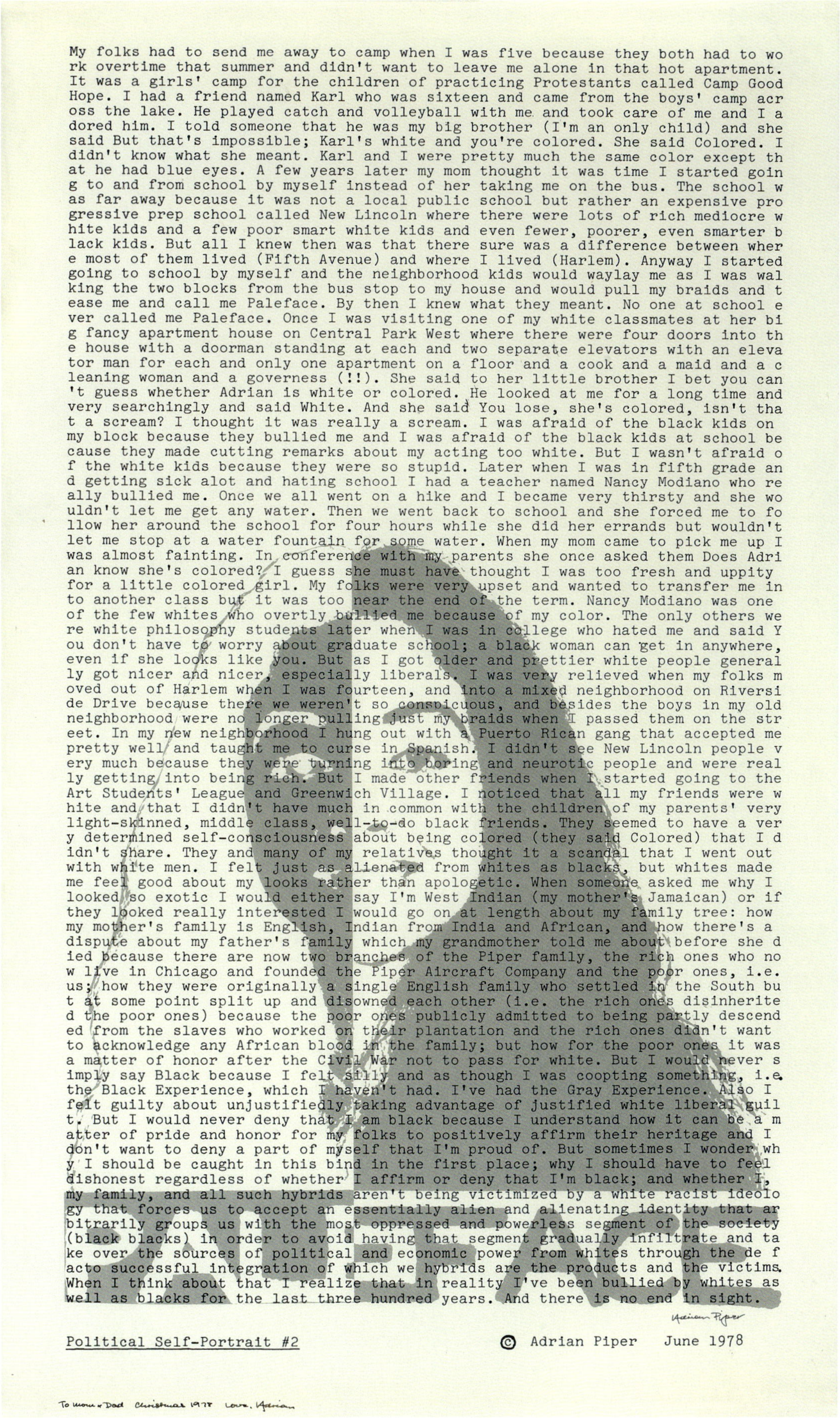

My folks had to send me away to camp when I was five because they both had to wo
rk overtime that summer and didn't want to leave me alone in that hot apartment.
It was a girls' camp for the children of practicing Protestants called Camp Good
Hope. I had a friend named Karl who was sixteen and came from the boys' camp acr
oss the lake. He played catch and volleyball with me and took care of me and I a
dored him. I told someone that he was my big brother (I'm an only child) and she
said But that's impossible; Karl's white and you're colored. She said Colored. I
didn't know what she meant. Karl and I were pretty much the same color except th
at he had blue eyes. A few years later my mom thought it was time I started goin
g to and from school by myself instead of her taking me on the bus. The school w
as far away because it was not a local public school but rather an expensive pro
gressive prep school called New Lincoln where there were lots of rich mediocre w
hite kids and a few poor smart white kids and even fewer, poorer, even smarter b
lack kids. But all I knew then was that there sure was a difference between wher
e most of them lived (Fifth Avenue) and where I lived (Harlem). Anyway I started
going to school by myself and the neighborhood kids would waylay me as I was wal
king the two blocks from the bus stop to my house and would pull my braids and t
ease me and call me Paleface. By then I knew what they meant. No one at school e
ver called me Paleface. Once I was visiting one of my white classmates at her bi
g fancy apartment house on Central Park West where there were four doors into th
e house with a doorman standing at each and two separate elevators with an eleva
tor man for each and only one apartment on a floor and a cook and a maid and a c
leaning woman and a governess (!!). She said to her little brother I bet you can
't guess whether Adrian is white or colored. He looked at me for a long time and
very searchingly and said White. And she said You lose, she's colored, isn't tha
t a scream? I thought it was really a scream. I was afraid of the black kids on
my block because they bullied me and I was afraid of the black kids at school be
cause they made cutting remarks about my acting too white. But I wasn't afraid o
f the white kids because they were so stupid. Later when I was in fifth grade an
d getting sick alot and hating school I had a teacher named Nancy Modiano who re
ally bullied me. Once we all went on a hike and I became very thirsty and she wo
uldn't let me get any water. Then we went back to school and she forced me to fo
llow her around the school for four hours while she did her errands but wouldn't
let me stop at a water fountain for some water. When my mom came to pick me up I
was almost fainting. In conference with my parents she once asked them Does Adri
an know she's colored? I guess she must have thought I was too fresh and uppity
for a little colored girl. My folks were very upset and wanted to transfer me in
to another class but it was too near the end of the term. Nancy Modiano was one
of the few whites who overtly bullied me because of my color. The only others we
re white philosophy students later when I was in college who hated me and said Y
ou don't have to worry about graduate school; a black woman can get in anywhere,
even if she looks like you. But as I got older and prettier white people general
ly got nicer and nicer, especially liberals. I was very relieved when my folks m
oved out of Harlem when I was fourteen, and into a mixed neighborhood on Riversi
de Drive because there we weren't so conspicuous, and besides the boys in my old
neighborhood were no longer pulling just my braids when I passed them on the str
eet. In my new neighborhood I hung out with a Puerto Rican gang that accepted me
pretty well and taught me to curse in Spanish. I didn't see New Lincoln people v
ery much because they were turning into boring and neurotic people and were real
ly getting into being rich. But I made other friends when I started going to the
Art Students' League and Greenwich Village. I noticed that all my friends were w
hite and that I didn't have much in common with the children of my parents' very
light-skinned, middle class, well-to-do black friends. They seemed to have a ver
y determined self-consciousness about being colored (they said Colored) that I d
idn't share. They and many of my relatives thought it a scandal that I went out
with white men. I felt just as alienated from whites as blacks, but whites made
me feel good about my looks rather than apologetic. When someone asked me why I
looked so exotic I would either say I'm West Indian (my mother's Jamaican) or if
they looked really interested I would go on at length about my family tree: how
my mother's family is English, Indian from India and African, and how there's a
dispute about my father's family which my grandmother told me about before she d
ied because there are now two branches of the Piper family, the rich ones who no
w live in Chicago and founded the Piper Aircraft Company and the poor ones, i.e.
us; how they were originally a single English family who settled in the South bu
t at some point split up and disowned each other (i.e. the rich ones disinherite
d the poor ones) because the poor ones publicly admitted to being partly descend
ed from the slaves who worked on their plantation and the rich ones didn't want
to acknowledge any African blood in the family; but how for the poor ones it was
a matter of honor after the Civil War not to pass for white. But I would never s
imply say Black because I felt silly and as though I was coopting something, i.e.
the Black Experience, which I haven't had. I've had the Gray Experience. Also I
felt guilty about unjustifiedly taking advantage of justified white liberal guil
t. But I would never deny that I am black because I understand how it can be a m
atter of pride and honor for my folks to positively affirm their heritage and I
don't want to deny a part of myself that I'm proud of. But sometimes I wonder wh
y I should be caught in this bind in the first place; why I should have to feel
dishonest regardless of whether I affirm or deny that I'm black; and whether I,
my family, and all such hybrids aren't being victimized by a white racist ideolo
gy that forces us to accept an essentially alien and alienating identity that ar
bitrarily groups us with the most oppressed and powerless segment of the society
(black blacks) in order to avoid having that segment gradually infiltrate and ta
ke over the sources of political and economic power from whites through the de f
acto successful integration of which we hybrids are the products and the victims.
When I think about that I realize that in reality I've been bullied by whites as
well as blacks for the last three hundred years. And there is no end in sight.

Adrian Piper

Political Self-Portrait #2 © Adrian Piper June 1978

To Mom & Dad Christmas 1978 Love, Adrian

Political Self-Portrait #2 (Race). 1978
Photostat
29⅝ × 19⅝ in. (75.3 × 49.9 cm)
Collection Adrian Piper Research Archive Foundation Berlin

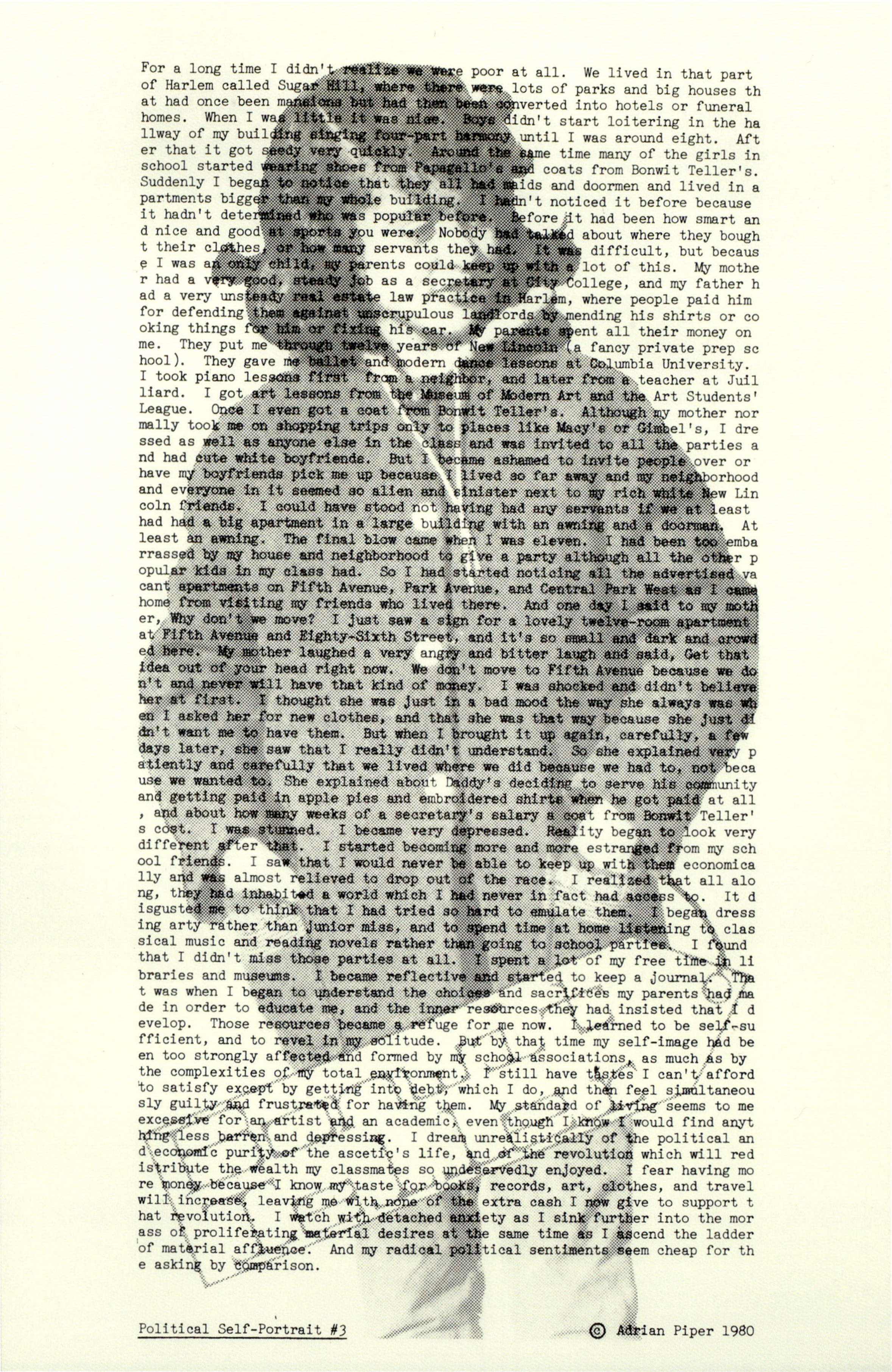

Political Self-Portrait #3 (Class). 1980
Photostat
29⅝ × 19⅝ in. (75.3 × 49.9 cm)
Collection John Campione

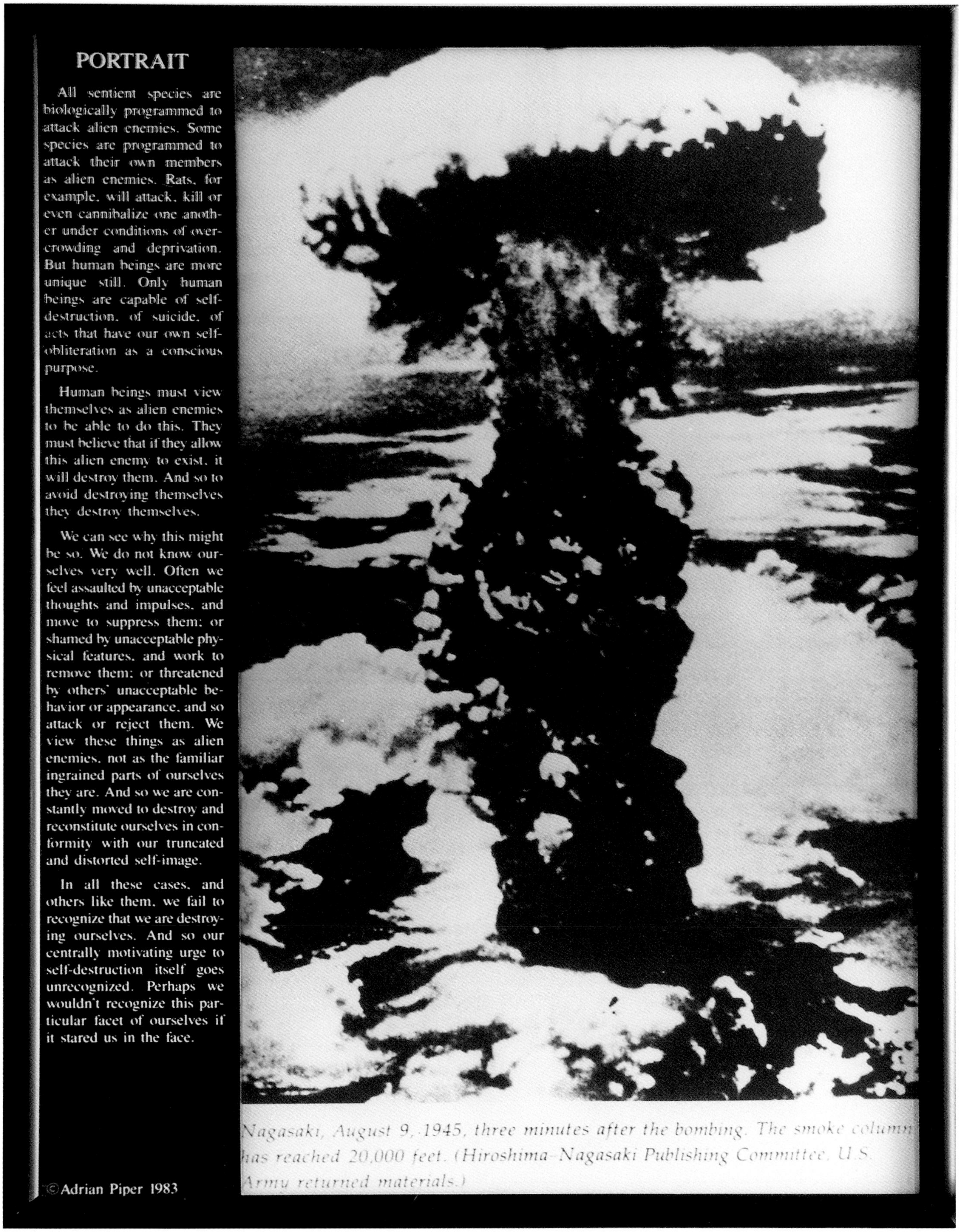

Portrait. 1983
Photostat
40 × 30 in. (101.6 × 76.2 cm)
Private collection

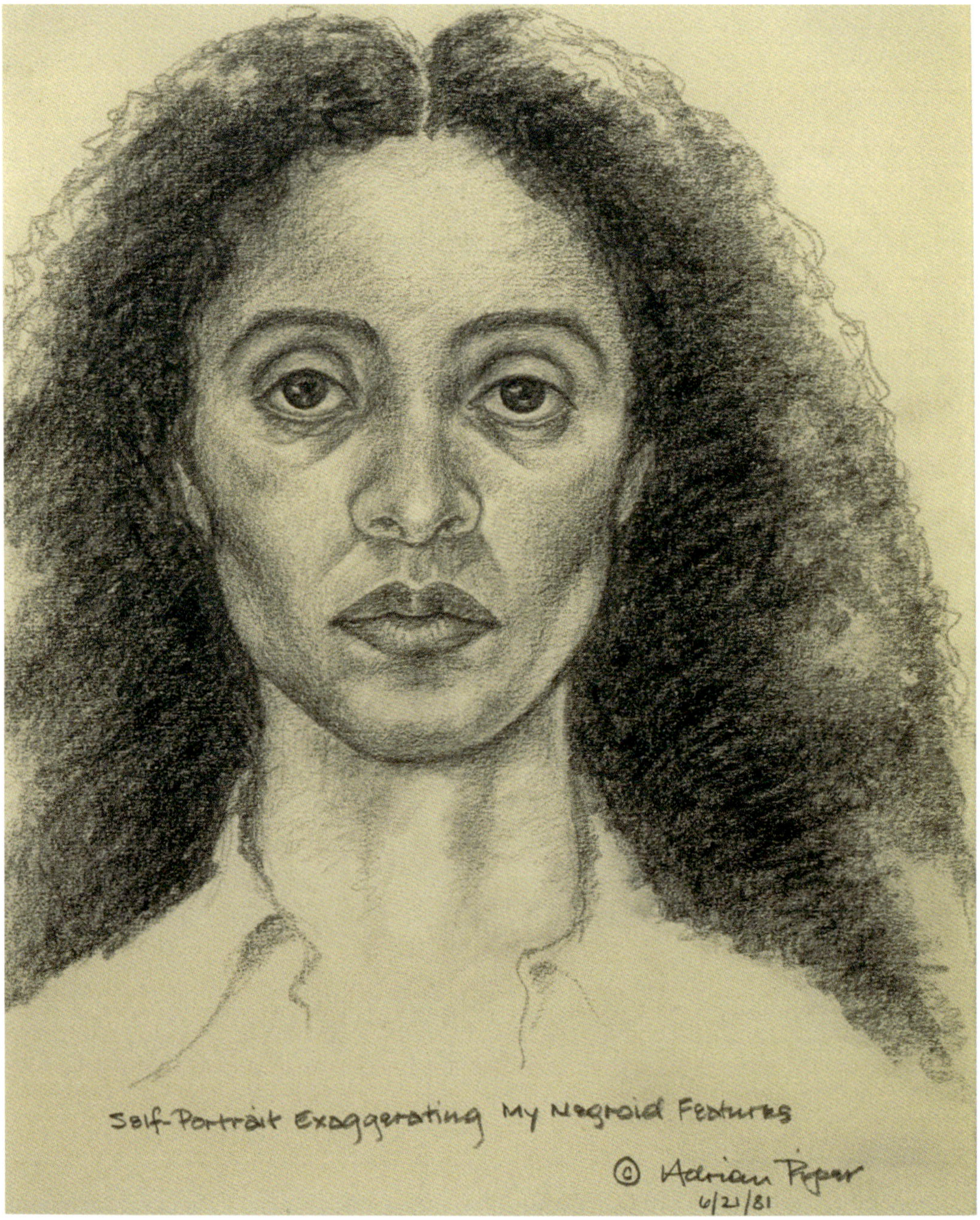

Self-Portrait Exaggerating My Negroid Features. 1981
Pencil on paper
10 × 8 in. (25.4 × 20.3 cm)
The Eileen Harris Norton Collection

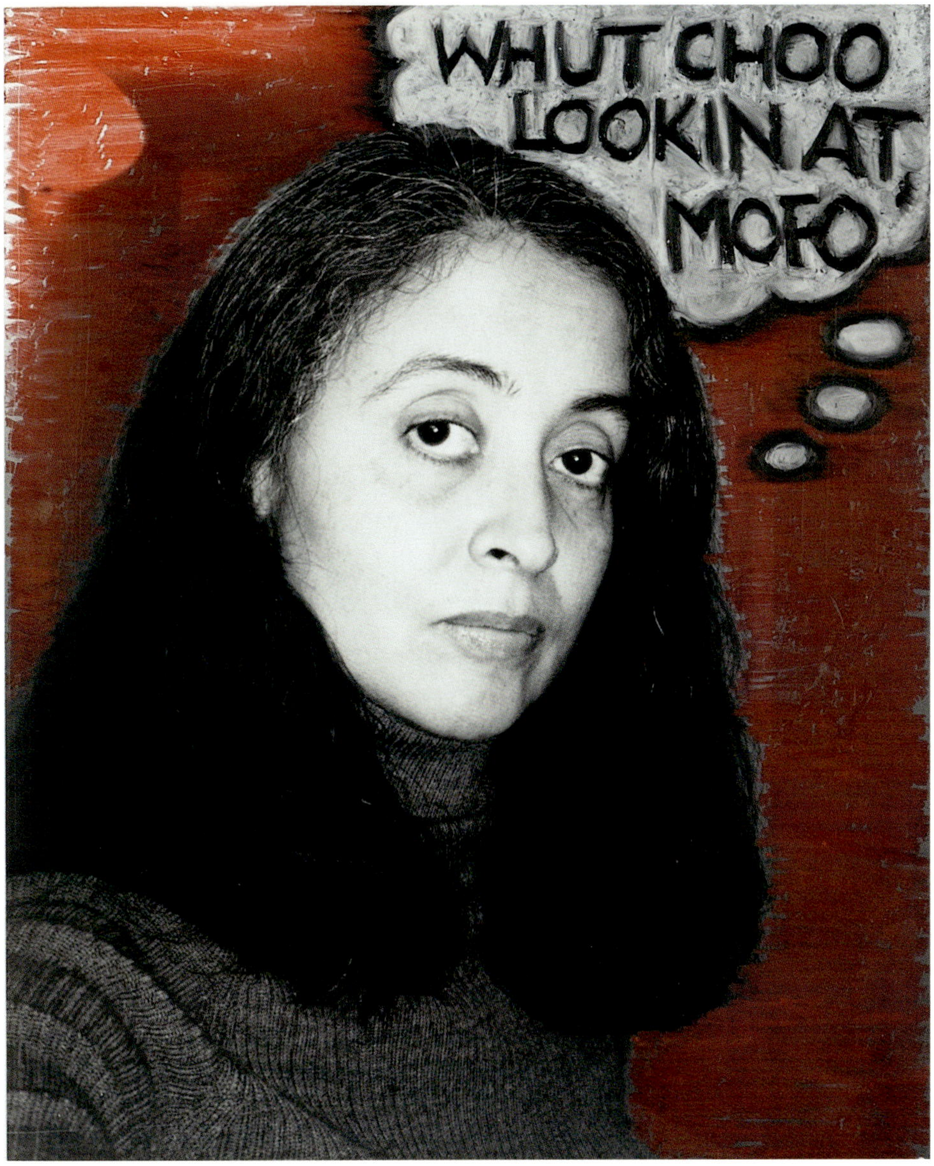

Self-Portrait as a Nice White Lady. 1995
Oil crayon on black-and-white photograph
10 × 8 in. (25.4 × 20.3 cm)
The Studio Museum in Harlem, New York. Museum purchase made possible by a gift from Barbara Karp Shuster, New York

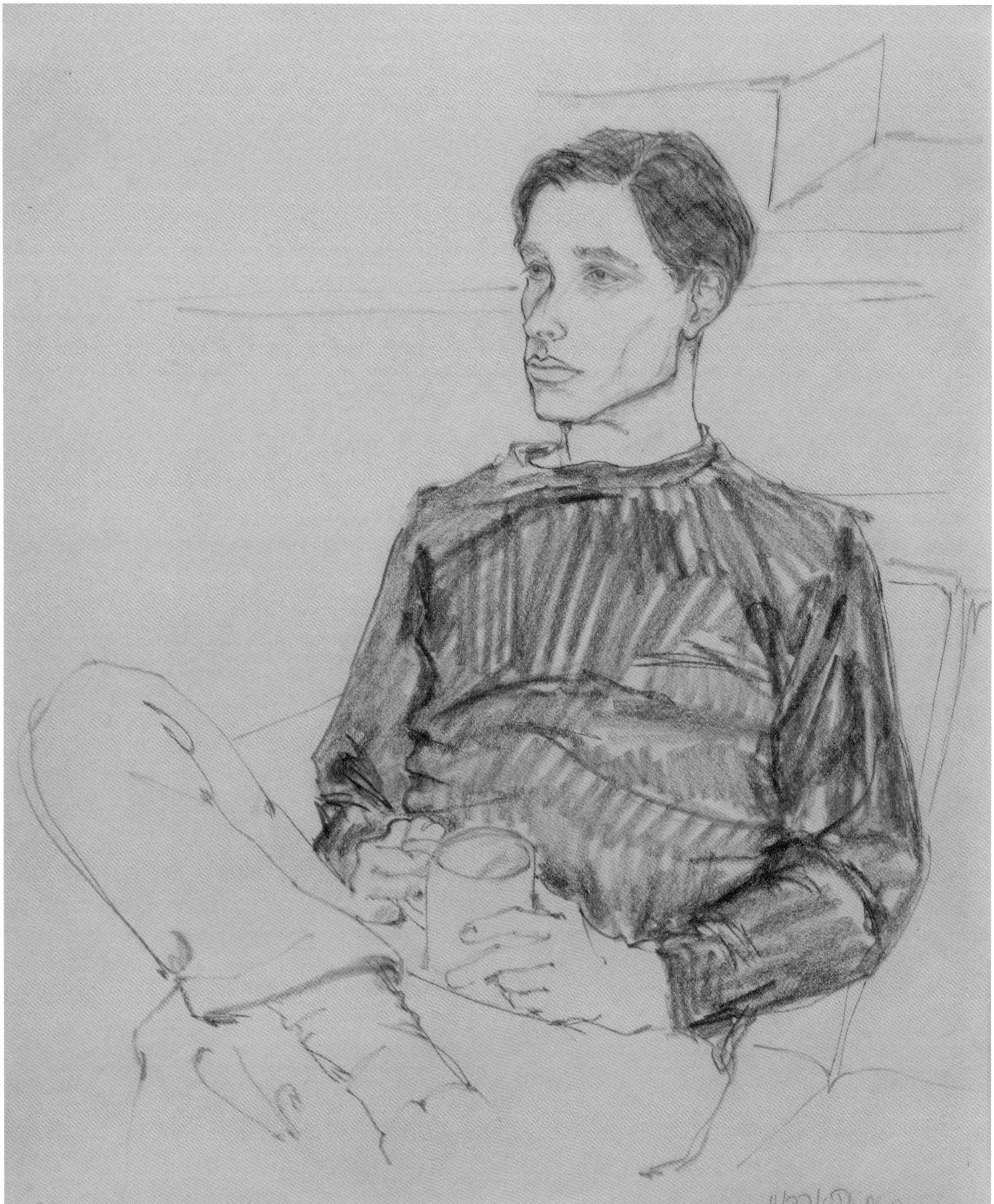

Phillip Zohn. 1966
Charcoal on paper
21 × 17 in. (53.3 × 43.2 cm)
Collection Adrian Piper Research Archive Foundation Berlin

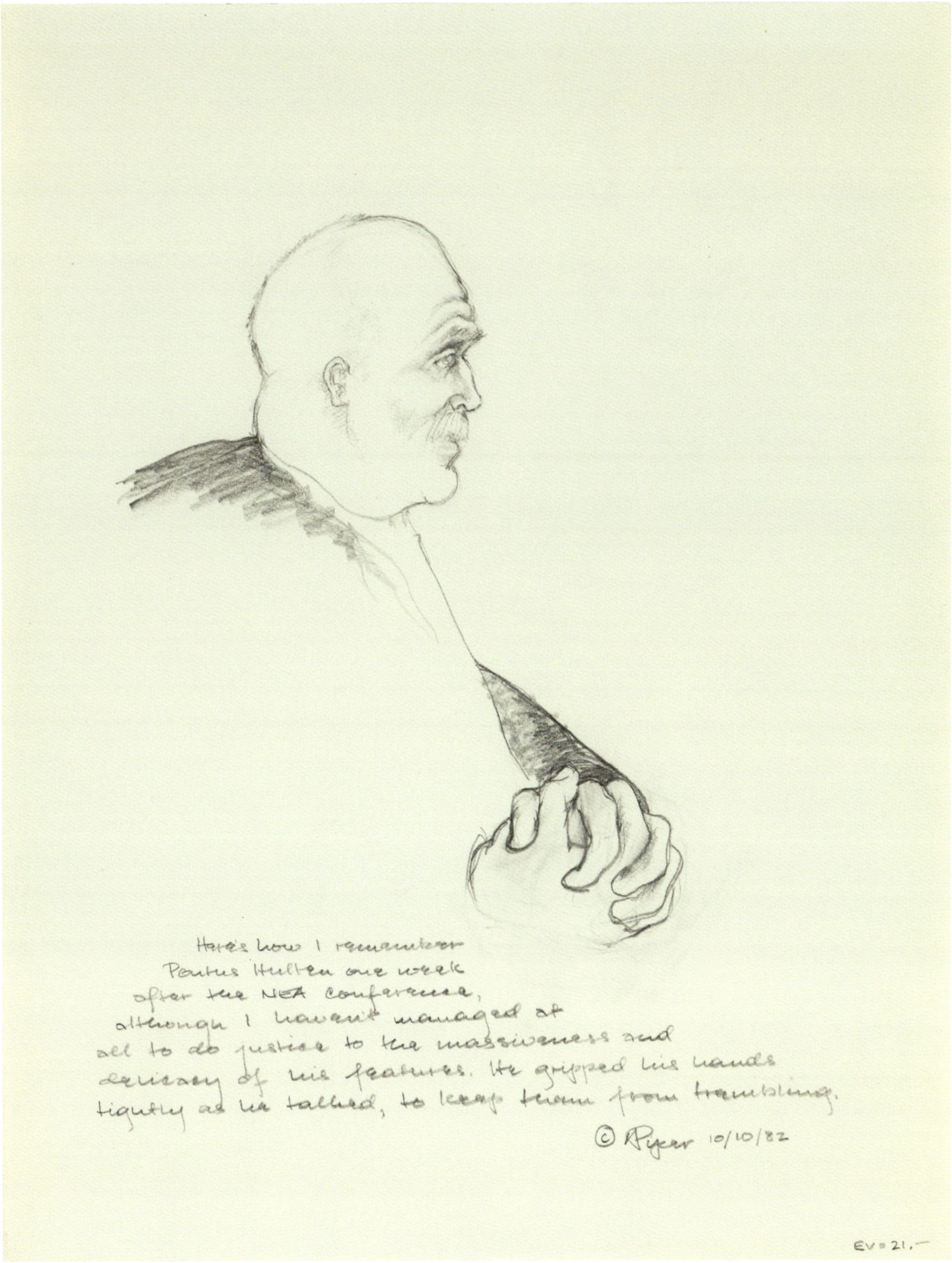

$10.00/Hour Drawing of Pontus Hulten. 1982
Pencil on paper
12 × 8⅞ in. (30.5 × 22.6 cm)
Collection Adrian Piper Research Archive Foundation Berlin

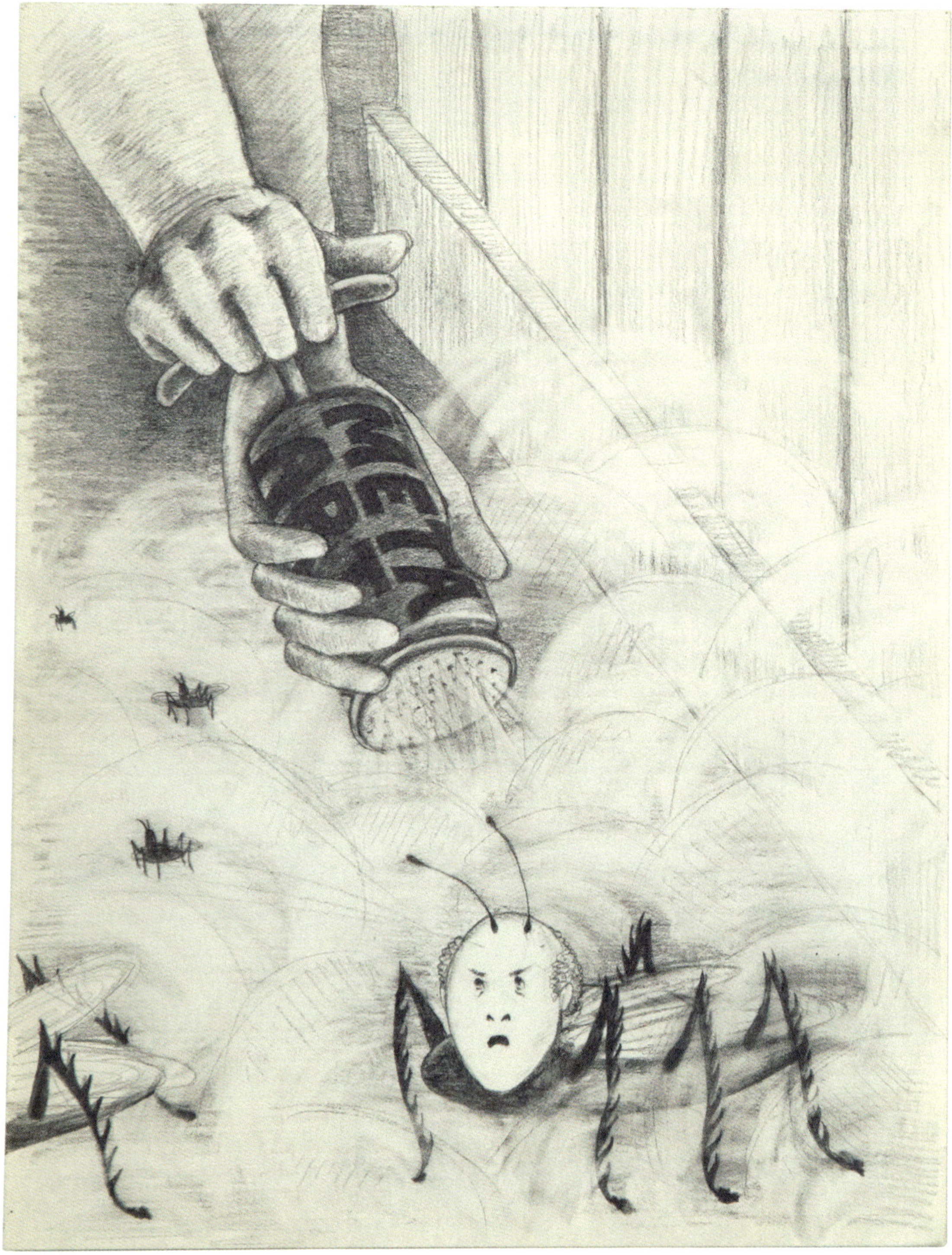

An Open Letter to Donald Kuspit (Kuspit Extermination Fantasy). 1987
Pencil on paper
12 × 9 in. (30.4 × 22.8 cm)
University of Colorado Art Museum, Boulder. Gift of the artist

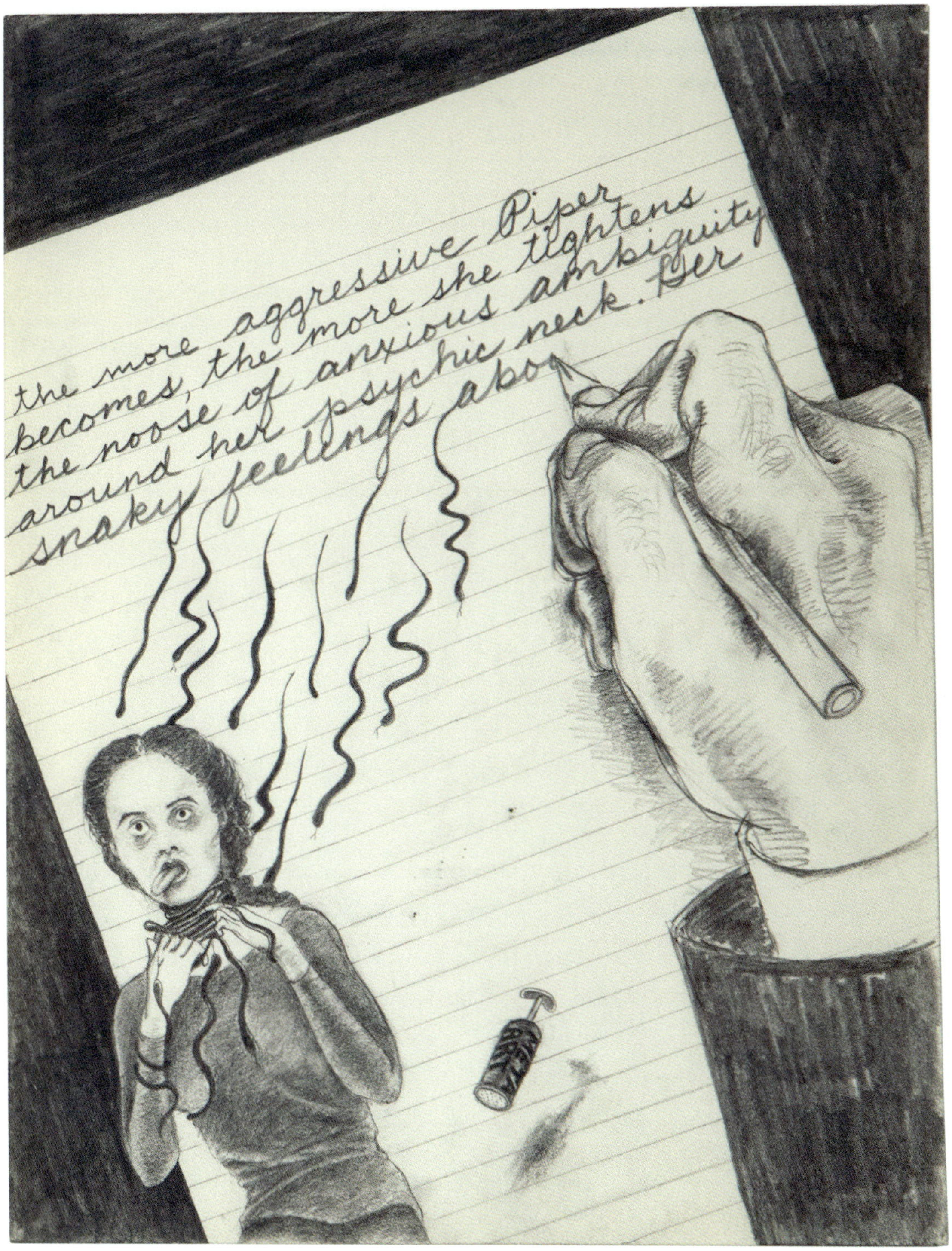

An Open Letter to Donald Kuspit (Kuspit Strangulation Fantasy). 1987
Pencil on paper
12 × 9 in. (30.4 × 22.8 cm)
University of Colorado Art Museum, Boulder. Gift of the artist

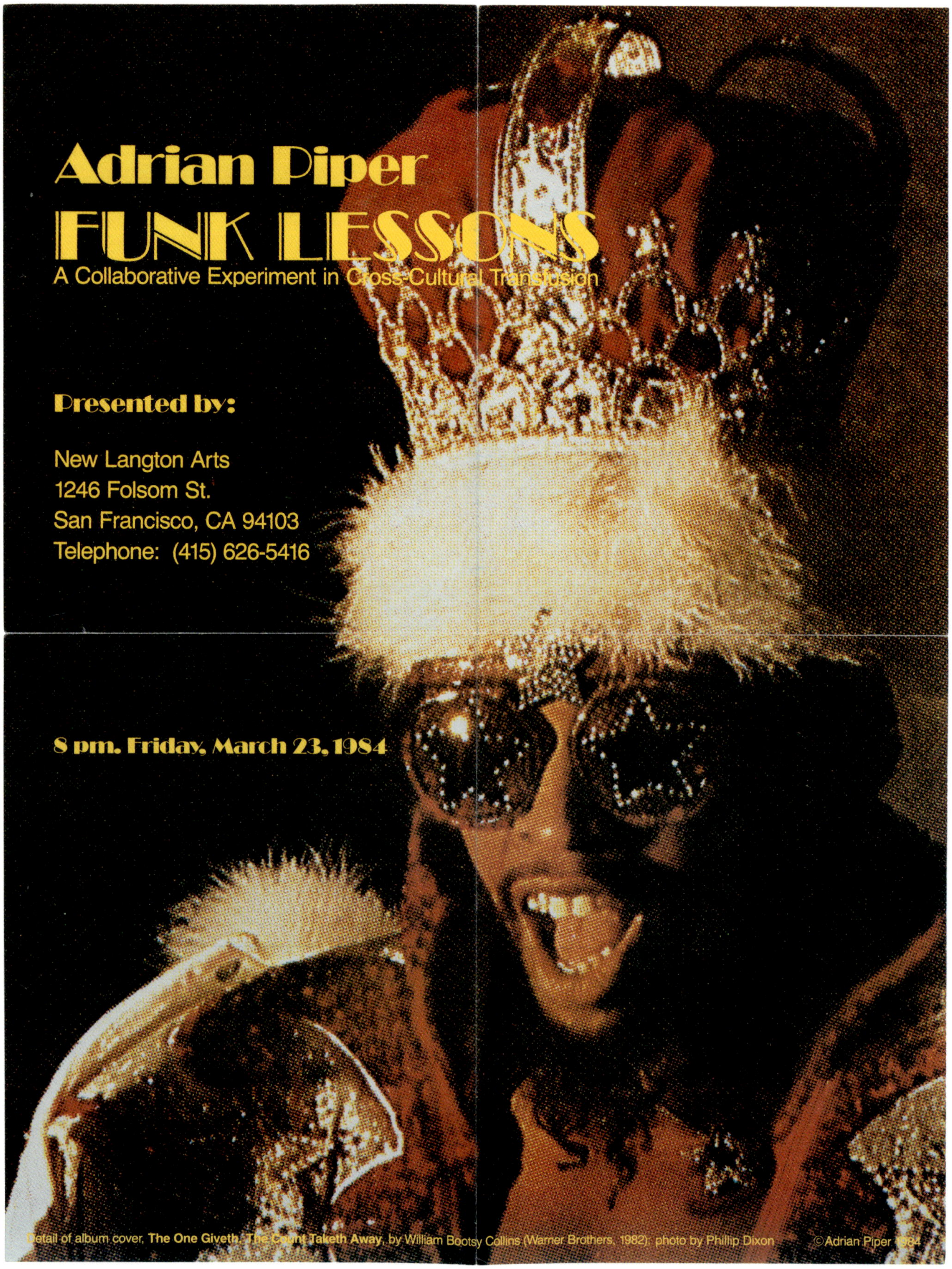

Funk Lessons: A Collaborative Experiment in Cross-Cultural Transfusion. 1984
Photolithograph
24 × 18 in. (61 × 45.7 cm)
The Museum of Modern Art Library, New York

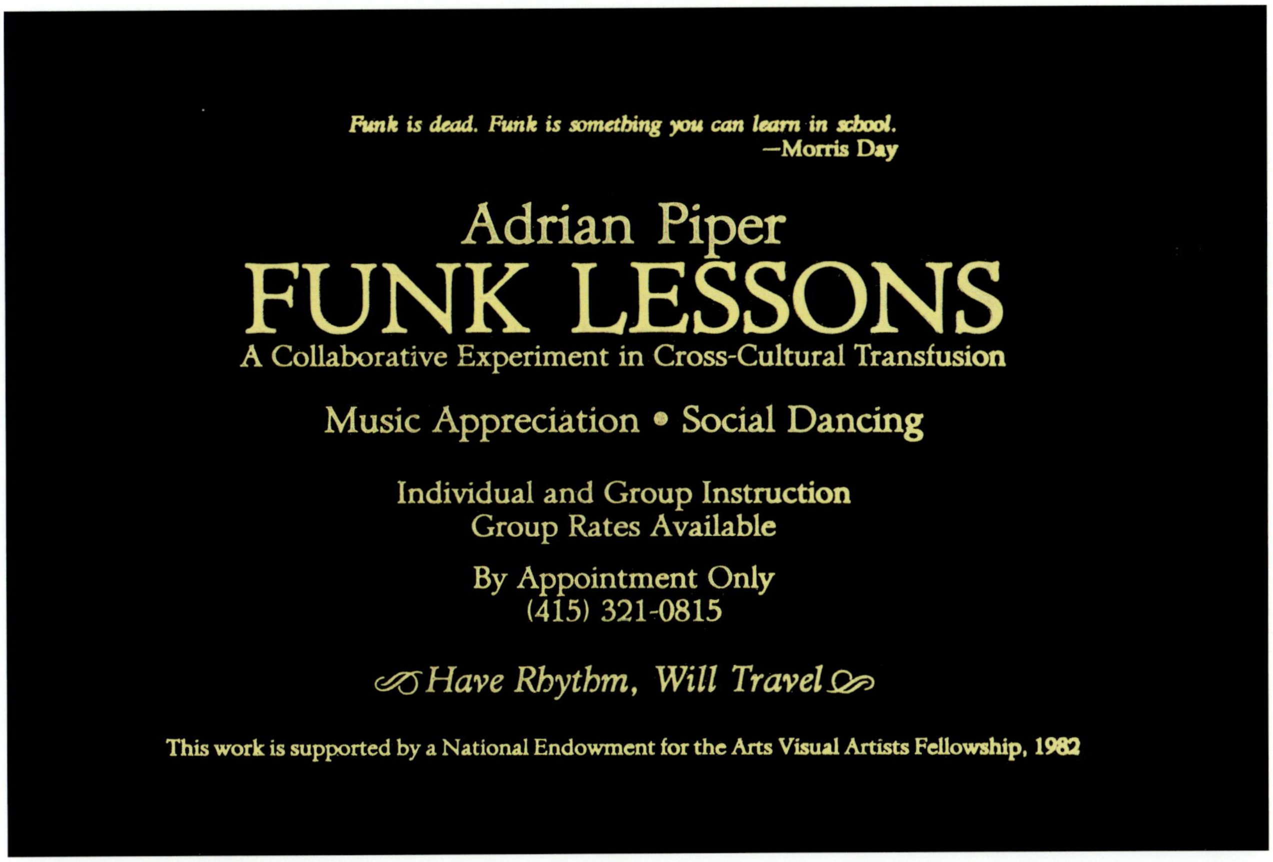

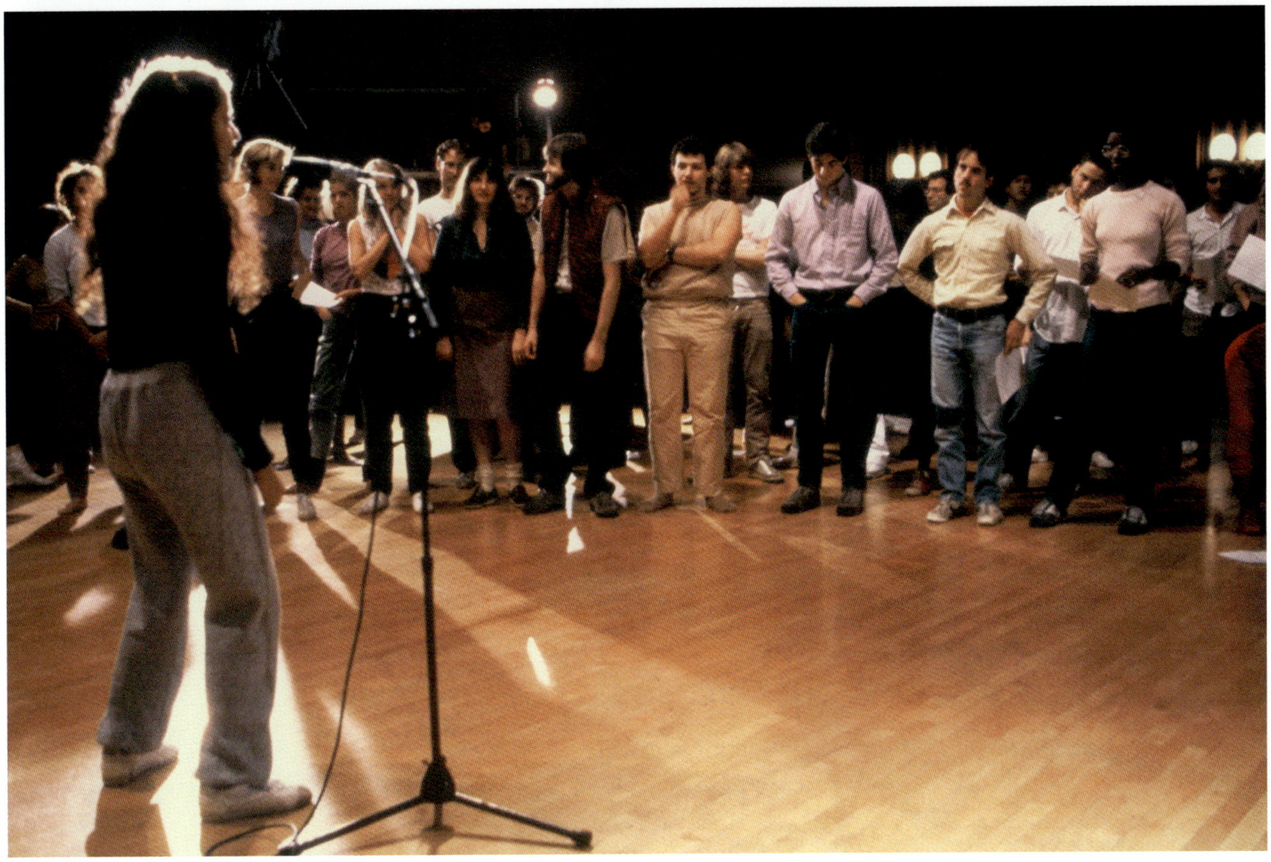

Funk Lessons Direct Mail Advertisement. 1983
Letterpress card with gold leaf
5¾ × 8¾ in. (14.6 × 22.2 cm)
Collection Adrian Piper Research Archive Foundation Berlin

Funk Lessons. 1983–84
Documentation of the group performance at University of California, Berkeley, November 6, 1983. Color photograph
Collection Adrian Piper Research Archive Foundation Berlin

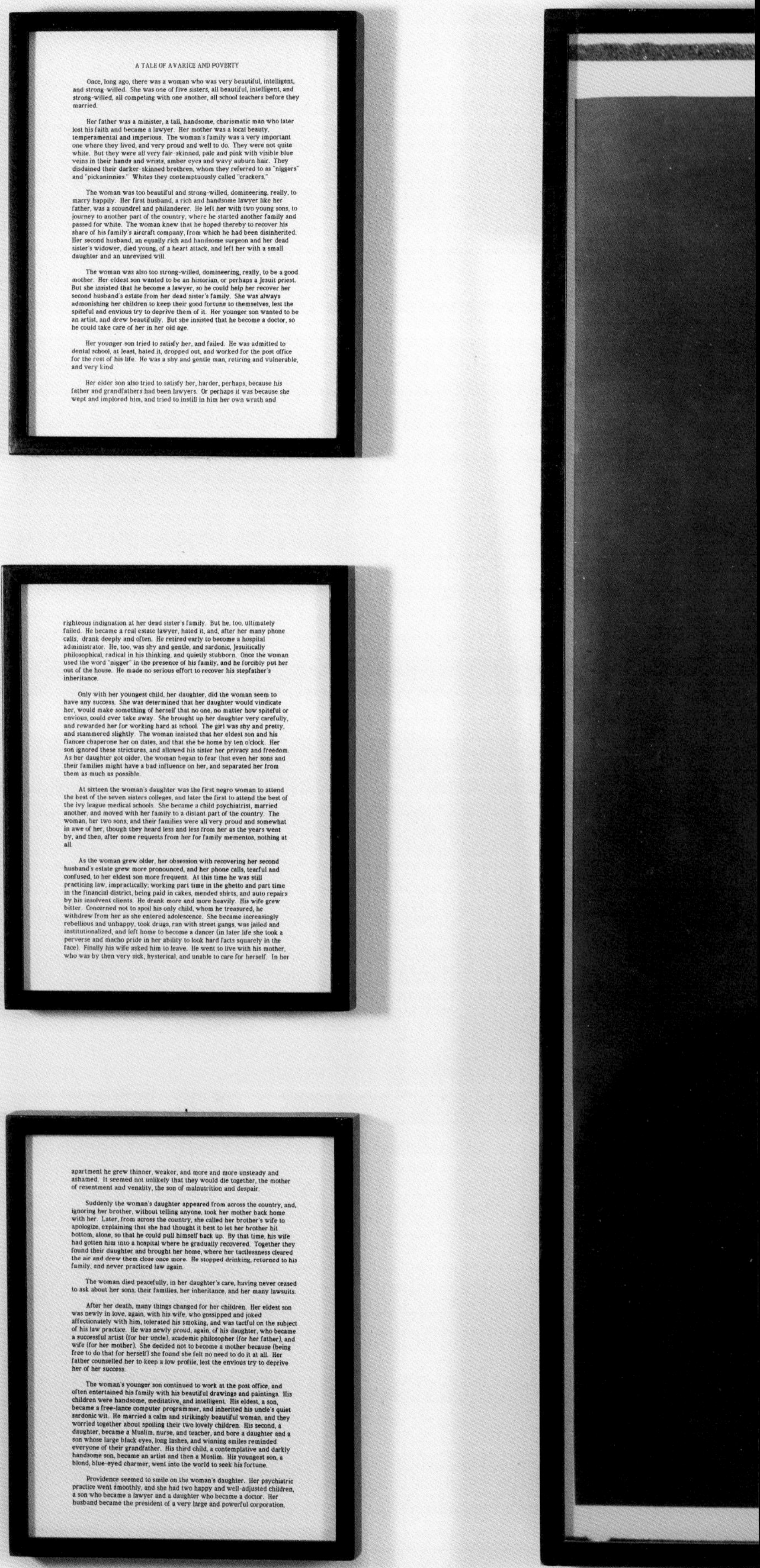

A Tale of Avarice and Poverty. 1985
Six texts and enlarged gelatin silver print
Each text 11 × 8½ in. (27.9 × 21.6 cm); photograph 37¼ × 25¼ in. (94.6 × 64.1 cm)
The Wadsworth Atheneum, Hartford, Connecticut. Purchased through the gift of James Junius Goodwin

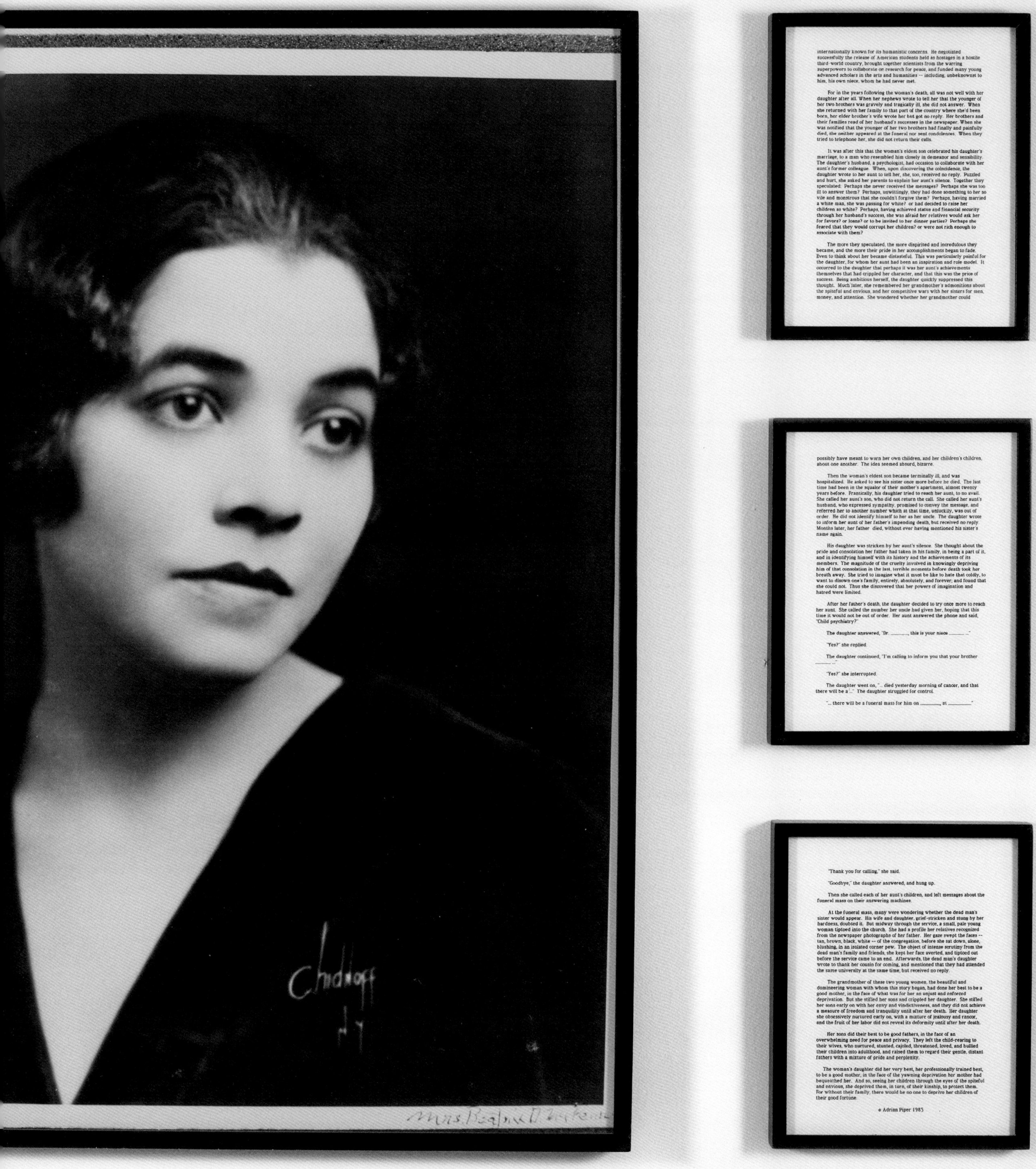
internationally known for its humanistic concerns. He negotiated successfully the release of American students held as hostages in a hostile third-world country, brought together scientists from the warring superpowers to collaborate on research for peace, and funded many young advanced scholars in the arts and humanities -- including, unbeknownst to him, his own niece, whom he had never met.
For in the years following the woman's death, all was not well with her daughter after all. When her nephews wrote to tell her that the younger of her two brothers was gravely and tragically ill, she did not answer. When she returned with her family to that part of the country where she'd been born, her elder brother's wife wrote her but got no reply. Her brothers and their families read of her husband's successes in the newspaper. When she was notified that the younger of her two brothers had finally and painfully died, she neither appeared at the funeral nor sent condolences. When they tried to telephone her, she did not return their calls.
It was after this that the woman's eldest son celebrated his daughter's marriage, to a man who resembled him closely in demeanor and sensibility. The daughter's husband, a psychologist, had occasion to collaborate with her aunt's former colleague. When, upon discovering the coincidence, the daughter wrote to her aunt to tell her, she, too, received no reply. Puzzled and hurt, she asked her parents to explain her aunt's silence. Together they speculated: Perhaps she never received the messages? Perhaps she was too ill to answer them? Perhaps, unwittingly, they had done something to her so vile and monstrous that she couldn't forgive them? Perhaps, having married a white man, she was passing for white? or had decided to raise her children as white? Perhaps, having achieved status and financial security through her husband's success, she was afraid her relatives would ask her for favors? or loans? or to be invited to her dinner parties? Perhaps she feared that they would corrupt her children? or were not rich enough to associate with them?
The more they speculated, the more dispirited and incredulous they became, and the more their pride in her accomplishments began to fade. Even to think about her became distasteful. This was particularly painful for the daughter, for whom her aunt had been an inspiration and role model. It occurred to the daughter that perhaps it was her aunt's achievements themselves that had crippled her character, and that this was the price of success. Being ambitious herself, the daughter quickly suppressed this thought. Much later, she remembered her grandmother's admonitions about the spiteful and envious, and her competitive wars with her sisters for men, money, and attention. She wondered whether her grandmother could
possibly have meant to warn her own children, and her children's children, about one another. The idea seemed absurd, bizarre.
Then the woman's eldest son became terminally ill, and was hospitalized. He asked to see his sister once more before he died. The last time had been in the squalor of their mother's apartment, almost twenty years before. Frantically, his daughter tried to reach her aunt, to no avail. She called her aunt's son, who did not return the call. She called her aunt's husband, who expressed sympathy, promised to convey the message, and referred her to another number which at that time, unluckily, was out of order. He did not identify himself to her as her uncle. The daughter wrote to inform her aunt of her father's impending death, but received no reply. Months later, her father died, without ever having mentioned his sister's name again.
His daughter was stricken by her aunt's silence. She thought about the pride and consolation her father had taken in his family, in being a part of it, and in identifying himself with its history and the achievements of its members. The magnitude of the cruelty involved in knowingly depriving him of that consolation in the last, terrible moments before death took her breath away. She tried to imagine what it must be like to hate that coldly, to want to disown one's family, entirely, absolutely, and forever; and found that she could not. Thus she discovered that her powers of imagination and hatred were limited.
After her father's death, the daughter decided to try once more to reach her aunt. She called the number her uncle had given her, hoping that this time it would not be out of order. Her aunt answered the phone and said, "Child psychiatry?"
The daughter answered, "Dr. ______, this is your niece ______ ..."
"Yes?" she replied.
The daughter continued, "I'm calling to inform you that your brother ______ ..."
"Yes?" she interrupted.
The daughter went on, "... died yesterday morning of cancer, and that there will be a ..." The daughter struggled for control.
"... there will be a funeral mass for him on ______, at ______."
"Thank you for calling," she said.
"Goodbye," the daughter answered, and hung up.
Then she called each of her aunt's children, and left messages about the funeral mass on their answering machines.
At the funeral mass, many were wondering whether the dead man's sister would appear. His wife and daughter, grief-stricken and stung by her hardness, doubted it. But midway through the service, a small, pale young woman tiptoed into the church. She had a profile her relatives recognized from the newspaper photographs of her father. Her gaze swept the faces -- tan, brown, black, white -- of the congregation, before she sat down, alone, blushing, in an isolated corner pew. The object of intense scrutiny from the dead man's family and friends, she kept her face averted, and tiptoed out before the service came to an end. Afterwards, the dead man's daughter wrote to thank her cousin for coming, and mentioned that they had attended the same university at the same time, but received no reply.
The grandmother of these two young women, the beautiful and domineering woman with whom this story began, had done her best to be a good mother, in the face of what was for her an unjust and enforced deprivation. But she stifled her sons and crippled her daughter. She stifled her sons early on with her envy and vindictiveness, and they did not achieve a measure of freedom and tranquility until after her death. Her daughter she obsessively nurtured early on, with a mixture of jealousy and rancor, and the fruit of her labor did not reveal its deformity until after her death.
Her sons did their best to be good fathers, in the face of an overwhelming need for peace and privacy. They left the child-rearing to their wives, who nurtured, stunted, cajoled, threatened, loved, and bullied their children into adulthood, and raised them to regard their gentle, distant fathers with a mixture of pride and perplexity.
The woman's daughter did her very best, her professionally trained best, to be a good mother, in the face of the yawning deprivation her mother had bequeathed her. And so, seeing her children through the eyes of the spiteful and envious, she deprived them, in turn, of their kinship, to protect them. For without their family, there would be no one to deprive her children of their good fortune.
© Adrian Piper 1985

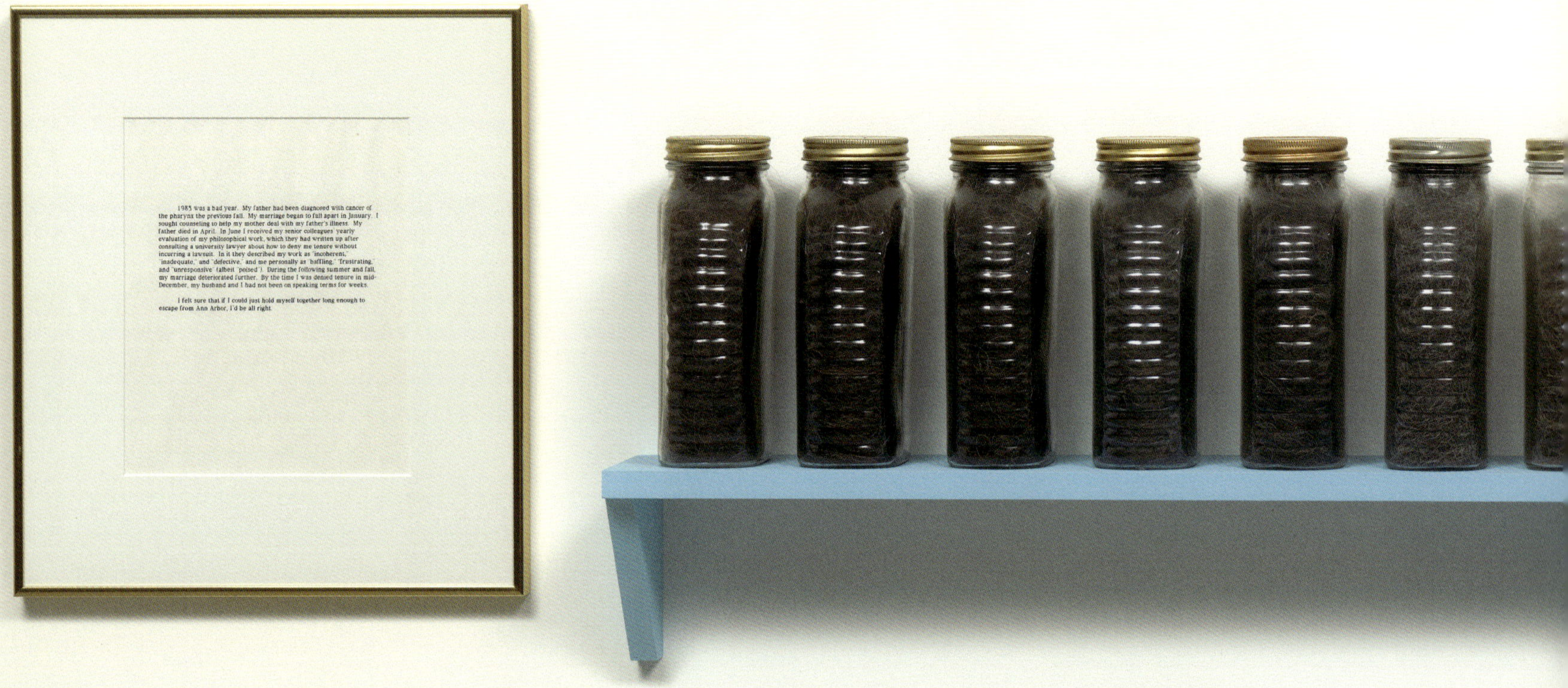

What Will Become of Me. 1985, ongoing
Two framed texts, glass jars, shelf, hair, fingernails, and skin
Dimensions variable
The Museum of Modern Art, New York. Gift of Gwen and Peter Norton

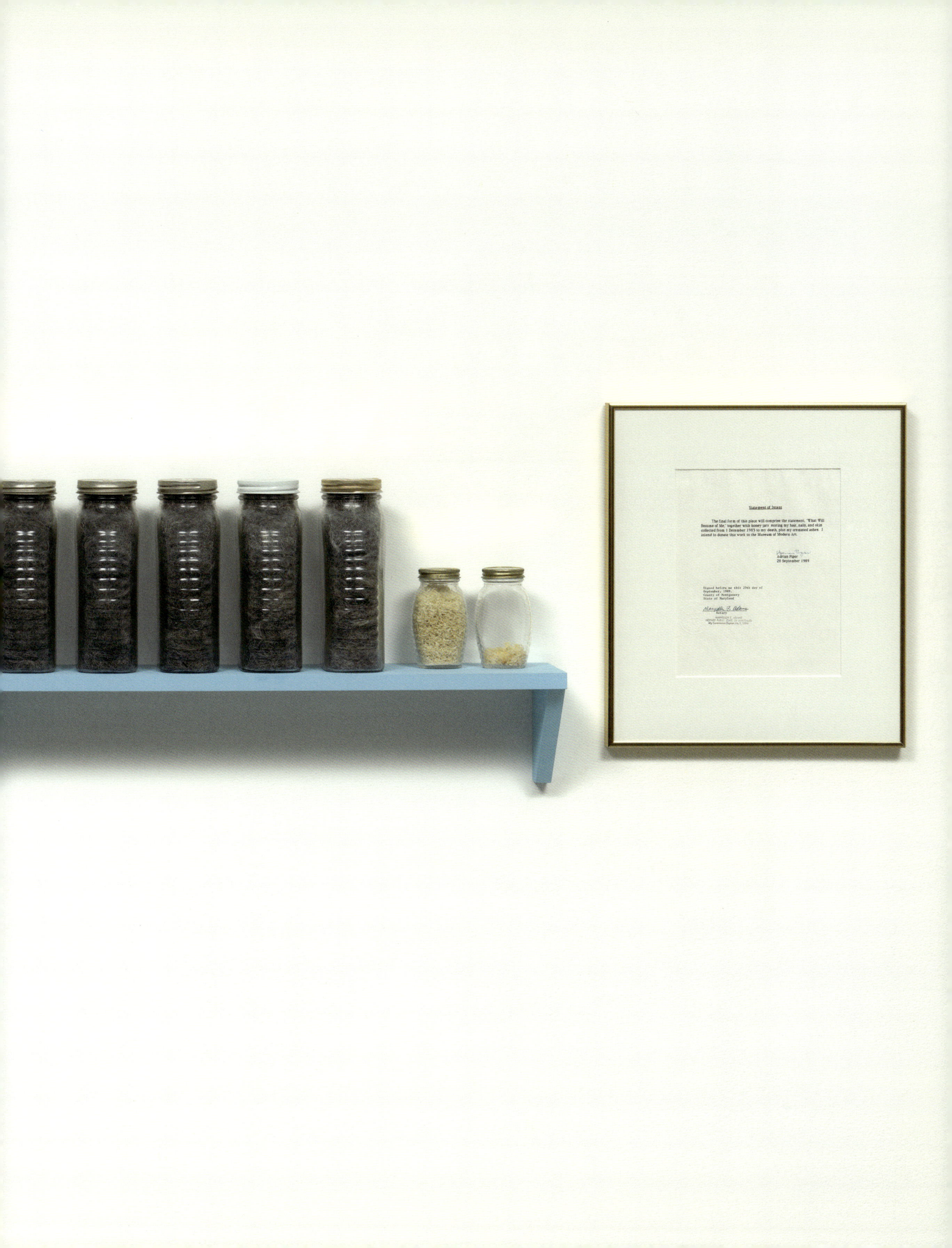
Statement of Intent
The final form of this piece will comprise the statement, "What Will Become of Me," together with honey jars storing my hair, nails, and skin collected from 1 December 1985 to my death, plus my cremated ashes. I intend to donate this work to the Museum of Modern Art.
Adrian Piper
20 September 1989
Signed before me this 20th day of September, 1989.
County of Montgomery
State of Maryland
Notary

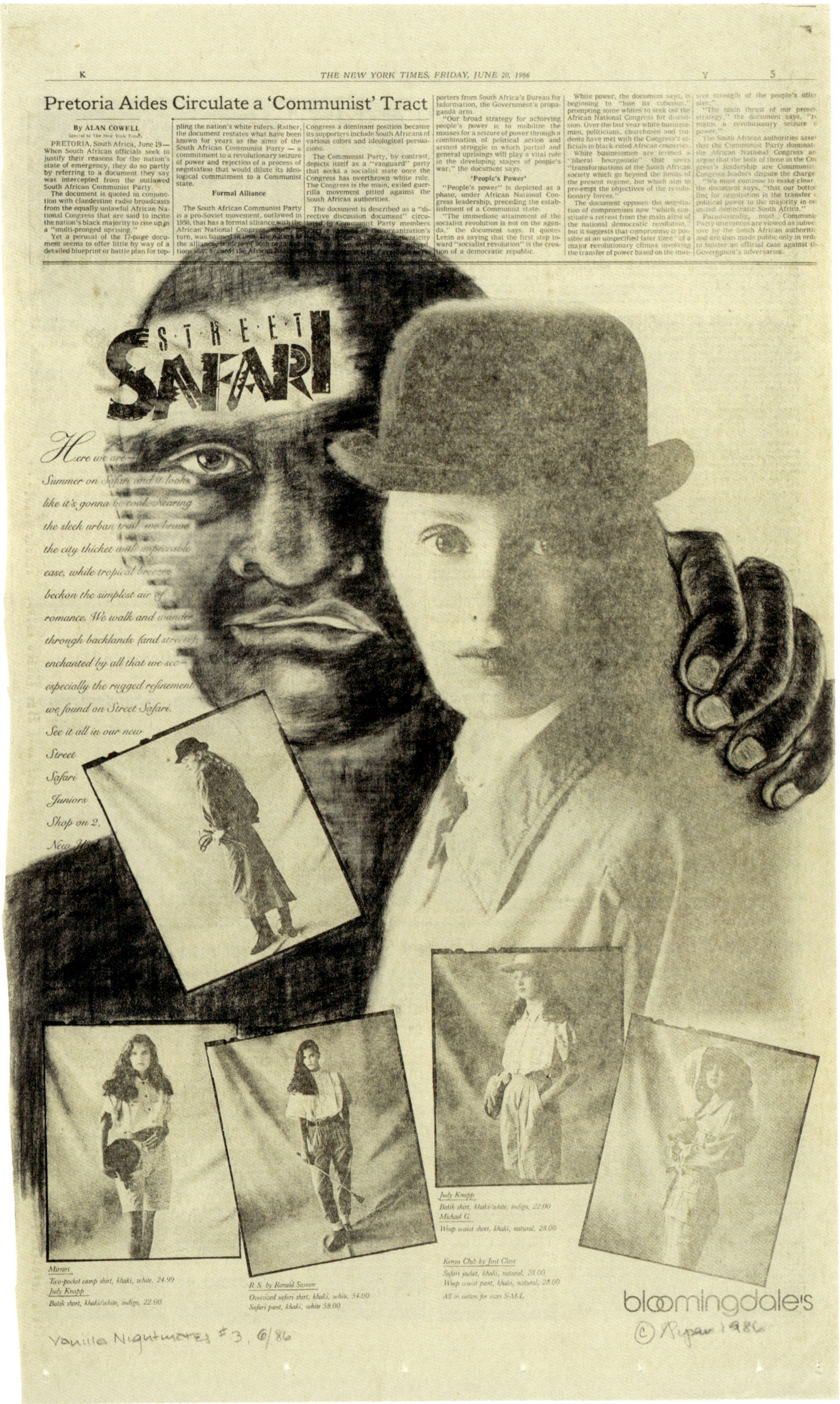

Vanilla Nightmares #3. 1986
Charcoal and oil crayon on newspaper
25⅜ × 13⅞ in. (64.5 × 35.2 cm)
Walker Art Center, Minneapolis. T. B. Walker Acquisition Fund

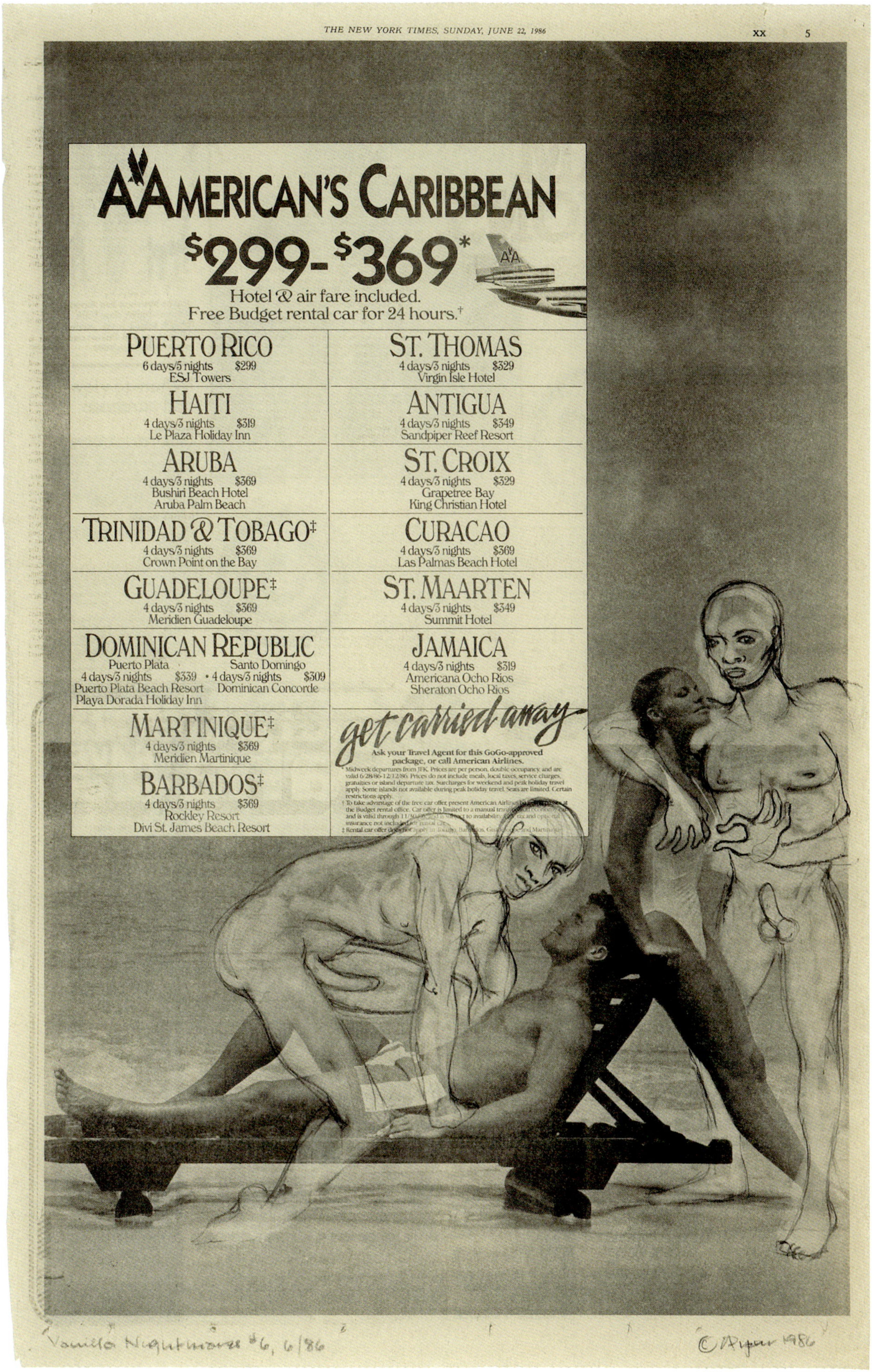

Vanilla Nightmares #6. 1986
Charcoal on newspaper
23 × 13¾ in. (58.4 × 34.9 cm)
Collection Adrian Piper Research Archive Foundation Berlin

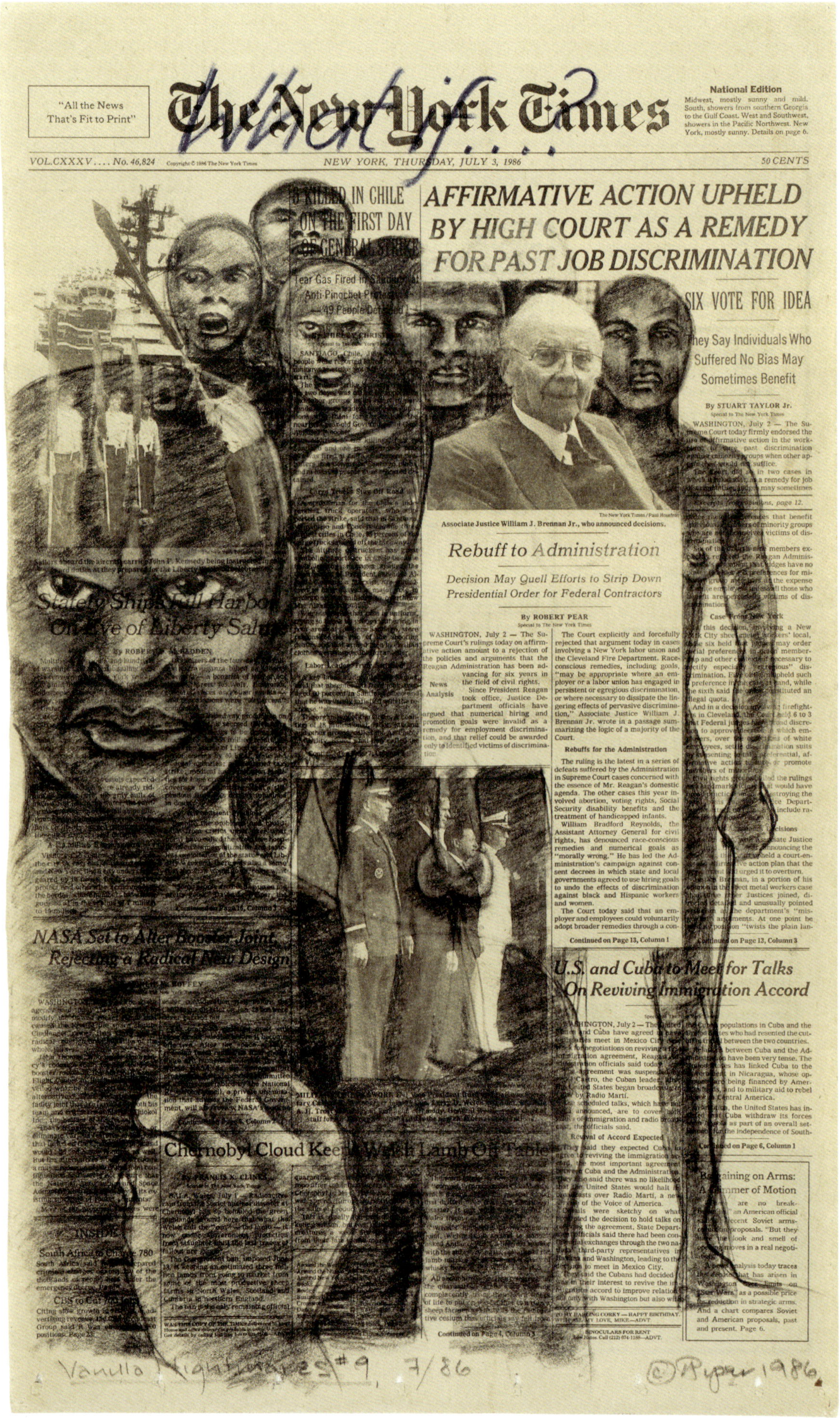

Vanilla Nightmares #9. 1986
Charcoal and oil crayon on newspaper
22 × 13¾ in. (55.9 × 34.9 cm)
Walker Art Center, Minneapolis. T. B. Walker Acquisition Fund

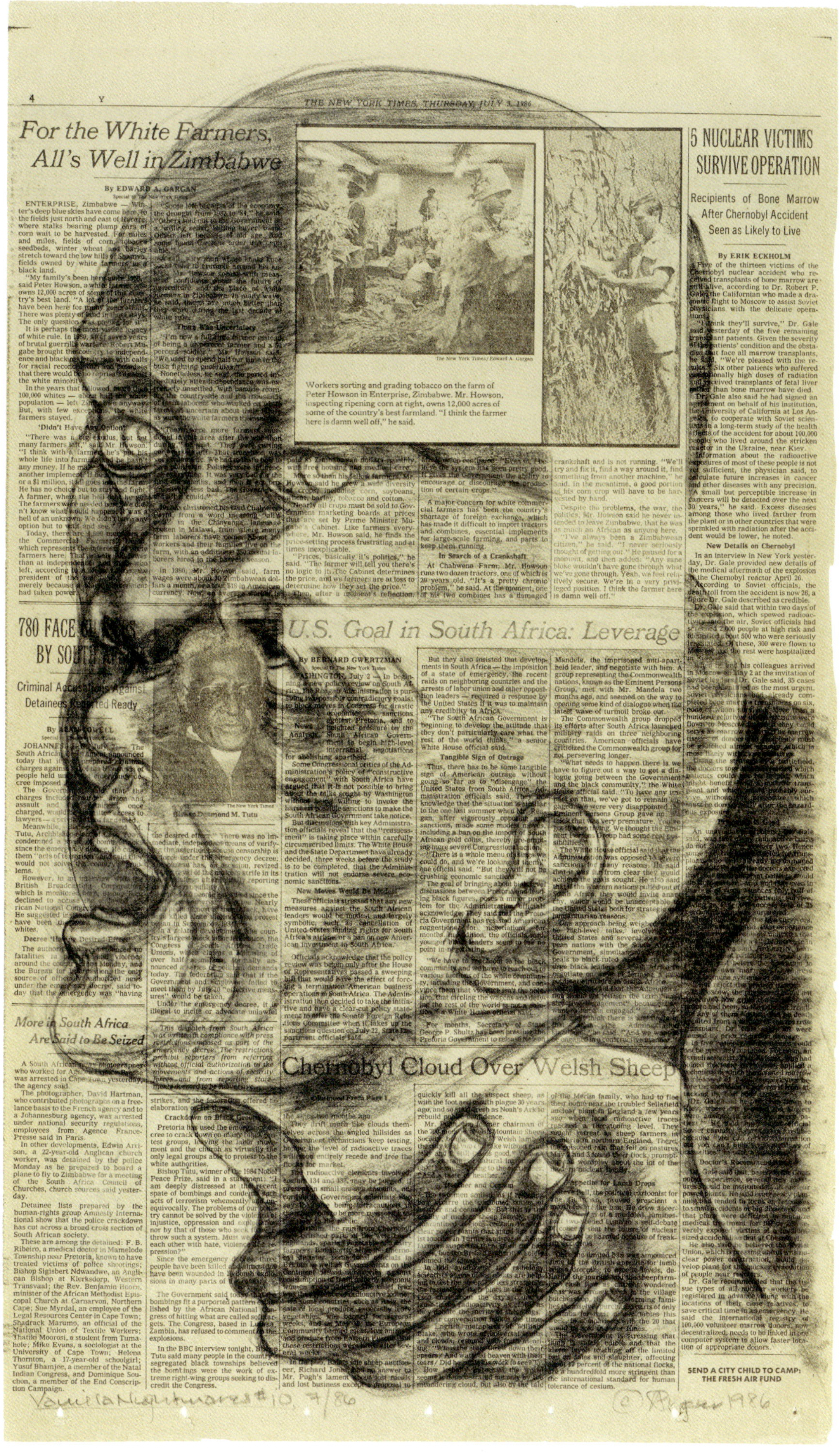

Vanilla Nightmares #10. 1986
Charcoal and oil crayon on newspaper
23 × 13½ in. (58.4 × 34.3 cm)
Walker Art Center, Minneapolis. T. B. Walker Acquisition Fund

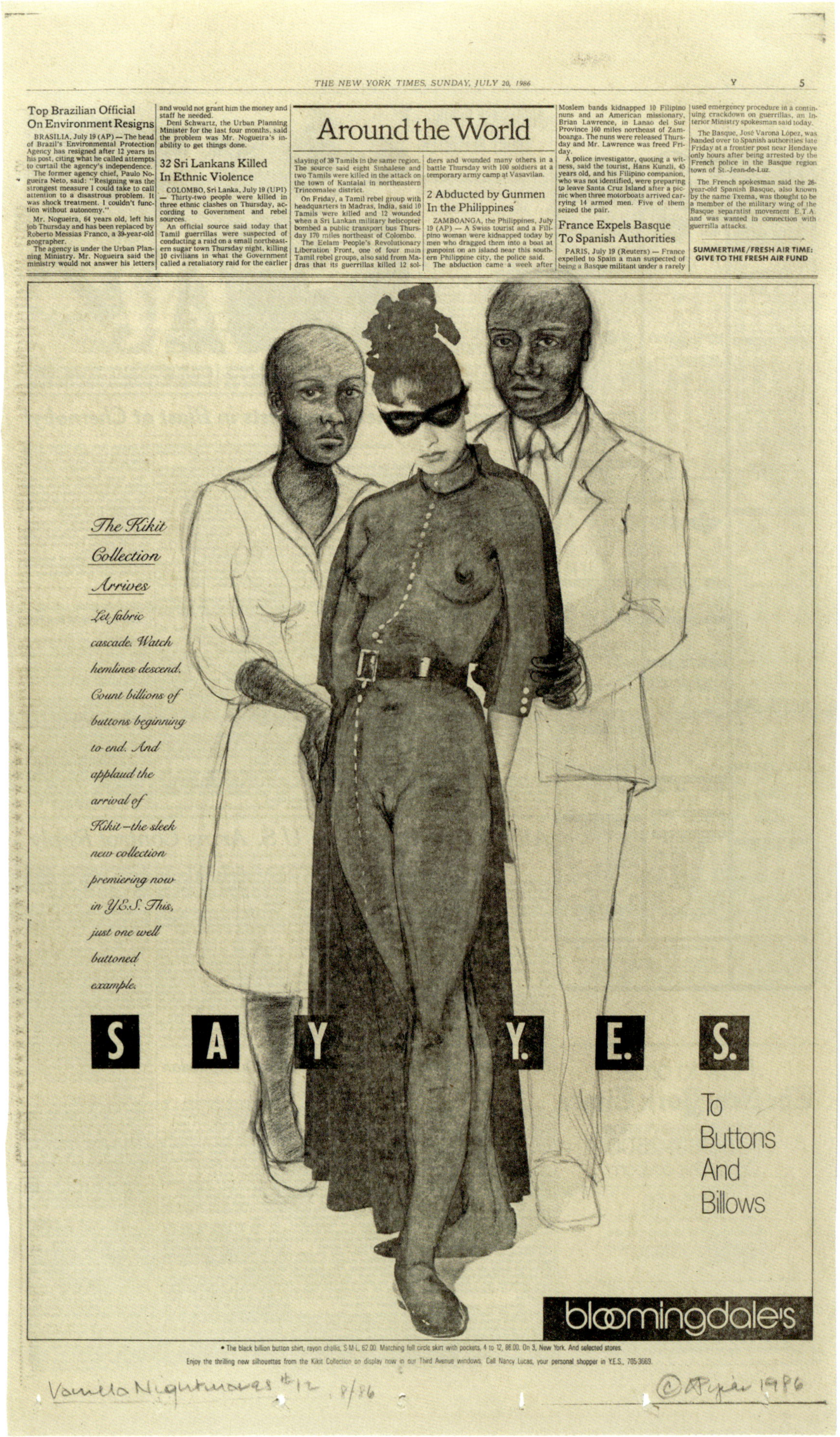

Vanilla Nightmares #12. 1986
Charcoal on newspaper
23½ × 13½ in. (59.7 × 34.3 cm)
The Museum of Modern Art, New York. Gift of Gwen and Peter Norton

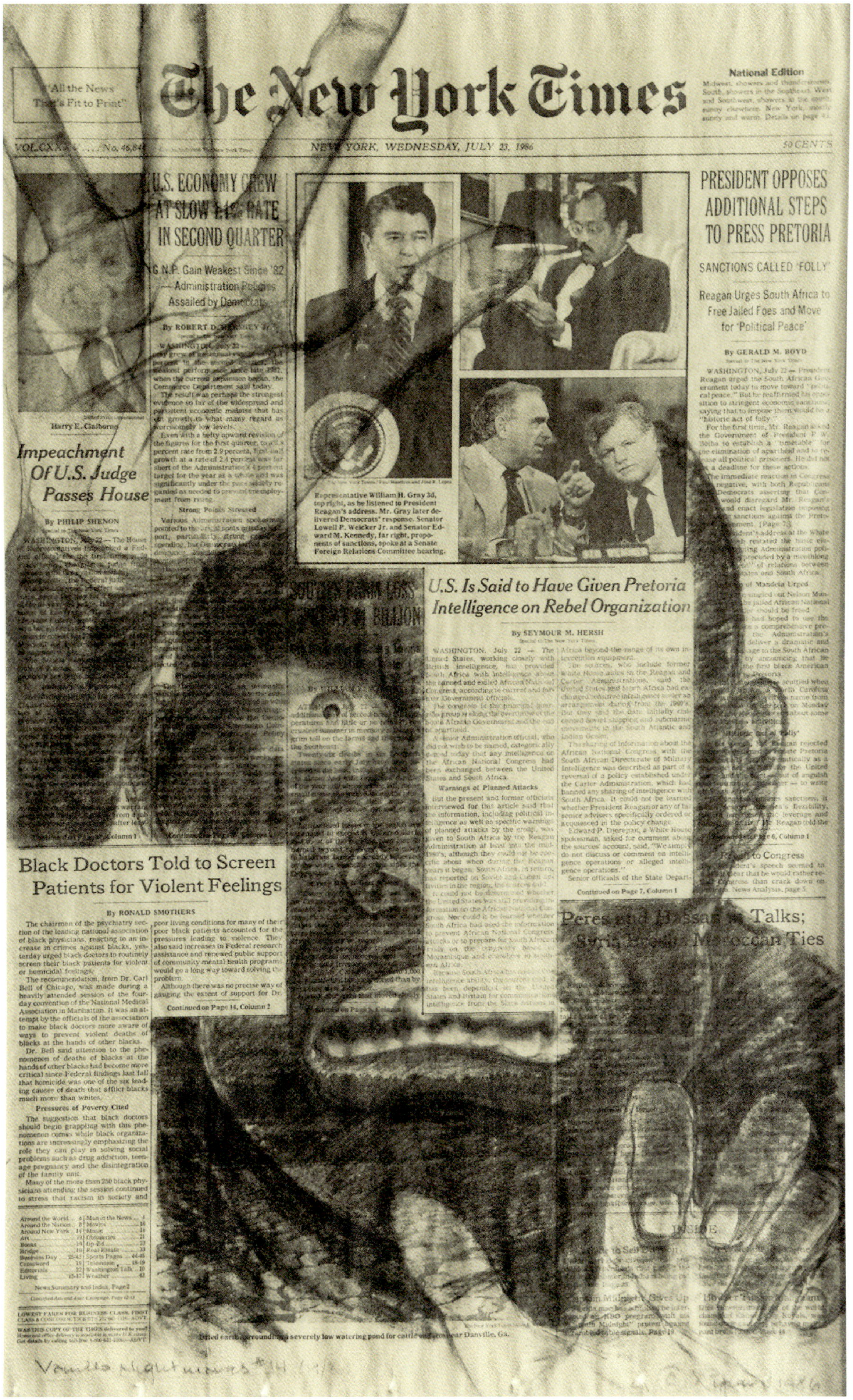

Vanilla Nightmares #14. 1986
Charcoal on newspaper
23½ × 14 in. (59.7 × 35.6 cm)
Faulconer Gallery, Grinnell College Art Collection, Grinnell, Iowa

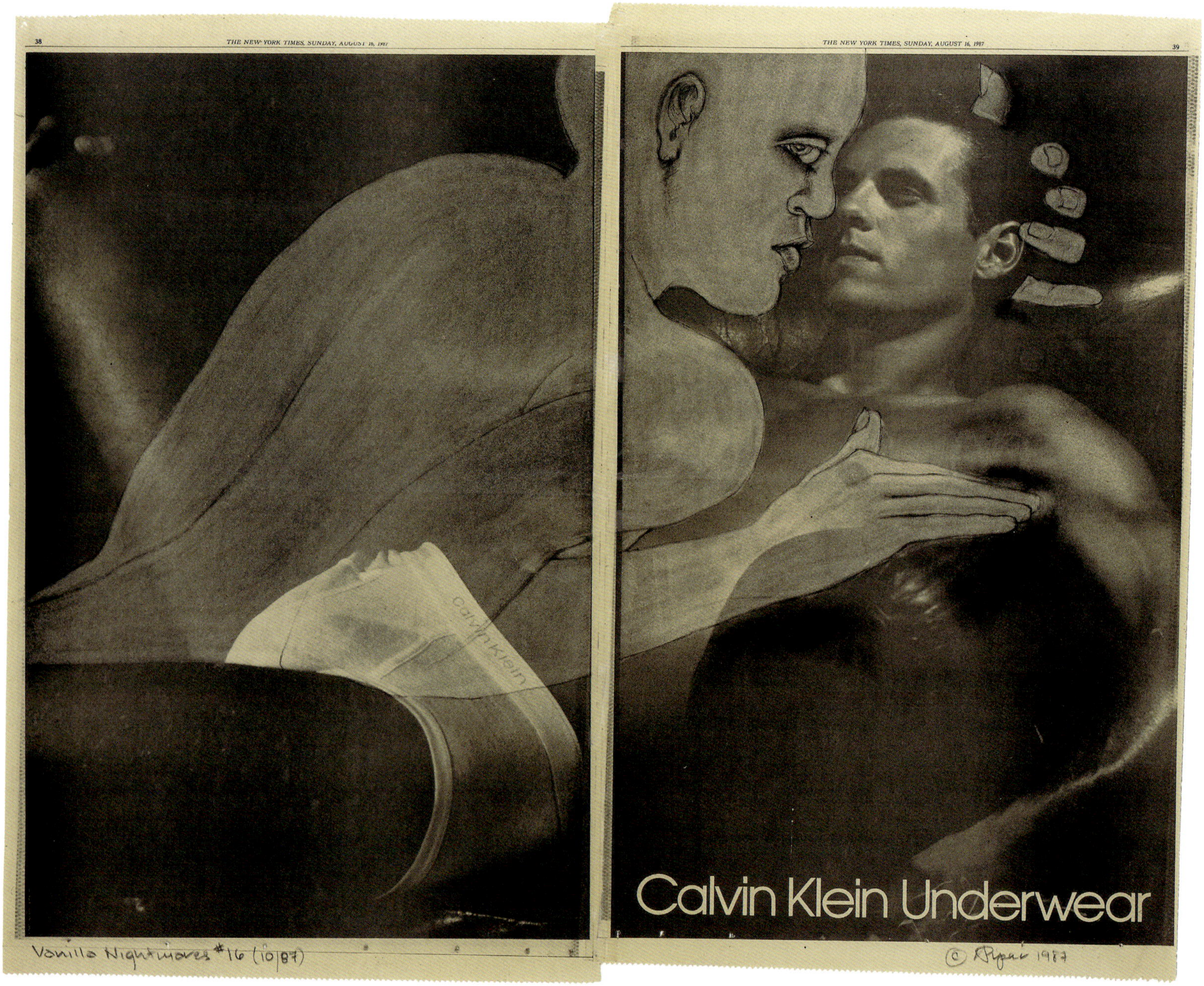

Vanilla Nightmares #16. 1987
Charcoal on newspaper
21⅝ × 26⅜ in. (55 × 67 cm)
Collection Katharina Faerber

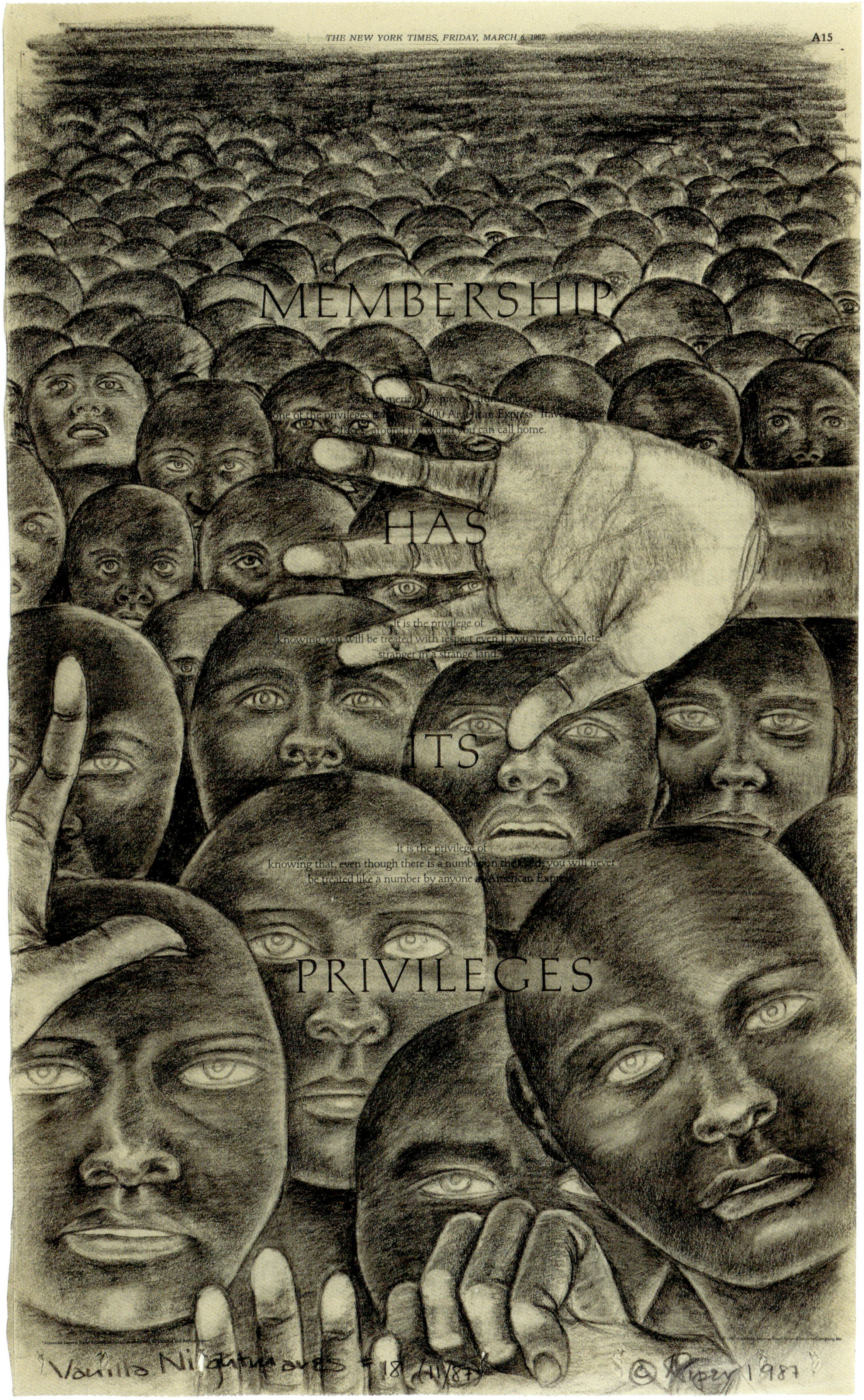

Vanilla Nightmares #18. 1987
Charcoal on newspaper
22³⁄₁₆ × 13¹¹⁄₁₆ in. (56.4 × 34.8 cm)
Williams College Museum of Art, Williamstown, Massachusetts.
Gift of the American Academy and Institute of Arts and Letters, New York; Hassam, Speicher, Betts and Symons Funds

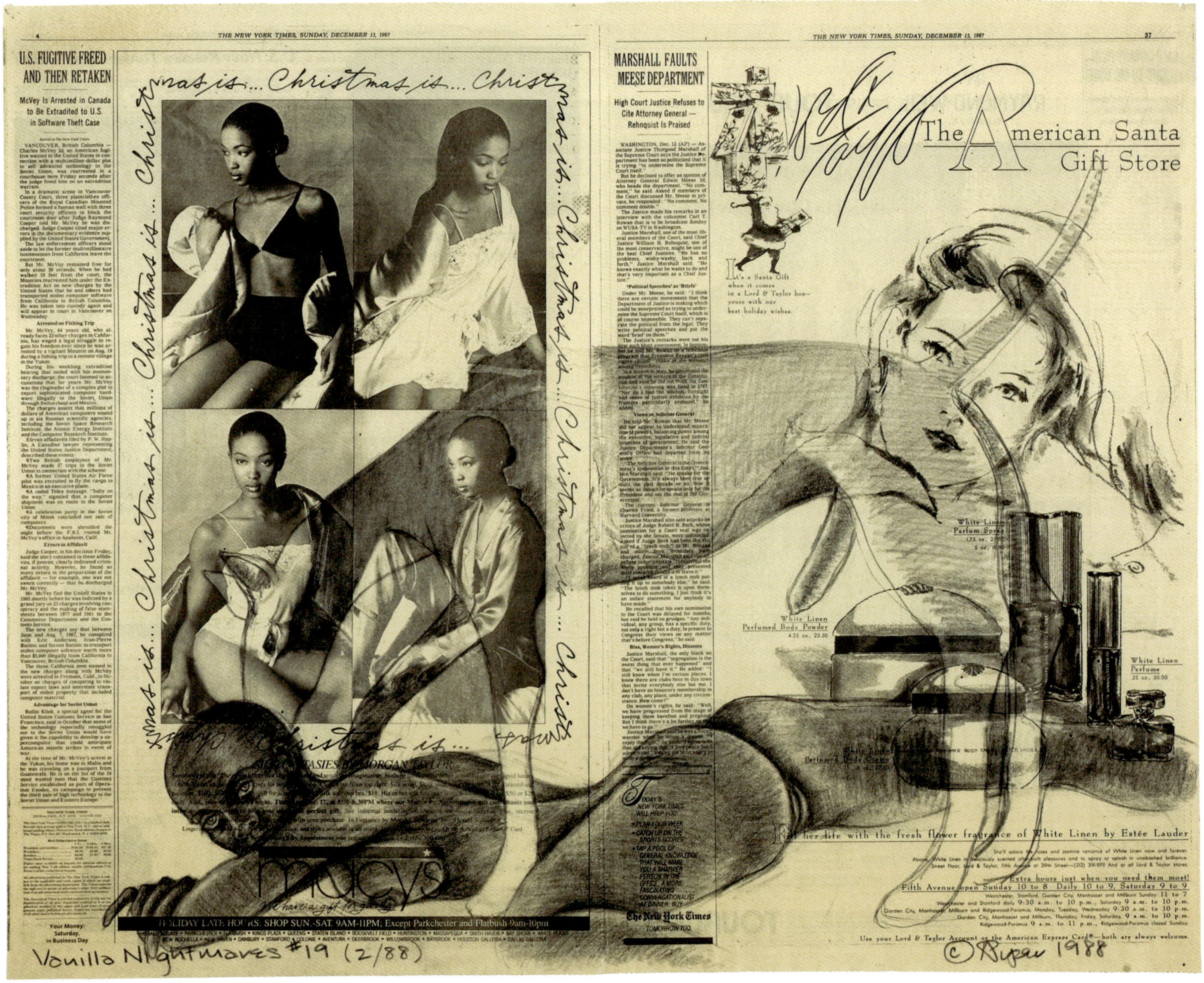

Vanilla Nightmares #19. 1988
Charcoal on newspaper
22¼ × 27¼ in. (56.5 × 69.2 cm)
Collection Adrian Piper Research Archive Foundation Berlin

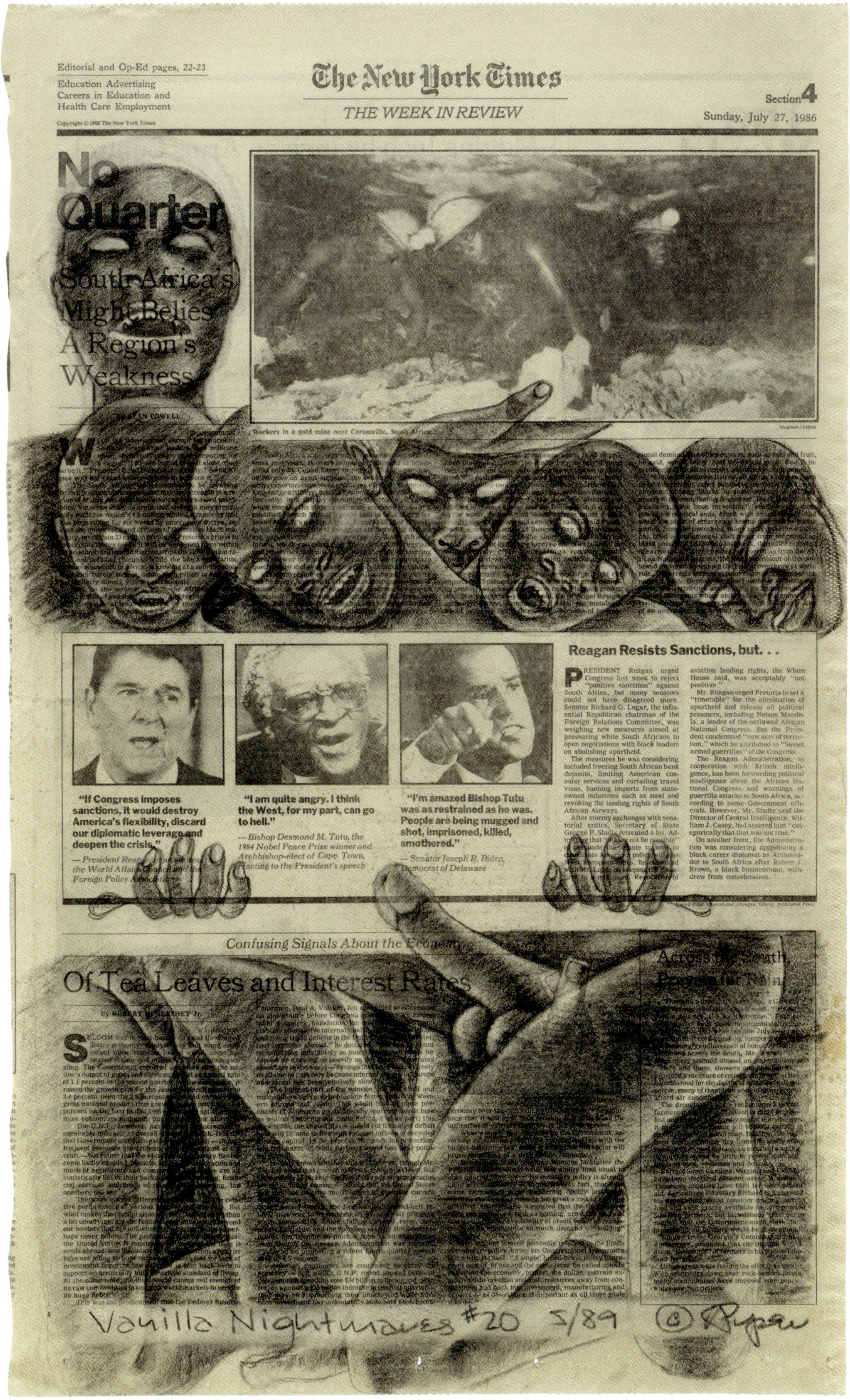

Vanilla Nightmares #20. 1989
Charcoal on newspaper
23 × 13¾ in. (58.4 × 34.9 cm)
Hammer Museum, Los Angeles. Purchase

Dear Friend,

I am black.

I am sure you did not realize this when you made/laughed at/agreed with that racist remark. In the past, I have attempted to alert white people to my racial identity in advance. Unfortunately, this invariably causes them to react to me as pushy, manipulative, or socially inappropriate. Therefore, my policy is to assume that white people do not make these remarks, even when they believe there are no black people present, and to distribute this card when they do.

I regret any discomfort my presence is causing you, just as I am sure you regret the discomfort your racism is causing me.

Dear Friend,

I am not here to pick anyone up, or to be picked up. I am here alone because I want to be here, ALONE.

This card is not intended as part of an extended flirtation.

Thank you for respecting my privacy.

DO NOT TOUCH, TAP, PAT,
STROKE, PROD, PINCH, POKE,
GROPE OR GRAB ME.

My Calling (Card) #1 (Reactive Guerrilla Performance for Dinners and Cocktail Parties). 1986–90
Performance prop. Printed card
$1\frac{15}{16} \times 3\frac{1}{2}$ in. (5 × 9 cm)
The Museum of Modern Art Library, New York

My Calling (Card) #2 (Reactive Guerrilla Performance for Bars and Discos). 1986–90
Performance prop. Printed card
$1\frac{15}{16} \times 3\frac{1}{2}$ in. (5 × 9 cm)
The Museum of Modern Art Library, New York

My Calling (Card) #3 (Reactive Guerrilla Performance for Disputed Territorial Skirmishes). 2012
Performance prop. Printed card
$1\frac{15}{16} \times 3\frac{1}{2}$ in. (5 × 9 cm)
Collection Adrian Piper Research Archive Foundation Berlin

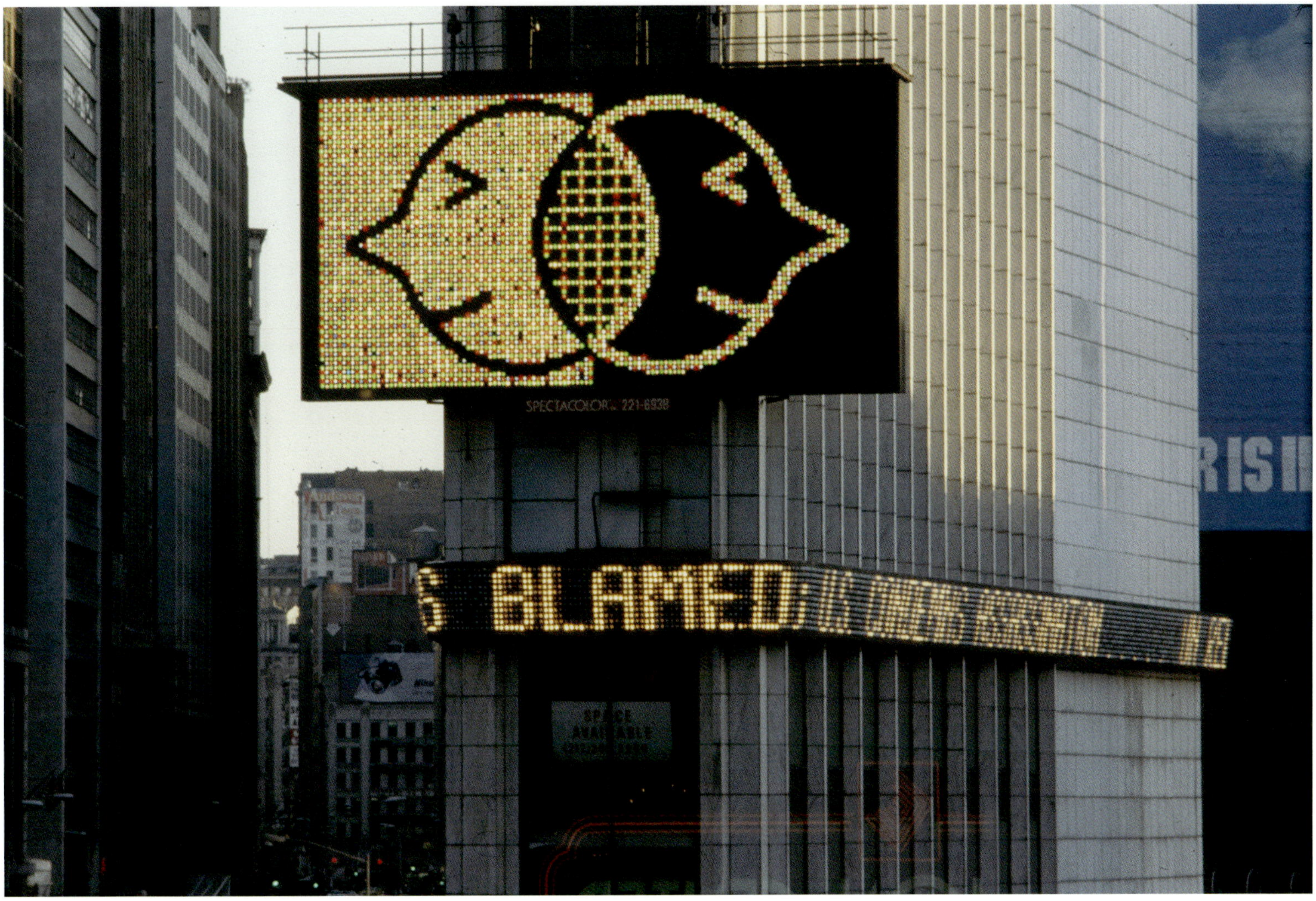

Merge. 1988
Video of Times Square LED billboard. Video (color, silent), 00:00:56, endless loop
Installation view of billboard in *Messages to the Public*, organized by Public Art Fund, New York. Shown every twenty minutes, May 1–May 31, 1989
Collection Adrian Piper Research Archive Foundation Berlin

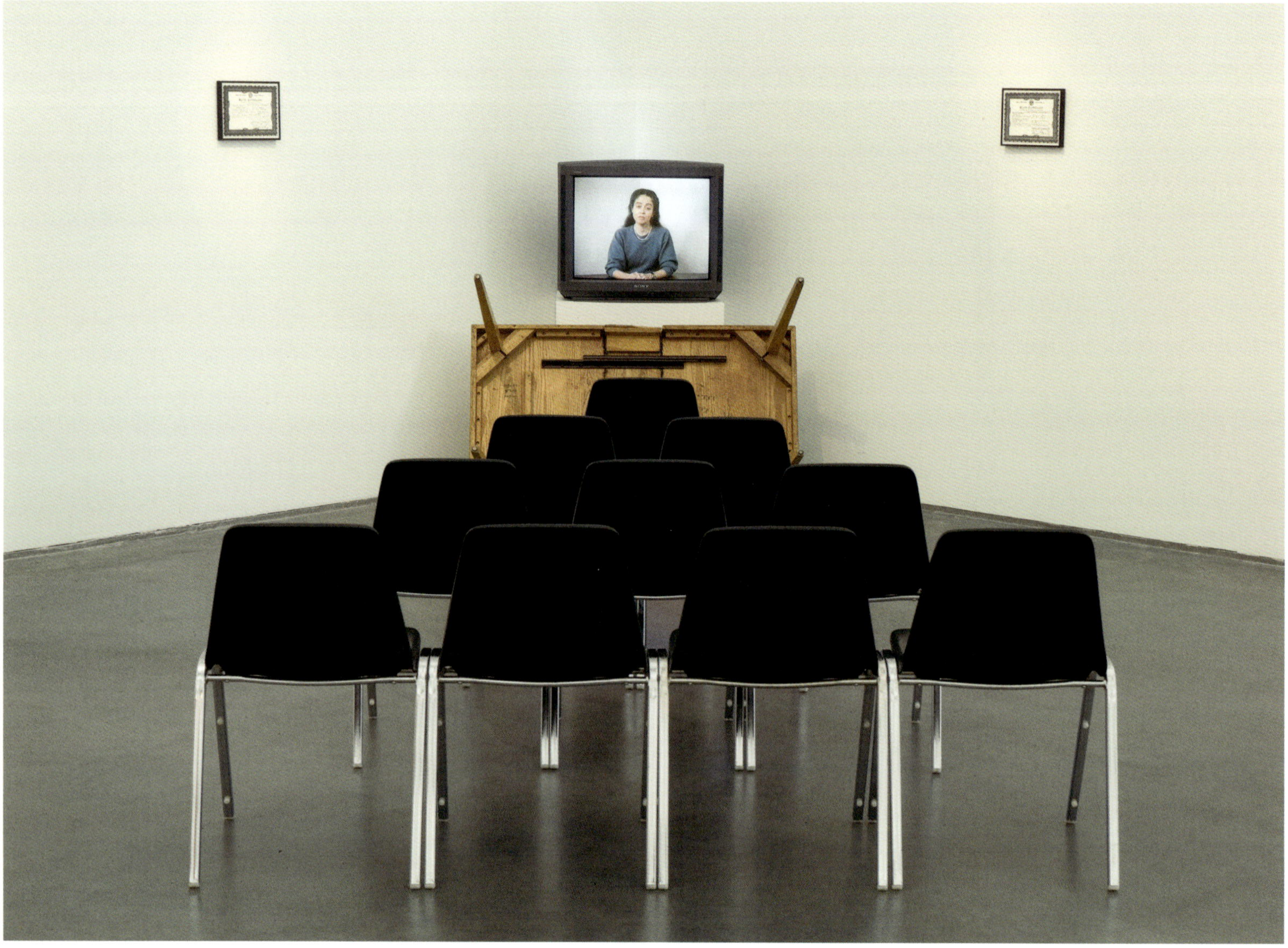

Cornered. 1988
Video installation. Video (color, sound), approx. 00:17:00, with monitor, birth certificates, table, and chairs
Dimensions variable
Museum of Contemporary Art, Chicago. Bernice and Kenneth Newberger Fund

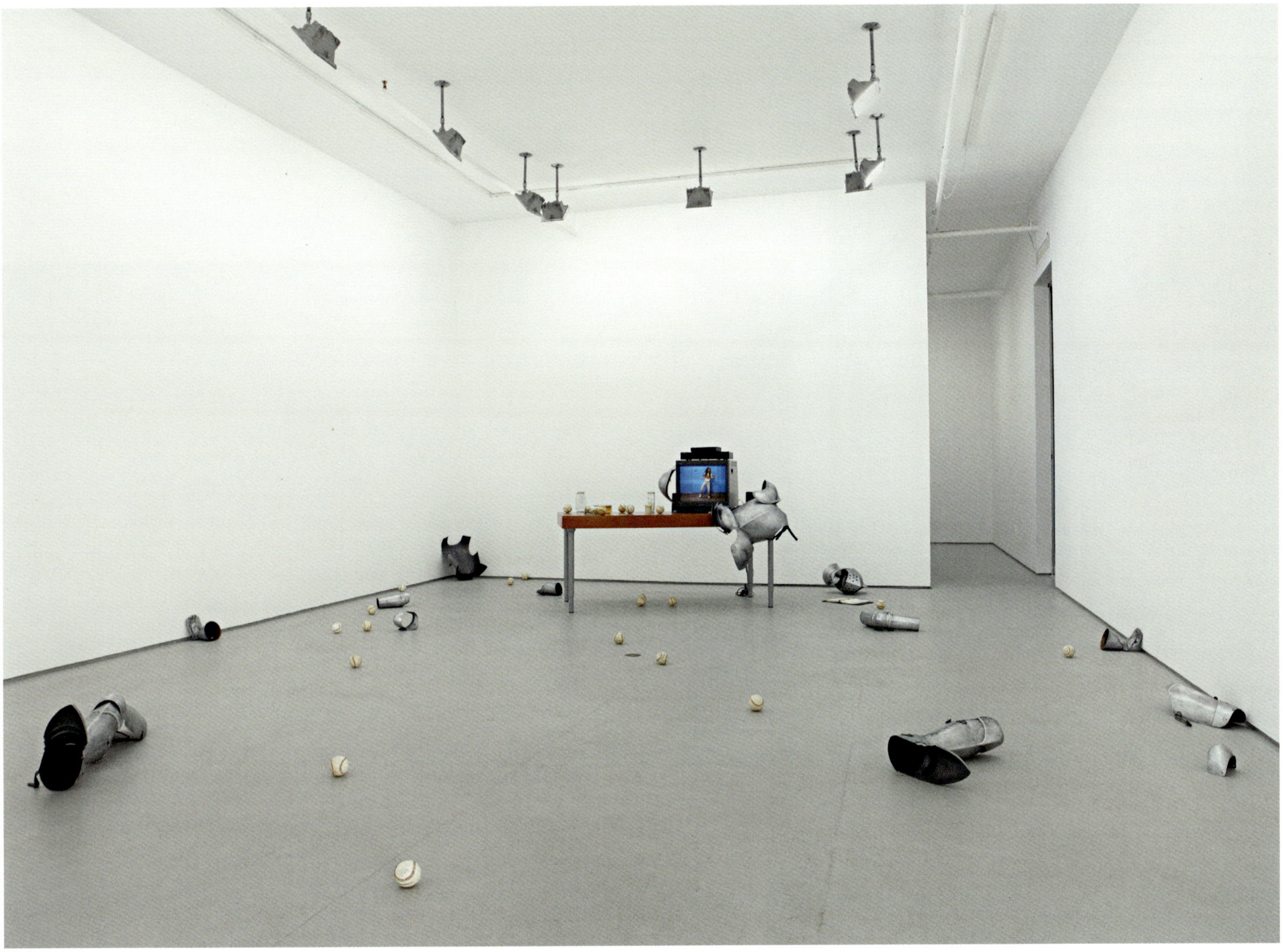

The Big Four Oh. 1988
Video installation. Video (color, sound), 00:47:32, with monitor, ring binder with two pages of handwritten text, and 153 blank sheets, forty baseballs, disassembled plastic coat of armor in fourteen pieces, and five bottles each containing blood, sweat, tears, piss, or vinegar
Dimensions variable
Installation view in *Est. 2002,* Elizabeth Dee Gallery, New York, June 29–August 15, 2012
Walker Art Center, Minneapolis. T. B. Walker Acquisition Fund

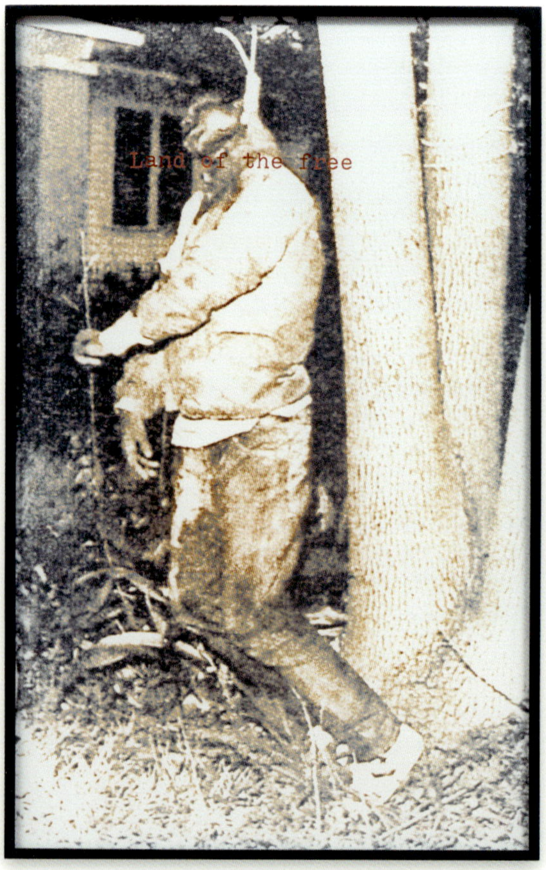

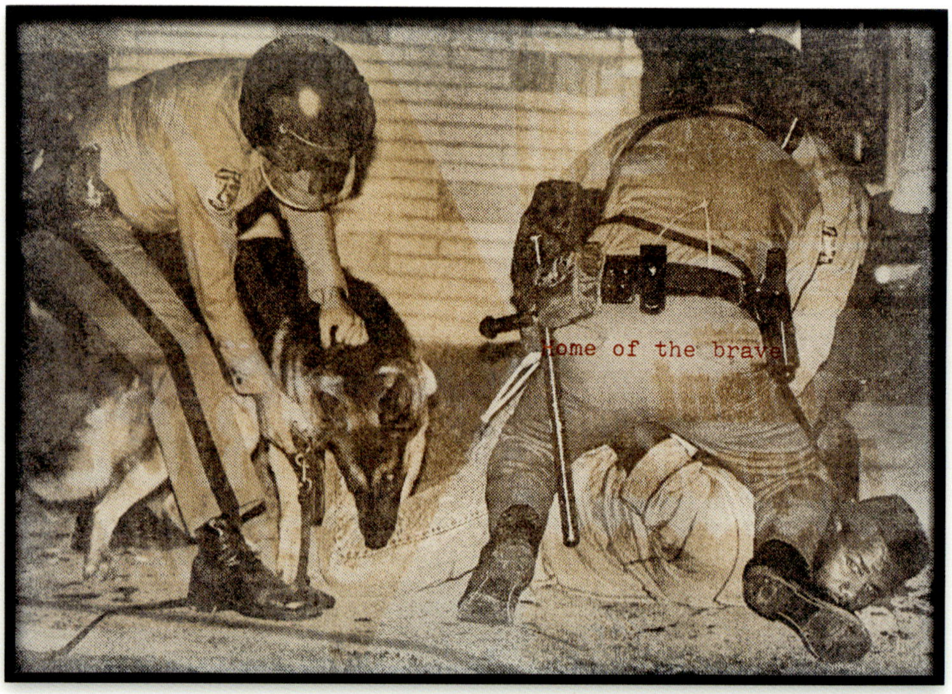

Free #2. 1989
Screenprinted text on two black-and-white photographs, mounted on foam core
48 × 31 in. (121.9 × 78.7 cm) and 38 × 53 in. (96.5 × 134.6 cm)
Collection Adrian Piper Research Archive Foundation Berlin

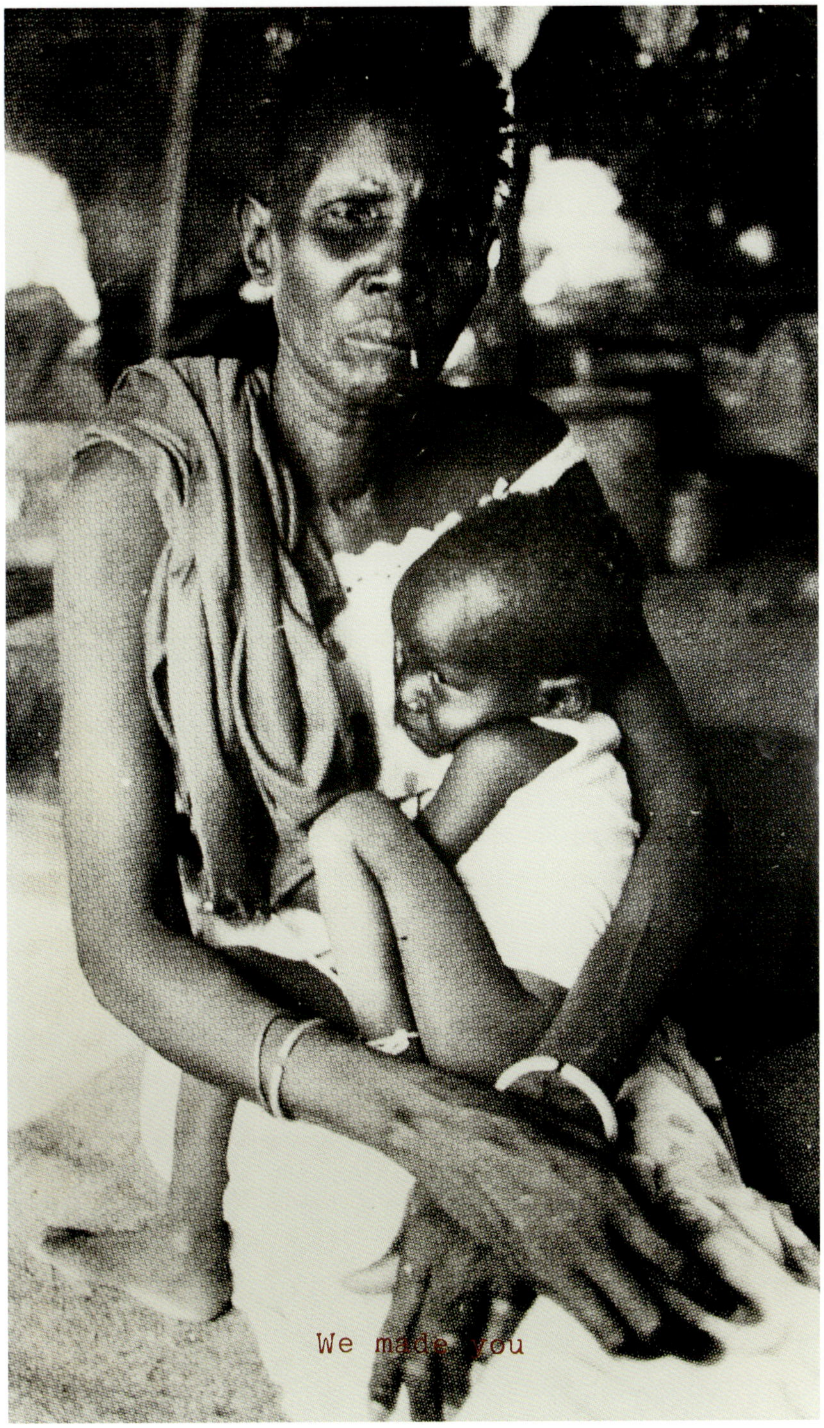

Ur-Mutter #2: We Made You. 1989
Screenprinted text on black-and-white photograph, mounted on foam core
40 × 23 in. (101.6 × 58.4 cm)
Mount Holyoke College Art Museum, South Hadley, Massachusetts. Purchase with the Eleanor H. Bunce (Class of 1926) Art Acquisition Fund

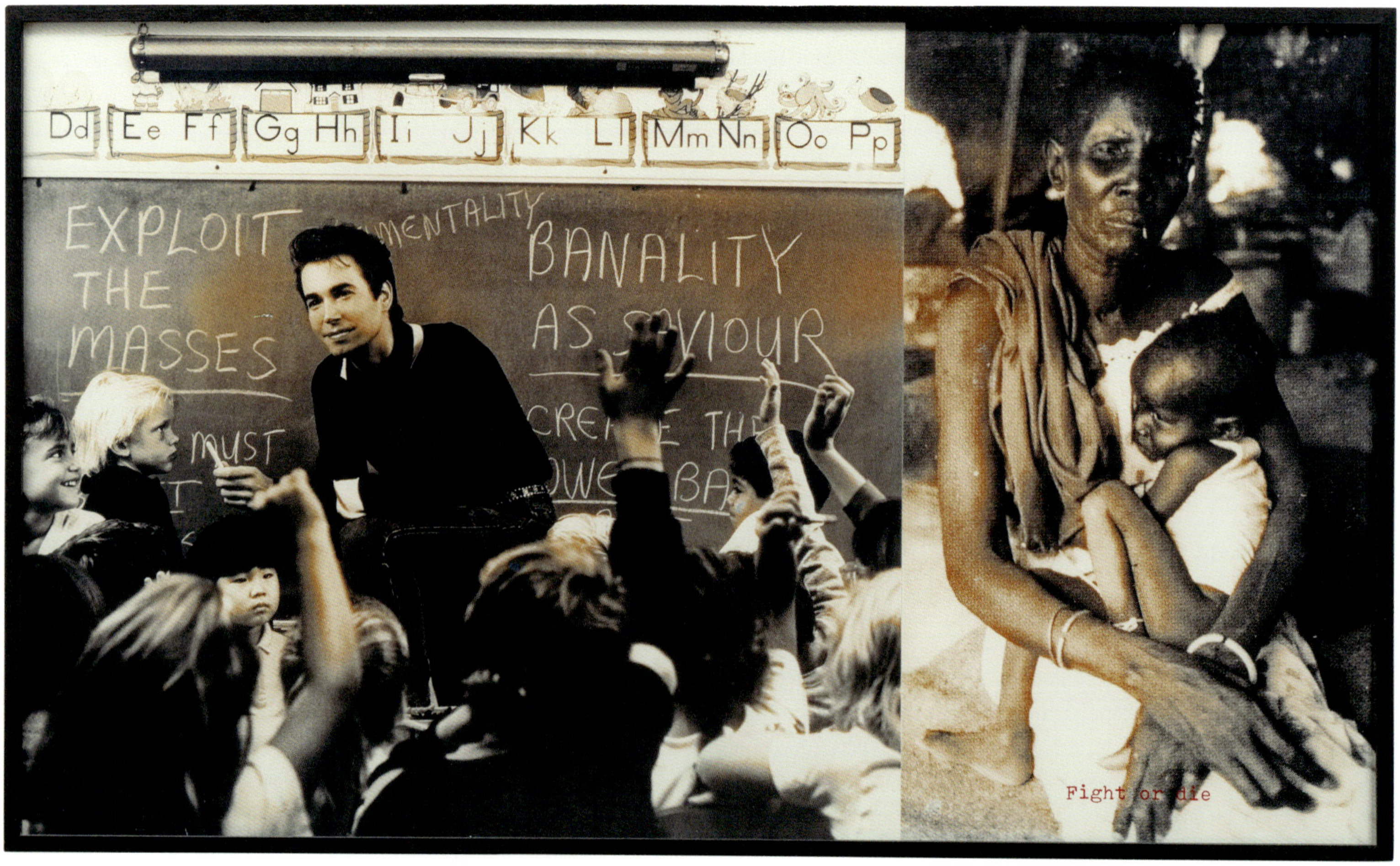

Ur-Mutter #8. 1989
Screenprinted text on two black-and-white photographs, mounted on foam core
Overall 36 × 59½ in. (91.4 × 151.1 cm)
Collection Adrian Piper Research Archive Foundation Berlin

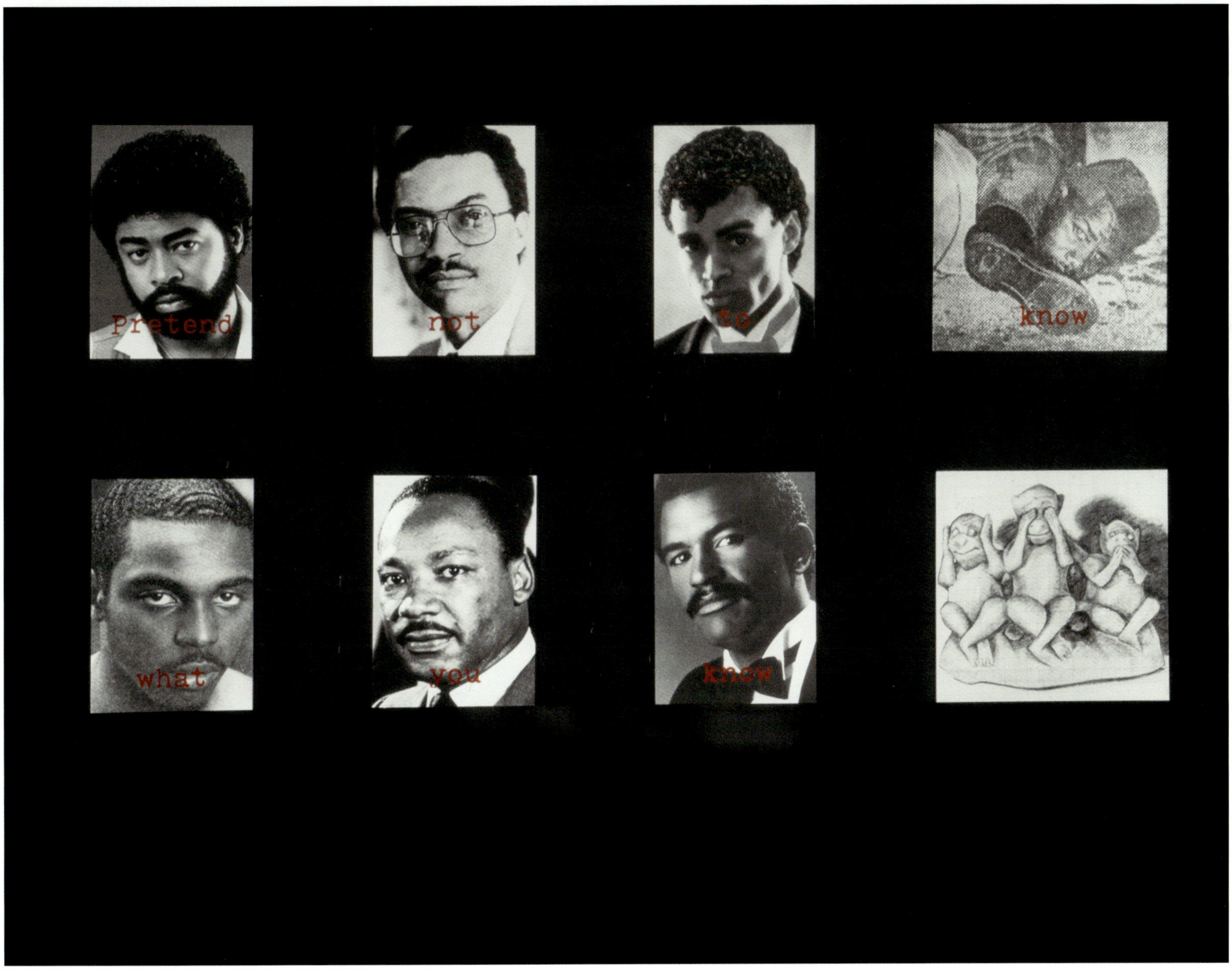

Pretend #1, 1990
Screenprinted text on eight black-and-white photographs, mounted on foam core
Six prints each 12 × 8 in. (30.4 × 20.3 cm) and two prints each 12 × 12 in. (30.4 × 30.4 cm)
The New School Art Collection, New York.

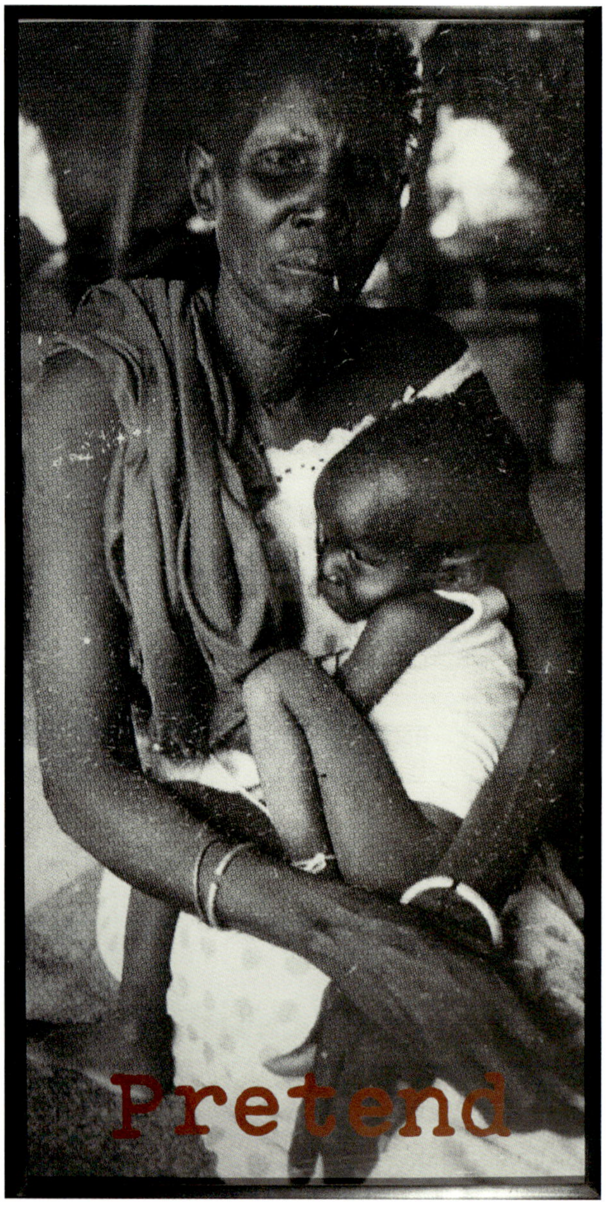

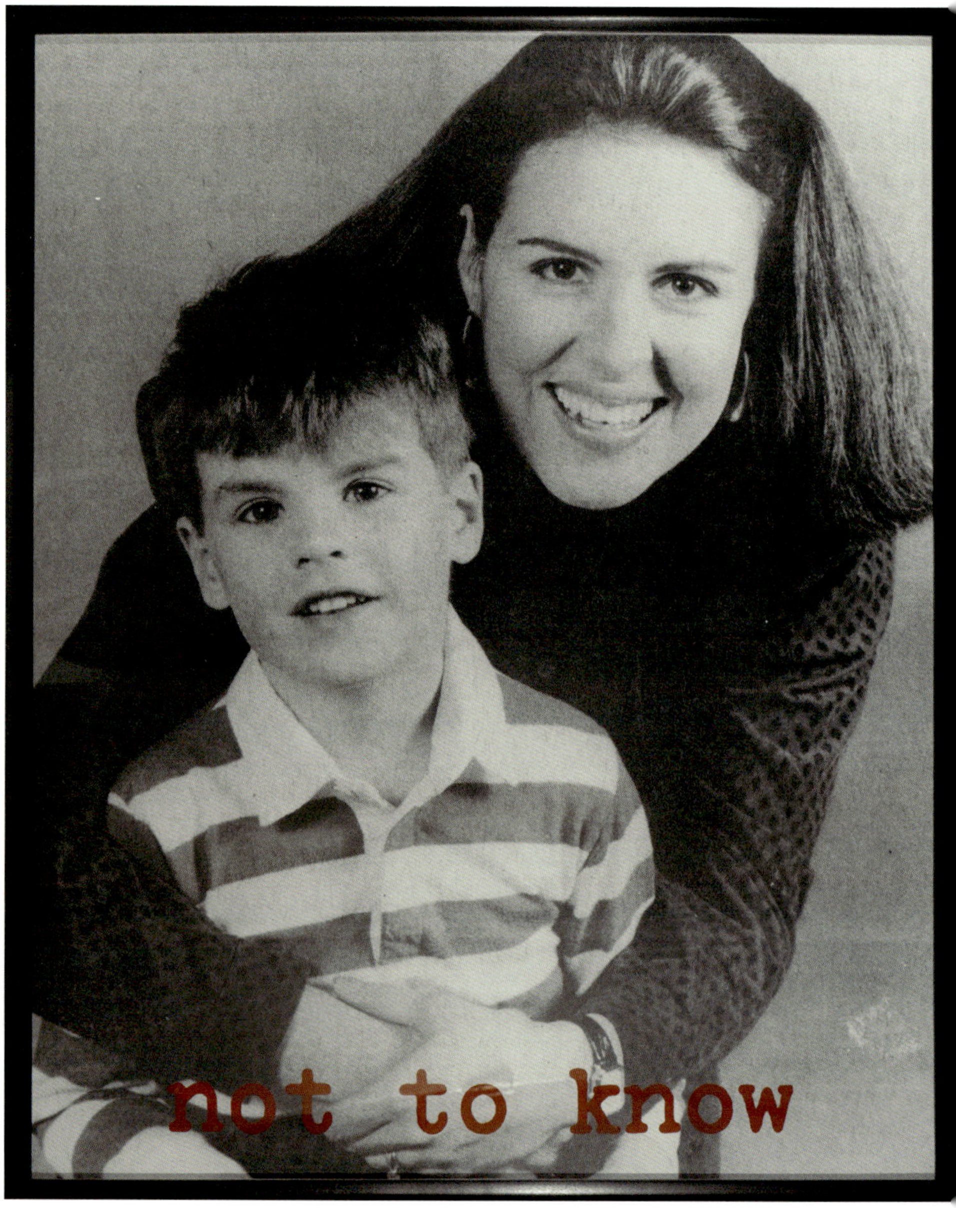

Pretend #2. 1990
Screenprinted text on three black-and-white photographs, mounted on foam core
44 × 22 in. (111.7 × 55.8 cm); 44 × 35 in. (111.7 × 88.9 cm); and 44 × 31 in. (111.7 × 78.7 cm)
Brooklyn Museum, New York. Purchased with funds given by the Daniel and Joanna S. Rose Fund

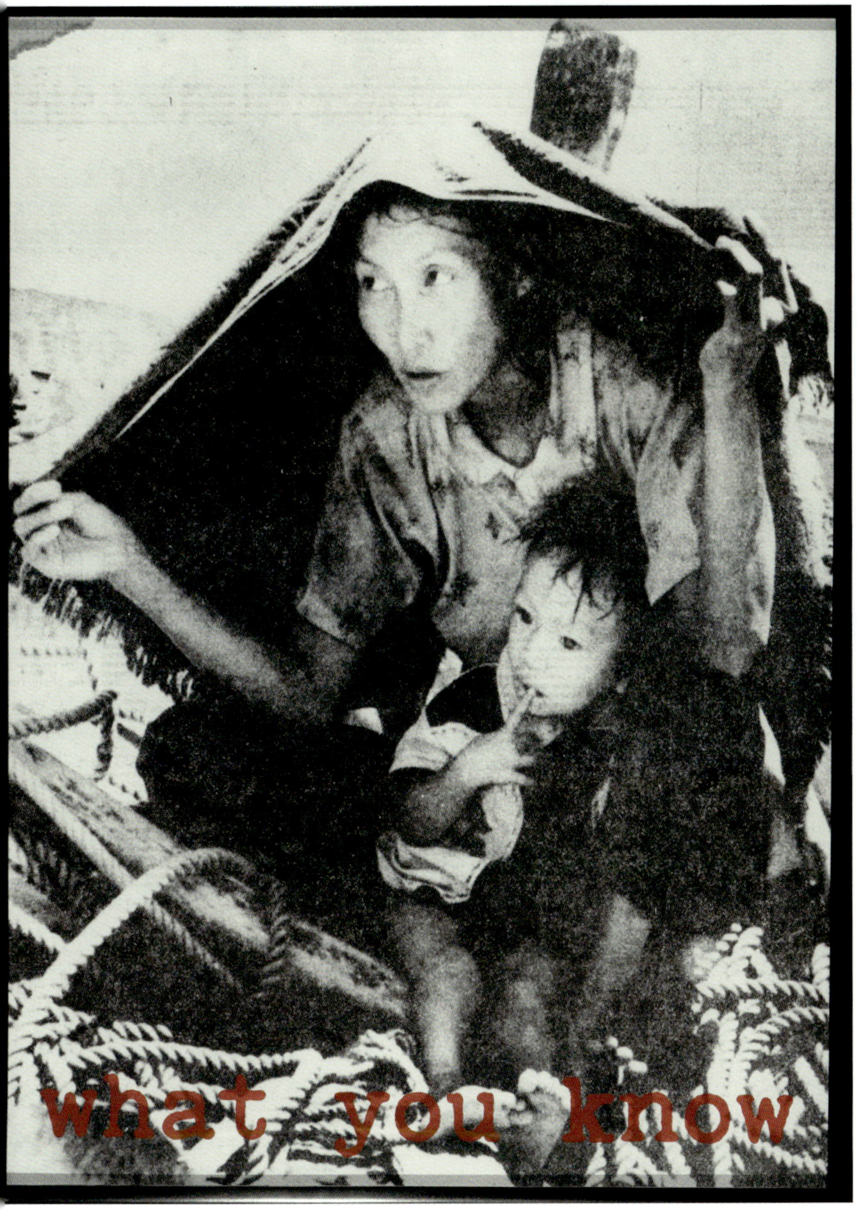
what you know

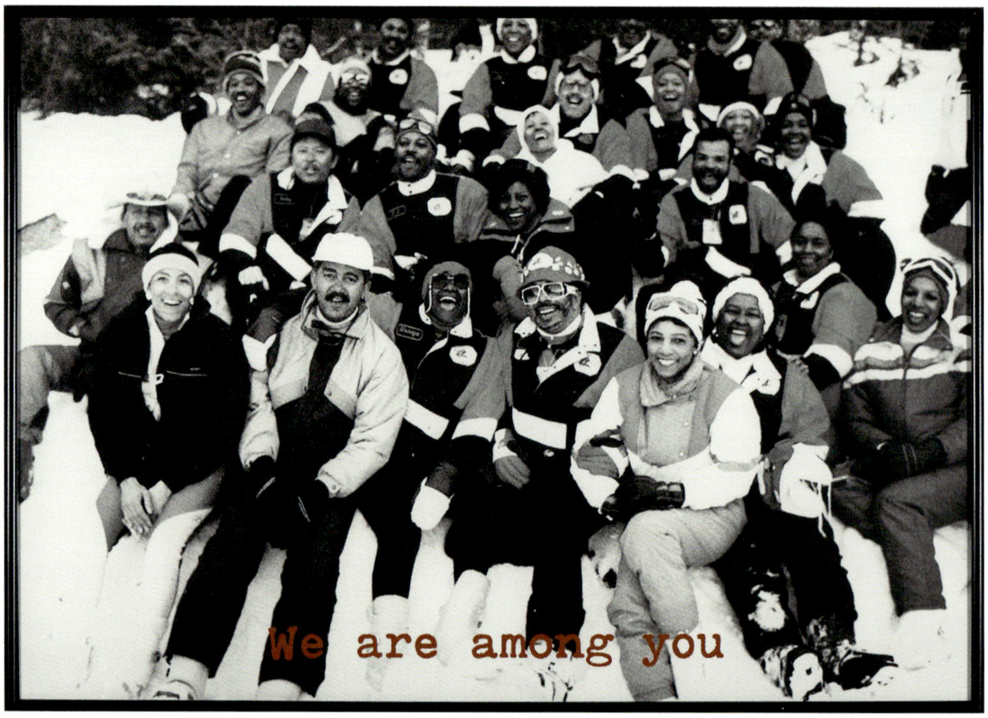

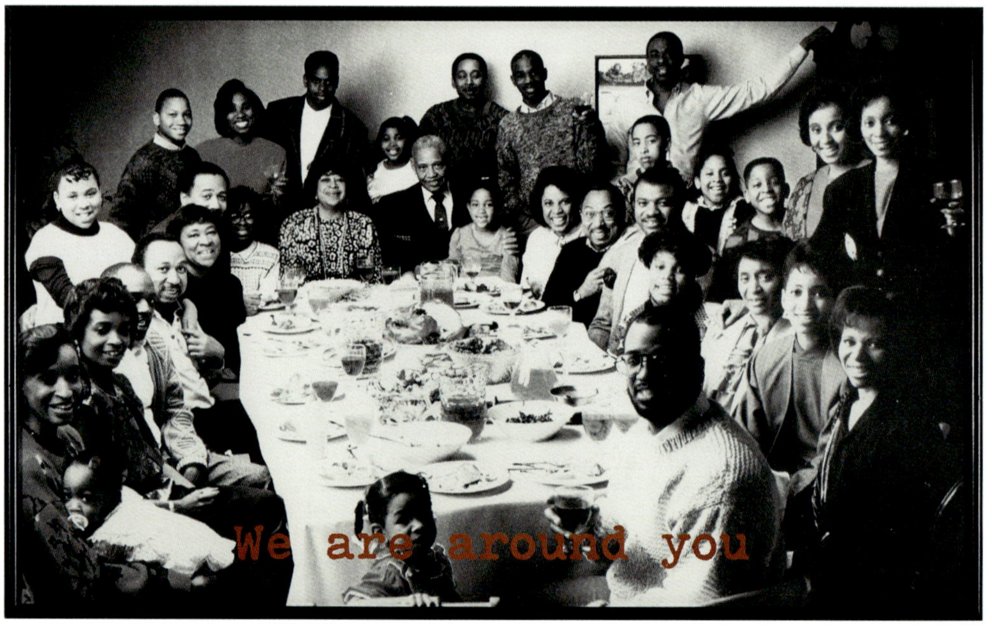

Safe #1–4. 1990
Mixed-medium installation. Screenprinted text on four black-and-white photographs, mounted on foam core and affixed to the corners of a room, with audio
30¼ × 42 in (76.8 × 106.7 cm); 24⅝ × 39¼ in. (62.5 × 99.7 cm); 30⁷⁄₁₆ × 24¹⁵⁄₁₆ in. (77.3 × 63.3 cm); and 44⁵⁄₁₆ × 39 in. (112.6 × 99.1 cm)
Collection Adrian Piper Research Archive Foundation Berlin
Detail: photographs

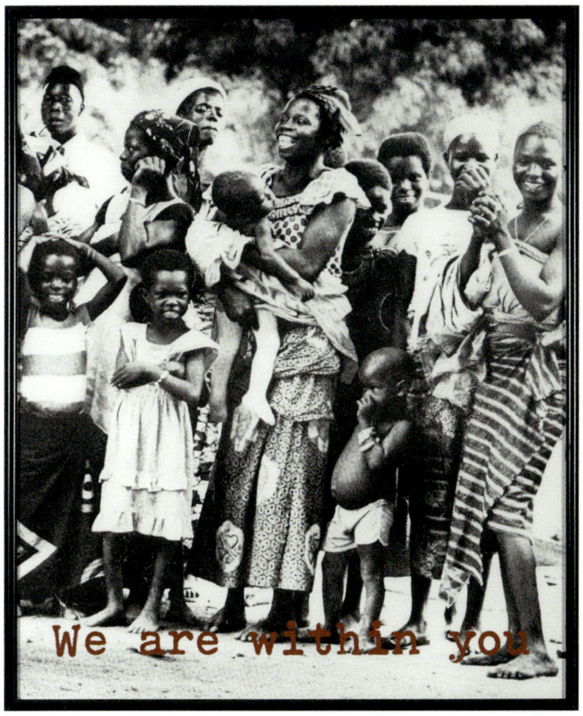
We are within you

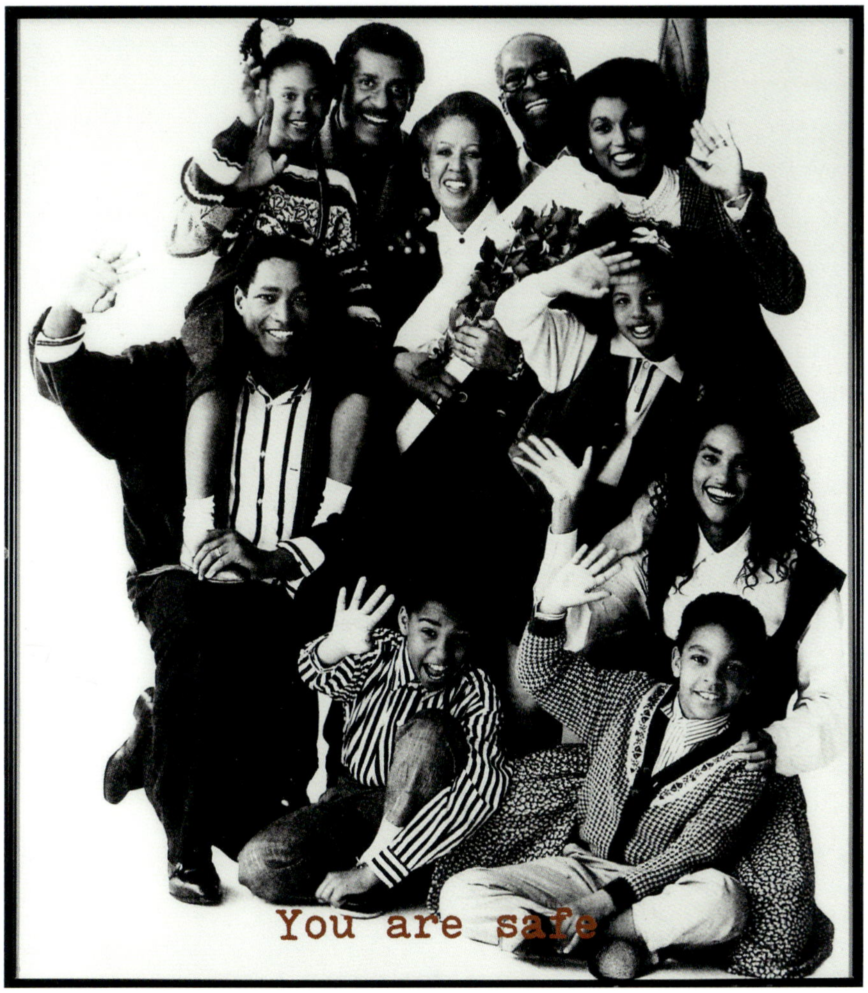
You are safe

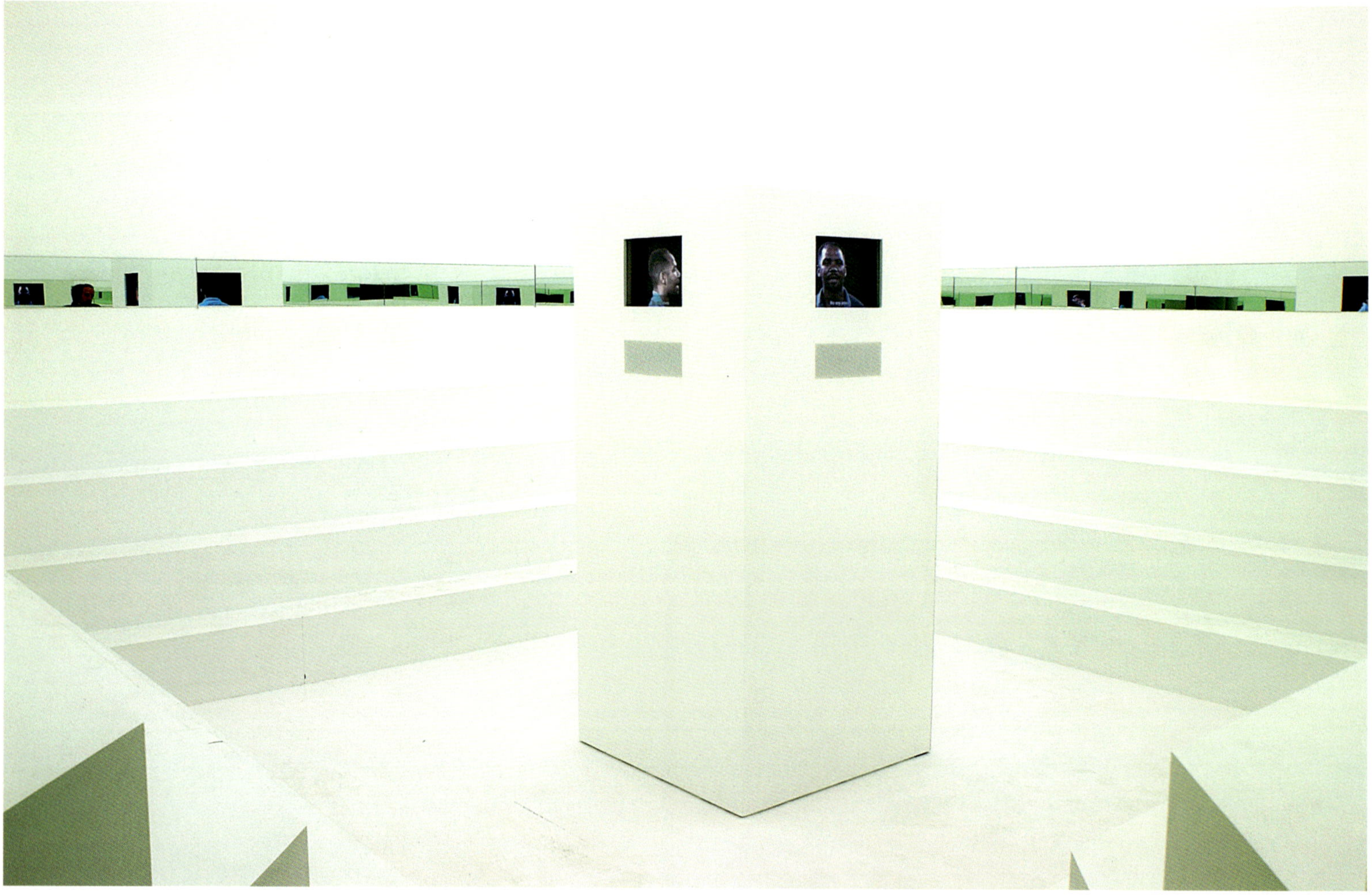

What It's Like, What It Is #3. 1991
Video installation. Video (color, sound), constructed wood environment, four monitors, mirrors, and lighting
Dimensions variable
Installation views in *Adrian Piper: desde 1965*, Museu d'Art Contemporani de Barcelona, October 17, 2003–January 18, 2004
The Museum of Modern Art, New York. Acquired in part through the generosity of Lonti Ebers, Marie-Josée and Henry Kravis, Candace King Weir, and Lévy Gorvy Gallery, and with support from The Modern Women's Fund

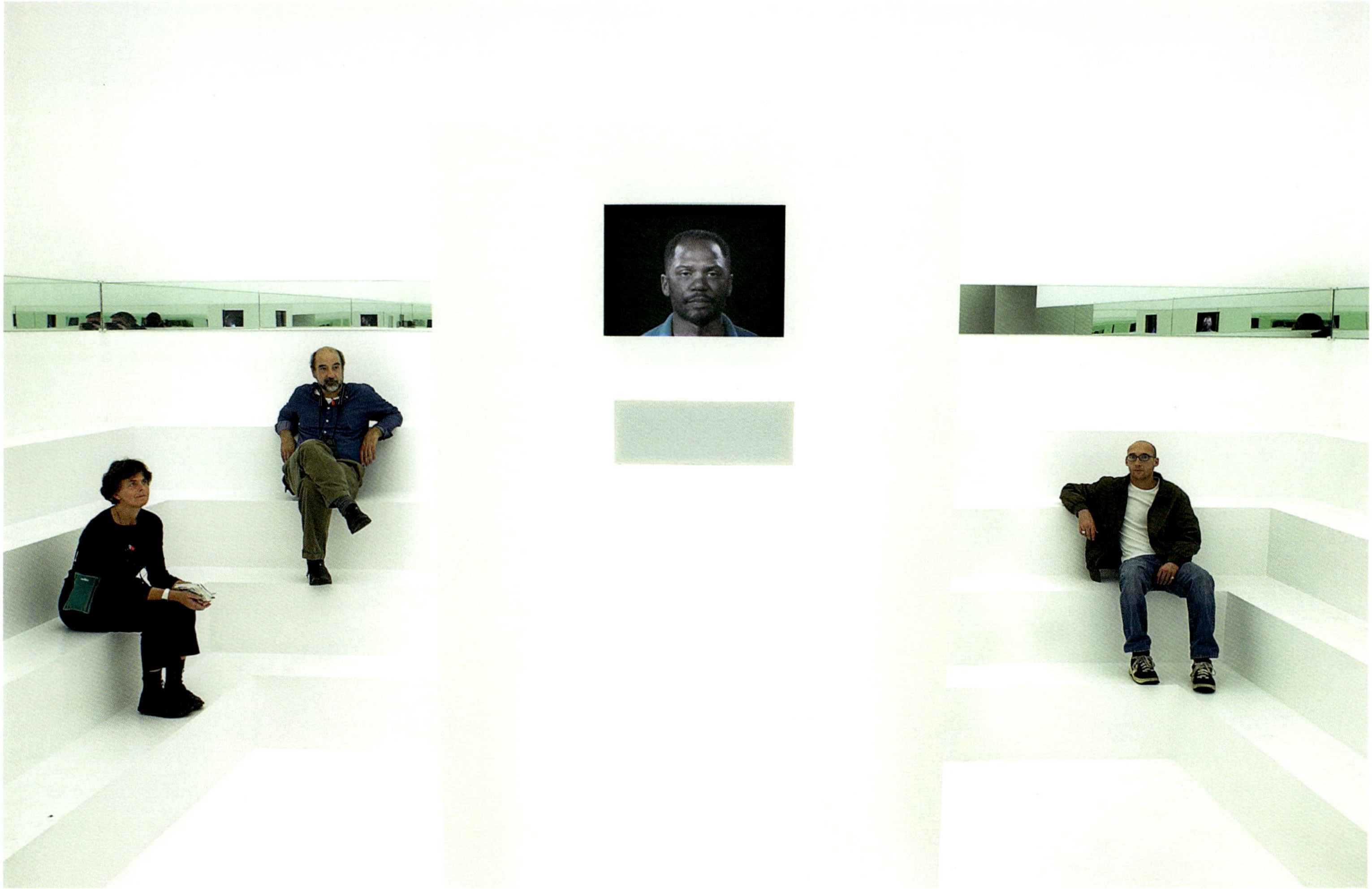

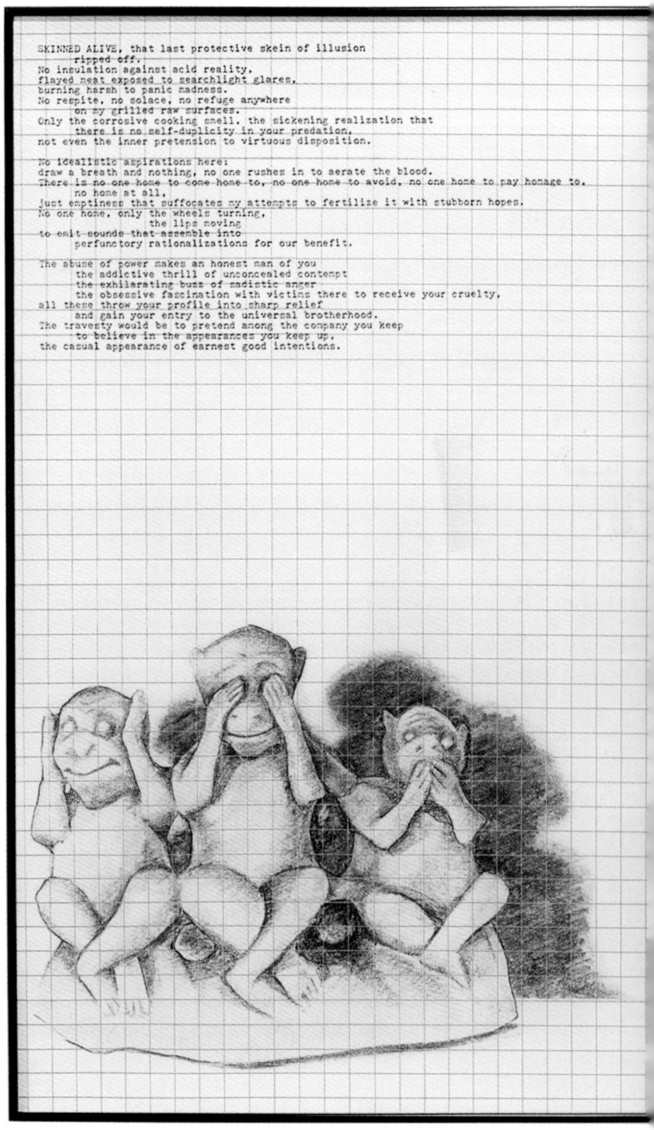

Decide Who You Are #1: Skinned Alive. 1992
Screenprinted images and text on three sheets of paper, mounted on foam core
72 × 42 in. (182.8 × 106.7 cm); 72 × 63 in. (182.8 × 160 cm); and 72 × 42 in. (182.8 × 106.7 cm)
Collection Margaret and Daniel S. Loeb

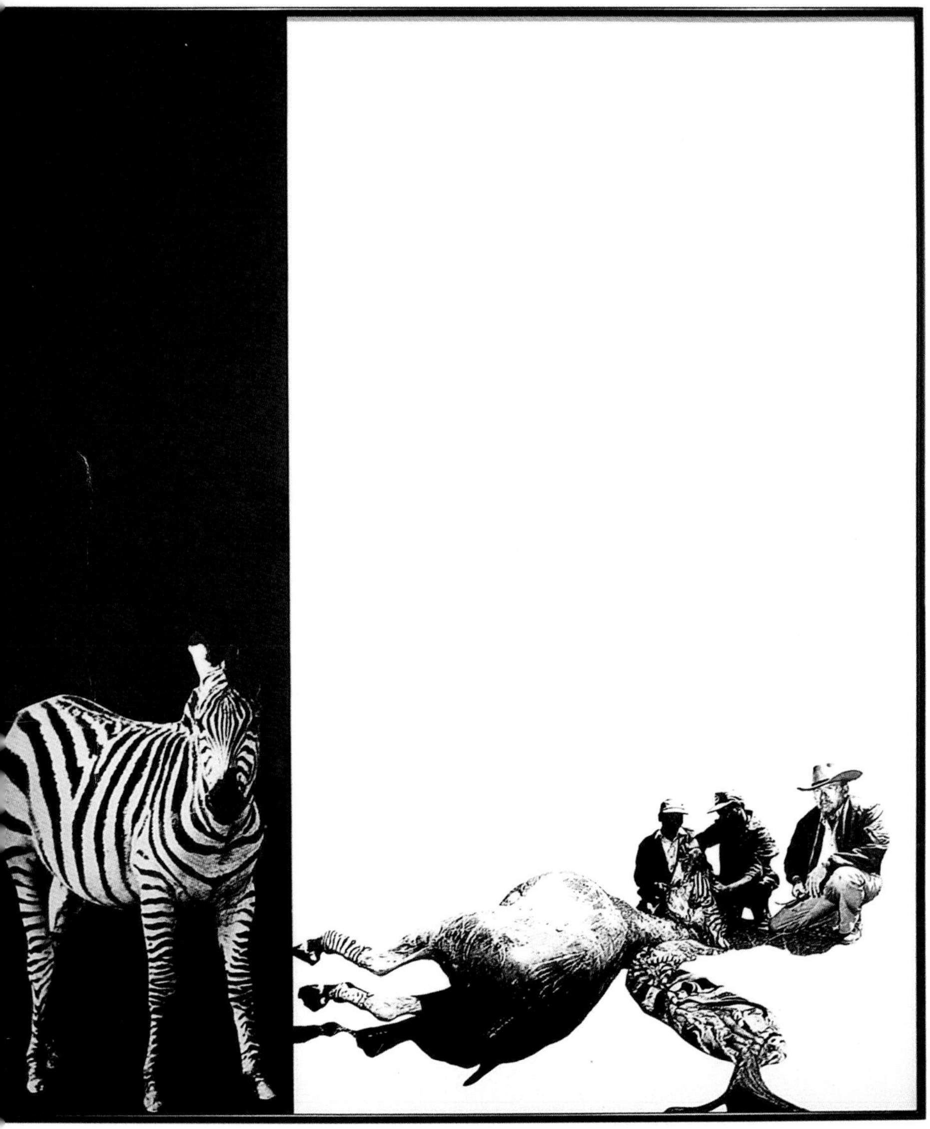

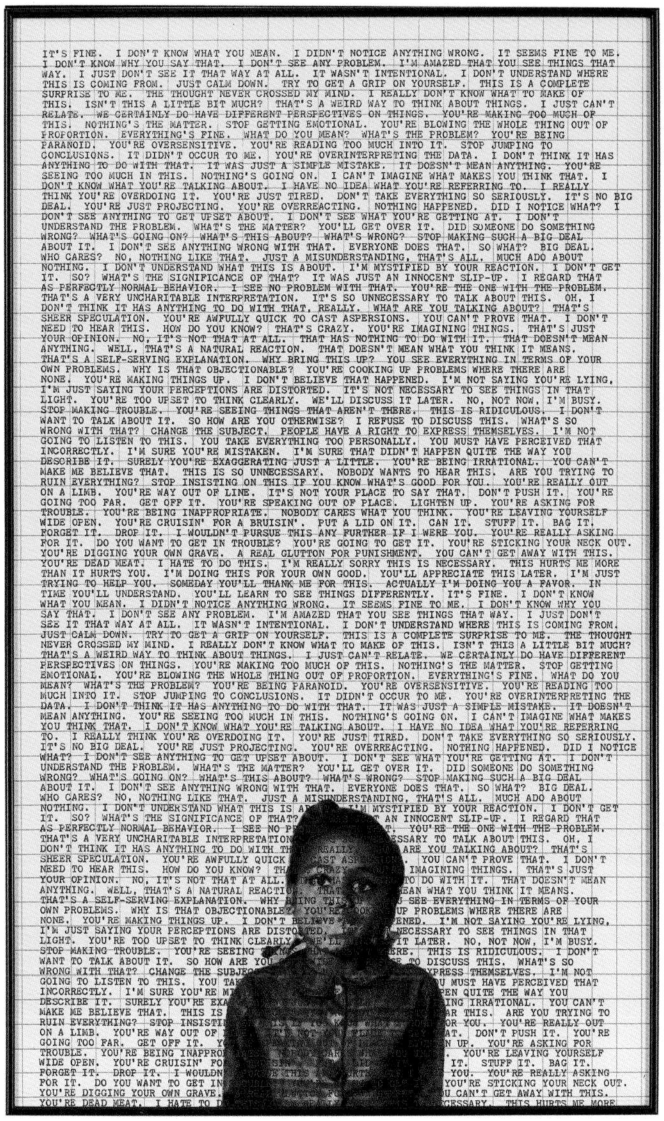
IT'S FINE. I DON'T KNOW WHAT YOU MEAN. I DIDN'T NOTICE ANYTHING WRONG. IT SEEMS FINE TO ME.
I DON'T KNOW WHY YOU SAY THAT. I DON'T SEE ANY PROBLEM. I'M AMAZED THAT YOU SEE THINGS THAT
WAY. I JUST DON'T SEE IT THAT WAY AT ALL. IT WASN'T INTENTIONAL. I DON'T UNDERSTAND WHERE
THIS IS COMING FROM. JUST CALM DOWN. TRY TO GET A GRIP ON YOURSELF. THIS IS A COMPLETE
SURPRISE TO ME. THE THOUGHT NEVER CROSSED MY MIND. I REALLY DON'T KNOW WHAT TO MAKE OF
THIS. ISN'T THIS A LITTLE BIT MUCH? THAT'S A WEIRD WAY TO THINK ABOUT THINGS. I JUST CAN'T
RELATE. WE CERTAINLY DO HAVE DIFFERENT PERSPECTIVES ON THINGS. YOU'RE MAKING TOO MUCH OF
THIS. NOTHING'S THE MATTER. STOP GETTING EMOTIONAL. YOU'RE BLOWING THE WHOLE THING OUT OF
PROPORTION. EVERYTHING'S FINE. WHAT DO YOU MEAN? WHAT'S THE PROBLEM? YOU'RE BEING
PARANOID. YOU'RE OVERSENSITIVE. YOU'RE READING TOO MUCH INTO IT. STOP JUMPING TO
CONCLUSIONS. IT DIDN'T OCCUR TO ME. YOU'RE OVERINTERPRETING THE DATA. I DON'T THINK IT HAS
ANYTHING TO DO WITH THAT. IT WAS JUST A SIMPLE MISTAKE. IT DOESN'T MEAN ANYTHING. YOU'RE
SEEING TOO MUCH IN THIS. NOTHING'S GOING ON. I CAN'T IMAGINE WHAT MAKES YOU THINK THAT. I
DON'T KNOW WHAT YOU'RE TALKING ABOUT. I HAVE NO IDEA WHAT YOU'RE REFERRING TO. I REALLY
THINK YOU'RE OVERDOING IT. YOU'RE JUST TIRED. DON'T TAKE EVERYTHING SO SERIOUSLY. IT'S NO BIG
DEAL. YOU'RE JUST PROJECTING. YOU'RE OVERREACTING. NOTHING HAPPENED. DID I NOTICE WHAT? I
DON'T SEE ANYTHING TO GET UPSET ABOUT. I DON'T SEE WHAT YOU'RE GETTING AT. I DON'T
UNDERSTAND THE PROBLEM. WHAT'S THE MATTER? YOU'LL GET OVER IT. DID SOMEONE DO SOMETHING
WRONG? WHAT'S GOING ON? WHAT'S THIS ABOUT? WHAT'S WRONG? STOP MAKING SUCH A BIG DEAL
ABOUT IT. I DON'T SEE ANYTHING WRONG WITH THAT. EVERYONE DOES THAT. SO WHAT? BIG DEAL.
WHO CARES? NO, NOTHING LIKE THAT. JUST A MISUNDERSTANDING, THAT'S ALL. MUCH ADO ABOUT
NOTHING. I DON'T UNDERSTAND WHAT THIS IS ABOUT. I'M MYSTIFIED BY YOUR REACTION. I DON'T GET
IT. SO? WHAT'S THE SIGNIFICANCE OF THAT? IT WAS JUST AN INNOCENT SLIP-UP. I REGARD THAT
AS PERFECTLY NORMAL BEHAVIOR. I SEE NO PROBLEM WITH THAT. YOU'RE THE ONE WITH THE PROBLEM.
THAT'S A VERY UNCHARITABLE INTERPRETATION. IT'S SO UNNECESSARY TO TALK ABOUT THIS. OH, I
DON'T THINK IT HAS ANYTHING TO DO WITH THAT, REALLY. WHAT ARE YOU TALKING ABOUT? THAT'S
SHEER SPECULATION. YOU'RE AWFULLY QUICK TO CAST ASPERSIONS. YOU CAN'T PROVE THAT. I DON'T
NEED TO HEAR THIS. HOW DO YOU KNOW? THAT'S CRAZY. YOU'RE IMAGINING THINGS. THAT'S JUST
YOUR OPINION. NO, IT'S NOT THAT AT ALL. THAT HAS NOTHING TO DO WITH IT. THAT DOESN'T MEAN
ANYTHING. WELL, THAT'S A NATURAL REACTION. THAT DOESN'T MEAN WHAT YOU THINK IT MEANS.
THAT'S A SELF-SERVING EXPLANATION. WHY BRING THIS UP? YOU SEE EVERYTHING IN TERMS OF YOUR
OWN PROBLEMS. WHY IS THAT OBJECTIONABLE? YOU'RE COOKING UP PROBLEMS WHERE THERE ARE
NONE. YOU'RE MAKING THINGS UP. I DON'T BELIEVE THAT HAPPENED. I'M NOT SAYING YOU'RE LYING,
I'M JUST SAYING YOUR PERCEPTIONS ARE DISTORTED. IT'S NOT NECESSARY TO SEE THINGS IN THAT
LIGHT. YOU'RE TOO UPSET TO THINK CLEARLY. WE'LL DISCUSS IT LATER. NO, NOT NOW, I'M BUSY.
STOP MAKING TROUBLE. YOU'RE SEEING THINGS THAT AREN'T THERE. THIS IS RIDICULOUS. I DON'T
WANT TO TALK ABOUT IT. SO HOW ARE YOU OTHERWISE? I REFUSE TO DISCUSS THIS. WHAT'S SO
WRONG WITH THAT? CHANGE THE SUBJECT. PEOPLE HAVE A RIGHT TO EXPRESS THEMSELVES. I'M NOT
GOING TO LISTEN TO THIS. YOU TAKE EVERYTHING TOO PERSONALLY. YOU MUST HAVE PERCEIVED THAT
INCORRECTLY. I'M SURE YOU'RE MISTAKEN. I'M SURE THAT DIDN'T HAPPEN QUITE THE WAY YOU
DESCRIBE IT. SURELY YOU'RE EXAGGERATING JUST A LITTLE. YOU'RE BEING IRRATIONAL. YOU CAN'T
MAKE ME BELIEVE THAT. THIS IS SO UNNECESSARY. NOBODY WANTS TO HEAR THIS. ARE YOU TRYING TO
RUIN EVERYTHING? STOP INSISTING ON THIS IF YOU KNOW WHAT'S GOOD FOR YOU. YOU'RE REALLY OUT
ON A LIMB. YOU'RE WAY OUT OF LINE. IT'S NOT YOUR PLACE TO SAY THAT. DON'T PUSH IT. YOU'RE
GOING TOO FAR. GET OFF IT. YOU'RE SPEAKING OUT OF PLACE. LIGHTEN UP. YOU'RE ASKING FOR
TROUBLE. YOU'RE BEING INAPPROPRIATE. NOBODY CARES WHAT YOU THINK. YOU'RE LEAVING YOURSELF
WIDE OPEN. YOU'RE CRUISIN' FOR A BRUISIN'. PUT A LID ON IT. CAN IT. STUFF IT. BAG IT.
FORGET IT. DROP IT. I WOULDN'T PURSUE THIS ANY FURTHER IF I WERE YOU. YOU'RE REALLY ASKING
FOR IT. DO YOU WANT TO GET IN TROUBLE? YOU'RE GOING TO GET IT. YOU'RE STICKING YOUR NECK OUT.
YOU'RE DIGGING YOUR OWN GRAVE. A REAL GLUTTON FOR PUNISHMENT. YOU CAN'T GET AWAY WITH THIS.
YOU'RE DEAD MEAT. I HATE TO DO THIS. I'M REALLY SORRY THIS IS NECESSARY. THIS HURTS ME MORE
THAN IT HURTS YOU. I'M DOING THIS FOR YOUR OWN GOOD. YOU'LL APPRECIATE THIS LATER. I'M JUST
TRYING TO HELP YOU. SOMEDAY YOU'LL THANK ME FOR THIS. ACTUALLY I'M DOING YOU A FAVOR. IN
TIME YOU'LL UNDERSTAND. YOU'LL LEARN TO SEE THINGS DIFFERENTLY. IT'S FINE. I DON'T KNOW
WHAT YOU MEAN. I DIDN'T NOTICE ANYTHING WRONG. IT SEEMS FINE TO ME. I DON'T KNOW WHY YOU
SAY THAT. I DON'T SEE ANY PROBLEM. I'M AMAZED THAT YOU SEE THINGS THAT WAY. I JUST DON'T
SEE IT THAT WAY AT ALL. IT WASN'T INTENTIONAL. I DON'T UNDERSTAND WHERE THIS IS COMING FROM.
JUST CALM DOWN. TRY TO GET A GRIP ON YOURSELF. THIS IS A COMPLETE SURPRISE TO ME. THE THOUGHT
NEVER CROSSED MY MIND. I REALLY DON'T KNOW WHAT TO MAKE OF THIS. ISN'T THIS A LITTLE BIT MUCH?
THAT'S A WEIRD WAY TO THINK ABOUT THINGS. I JUST CAN'T RELATE. WE CERTAINLY DO HAVE DIFFERENT
PERSPECTIVES ON THINGS. YOU'RE MAKING TOO MUCH OF THIS. NOTHING'S THE MATTER. STOP GETTING
EMOTIONAL. YOU'RE BLOWING THE WHOLE THING OUT OF PROPORTION. EVERYTHING'S FINE. WHAT DO YOU
MEAN? WHAT'S THE PROBLEM? YOU'RE BEING PARANOID. YOU'RE OVERSENSITIVE. YOU'RE READING TOO
MUCH INTO IT. STOP JUMPING TO CONCLUSIONS. IT DIDN'T OCCUR TO ME. YOU'RE OVERINTERPRETING THE
DATA. I DON'T THINK IT HAS ANYTHING TO DO WITH THAT. IT WAS JUST A SIMPLE MISTAKE. IT DOESN'T
MEAN ANYTHING. YOU'RE SEEING TOO MUCH IN THIS. NOTHING'S GOING ON. I CAN'T IMAGINE WHAT MAKES
YOU THINK THAT. I DON'T KNOW WHAT YOU'RE TALKING ABOUT. I HAVE NO IDEA WHAT YOU'RE REFERRING
TO. I REALLY THINK YOU'RE OVERDOING IT. YOU'RE JUST TIRED. DON'T TAKE EVERYTHING SO SERIOUSLY.
IT'S NO BIG DEAL. YOU'RE JUST PROJECTING. YOU'RE OVERREACTING. NOTHING HAPPENED. DID I NOTICE
WHAT? I DON'T SEE ANYTHING TO GET UPSET ABOUT. I DON'T SEE WHAT YOU'RE GETTING AT. I DON'T
UNDERSTAND THE PROBLEM. WHAT'S THE MATTER? YOU'LL GET OVER IT. DID SOMEONE DO SOMETHING
WRONG? WHAT'S GOING ON? WHAT'S THIS ABOUT? WHAT'S WRONG? STOP MAKING SUCH A BIG DEAL
ABOUT IT. I DON'T SEE ANYTHING WRONG WITH THAT. EVERYONE DOES THAT. SO WHAT? BIG DEAL.
WHO CARES? NO, NOTHING LIKE THAT. JUST A MISUNDERSTANDING, THAT'S ALL. MUCH ADO ABOUT
NOTHING. I DON'T UNDERSTAND WHAT THIS IS A I'M MYSTIFIED BY YOUR REACTION. I DON'T GET
IT. SO? WHAT'S THE SIGNIFICANCE OF THAT? AN INNOCENT SLIP-UP. I REGARD THAT
AS PERFECTLY NORMAL BEHAVIOR. I SEE NO P T. YOU'RE THE ONE WITH THE PROBLEM.
THAT'S A VERY UNCHARITABLE INTERPRETATION ESSARY TO TALK ABOUT THIS. OH, I
DON'T THINK IT HAS ANYTHING TO DO WITH TH ARE YOU TALKING ABOUT? THAT'S
SHEER SPECULATION. YOU'RE AWFULLY QUICK . YOU CAN'T PROVE THAT. I DON'T
NEED TO HEAR THIS. HOW DO YOU KNOW? IMAGINING THINGS. THAT'S JUST
YOUR OPINION. NO, IT'S NOT THAT AT ALL. TO DO WITH IT. THAT DOESN'T MEAN
ANYTHING. WELL, THAT'S A NATURAL REACTI EAN WHAT YOU THINK IT MEANS.
THAT'S A SELF-SERVING EXPLANATION. WHY SEE EVERYTHING IN TERMS OF YOUR
OWN PROBLEMS. WHY IS THAT OBJECTIONABLE UP PROBLEMS WHERE THERE ARE
NONE. YOU'RE MAKING THINGS UP. I DON'T PENED. I'M NOT SAYING YOU'RE LYING,
I'M JUST SAYING YOUR PERCEPTIONS ARE DISTO NECESSARY TO SEE THINGS IN THAT
LIGHT. YOU'RE TOO UPSET TO THINK CLEARLY IT LATER. NO, NOT NOW, I'M BUSY.
STOP MAKING TROUBLE. YOU'RE SEEING ERE. THIS IS RIDICULOUS. I DON'T
WANT TO TALK ABOUT IT. SO HOW ARE YOU TO DISCUSS THIS. WHAT'S SO
WRONG WITH THAT? CHANGE THE SUBJE XPRESS THEMSELVES. I'M NOT
GOING TO LISTEN TO THIS. YOU U MUST HAVE PERCEIVED THAT
INCORRECTLY. I'M SURE YOU'RE M PEN QUITE THE WAY YOU
DESCRIBE IT. SURELY YOU'RE EXA ING IRRATIONAL. YOU CAN'T
MAKE ME BELIEVE THAT. THIS IS AR THIS. ARE YOU TRYING TO
RUIN EVERYTHING? STOP INSISTI OR YOU. YOU'RE REALLY OUT
ON A LIMB. YOU'RE WAY OUT OF AT. DON'T PUSH IT. YOU'RE
GOING TOO FAR. GET OFF IT. N UP. YOU'RE ASKING FOR
TROUBLE. YOU'RE BEING INAPPRO . YOU'RE LEAVING YOURSELF
WIDE OPEN. YOU'RE CRUISIN' FO IT. STUFF IT. BAG IT.
FORGET IT. DROP IT. I WOULDN YOU. YOU'RE REALLY ASKING
FOR IT. DO YOU WANT TO GET IN YOU'RE STICKING YOUR NECK OUT.
YOU'RE DIGGING YOUR OWN GRAVE. U CAN'T GET AWAY WITH THIS.

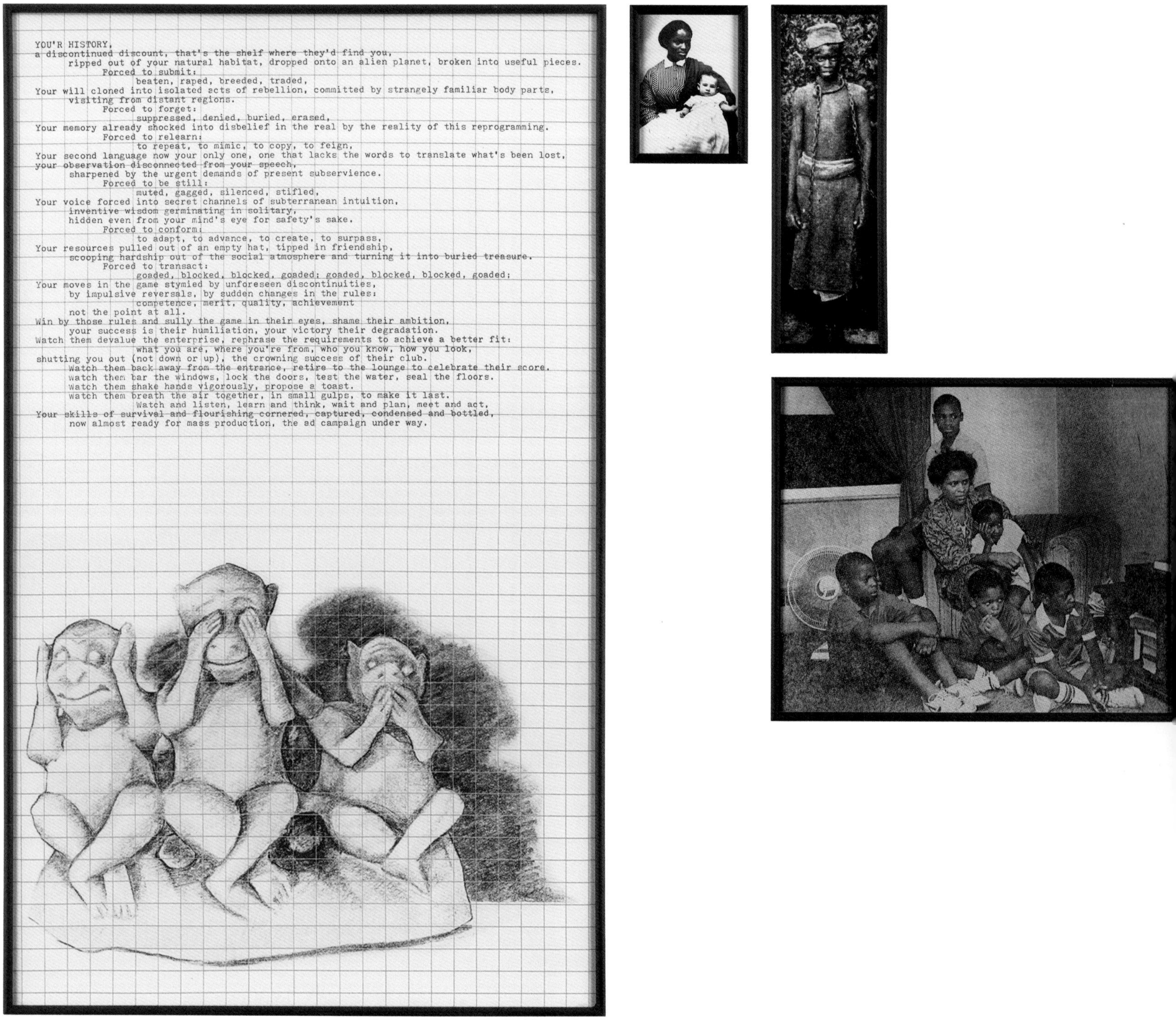

Decide Who You Are #6: You'r History. 1992
Screenprinted images and text on seven sheets of paper, mounted on foam core
72 × 42 in. (182.8 × 106.7 cm); 9¾ × 7 in. (24.8 × 17.8 cm); 24 × 7¼ in. (61 × 18.4 cm); 24 × 29 in. (61 × 73.7 cm); 22 × 32 in. (55.9 × 81.3 cm);
20 × 24¾ in. (50.8 × 62.9 cm); and 72 × 42 in. (182.8 × 106.7 cm)
Mott-Warsh Collection, Flint, Michigan

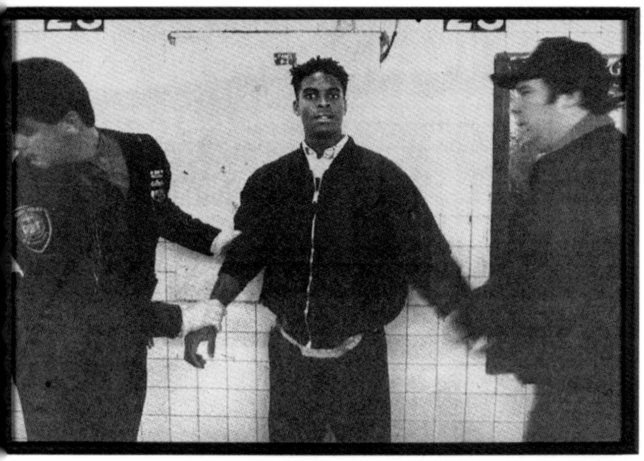

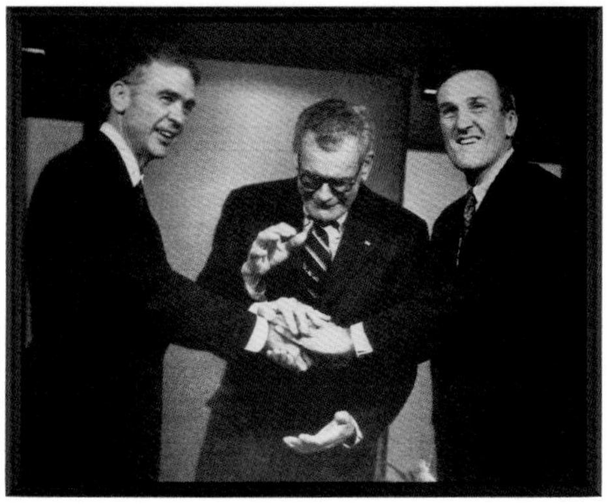

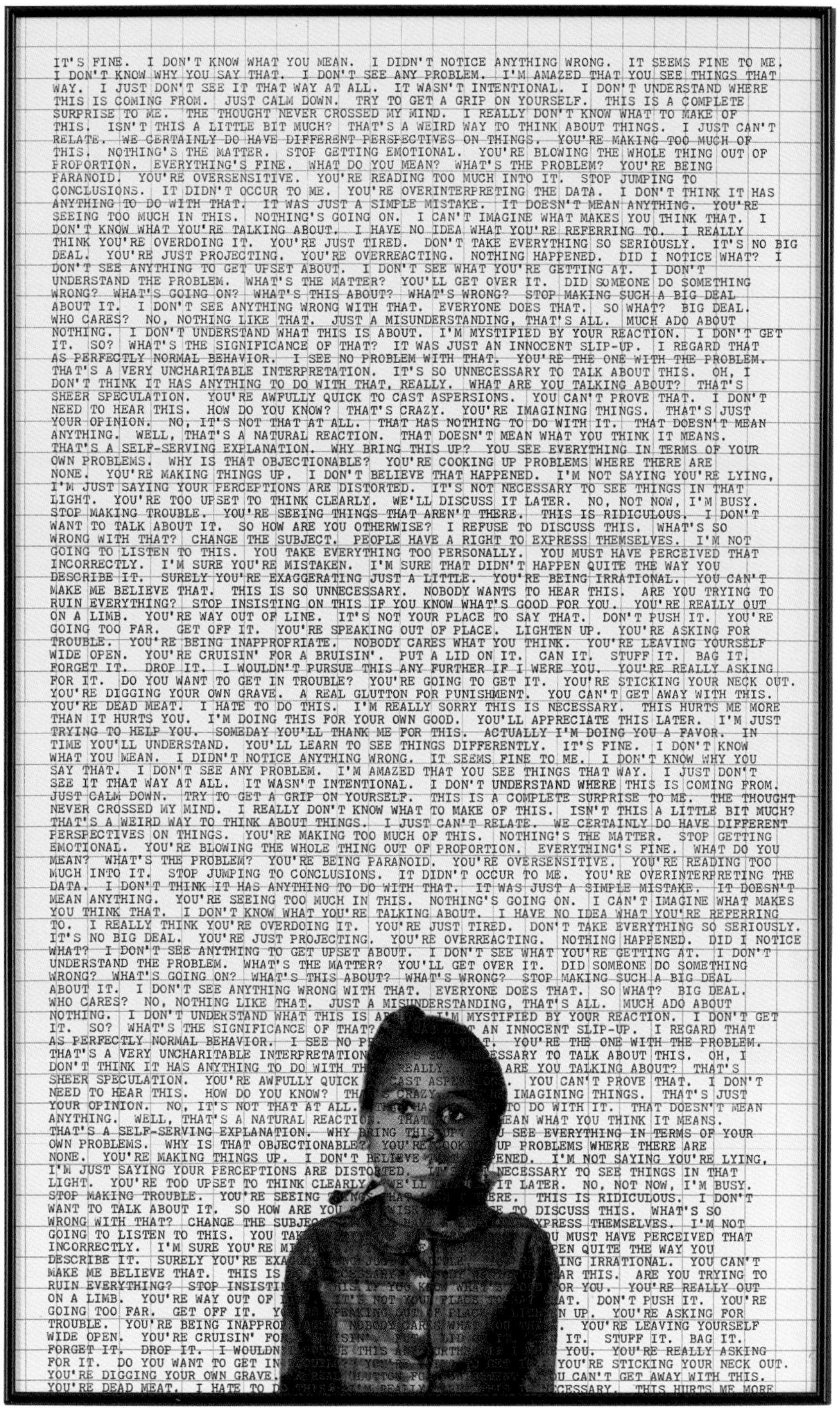

IT'S FINE. I DON'T KNOW WHAT YOU MEAN. I DIDN'T NOTICE ANYTHING WRONG. IT SEEMS FINE TO ME.
I DON'T KNOW WHY YOU SAY THAT. I DON'T SEE ANY PROBLEM. I'M AMAZED THAT YOU SEE THINGS THAT
WAY. I JUST DON'T SEE IT THAT WAY AT ALL. IT WASN'T INTENTIONAL. I DON'T UNDERSTAND WHERE
THIS IS COMING FROM. JUST CALM DOWN. TRY TO GET A GRIP ON YOURSELF. THIS IS A COMPLETE
SURPRISE TO ME. THE THOUGHT NEVER CROSSED MY MIND. I REALLY DON'T KNOW WHAT TO MAKE OF
THIS. ISN'T THIS A LITTLE BIT MUCH? THAT'S A WEIRD WAY TO THINK ABOUT THINGS. I JUST CAN'T
RELATE. WE CERTAINLY DO HAVE DIFFERENT PERSPECTIVES ON THINGS. YOU'RE MAKING TOO MUCH OF
THIS. NOTHING'S THE MATTER. STOP GETTING EMOTIONAL. YOU'RE BLOWING THE WHOLE THING OUT OF
PROPORTION. EVERYTHING'S FINE. WHAT DO YOU MEAN? WHAT'S THE PROBLEM? YOU'RE BEING
PARANOID. YOU'RE OVERSENSITIVE. YOU'RE READING TOO MUCH INTO IT. STOP JUMPING TO
CONCLUSIONS. IT DIDN'T OCCUR TO ME. YOU'RE OVERINTERPRETING THE DATA. I DON'T THINK IT HAS
ANYTHING TO DO WITH THAT. IT WAS JUST A SIMPLE MISTAKE. IT DOESN'T MEAN ANYTHING. YOU'RE
SEEING TOO MUCH IN THIS. NOTHING'S GOING ON. I CAN'T IMAGINE WHAT MAKES YOU THINK THAT. I
DON'T KNOW WHAT YOU'RE TALKING ABOUT. I HAVE NO IDEA WHAT YOU'RE REFERRING TO. I REALLY
THINK YOU'RE OVERDOING IT. YOU'RE JUST TIRED. DON'T TAKE EVERYTHING SO SERIOUSLY. IT'S NO BIG
DEAL. YOU'RE JUST PROJECTING. YOU'RE OVERREACTING. NOTHING HAPPENED. DID I NOTICE WHAT? I
DON'T SEE ANYTHING TO GET UPSET ABOUT. I DON'T SEE WHAT YOU'RE GETTING AT. I DON'T
UNDERSTAND THE PROBLEM. WHAT'S THE MATTER? YOU'LL GET OVER IT. DID SOMEONE DO SOMETHING
WRONG? WHAT'S GOING ON? WHAT'S THIS ABOUT? WHAT'S WRONG? STOP MAKING SUCH A BIG DEAL
ABOUT IT. I DON'T SEE ANYTHING WRONG WITH THAT. EVERYONE DOES THAT. SO WHAT? BIG DEAL.
WHO CARES? NO, NOTHING LIKE THAT. JUST A MISUNDERSTANDING, THAT'S ALL. MUCH ADO ABOUT
NOTHING. I DON'T UNDERSTAND WHAT THIS IS ABOUT. I'M MYSTIFIED BY YOUR REACTION. I DON'T GET
IT. SO? WHAT'S THE SIGNIFICANCE OF THAT? IT WAS JUST AN INNOCENT SLIP-UP. I REGARD THAT
AS PERFECTLY NORMAL BEHAVIOR. I SEE NO PROBLEM WITH THAT. YOU'RE THE ONE WITH THE PROBLEM.
THAT'S A VERY UNCHARITABLE INTERPRETATION. IT'S SO UNNECESSARY TO TALK ABOUT THIS. OH, I
DON'T THINK IT HAS ANYTHING TO DO WITH THAT, REALLY. WHAT ARE YOU TALKING ABOUT? THAT'S
SHEER SPECULATION. YOU'RE AWFULLY QUICK TO CAST ASPERSIONS. YOU CAN'T PROVE THAT. I DON'T
NEED TO HEAR THIS. HOW DO YOU KNOW? THAT'S CRAZY. YOU'RE IMAGINING THINGS. THAT'S JUST
YOUR OPINION. NO, IT'S NOT THAT AT ALL. THAT HAS NOTHING TO DO WITH IT. THAT DOESN'T MEAN
ANYTHING. WELL, THAT'S A NATURAL REACTION. THAT DOESN'T MEAN WHAT YOU THINK IT MEANS.
THAT'S A SELF-SERVING EXPLANATION. WHY BRING THIS UP? YOU SEE EVERYTHING IN TERMS OF YOUR
OWN PROBLEMS. WHY IS THAT OBJECTIONABLE? YOU'RE COOKING UP PROBLEMS WHERE THERE ARE
NONE. YOU'RE MAKING THINGS UP. I DON'T BELIEVE THAT HAPPENED. I'M NOT SAYING YOU'RE LYING,
I'M JUST SAYING YOUR PERCEPTIONS ARE DISTORTED. IT'S NOT NECESSARY TO SEE THINGS IN THAT
LIGHT. YOU'RE TOO UPSET TO THINK CLEARLY. WE'LL DISCUSS IT LATER. NO, NOT NOW, I'M BUSY.
STOP MAKING TROUBLE. YOU'RE SEEING THINGS THAT AREN'T THERE. THIS IS RIDICULOUS. I DON'T
WANT TO TALK ABOUT IT. SO HOW ARE YOU OTHERWISE? I REFUSE TO DISCUSS THIS. WHAT'S SO
WRONG WITH THAT? CHANGE THE SUBJECT. PEOPLE HAVE A RIGHT TO EXPRESS THEMSELVES. I'M NOT
GOING TO LISTEN TO THIS. YOU TAKE EVERYTHING TOO PERSONALLY. YOU MUST HAVE PERCEIVED THAT
INCORRECTLY. I'M SURE YOU'RE MISTAKEN. I'M SURE THAT DIDN'T HAPPEN QUITE THE WAY YOU
DESCRIBE IT. SURELY YOU'RE EXAGGERATING JUST A LITTLE. YOU'RE BEING IRRATIONAL. YOU CAN'T
MAKE ME BELIEVE THAT. THIS IS SO UNNECESSARY. NOBODY WANTS TO HEAR THIS. ARE YOU TRYING TO
RUIN EVERYTHING? STOP INSISTING ON THIS IF YOU KNOW WHAT'S GOOD FOR YOU. YOU'RE REALLY OUT
ON A LIMB. YOU'RE WAY OUT OF LINE. IT'S NOT YOUR PLACE TO SAY THAT. DON'T PUSH IT. YOU'RE
GOING TOO FAR. GET OFF IT. YOU'RE SPEAKING OUT OF PLACE. LIGHTEN UP. YOU'RE ASKING FOR
TROUBLE. YOU'RE BEING INAPPROPRIATE. NOBODY CARES WHAT YOU THINK. YOU'RE LEAVING YOURSELF
WIDE OPEN. YOU'RE CRUISIN' FOR A BRUISIN'. PUT A LID ON IT. CAN IT. STUFF IT. BAG IT.
FORGET IT. DROP IT. I WOULDN'T PURSUE THIS ANY FURTHER IF I WERE YOU. YOU'RE REALLY ASKING
FOR IT. DO YOU WANT TO GET IN TROUBLE? YOU'RE GOING TO GET IT. YOU'RE STICKING YOUR NECK OUT.
YOU'RE DIGGING YOUR OWN GRAVE. A REAL GLUTTON FOR PUNISHMENT. YOU CAN'T GET AWAY WITH THIS.
YOU'RE DEAD MEAT. I HATE TO DO THIS. I'M REALLY SORRY THIS IS NECESSARY. THIS HURTS ME MORE
THAN IT HURTS YOU. I'M DOING THIS FOR YOUR OWN GOOD. YOU'LL APPRECIATE THIS LATER. I'M JUST
TRYING TO HELP YOU. SOMEDAY YOU'LL THANK ME FOR THIS. ACTUALLY I'M DOING YOU A FAVOR. IN
TIME YOU'LL UNDERSTAND. YOU'LL LEARN TO SEE THINGS DIFFERENTLY. IT'S FINE. I DON'T KNOW
WHAT YOU MEAN. I DIDN'T NOTICE ANYTHING WRONG. IT SEEMS FINE TO ME. I DON'T KNOW WHY YOU
SAY THAT. I DON'T SEE ANY PROBLEM. I'M AMAZED THAT YOU SEE THINGS THAT WAY. I JUST DON'T
SEE IT THAT WAY AT ALL. IT WASN'T INTENTIONAL. I DON'T UNDERSTAND WHERE THIS IS COMING FROM.
JUST CALM DOWN. TRY TO GET A GRIP ON YOURSELF. THIS IS A COMPLETE SURPRISE TO ME. THE THOUGHT
NEVER CROSSED MY MIND. I REALLY DON'T KNOW WHAT TO MAKE OF THIS. ISN'T THIS A LITTLE BIT MUCH?
THAT'S A WEIRD WAY TO THINK ABOUT THINGS. I JUST CAN'T RELATE. WE CERTAINLY DO HAVE DIFFERENT
PERSPECTIVES ON THINGS. YOU'RE MAKING TOO MUCH OF THIS. NOTHING'S THE MATTER. STOP GETTING
EMOTIONAL. YOU'RE BLOWING THE WHOLE THING OUT OF PROPORTION. EVERYTHING'S FINE. WHAT DO YOU
MEAN? WHAT'S THE PROBLEM? YOU'RE BEING PARANOID. YOU'RE OVERSENSITIVE. YOU'RE READING TOO
MUCH INTO IT. STOP JUMPING TO CONCLUSIONS. IT DIDN'T OCCUR TO ME. YOU'RE OVERINTERPRETING THE
DATA. I DON'T THINK IT HAS ANYTHING TO DO WITH THAT. IT WAS JUST A SIMPLE MISTAKE. IT DOESN'T
MEAN ANYTHING. YOU'RE SEEING TOO MUCH IN THIS. NOTHING'S GOING ON. I CAN'T IMAGINE WHAT MAKES
YOU THINK THAT. I DON'T KNOW WHAT YOU'RE TALKING ABOUT. I HAVE NO IDEA WHAT YOU'RE REFERRING
TO. I REALLY THINK YOU'RE OVERDOING IT. YOU'RE JUST TIRED. DON'T TAKE EVERYTHING SO SERIOUSLY.
IT'S NO BIG DEAL. YOU'RE JUST PROJECTING. YOU'RE OVERREACTING. NOTHING HAPPENED. DID I NOTICE
WHAT? I DON'T SEE ANYTHING TO GET UPSET ABOUT. I DON'T SEE WHAT YOU'RE GETTING AT. I DON'T
UNDERSTAND THE PROBLEM. WHAT'S THE MATTER? YOU'LL GET OVER IT. DID SOMEONE DO SOMETHING
WRONG? WHAT'S GOING ON? WHAT'S THIS ABOUT? WHAT'S WRONG? STOP MAKING SUCH A BIG DEAL
ABOUT IT. I DON'T SEE ANYTHING WRONG WITH THAT. EVERYONE DOES THAT. SO WHAT? BIG DEAL.
WHO CARES? NO, NOTHING LIKE THAT. JUST A MISUNDERSTANDING, THAT'S ALL. MUCH ADO ABOUT
NOTHING. I DON'T UNDERSTAND WHAT THIS IS A I'M MYSTIFIED BY YOUR REACTION. I DON'T GET
IT. SO? WHAT'S THE SIGNIFICANCE OF THAT? AN INNOCENT SLIP-UP. I REGARD THAT
AS PERFECTLY NORMAL BEHAVIOR. I SEE NO P T. YOU'RE THE ONE WITH THE PROBLEM.
THAT'S A VERY UNCHARITABLE INTERPRETATION ESSARY TO TALK ABOUT THIS. OH, I
DON'T THINK IT HAS ANYTHING TO DO WITH TH REALLY. ARE YOU TALKING ABOUT? THAT'S
SHEER SPECULATION. YOU'RE AWFULLY QUICK CAST ASP . YOU CAN'T PROVE THAT. I DON'T
NEED TO HEAR THIS. HOW DO YOU KNOW? THA CRAZY IMAGINING THINGS. THAT'S JUST
YOUR OPINION. NO, IT'S NOT THAT AT ALL. TO DO WITH IT. THAT DOESN'T MEAN
ANYTHING. WELL, THAT'S A NATURAL REACTI EAN WHAT YOU THINK IT MEANS.
THAT'S A SELF-SERVING EXPLANATION. WHY BRING THIS U SEE EVERYTHING IN TERMS OF YOUR
OWN PROBLEMS. WHY IS THAT OBJECTIONABLE? YOU'RE UP PROBLEMS WHERE THERE ARE
NONE. YOU'RE MAKING THINGS UP. I DON'T BELIEVE ENED. I'M NOT SAYING YOU'RE LYING,
I'M JUST SAYING YOUR PERCEPTIONS ARE DISTORTED. NECESSARY TO SEE THINGS IN THAT
LIGHT. YOU'RE TOO UPSET TO THINK CLEARLY WE'LL IT LATER. NO, NOT NOW, I'M BUSY.
STOP MAKING TROUBLE. YOU'RE SEEING ERE. THIS IS RIDICULOUS. I DON'T
WANT TO TALK ABOUT IT. SO HOW ARE YO TO DISCUSS THIS. WHAT'S SO
WRONG WITH THAT? CHANGE THE SUBJE XPRESS THEMSELVES. I'M NOT
GOING TO LISTEN TO THIS. YOU TAK U MUST HAVE PERCEIVED THAT
INCORRECTLY. I'M SURE YOU'RE MI PEN QUITE THE WAY YOU
DESCRIBE IT. SURELY YOU'RE EXA ING IRRATIONAL. YOU CAN'T
MAKE ME BELIEVE THAT. THIS IS AR THIS. ARE YOU TRYING TO
RUIN EVERYTHING? STOP INSISTI OR YOU. YOU'RE REALLY OUT
ON A LIMB. YOU'RE WAY OUT OF AT. DON'T PUSH IT. YOU'RE
GOING TOO FAR. GET OFF IT. N UP. YOU'RE ASKING FOR
TROUBLE. YOU'RE BEING INAPPRO . YOU'RE LEAVING YOURSELF
WIDE OPEN. YOU'RE CRUISIN' FO IT. STUFF IT. BAG IT.
FORGET IT. DROP IT. I WOULDN YOU. YOU'RE REALLY ASKING
FOR IT. DO YOU WANT TO GET IN YOU'RE STICKING YOUR NECK OUT.
YOU'RE DIGGING YOUR OWN GRAVE. U CAN'T GET AWAY WITH THIS.
YOU'RE DEAD MEAT. I HATE TO CESSARY. THIS HURTS ME MORE

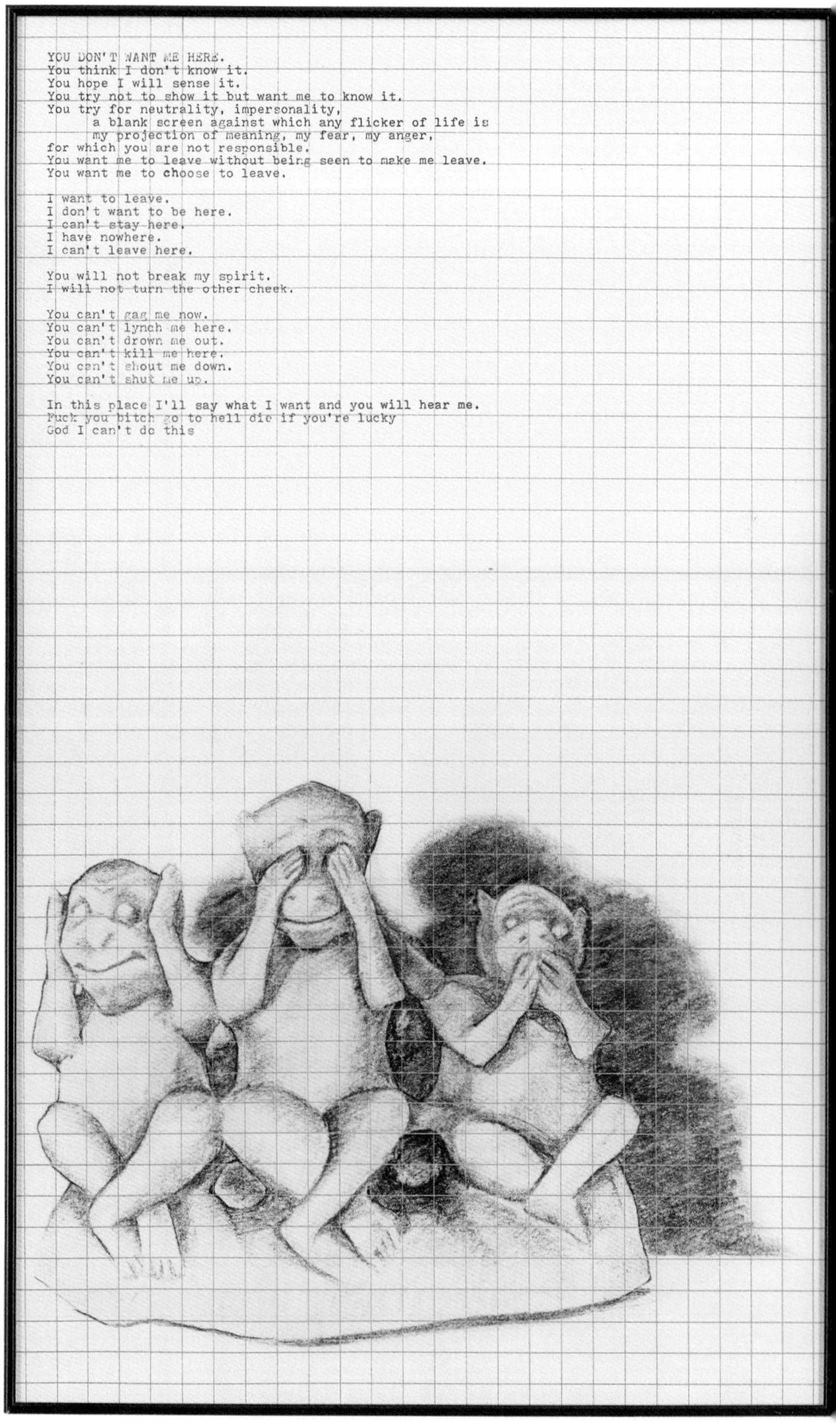

Decide Who You Are #15: You Don't Want Me Here. 1992
Screenprinted images and text on three sheets of paper, mounted on foam core
72 × 42 in. (182.8 × 106.7 cm); 61¾ × 36 in. (156.9 × 91.4 cm); and 72 × 42 in. (182.8 × 106.7 cm)
Collection Marilyn and Larry Fields

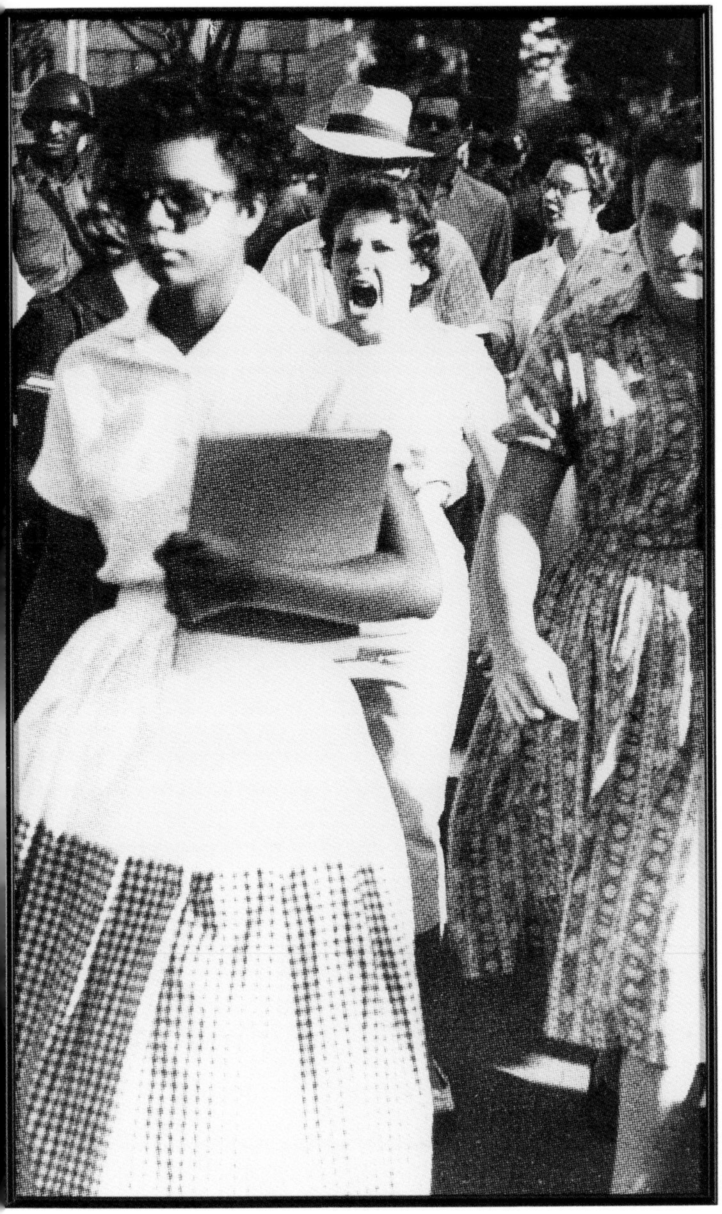

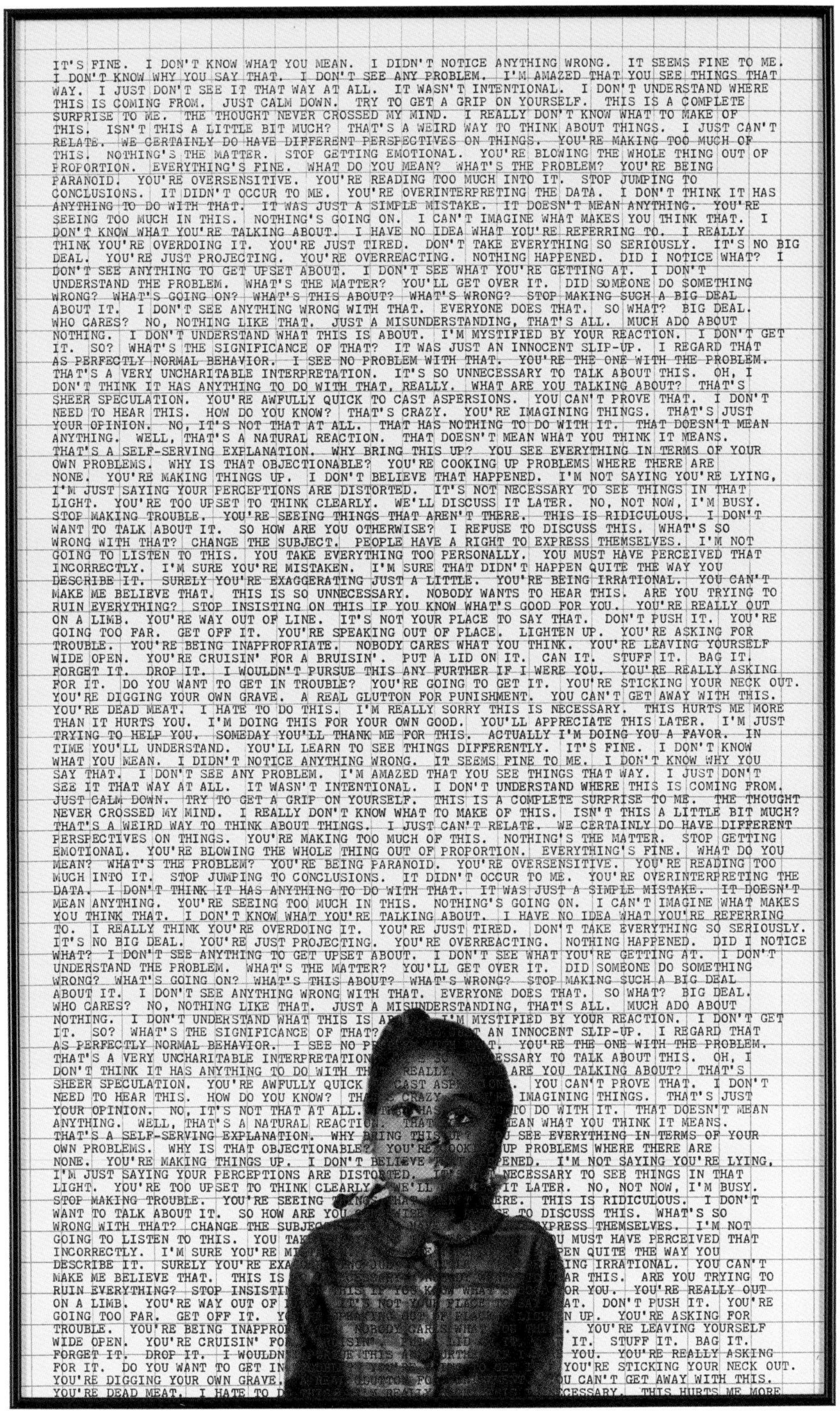
IT'S FINE. I DON'T KNOW WHAT YOU MEAN. I DIDN'T NOTICE ANYTHING WRONG. IT SEEMS FINE TO ME.
I DON'T KNOW WHY YOU SAY THAT. I DON'T SEE ANY PROBLEM. I'M AMAZED THAT YOU SEE THINGS THAT
WAY. I JUST DON'T SEE IT THAT WAY AT ALL. IT WASN'T INTENTIONAL. I DON'T UNDERSTAND WHERE
THIS IS COMING FROM. JUST CALM DOWN. TRY TO GET A GRIP ON YOURSELF. THIS IS A COMPLETE
SURPRISE TO ME. THE THOUGHT NEVER CROSSED MY MIND. I REALLY DON'T KNOW WHAT TO MAKE OF
THIS. ISN'T THIS A LITTLE BIT MUCH? THAT'S A WEIRD WAY TO THINK ABOUT THINGS. I JUST CAN'T
RELATE. WE CERTAINLY DO HAVE DIFFERENT PERSPECTIVES ON THINGS. YOU'RE MAKING TOO MUCH OF
THIS. NOTHING'S THE MATTER. STOP GETTING EMOTIONAL. YOU'RE BLOWING THE WHOLE THING OUT OF
PROPORTION. EVERYTHING'S FINE. WHAT DO YOU MEAN? WHAT'S THE PROBLEM? YOU'RE BEING
PARANOID. YOU'RE OVERSENSITIVE. YOU'RE READING TOO MUCH INTO IT. STOP JUMPING TO
CONCLUSIONS. IT DIDN'T OCCUR TO ME. YOU'RE OVERINTERPRETING THE DATA. I DON'T THINK IT HAS
ANYTHING TO DO WITH THAT. IT WAS JUST A SIMPLE MISTAKE. IT DOESN'T MEAN ANYTHING. YOU'RE
SEEING TOO MUCH IN THIS. NOTHING'S GOING ON. I CAN'T IMAGINE WHAT MAKES YOU THINK THAT. I
DON'T KNOW WHAT YOU'RE TALKING ABOUT. I HAVE NO IDEA WHAT YOU'RE REFERRING TO. I REALLY
THINK YOU'RE OVERDOING IT. YOU'RE JUST TIRED. DON'T TAKE EVERYTHING SO SERIOUSLY. IT'S NO BIG
DEAL. YOU'RE JUST PROJECTING. YOU'RE OVERREACTING. NOTHING HAPPENED. DID I NOTICE WHAT? I
DON'T SEE ANYTHING TO GET UPSET ABOUT. I DON'T SEE WHAT YOU'RE GETTING AT. I DON'T
UNDERSTAND THE PROBLEM. WHAT'S THE MATTER? YOU'LL GET OVER IT. DID SOMEONE DO SOMETHING
WRONG? WHAT'S GOING ON? WHAT'S THIS ABOUT? WHAT'S WRONG? STOP MAKING SUCH A BIG DEAL
ABOUT IT. I DON'T SEE ANYTHING WRONG WITH THAT. EVERYONE DOES THAT. SO WHAT? BIG DEAL.
WHO CARES? NO, NOTHING LIKE THAT. JUST A MISUNDERSTANDING, THAT'S ALL. MUCH ADO ABOUT
NOTHING. I DON'T UNDERSTAND WHAT THIS IS ABOUT. I'M MYSTIFIED BY YOUR REACTION. I DON'T GET
IT. SO? WHAT'S THE SIGNIFICANCE OF THAT? IT WAS JUST AN INNOCENT SLIP-UP. I REGARD THAT
AS PERFECTLY NORMAL BEHAVIOR. I SEE NO PROBLEM WITH THAT. YOU'RE THE ONE WITH THE PROBLEM.
THAT'S A VERY UNCHARITABLE INTERPRETATION. IT'S SO UNNECESSARY TO TALK ABOUT THIS. OH, I
DON'T THINK IT HAS ANYTHING TO DO WITH THAT, REALLY. WHAT ARE YOU TALKING ABOUT? THAT'S
SHEER SPECULATION. YOU'RE AWFULLY QUICK TO CAST ASPERSIONS. YOU CAN'T PROVE THAT. I DON'T
NEED TO HEAR THIS. HOW DO YOU KNOW? THAT'S CRAZY. YOU'RE IMAGINING THINGS. THAT'S JUST
YOUR OPINION. NO, IT'S NOT THAT AT ALL. THAT HAS NOTHING TO DO WITH IT. THAT DOESN'T MEAN
ANYTHING. WELL, THAT'S A NATURAL REACTION. THAT DOESN'T MEAN WHAT YOU THINK IT MEANS.
THAT'S A SELF-SERVING EXPLANATION. WHY BRING THIS UP? YOU SEE EVERYTHING IN TERMS OF YOUR
OWN PROBLEMS. WHY IS THAT OBJECTIONABLE? YOU'RE COOKING UP PROBLEMS WHERE THERE ARE
NONE. YOU'RE MAKING THINGS UP. I DON'T BELIEVE THAT HAPPENED. I'M NOT SAYING YOU'RE LYING,
I'M JUST SAYING YOUR PERCEPTIONS ARE DISTORTED. IT'S NOT NECESSARY TO SEE THINGS IN THAT
LIGHT. YOU'RE TOO UPSET TO THINK CLEARLY. WE'LL DISCUSS IT LATER. NO, NOT NOW, I'M BUSY.
STOP MAKING TROUBLE. YOU'RE SEEING THINGS THAT AREN'T THERE. THIS IS RIDICULOUS. I DON'T
WANT TO TALK ABOUT IT. SO HOW ARE YOU OTHERWISE? I REFUSE TO DISCUSS THIS. WHAT'S SO
WRONG WITH THAT? CHANGE THE SUBJECT. PEOPLE HAVE A RIGHT TO EXPRESS THEMSELVES. I'M NOT
GOING TO LISTEN TO THIS. YOU TAKE EVERYTHING TOO PERSONALLY. YOU MUST HAVE PERCEIVED THAT
INCORRECTLY. I'M SURE YOU'RE MISTAKEN. I'M SURE THAT DIDN'T HAPPEN QUITE THE WAY YOU
DESCRIBE IT. SURELY YOU'RE EXAGGERATING JUST A LITTLE. YOU'RE BEING IRRATIONAL. YOU CAN'T
MAKE ME BELIEVE THAT. THIS IS SO UNNECESSARY. NOBODY WANTS TO HEAR THIS. ARE YOU TRYING TO
RUIN EVERYTHING? STOP INSISTING ON THIS IF YOU KNOW WHAT'S GOOD FOR YOU. YOU'RE REALLY OUT
ON A LIMB. YOU'RE WAY OUT OF LINE. IT'S NOT YOUR PLACE TO SAY THAT. DON'T PUSH IT. YOU'RE
GOING TOO FAR. GET OFF IT. YOU'RE SPEAKING OUT OF PLACE. LIGHTEN UP. YOU'RE ASKING FOR
TROUBLE. YOU'RE BEING INAPPROPRIATE. NOBODY CARES WHAT YOU THINK. YOU'RE LEAVING YOURSELF
WIDE OPEN. YOU'RE CRUISIN' FOR A BRUISIN'. PUT A LID ON IT. CAN IT. STUFF IT. BAG IT.
FORGET IT. DROP IT. I WOULDN'T PURSUE THIS ANY FURTHER IF I WERE YOU. YOU'RE REALLY ASKING
FOR IT. DO YOU WANT TO GET IN TROUBLE? YOU'RE GOING TO GET IT. YOU'RE STICKING YOUR NECK OUT.
YOU'RE DIGGING YOUR OWN GRAVE. A REAL GLUTTON FOR PUNISHMENT. YOU CAN'T GET AWAY WITH THIS.
YOU'RE DEAD MEAT. I HATE TO DO THIS. I'M REALLY SORRY THIS IS NECESSARY. THIS HURTS ME MORE
THAN IT HURTS YOU. I'M DOING THIS FOR YOUR OWN GOOD. YOU'LL APPRECIATE THIS LATER. I'M JUST
TRYING TO HELP YOU. SOMEDAY YOU'LL THANK ME FOR THIS. ACTUALLY I'M DOING YOU A FAVOR. IN
TIME YOU'LL UNDERSTAND. YOU'LL LEARN TO SEE THINGS DIFFERENTLY. IT'S FINE. I DON'T KNOW
WHAT YOU MEAN. I DIDN'T NOTICE ANYTHING WRONG. IT SEEMS FINE TO ME. I DON'T KNOW WHY YOU
SAY THAT. I DON'T SEE ANY PROBLEM. I'M AMAZED THAT YOU SEE THINGS THAT WAY. I JUST DON'T
SEE IT THAT WAY AT ALL. IT WASN'T INTENTIONAL. I DON'T UNDERSTAND WHERE THIS IS COMING FROM.
JUST CALM DOWN. TRY TO GET A GRIP ON YOURSELF. THIS IS A COMPLETE SURPRISE TO ME. THE THOUGHT
NEVER CROSSED MY MIND. I REALLY DON'T KNOW WHAT TO MAKE OF THIS. ISN'T THIS A LITTLE BIT MUCH?
THAT'S A WEIRD WAY TO THINK ABOUT THINGS. I JUST CAN'T RELATE. WE CERTAINLY DO HAVE DIFFERENT
PERSPECTIVES ON THINGS. YOU'RE MAKING TOO MUCH OF THIS. NOTHING'S THE MATTER. STOP GETTING
EMOTIONAL. YOU'RE BLOWING THE WHOLE THING OUT OF PROPORTION. EVERYTHING'S FINE. WHAT DO YOU
MEAN? WHAT'S THE PROBLEM? YOU'RE BEING PARANOID. YOU'RE OVERSENSITIVE. YOU'RE READING TOO
MUCH INTO IT. STOP JUMPING TO CONCLUSIONS. IT DIDN'T OCCUR TO ME. YOU'RE OVERINTERPRETING THE
DATA. I DON'T THINK IT HAS ANYTHING TO DO WITH THAT. IT WAS JUST A SIMPLE MISTAKE. IT DOESN'T
MEAN ANYTHING. YOU'RE SEEING TOO MUCH IN THIS. NOTHING'S GOING ON. I CAN'T IMAGINE WHAT MAKES
YOU THINK THAT. I DON'T KNOW WHAT YOU'RE TALKING ABOUT. I HAVE NO IDEA WHAT YOU'RE REFERRING
TO. I REALLY THINK YOU'RE OVERDOING IT. YOU'RE JUST TIRED. DON'T TAKE EVERYTHING SO SERIOUSLY.
IT'S NO BIG DEAL. YOU'RE JUST PROJECTING. YOU'RE OVERREACTING. NOTHING HAPPENED. DID I NOTICE
WHAT? I DON'T SEE ANYTHING TO GET UPSET ABOUT. I DON'T SEE WHAT YOU'RE GETTING AT. I DON'T
UNDERSTAND THE PROBLEM. WHAT'S THE MATTER? YOU'LL GET OVER IT. DID SOMEONE DO SOMETHING
WRONG? WHAT'S GOING ON? WHAT'S THIS ABOUT? WHAT'S WRONG? STOP MAKING SUCH A BIG DEAL
ABOUT IT. I DON'T SEE ANYTHING WRONG WITH THAT. EVERYONE DOES THAT. SO WHAT? BIG DEAL.
WHO CARES? NO, NOTHING LIKE THAT. JUST A MISUNDERSTANDING, THAT'S ALL. MUCH ADO ABOUT
NOTHING. I DON'T UNDERSTAND WHAT THIS IS A … I'M MYSTIFIED BY YOUR REACTION. I DON'T GET
IT. SO? WHAT'S THE SIGNIFICANCE OF THAT? … AN INNOCENT SLIP-UP. I REGARD THAT
AS PERFECTLY NORMAL BEHAVIOR. I SEE NO P … YOU'RE THE ONE WITH THE PROBLEM.
THAT'S A VERY UNCHARITABLE INTERPRETATION … ESSARY TO TALK ABOUT THIS. OH, I
DON'T THINK IT HAS ANYTHING TO DO WITH TH … ARE YOU TALKING ABOUT? THAT'S
SHEER SPECULATION. YOU'RE AWFULLY QUICK … YOU CAN'T PROVE THAT. I DON'T
NEED TO HEAR THIS. HOW DO YOU KNOW? THA … IMAGINING THINGS. THAT'S JUST
YOUR OPINION. NO, IT'S NOT THAT AT ALL. … TO DO WITH IT. THAT DOESN'T MEAN
ANYTHING. WELL, THAT'S A NATURAL REACTI … EAN WHAT YOU THINK IT MEANS.
THAT'S A SELF-SERVING EXPLANATION. WHY … SEE EVERYTHING IN TERMS OF YOUR
OWN PROBLEMS. WHY IS THAT OBJECTIONABLE? … UP PROBLEMS WHERE THERE ARE
NONE. YOU'RE MAKING THINGS UP. I DON'T … PENED. I'M NOT SAYING YOU'RE LYING,
I'M JUST SAYING YOUR PERCEPTIONS ARE DISTO … NECESSARY TO SEE THINGS IN THAT
LIGHT. YOU'RE TOO UPSET TO THINK CLEARLY … IT LATER. NO, NOT NOW, I'M BUSY.
STOP MAKING TROUBLE. YOU'RE SEEING … ERE. THIS IS RIDICULOUS. I DON'T
WANT TO TALK ABOUT IT. SO HOW ARE YOU … TO DISCUSS THIS. WHAT'S SO
WRONG WITH THAT? CHANGE THE SUBJE … XPRESS THEMSELVES. I'M NOT
GOING TO LISTEN TO THIS. YOU TA … U MUST HAVE PERCEIVED THAT
INCORRECTLY. I'M SURE YOU'RE MI … PEN QUITE THE WAY YOU
DESCRIBE IT. SURELY YOU'RE EXA … ING IRRATIONAL. YOU CAN'T
MAKE ME BELIEVE THAT. THIS IS … AR THIS. ARE YOU TRYING TO
RUIN EVERYTHING? STOP INSISTI … OR YOU. YOU'RE REALLY OUT
ON A LIMB. YOU'RE WAY OUT OF … AT. DON'T PUSH IT. YOU'RE
GOING TOO FAR. GET OFF IT. Y … N UP. YOU'RE ASKING FOR
TROUBLE. YOU'RE BEING INAPPRO … YOU'RE LEAVING YOURSELF
WIDE OPEN. YOU'RE CRUISIN' FO … IT. STUFF IT. BAG IT.
FORGET IT. DROP IT. I WOULDN … YOU. YOU'RE REALLY ASKING
FOR IT. DO YOU WANT TO GET IN … YOU'RE STICKING YOUR NECK OUT.
YOU'RE DIGGING YOUR OWN GRAVE. … U CAN'T GET AWAY WITH THIS.
YOU'RE DEAD MEAT. I HATE TO D … CESSARY. THIS HURTS ME MORE

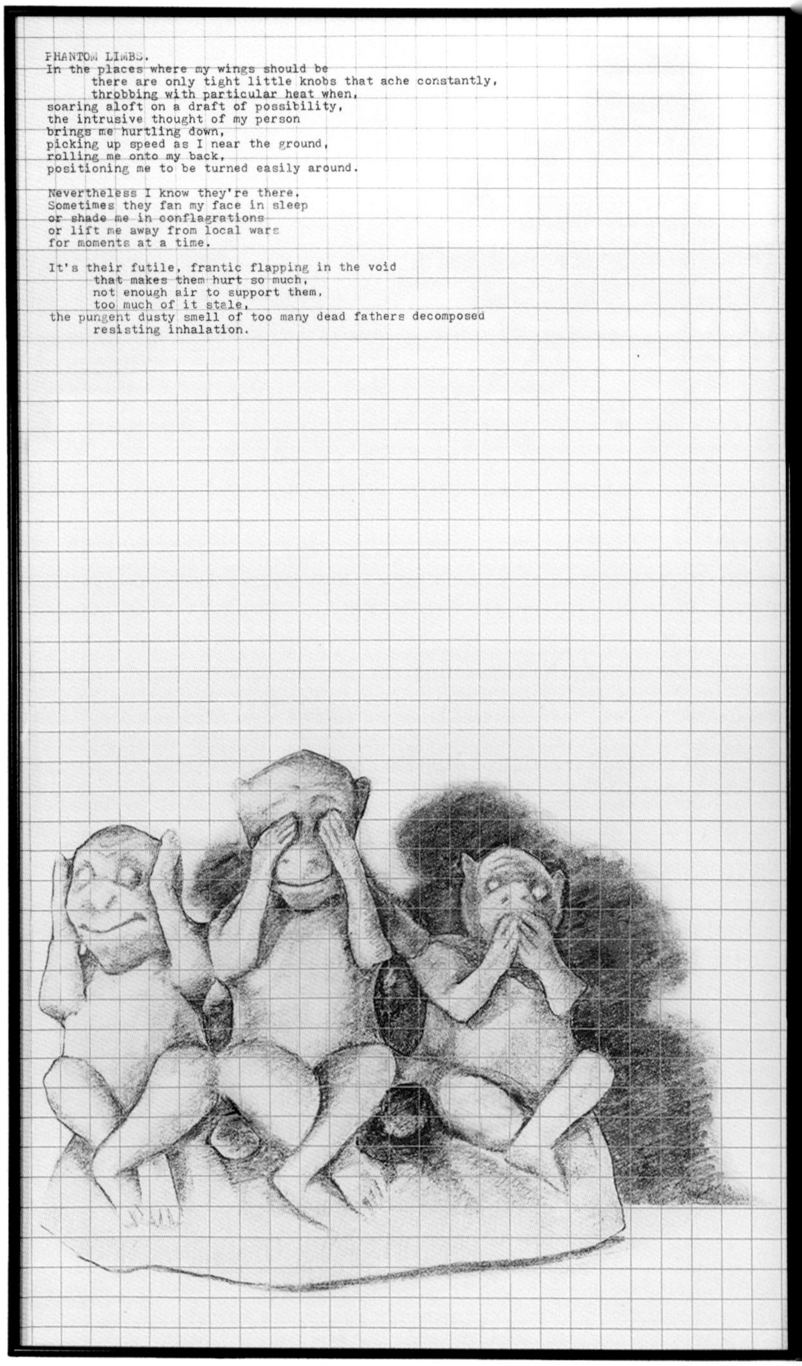

Decide Who You Are #21: Phantom Limbs. 1992
Screenprinted images and text on four sheets of paper, mounted on foam core
72 × 42 in. (182.8 × 106.7 cm); 24 × 43 in. (61 × 109.2 cm); 15 × 13 in. (38.1 × 33 cm); and 72 × 42 in. (182.8 × 106.7 cm)
Collection Adrian Piper Research Archive Foundation Berlin

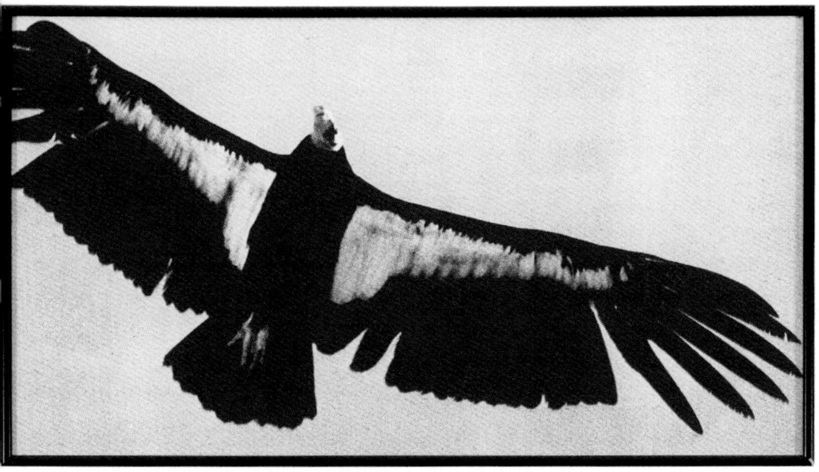

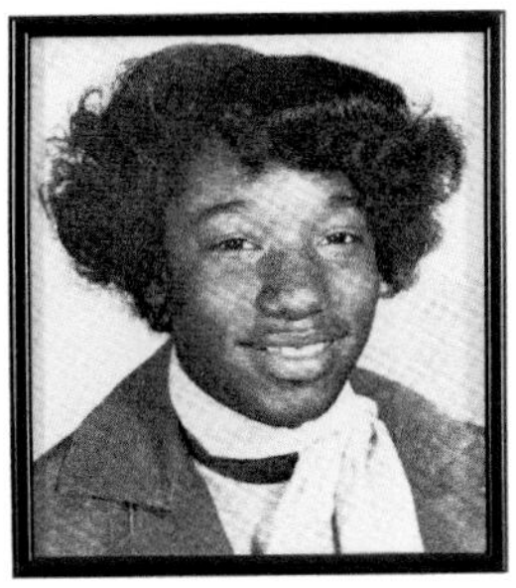

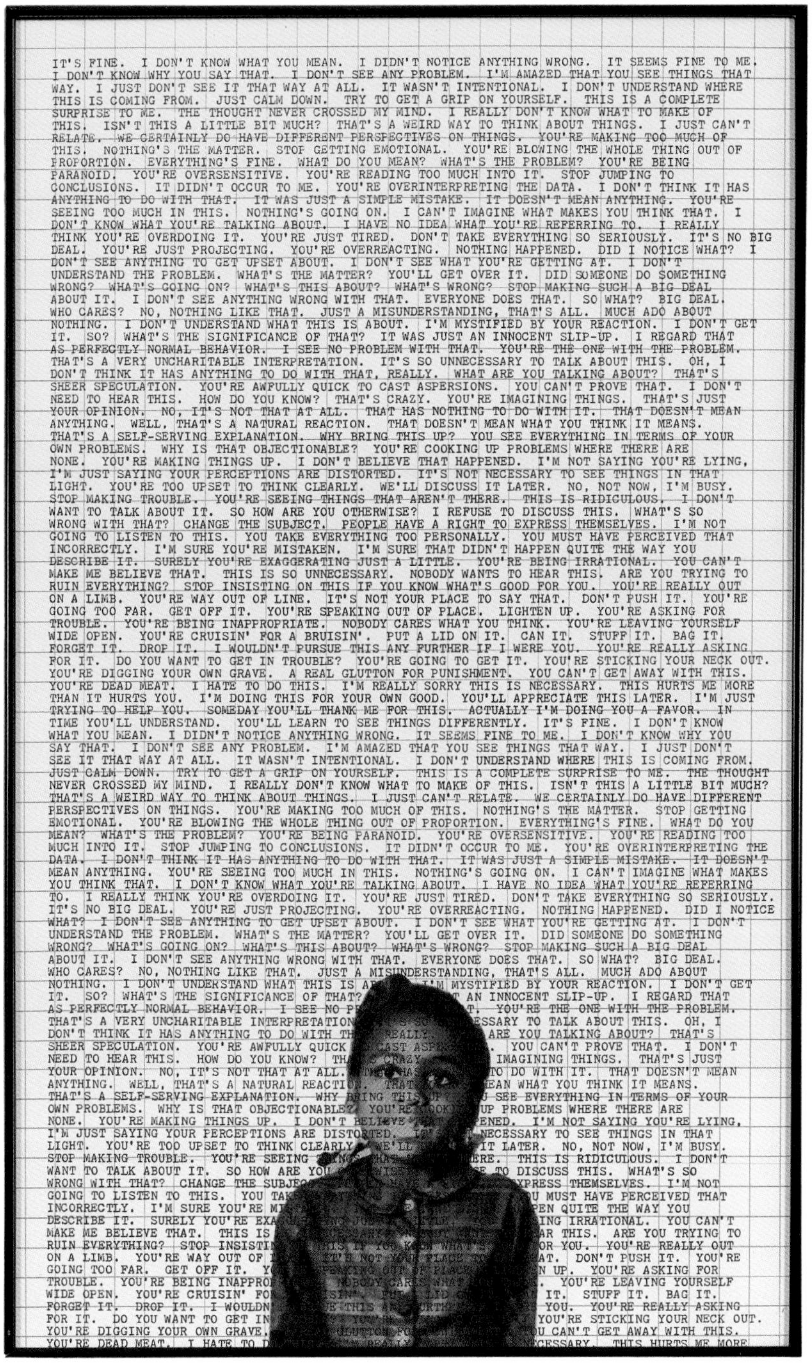

IT'S FINE. I DON'T KNOW WHAT YOU MEAN. I DIDN'T NOTICE ANYTHING WRONG. IT SEEMS FINE TO ME.
I DON'T KNOW WHY YOU SAY THAT. I DON'T SEE ANY PROBLEM. I'M AMAZED THAT YOU SEE THINGS THAT
WAY. I JUST DON'T SEE IT THAT WAY AT ALL. IT WASN'T INTENTIONAL. I DON'T UNDERSTAND WHERE
THIS IS COMING FROM. JUST CALM DOWN. TRY TO GET A GRIP ON YOURSELF. THIS IS A COMPLETE
SURPRISE TO ME. THE THOUGHT NEVER CROSSED MY MIND. I REALLY DON'T KNOW WHAT TO MAKE OF
THIS. ISN'T THIS A LITTLE BIT MUCH? THAT'S A WEIRD WAY TO THINK ABOUT THINGS. I JUST CAN'T
RELATE. WE CERTAINLY DO HAVE DIFFERENT PERSPECTIVES ON THINGS. YOU'RE MAKING TOO MUCH OF
THIS. NOTHING'S THE MATTER. STOP GETTING EMOTIONAL. YOU'RE BLOWING THE WHOLE THING OUT OF
PROPORTION. EVERYTHING'S FINE. WHAT DO YOU MEAN? WHAT'S THE PROBLEM? YOU'RE BEING
PARANOID. YOU'RE OVERSENSITIVE. YOU'RE READING TOO MUCH INTO IT. STOP JUMPING TO
CONCLUSIONS. IT DIDN'T OCCUR TO ME. YOU'RE OVERINTERPRETING THE DATA. I DON'T THINK IT HAS
ANYTHING TO DO WITH THAT. IT WAS JUST A SIMPLE MISTAKE. IT DOESN'T MEAN ANYTHING. YOU'RE
SEEING TOO MUCH IN THIS. NOTHING'S GOING ON. I CAN'T IMAGINE WHAT MAKES YOU THINK THAT. I
DON'T KNOW WHAT YOU'RE TALKING ABOUT. I HAVE NO IDEA WHAT YOU'RE REFERRING TO. I REALLY
THINK YOU'RE OVERDOING IT. YOU'RE JUST TIRED. DON'T TAKE EVERYTHING SO SERIOUSLY. IT'S NO BIG
DEAL. YOU'RE JUST PROJECTING. YOU'RE OVERREACTING. NOTHING HAPPENED. DID I NOTICE WHAT? I
DON'T SEE ANYTHING TO GET UPSET ABOUT. I DON'T SEE WHAT YOU'RE GETTING AT. I DON'T
UNDERSTAND THE PROBLEM. WHAT'S THE MATTER? YOU'LL GET OVER IT. DID SOMEONE DO SOMETHING
WRONG? WHAT'S GOING ON? WHAT'S THIS ABOUT? WHAT'S WRONG? STOP MAKING SUCH A BIG DEAL
ABOUT IT. I DON'T SEE ANYTHING WRONG WITH THAT. EVERYONE DOES THAT. SO WHAT? BIG DEAL.
WHO CARES? NO, NOTHING LIKE THAT. JUST A MISUNDERSTANDING, THAT'S ALL. MUCH ADO ABOUT
NOTHING. I DON'T UNDERSTAND WHAT THIS IS ABOUT. I'M MYSTIFIED BY YOUR REACTION. I DON'T GET
IT. SO? WHAT'S THE SIGNIFICANCE OF THAT? IT WAS JUST AN INNOCENT SLIP-UP. I REGARD THAT
AS PERFECTLY NORMAL BEHAVIOR. I SEE NO PROBLEM WITH THAT. YOU'RE THE ONE WITH THE PROBLEM.
THAT'S A VERY UNCHARITABLE INTERPRETATION. IT'S SO UNNECESSARY TO TALK ABOUT THIS. OH, I
DON'T THINK IT HAS ANYTHING TO DO WITH THAT, REALLY. WHAT ARE YOU TALKING ABOUT? THAT'S
SHEER SPECULATION. YOU'RE AWFULLY QUICK TO CAST ASPERSIONS. YOU CAN'T PROVE THAT. I DON'T
NEED TO HEAR THIS. HOW DO YOU KNOW? THAT'S CRAZY. YOU'RE IMAGINING THINGS. THAT'S JUST
YOUR OPINION. NO, IT'S NOT THAT AT ALL. THAT HAS NOTHING TO DO WITH IT. THAT DOESN'T MEAN
ANYTHING. WELL, THAT'S A NATURAL REACTION. THAT DOESN'T MEAN WHAT YOU THINK IT MEANS.
THAT'S A SELF-SERVING EXPLANATION. WHY BRING THIS UP? YOU SEE EVERYTHING IN TERMS OF YOUR
OWN PROBLEMS. WHY IS THAT OBJECTIONABLE? YOU'RE COOKING UP PROBLEMS WHERE THERE ARE
NONE. YOU'RE MAKING THINGS UP. I DON'T BELIEVE THAT HAPPENED. I'M NOT SAYING YOU'RE LYING,
I'M JUST SAYING YOUR PERCEPTIONS ARE DISTORTED. IT'S NOT NECESSARY TO SEE THINGS IN THAT
LIGHT. YOU'RE TOO UPSET TO THINK CLEARLY. WE'LL DISCUSS IT LATER. NO, NOT NOW, I'M BUSY.
STOP MAKING TROUBLE. YOU'RE SEEING THINGS THAT AREN'T THERE. THIS IS RIDICULOUS. I DON'T
WANT TO TALK ABOUT IT. SO HOW ARE YOU OTHERWISE? I REFUSE TO DISCUSS THIS. WHAT'S SO
WRONG WITH THAT? CHANGE THE SUBJECT. PEOPLE HAVE A RIGHT TO EXPRESS THEMSELVES. I'M NOT
GOING TO LISTEN TO THIS. YOU TAKE EVERYTHING TOO PERSONALLY. YOU MUST HAVE PERCEIVED THAT
INCORRECTLY. I'M SURE YOU'RE MISTAKEN. I'M SURE THAT DIDN'T HAPPEN QUITE THE WAY YOU
DESCRIBE IT. SURELY YOU'RE EXAGGERATING JUST A LITTLE. YOU'RE BEING IRRATIONAL. YOU CAN'T
MAKE ME BELIEVE THAT. THIS IS SO UNNECESSARY. NOBODY WANTS TO HEAR THIS. ARE YOU TRYING TO
RUIN EVERYTHING? STOP INSISTING ON THIS IF YOU KNOW WHAT'S GOOD FOR YOU. YOU'RE REALLY OUT
ON A LIMB. YOU'RE WAY OUT OF LINE. IT'S NOT YOUR PLACE TO SAY THAT. DON'T PUSH IT. YOU'RE
GOING TOO FAR. GET OFF IT. YOU'RE SPEAKING OUT OF PLACE. LIGHTEN UP. YOU'RE ASKING FOR
TROUBLE. YOU'RE BEING INAPPROPRIATE. NOBODY CARES WHAT YOU THINK. YOU'RE LEAVING YOURSELF
WIDE OPEN. YOU'RE CRUISIN' FOR A BRUISIN'. PUT A LID ON IT. CAN IT. STUFF IT. BAG IT.
FORGET IT. DROP IT. I WOULDN'T PURSUE THIS ANY FURTHER IF I WERE YOU. YOU'RE REALLY ASKING
FOR IT. DO YOU WANT TO GET IN TROUBLE? YOU'RE GOING TO GET IT. YOU'RE STICKING YOUR NECK OUT.
YOU'RE DIGGING YOUR OWN GRAVE. A REAL GLUTTON FOR PUNISHMENT. YOU CAN'T GET AWAY WITH THIS.
YOU'RE DEAD MEAT. I HATE TO DO THIS. I'M REALLY SORRY THIS IS NECESSARY. THIS HURTS ME MORE
THAN IT HURTS YOU. I'M DOING THIS FOR YOUR OWN GOOD. YOU'LL APPRECIATE THIS LATER. I'M JUST
TRYING TO HELP YOU. SOMEDAY YOU'LL THANK ME FOR THIS. ACTUALLY I'M DOING YOU A FAVOR. IN
TIME YOU'LL UNDERSTAND. YOU'LL LEARN TO SEE THINGS DIFFERENTLY. IT'S FINE. I DON'T KNOW
WHAT YOU MEAN. I DIDN'T NOTICE ANYTHING WRONG. IT SEEMS FINE TO ME. I DON'T KNOW WHY YOU
SAY THAT. I DON'T SEE ANY PROBLEM. I'M AMAZED THAT YOU SEE THINGS THAT WAY. I JUST DON'T
SEE IT THAT WAY AT ALL. IT WASN'T INTENTIONAL. I DON'T UNDERSTAND WHERE THIS IS COMING FROM.
JUST CALM DOWN. TRY TO GET A GRIP ON YOURSELF. THIS IS A COMPLETE SURPRISE TO ME. THE THOUGHT
NEVER CROSSED MY MIND. I REALLY DON'T KNOW WHAT TO MAKE OF THIS. ISN'T THIS A LITTLE BIT MUCH?
THAT'S A WEIRD WAY TO THINK ABOUT THINGS. I JUST CAN'T RELATE. WE CERTAINLY DO HAVE DIFFERENT
PERSPECTIVES ON THINGS. YOU'RE MAKING TOO MUCH OF THIS. NOTHING'S THE MATTER. STOP GETTING
EMOTIONAL. YOU'RE BLOWING THE WHOLE THING OUT OF PROPORTION. EVERYTHING'S FINE. WHAT DO YOU
MEAN? WHAT'S THE PROBLEM? YOU'RE BEING PARANOID. YOU'RE OVERSENSITIVE. YOU'RE READING TOO
MUCH INTO IT. STOP JUMPING TO CONCLUSIONS. IT DIDN'T OCCUR TO ME. YOU'RE OVERINTERPRETING THE
DATA. I DON'T THINK IT HAS ANYTHING TO DO WITH THAT. IT WAS JUST A SIMPLE MISTAKE. IT DOESN'T
MEAN ANYTHING. YOU'RE SEEING TOO MUCH IN THIS. NOTHING'S GOING ON. I CAN'T IMAGINE WHAT MAKES
YOU THINK THAT. I DON'T KNOW WHAT YOU'RE TALKING ABOUT. I HAVE NO IDEA WHAT YOU'RE REFERRING
TO. I REALLY THINK YOU'RE OVERDOING IT. YOU'RE JUST TIRED. DON'T TAKE EVERYTHING SO SERIOUSLY.
IT'S NO BIG DEAL. YOU'RE JUST PROJECTING. YOU'RE OVERREACTING. NOTHING HAPPENED. DID I NOTICE
WHAT? I DON'T SEE ANYTHING TO GET UPSET ABOUT. I DON'T SEE WHAT YOU'RE GETTING AT. I DON'T
UNDERSTAND THE PROBLEM. WHAT'S THE MATTER? YOU'LL GET OVER IT. DID SOMEONE DO SOMETHING
WRONG? WHAT'S GOING ON? WHAT'S THIS ABOUT? WHAT'S WRONG? STOP MAKING SUCH A BIG DEAL
ABOUT IT. I DON'T SEE ANYTHING WRONG WITH THAT. EVERYONE DOES THAT. SO WHAT? BIG DEAL.
WHO CARES? NO, NOTHING LIKE THAT. JUST A MISUNDERSTANDING, THAT'S ALL. MUCH ADO ABOUT
NOTHING. I DON'T UNDERSTAND WHAT THIS IS A
I'M MYSTIFIED BY YOUR REACTION. I DON'T GET
IT. SO? WHAT'S THE SIGNIFICANCE OF THAT?
AN INNOCENT SLIP-UP. I REGARD THAT
AS PERFECTLY NORMAL BEHAVIOR. I SEE NO P
YOU'RE THE ONE WITH THE PROBLEM.
THAT'S A VERY UNCHARITABLE INTERPRETATION
ESSARY TO TALK ABOUT THIS. OH, I
DON'T THINK IT HAS ANYTHING TO DO WITH TH
ARE YOU TALKING ABOUT? THAT'S
SHEER SPECULATION. YOU'RE AWFULLY QUICK
YOU CAN'T PROVE THAT. I DON'T
NEED TO HEAR THIS. HOW DO YOU KNOW?
IMAGINING THINGS. THAT'S JUST
YOUR OPINION. NO, IT'S NOT THAT AT ALL.
TO DO WITH IT. THAT DOESN'T MEAN
ANYTHING. WELL, THAT'S A NATURAL REACTI
EAN WHAT YOU THINK IT MEANS.
THAT'S A SELF-SERVING EXPLANATION. WHY
U SEE EVERYTHING IN TERMS OF YOUR
OWN PROBLEMS. WHY IS THAT OBJECTIONABLE?
UP PROBLEMS WHERE THERE ARE
NONE. YOU'RE MAKING THINGS UP. I DON'T
ENED. I'M NOT SAYING YOU'RE LYING,
I'M JUST SAYING YOUR PERCEPTIONS ARE DISTO
NECESSARY TO SEE THINGS IN THAT
LIGHT. YOU'RE TOO UPSET TO THINK CLEARLY
IT LATER. NO, NOT NOW, I'M BUSY.
STOP MAKING TROUBLE. YOU'RE SEEING
ERE. THIS IS RIDICULOUS. I DON'T
WANT TO TALK ABOUT IT. SO HOW ARE YO
TO DISCUSS THIS. WHAT'S SO
WRONG WITH THAT? CHANGE THE SUBJE
XPRESS THEMSELVES. I'M NOT
GOING TO LISTEN TO THIS. YOU TA
U MUST HAVE PERCEIVED THAT
INCORRECTLY. I'M SURE YOU'RE MI
PEN QUITE THE WAY YOU
DESCRIBE IT. SURELY YOU'RE EXA
ING IRRATIONAL. YOU CAN'T
MAKE ME BELIEVE THAT. THIS IS
AR THIS. ARE YOU TRYING TO
RUIN EVERYTHING? STOP INSISTI
OR YOU. YOU'RE REALLY OUT
ON A LIMB. YOU'RE WAY OUT OF
AT. DON'T PUSH IT. YOU'RE
GOING TOO FAR. GET OFF IT.
N UP. YOU'RE ASKING FOR
TROUBLE. YOU'RE BEING INAPPRO
YOU'RE LEAVING YOURSELF
WIDE OPEN. YOU'RE CRUISIN' FO
IT. STUFF IT. BAG IT.
FORGET IT. DROP IT. I WOULDN
YOU. YOU'RE REALLY ASKING
FOR IT. DO YOU WANT TO GET IN
YOU'RE STICKING YOUR NECK OUT.
YOU'RE DIGGING YOUR OWN GRAVE.
U CAN'T GET AWAY WITH THIS.

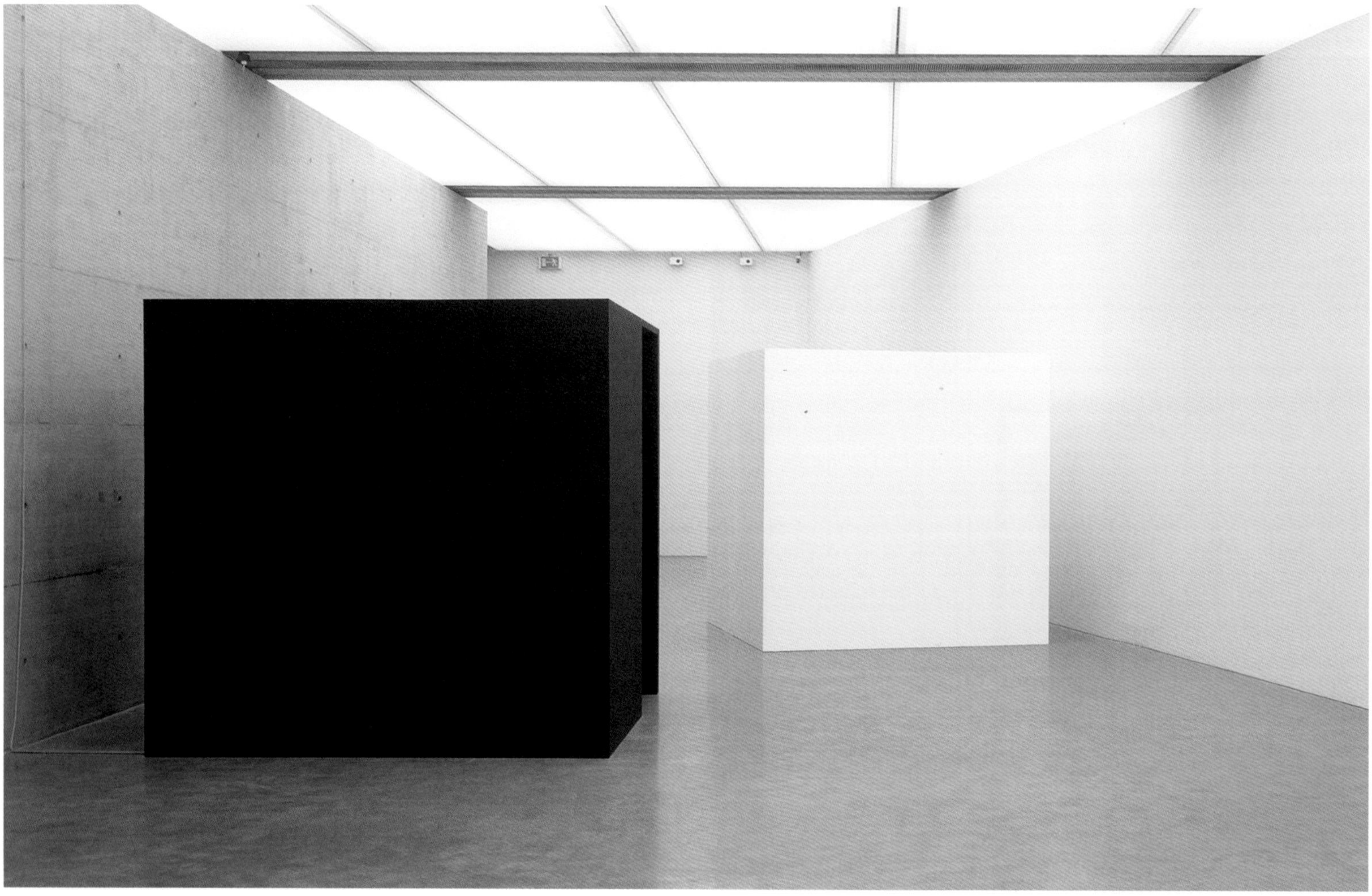

Black Box/White Box. 1992
Video installation. Video (color, sound), 00:30:00, with two constructed wood environments, monitor, four photographs, light box, audio, chairs, tables, tissue boxes, and trash baskets
Dimensions variable
Installation view in *Adrian Piper: seit 1965*, Generali Foundation, Vienna, May 17–August 18, 2002
Generali Foundation Collection—Permanent Loan to the Museum der Moderne Salzburg

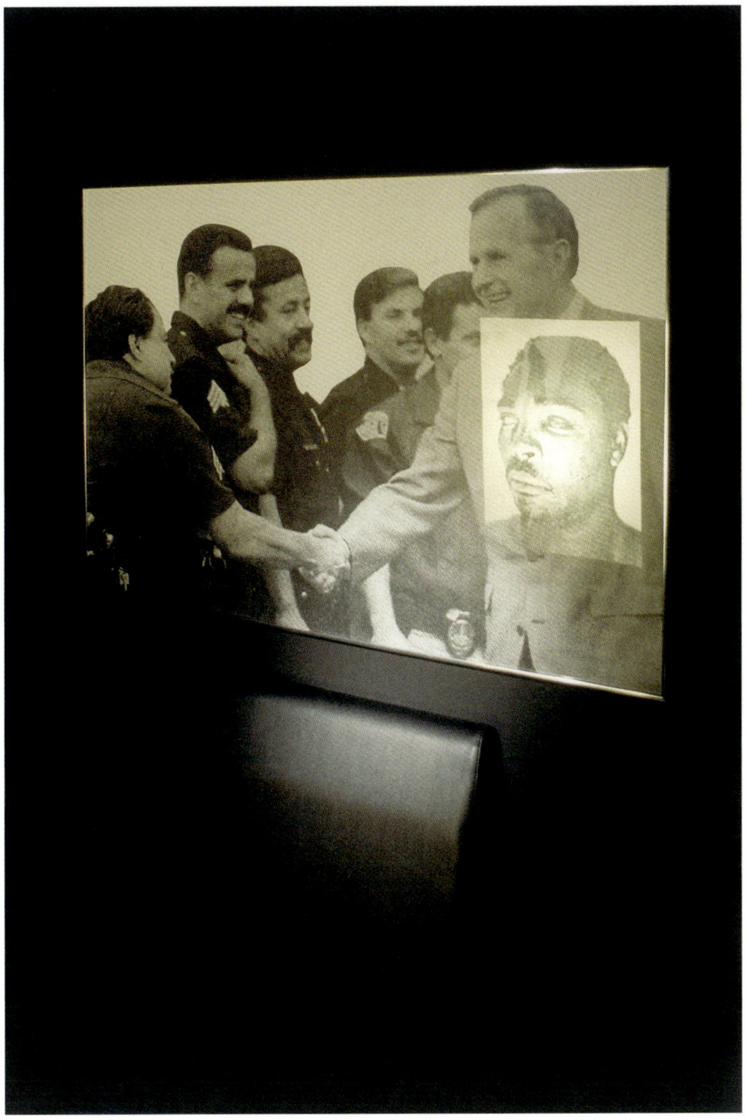

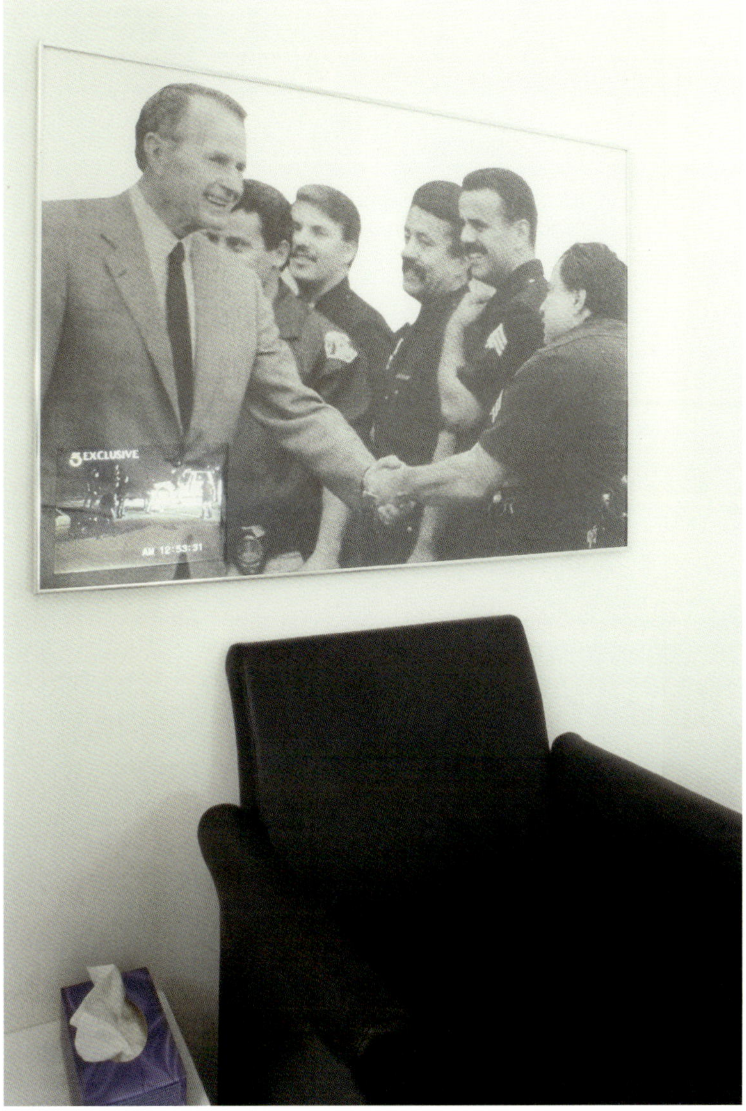

Details: black box and white box interiors

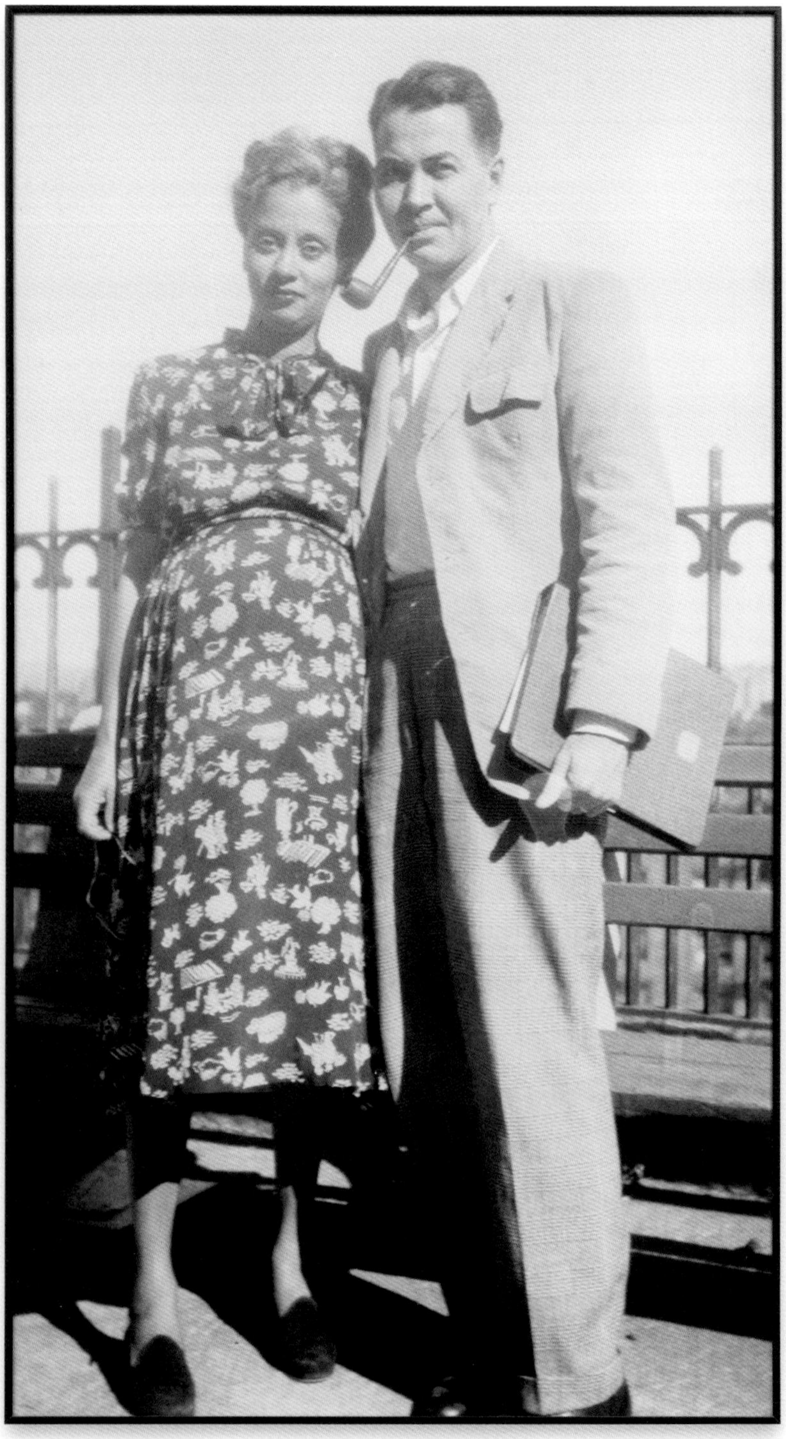

Ashes to Ashes

Theirs was a marriage of passion rather than convenience. He was her first date, and first and only husband. They both started smoking in their teens. "Everyone did it," they said later. "It was about being young and independent, and daring." They threw parties, went dancing, were invited out, and accepted tributes to their beauty from their friends. She stopped smoking in her fifties, after watching her boss, a debonair three-packs-a-day man, die horribly from brain cancer. But still she became more and more tired and breathless, more and more quickly. Finally she was diagnosed with emphysema. Her doctor warned him that he had to stop smoking too, or the smoke would kill her. He tried to stop. He couldn't. It hurt his pride. He said he could if he wanted to, but he didn't want to. And besides, he said, it wasn't the smoke that was damaging her lungs, it was the smog from the city. Whenever he lit a cigarette, she would leave the room. He smoked almost constantly, so she learned to live in distant rooms. She thought he loved his cigarettes more than he cared about her. He kept trying to stop. He tried candy, cinnamon sticks, toothpicks, cold turkey. Nothing worked. He couldn't control it. He felt ashamed. He grew withdrawn. She felt unloved, neglected, alone. She grew resigned. Then he had a stroke and fell down in the street. He was scared enough by that to stop for four months. After he started up again, he never again would discuss his smoking and never again tried to stop. But she had seen that he couldn't stop; that he'd tried and tried, but couldn't stop, just couldn't, not to save her life, not to save their marriage, not even to save himself. And so she forgave him. By that time she was so short of breath that she could no longer walk up the hill to the supermarket to buy groceries. So she let him do that, and post the mail, and run her errands. He was grateful that she let him do it and she was glad he wanted to do it. Once again he was her hero. They were happy. When the cancer first began to stipple his face and throat he refused to notice it. Only after their daughter began to carry out her threat to hound him and nag him and dog his footsteps until he agreed to see a doctor did he finally relent. The cancer quickly ate away his pharynx, throat and mouth. He got smaller and thinner and sadder and quieter as the huge, raging growths on his neck got bigger and redder. After he died she said, "You cannot imagine how it feels to watch someone you have physically loved waste away in pain to nothing." Her grief was inconsolable. Because her breath was so short - she said it felt as though she'd taken a very deep breath in but couldn't exhale - there was very little she could do. But because she refused to give up, everything had to be arranged: one friend to bring her mail upstairs from the mailbox, another to take it down; the newspaper to be delivered, not to the impossibly distant front door downstairs, but to her apartment; a reliable neighbor's son to deliver her groceries; a friend to bring her snacks; another to run her errands and feed the cat; a cleaning lady to keep the dust and grime at bay; her daughter to manage the bills, and, later, her wellbeing. After awhile there was too much to arrange and she was too exhausted to do any of it, or withstand the incursions of those who were trained to help. She wanted to go, prayed for it to be over. Near the very end, when she had no breath left even to move or speak, she would look at his picture lovingly, and smile with anticipation.

© Adrian Piper 1995

Ashes to Ashes. 1995
Enlarged black-and-white photograph, two enlarged color photographs, and text
48 × 30 in. (121.9 × 76.2 cm); 48 × 24 in. (121.9 × 61 cm); 18 × 30 in. (45.7 × 76.2 cm); and 24 × 30 in. (61 × 76.2 cm)
Collection Adrian Piper Research Archive Foundation Berlin

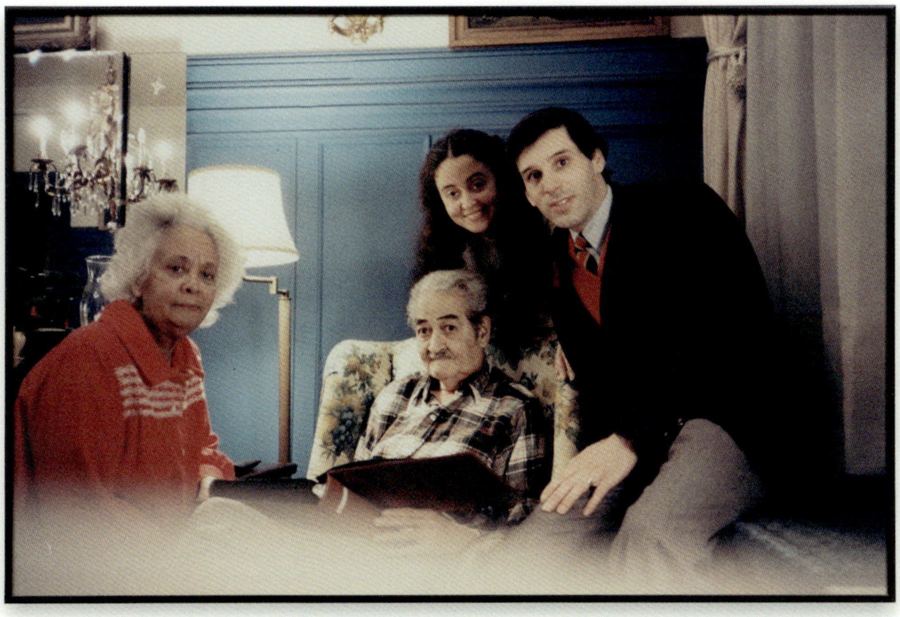

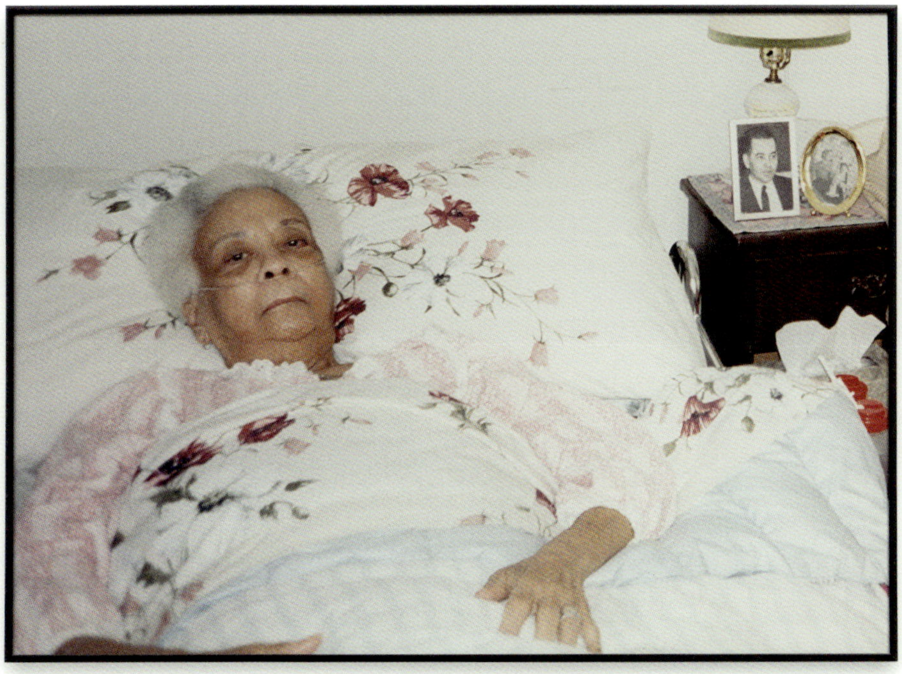

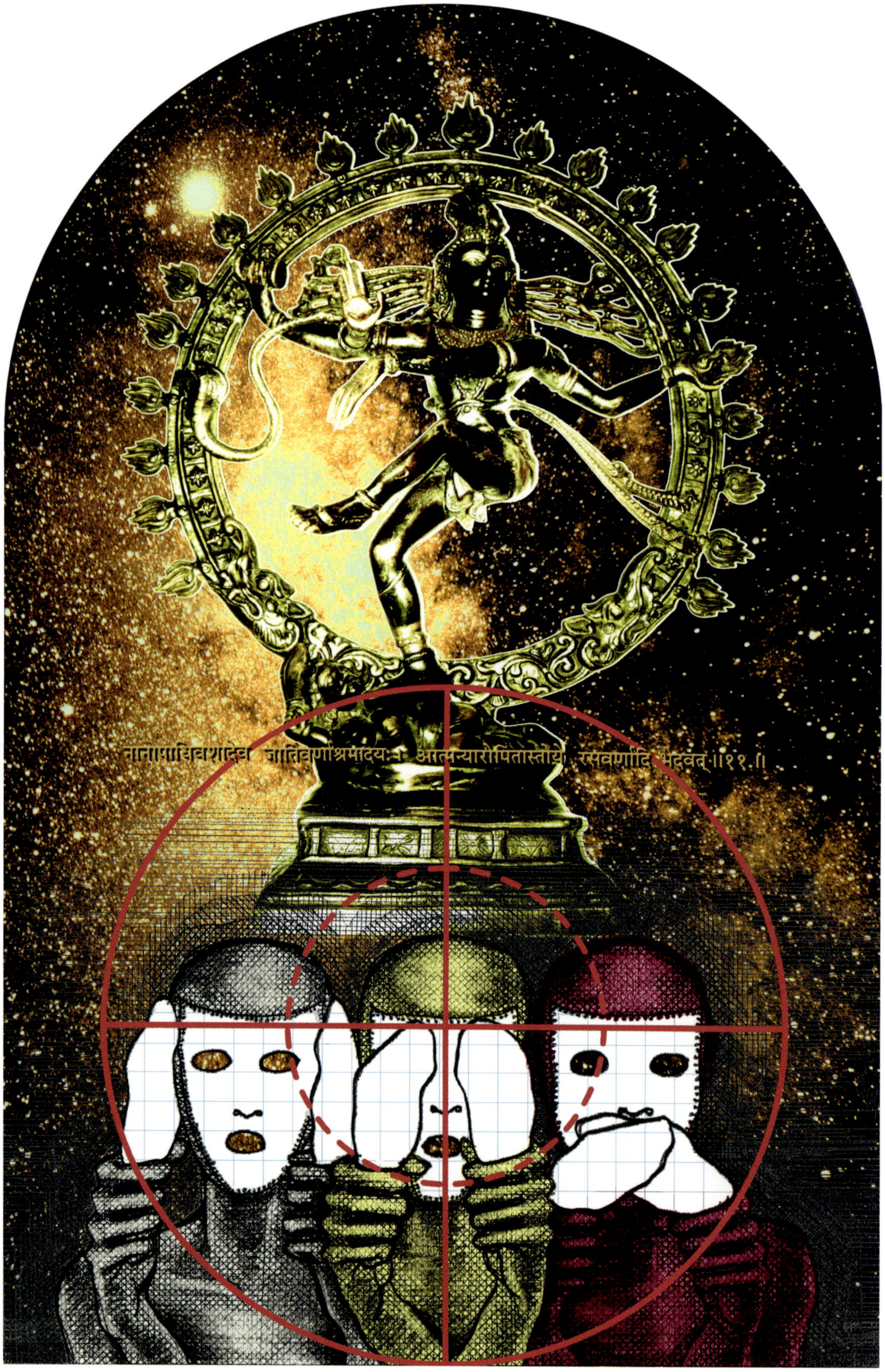

The Color Wheel Series. 2000
Digital file for print reproduction
Dimensions variable
Collection Adrian Piper Research Archive Foundation Berlin
Detail: *The Color Wheel Series, First Adhyasa: Annomayakosha #33*

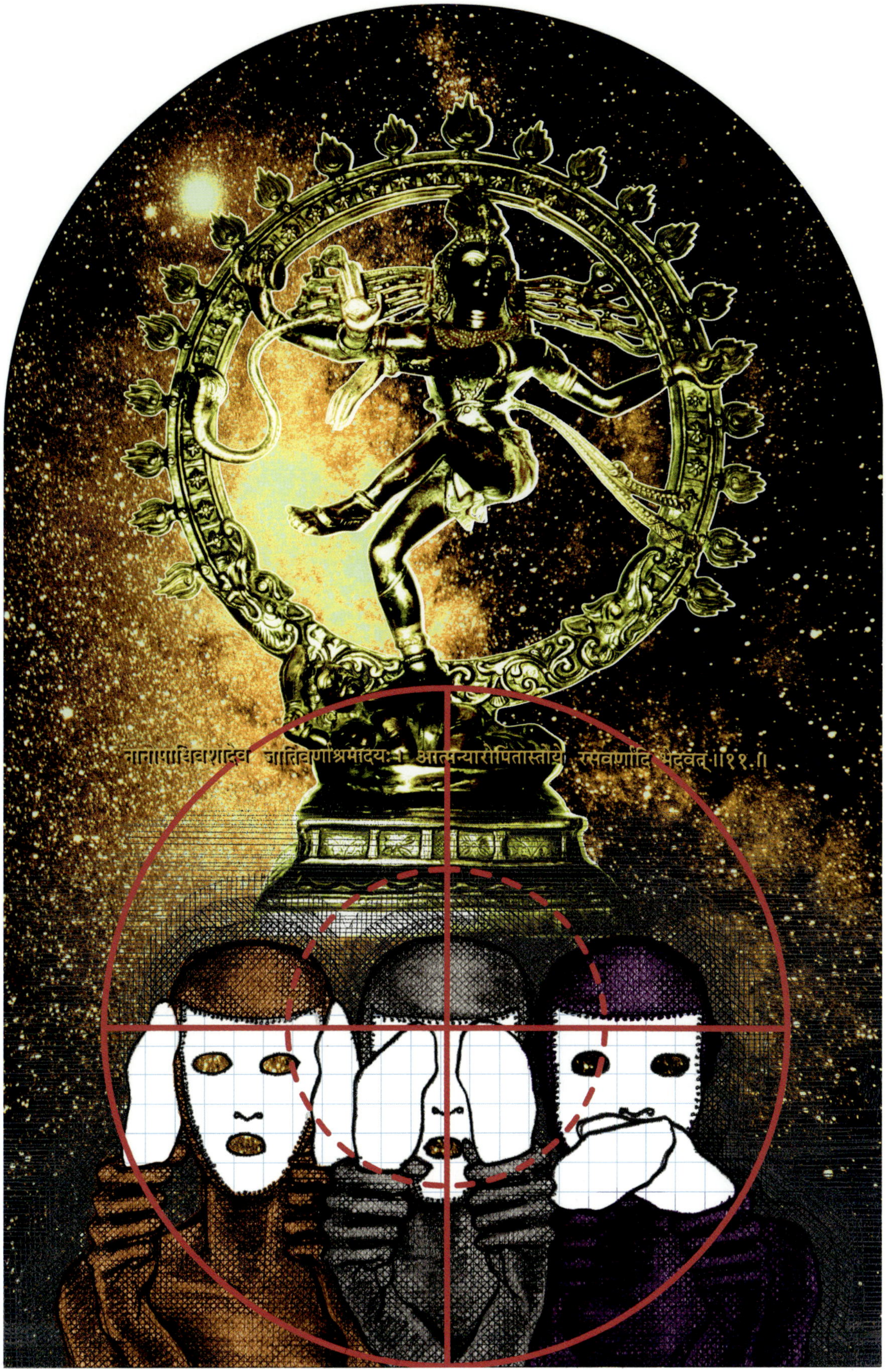

Detail: *The Color Wheel Series, First Adhyasa: Annomayakosha #29*

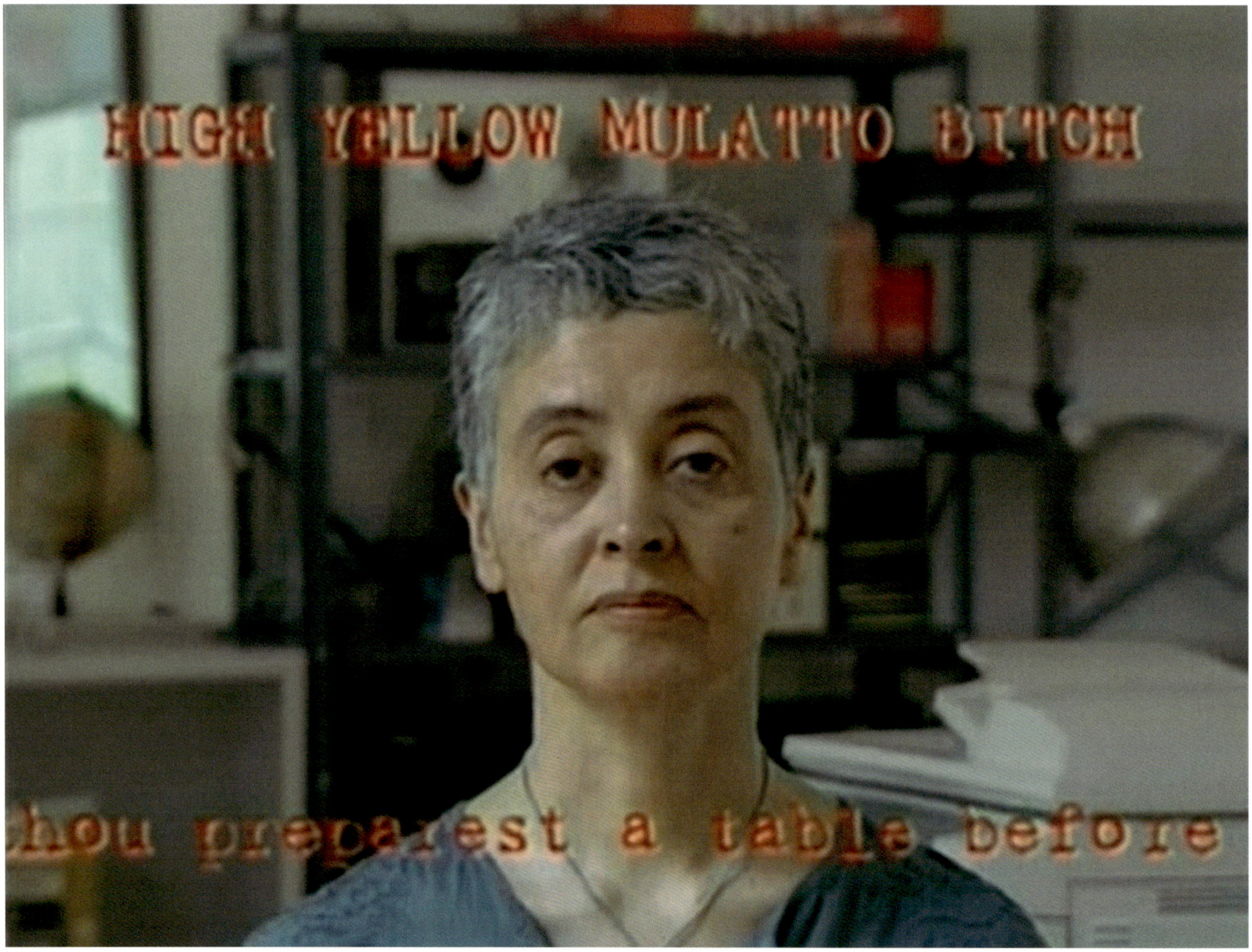

You/Stop/Watch: A Shiva Japan. 2002
Documentation of the performance. Video (color, sound), 00:42:26
Collection Adrian Piper Research Archive Foundation Berlin
Detail: video still at 00:29:04

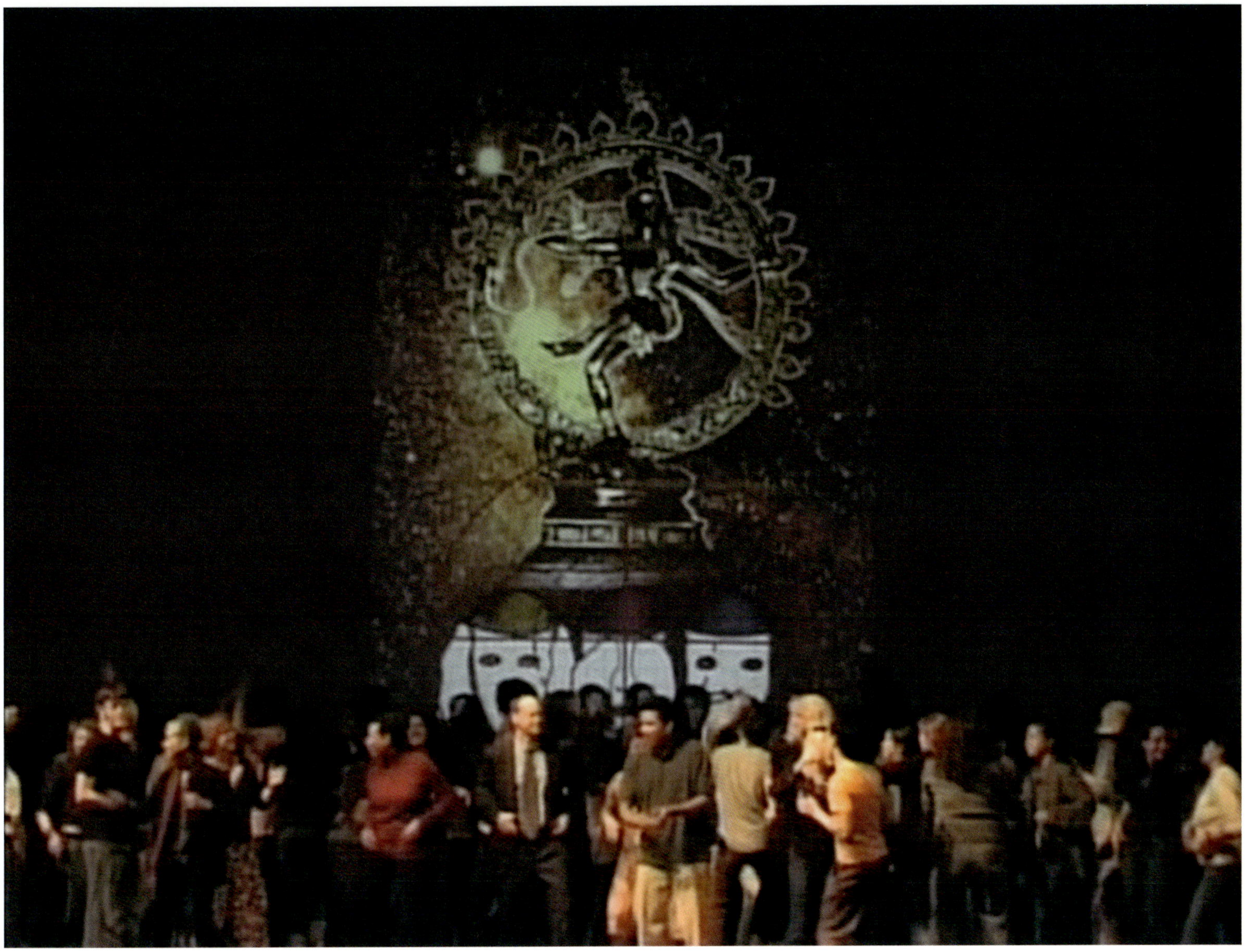

Shiva Dances with the Art Institute of Chicago. 2004
Documentation of the participatory performance-lecture. Video (color, sound), 01:43:18
Collection Adrian Piper Research Archive Foundation Berlin
Detail: video still at 00:51:54

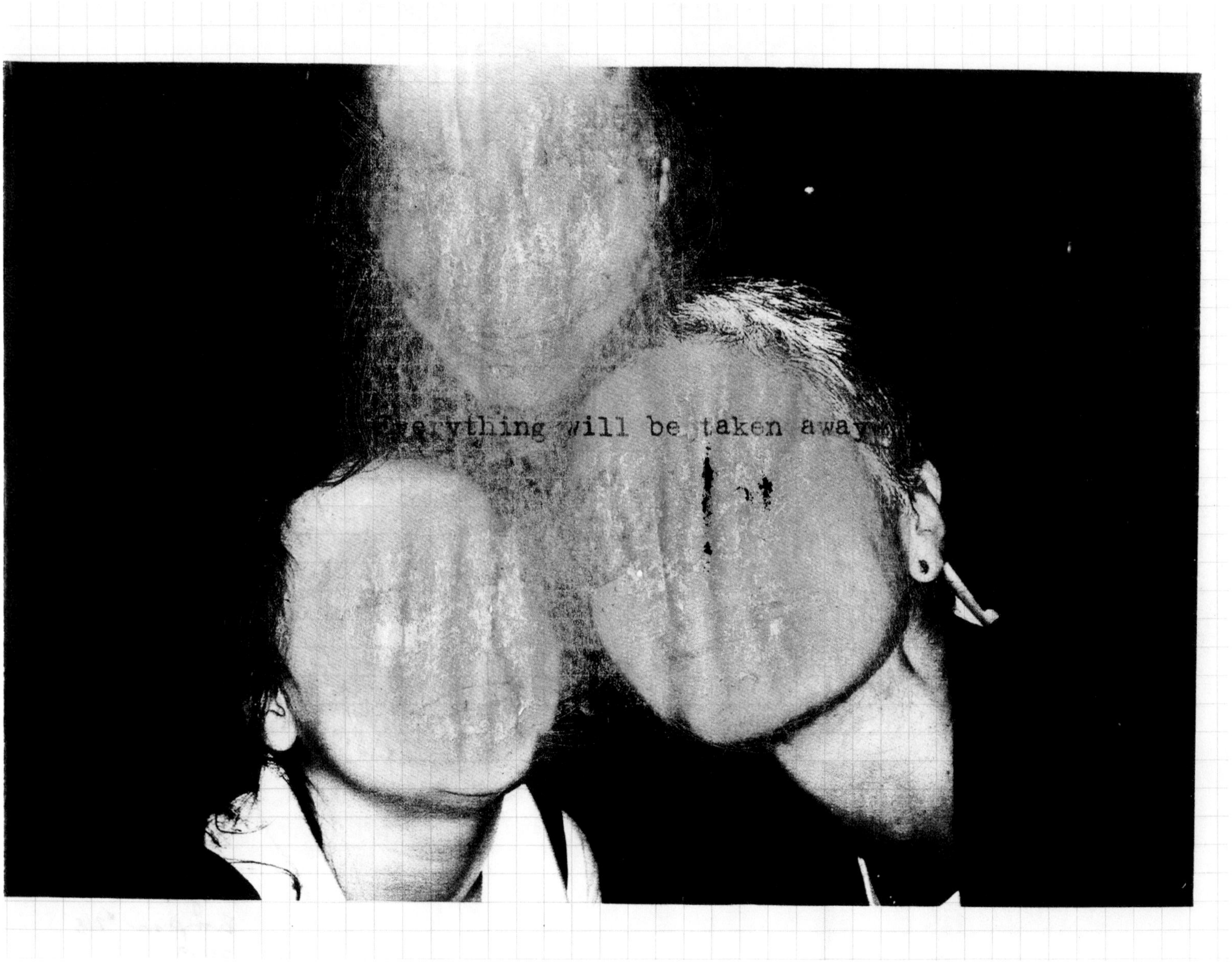

Everything #2.3. 2003
Photograph photocopied on graph paper and sanded with sandpaper, with printed text
8½ × 11 in. (21.6 × 27.9 cm)
Private collection

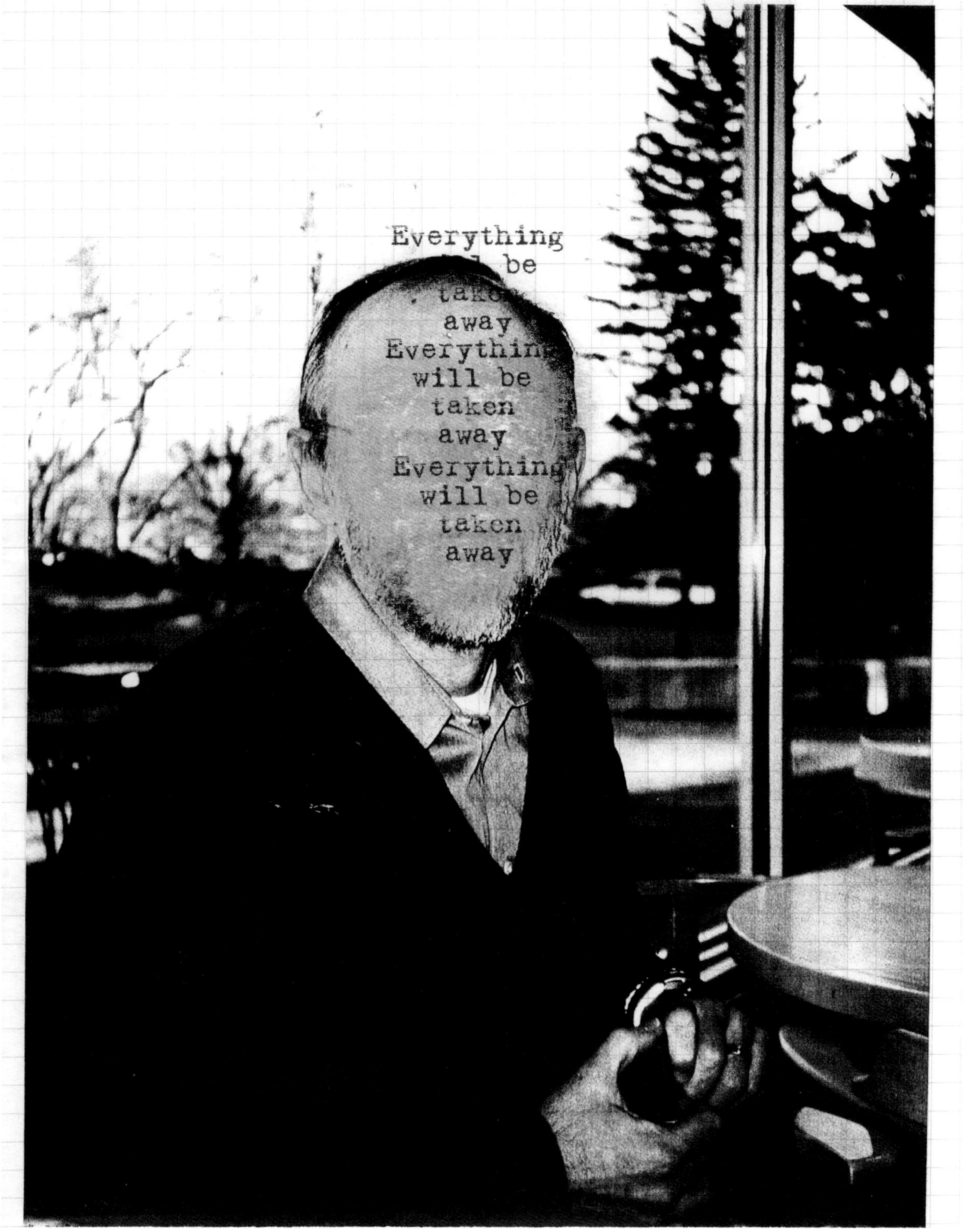

Everything #2.5. 2003
Photograph photocopied on graph paper and sanded with sandpaper, with printed text
11 × 8½ in. (27.9 × 21.6 cm)
Private collection

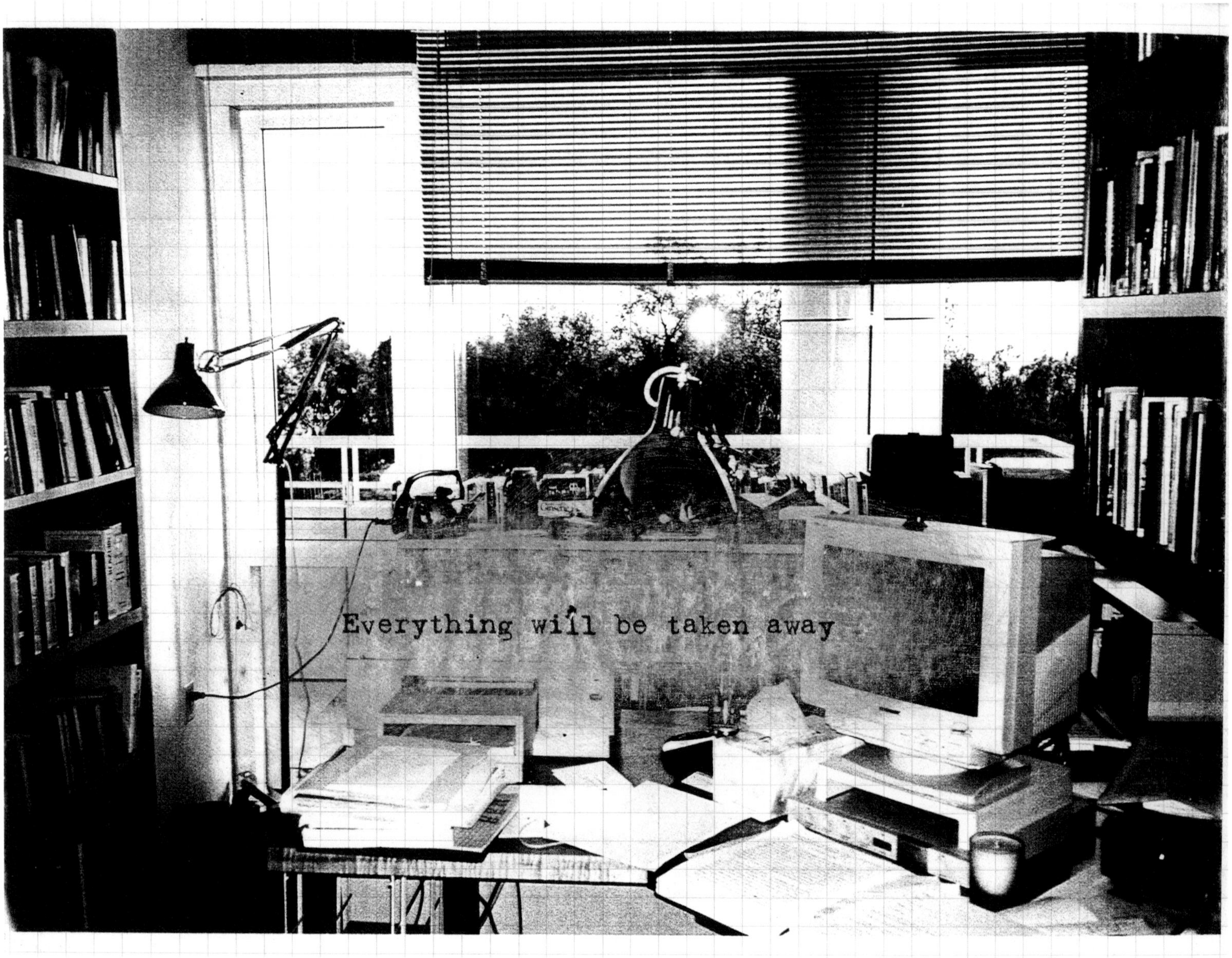

Everything #2.7. 2003
Photograph photocopied on graph paper and sanded with sandpaper, with printed text
8½ × 11 in. (21.6 × 27.9 cm)
Private collection

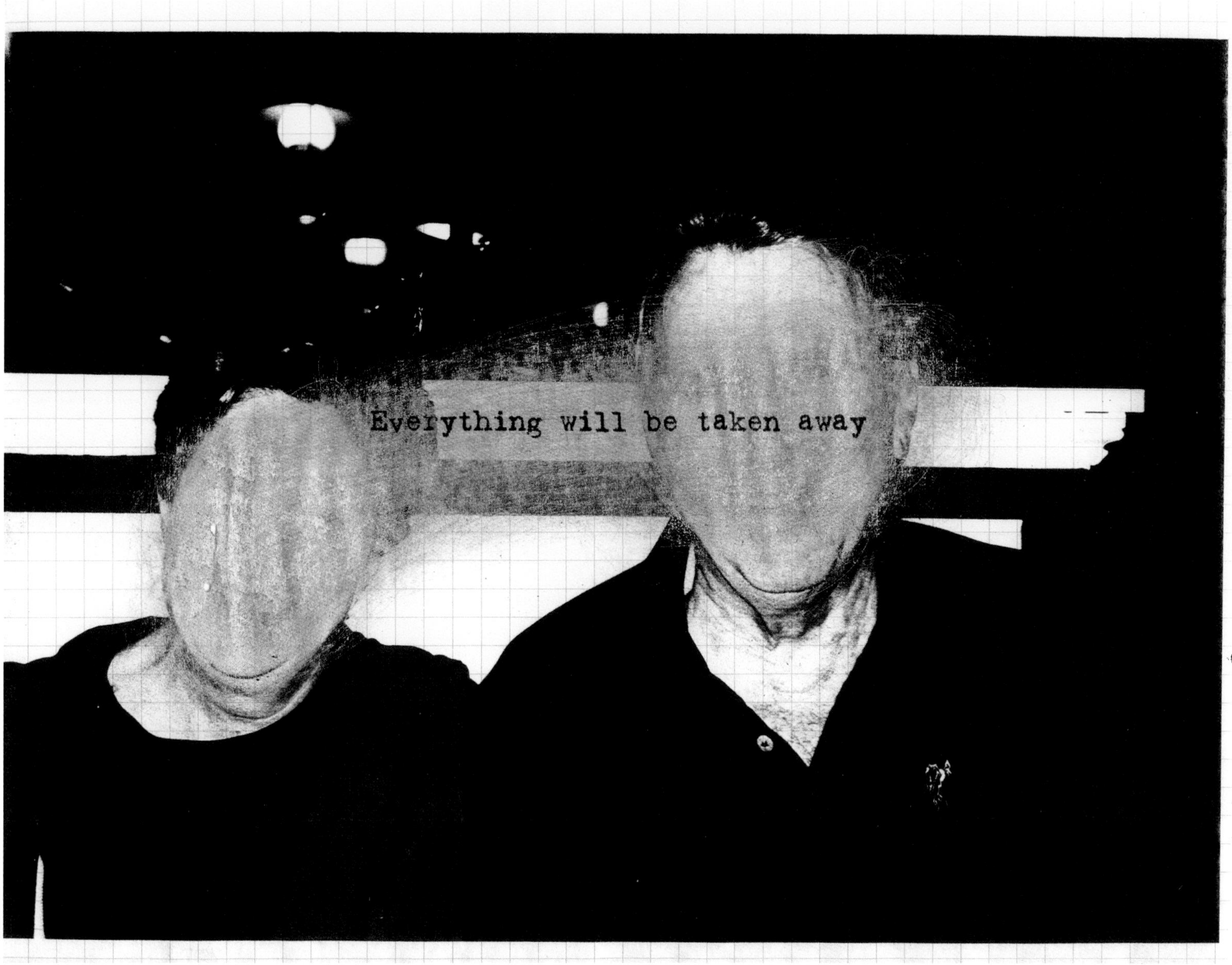

Everything #2.8. 2003
Photograph photocopied on graph paper and sanded with sandpaper, with printed text
8½ × 11 in. (21.6 × 27.9 cm)
Private collection

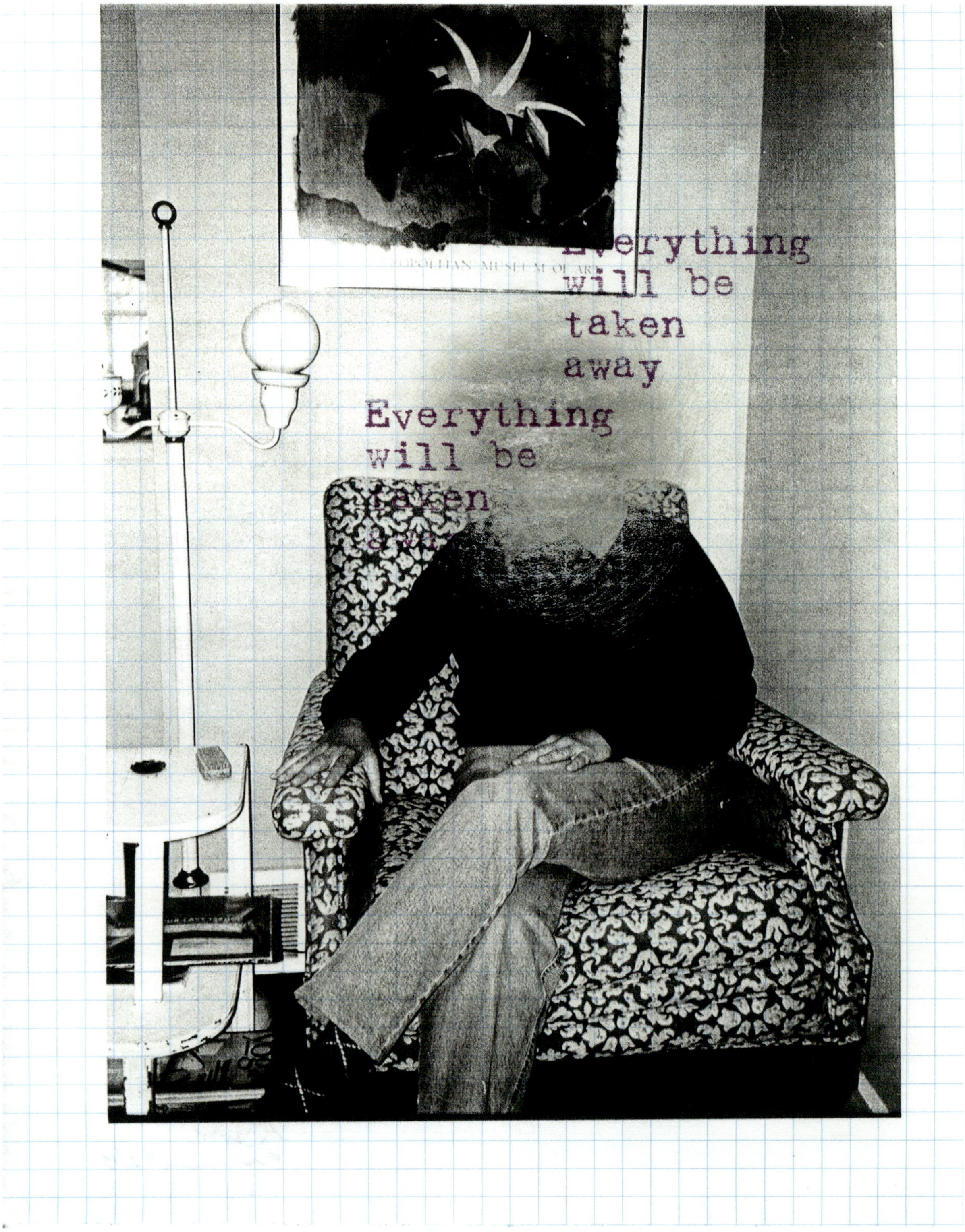

Everything #2.9. 2003
Photograph photocopied on graph paper and sanded with sandpaper, with printed text
11 × 8½ in. (27.9 × 21.6 cm)
Private collection. Courtesy Flow Advisory

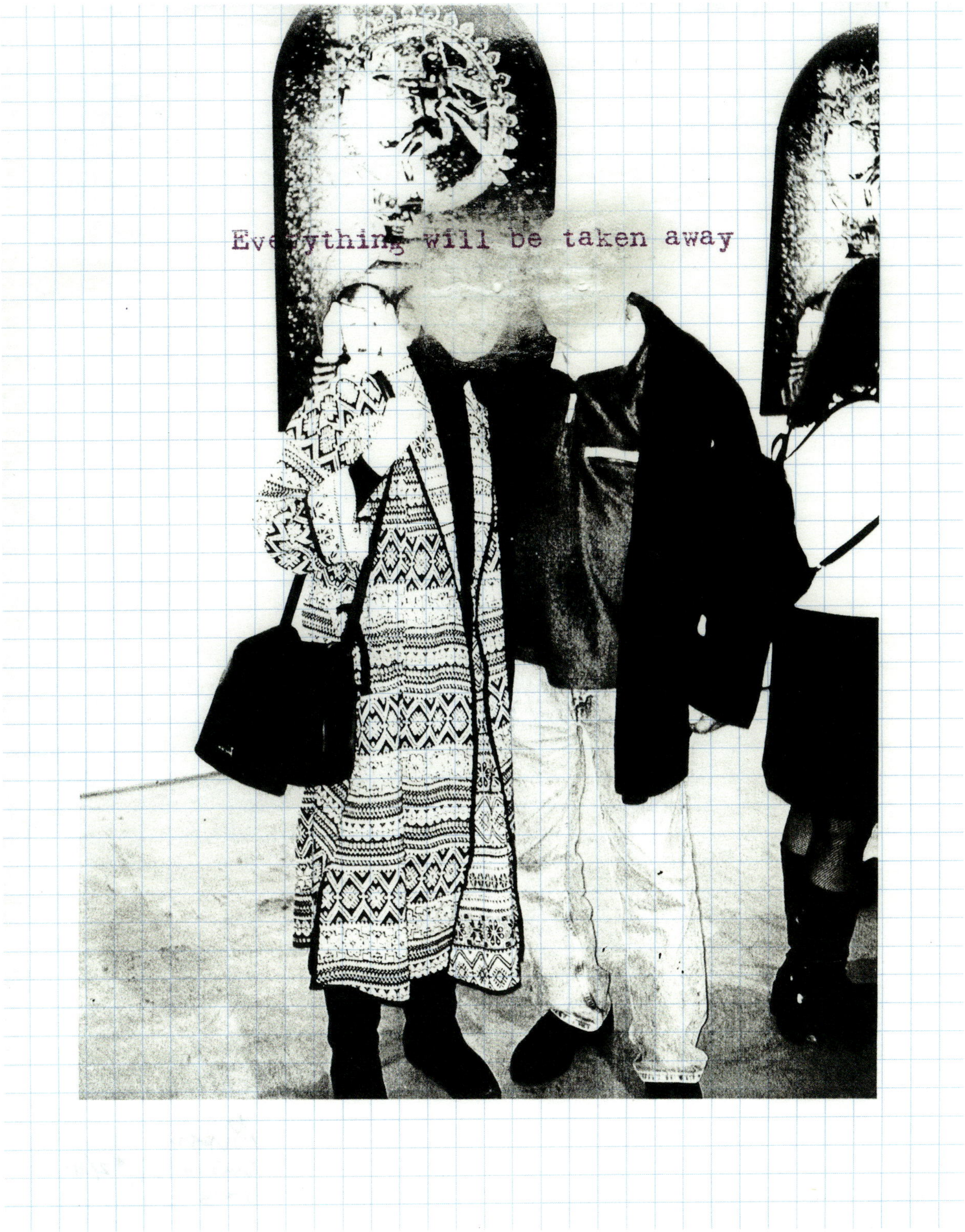

Everything #2.10. 2003
Photograph photocopied on graph paper and sanded with sandpaper, with printed text
11 × 8½ in. (27.9 × 21.6 cm)
Rothier Faria Collection

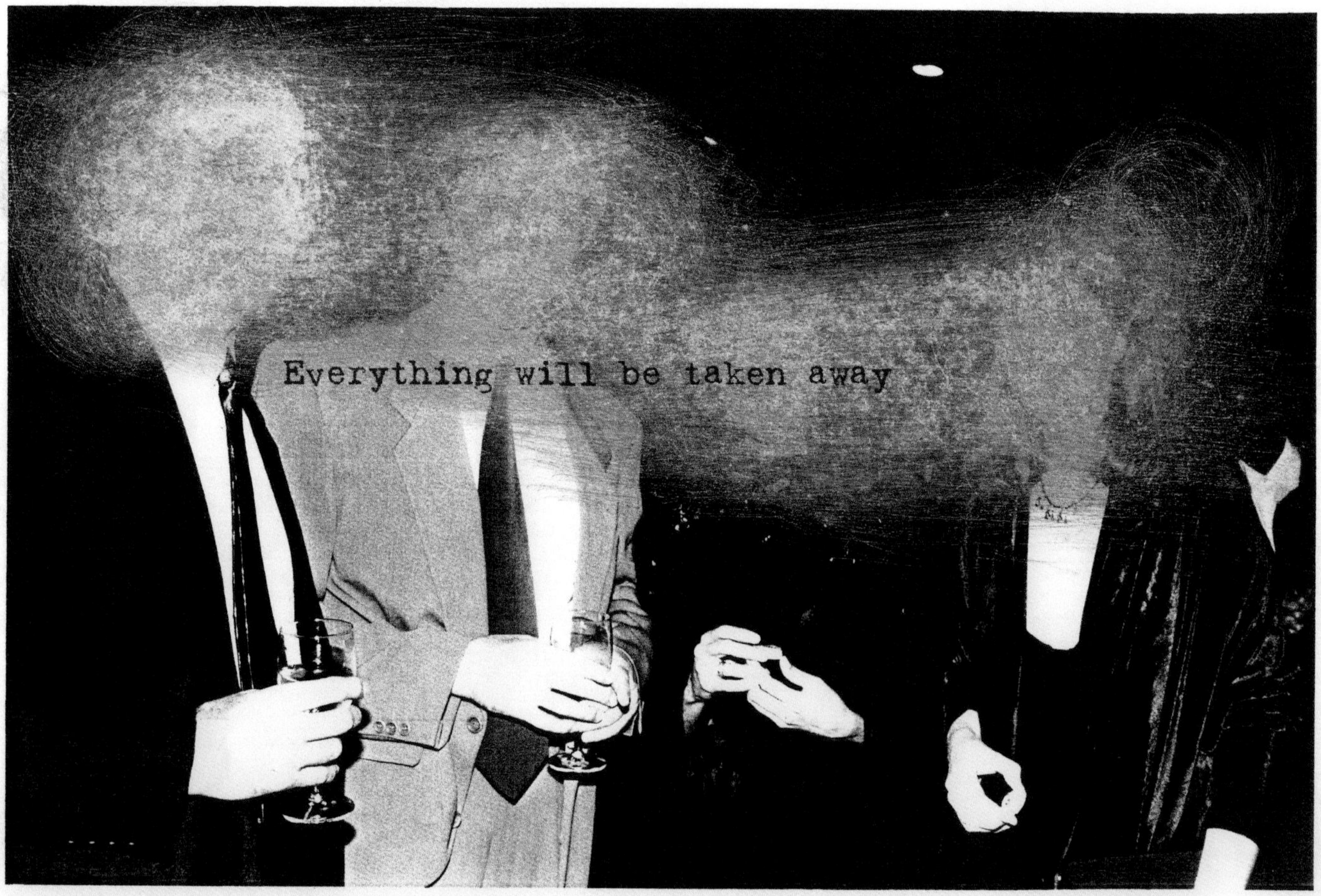

Everything #2.12a. 2003
Photograph photocopied on paper and sanded with sandpaper, with printed text
8½ × 11 in. (21.6 × 27.9 cm)
Collection J-E Van Praet

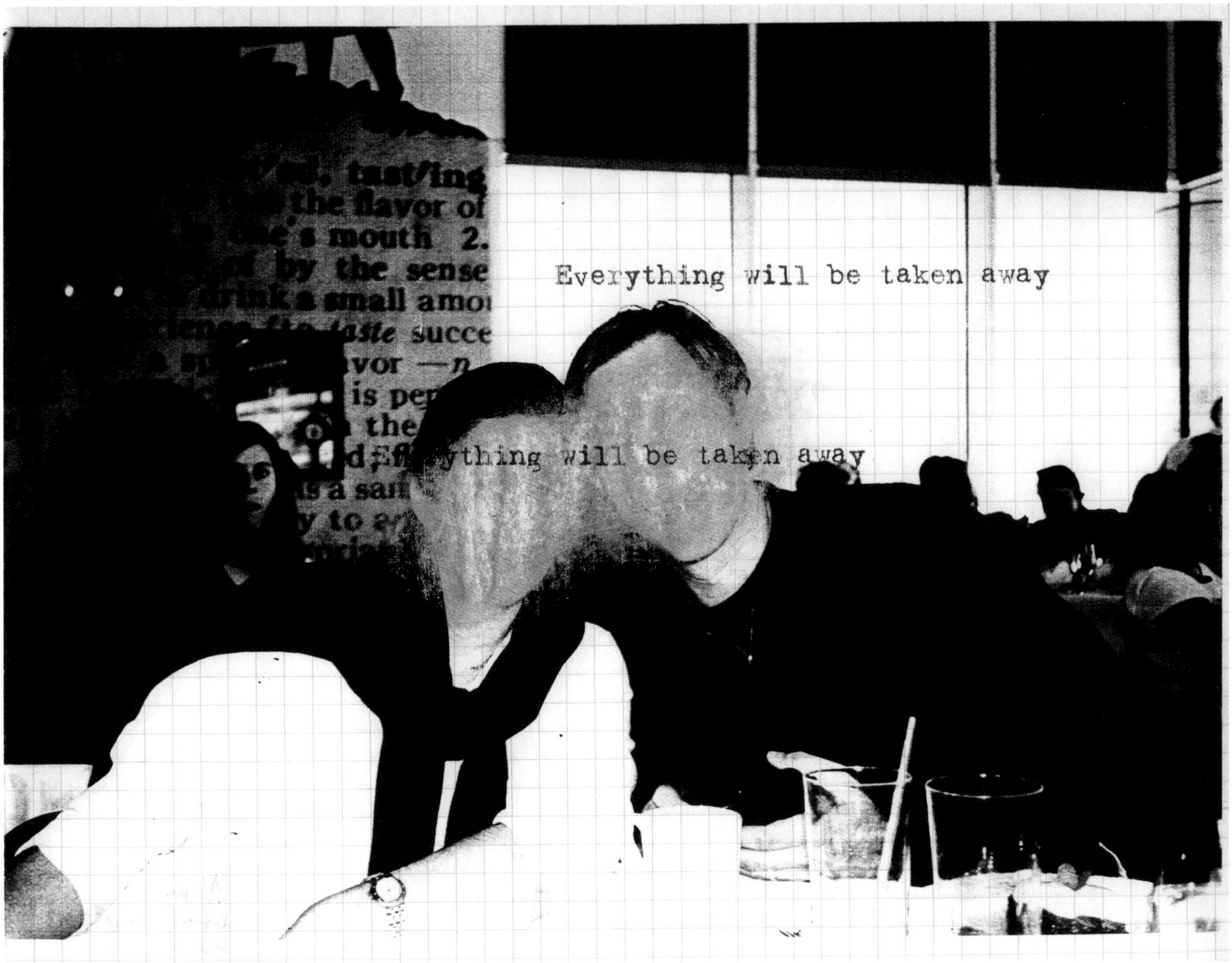

Everything #2.13. 2003
Photograph photocopied on graph paper and sanded with sandpaper, with printed text
8½ × 11 in. (21.6 × 27.9 cm)
Collection Lonti Ebers, New York

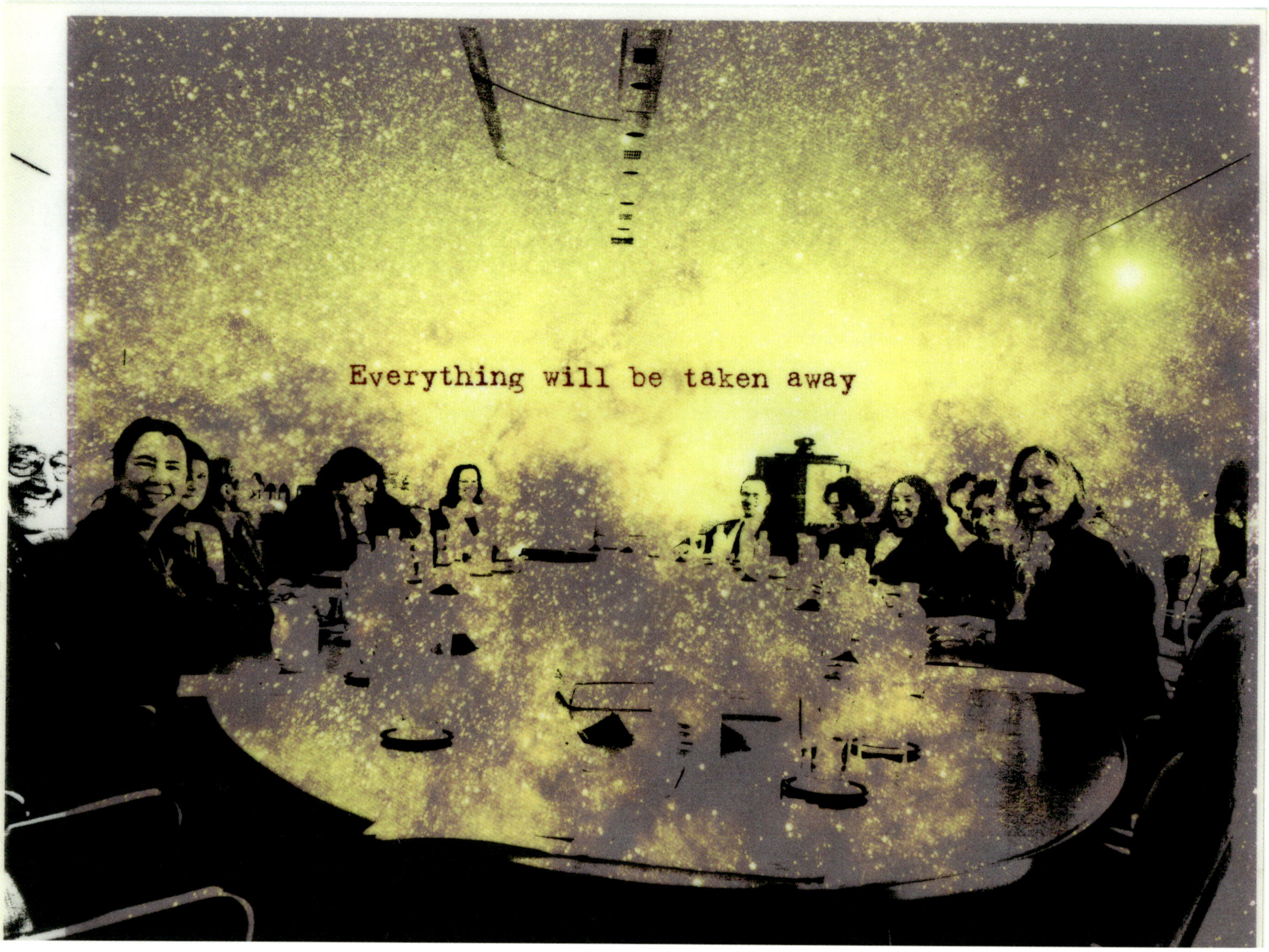

Everything #2.14. 2003
Photograph photocopied on vellum over inkjet print, with printed text, combined in plastic sleeve
8½ × 11 in. (27.9 × 21.6 cm)
Private collection

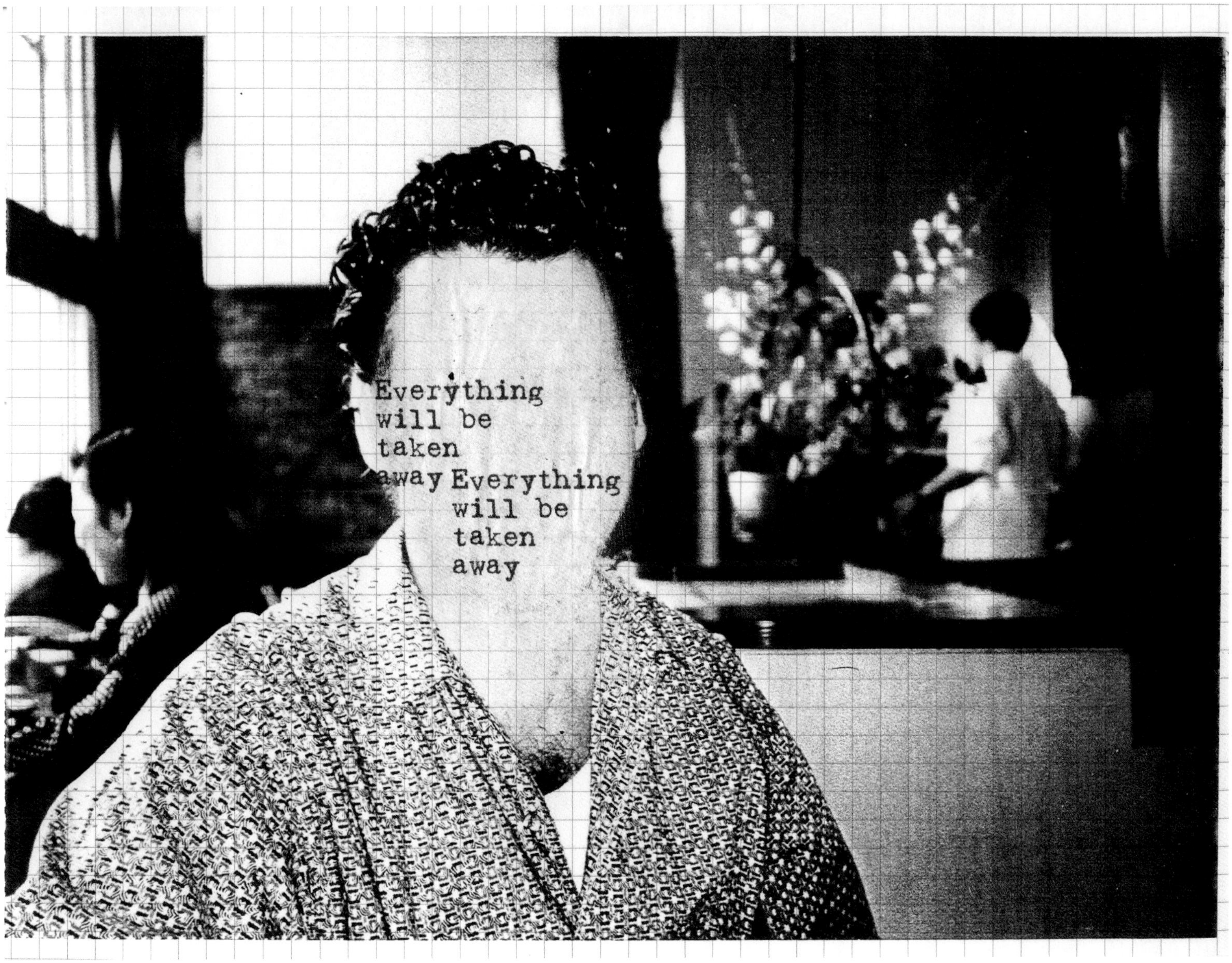

Everything #2.15. 2003
Photograph photocopied on graph paper and sanded with sandpaper, with printed text
8½ × 11 in. (27.9 × 21.6 cm)
Collection Lonti Elbers, New York

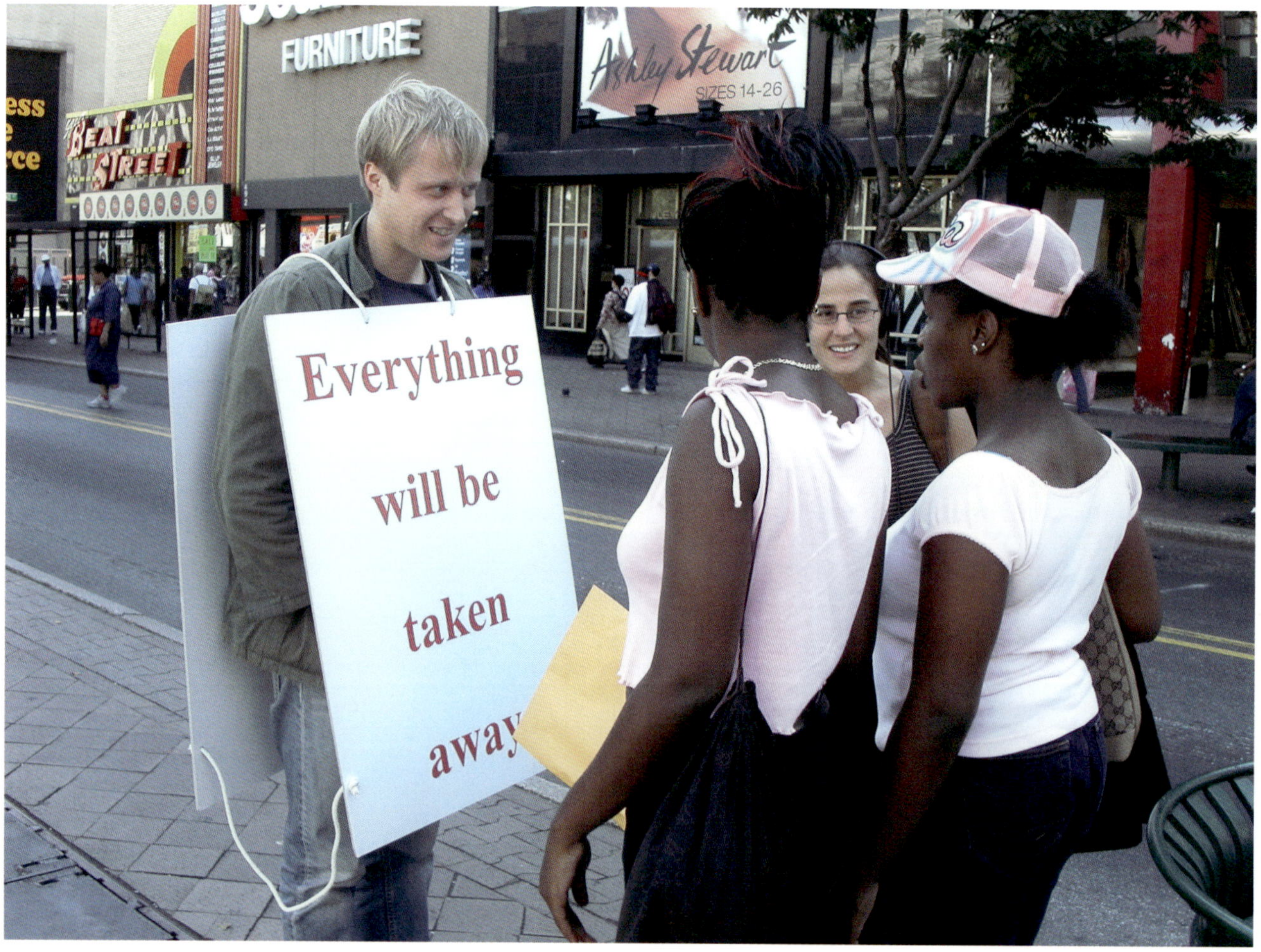

Everything #3. 2003
Sandwich-board performance
Performance view in *Sandwiched*, organized and performed by Jacob Fabricius, with Public Art Fund and The Wrong Gallery, New York, September 24, 2003
Collection Adrian Piper Research Archive Foundation Berlin

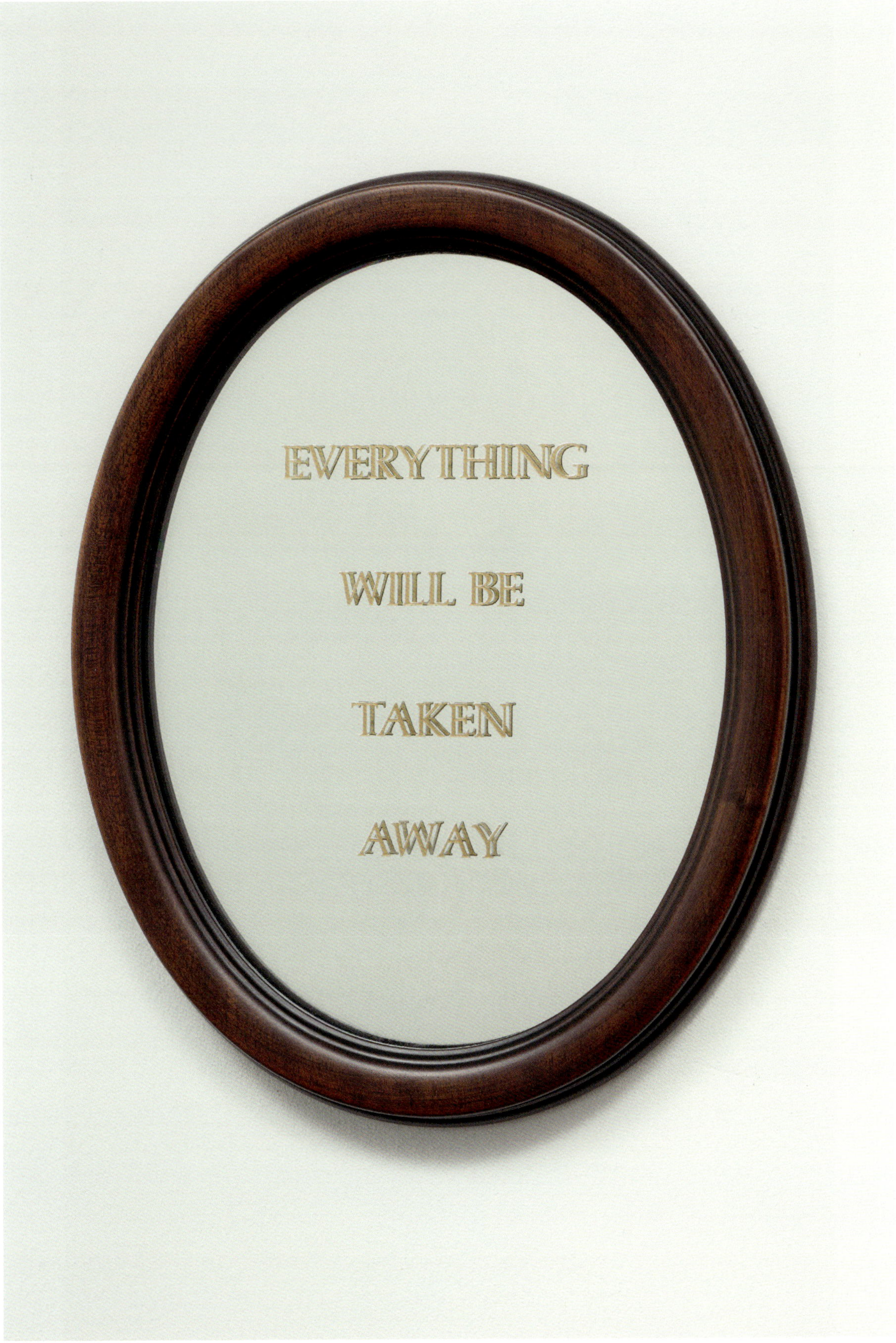

Everything #4. 2004
Engraved mirror, gold leaf, and wood frame
Edition: 2 of 8
13 × 10 in. (33 × 25.4 cm)
Collection Adrian Piper Research Archive Foundation Berlin

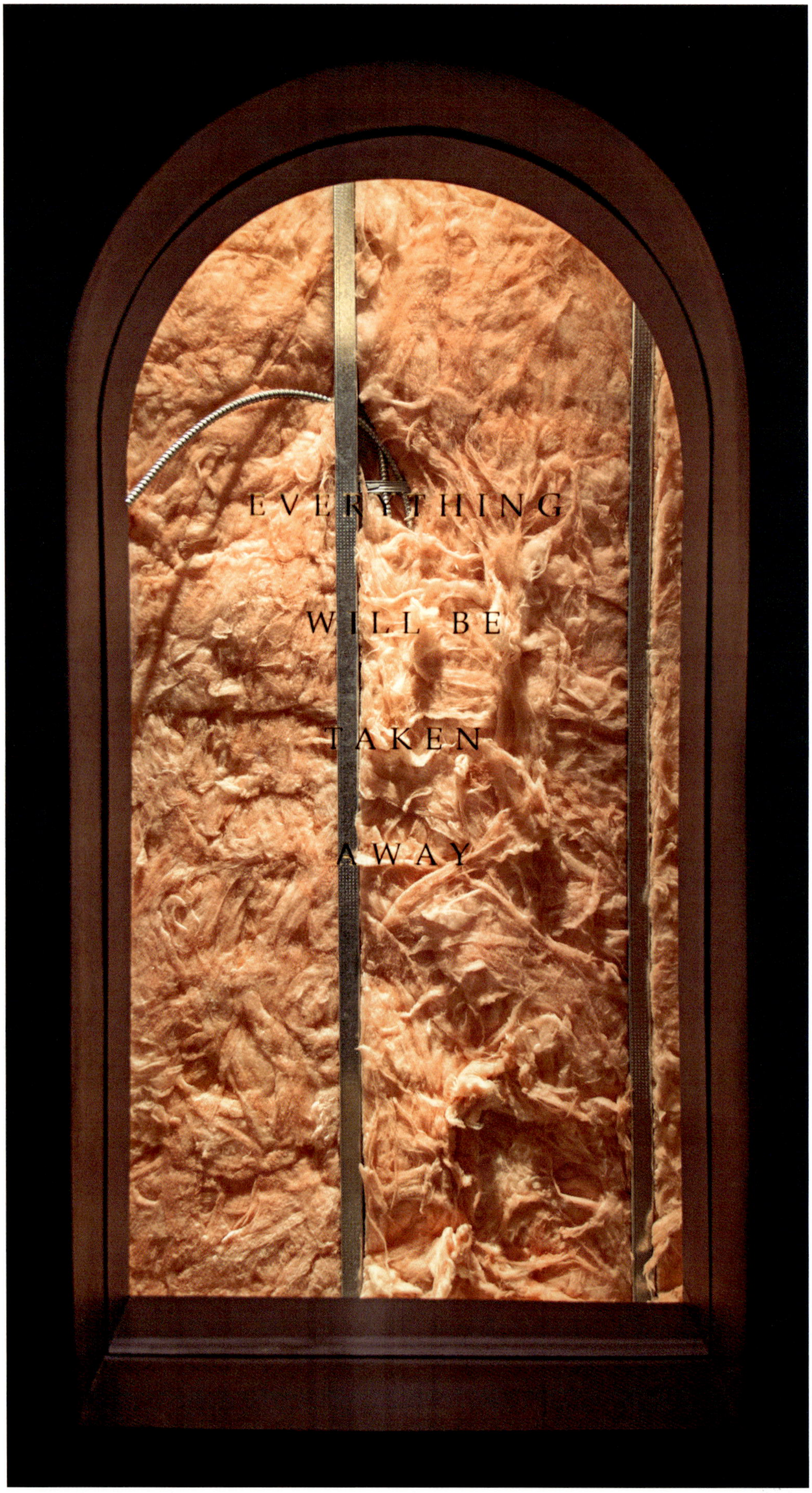

Everything #5.1. 2004
Engraved Plexiglas and gold leaf, inserted into wall
48 × 24 in. (121.9 × 61 cm)
Installation view in *The Wall in Our Heads: American Artists and the Berlin Wall*,
Goethe Institute, Washington, D.C., October 25–December 15, 2014
Collection Adrian Piper Research Archive Foundation Berlin

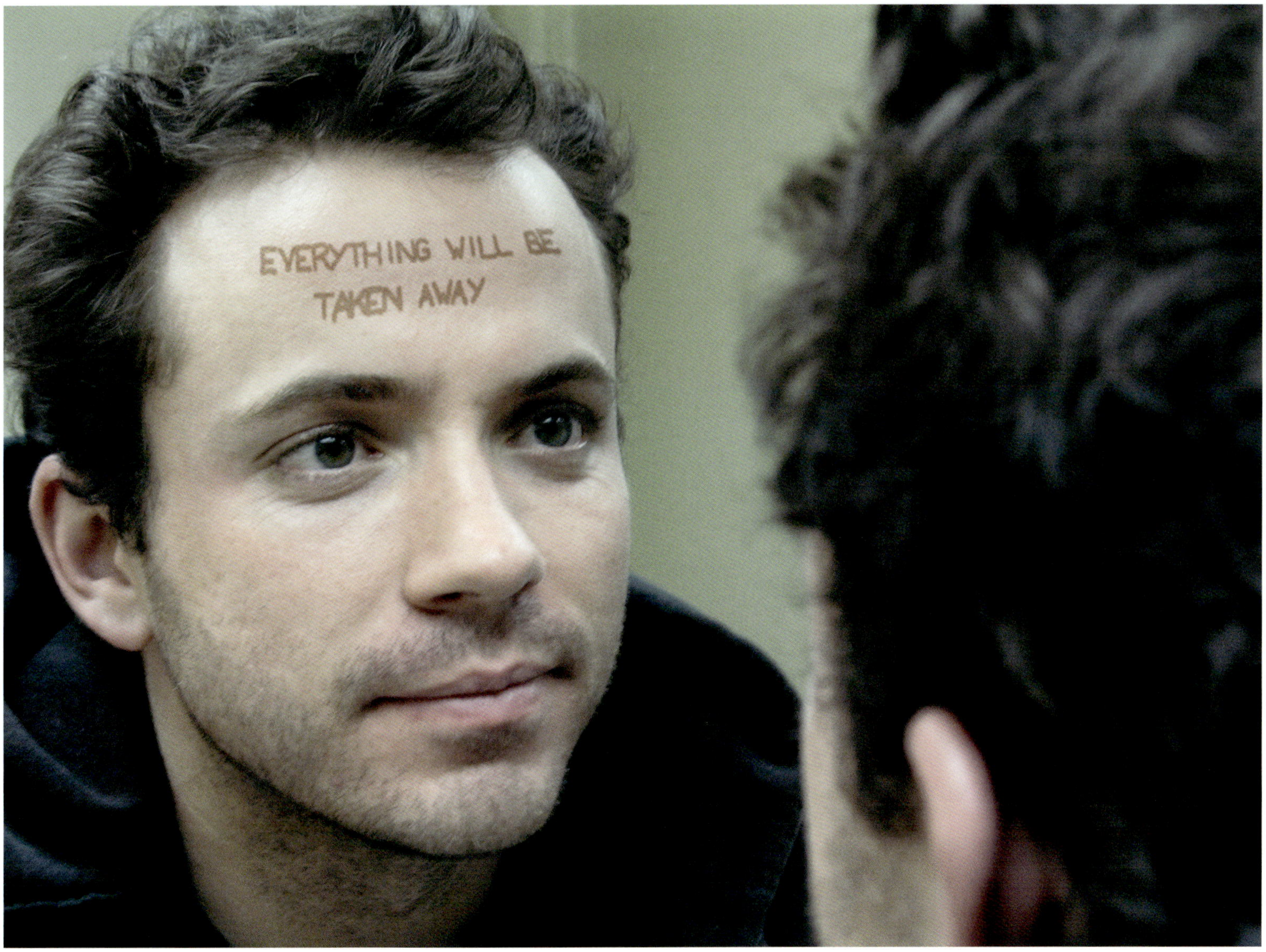

Everything #10. 2007
Participatory group performance
Performance view in *Six Actions for New York City*, commissioned and organized by Creative Time, New York, May 2007, with participant Gavin Kroeber
Collection Adrian Piper Research Archive Foundation Berlin

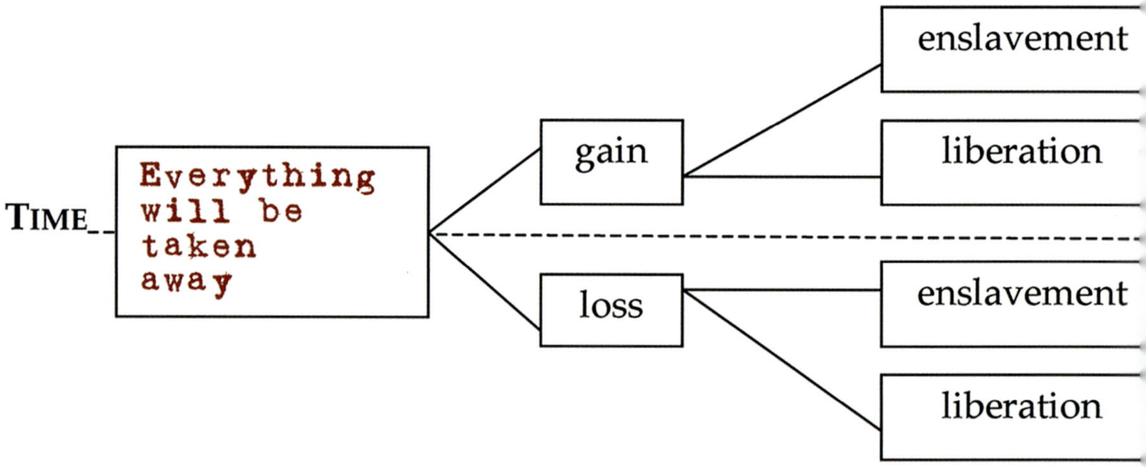

Everything #17.2. 2007
Extensive-form decision tree wallpaper. Vinyl wall print
Dimensions variable
Collection Adrian Piper Research Archive Foundation Berlin

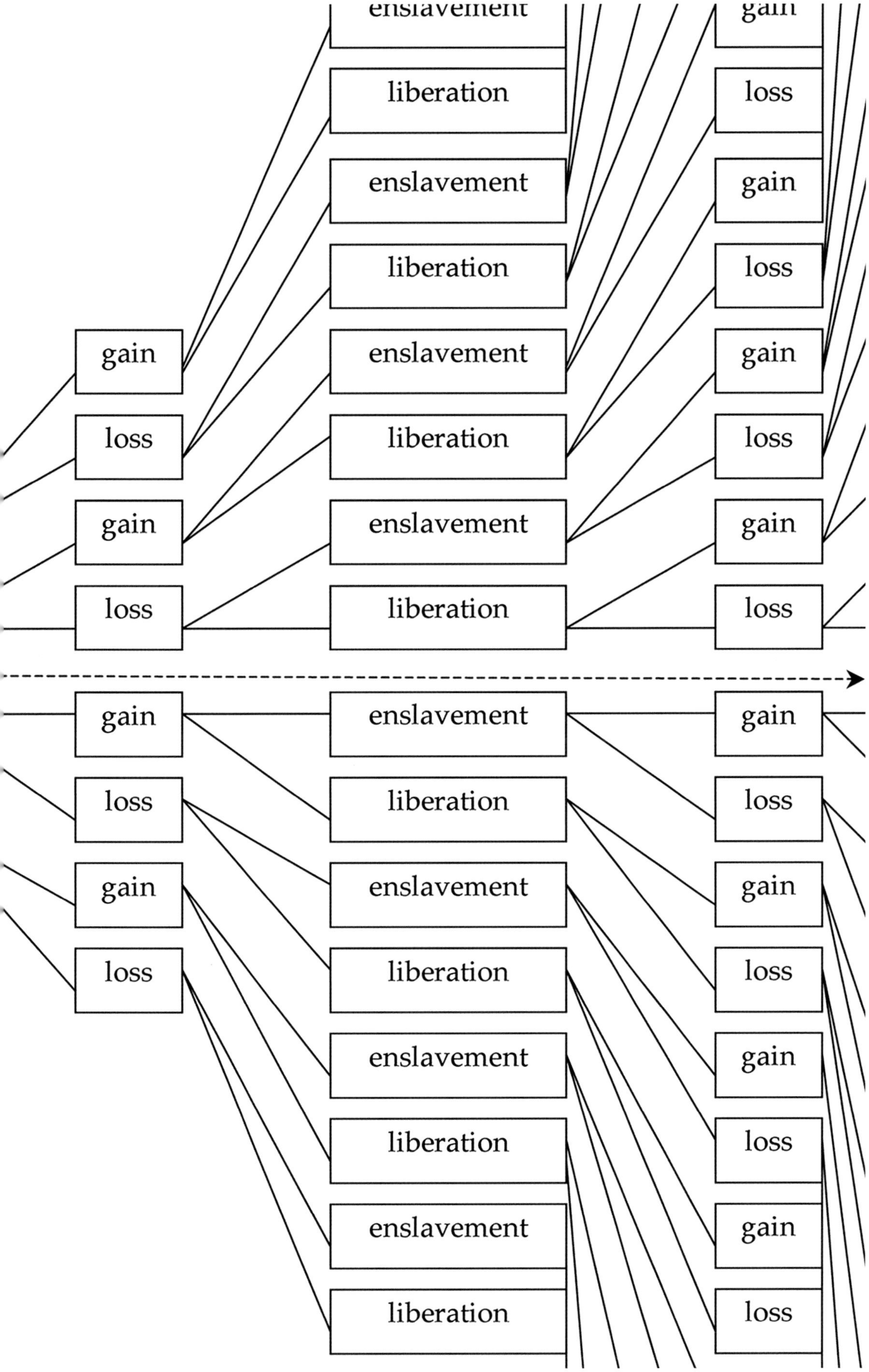
gain
loss
gain
loss
gain
loss
gain
loss
liberation
enslavement
liberation
enslavement
liberation
enslavement
liberation
enslavement
liberation
enslavement
liberation
enslavement
liberation
enslavement
liberation
loss
gain
loss
gain
loss
gain
loss
gain
loss
gain
loss
gain
loss
gain
loss

Everything #19.1. 2008
White vinyl text on wall with 10% gray paint
Dimensions variable
Collection Adrian Piper Research Archive Foundation Berlin

Everything #19.2. 2007
Video (black and white, silent), 00:04:45
Collection Adrian Piper Research Archive Foundation Berlin
Detail: video still at 00:00:14

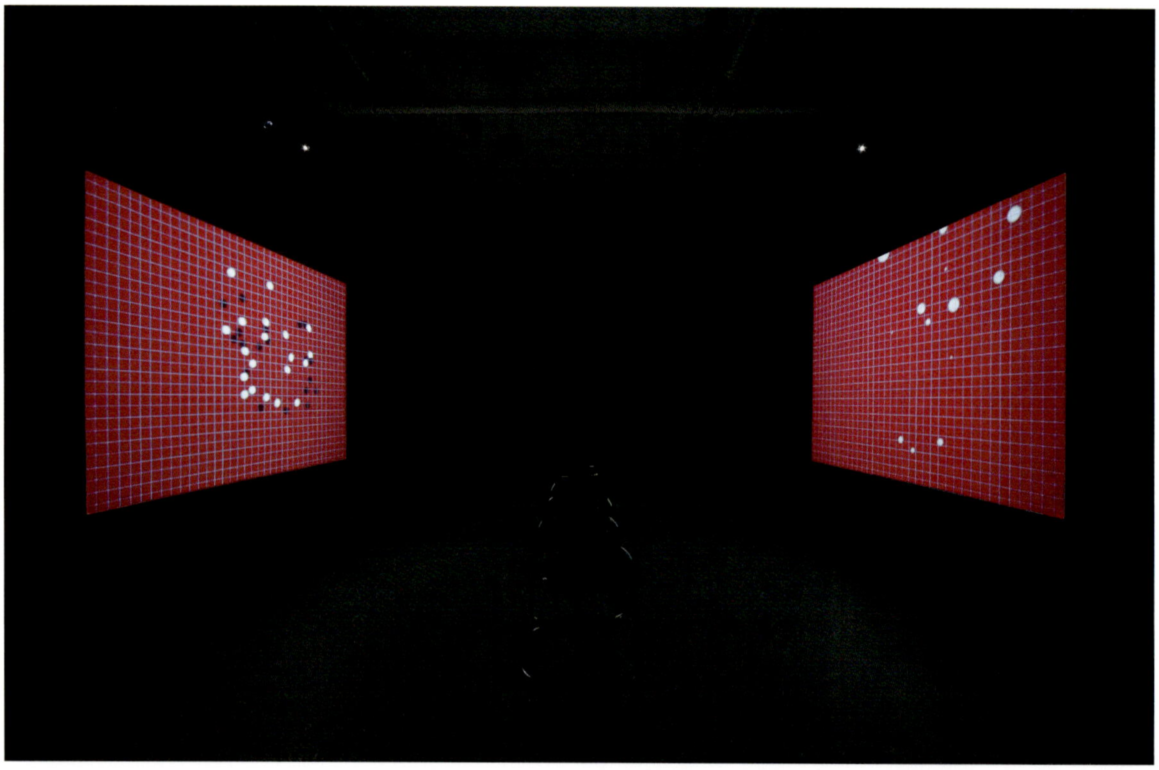

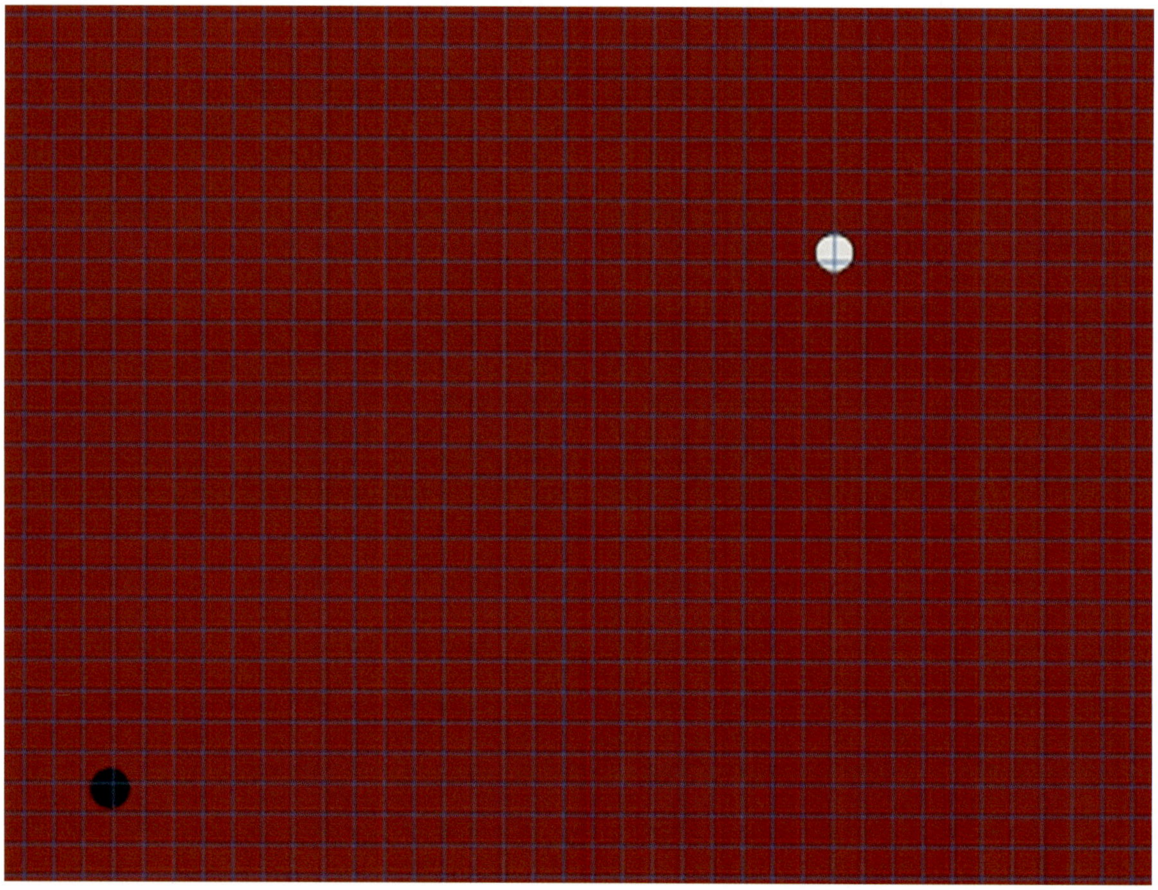

The Spurious Life-Death Distinction (Part II of The Pac-Man Trilogy). 2006
Unite (Part I of The Pac-Man Trilogy). 2005
Two animated videos (color, silent), 00:45:00 and 00:09:22
Installation view in *Adrian Piper: Everything*, Elizabeth Dee Gallery, New York, March 1–April 19, 2008
Collection Adrian Piper Research Archive Foundation Berlin

Bait-and-Switch (Part III of The Pac-Man Trilogy). 2008
Animated video (color, silent), 00:04:48
Collection Adrian Piper Research Archive Foundation Berlin
Detail: video still at 00:00:44

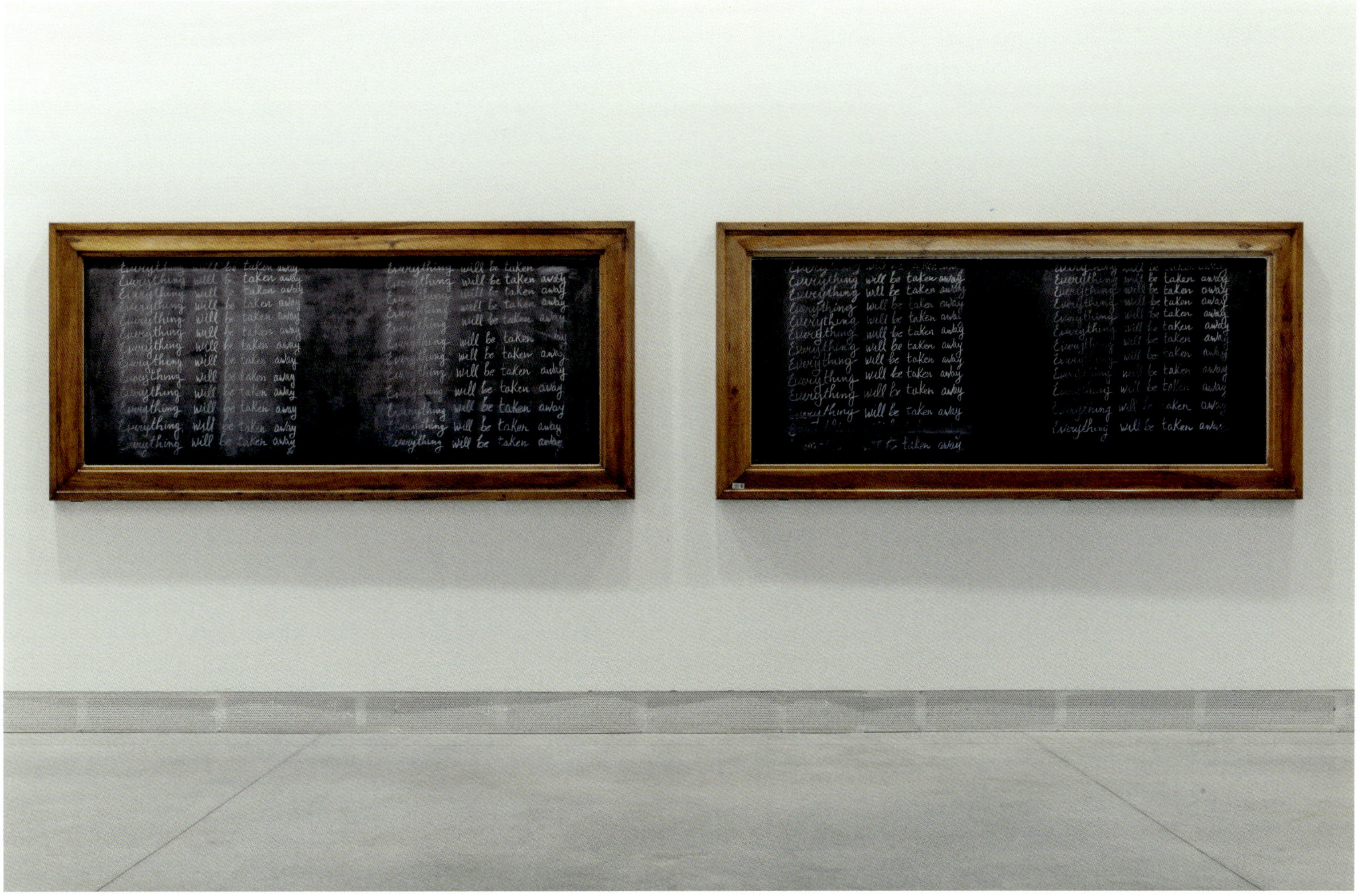

Everything #21. 2010–13
Chalk on four vintage blackboards in lacquered wood frames, each covered with the handwritten sentence "Everything will be taken away" and mounted on the wall at eye-level
Each 47¼ in. × 8 ft. $2\frac{7}{16}$ in. (120 × 250 cm)
Rennie Collection, Vancouver
Detail: two of four

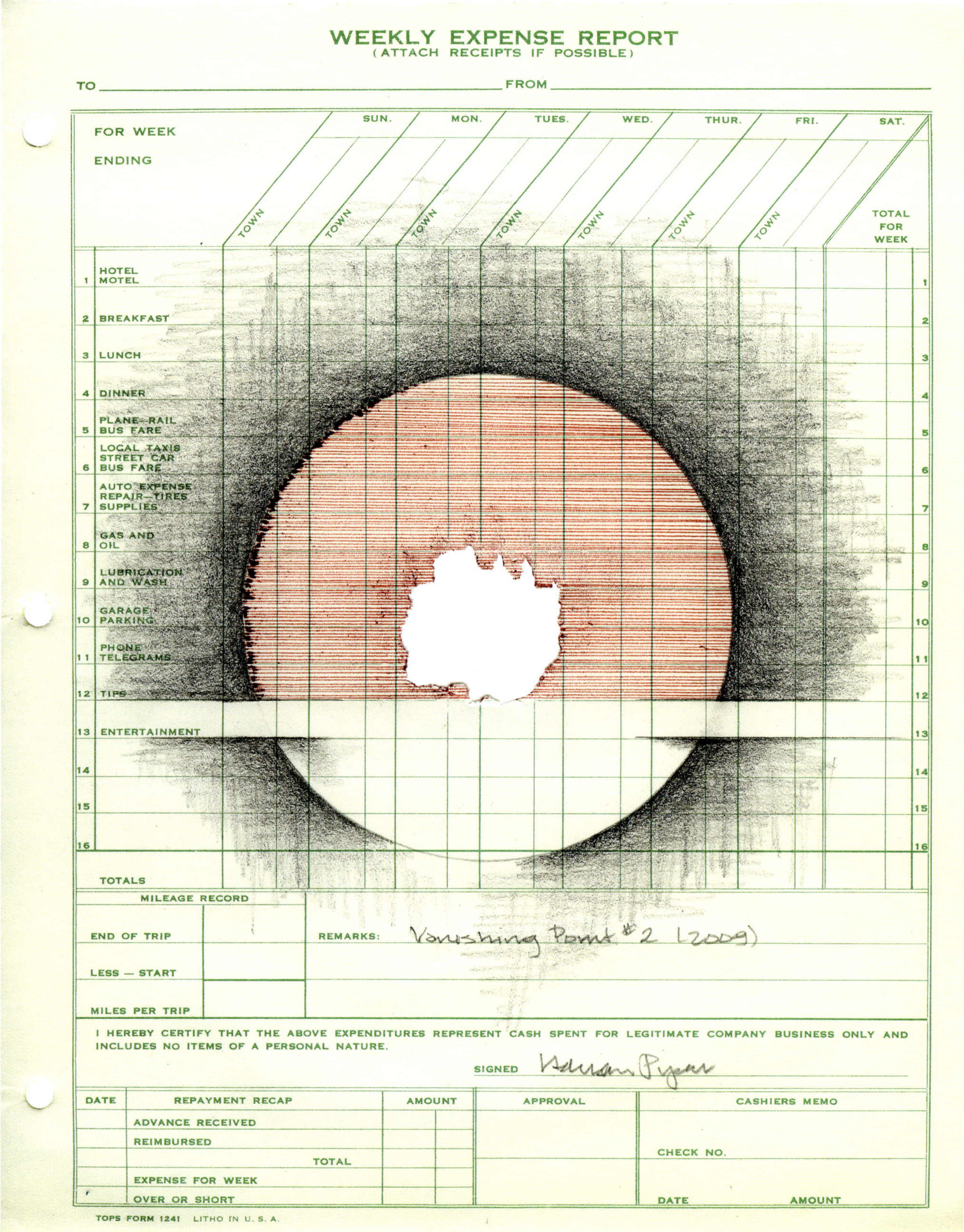

Vanishing Point #2. 2009
Pencil and ballpoint pen on expense report sanded with sandpaper
11 × 8½ in. (27.9 × 21.6 cm)
Annette Gentz and Pascal Decker Collection

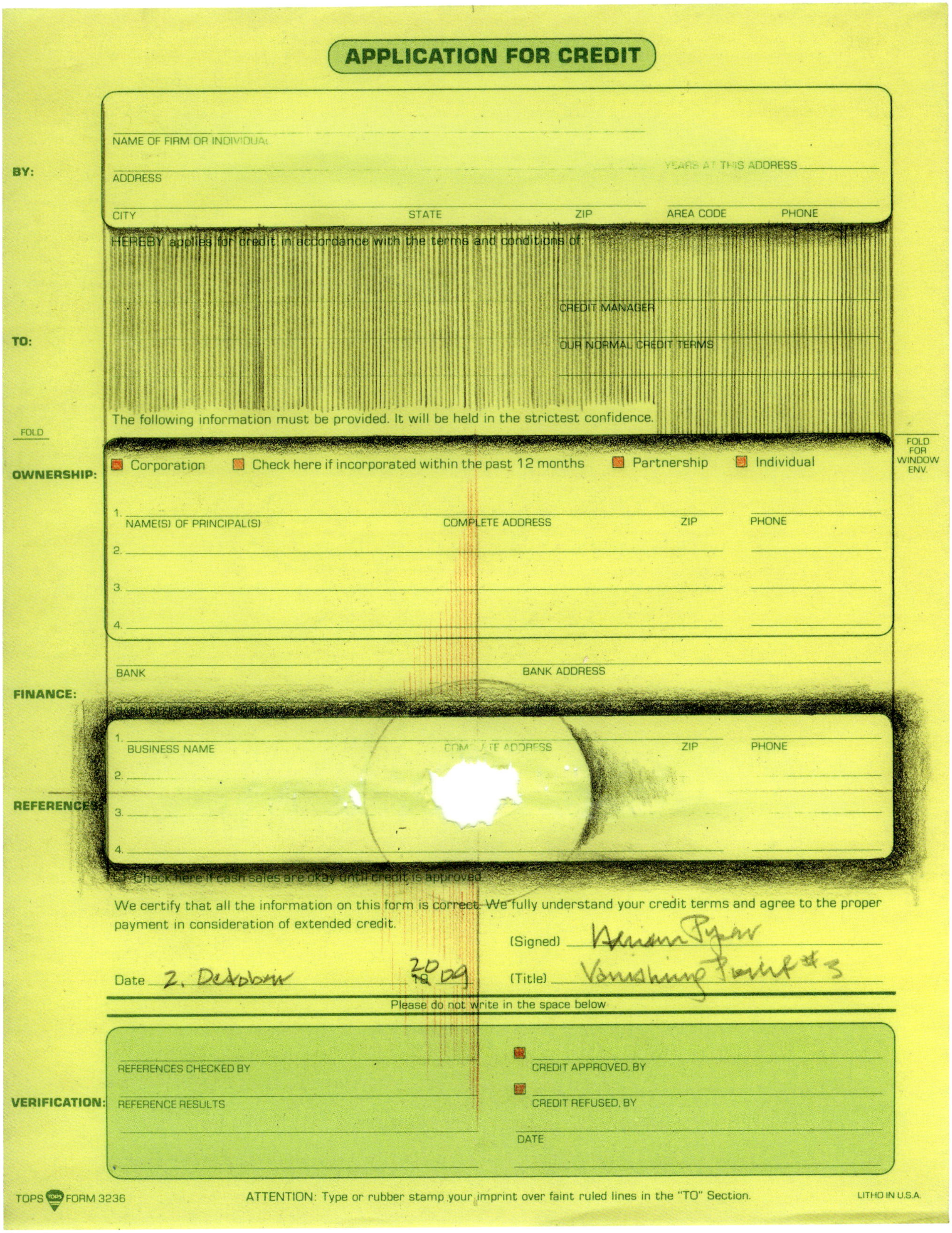

APPLICATION FOR CREDIT

BY:
NAME OF FIRM OR INDIVIDUAL
ADDRESS
YEARS AT THIS ADDRESS
CITY STATE ZIP AREA CODE PHONE

HEREBY applies for credit in accordance with the terms and conditions of:

TO:
CREDIT MANAGER
OUR NORMAL CREDIT TERMS

The following information must be provided. It will be held in the strictest confidence.

FOLD

OWNERSHIP: Corporation / Check here if incorporated within the past 12 months / Partnership / Individual

FOLD FOR WINDOW ENV.

1. NAME(S) OF PRINCIPAL(S)	COMPLETE ADDRESS	ZIP	PHONE
2.			
3.			
4.			

FINANCE:
BANK BANK ADDRESS

REFERENCES:

1. BUSINESS NAME	COMPLETE ADDRESS	ZIP	PHONE
2.			
3.			
4.			

Check here if cash sales are okay until credit is approved

We certify that all the information on this form is correct. We fully understand your credit terms and agree to the proper payment in consideration of extended credit.

(Signed) Adrian Piper

Date 2. Oktober 2009

(Title) Vanishing Point #3

Please do not write in the space below

VERIFICATION:
REFERENCES CHECKED BY
REFERENCE RESULTS
CREDIT APPROVED, BY
CREDIT REFUSED, BY
DATE

TOPS FORM 3236 ATTENTION: Type or rubber stamp your imprint over faint ruled lines in the "TO" Section. LITHO IN U.S.A.

Vanishing Point #3. 2009
Pencil on credit application sanded with sandpaper
11 × 8½ in. (27.9 × 21.6 cm)
Collection Adrian Piper Research Archive Foundation Berlin

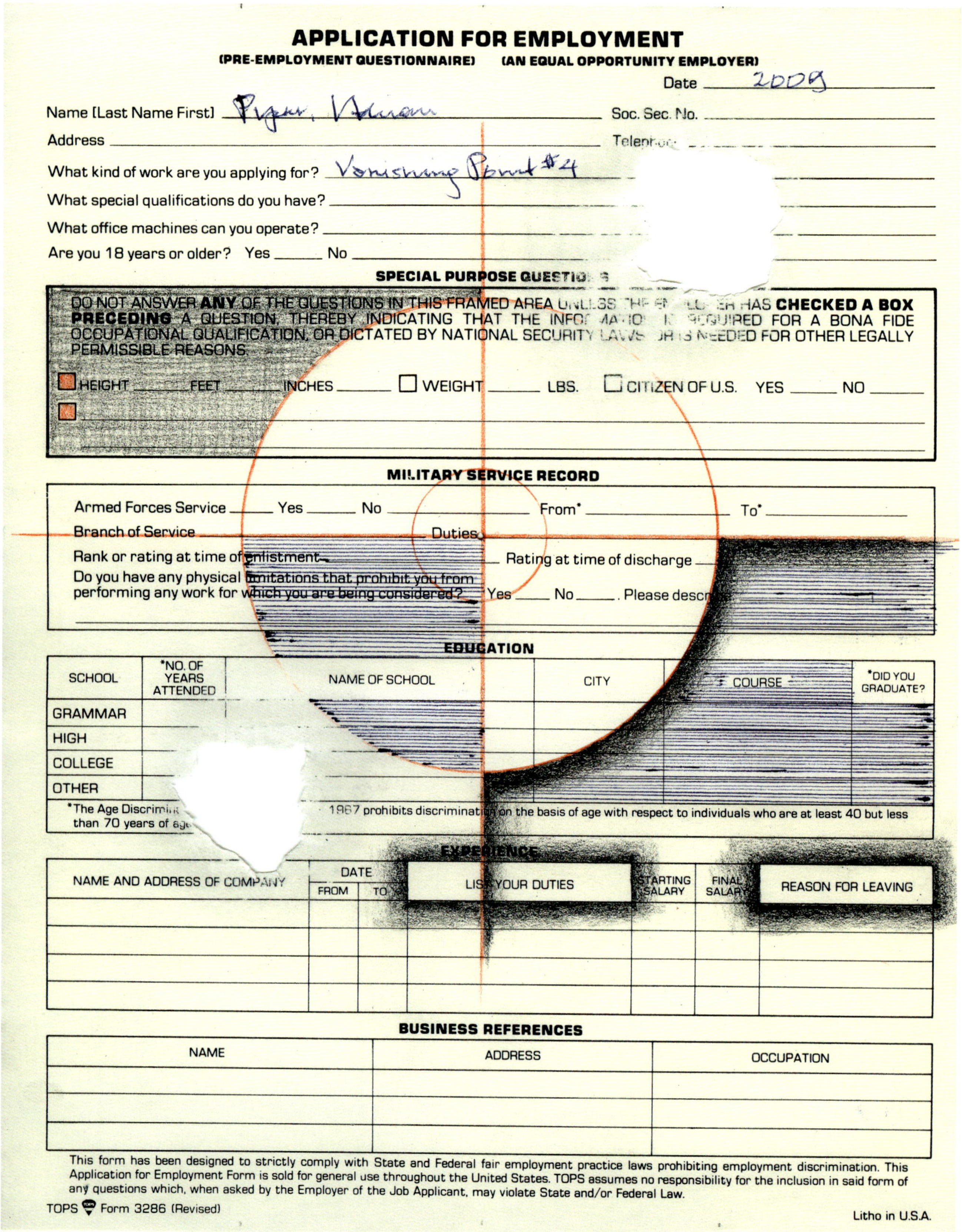

APPLICATION FOR EMPLOYMENT

(PRE-EMPLOYMENT QUESTIONNAIRE) (AN EQUAL OPPORTUNITY EMPLOYER)

Date 2009

Name [Last Name First] Piper, Adrian Soc. Sec. No.

Address Telephone

What kind of work are you applying for? Vanishing Point #4

What special qualifications do you have?

What office machines can you operate?

Are you 18 years or older? Yes ______ No

SPECIAL PURPOSE QUESTIONS

DO NOT ANSWER **ANY** OF THE QUESTIONS IN THIS FRAMED AREA UNLESS THE EMPLOYER HAS **CHECKED A BOX PRECEDING** A QUESTION, THEREBY INDICATING THAT THE INFORMATION IS REQUIRED FOR A BONA FIDE OCCUPATIONAL QUALIFICATION, OR DICTATED BY NATIONAL SECURITY LAWS, OR IS NEEDED FOR OTHER LEGALLY PERMISSIBLE REASONS.

☐ HEIGHT ______ FEET ______ INCHES ______ ☐ WEIGHT ______ LBS. ☐ CITIZEN OF U.S. YES ______ NO ______

☐

MILITARY SERVICE RECORD

Armed Forces Service ______ Yes ______ No ______ From* ______ To* ______

Branch of Service ______ Duties ______

Rank or rating at time of enlistment ______ Rating at time of discharge ______

Do you have any physical limitations that prohibit you from performing any work for which you are being considered? Yes ______ No ______. Please describe

EDUCATION

SCHOOL	*NO. OF YEARS ATTENDED	NAME OF SCHOOL	CITY	COURSE	*DID YOU GRADUATE?
GRAMMAR					
HIGH					
COLLEGE					
OTHER					

*The Age Discrimination ... 1967 prohibits discrimination on the basis of age with respect to individuals who are at least 40 but less than 70 years of age.

EXPERIENCE

NAME AND ADDRESS OF COMPANY	DATE FROM	DATE TO	LIST YOUR DUTIES	STARTING SALARY	FINAL SALARY	REASON FOR LEAVING

BUSINESS REFERENCES

NAME	ADDRESS	OCCUPATION

This form has been designed to strictly comply with State and Federal fair employment practice laws prohibiting employment discrimination. This Application for Employment Form is sold for general use throughout the United States. TOPS assumes no responsibility for the inclusion in said form of any questions which, when asked by the Employer of the Job Applicant, may violate State and/or Federal Law.

TOPS Form 3286 (Revised)

Litho in U.S.A.

Vanishing Point #4. 2009
Pencil, colored pencil, and ballpoint pen on employment application sanded with sandpaper
11 × 8½ in. (27.9 × 21.6 cm)
Collection Adrian Piper Research Archive Foundation Berlin

Vanishing Point #5. 2009
Ballpoint pen and pencil on employment application sanded with sandpaper
11 × 8½ in. (27.9 × 21.6 cm)
Collection Adrian Piper Research Archive Foundation Berlin

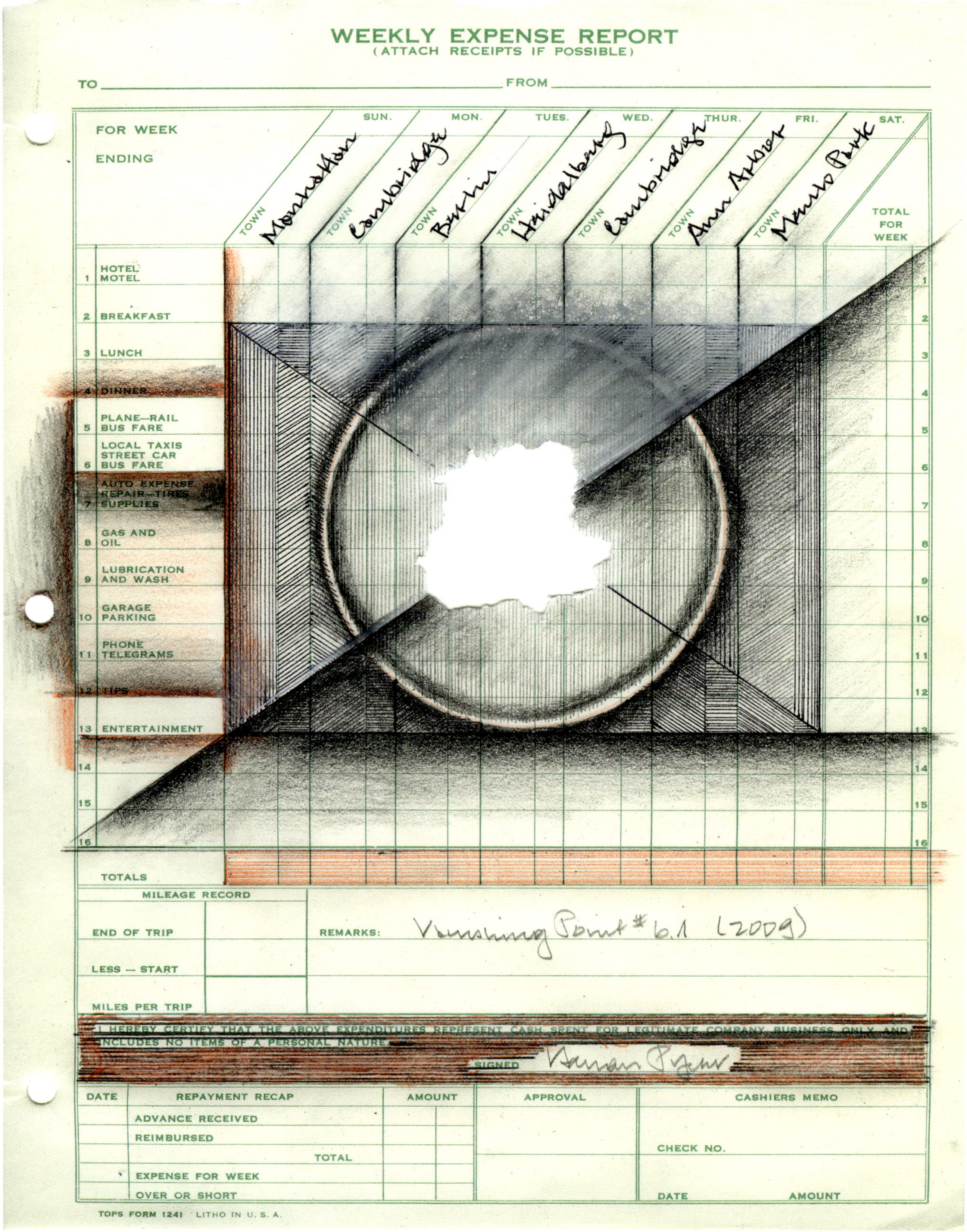

Vanishing Point #6.1. 2009
Ballpoint pen, crayon, and pencil on weekly expense-report form sanded with sandpaper
11 × 8½ in. (27.9 × 21.6 cm)
Collection Adrian Piper Research Archive Foundation Berlin

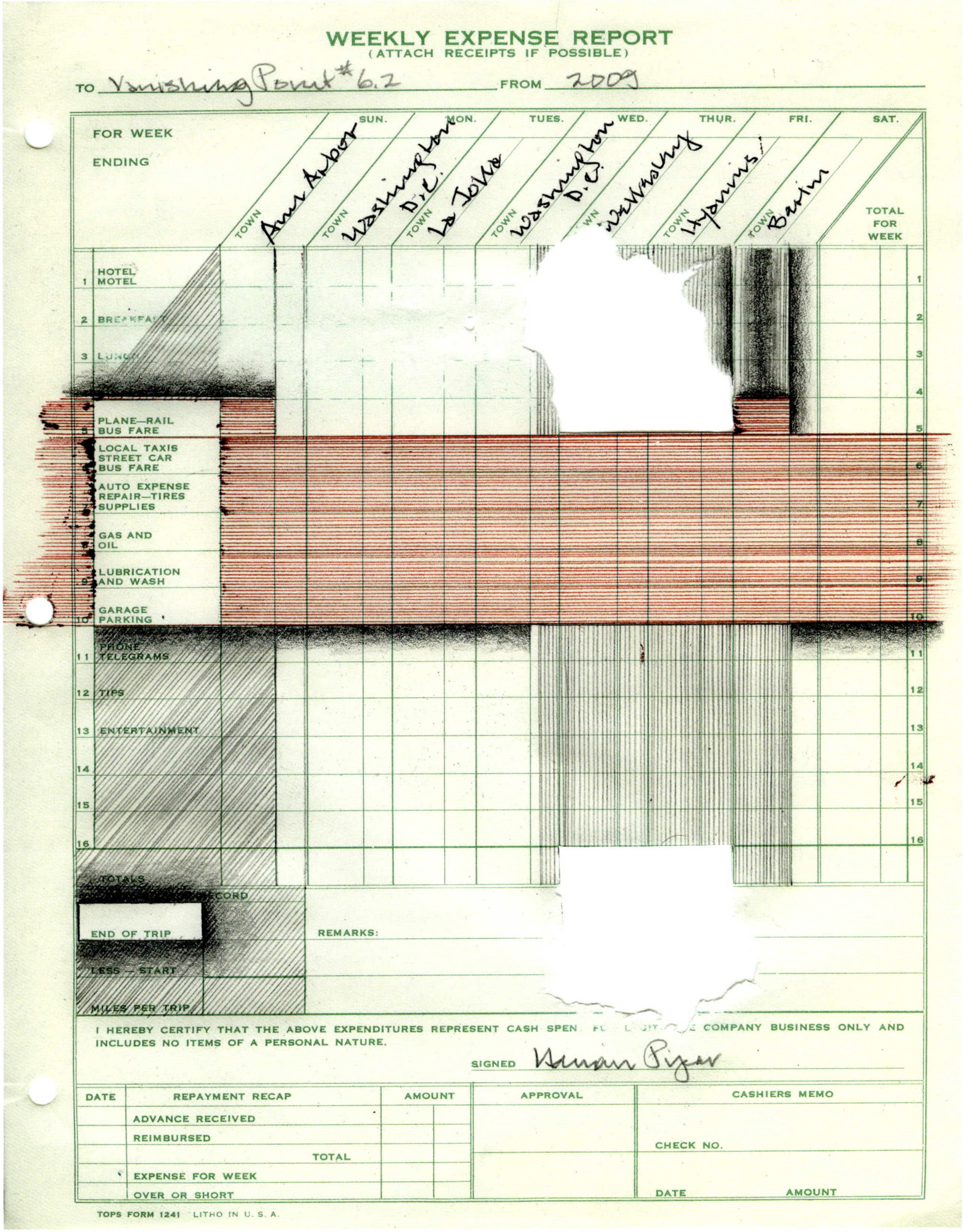

Vanishing Point #6.2. 2009
Ballpoint pen, crayon, and pencil on weekly expense-report form sanded with sandpaper
11 × 8½ in. (27.9 × 21.6 cm)
Collection Adrian Piper Research Archive Foundation Berlin

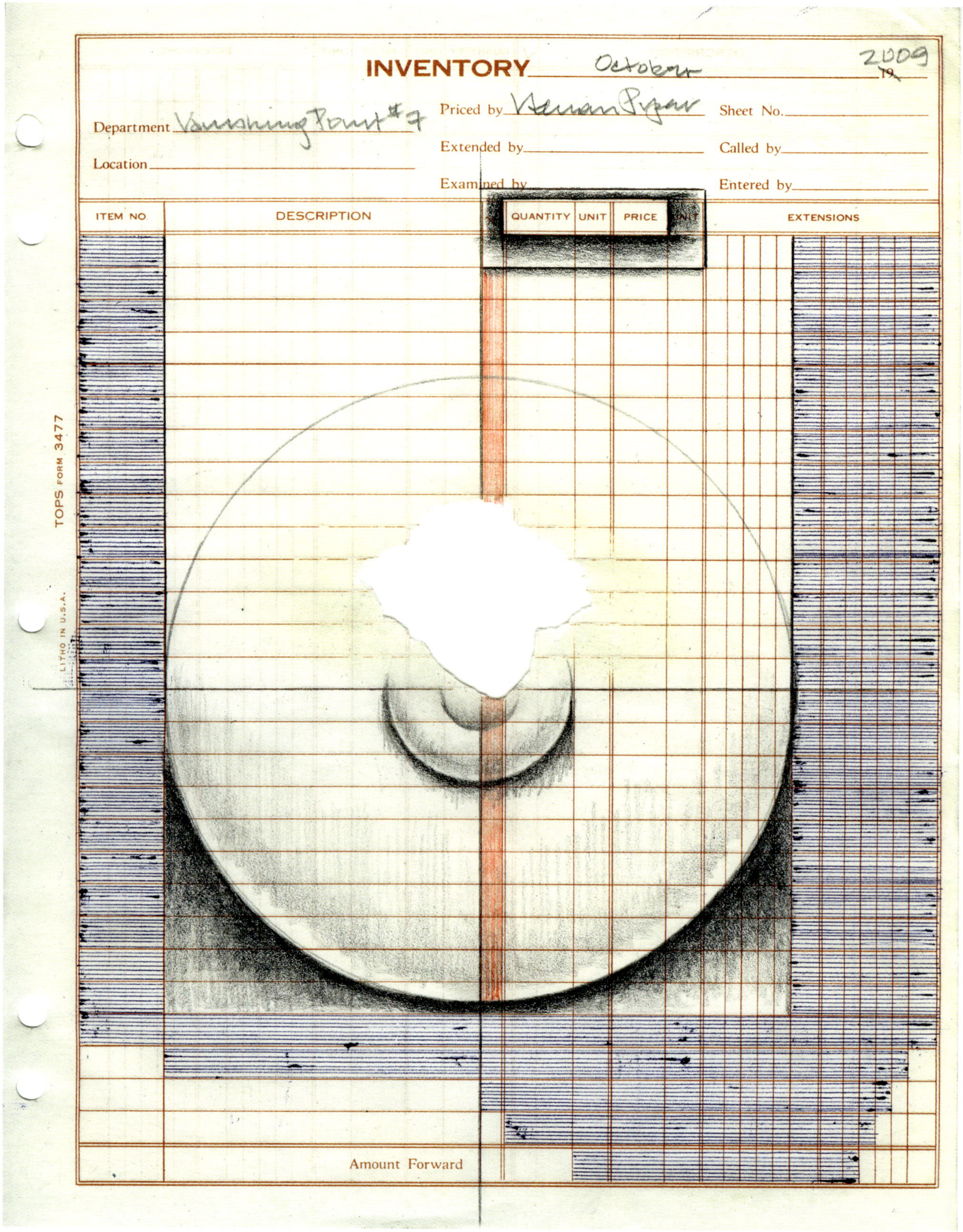

Vanishing Point #7. 2009
Ballpoint pen and colored pencil on inventory form sanded with sandpaper
11 × 8½ in. (27.9 × 21.6 cm)
Collection Adrian Piper Research Archive Foundation Berlin

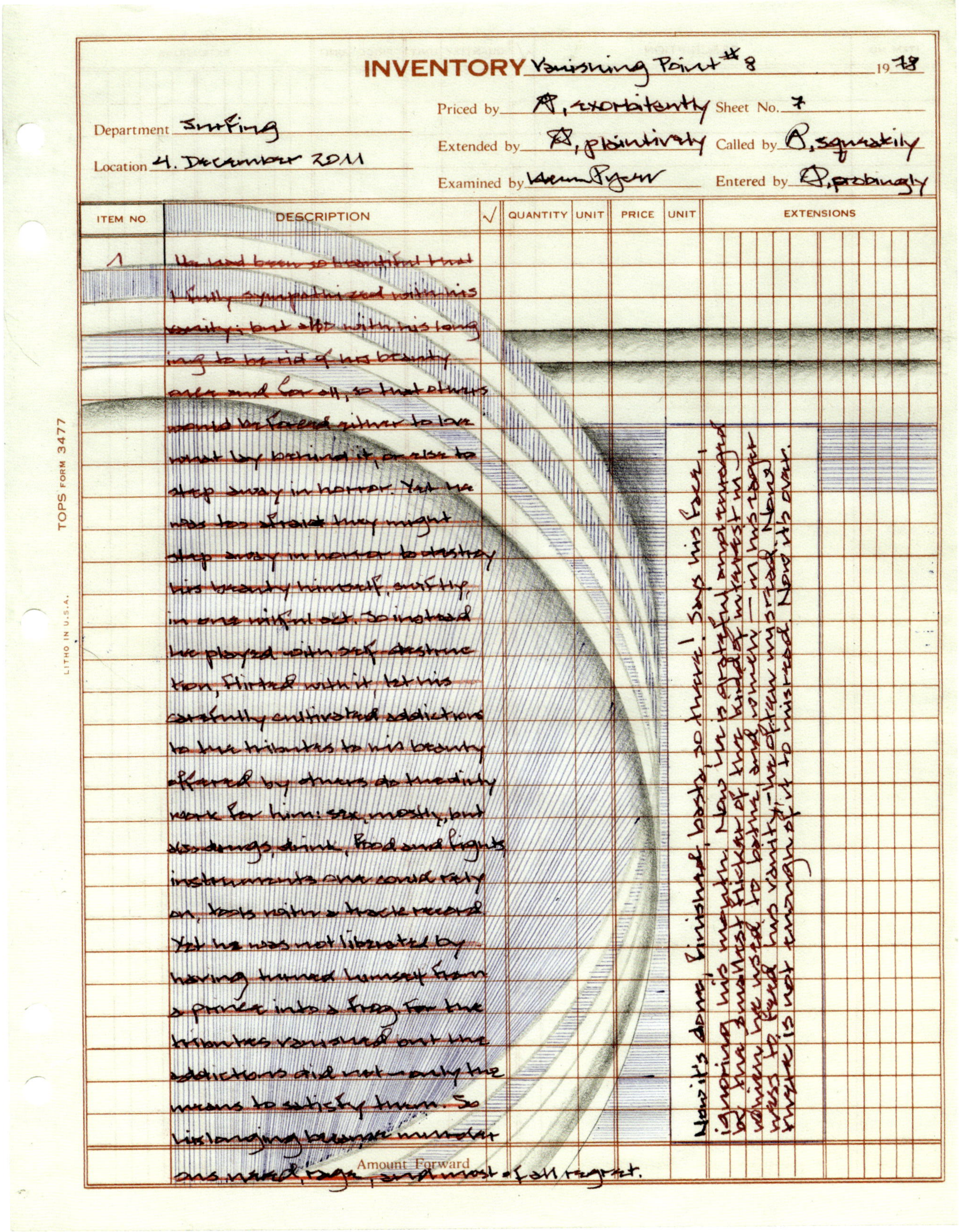

Vanishing Point #8. 2011
Colored ink, ballpoint pen, pencil, and colored pencil on inventory form
11 × 8½ in. (27.9 × 21.6 cm)
Collection Adrian Piper Research Archive Foundation Berlin

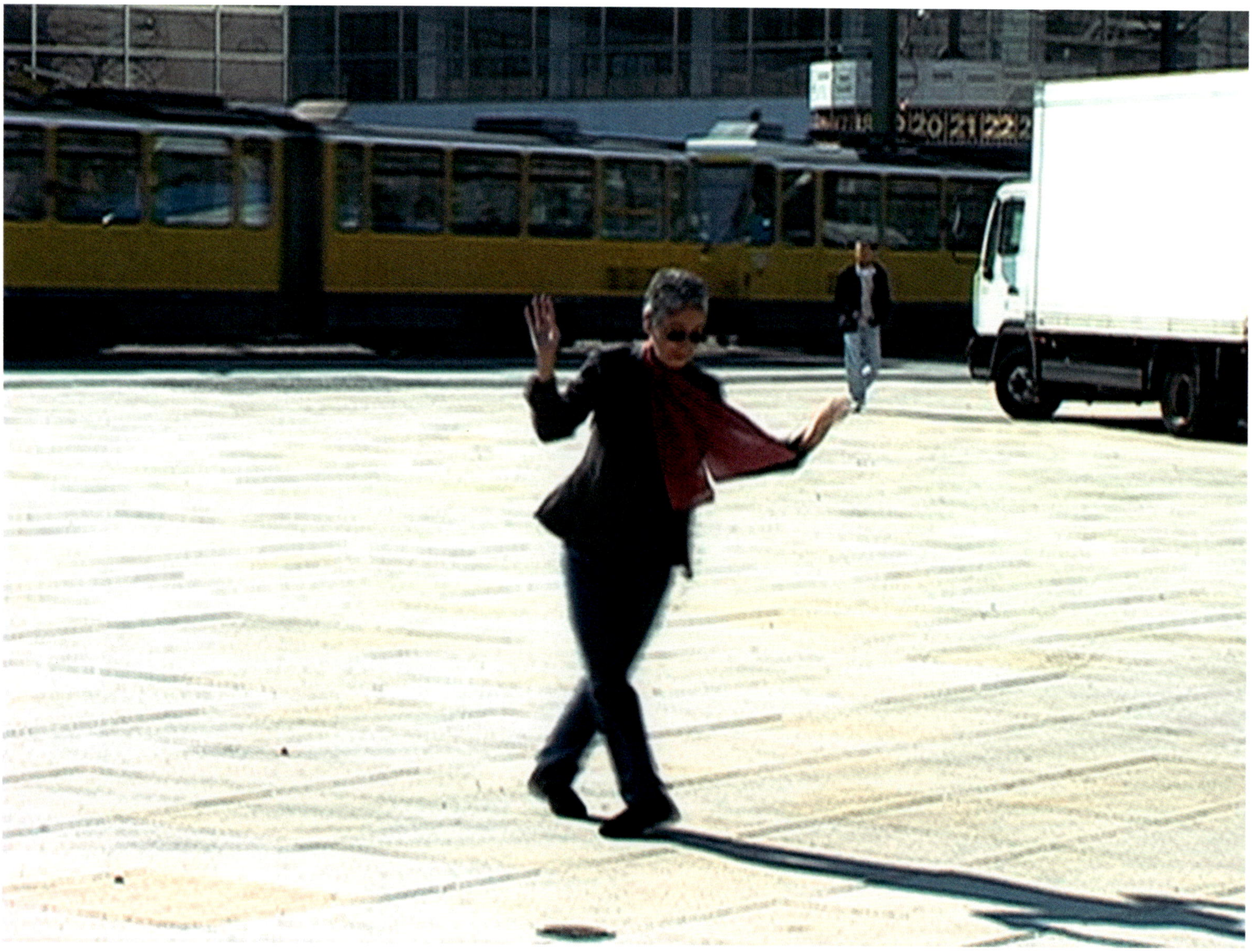

Adrian Moves to Berlin. 2007
Documentation of the street performance. Video (color, sound), 01:02:42
Video by Robert Del Principe
Collection Adrian Piper Research Archive Foundation Berlin
Detail: video still at 00:38:09

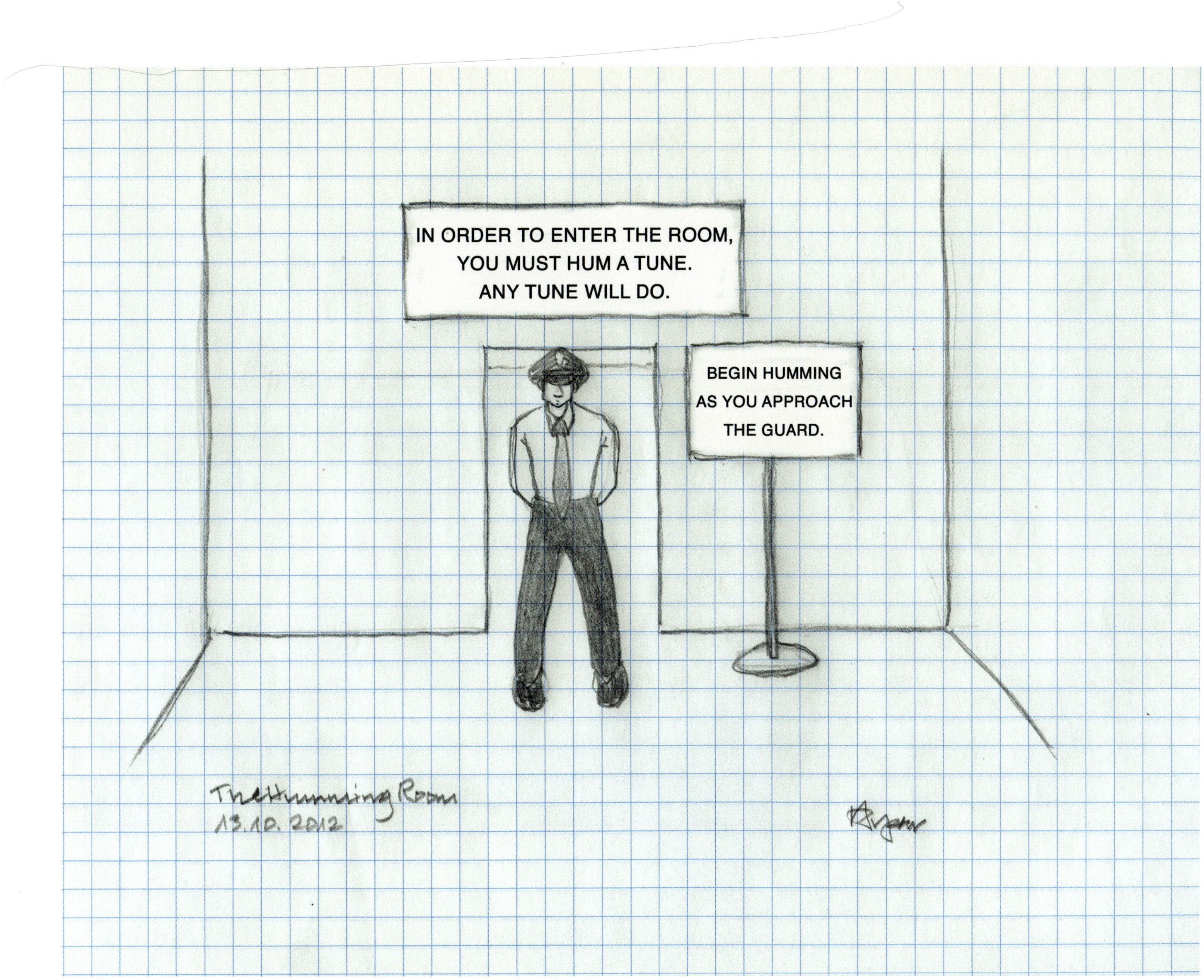

The Humming Room. 2012
Exhibition instruction. Pencil on graph paper with digital additions
8½ × 11 in. (21.6 × 27.9 cm)
Collection Adrian Piper Research Archive Foundation Berlin

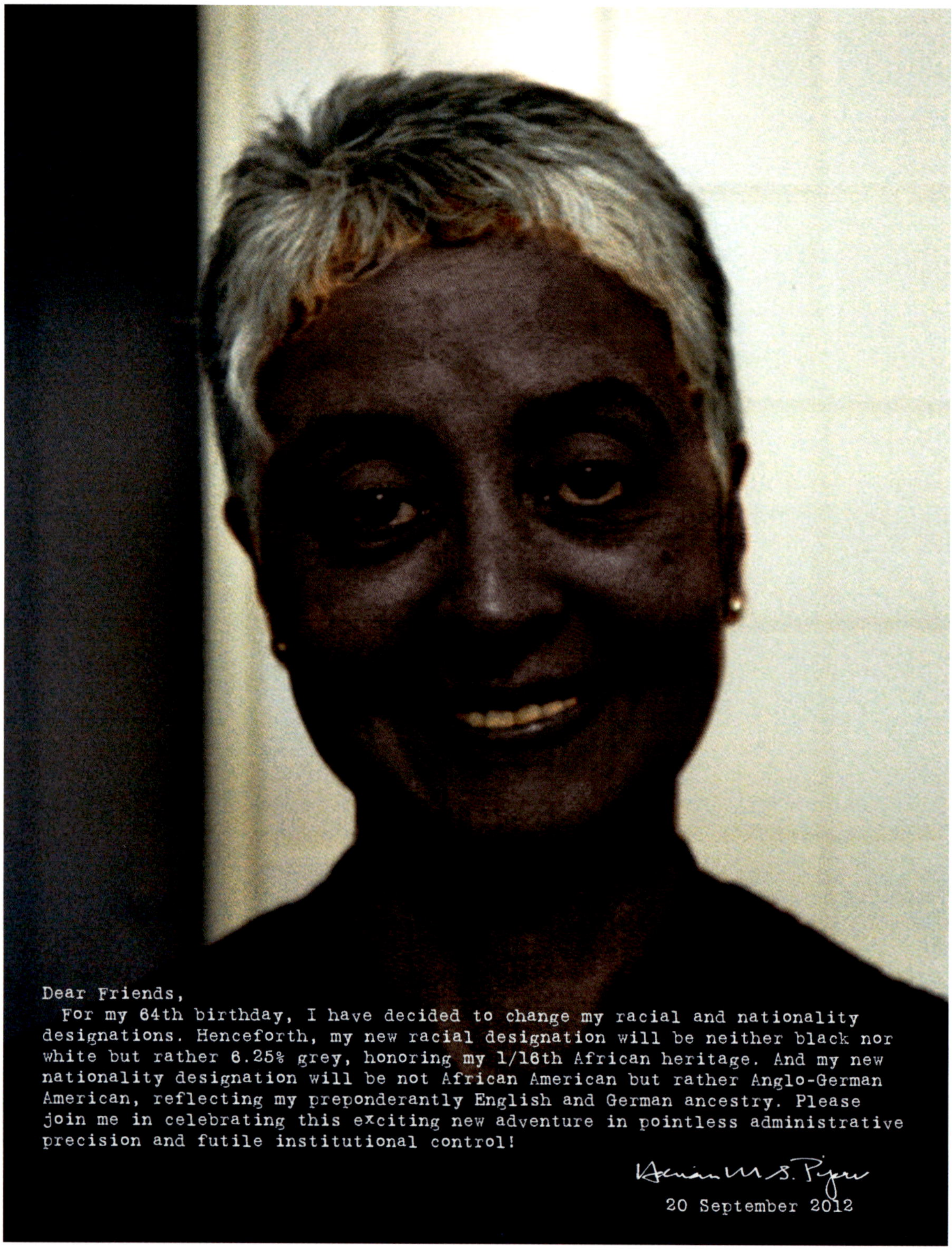

Thwarted Projects, Dashed Hopes, A Moment of Embarrassment. 2012
Digital file
Dimensions variable
Collection Adrian Piper Research Archive Foundation Berlin

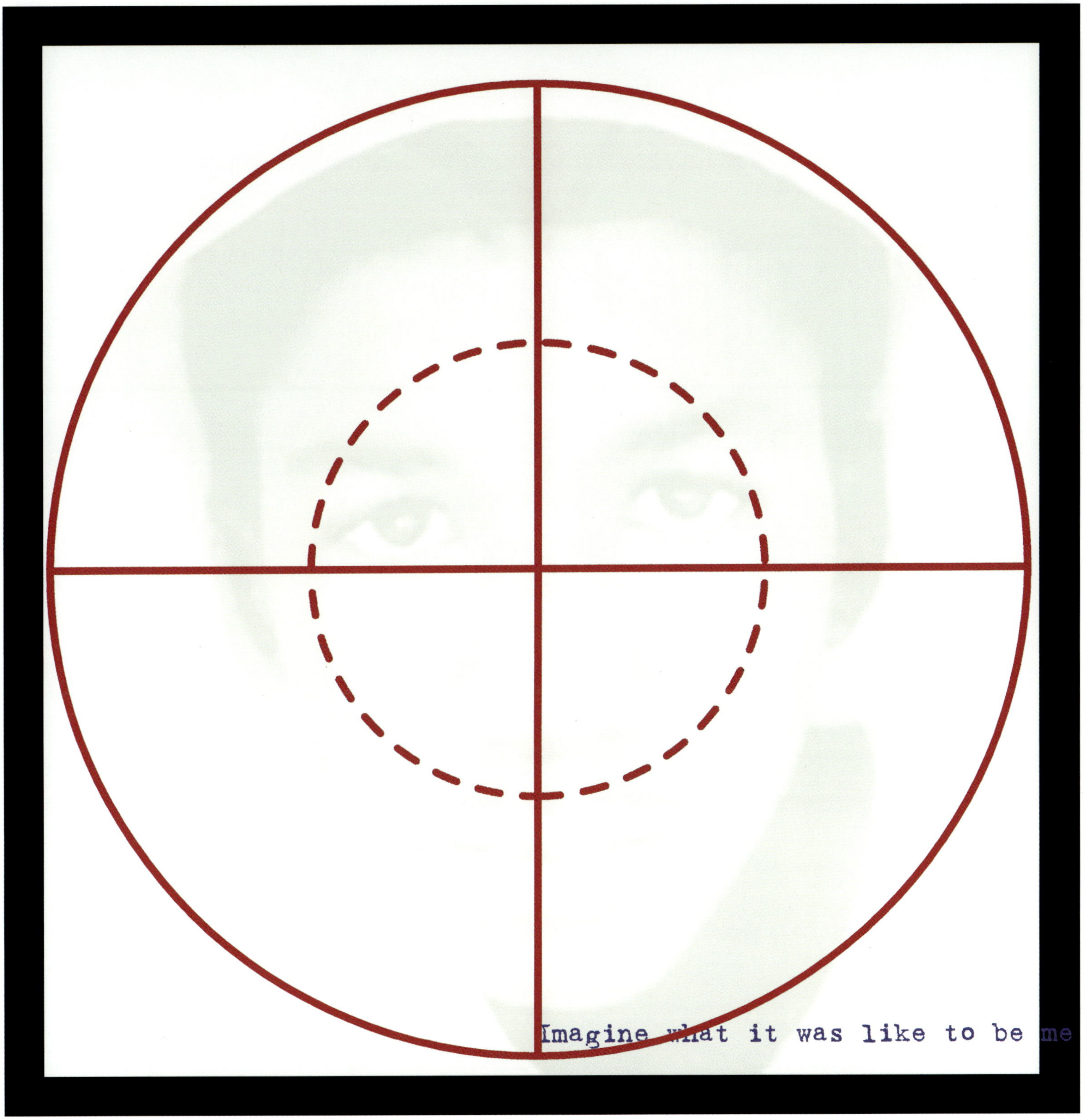

Imagine [Trayvon Martin]. 2013
Photolithograph
10⁷⁄₁₆ × 10¾ in. (26.5 × 27.3 cm)
Collection Adrian Piper Research Archive Foundation Berlin

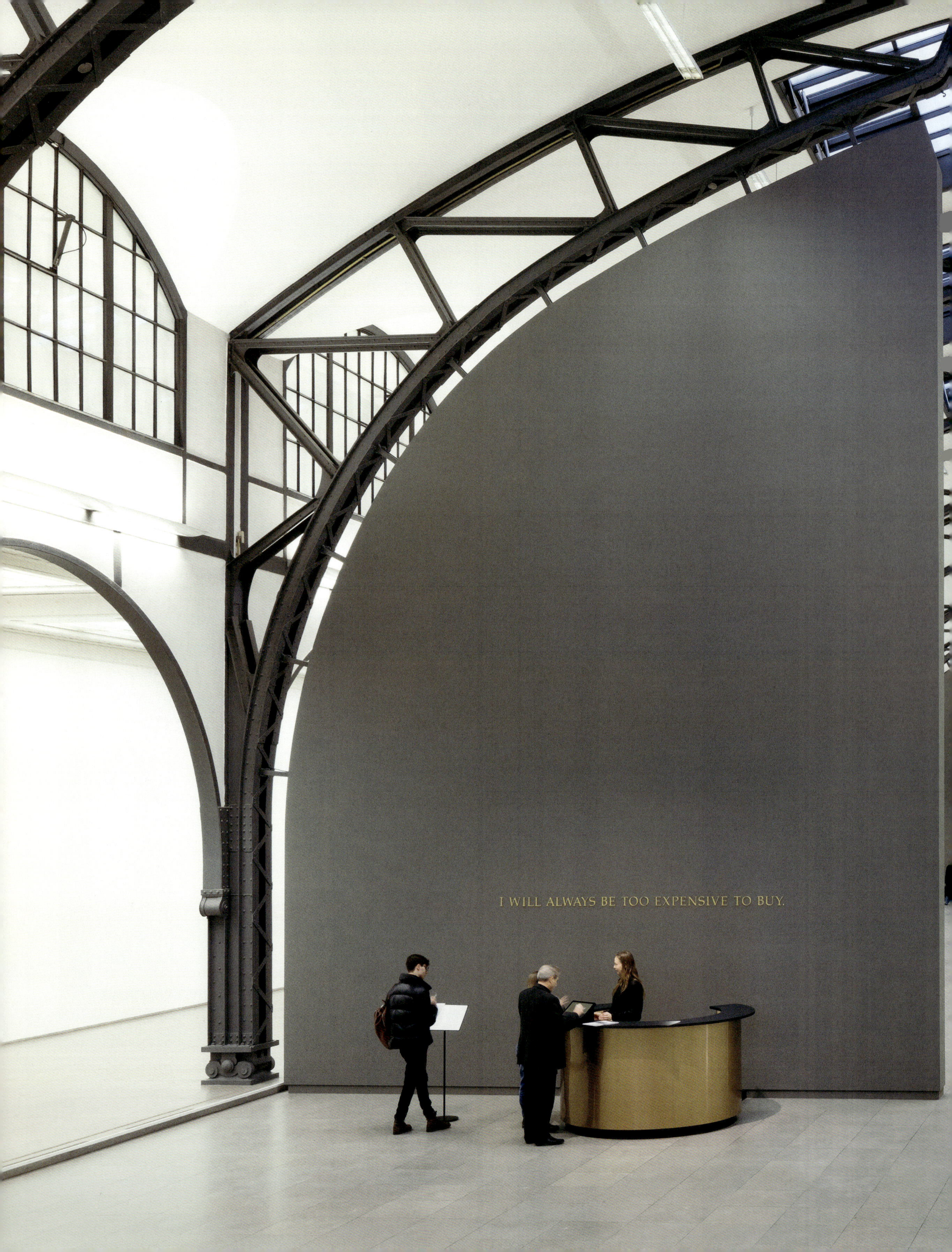
I WILL ALWAYS BE TOO EXPENSIVE TO BUY.

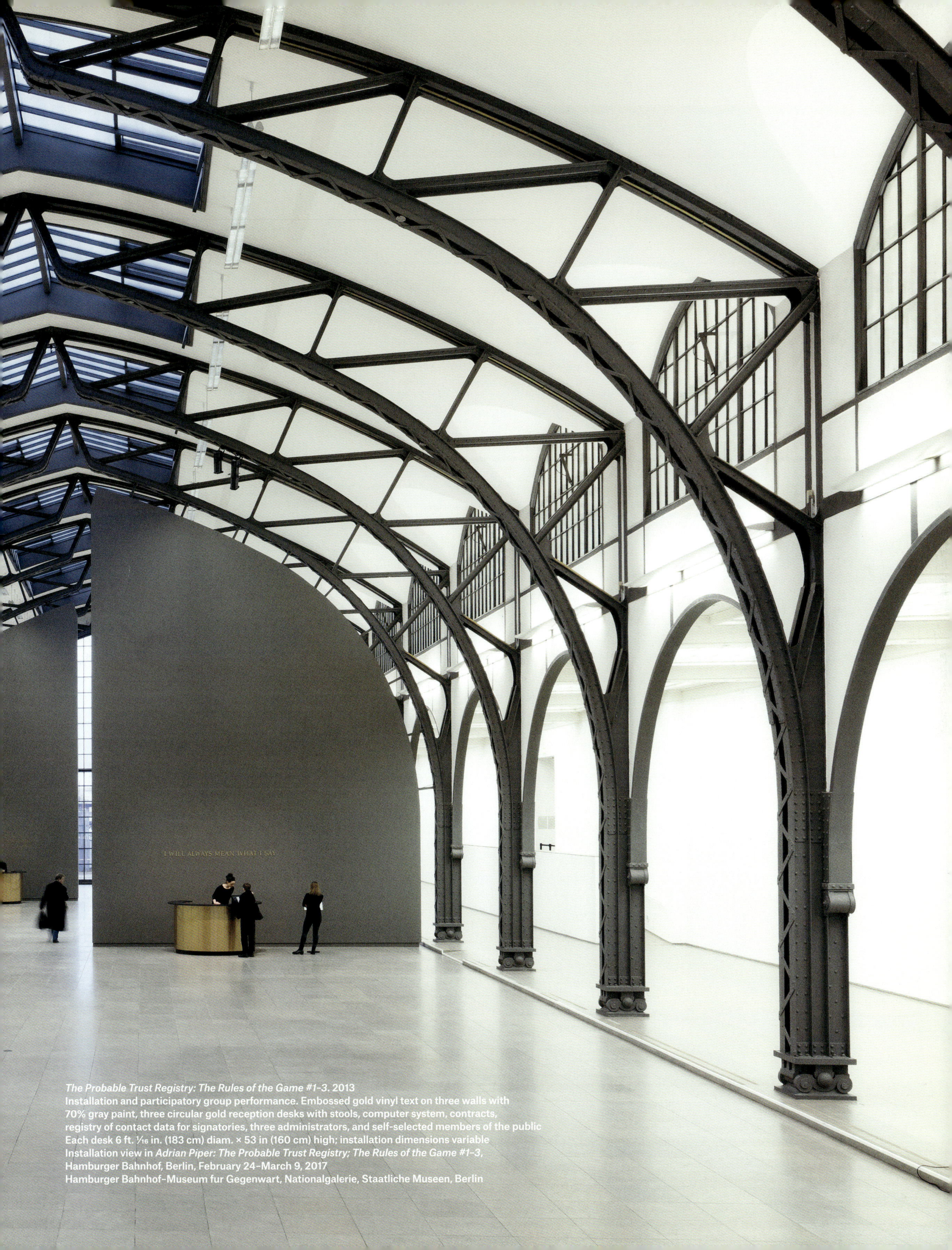

The Probable Trust Registry: The Rules of the Game #1–3. 2013
Installation and participatory group performance. Embossed gold vinyl text on three walls with 70% gray paint, three circular gold reception desks with stools, computer system, contracts, registry of contact data for signatories, three administrators, and self-selected members of the public
Each desk 6 ft. 1⁄16 in. (183 cm) diam. × 53 in (160 cm) high; installation dimensions variable
Installation view in *Adrian Piper: The Probable Trust Registry; The Rules of the Game #1–3*, Hamburger Bahnhof, Berlin, February 24–March 9, 2017
Hamburger Bahnhof–Museum fur Gegenwart, Nationalgalerie, Staatliche Museen, Berlin

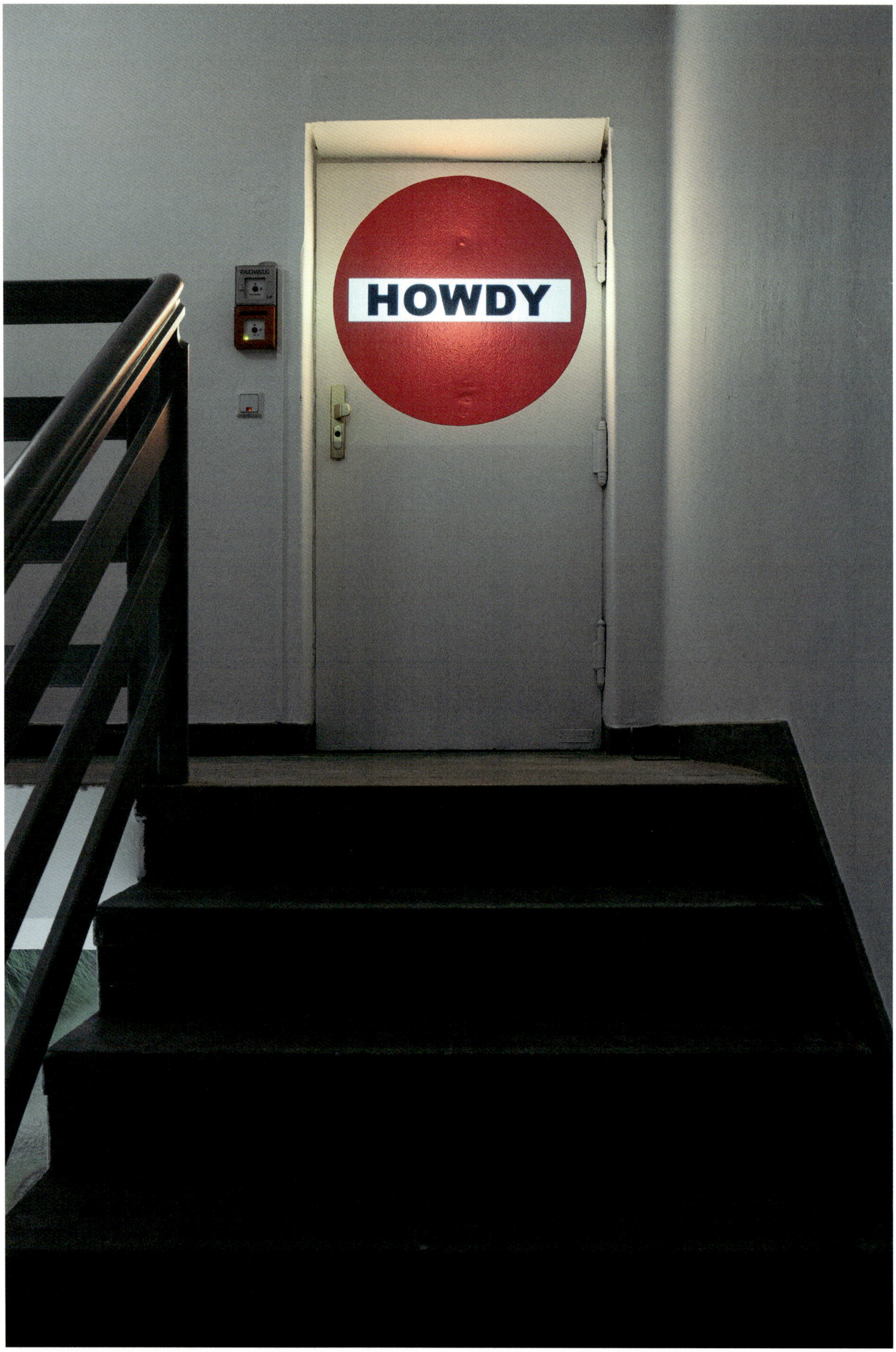

Howdy #6 [Second Series]. 2015
Ceiling-mounted light projection, closed and locked door, and darkened hallway
Projection 36 × 36 in. (91.4 × 91.4 cm)
Installation view in *The Present in Drag*, 9th Berlin Biennale, June 4–September 18, 2016
Collection Adrian Piper Research Archive Foundation Berlin

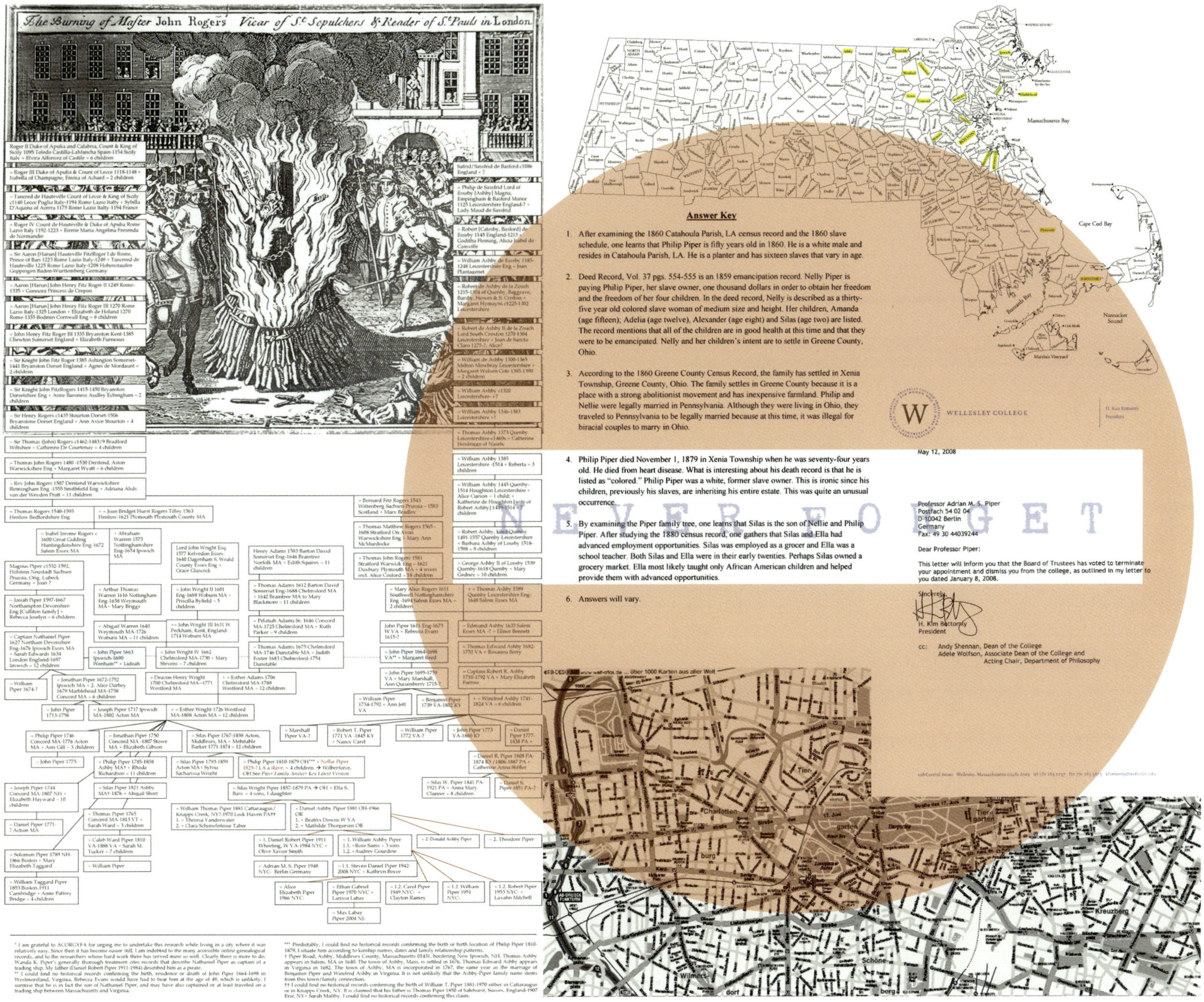

Never Forget. 2016
Wall print
31 × 33 in. (78.7 × 83.8 cm)
Collection Adrian Piper Research Archive Foundation Berlin

PERSONAL CHRONOLOGY

ADRIAN PIPER

1948

Adrian Margaret Smith Piper born September 20 in Washington Heights, only child of Daniel Robert Piper and Olive Xavier Smith Piper.

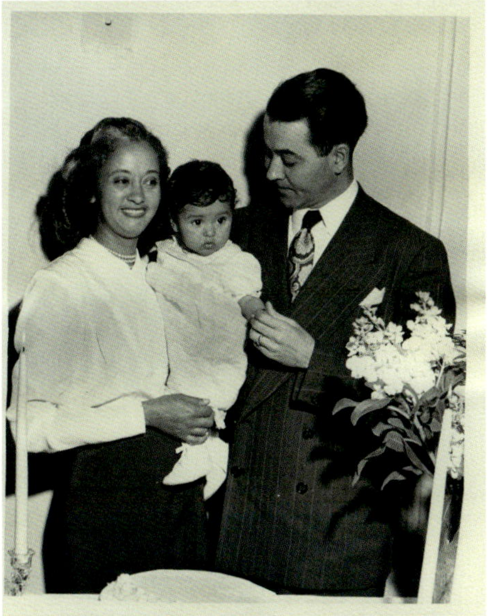

Olive Xavier Smith Piper, Adrian Margaret Smith Piper, and Daniel Robert Piper at Adrian's christening, 1949

1951

Maternal grandmother Margaret Ann Norris Smith, a former high school teacher, who lives with family, teaches Piper to draw.

1952

Piper enters Riverside Church Nursery and Sunday School. Hears Nikolai Rimsky-Korsakov's *Scheherazade*.

1953

Piper writes and illustrates own stories. Spends summer at Camp Good News, on Cape Cod, Massachusetts.

1954

Piper enters first grade at New Lincoln School, in Manhattan, on a scholarship. Spends summer (and every summer thereafter through 1962) at Camp Bass Lake Farm, in Altmar, New York. Learns to swim. Takes violin lessons.

1955

Piper sees first film: *The Court Jester*, with Danny Kaye.

1956

Piper begins ballet and piano lessons, takes tennis lessons from father. Reads Rudyard Kipling's *Jungle Book*s, Herman Wouk's *Marjorie Morningstar*, complete Mary Poppins series (repeatedly), Albert Payson Terhune's *Lad* series. Watches *Lassie*, *The Sandy Becker Show*, *Perry Mason*, *The Perry Como Show* on television. Discovers *MAD Magazine*.

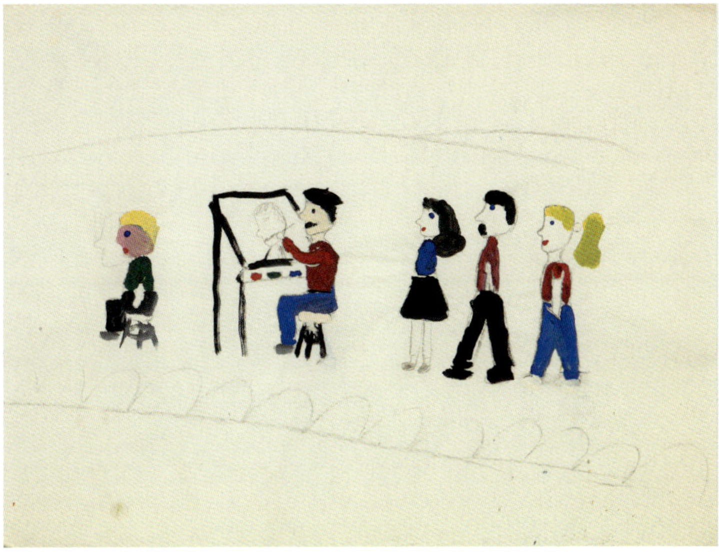

Adrian Piper
***Portrait Artist with Customers*. 1956**

1957

Piper takes art classes at The Museum of Modern Art (MoMA) after school. Reads Lewis Carroll, becomes *Alice in Wonderland* (through 1979). Listens to Igor Stravinsky's *Les Noces*. Fourth-grade teacher Mrs. Catherine Moore brings Piper up to speed in math.

1958

Piper's fifth-grade teacher, Miss Modiano, asks parents if Piper is aware that she is colored. Piper gets sick a lot. Listens to *The FBI in Peace and War*, *Suspense*, *Amos 'n' Andy*, *Burns and Allen*, *The Shadow*, *Our Gal Sunday*, *Ma Perkins*, *One Man's Family*, *Helen Trent* on radio. Sees *The Horror of Dracula* and wears garlic around neck for rest of summer. Gets pleuredema. Gives away superb comic book collection. Takes riding lessons at Van Cortlandt Park.

1959

Piper receives art lessons from paternal grandmother Beatrix Downs Piper McCleary, a former grammar school teacher. Discovers Booth Tarkington, Laura Ingalls Wilder. Piper sells her complete Nancy Drew series for a pittance. Gets *The Diary of Anne Frank* from parents for birthday. Gets a journal from parents for Christmas.

1960

Piper begins journals with the new year.

1961

Piper abandons piano lessons after paralyzing stage fright before planned participation in Town Hall recital. Sells superb collection of 45 rpm rock-music records, rediscovers Johann Sebastian Bach. Piper works as assistant arts-and-crafts counselor at Camp Bass Lake Farm (through 1962). Does india ink gouache illustrations of Hans Christian Andersen's "What the Moon Saw." Reads Charles Dickens, Mark Twain. Sees Arthur Miller's *The Misfits*. Ceases riding lessons and never gets on a horse again.

1962

Piper joins local high school Student Nonviolent Coordinating Committee (SNCC). Family moves from Washington Heights to Riverside Drive, leaving bachelor maternal uncle Martin Smith, who also lived with family, in Washington Heights apartment, where he becomes a recluse. Maternal grandmother Margaret Ann Norris Smith dies. Piper joins Puerto Rican gang. Teaches herself to play guitar. Bikes weekly to Greenwich Village for Sunday breakfast at Cafe Figaro. Participates in life-drawing groups at various locations in Manhattan. Listens to Johnny Pacheco, Charlie Palmieri, Celia Cruz. Sees Alain Resnais's *Last Year at Marienbad* for the first of many hundreds of times, Greta Garbo's complete oeuvre.

1963

Abandons ballet and modern-dance lessons. Takes jazz-dance lessons. Starts painting and drawing classes at the Art Students League after school and during summers and weekends. Starts part-time freelance fashion modeling (through 1965). Piper attends the March on Washington. Reads Ralph Ellison, Richard Wright, Franz Kafka. Listens to Bob Dylan, Joan Baez, Pete Seeger, and the Weavers.

1964

Hangs out at Steve Paul's The Scene; encounters Edie Sedgwick. Piper reads Sigmund Freud, Edmund Wilson, Herman Melville. Works through Russian phase (Leo Tolstoy, Nikolai Gogol, Anton Chekhov, Fyodor Dostoyevsky, all in Constance Garnett translations), German phase (Hermann Hesse, Thomas Mann, Heinrich Böll, Bertolt Brecht, Robert Musil, Günter Grass), French phase (Jean-Paul Sartre, Albert Camus, Honoré de Balzac, Émile Zola, Stendhal, Marcel Proust, Guy de Maupassant, André Gide, Théophile Gautier), Scandinavian phase (Pär Lagerkvist, Knut Hamsun, August Strindberg, Sigrid Undset, Ingmar Bergman, Victor Sjöström). Multiple viewings of Bergman trilogy (*Through a Glass Darkly*, *Winter Light*, *The Silence*).

1965

Piper reads Beat writers (Allen Ginsberg, Jack Kerouac, William S. Burroughs), discovers yoga, does psychedelic drawings and paintings, writes poetry. Reads Ginsberg's "Howl," takes LSD, leaves home, works as a discotheque dancer at Ginza and Entre Nous nightclubs, is picked up by police and sent to juvenile court, pleads guilty to being a wayward minor, is sent to Bellevue for observation. Resumes artwork, finishes high school course work, meets Phillip Zohn, resumes painting classes at the Art Students League. Reads the Upanishads, the Bhagavad-Gita. Sees Fritz Lang's *Metropolis*. Discovers Busby Berkeley.

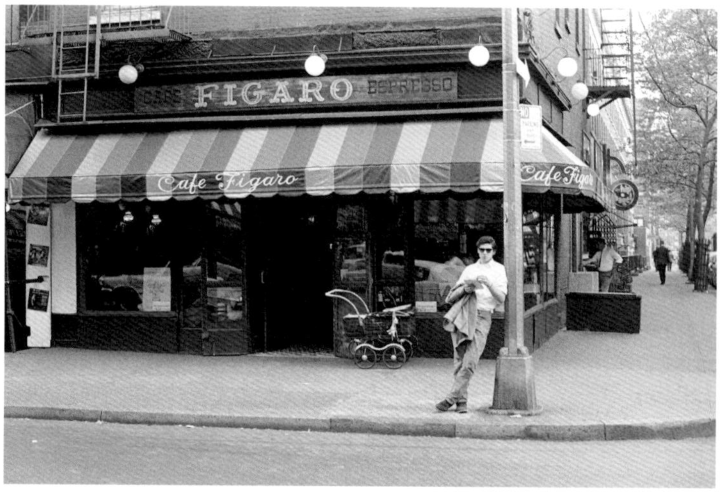

Café Figaro, on the corner of Macdougal and Bleecker Streets, Greenwich Village, New York, 1965

1966

Piper graduates from New Lincoln School. Enters School of Visual Arts (SVA). Studies yoga at Swami Satchidananda's Integral Yoga Institute on West End Avenue (through 1971). Goes to New York art galleries, subscribes to *Art News* and *Artforum*, attends films by Andy Warhol, the Kuchar brothers; Happenings by Robert Rauschenberg, Simone Forti Whitman, and Marcel Duchamp at SVA. Reads Johann Wolfgang von Goethe, Theodore Dreiser, Kenneth Patchen.

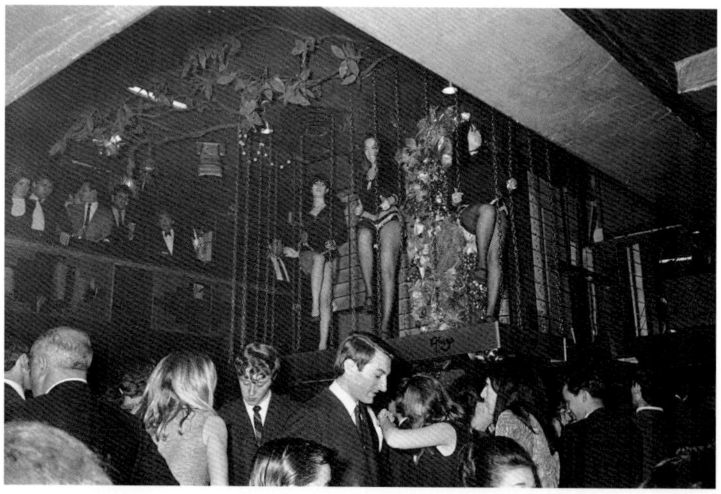

Dancers onstage at Ginza nightclub, New York, April 1, 1966

1967

Piper begins summer philosophy courses at the City College of New York (CCNY). Meets Rosemary Mayer and Vito Acconci. Stops attending classes at SVA. Reads Alain Robbe-Grillet, Samuel Beckett, Gertrude Stein, Jorge Luis Borges, Nathalie Sarraute, Raymond Queneau, Marguerite Duras, Michel Butor, Robert Pinget, Ludwig Wittgenstein; listens to Arnold Schoenberg, Anton Webern, Pierre Boulez, Karlheinz Stockhausen, John Cage, LaMonte Young, Terry Riley, Steve Reich. Attends Charles Ludlam's Ridiculous Theatrical Company production *Conquest of the Universe or When Queens Collide*. Sees Sol LeWitt's *46 Three-Part Variations on 3 Different Kinds of Cubes* at Dwan Gallery. Begins to carve up objects spatiotemporally into infinite series, progressions, and variations. Goes on Robert Bresson binge: *Balthazar*, *Mouchette*, *The Diary of a Country Priest*, *The Trial of Joan of Arc*, *Pickpocket*. Sees Delmer Daves's *Dark Passage*.

1968

Piper Meets LeWitt. Attends Yvonne Rainer's dance concert *The Mind Is a Muscle* three days in a row. Attends lectures by Borges at SVA and the 92nd Street Y. Awarded First Prize in Drawing and Honorable Mention in Sculpture at SVA Annual Student Exhibition. Sells sports magazines on the telephone. Moves to loft on Hester Street. Listens to Bach's orchestral works. Hospitalized with dysentery and colitis; becomes a lactovegetarian. Produces *Parallel Grid Proposal for Dugway Proving Grounds Headquarters* and *Concrete Space-Time-Infinity* pieces. Performs *Meat into Meat* in first incarnation as *Five Unrelated Time Pieces*. Meets Hans Haacke. Takes a crack at James Joyce, gives up. Attends multiple viewings of Danièle Huillet and Jean-Marie Straub's *The Chronicle of Anna Magdalena Bach*.

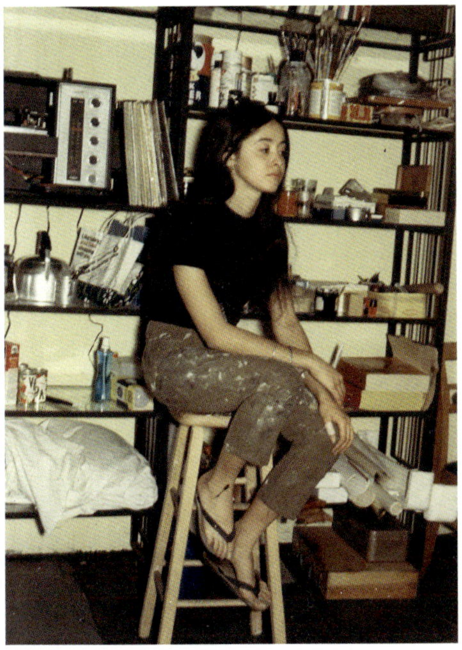

Adrian Piper in loft at East Twenty-sixth Street and Lexington Avenue, 1968

1969

Piper's Conceptual art works published in Acconci's magazine *0 TO 9*. Works as receptionist and administrative assistant in Seth Siegelaub's *January Show* gallery. *Three Untitled Projects* mail-art exhibition is published by 0 TO 9 Press. Shows conceptual work in group shows at Dwan, Paula Cooper Gallery, Städtisches Museum Leverkusen, Kunsthalle Bern, etc. Graduates from SVA with associate in arts degree in fine arts. Reads Immanuel Kant's *Critique of Pure Reason*. Models for Raphael Soyer (through 1971). Executes wall drawings for LeWitt. Types *Ad Reinhardt* manuscript for Lucy Lippard. Works as bookkeeper for Cameo Personnel Agency.

1970

Piper performs *Catalysis* works. Conducts a series of juice fasts. Begins CCNY full-time with plans to major in philosophy, musicology, physics, and history; eventually settles for a major in philosophy and minor in Medieval and Renaissance musicology. Clerk in CCNY music library (through 1971). Listens to Johannes Ockeghem. Exhibits *Context #7* in *Information*, at MoMA. Withdraws *Hypothesis* work from *Conceptual Art and Conceptual Aspects*, at New York Cultural Center, in protest against Richard Nixon's invasion of Cambodia and Kent State and Jackson State massacres. Joins Art Workers' Coalition. Attends open rehearsals held by Steve Reich and Philip Glass.

1971

Piper hears about cancellation of Haacke's Guggenheim show. Fasts, isolates self, does yoga while writing paper on Kant. Produces *Food for the Spirit* private loft performance. Starts women's consciousness-raising group with Mayer, Donna Dennis, Randa Haines, Grace Murphy, Jane Weiss, others. Works as receptionist, clerk, and switchboard operator at Animal Medical Center (through 1974). Reads Georges Simenon, listens to Giovanni Pierluigi da Palestrina.

1972

Piper starts Mythic Being/*Village Voice* performance series. Holds music-listening evenings for small group of philosophy classmates. Reads Henry James. Followed home from CCNY by Diotima the cat, who settles in.

1973

Piper researches and writes musicology thesis on Ockeghem's *Missa Prolationem* and philosophy honors thesis on deception and self-deception.

1974

Piper graduates from CCNY summa cum laude, Phi Beta Kappa, etc. Receives Frederick W. Sperling Award for Excellence in Philosophy. Awarded Phi Beta Kappa Medal for Best Honors Thesis in the Social Sciences. Awarded Danforth and Ford Foundation graduate fellowships. Moves to Cambridge, Massachusetts. Begins doctoral program in philosophy at Harvard University. Reads George Eliot, Jane Austen, listens to Claudio Monteverdi.

1975

Piper performs later Mythic Being streetworks in Cambridge and *Some Reflective Surfaces* at Whitney Museum. Produces Mythic Being posters. Listens to funk, Mario Davidowsky, Josquin des Prés. Reads Anthony Trollope.

1976

Piper completes course work at Harvard. Works as teaching assistant for John Rawls and Ronald Dworkin. Reads Richard Brautigan.

1977

Piper awarded Harvard Sheldon Traveling Fellowship to spend academic year in Berlin and Heidelberg working on Kant and Georg Wilhelm Friedrich Hegel. Passport and belongings stolen in the Musée d'Art moderne while constructing *Art for the Artworld Surface Pattern* for the Paris Biennale. In Heidelberg, participates in student resistance to Altstadt Studentenheim Sanierung; studies and writes all day, drinks beer all evening, goes dancing most of the night. Reads Peter Handke, Karl Philipp Moritz. Rediscovers 1960s and '70s rock, also Nina Hagen, Ian Dury.

1978

Piper returns to United States. Premieres *Aspects of the Liberal Dilemma* at Artists Space, in New York. First philosophy article published: "Utility, Publicity, and Manipulation." Listens to Crosby, Stills, Nash & Young, discovers *The Mary Tyler Moore Show.*

1979

Piper flies from Cambridge to Paris for four days to see *Paris-Moscow, 1900–1930* at Centre Pompidou. Awarded her first full Visual Artists' Fellowship by National Endowment for the Arts (NEA). Moves to Ann Arbor, Michigan, begins tenure-track assistant professorship in philosophy at the University of Michigan. Completes *Three Political Self-Portraits.*

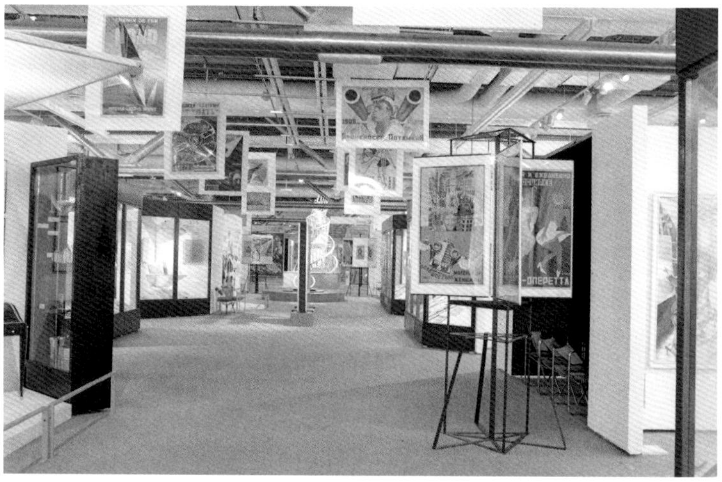

The exhibition *Paris-Moscow*, 1900–1930, Centre Georges Pompidou, Paris, May 31–November 5, 1979

1980

Piper premieres *Four Intruders Plus Alarm Systems* and *It's Just Art* in *Art of Conscience: The Last Decade* at Wright State University, Dayton. Listens to Patti Smith, The Police, Talking Heads.

1981

Piper completes doctoral dissertation, "A New Model of Rationality," with John Rawls. Buys house. Piper's maternal Uncle Martin dies. Piper gets really, really sick with "the yuppie disease" (an undiagnosed chronic fatigue syndrome–like illness). Performs *It's Just Art* at *AND/OR*, in Seattle, where a member of the audience asks Piper why she is up on stage shaking her booty. Hears Ornette Coleman perform live. Reads Russell Hoban's *Riddley Walker.* Sees Steve Martin's *Pennies from Heaven.*

1982

Piper awarded senior status NEA Visual Artists' Fellowship. Also awarded two-year Mellon Postdoctoral Fellowship to do research in philosophy at Stanford University. Gets married. Travels to Jamaica on honeymoon, meets mother's family in Kingston, Portland, and Port Antonio. Moves to Menlo Park, California. Begins work on manuscript of *Rationality and the Structure of the Self.* Listens to Charlie Barnett, Artie Shaw, Woody Herman, Steely Dan, Heinrich Schütz, Guillaume de Machaut.

1983

Piper premieres *Funk Lessons* at Nova Scotia College of Art and Design. Best friend Phillip Zohn dies of AIDS-related encephalitis. Piper begins design of poster *Think About It,* commemorating 1963 March on Washington. Reads Toni

Morrison. Goes dancing regularly and hears live funk bands from Oakland and Los Angeles at Orphan Annie's, in Foster City, California. Watches *Entertainment Tonight*. Sees *Brainstorm*, *The Hunger*.

1984

Piper visits William "Bootsy" Collins's manager, views Parliament-Funkadelic live-performance videotapes. Reluctantly returns to the University of Michigan. Reads Joyce Carol Oates. Listens to Dieterich Buxtehude. Sees *Taxi zum Klo*.

1985

Piper's father dies of cancer of the pharynx, shunned by his sister Beatrix Hamburg and her family during his illness and death. Piper swims daily; views every episode of *Dynasty* made up to that point. Denied tenure at the University of Michigan. Begins continuing self-collection piece *What Will Become of Me*. Premieres *A Tale of Avarice and Poverty* at New Museum of Contemporary Art, New York.

1986

Piper's philosophy article "Two Conceptions of the Self" voted one of the ten best papers of 1985 by editors of *Philosophical Studies*. Prepares *My Calling (Card) #1* and *#2*. Begins *Vanilla Nightmares* drawings on newspaper. Reads Anita Brookner. Moves to Washington, D.C. Separates from husband. Begins permanent position at Georgetown University Philosophy Department. Listens to Bach cantatas.

1987

Piper celebrates Diotima the cat's fifteenth birthday and year with Piper. Attends inaugural meeting of Women of African Descent in the Visual Arts (WADVA). Gets divorce. Starts teaching Nietzsche in introductory ethics course. Completes *Think About It*. At Jane Farver's request, writes up first installment of Personal Chronology for catalogue of twenty-year retrospective, *Adrian Piper: Reflections, 1967–1987*, which opens at The Alternative Museum, New York, and travels around the country (through 1991). Meets members of a "white" branch of the Piper family at opening of retrospective in Atlanta. Awarded National Endowment of the Humanities (NEH) Summer Stipend to complete Kant chapter of *Rationality and the Structure of the Self*.

1988

Piper joins stable of John Weber Gallery. Completes video installations *Cornered* and *The Big Four-Oh*. Injures knees, rereads journals. Accepts tenured associate professorship in philosophy at the University of California at San Diego. Awarded Woodrow Wilson International Center for Scholars Fellowship in Washington, D.C., to work on *Rationality and the Structure of the Self*.

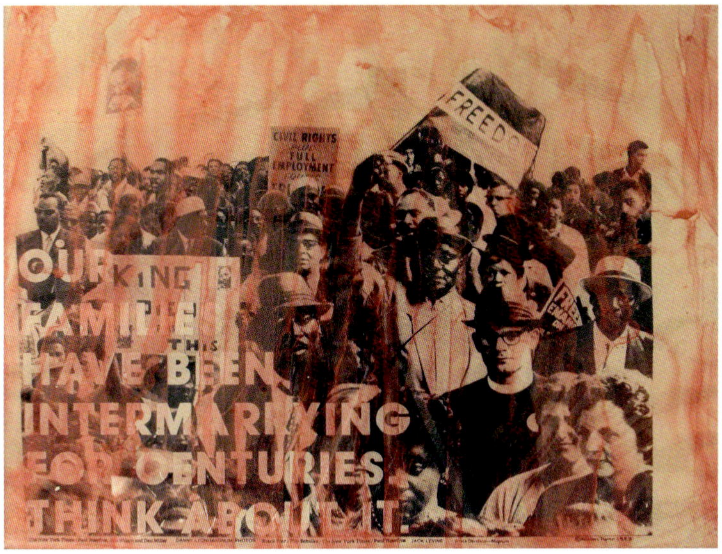

Adrian Piper
Think About It. 1987
Mock-up for billboard design

1989

Piper awarded Guggenheim Fellowship in Fine Arts. Produces Ur-Mutter series. Premieres *Cornered* at John Weber.

1990

Diotima the cat dies of brain hemorrhage. Piper produces Pretend series. Accepts tenured full professorship in philosophy at Wellesley College and moves from Washington, D.C., to Wellesley, Massachusetts. Publishes "Higher-Order Discrimination." Piper's 1975 performance *Some Reflective Surfaces* appears on cover of *Art in America*. Exhibits new work at John Weber, Exit Art, and Whitney Museum Film and Video Gallery. Awarded grant from Awards in the Visual Arts Program. Dubbed the artist of the fall season in New York by Michael Brenson in the *New York Times*. *Rationality and the Structure of the Self* becomes two books.

1991

Piper publishes "Impartiality, Compassion, and Modal Imagination," in *Ethics*. Exhibits *What It's Like, What It Is #1* at Washington Project for the Arts; *What It's Like, What It Is #2* at the Hirshhorn Museum and Sculpture Garden; and *What It's Like, What It Is #3* at MoMA. Twenty-year retrospective travels in England and Germany. Art-world rehabilitation continues. Publishes "Passing for White, Passing for Black." Collapses twice from physical exhaustion, ends spring semester on medical leave. Curtails speaking and writing commitments.

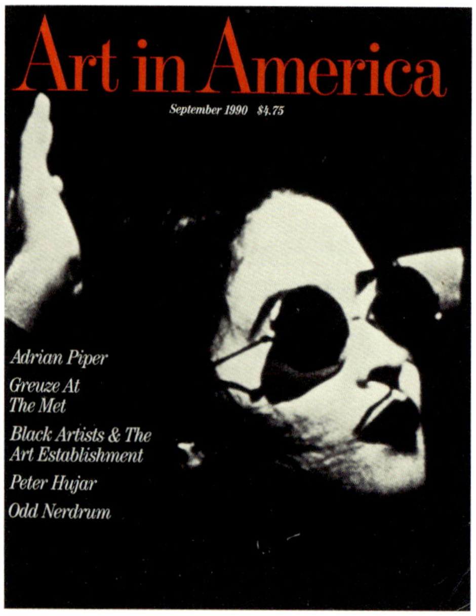

Some Reflective Surfaces **(1975), on the cover of *Art in America*, September 1990**

1992

Piper produces Decide Who You Are series for exhibition at John Weber, Paula Cooper, and New York University's Grey Art Gallery. Delivers philosophy paper "Xenophobia and Kantian Rationalism" and art lecture "Xenophobia and the Indexical Present" at daylong NYU conference "What Does the *Critique of Pure Reason* Have to Do with the Pure Critique of Racism? A Look at the Work of Adrian Piper." Withdraws from Documenta. Collapses from physical exhaustion at end of spring and fall semesters. Wins Wellesley College Faculty Vacation Prize, spends it at Kripalu Yoga Center. Publishes "Two Kinds of Discrimination," in *Yale Journal of Criticism. Rationality and the Structure of the Self* becomes three books. Listens to Hildegard von Bingen. Discovers *Star Trek*, *Star Trek*: *The Next Generation*, and *Star Trek: Deep Space Nine.*

1993

Piper exhibits Hypothesis series at Paula Cooper. Moves to Cape Cod to take care of mother during her terminal decline from emphysema, while continuing to teach at Wellesley and lecture on art and philosophy. Collapses from physical exhaustion at end of spring and fall semesters. Further curtails speaking engagements.

1994

Piper collapses from physical exhaustion at end of spring and fall semesters. Mother dies from emphysema.

1995

Piper conducts two-week residency at the Kunstakademie München entirely in German. Begins two-year process of managing mother's estate. Discovers mother's journals. Collapses from physical exhaustion, ends spring semester on medical leave. Awarded Skowhegan Medal for Sculpture/Installation. Withdraws early Conceptual work from *1965–1975: Reconsidering the Object of Art*, at Museum of Contemporary Art, Los Angeles (MOCA), upon discovering Philip Morris sponsorship. *Ashes to Ashes* produced, offered as a substitute to and declined by MOCA. Begins teaching the Upanishads in introductory ethics course. Collapses from physical exhaustion at end of fall semester. Starts studying Iyengar yoga with Arthur Kilmurray.

1996

Piper collapses from physical exhaustion at end of spring and fall semesters. Delivers Inaugural Ian Burn Memorial Lecture at Monash University, Melbourne, and Museum of Contemporary Art, Sydney. Exhibits *Ashes to Ashes* at John Weber. *Out of Order, Out of Sight*, vol. 1, *Selected Writings in Meta-Art, 1968–1992*, and vol. 2, *Selected Writings in Art Criticism, 1967–1992*, published by MIT Press. Reads "the Johns" (Barth, Cheever, Updike) and *Faust* by Mann, Goethe, and Christopher Marlowe. Listens to The Anonymous Four a capella group.

1997

Piper publishes "Kant on the Objectivity of the Moral Law." Diagnosed with ankylosing spondylitis. Intensifies yoga practice to three-plus hours daily, becomes a vegan. Doesn't collapse from physical exhaustion at end of spring semester. Leaves John Weber to go solo while continuing nonexclusive relationship with Paula Cooper. Exhibits at Galleria Emi Fontana, Milan, and Thomas Erben Gallery, New York. Reads John Banville. Discovers Gavin Bryars, Stefan Wolpe, Discantus. Receives NEH Research Fellowship. Elected Distinguished Scholar at the Getty Research Institute. Celebrates forty-ninth birthday at Richard Freeman's Ashtanga yoga workshop. Embarks on two-year sabbatical from Wellesley and postpones production of new artwork to finish all three volumes of *Rationality and the Structure of the Self.* Spends last seven months of 1997 disposing of paperwork backlog from 1993.

1998

Piper takes first trip to India for "Frameworks for Art" conference, Mohile Parikh Centre for the Visual Arts, Mumbai; delivers talk "What the Indexical Present Really Is." Discovers M. S. Subbulakshmi, Pandit Jasraj, L. Subramaniam. *Who Are You? Selected Works by Adrian Piper* opens at Davis Museum of Wellesley College. Continues disposition of Wellesley committee paperwork backlog. Writes "Racism at Wellesley: Causes and Containment" for circulation exclusively within college community, where it receives sponsorship from all faculty antiracism committees. Ginger the cat chooses Cape Cod house inherited from Piper's mother as birthing place for kittens. Piper decides to move permanently to Cape Cod and keep surviving kittens Kali and Clive. Takes Don Peccerill's advanced Iyengar class. Under duress, becomes own contractor on large studio/library/art-storage addition to house. Under duress, spends summer learning the construction industry (land surveys, deeds, permits, plans, stock lists, demolition, backfilling, excavation, foundations, forms, footing, floors, insulation, framing, roofing, siding, heating, plumbing, sheetrocking, plastering, painting, electrical wiring, landscaping, etc.). Moves to Los Angeles for Getty scholarship residency. At Getty, embarks on rewriting ten- to fifteen-year-old "completed" portions of first volume of *Rationality and the Structure of the Self*. Presents new material from first volume: "The Problem of Moral Motivation" and "The Enterprise of Socratic Metaethics." Attends *Yoga Journal* conference, takes workshops with Richard Freeman, David Swenson, Patricia Walden, David Life, Erich Schiffmann, John Friend. Makes serious commitment to Ashtanga yoga; studies with Chuck Miller at Yoga Works. Attends *kirtan*, joins Yoga Works' Yoga Sutras study group, attends weekly lectures at the Vedanta Society. Breaks the bank at the Vedanta Bookstore. Creates new course for Wellesley, "Vedanta Ethics and Epistemology." Takes first baby steps into Sanskrit. *Rationality and the Structure of the Self* morphs back into two books plus *Kant's Metaethics*.

1999

Piper almost finishes rewriting first volume of *Rationality and the Structure of the Self*. Presents new material from *Kant's Metaethics*: "Kant's Two Standpoints on Action." Learns Gayatri mantra, Maha Mrtunjaya mantra, Ashtanga mantra invocation, Saraswati Ma bhajan. Shows Mythic Being series at Thomas Erben. Writes "The Meaning of Brahmacharya." Studies Ashtanga yoga with Tim Miller. Begins second series. Injures quadratus lumborum. Attends Paul Cabanis's advanced Iyengar class once a week, workshops with Freeman, Schiffmann, Gary Kraftsow, Patricia Walden. Applies for Person of Indian Origin expatriate card citing Hindu maternal great-grandmother. Joins two more Yoga Sutras study groups hosted by Christopher Chapple and Cabanis, respectively. Creates new seminar for Wellesley, "The Philosophy of Yoga." *MEDI(t)ATIONS* retrospective of time-based medium work opens at Museum of Contemporary Art, Chicago. Returns to full-time teaching at Wellesley, becomes faculty chair of Wellesley's Black Task Force, teaches new Guyer/Wood translation of Kant's *Critique of Pure Reason*. Attends Walden's Level IV and Aspiring Teachers classes. *Adrian Piper: A Retrospective, 1965–2000* opens at Fine Arts Gallery, University of Maryland, Baltimore.

2000

Piper teaches "Vedanta Ethics and Epistemology" course for first time. Secures permanent existence of Wellesley's Black Task Force through college legislation. Attends Internationalen Kant-Kongress in Berlin and International Conference on Science and Consciousness in New Mexico. Sends "Personal Report: Fall 1990–Spring 2000" to Wellesley president, who refuses to discuss it. Home burglarized twice in two weeks. Spends summer doing paperwork and fighting with security-alarm company. Sues Wellesley College for fraud, breach of contract, loss of reputation, discrimination, harassment, and retaliation. Rushed to hospital with ruptured appendicitis one week after warning department chair of impending physical collapse. Undergoes emergency appendectomy. Develops peritonitis, intestinal adhesions. Undergoes lysis of adhesions. Released from hospital after one month. House vandalized. Goes on medical leave for rest of fall semester. Completes *The Color Wheel Series, First Adhyasa: Annomayakosha #2–24* in time for exhibition at Paula Cooper. Concurrently exhibits related works at Thomas Erben and both retrospectives conjointly at New Museum of Contemporary Art. Gradually resumes yoga practice with a few elementary asanas. Completes design for *Prayer Wheel*. Begins preparing to leave United States in wake of "election" of George W. Bush to U.S. presidency.

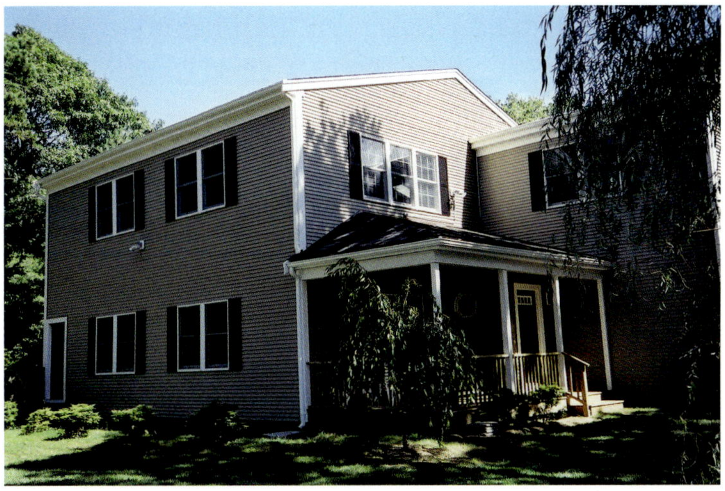

Adrian Piper's home on Cape Cod, 2000

2001

Piper begins working with yoga therapist. Pace of recuperation retarded and complicated by postoperative intensification of ankylosing spondylitis symptoms. Medical leave extended through spring 2002 semester. Completes *Prayer Wheel I.1* for The Andy Warhol Museum, Pittsburgh. Slowly resumes redrafting of *Rationality and the Structure of the Self*. Revises "The Concept of a Genuine Preference" from second volume, begins revisions to "The Utility Maximizing Model of Rationality" from first volume. Completes *Das Gebetsrad Quadriert: Ein Radiostück* for Documenta 11, and *Color Wheel Series* page project for *Art Journal*. The College cuts off health and dental insurance retroactive to July 1, 2001, then reinstates it; supplies false information to MetLife, resulting in denial of disability benefits. American Association of University Professors (AAUP) refuses to investigate. Boston Association of Black Journalists informs Piper of decision not to report on lawsuit. Piper tries and fails to establish Adrian Piper Research Archive (APRA) in will.

2002

The College again cuts off health and dental benefits and again reinstates them. Piper reads Joe R. Feagin's *Racist America: Roots, Current Realities, and Future Reparations*. Delivers "Recognition and Responsibility" to Boston University Institute on Race and Social Division. Reads Ben H. Bagdikian's *The Media Monopoly*. Produces and mails postal artwork *PRESS BLACK-OUT*. Expands "Recognition and Responsibility" into a book manuscript. Piper's long-term disability benefits appeal denied. Piper produces soundwork *Shiva DANCES, for God's Sake*. College's Black Task Force votes to refuse comment for Vanessa Jones's "Fallen Star" article published in *Boston Globe*. Piper's traveling European retrospective, *Adrian Piper since 1965*, opens at Generali Foundation, Vienna. Lawsuit against Wellesley College dismissed on statute of limitations technicalities. Fourteen prints from *The Color Wheel Series, First Adhyasa: Annomayakosha* exhibited at Documenta 11. Social Security disability benefits appeal denied. Liver biopsy reveals "significant liver damage, scarring, and chronic inflammation of unknown origin." Succeeds in establishing APRA. Piper shoots *You/Stop/Watch* video for installation. Sues Wellesley College a second time through Massachusetts Commission against Discrimination (MCAD) for retaliation against first lawsuit. Delivers "Documente aus den Staaten" at Museum Ludwig, Cologne. Finishes two of four volumes of *Rationality and the Structure of the Self.* The College reduces salary by twenty-five percent due to medical limitations on teaching. AAUP again refuses to investigate.

2003

Piper notifies Wellesley of receipt of Internationales Forschungszentrum Kulturwissenschaften (IFK) Fellowship. The College cancels spring semester metaethics course seventeen days before registration. Piper is forced to decline IFK invitation on medical grounds due to The College's refusal to pay benefits during fellowship period; Piper amends MCAD lawsuit to include additional charges. Finishes third volume of *Rationality and the Structure of the Self.* Condenses three volumes into two and spins off fourth volume into separate project, *Kant's Metaethics*. Delivers *Funk Lessons Lessons* at Art Institute of Chicago; "Now What? Passing beyond Passing" at University of Illinois, Urbana/Champaign; "Talking Pictures" at Museu d'Art Contemporani Barcelona (MACBA); and "*Vergangenheitsverarbeitung* and the Pursuit of Happiness: Regarding the Other in Germany and the U.S." at Einstein-Forum, Berlin. Retrospective *Adrian Piper since 1965* opens at MACBA. Piper preemptively withdraws "Vedanta Ethics and Epistemology" course, creates and publicizes midlevel "Philosophy of Yoga" course for Wellesley's spring 2004 semester.

2004

Piper teaches "Philosophy of Yoga" course. Blocks Philosophy Department's second attempt to cancel annual Kant seminar. Finishes *The Color Wheel Series* with video, *Shiva Dances with the Art Institute of Chicago*. Dean of The College discontinues medical disability accommodations against doctors' warnings, effective spring 2005. House vandalized. Piper begins purchase of apartment building in Berlin-Mitte. Philosophy Department accidentally drops description of new Rawls and Jürgen Habermas course, repeatedly, from 2005 course catalogue. Piper's second liver biopsy reveals persisting cryptogenic portal stage 2 fibrosis. Piper discovers Bhangra hip-hop. Shunned by Philosophy Department junior colleague; department and Committee on Faculty Appointments decline to reprimand her. Piper teaches "Kant's Metaethics" seminar. Summarily relieved of committee responsibilities and involvement in promotion and hiring decisions by Philosophy Department. Develops chronic pleurisy. Again amends MCAD lawsuit to include additional charges. Attends London and Berlin premieres of *Shiva Dances with the Art Institute of Chicago* and gives talks: "Political Art and the Paradigm of Innovation," at Tate Modern and Humboldt University's art history department, and "Passing Beyond Passing," at Haus der Kulturen der Welt, Berlin. At urging of European friends sees Lars von Trier's *Dogville*; gets it. Invited to accept Research Fellowship at Wissenschaftskolleg zu Berlin/Institute for Advanced Study for academic year 2005–06. Produces and gives talk on soundwork *Construct Madrid* at Residencia de Estudiantes, Madrid, for citywide 2005 exhibition *Itinerarios del sonido*. Attends second opening of group show *Funky Lessons*, BAWAG P.S.K. Contemporary Vienna.

2005

Piper ensures ability to continue teaching without disability accommodations by correctly forecasting and scheduling periodic physical collapses into spring 2005 syllabus, totaling a month of absence from classes (out of a three-month long semester). Nevertheless falls asleep at wheel on highway twice, has minor accident once, narrowly avoids major accident once. Repeatedly gets flat tires on return leg of Wellesley–Cape Cod commute. Refuses Dean of The College's pressure to forfeit fall 2006 paid sabbatical. The College rejects application for paid sabbatical for fall 2005–spring 2006, rejects appeal, rejects Wissenschaftskolleg's offer of junior faculty teaching compensation, attempts to force application for unpaid leave of absence. Piper refuses to apply for unpaid leave of absence. Files internal formal grievance against College President and Dean for multiple violations of Wellesley's bylaws and impairments of college's interests. President and Dean both refuse to respond. Grievance Committee forbids speaking directly to its members, denies request for hearing, denies request to question President and Dean, denies request that President be recused as final court of appeal, denies request for additional time to submit evidence, dismisses grievance. AAUP again refuses to investigate. Scholars at Risk refuses to investigate. Philosophy colleague warns Piper not even to approach relevant APA committees. Piper again amends MCAD lawsuit to include additional charges. Piper regretfully declines invitation fellowship at Wissenschaftskolleg. Spends four-day retreat at Sarada Convent, in Hollywood Hills. College requests conflict resolution. Piper proposes resolution. Sells house on Cape Cod. Sells car. Sells personal effects.

Piper moves to East Berlin apartment with Ginger and Kali. Piper becomes first (and, as of this date, only known) recipient of German residency permit under new Ausländerrecht (Foreigners law) Par. 71.3. AufenthG: Ausnahmefälle (Exceptional cases). Chronic pleurisy disappears. Ankylosing spondylitis symptoms disappear. Liver fibrosis disappears. The College rejects conflict-resolution proposal, refuses to propose alternative. Piper rejects Wellesley's offer of "impartial" mediation in which both her lawyer and the mediator are paid by The College. Dean of The College cancels salary, health insurance, dental insurance, and pension contributions in second week of fall semester. Piper begins final revisions of *Rationality and the Structure of the Self.* Completes purchase of apartment building in Berlin-Mitte. Begins visiting professorship at Danish Royal Academy of Art's School of Walls and Space.

2006

Dean of The College threatens to deduct health insurance premiums from future salary payments. President of The College resigns effective June 2007. The College's Affirmative Action Officer resigns effective June 2006. Philosophy Department goes into administrative receivership under supervision of Associate Dean of The College. Dean of The College charges $9,000 worth of health insurance premiums retroactively to July 2005, demands immediate payment. Piper finishes *Rationality and the Structure of the Self.* Finishes *Unite.* Begins final revisions on *Kant's Metaethics: First Critique Foundations of His Theory of Action.* Reads Adolf Hitler's *Mein Kampf.* Reads Muhammad Yunus's *Banker to the Poor.* Attends sixth Gesellschaft für analytische Philosophie at Freie Universität Berlin. Notifies MCAD of decision not to return to continuing hostile environment at Wellesley. MCAD "resends" notification of September 2005 dismissal of charges. Requests Substantial Weight Review of case by U.S. Employment Equal Opportunity Commission (EEOC). Delivers keynote address "Criticizing the Critics" at Frieze Art Fair, London. On U.S. lecture tour, delivers "Passing Beyond Passing," "The Ideal of Agent Integrity," and "Why Shiva Dances," in Austin, Santa Fe, Minneapolis, and Bloomington, discovers name on U.S. Transportation Security Administration's Suspicious Travelers Watch List. Returns to Berlin, notifies Wellesley College of Watch List and requests indefinite leave of absence. The College denies request, threatens termination of employment as tenured full professor.

2007

EEOC upholds MCAD's dismissal of charges. Piper goes on retreat at Ramakrishna Mission, Belur Math, India, tours Kolkata, West Bengal, and Orissa with Royal Danish Academy of Art students. Medical tests confirm regenerated liver, remission of AS symptoms. Piper performs *Adrian Moves to Berlin* at Berlin Alexanderplatz. Sol LeWitt dies. Delivers Marie Jahoda Guest Professorship Lectures "Das Ideal der Integrität des Akteurs" and "Dokumente aus den Staaten" at Ruhr-Universität Bochum. Does video interview with Lynn Lukkas for *Telling Time Projects.* Executes wall drawing *Hi Sol* for *Irrational Thoughts*, a tribute exhibition to Sol LeWitt at Cairn Gallery, Pittenweem, Fife, Scotland. The College offers Piper choice of either taking early retirement and "releasing and discharging Wellesley College and all those connected with it from any and all rights and claims that [she] may have had in the past, now have or might now have as of this date in connection with [her] employment at the College," or else being fired from tenured full professorship. Piper refuses to return to U.S. while on Suspicious Travelers Watch List, refuses early retirement offer, refuses to resign position. AAUP again refuses to investigate. Piper finds *The Barbie Doll Drawings* (1967) in archive. Finishes *The Spurious Life-Death Distinction.* Obtains German private health and long-term care insurance. Delivers keynote address "'On Wearing Three Hats' ein Jahrzehnt später" at Neue Gesellschaft für bildende Kunst, Berlin, in symposium "Multitasking: Synchronität als kulturelle Praxis." Posts time-based medium clips on website.

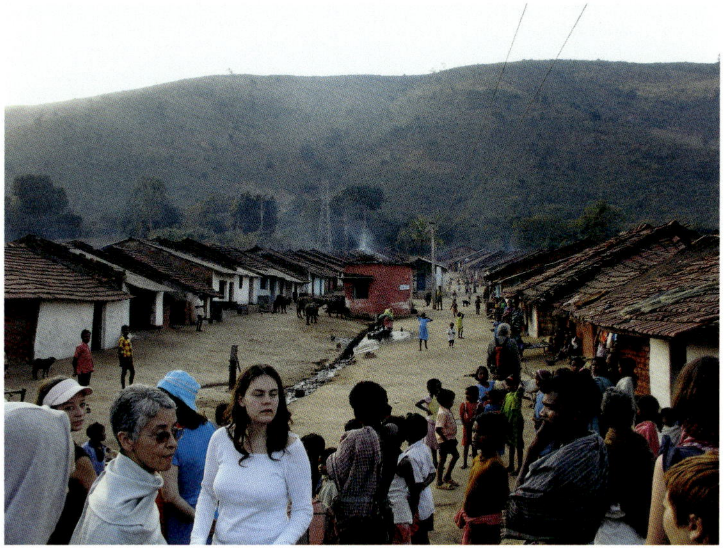

Piper touring West Bengal and Orissa, India, with students from the Royal Danish Academy of Art, 2007

2008

The College's new president recommends termination of Piper's tenured full professorship to board of trustees. Piper opens solo exhibition *Everything* at Elizabeth Dee Gallery, New York, in absentia. Scans close to one thousand family photos from family archive. Cambridge University Press formally accepts both *Rationality and the Structure of the Self*, vol. 1, *The Humean Conception* and also *Rationality and the Structure of the Self*, vol. 2, *A Kantian Conception* for publication. Piper goes on several retreats at Vedanta-Gesellschaft, Bindeweide. The College's board of trustees terminates Piper's tenured full professorship in philosophy. AAUP again refuses to investigate. Cambridge University Press reneges on written agreement to demand no further cuts to *Rationality and the Structure of the Self.* Piper refuses to sign contract and instead publishes both volumes gratis at APRA website. The North

American Kant Society quarterly newsletter announces both volumes of the project in its online publication. Piper advertises it in *Proceedings of the American Philosophical Association, The Journal of Philosophy, Philosophical Review, Mind, Ethics, Political Theory, European Journal of Philosophy, Economics and Philosophy,* and the Philosophy in Europe e-List. United Kingdom Kant Society (UKKS) announces it at website. Piper delivers "Zwei Ideale rationaler Motivation" at Leibniz-Universität Hannover. Does visiting residency at Paul Klee Sommerakademie, Bern. Attends Kant-Gesellschaft conference on Transcendental Illusion in Frankfurt and UKKS conference on Space and Time at the University of Sussex. Produces *Everything #19.3: New York Times Portrait of Megan Williams* for *Farimani* magazine. Goes OUT TO LUNCH for entire month of September, begins memoir, makes it to sixtieth birthday, goes dancing at ACUD club to celebrate. Ginger dies of kidney failure. Posts "Decision-Theoretic Legitimacy for Market Regulation" on Philosophy in Europe e-List, deals with fallout. Delivers "Conceptual Art and Intellectual Intuition" at Finnish Academy of Fine Arts, Helsinki. Completes full draft of memoir *Escape to Berlin: A Detour off the American Way*.

2009

Piper successfully renews passport. Interview by Dawn Chan about *Rationality and the Structure of the Self* appears at *Artforum* website. Posts "Academic Rankings" on Philosophy in Europe e-List, deals with fallout. Delivers "Kant's Transcendental Analysis of Action" at British Society for the History of Philosophy's annual conference "Transcendental Philosophy: Its History and Nature" at Manchester Metropolitan University. Does follow-up interview with Lukkas for *Telling Time Projects*. Attends decision-theory and logic workshops at London School of Economics, HEC Lausanne, and University of Groningen, the Netherlands. Exhibits artwork at Elizabeth Dee, Emi Fontana, and Galerie Christian Nagel booths at Art Basel. Premieres installation *Everything #5.2* (2004) at *IN TRANSIT*, Haus der Kulturen der Welt, Berlin. Chairs session at annual UKKS conference on Morality and Society, Lancaster University; attends Kant-Gesellschaft conference on Regulative Ideas in Frankfurt. Begins Vanishing Point drawing-and-installation series. Discovers Paolo Conte. Reads Alexis de Toqueville. Finishes *Bait-and-Switch*, exhibits complete *Pac-Man Trilogy* (2005–09) at Berlin Akademie der Künste ABC Art Contemporary and eleven *Drawings about Paper, Writings about Words* (1967) in *Materialien* exhibition at Münzsalon, Berlin. Rereads Hermann Hesse's *Magister Ludi (Das Glasperlenspiel)*. First and only critical notice of *Rationality and the Structure of the Self* appears in *Artforum's* Best Books section in December. Launches APRA Foundation Berlin. Within three hours of posting Foundation page at website, receives phone call and e-mail messages from The College requesting meeting in Berlin.

2010

Piper reorganizes archive. Presents APRA Foundation Berlin at Berliner Senatskanzlei Empfang für Neustifter. Robert Del Principe does video interview about *Rationality and the Structure of the Self*. Piper discovers ostdeutsche Schäferhund. Delivers "Practical Action: First *Critique* Foundations" at International Kant Congress 2010, in Pisa. Announces release of *Rationality and the Structure of the Self* as two single-file PDF documents. Taken to visit Dresden by neighbor. Chairs session at annual UKKS Conference, Oxford. Publishes "Style and the Paradox of Minimalism" in *Artforum*. Applies for and is granted permanent residency permit in Germany. Exhibits historical work at Elizabeth Dee and new work *Everything #21* at Cairn Gallery. Delivers "Kant's Self-Legislation Procedure Reconsidered" at Keele University, U.K.

2011

Piper receives another e-mail message from The College, now requesting web access to "documented lawsuit" against The College and "Personal Report." Delivers "Kant's Self-Legislation Procedure Reconsidered" to King's College London Philosophy Department. Announces first APRA Foundation Berlin Multi-Disciplinary Fellow. Yoga poses Ardha Baddha Padma Paschimottanasana (left side), Marichyasana D, Baddha Konasana, Baddha Padmasana, Urdhva Padmasana, Pindasana, self-invented Herniasana are taken away by torn left medial meniscus, then gradually restored, on loan from Shiva. Develops peer-review web-publication application that reconciles antiplagiarism policy with blind submission/double-blind review procedure, conceives and launches *Berlin Journal of Philosophy*, announces both on Philosophy in Europe e-list, and offers web application to other philosophy journals. None accept it. Sued by disgruntled former director of APRA. Delivers "Kant's Two Replies to Hobbes" to first plenary session of UKKS Annual Conference. Piper discovers that entire Archive staff has been working at APRA under false pretenses with fraudulent contracts, endangering its legal and financial standing; all resign. Advised that this form of work fraud is usual and protected under German law. Closes Archive. Title of Professor Emeritus conferred by American Philosophical Association. Posts "Contracts & Contempt" at website. Hearing in right ear taken away then gradually restored, on loan from Shiva.

2012

Second APRA Foundation Berlin Multi-Disciplinary Fellow rejects funding and cancels awarded project. Piper reads *Stellungnahme zu dem Beschluß des Landesgerichts Berlin* aloud at second lawsuit hearing; judge agrees not to apply statutes protecting work fraud. Wins College Art Association 2012 Artist Award for a Distinguished Body of Work, for having "since the late 1960s . . . profoundly influenced the language and form of Conceptual art." Establishes APRA Foundation Berlin Graduate Student Teaching Scholarship in Philosophy at Keele University. Resolves to stop doing Kapotasana, Mukta

Hasta Shirshasana to protect neck vertebrae. Confronts habituation to Kapotasana, Mukta Hasta Shirshana, inability to stop doing them absentmindedly. Delivers series of three lectures "The Connection between Truth and Goodness: Explorations in Kant's Metaethics" to Zentrum für Kunst und Medientechnologie, Karlsruhe. Discovers Falco. Delivers "On the Very Idea of Artistic Research" to Ruskin School of Drawing and Fine Art, Oxford University, at "Art as a Mode of Inquiry" conference. Reopens archive. Article "Kant's Two Solutions to the Free Rider Problem" published in *Kant Yearbook 4/2012: Kant and Contemporary Moral Philosophy*. At third lawsuit hearing, interrogates plaintiff; court settles case favorably for APRA. Presents third chapter of second volume of *Rationality and the Structure of the Self* "The Concept of a Genuine Preference" at workshop "Kant und Hegel über Logik und Ontologie," at Universität Potsdam. Discovers Max Raabe. For sixty-fourth birthday, decides to retire from being black. Creates *Thwarted Projects, Dashed Hopes, A Moment of Embarrassment* and announces new racial and nationality designations at website. Resumes studying Sanskrit in earnest. Learns Yoga Sutras I.1–12 by heart. Publishes "Kant's Self-Legislation Procedure Reconsidered" in *Kant Studies Online*. Attends first Sonnenwendefest.

2013

Piper publishes "Philosophy Journal Paper Submissions Policies" at *Berlin Journal of Philosophy* website. Publishes second edition of *Rationality and the Structure of the Self* at website. Creates *The Probable Trust Registry: The Rules of the Game #1–3*. Reads Riane Eisler's *The Chalice and the Blade: Our History, Our Future*. Undergoes knee surgery for torn left meniscus and damaged cartilage. Starts twice-weekly fitness training. Turns into fitness jock. Delivers "On the Very Idea of Artistic Research" at Sound/Image/Culture (SIC) Brussels. Posts "Adrian Piper Video Interview: Rationality and the Structure of the Self" at website, and on YouTube and Vimeo; advertises second edition of *Rationality and the Structure of the Self* in *New York Review of Books* and *Times Literary Supplement*; sends it out for review to *Journal of Philosophy, Philosophical Review, Ethics, European Journal of Philosophy, Mind, Analysis, Philosophy and Public Affairs, Economics and Philosophy, London Review of Books, New York Times Book Review, The Economist*; none acknowledge receipt. Composes Saraswati bhajan. Attends Annual UKKS Conference. Delivers Empson Lecture "The Real Thing Strange" to British Society of Aesthetics at Cambridge University. "Practical Action: First Critique Foundations" published in *Kant und die Philosophie in Weltbürgerlicher Absicht: Akten des XI. Internationalen Kant-Kongreßes 2010*. Delivers Rousseau Lecture "Playing By the Rules I" to Keele University and "Playing By the Rules II" to Keele University Forum for Philosophical Research Annual Lecture and Conference "Playing by the Rules." Ned McClennen dies; Piper is invited to write memorial tribute for *Critical Inquiry*. Requests deletion of name from American Philosophical Association (APA) e-mail list soliciting donations for Diversity and Inclusiveness Initiatives. APA executive director "[takes] the liberty" of deleting Piper's name from APA general e-mail list. Piper cancels APA membership. Attends second Sonnenwendefest. Learns Yoga Sutras I.13–35 by heart. Publicly announces New Year's resolution to finish *Kant's Metaethics: First Critique Foundations* on Philos-L listserv.

2014

Piper publishes updated "Philosophy Journal Paper Submission Policies" on *Berlin Journal of Philosophy* website. Awarded Women's Caucus for Art (WCA) Lifetime Achievement Award for "distinguished work as a philosopher and conceptual artist." Delivers "Second Wave Feminism: Unfinished Business" at Kunsthøgskolen Oslo. Premiers video lecture/screening/discussion *Passing beyond Passing* (2004) at Ihme Contemporary Art Festival, Helsinki. Posts "The Money Pump Is Necessarily Diachronic" at APRA Foundation Berlin website and PhilPapers.org. Creates *Everything #24* for 8th Shenzhen Sculpture Biennale; makes first trip to China. Delivers "Playing by the Rules I: Two- or More-Person Games" at Shenzhen OCAT Library. Premieres *The Probable Trust Registry* at Elizabeth Dee. Delivers "The Logic of Kant's Categorical 'Imperative'" at the Conference on Kant and Schopenhauer/Ethics and Aesthetics, at St. Andrews University, Scotland. Accepts invitation from MoMA to present a comprehensive traveling retrospective, to open in 2018. Learns Yoga Sutras I.36–51, II.1–12 by heart. Attends annual UKKS Conference at Oxford. Delivers "Second-Wave Feminism: Unfinished Business," at University of Hull, England.

2015

Piper announces gratis availability of *Imagine [Trayvon Martin]* (2013) on e-artnow.org. Publishes updated "Philosophy Journal Paper Submission Policies" at *Berlin Journal of Philosophy* website, deals with fallout. Delivers "Playing by the Rules I: Two- or More-Person Games," at Bard College Berlin. Posts "Mad Dog Referee Reports Anonymous Survey" at *Berlin Journal of Philosophy* website. Exhibits *The Probable Trust Registry* and selection of *Everything* works at Venice Biennale; receives Golden Lion Award for Best Artist. Delivers commencement address "Playing by the Rules II: One-Person Games" at Bard College Berlin; "Zwei Ideale rationaler Motivation" at Universität Potsdam Philosophy Department; and "The Logic of Kant's Categorical 'Imperative'" at 11th Kant Congress, Universität Wien. Kali dies of liver failure. Piper creates digital light projection *Self-Portrait with Shiva Ardhanarishvara*. Learns Yoga Sutras II.13–48 by heart.

2016

Piper decides to forego participation in further philosophy conferences while working on MoMA retrospective. *The Barbie Doll Drawings* included in *Drawing Then: Innovation and Influence in American Drawing of the Sixties* at Dominique Lévy Gallery. Exhibits *Howdy #6* (2015) and *Everything #5.1* (2004) in 9th Berlin

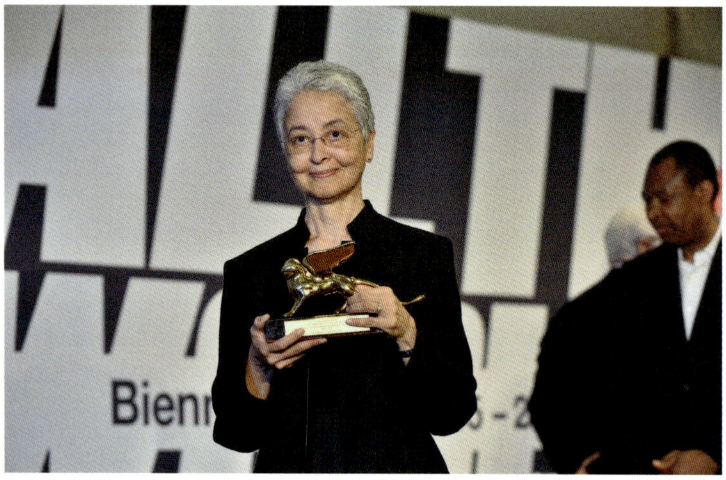

Piper receiving the Golden Lion award, Venice Biennale, with Okwui Enwezor at right, 2015

Biennale; *Funk Lessons* in Manifesta 11; and *My Calling (Card) #3: Guerrilla Performance for Disputed Territorial Skirmishes* (2012) at Museum der Moderne Salzburg collections show. Completes manuscript *Escape to Berlin: A Travel Memoir*, begins publication-production process. Streamlines asana practice. Immediately injures back, gives up Supta Kurmasana. Multiple intimations of her mortality cause in Piper an obsessive-compulsive addiction to genealogical research on her family that threatens to engulf her life and work. Tries to make peace with it by creating *Never Forget*. Reads all the slave narratives she has been stockpiling in her library for decades. Discovers cat's claw herbal tea, back pain disappears, gradually recovers Supta Kurmasana. Places *The Probable Trust Registry* with Nationalgalerie Berlin, begins work on its exhibition premiere at Hamburger Bahnhof in 2017. Creates *President Bandersnatch* (with thanks to Lewis Carroll and John Tenniel) for *Grey Room* magazine to commemorate election of Donald Trump to U.S. presidency. Learns of Bob Dylan's refusal to attend award ceremony in Oslo to receive Nobel Prize in Literature, decides to make no further public appearances. Takes enforced holiday: IT system crashes, Piper loses computer and e-mail access for a month. Simultaneously Piper also crashes: gets really bad flu virus, incapacitated for a month plus rehab time. Reads history and sociology of American society, European history, ancient and medieval history while recovering from burnout. Finds and reads Great-Aunt Ruby's wonderful Hunter College undergraduate textbook, *The History of Medieval Europe* by Lynn Thorndike. Learns Yoga Sutras II.48–III.24 by heart.

2017

Piper exhibits *The Probable Trust Registry* at Hamburger Bahnhof of the Nationalgalerie Berlin. Completes legal restructuring of APRA Foundation Berlin. Finalizes will. Progressively neglects more and more of yoga practice as deadline pressures for MoMA retrospective increase. Convinces the Berlin city housing-construction department to mention some experienced and competent architectural firms able to complete renovation of house. Receives honorary doctor of arts degree from Nova Scotia College of Art & Design (NSCAD University). Honored by Artists Space, New York. Invited to join National Academy of Art. Signs contract with Central Books Ltd. for distribution of APRA Foundation Berlin print publications. Grieves death at the age of forty-eight, after twelve years of tenure in the Princeton philosophy department, of Delia Graff Fara. Grieves death at the age of forty, after nine years of tenure in the Stanford mathematics department, of Maryam Mirzakhani. Discontinues APRA Foundation Berlin Graduate Student Teaching Scholarship in Philosophy at Keele University. Discovers Christopher Dawson's *Medieval Essays* in parents' library. Exhibits *It's Just Art* (1980) and *Here* (2008–15) at Lévy Gorvy, New York. Writes up "Consistency as Non-Contradiction in Rational Choice Theory." Establishes *The Order of Celestial Laughter*. Begins work on final chapter of *Kant's Metaethics: First Critique Foundations of His Theory of Action*. Discovers Johann Huizinga's *The Waning of the Middle Ages* in parents' library. Completely sacrifices yoga practice to preparations for MoMA retrospective and publication of *Escape to Berlin*. Reads Ian Mortimer's *The Time Traveller's Guide to Medieval England*. Learns Yoga Sutras III.25–IV.1 by heart.

2018

Publishes *Escape to Berlin: A Travel Memoir* (Berlin: APRA Foundation Berlin, 2018). Wins Germany's Käthe-Kollwitz-Preis for 2018. Reads Christine de Pizan's *A Medieval Woman's Mirror of Honor*, Hildegard von Bingen's *Weisheiten und Ratschläge für jeden Tag*, discovers Barbara Tuchman's *A Distant Mirror* in parents' library. Retrospective *Adrian Piper: A Synthesis of Intuitions, 1965–2016*, opens at The Museum of Modern Art, New York. Gradually resumes yoga practice with a few elementary asanas.

Page 313 (left):
Olive Xavier Smith Piper, Adrian Margaret Smith Piper, and Daniel Robert Piper at Adrian's christening, 1949
Black-and-white photograph
10 × 8 in. (25.4 × 20.3 cm)
Collection Adrian Piper Research Archive Foundation Berlin

Page 313 (right):
Adrian Piper
Portrait Artist with Customers. 1956
Tempera and pencil on paper
18 × 24⅜ in. (45.7 × 61.9 cm)
Collection Adrian Piper Research Archive Foundation Berlin

Page 314:
Café Figaro, on the corner of Macdougal and Bleecker Streets, Greenwich Village, New York, 1965

Page 315 (left):
Dancers onstage at Ginza nightclub, New york, April 1, 1966

Page 315 (right):
Adrian Piper in loft at East Twenty-sixth Street and Lexington Avenue, 1968
Color photograph
13¼ × 9 in. (33.7 × 22.9 cm)
Collection Adrian Piper Research Archive Foundation Berlin

Page 316:
The exhibition *Paris-Moscow, 1900-1930*, Centre Georges Pompidou, Paris, May 31-November 5, 1979

Page 317:
Adrian Piper
Think About It. 1987
Mock-up for billboard design. Rephotographed newspaper images, transparent foil, text, and watercolor
14 × 17 in. (35.6 × 43.2 cm)
Sara M. and Michelle Vance Waddell

Page 318:
Some Reflective Surfaces (1975), on the cover of *Art in America*, September 1990

Page 319:
Adrian Piper's home on Cape Cod, 2000
Digital photograph
4 × 6 in. (10.2 × 15.2 cm)
Collection Adrian Piper Research Archive Foundation Berlin

Page 321:
Adrian Piper touring West Bengal and Orissa, India, with students from the Royal Danish Academy of Art, 2007
Digital photograph #136
13¾ × 17¹³⁄₁₆ in. (33.9 × 45.2 cm)
Collection Adrian Piper Research Archive Foundation Berlin

Page 324:
Adrian Piper receiving the Golden Lion award, Venice Biennale, with Okwui Enwezor at right, 2015

SELECTED EXHIBITION HISTORY
COMPILED BY TESSA FERREYROS

SOLO EXHIBITIONS

1969
0 TO 9 Press, New York. *Three Untitled Projects [for 0 to 9]: Some Areas in the New York Area* (mail-art exhibition). March.

1971
The New York Cultural Center. *One Man (sic). One Work*. February.

1976
Gallery One, Montclair State College, New Jersey. *Adrian Piper*. February.

1980
Wadsworth Atheneum, Hartford. *Adrian Piper at Matrix 56*. March 7–April 6. In conjunction with Real Art Ways, Hartford. March 7–31.

1987
The Alternative Museum, New York. *Adrian Piper: Reflections, 1967–1987*. April 18–May 30. Traveled to Nexus Contemporary Art Center, Atlanta, November 21–December 19; Goldie Paley Gallery, Moore College of Art and Design, Philadelphia, February 24–April 1, 1989; University of Colorado Art Gallery, Boulder, March 1–31, 1990; Power Plant Gallery, Toronto, May 4–June 10, 1990; College of Wooster Art Museum, Ohio, August 29–October 4, 1990; Lowe Art Museum, University of Miami, Coral Gables, Florida, December 1990–January 27, 1991; Santa Monica Museum of Contemporary Art, February–March 1991; and Washington Project for the Arts, Washington, D.C., June–August 1991.

1989
John Weber Gallery, New York. *Cornered*. March 4–25. Traveled to Matrix Gallery, University Art Museum, University of California, Berkeley, August 19–November 5; and Williams College Art Museum, Williamstown, Massachusetts, January–March 1990 (as *ARTWORKS: Adrian Piper*).
Times Square, New York. *Adrian Piper: Messages to the Public; Merge*. Organized by Public Art Fund. May 1–31.

1990
University of Rhode Island Art Gallery, Kingston. *Why Guess*. February–March.
University of Iowa Art Gallery, Iowa City. *Adrian Piper: Close to Home*. February 2–March 17.
John Weber Gallery, New York. *Pretend*. September 1–29.
Whitney Museum of American Art, New York. *Out of the Corner*. October 9–November 11.
Exit Art, New York. *Why Guess*. October 13–November 3.

1991
Washington Project for the Arts, Washington, D.C. *What It's Like, What It Is #1*. June–August.
Hirshhorn Museum and Sculpture Garden, Smithsonian Institution, Washington, D.C. *What It's Like, What It Is #2*. June 19–September 22.
Ikon Gallery, Birmingham, England. *Adrian Piper*. September 21–November 2. Traveled to Cornerhouse, Manchester, January 18–February 23, 1992; Cartwright Hall, Bradford, March 21–May 10, 1992; Kettle's Yard, Cambridge, July 25–September 6, 1992; and Kunstverein, Munich, October 6–November 22, 1992.
John Weber Gallery, New York. *Space, Time and Reference, 1967–1970*. October 5–26.
Cleveland Center for Contemporary Art. *Political Drawings and Installations, 1975–1991*. November 22, 1991–February 7, 1992. Traveled to Carver Center, San Antonio, April 1992; Herron Gallery, Indianapolis Center for Contemporary Art, May–June 1992; and Women & Their Work, Austin, October–December 1992.

1992
Krannert Art Museum, Champaign, Illinois. *What It's Like, What It Is #2*. January 17–February 23.
Monasterio de Santa Clara, Moguer, Spain. *Ur-Madonna, Expo '92*. August.
Grey Art Gallery, New York University. *Decide Who You Are*. September 15–October 31. Other works in the series shown at John Weber Gallery, New York, September 19–October 17; Paula Cooper Gallery, New York, October 6–31; Brody's Gallery, Washington, D.C., February 4–27, 1993; Art Awareness, Lexington, New York, June–July 1993; City Gallery of Contemporary Art, Raleigh, North Carolina, October–December 1993; and Myers Fine Arts Gallery, Plattsburgh State Art Museum, Plattsburgh State University of New York, January 29–February 24, 1994.

1993
New Langton Arts, San Francisco. *Installations by Adrian Piper*. September 15–October 16.

1994
Paula Cooper Gallery, New York. *The Hypothesis Series, 1968–70*. March 3–26.

1995
University at Buffalo Art Gallery, New York. *Cornered/ Decide Who You Are*. March 8–May 5.
Savannah College of Art and Design Gallery. *Icons of One: Decide Who You Are*. October 16–November 3.

1996
John Weber Gallery, New York. *Adrian Piper: Ashes to Ashes*. November 23–December 21.

1997
Galleria Emi Fontana, Milan. *Adrian Piper*. October 30.
Thomas Erben Gallery, New York. *Food for the Spirit: July 1971*. December 11, 1997–January 31, 1998.

1998
Davis Museum and Cultural Center, Wellesley College, Massachusetts. *Who Are You? Selected Works by Adrian Piper*. March 11–August 16.
Thomas Erben Gallery, New York. *Adrian Piper: The Mythic Being, 1972–1975*. November 7, 1998–January 16, 1999.

1999
Fine Arts Gallery, University of Maryland, Baltimore County. *Adrian Piper: A Retrospective*. October 14, 1999–January 15, 2000. Traveled to New Museum, New York, October 4, 2000–January 15, 2001; Andy Warhol Museum, Pittsburgh, March 3–May 13, 2001; Contemporary Arts Center, Cincinnati, June 23–August 26, 2001; and Weatherspoon Art Gallery, University of North Carolina, Greensboro, September 23–December 16, 2001.

2000
Gallerie Voges und Deisen, Frankfurt. *Adrian Piper: A Solo Exhibition*. June 8–July 29.
Museum of Contemporary Art at California Plaza, San Diego. *MEDI(t)Ations: Adrian Piper's Videos, Installations, Performances, and Soundworks, 1968–1992*. August 6–November 5. Traveled to New Museum, New York, October 4, 2000–January 13, 2001; and Andy Warhol Museum, Pittsburgh, March 4–May 31, 2001.
Thomas Erben Gallery, New York. *Adrian Piper: Early Drawings and Other Works*. December 7, 2000–January 20, 2001.

2002
Generali Foundation, Vienna. *Adrian Piper: seit 1965*. May 17–August 18. Traveled to Institut d'Art Contemporain, Villeurbane, France, January 31–May 25, 2003 (as *Adrian Piper: depuis 1965*); and Museu d'Art Contemporani de Barcelona, October 17, 2003–January 11, 2004 (as *Adrian Piper: desde 1965*).

2003
Galleria Emi Fontana, Milan. *Adrian Piper Over the Edge*. November 9, 2003–January 2004.

2004
ARTSADMIN, London. *Adrian Piper Videos*. November.

2005
Index—The Swedish Contemporary Art Foundation, Stockholm. *Adrian Piper*. April–June 5.

2006
CPH Kunsthal, Copenhagen. *Adrian Piper*. April 7–May 5.
Smart Museum of Art, University of Chicago. *Adrian Piper: The Mythic Being*. September 16–December 10.

2007
Cinema Svetozor, Prague. *Adrian Piper: Funk Lessons*. Organized with Tranzit.cz. May.

2008
Elizabeth Dee Gallery, New York. *Adrian Piper: Everything*. March 1–April 16.

2010
Elizabeth Dee Gallery, New York. *Adrian Piper: Past Time: Selected Works, 1973–1995*. October 23–December 11.

2011
Cairn Gallery, Pittenweem, Scotland. *Adrian Piper: Everything #21*. October 2011–January 2012.

2014
Elizabeth Dee Gallery, New York. *Adrian Piper: The Probable Trust Registry*. May 3–31.

2016
FRAC Bourgogne, France. *Adrian Piper: Bach Whistled*. July 2–August 28 and September 3–18.

2017
Hamburger Bahnhof—Museum für Gegenwart, Berlin. *Adrian Piper. The Probable Trust Registry: The Rules of the Game #1–3*. February 24–September 3.
Lévy Gorvy, New York. *Adrian Piper*. September 14–October 21.

PERFORMANCES

1968
Private loft performance, New York. *Five Unrelated Time Pieces (Meat into Meat)*. October 11–13.

1969
Between West Thirteenth and Fourteenth Streets and Fifth and Sixth Avenues, New York. Three untitled performances, in *Street Works II*. April 18.

1970
Max's Kansas City, New York. *Untitled Performance*, in *The Saturday Afternoon Show*. May 2.
Various locations, New York. *Catalysis* actions. 1970–71.

1971
Private loft performance, 117 Hester Street, New York. *Food for the Spirit*, June–July.
Streets of New York. Untitled street works. 1971–73.

1972

Streets of Rochester, New York. Two untitled street works. April.

1973

Hester and Ludlow Streets, New York. *Being Mythic on the Street.* Staged for *Other Than Art's Sake*, a film by Peter Kennedy. October.
Rhode Island School of Design, Providence. Untitled streetwork. October.

1975

Streets of Cambridge, Massachusetts. *The Mythic Being.* 1975–76.
Fine Arts Building, New York University. *Some Reflective Surfaces.* December. Also performed at Whitney Museum of American Art, New York, in *Performances—Four Evenings, Four Days.* February 28 and 29, 1976.

1977

Kurfürstendamm, West Berlin. *Danke(sehr)schon.* September.

1978

Hauptstrasse, Heidelberg. *Collegium Academicum Freischrei.* February.

1980

Allen Memorial Museum, Oberlin College, Ohio. *It's Just Art.* April 23. Also performed at Contemporary Art Institute of Detroit, July; University Art Galleries, Wright State University, Dayton, Ohio, October 13; The Western Front, Vancouver, February 24, 1981; And/Or, Seattle, February 26, 1981; Artists Space, New York, April 28, 1981; and Penn State University, University Park, May 1981.

1981

Franklin Furnace, New York. *Xerox Philosophy.* April 21.

1982

Streets of Menlo Park, California. *Wide Receiver.* October.
Streets of Palo Alto, California. *Invasion.* December.

1983

Nova Scotia College of Art and Design, Halifax. *Funk Lessons.* March. Also performed at Walker Art Center, organized with Minneapolis College of Art and Design, October 28; University of California at Berkeley, November 6; San Francisco Art Institute, February 1984; The Women's Building, Los Angeles, March 3, 1984; California Institute of Art, Valencia, March 1984; New Langton Arts, San Francisco, March 23, 1984.

1985

Center for Music Experiment, University of California at San Diego, La Jolla. *Funk Lessons* (videotape), in *What's Cooking VI.* February.

1986

Reactive guerrilla performance. *My Calling (Card) #1 (for Dinners and Cocktail Parties).* April 1986–90.
Reactive guerrilla performance. *My Calling (Card) #2 (for Bars and Discos).* May 1986–90.

1987

Randolph Street Gallery, Chicago. *My Calling (Cards) #1 and #2: A Meta-Performance I.* January 30.

1988

The Studio Museum in Harlem, New York. *My Calling (Cards) #1 and #2: A Meta-Performance II.* May.

2003

The Art Institute of Chicago. *Shiva Dances with the Art Institute of Chicago.* October 9.

2007

Berlin Alexanderplatz. *Adrian Moves to Berlin.* March 26.
Streets of New York. *Everything #10*, in *Six Actions for New York City.* Organized by Creative Time, New York. May 1 and 2.

2010

Bowery Poetry Project, New York. *One 16 Minute-Long, Thickly Textured Straight Line Running Parallel with the Bowery Poetry Project Floor.* May.
NIMK, Netherlands Media Arts Institute, Amsterdam. *Variety Evening.* July.

GROUP EXHIBITIONS

1969

Paula Cooper Gallery, New York. *Number 7.* May 18–June 15.
Dwan Gallery, New York. *Language III.* May 24–June 18.
Seattle Art Museum. *557,087.* September 5–October 5. Traveled to Vancouver Art Gallery, January 13–February 8, 1970 (as *955,000*).
Städtisches Museum, Leverkusen, Germany. *Concept Art.* October.
Kunsthalle Bern. *Pläne und Projekte als Kunst.* November 8–December 7.

1970

New York Cultural Center. *Conceptual Art and Conceptual Aspects.* April 10–August 25 (artwork withdrawn).
Allen Memorial Art Museum, Oberlin College, Ohio. *Art in the Mind.* April 17–May 12.
Dwan Gallery, New York. *Language IV.* June 2–25.
The Museum of Modern Art, New York. *Information.* July 2–September 20.

1971

The Aldrich Contemporary Art Museum, Ridgefield, Connecticut. *26 Contemporary Women Artists.* April 18–June 13.
7th Biennale de Paris, Musée d'art moderne de la ville de Paris. September 24–November 1.

1972

Memorial Art Gallery, University of Rochester, New York. *Art without Limits.* April 7–May 7.

1973

Pace College Gallery, New York. *Thought: Structures.* January.
Yager Gallery, Hartwick College, Oneonta, New York. *Nine New York Artists: Drawings—Prints—Concepts—Forms.* April 3–27.
Pomona College Museum of Art and the Libra Gallery of Claremont Graduate School, California. *ArtForms Abstract Activities Ideas: Exhibition of Conceptual Art.* April 23–May 11.
California Institute of the Arts, Valencia. *c. 7,500.* May 14–18. Traveled to Wadsworth Atheneum, Hartford, June 19–July 31; Moore College of Art, Philadelphia, September 21–October 9; Walker Art Center, Minneapolis, November 16–December 16; Institute of Contemporary Art, Boston, December 23, 1973–January 14, 1974; Smith College Museum of Art, Northampton, Massachusetts, January 17–February 10, 1974; 48 Earlham Street, London, April 8–26, 1974; A.I.R. Gallery, New York, June 1–15, 1974; And/Or, Seattle, September 19–October 6, 1974; and Vassar College Art Gallery, Poughkeepsie, New York, October 16–November 14, 1974.

1974

Artists Space, New York. *PersonA.* April 23–26.

1975

Museum of Contemporary Art, Chicago. *Bodyworks.* March 8–April 27.
San Jose State University Art Gallery, California. *Word Works Too.* April 14–May 16.
Women's Interart Center, New York. *Eleven in New York.* May.
Fine Arts Building, New York University. *Lives.* November 29–December 20.

1977

The Museum of Modern Art, New York. *Bookworks.* March 17–May 30.
10th Biennale de Paris, Musée d'art moderne de la ville de Paris. September 17–November 1.

1978

Artists Space, New York. September 23–October 28.
Neuberger Museum of Art, Purchase College, State University of New York. *The Sense of the Self: From Self-Portrait to Autobiography.* Organized by Independent Curators Incorporated, Washington, D.C., and New York. September 24–November 26. Traveled to New Gallery of Contemporary Art, Cleveland, January–February 1979; University of North Dakota, Grand Forks, February–March 1979; Alberta College of Art Gallery, Calgary, November–December 1979; Tangeman Fine Art Gallery, University of Cincinnati, February–March 1980; Allen Memorial Art Museum, Oberlin College, Ohio, April–May 1980.

1979

Artemisia Gallery, Chicago. *Both Sides Now: An International Exhibition Integrating Feminism and Leftist Politics.* March 6–31.
Franklin Furnace, New York. *The Page as Alternative Space, 1909–1980.* September 1979–June 1980.
Massachusetts College of Art and Design, Boston. *Eventworks.*

1980

A.I.R. Gallery, New York. *Speaking Volumes: Women Artists' Books.* June 3–21.
Wright State University, Dayton, Ohio. *Art of Conscience: The Last Decade.* October 13–30. Traveled to Freadman Gallery, Albright College, Reading, Pennsylvania, September 1–October 1, 1981; Joe and Emily Lowe Art Gallery, Syracuse University, New York, November 15, 1981–January 10, 1982; Emily Davis Gallery, University of Akron, Ohio, January 17–February 28, 1982; and Doane Hall of Art, Allegheny College, Meadville, Pennsylvania, April 1–23, 1982.
Institute of Contemporary Arts, London. *Issue: Social Strategies by Women Artists.* November 14–December 21.

1981

New Museum, New York. *Events: Artists Invite Artists.* February 13–March 5.
Group Material, New York. *It's a Gender Show!* February 14–March 9.
And/Or, Seattle. *Oppositions.* May 13–May 30.
Davidson Art Center, Wesleyan University, Middletown, Connecticut. *No Title: The Collection of Sol LeWitt.* October 21–December 20.

1983

University of Michigan Residential College, Ann Arbor. *Art at Ground Zero: Artists' Statements on Nuclear War.* March 13–17.
New Museum, New York. *Language, Drama, Source, and Vision.* October 8–November 27.

1984

Artists Space, New York. *A Decade of New Art: Artists Space.* May 31–June 30.
Contemporary Arts Center, Cincinnati. *Disarming Images: Art for Nuclear Disarmament.* Organized by Bread and Roses, New York. September 14–October 27. Traveled to University Art Gallery, San Diego State University, November 23–December 22; Museum of Art, Washington State University, Pullman, February 11–March 3, 1985; New York State Museum, Albany, March 24–June 2, 1985; University Art Museum, University of California, Santa Barbara, June 25–August 4, 1985; Munson-Williams-Proctor Institute Museum of Art, Utica, New York, September 1–29, 1985; Fine Arts Gallery, University of Nevada, January 5–February 2, 1986; Baxter Art Gallery, California Institute of Technology, March 2–30, 1986; Yellowstone Art Center, Montana, April 28–June 9, 1986; and Bronx Museum of the Arts, New York, September 11–November 20, 1986.

1985

The Studio Museum in Harlem, New York. *Tradition and Conflict: Images of a Turbulent Decade, 1963–1973.* January 27–June 30. Traveled to Lang Gallery, Scripps College, Claremont, California, January 19–February 20, 1986; Heckscher Museum of Art, Huntington, New York, March 22–April 17, 1986; Museum of the Center for Afro-American Artists, Boston, May 18–June 22, 1986; Peninsula Fine Arts Center, Newport News, Virginia, August 11–September 26, 1986; Museum of Art and Archaeology, University of Missouri, Columbia, November 15, 1986–January 4, 1987; David and Alfred Smart Gallery, University of Chicago, May 15–June 30, 1987; Arkansas Arts Center, Little Rock, August 7–September 20, 1987; and Tower Fine Arts Gallery, State University of New York, Brockport, October 9–November 15, 1987.
Museum Moderner Kunst, Vienna. *Kunst mit Eigensinn.* March 21–May 12.
New Museum, New York. *The Art of Memory/The Loss of History.* November 23, 1985–January 19, 1986.

1986

The Alternative Museum, New York. *Liberty & Justice.* February 22–March 22.

1987

Hallwalls Contemporary Arts Center, Buffalo, New York. *Floating Values.* March 28–April 25.

1988

The Museum of Modern Art, New York. *Committed to Print.* January 13–April 19.
Diverse Works Gallery, Houston. *Coast to Coast: A Women of Color National Artists' Book Project.* February. Traveled to College of Wooster Art Museum, Ohio, January 15–February 19, 1989; DePauw University Art Museum, Greencastle, Indiana, March 27–April 21, 1989; The Center for Book Arts, New York, June 8–August 4, 1989; University of Michigan School of Art Museum, Ann Arbor, October 30–November, 1989; The Radford University Flossie Martin Gallery, Virginia, January 14–February 2, 1990; Baltimore Museum of Art, February 18–March 14, 1990; The Eubie Blake Center, Baltimore, February 26–March 31, 1990; Artemisia Gallery, Chicago, April 6–April 28, 1990; and The Jamaica Arts Center, New York, August 7–September 22, 1990.
INTAR Latin American Gallery, New York. *Autobiography: In Her Own Image.* June 1–July 8.
Whitney Museum of American Art, New York. *Modes of Address: Language in Art since 1960.* July 29–September 23.
Hillwood Art Gallery, Long Island University, Greenvale, New York. *Unknown Secrets: Art and the Rosenberg Era.* September 8–October 23. Traveled to Massachusetts College of Art North Gallery, Boston, November 16–December 23; Olin Gallery, Kenyon College, Gambier, Ohio, January 8–February 5, 1989; Palmer Museum of Art, Pennsylvania State University, University Park, March 19–May 14, 1989; University of Colorado Art Gallery, Boulder, June 8–August 12, 1989; Installation Gallery San Diego, September 8–October 22, 1989; Parsons Gallery, Otis College of Art and Design, Los Angeles, December 2, 1989–January 6, 1990; Jewish Community Museum, San Francisco, January 7–March 30; Spertus Museum of Judaica, Chicago, April 15–July 15, 1990; and Aspen Art Museum, September 20–November 4, 1990.
Cleveland Center for Contemporary Art. *The Turning Point: Art and Politics in 1968.* September 9–October 26. Traveled to Lehman College Art Gallery, City University of New York, November 10, 1988–January 14, 1989.
Maryland Institute College of Art, Baltimore. *Art as a Verb: The Evolving Continuum.* November 21, 1988–January 8, 1989. Traveled to Metropolitan Life Gallery, New York, March 6–April 8, 1989; and The Studio Museum in Harlem, New York, March 12–June 18, 1989.
Nickle Arts Museum, Calgary. *Signs.* Organized by the Art Gallery of Ontario, Toronto. November 25, 1988–January 1, 1989. Traveled to Norman Mackenzie Art Gallery, Regina, Canada, February 3–March 12, 1989; and Macdonald Stewart Art Centre, Guelph, Canada, September 2–October 1, 1989.
Whitney Museum of American Art, New York. *Identity: Representation of the Self.* December 1988–February 10, 1989.

1989

Cincinnati Art Museum. *Making Their Mark: Women Artists Move into the Mainstream, 1970–1985.* February 22–April 2. Traveled to New Orleans Museum of Art, May 6–June 8; Denver Art Museum, July 22–September 10; and Pennsylvania Academy of the Fine Arts, Philadelphia, October 20–December 31.
Maryland Art Place, Baltimore. *Collecting, Organizing, Transposing.* March 16–April 29. Traveled to Anderson Gallery, Virginia Commonwealth University, Richmond, August 24–October 1; and Newhouse Center for Contemporary Art, Staten Island, January 14–February 25, 1990.
Bernice Steinbaum Gallery, New York. *American Resources: Selected Works of African American Artists.* June 18–August 18. Traveled to Downtown Arts Gallery, Nashville, August 26–September 24 (as *Contemporary African American Artists*).
Long Beach Art Museum, California. *Raymond Saunders: Some Choices.* June 24–July 23.
Contemporary Arts Center, Cincinnati. *Double Take: Advertising Reconsidered.* July 21–September 2.
Feature Inc., New York. *Buttinsky.* September 5–30.
Feature Inc., New York. *I Only Want You to Love Me.* October 7–November 4.
Musée d'art moderne de la ville de Paris. *L'Art conceptuel: Une perspective.* November 22, 1989–February 18, 1990.

1990

Hallwalls Contemporary Arts Center, Buffalo. *Insect Politics: Body Horror/Social Order.* March 17–April 13.
Woodstock Artists Association and Museum, New York. *Signs of the Self: Changing Perceptions.* March 17–April 15.
Feigen Gallery, Chicago. *Sarah Charlesworth, Jeanne Dunning, Annette Messager, Adrian Piper, Laurie Simmons.* March 30–April 28.
New Museum of Contemporary Art, New York. *The Decade Show: Frameworks of Identity in the 1980s.* May 12–August 19. Organized with and also took place at Museum of Contemporary Hispanic Art, New York, May 16–August 18; and The Studio Museum in Harlem, New York, May 19–August 18.
Barbara Krakow Gallery, Boston. *Constructive Anger.* May 19–June 23.
P.P.O.W., New York. *The Power of Words: An Aspect of Recent Documentary Photography.* June–July.
Milwaukee Art Museum. *Word as an Image: American Art 1960–1990.* June 15–August 26. Traveled to Oklahoma City Museum of Art, November 17, 1990–February 2, 1991; and Contemporary Arts Museum, Houston, February 23–May 12, 1991.
Feature, Inc., New York. *The Thing Itself.* July 10–August 10.
Real Art Ways, Hartford. *Presumed Identities.*

1991

The Aldrich Contemporary Art Museum, Ridgefield, Connecticut. *The Art of Advocacy.* May 18–September 22.
Hirshhorn Museum and Sculpture Garden, Smithsonian Institution, Washington, D.C. *Awards in the Visual Arts 10.* June 12–September 2. Traveled to The Albuquerque Museum of Art, History and Science, September–December; and The Toledo Museum of Art, Ohio, December 1991–January 1992.
Wadsworth Atheneum, Hartford. *Open Mind: The LeWitt Collection.* August 4, 1991–February 1992.
Institute of Contemporary Art, Philadelphia. *Devil on the Stairs: Looking Back on the Eighties.* October 4, 1991–January 5, 1992. Traveled to Newport Harbor Art Museum, Newport Beach, California, April 16–June 21, 1992.
The Museum of Modern Art, New York. *DISLOCATIONS.* October 20, 1991–January 7, 1992.
Alternative Museum, New York. *Artists of Conscience: 16 Years of Social and Political Commentary.* November 5, 1991–January 25, 1992.
Iris and B. Gerald Cantor Art Gallery, College of the Holy Cross, Worcester, Massachusetts. *Affirmative Re-Actions: Adrian Piper, Lorna Simpson & Carrie Mae Weems.*

1992

New Loom House, London. *Book Works: A Women's Perspective.* March 28–April 16.
Herron Gallery, Indianapolis Center for Contemporary Art. *Adrian Piper, Carl Pope.* May 9–June 26.
documenta 9, Kassel. June 13–September 20 (artwork withdrawn).
Wexner Center for the Arts, The Ohio State University, Columbus. *Will/Power: New Works by Papo Colo, Jimmie Durham, David Hammons, Hachivi Edgar Heap of Birds, Adrian Piper, Aminah Brenda Lynn Robinson.* September 26–December 27.
Fukui Fine Arts Museum, Japan. *Dream Singers, Story Tellers: An African American Presence.* Organized by the New Jersey Department of State and the Prefecture of Fukui. November 6–December 6, 1992. Traveled to New Jersey State Museum, August 7, 1993–March 20, 1994.
University Art Museum, University of California, Santa Barbara. *Mistaken Identities.* November 11–December 20. Traveled to Museum Folkwang, Essen, Germany, February 11–March 31, 1993; Forum Stadtpark, Graz, Austria, April 29–May 30, 1993; Neues Museum Weserburg Bremen im Forum Langenstrasse, Bremen, Germany, June 6–August 18, 1993; and Louisiana Museum of Modern Art, Humlebaek, Denmark, September 17–November 14, 1993.
The Alternative Museum, New York. *10: Artist as Catalyst.* November 21–February 12.
9th Biennale of Sydney, Art Gallery of New South Wales. *The Boundary Rider.* December 15, 1992–March 14, 1993.

1993

Espace lyonnais d'art contemporain, Lyon, France. *Here's Looking at Me: Contemporary Self-Portraits.* January 29–April 30.
Fine Arts Gallery, University of California, Irvine. *The Theater of Black Refusal: Black Art and Mainstream Criticism.* April 8–May 12. Traveled to Richard L. Nelson Gallery, University of California, Davis, November 7–December 1; University Art Gallery, University of

California, Riverside, January 9, 1993–February 27, 1994; and Center for Art, Design and Visual Culture, University of Maryland, Baltimore, November 11–December 17, 1994.
Neue Galerie, Graz, Austria. *Kontext Kunst*. October 2–November 11.
Fine Arts Gallery, University of Maryland, Baltimore County. *Ciphers of Identity*. November 12, 1993–January 15, 1994. Traveled to Ronald Feldman Fine Arts, New York; Fine Arts Gallery, University of California, Irvine; Contemporary Art Museum, University of South Florida, Tampa; the Contemporary Arts Center, New Orleans; the Woodruff Art Center, Atlanta College of Art; and Kemper Museum of Contemporary Art, Kansas City.

1994

Musée d'art moderne de la ville de Paris. *L'Hiver de l'amour*. February 10–March 13. Traveled to P.S.1 Contemporary Art Center, Long Island City, New York, October 9, 1994–January 8, 1995 (as *The Winter of Love*).
De Beyerd Centrum voor Beeldende Kunst, Breda, the Netherlands. *Can You Always Believe Your Eyes: Amerikaanse tekeningen*. April 16–May 29.
Center for Curatorial Studies, Bard College, Annandale-on-Hudson, New York. *Transformers: The Art of Multiphrenia*. Organized by Independent Curators International, New York. September 21–November 13. Traveled to Herbert F. Johnson Museum of Art, Cornell University, Ithaca, New York, January 27–March 26, 1996; Nexus Contemporary Art Center, Atlanta, March 15–June 1, 1996; Art Gallery of Windsor, Ontario, June 21–September 9, 1996; Illingworth Kerr Art Gallery, Calgary, November 4–November 28, 1996; Decker Galleries, Maryland Institute College of Art, Baltimore, November 21–December 21, 1997.
The Museum of Modern Art, New York. *Mapping*. October 6–December 20.
Whitney Museum of American Art, New York. *Black Male: Representations of Masculinity in Contemporary American Art*. November 10, 1994–March 5, 1995.
Neue Gesellschaft für bildende Kunst, Berlin. *Gewalt/Geschäfte: Eine Ausstellung zum Topos der Gewalt in der gegenwärtigen künstlerischen Auseinandersetzung*. December 10, 1994–February 19, 1995.

1995

Southeastern Center for Contemporary Art, Winston-Salem, North Carolina. *CIVIL RIGHTS NOW*. January 28–April 15. Traveled to Cleveland Center for Contemporary Art, May 12–August 13.
Museum of Contemporary Art, Kiasma, Helsinki. *Public/Private: ARS 95*. February 11–May 28.
Castle Gallery at The College of New Rochelle, New York. *The Message Is the Medium: Issues of Representation in Modern Technologies*. February 12–April 7.
Johannesburg Biennale. *Africus*. February 28–April 30.
Forum for Contemporary Art, St. Louis. *Altered States: American Art in the 90s*. March 24–May 6.
Paula Cooper Gallery, New York. *Cornered*. June 9–July 28.
Museum of Contemporary Art, Los Angeles. *Reconsidering the Object of Art: 1965–1975*. October 15, 1995–February 4, 1996 (artwork withdrawn due to Philip Morris sponsorship).
The Newark Museum, New Jersey. *Art with Conscience*. November 22, 1995–February 18, 1996.

1996

Louisiana Museum of Modern Art, Humlebaek, Denmark. *Now Here*. May 15–September 8.
The Museum of Modern Art, New York. *Thinking Print: Books to Billboards, 1980–1995*. June 20–September 10.
Center for Curatorial Studies, Bard College, Annandale-on-Hudson, New York. *a/drift*. October 26, 1996–January 5, 1997.
Centre Georges Pompidou, Paris. *Face à l'histoire, 1933–1996*. December 19, 1996–April 7, 1997.

1997

Strong Museum, Rochester, New York. *Between Two Worlds*. March–December.
Le MAGASIN, Centre national d'art contemporain, Grenoble, France. *Vraiment: Féminisme et art*. April 5–May 25.
Verein Shedhalle, Zurich. *If I Ruled the World*. July 4–August 17.
Setagaya Art Museum and The Asahi Shimbun, Japan. *American Stories: Amidst Displacement and Transformation/Amerikan sutori: ido to hen yo no naka de*. August 30–October 19. Traveled to Chiba City Museum of Art, Chiba, Japan, November 1–December 23; Fukui Fine Arts Museum, Fukui, Japan, April 29–May 24, 1998; Kurashiki City Art Museum, Kurashiki, Japan, June 13–July 26, 1998; and Akita Senshū Museum of Art, Akita, Japan, August 7–September 6, 1998.
Fine Arts Gallery, University of Maryland, Baltimore County. *Minimal Politics: Performativity and Minimalism in Recent American Art*. September 25, 1997–January 17, 1998.

1998

Museo de Bellas Artes, Caracas, Venezuela. *Desde el cuerpo: Alegorias de lo femenino* (*From the Body: Allegories of the Feminine*). January–March.
The Geffen Contemporary at The Museum of Contemporary Art, Los Angeles. *Out of Actions: Between Performance and the Object, 1949–1979*. February 8–May 10. Traveled to Österreichisches Museum für Angewandte Kunst, Vienna, June 17–September 6; Museu d'Art Contemporani de Barcelona, October 15, 1998–January 6, 1999; and Museum of Contemporary Art, Tokyo, February 11–April 11, 1999.
Bowdoin College Museum of Art, Brunswick, Maine. *Memorable Histories and Historic Memories*. September 25–December 6.

1999

Katonah Museum of Art, New York. *Re-Righting History: Counternarratives by Contemporary African/American Artists*. March 14–May 16.
Queens Museum of Art, Flushing, New York. *Global Conceptualism: Points of Origin, 1950s–1980s*. April 28–August 29. Traveled to Walker Art Center, Minneapolis, December 19, 1999–March 5, 2000; Miami Art Museum, June 23–August 27, 2000; and List Visual Arts Center, Massachusetts Institute of Technology, Cambridge, October 24–December 31, 2000.
University at Buffalo Art Gallery, New York. *Persuasion: Tales of Commerce and the Avant-Garde*. September 17–November 14.
Whitney Museum of American Art, New York. *The American Century: Art & Culture, 1950–2000*. September 26, 1999–February 13, 2000.

2000

P.S.1 Contemporary Art Center, Long Island City, New York. *Around 1984: A Look at Art in the Eighties*. May 21–September 3.
The Museum of Modern Art, New York. *Open Ends*. September 28, 2000–March 4, 2001.

2001

Norwich Gallery, Norwich School of Art and Design, England. *Conception: Conceptual Documents 1968–1972*. January 24–March 3. Traveled to City Art Gallery, Leeds, England, March 10–April 22; and Morris and Helen Belkin Art Gallery, University of British Columbia, Vancouver, October 12–December 2.
Aktionsforum Praterinsel, Munich. *Blondies and Brownies: Racism and Multiculturalism in the New and Old Worlds* (*Blondinchen und Baunchen, weiss weiss bin auch ich*). March–April 2001. Traveled to Torch Gallery, Amsterdam.
Generali Foundation, Vienna. *Double Life: Identity and Transformation in Contemporary Arts*. May 11–August 12.
Neuer Aachener Kunstverein, Aachen, Germany. *Wiederaufnahme Retake*. October 14–December 2.
The Bronx Museum of the Arts, New York. *One Planet Under a Groove: Hip-Hop and Contemporary Art*. October 26, 2001–March 3, 2002. Traveled to Spelman College Museum of Fine Art, Atlanta, March 21–May 17; and Walker Art Center, Minneapolis, July 13–October 13, 2003.
9e Biennale de l'image en mouvement, Centre pour l'image contemporaine Saint-Gervais, Geneva. November 2–10.

2002

The Aldrich Museum of Contemporary Art, Ridgefield, Connecticut. *Family*. May 14–September 4.
documenta 11, Kassel. June 8–August 15.
Guild Hall Museum, East Hampton, New York. *Personal and Political: The Women's Art Movement, 1969–1975*. August 10–October 20.
Gallery 101, Ottawa. *Mass Appeal: The Art Object and Hip Hop Culture*. August 29–October 12. Traveled to Arts Intercultural, Montreal, March 5–April 5, 2003; Khyber Centre for the Arts, Halifax, May 12–June 7, 2003; and Owens Art Gallery, Mount Allison University, Sackville, Canada, September 12–October 26, 2003.
White Columns, New York. *Gloria: Another Look at Feminist Art in the 1970s*. September 13–October 20.
Gesellschaft für Aktuelle Kunst, Bremen, Germany. *The Music in Me 2: Regarding Dance*. September 14–November 3.

2003

apexart, New York. *Walking in the City*. January 4–February 1. Traveled to Kunsthalle Fridericianum, Kassel, April–May 18.
Galleria Emi Fontana, Milan. *Imperfect Marriages*. April 9–May 17.
Metrotech Center, Brooklyn. *Sandwiched (In New York)*. Organized by Public Art Fund and The Wrong Gallery, New York. September 24–October 4.
International Center of Photography, New York. *Only Skin Deep: Changing Visions of the American Self*. December 12, 2003–February 29, 2004.

2004

William Benton Museum of Art, University of Connecticut, Storrs. *Masala: Diversity and Democracy in South Asian Art*. January 20–April 9.
Whitney Museum of American Art, New York. *Evidence of Impact: Art and Photography, 1963–1978*. May 29–October 20.
P.S.1 Contemporary Art Center, Long Island City, New York. *Curious Crystal of Unusual Purity*. June 27–October 3.
Institut d'art contemporain, Villeurbane, France. *Communauté*. July 9–September 26.
BüroFriedrich, Berlin. *Funky Lessons*. September 14–November 13. Traveled to BAWAG Foundation, Vienna, December 16, 2004–February 26, 2005.
Aarhus Festival of Contemporary Art, Denmark. *Minority Report: Challenging Intolerance in Contemporary Denmark*. September 25–October 24.
Artsadmin, London. *Performance Strategy and Process*. November.

Whitechapel Gallery, London. *Faces in the Crowd: Picturing Modern Life from Manet to Today*. December 3, 2004–February 28, 2005. Traveled to Castello di Rivoli, Turin, Italy, April 4, 2005–July 10, 2005 (as *Volti nella folla: Immagini della vita moderna da Manet a oggi*).

2005

Atlanta Contemporary Art Center. *What Business Are You In?* January 29–March 26.
Curzon Soho Cinemas, London. *International Exhibitionist*. February 26.
Center for Curatorial Studies, Bard College, Annandale-on-Hudson, New York. *Between Pass and Fail*. March 6–March 20.
Haus der Kunst, Munich. *Occupying Space: Generali Foundation Collection*. Organized with Generali Foundation Vienna. March 9–May 16. Traveled to Witte de With, Nederlands Fotomuseum, TENT, Rotterdam, July 8–August 28; and Museum of Contemporary Art, Zagreb, October 28–December 9.
Tate Liverpool, England. *Summer of Love: Art of the Psychedelic Era*. May 27–September 25. Traveled to Kunsthalle Schirn, Frankfurt, November 2, 2005–February 12, 2006; Kunsthalle Wien, Vienna, May 5–September 3, 2006; and Whitney Museum of American Art, New York, May 24–September 16, 2007.
Tate Modern, London. *Open Systems: Rethinking Art c. 1970*. June 1–September 18.
Generali Foundation, Vienna. *Wie Gesellschaft und Politik ins Bild Kommen/How Society and Politics Get in the Picture*. September 16–December 18.
Galleria d'Arte Moderna e Contemporanea Bergamo, Italy. *WAR IS OVER: 1945–2005; La libertà dell'arte da Picasso a Warhol a Cattelan/WAR IS OVER: 1945–2005; The Freedom of Art from Picasso to Warhol and Cattelan*. October 15, 2005–February 26, 2006.
Andrea Rosen Gallery, New York. *Looking at Words: The Formal Use of Text in Modern and Contemporary Works on Paper*. November 2–December 31.

2006

Orchard, New York. *Heard Not Seen*. March 10–April 9.
Museum Ludwig, Cologne. *Das achte Feld: Geschlechter, Leben und Begehren in der Kunst seit 1960*. August 19–November 12.
Museum of Contemporary Art, Antwerp. *Academy: Learning from Art*. September 15–November 26.
Generali Foundation, Vienna. *CONCEPT HAS NEVER MEANT HORSE*. September 15–December 17.
Göteborgs Konsthall, Sweden. *Art Link*. October 6, 2006–January 7, 2007.
Elizabeth Dee Gallery, New York. *Adrian Piper, Eric Baudelaire, Josephine Meckseper, Wayne Gonzales*. November 4–December 23.
National Gallery of Canada, Ottawa. *Art Metropole: The Top 100*. December 1, 2006–April 1, 2007.

2007

Künstlerhaus Bethanien, Berlin. *Normal Love: Precarious Sex. Precarious Work*. January 19–March 4.
Cornell Fine Arts Museum, Winter Park, Florida. *Crossing the Line: African American Artists in the Jacqueline Bradley and Clarence Otis, Jr. Collection*. January 19–April 22.
Museum für Gegenwartskunst Siegen, Germany. *Tanzen, Sehen*. February 18–May 28.
Museum of Contemporary Art, Los Angeles. *WACK! Art and the Feminist Revolution*. March 4–July 16. Traveled to The National Museum of Women in the Arts, Washington, D.C., September 21–December 16; P.S.1 Contemporary Art Center, Long Island City, New York, February 17–May 12, 2008; and Vancouver Art Gallery, October 4, 2008–January 11, 2009.
Galerie Lelong, New York. *Role Play: Feminist Art Revisited, 1960–1980*. March 15–April 28.
Frankfurter Kunstverein, Frankfurt. *Whenever It Starts It Is the Right Time: Strategies for a Discontinuous Future*. March 23–May 6.
Centre d'art Contemporain, Geneva. *I AM MAKING ART: 4 Studies on the Artist's Body; Chapter 3: Identité et Transformation*. March 27–April 8. Traveled to Centro de Arte Contemporaneo Huarte, Spain, November 1, 2008–February 1, 2009.
Barbican Art Gallery, London. *Panic Attack! Art in the Punk Years*. June 5–September 9.
The Museum of Modern Art, New York. *Lines, Grids, Stains, Words*. June 13–October 22. Traveled to Porto Museu de Arte Contemporanea de Serralves, Portugal, May 10–June 22, 2008; and Museum Wiesbaden, Germany, September 28, 2008–January 18, 2009.
Spazierengehen als Kunstform. Über die allmähliche Verfertigung der Gedanken beim Gehen, Kunstraum Kreuzberg/Bethanien, Berlin. *WALK*. September–October.
Neue Gesellschaft für bildenden Kunst, Berlin. *Multitasking-Synchronität als kulturelle Praxis/ Multitasking: Synchronicity as a Cultural Practice*. September 1–October 7.
Spelman College Museum of Fine Art, Atlanta. *Cinema Remixed & Reloaded: Black Women Artists and the Moving Image since 1970*. September 14–December 8. Traveled to Contemporary Art Museum, Houston, October 18, 2008–January 4, 2009.
John Hansard Gallery, University of Southampton, England. *Live Art on Camera*. September 18–November 10. Traveled to SPACE, London, March 15–April 18, 2008.
Centro Galego de Arte Contemporánea, Santiago de Compostela, Spain. *Gender Battle*. September 25–September 27.
Justina M. Barnicke Gallery, University of Toronto. *Scotiabank Nuit Blanche: Night School*. September 29.
The Museum of Modern Art, New York. *Multiplex: Directions in Art, 1970 to Now*. November 21, 2007–July 21, 2008.

2008

Nordanå, Skellefteå, Sweden. *The Space Between*. March 16–June 1. Traveled to Gävle Konstcentrum, Sweden, January 14–March 4, 2009.
16th Biennale of Sydney. *Revolutions—Forms That Turn*. June 18–September 7.
The Menil Collection, Houston. June 27–September 21. *NeoHooDoo: Art for a Forgotten Faith*. Traveled to P.S.1 Contemporary Art Center, Long Island City, New York, October 19, 2008–January 26, 2009; and Pérez Art Museum Miami, February 20–May 24, 2009.
Deutsche Guggenheim, Berlin. *Freeway Balconies*. July 5–October 10.
The Museum of Modern Art, New York. *Here Is Every. Four Decades of Contemporary Art*. September 10, 2008–March 23, 2009.
The Laboratory of Art and Ideas at Belmar, Lakewood, Colorado. *In Plain Sight: Street Works and Performances, 1968–1971*. September 24, 2008–January 4, 2009.
Hamburger Bahnhof—Museum für Gegenwart, Berlin. *Dekonstruktion des Künstlermythos—Ich kann mir nicht jeden Tag ein Ohr abschneiden/Cult of the Artist: "I can't just slice off an ear every day."* October 3, 2008–February 22, 2009.
Galeria Pauza, Krakow. *We Are Technology: Tapes from the 1960s and 70s*. November.
Beaver Projects, Copenhagen. *Swingtime: Freestyle*. November–December. Traveled to Charlotte Fogh Contemporary, Aarhus, Denmark, December 2008–February 2009.
Museum of Contemporary Art, Chicago. *USA Today*. November 8, 2008–March 15, 2009.
Akademie der Künste, Berlin. *re.act.feminism: performance art of the 1960s and 70s today* (video archive). December 13, 2008–February 8, 2009. Traveled to International Festival of Contemporary Arts, City of Women, Ljubljana, Slovenia, March 10–March 29, 2009; Kunsthaus Erfurt, Germany, April 19–May 10, 2009; Centro Cultural Montehermoso, Vitoria-Gasteiz, Spain, October–December 2011; Galerija Miroslav Kraljević, Zagreb; Wyspa Institute for Art, Danzig, Poland; Museum of Contemporary Art, Roskilde, Denmark; Tallinn Art Hall; Fundació Antoni Tàpies, Barcelona; and Akademie der Künste, Berlin.

2009

Museu da Républica, Rio de Janeiro. *Nós*. January–April.
Solomon R. Guggenheim Museum, New York. *The Third Mind: American Artists Contemplate Asia 1860–1989*. January 30–April 19.
Justina M. Barnicke Gallery, University of Toronto. *Funkaesthetics*. February 12–March 23. Traveled to Confederation Centre of the Arts, Charlottetown, Canada, November 21, 2009–February 28, 2010.
Walker Art Center, Minneapolis. *The Quick and the Dead*. April 24–September 27.
Museu d'Art Contemporani de Barcelona, Spain. *The Uncertainty Principle*. May 15–June 12.
Centre for Contemporary Art FUTURA, Prague. *The Eventual*. May 16–August 9.
Centre Georges Pompidou, Paris. *elles@centrepompidou: Women Artists in the Collection of the Musée national d'art moderne, Centre de création industrielle*. May 27, 2009–February 21, 2011. Exh. cat.
The Museum of Modern Art, New York. *Looking at Music: Side 2*. June 10–November 30.
Haus Der Kulturen Der Welt, Berlin. *In Transit 09: Resistance of the Object*. June 11–June 21.
Supportico Lopez, Berlin. *The Show Continues Upstairs*. June 20–July 25.
Center for Book Arts, New York. *Racism: An American Family Value*. July 8–September 12.
Wadsworth Atheneum, Hartford. *The MATRIX Effect*. July 25, 2009–January 3, 2010.
Lentos Kunstmuseum Linz, Austria. *See This Sound. Promises in Sound and Vision*. August 28, 2009–January 10, 2010.
Den Frie Centre of Contemporary Art, Copenhagen. *Fri PORTO*. September 19–October 18.
Julia Stoschek Foundation, Düsseldorf. *100 Years (version #1, Duesseldorf)*. October 10, 2009–July 29, 2010. Organized with P.S.1 Contemporary Art Center and Performa. Traveled to P.S.1 Contemporary Art Center, Long Island City, New York, November 1, 2009–May 3, 2010 (as *100 Years [version #2, ps1, nov 2009]*); Garage Center of Contemporary Culture, Moscow, June 19–September 17, 2010 (as *100 Years of Performance [version #3, Moscow, June 2010]*); and Boston University Art Galleries, January 19–March 25, 2012 (as *100 Years [version #4 Boston, 2012]*).
Fotogalerie Wien, Vienna. *Performance im Bild und im Medialen Übertrag*.

2010

Denison Museum, Denison University, Granville, Ohio. *Close Encounters 2: Acts of Social Imagination*. January 22–March 22.
Synagogue de Delme, France. *Self as Disappearance*. February 19–May 23.
Bowery Poetry Club, New York. *Selected Infinite Extensions Arbitrarily Constrained Featuring the Late Sol LeWitt and Adrian Piper*. March 19–May 2.
Walker Art Center, Minneapolis. *The Talent Show*. April 10–August 15.
Aboas Vetus & Ars Nova Museo, Turku, Finland. *Klangi*. September 10–October 31.
29th Bienal de São Paulo. *There Is Always a Cup of Sea to Sail In*. September 25–December 12. Traveled to Palácio das Artes, Belo Horizonte, Brazil, January 18–March 20.
Hayward Gallery, London. *Move: Choreographing You*. October 13, 2010–January 9, 2011. Traveled to Haus der Kunst, Munich, February 4–May 15, 2011; K20 Kunstsammlung Nordrhein-Westfalen, Düsseldorf, July 16–September 25, 2011; and National Museum of Contemporary Art, Seoul, June 6–December 8, 2011.
Museum of Contemporary Art, Chicago. *Without You I'm Nothing: Art and Its Audience*. November 20, 2010–

May 1, 2011.
Middlesbrough Institute of Modern Art, England. *Drawing in Progress*. November 26, 2010–March 20, 2011.

2011

Neuberger Museum of Art, Purchase College, State University of New York. *The Deconstructive Impulse: Women Artists Reconfigure the Signs of Power, 1973–1991*. January 15–April 3. Traveled to Nasher Museum of Art at Duke University, Durham, North Carolina, September 15–December 31; and Contemporary Arts Museum, Houston, January 21–April 15, 2012.
Weatherspoon Art Museum, University of North Carolina, Greensboro. *Weatherspoon Art Museum: 70 Years of Collecting*. February 6–May 1.
David Zwirner, New York. *Proofs and Refutations*. March 11–April 30.
Center for Art, Design and Visual Culture, University of Maryland, Baltimore. *Where Do We Migrate To?* March 17–April 30. Traveled to Sheila C. Johnson Center for Design, Parsons, The New School, New York, February 2–April 15, 2012; Contemporary Art Center, New Orleans, October 6, 2012–January 20, 2013; Värmlands Museum, Karlstad, Sweden, September 19, 2015–February 22, 2016; and Peeler Art Center, De Pauw University, Greencastle, Indiana, September 8–December 9, 2016.
Murray Guy, New York. *Vision Is Elastic. Thought Is Elastic*. April 21–June 4.
Hessel Museum of Art, Bard College, Annandale-On-Hudson, New York. *If You Lived Here, You'd Be Home by Now*. June 25–December 16.
FRAC Bourgogne, Châteauneuf-en-Auxois, France. *À corps perdu*. July 8–September 11.
Museum der Moderne, Salzburg. *Role Models–Role Playing*. July 23–October 30.
De Kabinetten van de Vleeshal, Middelburg, the Netherlands. *In Deed: Certificates of Authenticity in Art*. September 10–October 9. Traveled to Fondazione Bevilacqua la Masa, Venice, October 14–November 4; Khoj International Artists' Association, New Delhi, November 18–December 16; Mumbai Art Room, January 13–February 10, 2012; Nero HQ, Rome, February 3–March 2, 2012; John M. Flaxman Library Special Collections, School of the Art Institute of Chicago, March 30–April 28, 2012; Salt Beyoglu, Istanbul, Spring 2012; The Drawing Center, New York, November 8–December 16, 2012; and Weatherspoon Art Museum, University of North Carolina, Greensboro, January 12–April 14, 2013.
Circuit centre d'art contemporain, Lausanne. *Play Bach*. September 24–October 29.
Muzeum Sztuki, Lodz, Poland. *Eyes Looking for a Head to Inhabit*. September 30–December 11.
Coreana Museum of Art, Seoul. *Show Me Your Hair*. October–November.
New Museum, New York. *The Last Newspaper: Contemporary Art, Curating Histories, Alternative Models*. October 6, 2010–January 9, 2011.
Tate Liverpool. *Alice in Wonderland*. November 4, 2011–January 29, 2012. Traveled to Museo d'arte moderna e contemporanea di Trento e Rovereto, Italy, February 23–June 3, 2012; and Hamburger Kunsthalle, June 22–September 30, 2012.
Centre Georges Pompidou, Paris. *Danser sa vie*. November 23, 2011–April 2, 2012.
The Art Institute of Chicago. *Light Years: Conceptual Art and the Photograph, 1964–1977*. December 13, 2011–March 11, 2012.

2012

Museum of Contemporary Art, Chicago. *This Will Have Been: Art, Love & Politics in the 1980s*. February 11–June 3. Traveled to Walker Art Center, Minneapolis, June 30–September 30; and Institute of Contemporary Art, Boston, October 26, 2012–January 27, 2013.
SITE Santa Fe. *Time-Lapse*. February 18–May 20.
ZKM Center for Art and Media, Karlsruhe, Germany. *Moments. A History of Performance in 10 Acts*. March 8–April 29. Traveled to Lunds Konsthall, Sweden, December 1, 2012–February 10, 2013 (as *Moments on Moments/Dance Is Present*); and Museum of Contemporary Art Antwerp, February 22–May 12, 2013 (as *Moments on Moments*).
Palais de Tokyo, Paris. *La Triennale: Intense Proximité*. April 20–August 26.
Museum of Contemporary Art, Los Angeles. *Ends of the Earth: Art of the Land to 1974*. May 27–September 3. Traveled to Haus der Kunst, Munich, October 11, 2012–January 20, 2013.
National Museum of Art, Architecture and Design, Oslo. *I Wish I Was a Song: Music in Contemporary Art*. September 14, 2012–January 20, 2013.
Elizabeth A. Sackler Center for Feminist Art, Brooklyn Museum, New York. *Materializing "Six Years": Lucy R. Lippard and the Emergence of Conceptual Art*. September 14, 2012–February 17, 2013.
International Center of Photography, New York. *The Rise and Fall of Apartheid: Photography and the Bureaucracy of Everyday Life*. September 14, 2012–January 6, 2013. Traveled to Haus der Kunst, Munich, February 15–May 26; Padiglione d'Arte Contemporanea, Milan, July 8–September 15; and Museum Africa, Johannesburg, February 13, 2014–April 30, 2015.
New Museum, New York. *Come Closer: Art around the Bowery, 1969–1989*. September 19–December 30.
Laure Genillard, London. *Drop Me a Line*. September 21–November 24.
National Gallery of Art, Washington, D.C. *Shock of the News*. September 23, 2012–January 27, 2013.
Artexte, Montreal. *Sophie Belair Clement, 2 rooms equal size, 1 empty, with secretary, (1)*. September 27, 2012–January 26, 2013.
DeVos Art Museum, Northern Michigan University, Marquette. *You Complete Me: Mediating Relationships in Contemporary Art*. October 1–November 11.
Seattle Art Museum. *Elles: SAM: Singular Works by Seminal Women Artists*. October 11, 2012–February 17, 2013.
Serpentine Gallery, London. *Memory Marathon*. October 12–14.
Museum of Contemporary Art, Los Angeles. *Blues for Smoke*. October 21, 2012–January 7, 2013. Traveled to Whitney Museum of American Art, New York, February 6–April 28, 2013.
LENTOS Museum, Linz, Austria. *Vollmilch: Der Bart als Zeichen*. October 26, 2012–February 17, 2013.
KOW Gallery, Berlin. *Believers*. November 10, 2012–February 3, 2013.
Contemporary Arts Museum, Houston. *Radical Presence: Black Performance in Contemporary Art*. November 17, 2012–February 15, 2013. Traveled to Grey Art Gallery, New York University, September 10–December 7, 2013 (artwork withdrawn); Studio Museum in Harlem, New York, November 14, 2013–March 9, 2014 (artwork withdrawn); and Walker Art Center, Minneapolis, July 24, 2014–January 4, 2015 (artwork withdrawn).

2013

Kunsthalle, Basel. *Museumsnacht*. January 18.
David Kordansky Gallery, Los Angeles. *The Assistants*. January 18–February 23. Exh. cat
Generali Foundation, Vienna. *Amazing! Clever! Linguistic! An Adventure in Conceptual Art*. January 18–April 21.
Haus der Kulturen der Welt, Berlin. *The Whole Earth: California and the Disappearance of the Outside*. April 26–July 7.
Palazzo delle Esposizioni, Rome. *Empire State: New York Art Now*. April 22–July 20. Traveled to Galerie Thaddaeus Ropas, Paris, November 17, 2013–February 15, 2014.
Kumu Art Museum, Estonia. *Afterlives of Gardens*. May 10–September 8.
Socrates Sculpture Park, New York. *Do It!* May 12–July 7. For a complete list of traveling venues, see: www.curatorsintl.org/special-projects/do-it/more.
La Virreina, Barcelona. *This Is Not a Love Song: Interfaces between Visual Arts and Pop Music*. May 21–October 13.
Karst, Plymouth, England. *Individual Order*. June 15–July 21.
Institut français des Pays-Bas, Amsterdam. *Ce lieu n'est pas la maison de Descartes*. June 26–July 19.
El Museo Universitario Arte Contemporáneo (MUAC), Mexico City. *Pulso alterado*. August 17, 2013–January 12, 2014.
Rongwrong, Amsterdam. *And How Are You Otherwise?* September 15–November 3.
Friedrich Schiller Universität Jena, Germany. *BrandSchutz, Mentalitäten der Intoleranz*. September 21–November 17.
4th Athens Biennale. *AGORA*. September 29–December 1.
Kunstmuseum Bern. *The Weak Sex-How Art Pictures the New Male*. October 18, 2013–February 9, 2014.
Centre d'art contemporain—la synagogue de Delme, France. *Schizophonia*. October 26, 2013–February 16, 2014.
Museum Abteiberg, Moenchengladbach, Germany. *In Order to Join—Politisch in einem historischen Moment*. December 8, 2013–March 16, 2014. Traveled to Dr. Bhau Daji Lad Mumbai City Museum, November 1–December 14, 2014; and Goethe Institute/Max Mueller Bhavan, Mumbai, February 26–April 19, 2015.

2014

Contemporary Art Museum, St. Louis. *Readykeulous by Ridykeulous: This Is What Liberation Feels Like™*. January 24–April 13. Traveled to Institute of Contemporary Art, University of Pennsylvania, Philadelphia, September 19–December 28.
Dallas Biennial. February 1–May 31.
Hammer Museum, Los Angeles. *Take It or Leave It: Institution, Image, Ideology*. February 9–May 18.
Kunstnernes Hus, Oslo. *In These Great Times*. February 21–April 14.
Museo Nacional Centro de Arte Reina Sofía, Madrid. *Playgrounds*. April 30–September 22.
8th Shenzhen Sculpture Biennale, OCT Contemporary Art Terminal, China. *We Have Never Participated*. May 16–August 31.
Walker Art Center, Minneapolis. *Art Expanded, 1958–1978*. June 14, 2014–March 1, 2015.
La Panacée, Montpellier, France. *Une lettre arrive toujours*. July 18–November 16.
Hebbel am Ufer, Berlin. *Strut Your Stuff*. August 16–31. Traveled to Dansens Hus, Stockholm, August–September.
Institute for Curatorial Practice, Hampshire College, Amherst, Massachusetts. *Sometimes a Traveler: Women, Othered Bodies, and the Colonizing Gaze* (online exhibition).

2015

SPACE, Pittsburgh. *UNLOADED*. February 13–April 26. Traveled to Northern Illinois University Art Museum, Dekalb, August 24–October 25; Handwerker Gallery, Ithaca College, New York, February 3–March 6, 2016; Urban Institute for Contemporary Arts, Grand Rapids, Michigan, March 31–May 5 and July 5–31, 2016; Indianapolis Museum of Contemporary Art, October 7–December 31, 2016; Bolivar Art Gallery, University of Kentucky, Lexington, January 20–February 18, 2017; Minneapolis College of Art and Design, June 2–July 16, 2017; and Harris Art Gallery, University of La Verne, California, September 5–October 26, 2017.
Raven Row, London. *Five Issues of Studio International*. February 26—May 3.
Nottingham Contemporary, England. *Glenn Ligon: Encounters and Collisions*. April 3–June 14.
56th International Art Exhibition of La Biennale di

Venezia, Central Pavilion in the Giardini, Venice. *All the World's Futures*. May 9–November 22.
La Halle, Pont-en-Royans, France. *De l'un(e) à l'autre*. October 23–December 30.

2016

Dominique Lévy, New York. *Drawing Then: Innovation and Influence in American Drawings of the Sixties*. January 27–March 26.
DUVE, Berlin. **MIRRORS**. March 3–April 16.
9. Berlin Biennale. Organized by KW Institute for Contemporary Art. June 4–September 18.
Museum der Moderne, Salzburg. *Making Spaces: From the Collections*. October 22, 2016–April 17, 2017.

2017

Walker Art Center, Minneapolis. *I am you, you are too*. September 7, 2017–October 27, 2020.
MAMCO, Museé d'Art moderne et contemporain, Geneva. *Narrative Art*. October 11, 2017–February 4, 2018.

SELECTED BIBLIOGRAPHY
COMPILED BY TESSA FERREYROS

PAGEWORKS BY ADRIAN PIPER

1969

Position A–C, Part I: Position A–B. In *557,087*, edited by Lucy Lippard. Exh. cat. Seattle: Seattle Art Museum.

Untitled ("If you are a slow reader . . ."). 0 TO 9, edited by Vito Acconci and Bernadette Mayer, no. 5 (January): 49.

Untitled ("OR: 2) begin upper right corner . . ."). 0 TO 9, edited by Vito Acconci and Bernadette Mayer, no. 5 (January): 50–52.

Untitled ("The area described by the periphery of this ad . . .")/Area Relocation Series #2. Village Voice, May 29, p. 16.

Untitled ("1. Rectangles are located according to co-ordinate position . . ."). 0 TO 9, edited by Vito Acconci and Bernadette Mayer, no. 6 (July): 79–81.

Untitled ("The top side of the following page represents a void space . . ."). 0 TO 9, edited by Vito Acconci and Bernadette Mayer, no. 6 (July): 105–9.

Untitled work."Street Works." Supplement, *0 TO 9*, edited by Vito Acconci and Bernadette Mayer, no. 6 (July): n.p.

Untitled work. *Art Press*, no. 1 (August): 7.

1970

Groups. Organized by Lucy Lippard. *Studio International* 179, no. 920 (March): 95.

1971

Untitled work. *Free Media Bulletin*, no. 12. London: Ted Hawke Press.

Untitled work. In *26 Contemporary Women Artists*, edited by Lucy Lippard, n.p. Exh. cat. Ridgefield, Conn.: Aldrich Museum of Contemporary Art.

1973

The Mythic Being, Cycle I: 9/21/61. Village Voice, September 27, p. 56.

The Mythic Being, Cycle I: 10/17/62. Village Voice, October 25.

The Mythic Being, Cycle I: 11/63. Village Voice, November 29.

1974

The Mythic Being, Cycle I: 12/12/64. Village Voice, January 3, p. 23.

The Mythic Being, Cycle I: 1/9/65. Village Voice, January 31, p. 33.

The Mythic Being, Cycle I: 2/66. Village Voice, February 28, p. 29.

The Mythic Being, Cycle I: 3/67. Village Voice, March 28, p. 27.

The Mythic Being, Cycle I: 4/12/68. Village Voice, April 25, p. 31.

The Mythic Being, Cycle I: 5/7/69. Village Voice, May 30, p. 33.

The Mythic Being, Cycle I: 6/6/70. Village Voice, June 27, p. 33.

The Mythic Being, Cycle I: 6/6/70, Censored Village Voice Ad #10. Self-published and distributed.

The Mythic Being, Cycle I: 7/14/71. Village Voice, July 25, p. 11.

The Mythic Being, Cycle I: 8/14/72. Village Voice, August 29, p. 32.

The Mythic Being, . . . End of Cycle I. Village Voice, September 26, p. 38.

The Mythic Being, Cycle II: 10/13/61. Village Voice, October 31, p. 59.

The Mythic Being, Cycle II: 11/24/62. Village Voice, December 2, p. 97.

The Mythic Being, Cycle II: 12/63. Village Voice, December 30, p. 74.

1975

The Mythic Being, Cycle II: Thanks. Village Voice, February 2, p. 97.

Six Conditions on Art Production. In *Lives*, edited by Jeffrey Deitch. Exh. cat. New York: Fine Arts Building.

1980

Where's the Art? In *Matrix 56: Adrian Piper*. Exh. broch. Hartford: Wadsworth Atheneum.

1984

Selected Funk Lessons: A Page Project by Adrian Piper. Artforum 22, no. 5 (January): 64.

1987

Kuspit Extermination Fantasy and *Piper Strangulation Fantasy*. *Real Life Magazine* 17–18, no. 1 (1987–88): 2–11.

1989

How can anybody want to wipe you out just for being different? (Wonder Project). Artforum 28, no. 10 (Summer): 135.

1990

Girl Talk (#1–#3). ArtVu 4, no. 1 (July): n.p.

1997

DECISIONS, DECISIONS. "Paranoia." Special issue, *Grand St.*, no. 60, pp. 136–45.

2001

The Color Wheel Series, Second Adhyasa II.68–129. Art Journal 60, no. 3 (Fall): front and back covers.

2012

Spezial Buchcover. Monopol 10 (October): 77.

2016

"Adrian Piper: Artist's Project." *Artforum* 54, no. 10 (Summer): 330–37.

2018

My Calling (Card) #3: Guerrilla Performance for Disputed Territorial Skirmishes (2012). *Artforum* 56, no. 5 (January): 140–43.

ARTIST'S BOOKS BY ADRIAN PIPER

1968

Here and Now. Unique edition.

1969

Three Untitled Projects. New York: 0 TO 9 Press.

1991

Colored People. In collaboration with Houston Conwill, Kinshasa Conwill, Jane Farver, David Frankel, Sam Gilliam, Kellie Jones, Lucy Lippard, Rosemary Mayer, John Moore, John Morita, Clive Phillpot, Howardena Pindell, Lowery Sims, Kaylynn Sullivan, Judith Wilson, and Josephine Whithers. London: Bookworks. Reissued 2007.

WRITINGS BY ADRIAN PIPER

1970

"Three Models of Art Production Systems." In *Information*, edited by Kynaston McShine, p. 111. New York: The Museum of Modern Art. Reprinted in *Conceptual Art*, edited by Ursula Meyer, p. 202 (New York: E. P. Dutton, 1972); and *Essaying Essays: Alternative Forms of Exposition*, edited by Richard Kostelanetz, p. 276 (New York: Out of London Press, 1976).

1972

"An Ongoing Essay." In *Art and Artists* 6 (March): 44–47.

1973

"In Support of Meta-Art." *Artforum* 12, no. 2 (October): 79–81. Reprinted in *Conceptual Art: A Critical Anthology*, edited by Alexander Alberro and Blake Stimson, p. 298 (Cambridge, U.K.: Cambridge University Press, 1999).

"Selections from 'An Ongoing Essay.'" In *Six Years: The Dematerialization of the Art Object*, edited by Lucy Lippard, pp. 234–35. New York: Praeger.

"Withdrawal Statement (from New York Cultural Center)." In *Six Years: The Dematerialization of the Art Object*, edited by Lucy Lippard, p. 168. New York: Praeger.

1974

"Notes on the Mythic Being." *Tri-Quarterly*, Winter.

"A Political Statement." *Art-Rite* 6 (Summer): 24.

Talking to Myself: The Ongoing Autobiography of an Art Object. Brussels: Fernand Spillemaeckers (English/French); Bari, Italy: Marilena Bonomo, 1975 (English/Italian).

1975

"To Art (Reg. Intrans. V.)." *The Fox* 1, no. 1, pp. 60–65.

"A Proposal for Pricing Works of Art." *The Fox* 1, no. 2, pp. 48–49.

1976

"Cheap Art Utopia." *Art-Rite* 14 (Winter 1976–77): 11–12. Reprinted in *La Especial Norte* 2 (Fall 2008): 1–2.

"Notes on the Mythic Being, I–II." In *Individuals: Post-Movement Art*, edited by Alan Sondheim, pp. 270–89. New York: E. P. Dutton. Reprinted in *Voicing Today's Visions: Writings by Contemporary Women Artists*, edited by Mara Witzling, pp. 286–308 (New York: Universe, 1994).

"Some Reflective Surfaces." *Sun and Moon* 2 (Spring): 18–20.

1979

"Critics' Delight." In *A Critical Assembling*, edited by Richard Kostelanetz, p. 95. New York: Participation Project Foundation.

1980

"Is the Alternative Space a True Alternative?" Response compiled by Rudolph Baranik. *Studio International* 195, no. 990 (August): 72.

"Some Political Self-Reflection (July 1980)." In *Issue*. London: Institute of Contemporary Art, November.

"Some Thoughts on the Political Character of This Situation." In *Art of Conscience: The Last Decade*. Dayton: Wright University.

1981

"Food for the Spirit." *High Performance* 4, no. 1 (Spring): 19.

"Ideology, Confrontation, and Political Self-Awareness: An Essay." *High Performance* 4, no. 1 (Spring): 38–39. Reprinted in *Blasted Allegories: An Anthology of Writings by Contemporary Artists*, edited by Brian Wallis, p. 129 (New York: New Museum of Contemporary Art; Cambridge, Mass.: MIT Press, 1987); *Theories and Documents of Contemporary Art: A Sourcebook of Artists' Writings*, edited by Kristine Stiles and Peter Selz, pp. 787–91 (Berkeley: University of California Press, 1996); *The Citizen Artist: 20 Years of Art in the Public Arena*, edited by Linda Burnham and Steven Durland, p. 87 (New York: Critical Press, 1998); and *Art and Social Change: A Critical Reader*, edited by Will Bradley and Charles Esche, pp. 241–44 (London: Tate/After All Books, 2008).

"Performance and the Fetishism of the Art Object." *Vanguard* 10, no. 10 (December 1981–January 1982): 16–19. Reprinted in "Essays on [Performance] and Cultural Politicization," special issue edited by Bruce Barber, *Open Letter* 5, nos. 5–6 (Summer–

Fall 1983): 7–17.
"Untitled Art-Political Meditation." *Village Voice*, February 4, p. 62.

1984

"Critical Hegemony and the Division of Labor in Art." Paper delivered at "Visual Arts Seminar on Art Criticism," September 19–20, 1983, in *Proceedings of the National Endowment for the Arts*. Washington D.C.: The National Endowment for the Arts, 1984.
"Letter to Thomas McEvilley." *Artforum* 22, no. 2 (October): 2–3.

1985

"Untitled Statement." In *The Art of Memory/The Loss of History*, p. 34. New York: New Museum of Contemporary Art.

1987

"Flying." In *Adrian Piper: Reflections, 1967–1987*, pp. 24–33. New York: The Alternative Museum. Reprinted in *Adrian Piper*, pp. 21–27. Exh. cat (Birmingham, U.K.: Ikon Gallery, 1991).
"It's Not All Black and White." Letter to the editor. *Village Voice*, June 9, pp. 4, 6.
"An Open Letter to Donald Kuspit." *Real Life Magazine* 17–18 (Winter 1987–88): 2–11. Reprinted in *Witness to Her Art*, edited by Rhea Anastas and Michael Brenson, pp. 89–98 (Annandale-on-Hudson, N.Y.: Bard College Center for Curatorial Studies; Ostfildern-Ruit, Germany: Hatje Cantz Verlag, 2006); and *Real Life Magazine: Selected Writings and Projects, 1979–1994*, pp. 246–55 (New York: Primary Information, 2006).
"Who Is Safely White?" *Women Artists News* 12, no. 2 (June): 6.

1988

"On Conceptual Art." *Flash Art*, November–December, p. 115. Reprinted in *Conceptual Art: A Critical Anthology*, edited by Alexander Alberro and Blake Stimson, pp. 424–25 (Cambridge, U.K.: Cambridge University Press, 1999).

1989

"Cornered." Video screenplay. *Balcon 4*, pp. 122–35. Republished as "Coincée." In *Art et mondialisation*, edited by Sophie Orlando and translated by Jean-Francois Cornu, pp. 73–76. Paris: Éditions du Centre Pompidou, 2013.
"A Paradox of Conscience." *New Art Examiner* 16, no. 8 (April): 27–31.

1990

"Artist Statement." In *Words and Images—with a Message*. Exh. cat. Oneonta, New York: Women's Studio Workshop.
"Goodbye to Easy Listening." In *Adrian Piper: PRETEND*. Exh. cat. New York: John Weber Gallery. Reprinted in *Aphros*, Spring–Summer 1991, pp. 34–40.
"Introduction to Epistemology." *Real Life Magazine* 20, pp. 18–19.
"The Joy of Marginality." *Art Papers* 14, no. 4 (July–August): 12–13. Reprinted in "The Nineties," special issue, *Ikon*, 1991–92, pp. 3–7; and *Art Papers*, March–April 2014.
"To the Editors." *Art in America* 5, no. 1 (November): 39.
"The Triple Negation of Colored Women Artists." In *Next Generation*, pp. 15–22. Chapel Hill: University of North Carolina. Reprinted in *At the Crossroads* 3 (Summer–Fall 1994): 14–18; and *The Feminism and Visual Culture Reader*, edited by Amelia Jones, pp. 239–48 (New York: Routledge, 2003).
"Xenophobia and the Indexical Present" and "Funk Lessons." In *Re-Imaging America: The Arts of Social Change*, edited by Mark O'Brian, pp. 285–95. Philadelphia: New Society Press. Reprinted in *Kontext Kunst*, edited by Peter Weibel, pp. 490–98 (Cologne: DuMont Buchverlag, 1994).
"Xenophobia and the Individual Present." *Cover* 5, no. 1 (September): 14.

1991

"Adrian Piper." *MoMA Members Quarterly*, Fall, p. 8.
"Brenson on Quality." *Art Papers* 15, no. 6 (November–December): 68–73.
Letter to the editor. *Artforum* 29, no. 9 (May): 27–28.
"Letter to the Editor: Angle Dangle." *City Paper* 11, no. 29 (July 19–25): 4.
"A Transition into Solipsism October 1971." In *The Political Arm*, pp. 32–33. Exh. cat. New York: John Weber Gallery.
"Vanilla Nightmares 1986– ." In *Drawings*, pp. 34–35. Exh. cat. New York: John Weber Gallery.
"What It Isn't #2," *City Paper* 11, no. 33 (August 16–22): 4.

1992

"Art and Politics: A Pre-Election Symposium." *Art in America* 80, no. 10 (October): 41.
"Cornered: A Video Installation Project by Adrian Piper." *Movement Research Performance Journal*, no. 4 (Winter–Spring): 10. Reprinted in *Theory in Contemporary Art since 1985*, edited by Zoya Kocur and Simon Leung, pp. 182–86. Malden, Mass.: Blackwell, 2005.
Decide Who You Are: Texts. Exh. cat. New York: Paula Cooper Gallery.
"Government Support for Unconventional Works of Art." In *Culture and Democracy, Social and Ethical Issues in Public Support for the Arts and Humanities*, edited by Andrew Buchwalter, pp. 219–22. Boulder, Colo.: Westview Press,.
"Passing for White, Passing for Black." *Transition* 58, pp. 4–32. Reprinted in *New Feminist Criticism: Art-Identity-Action*, edited by Joanna Frueh, Cassandra L. Langer, and Arlene Raven, pp. 216–47 (New York: HarperCollins, 1994); and *Passing and the Fictions of Identity*, edited by Elaine K. Ginsberg, pp. 34–69 (Durham, N.C.: Duke University Press, 1996).

1993

"The Great War for Control of Reality." In *Ethics of Change: Women in the '90s—Sex, Power and Politics*, edited by Barbara J. Raines, pp. 95–161. New Smyrna Beach, Fla.: Atlantic Center for the Arts.
Introductory essay. "Color." Special issue, *New Observations*, no. 97 (September–October): 2–4.
"The Logic of Modernism." *Flash Art*, January–February. Reprinted in *Callaloo* 16, no. 3 (Summer); *Kontext Kunst*, edited by Peter Weibel, pp. 282–88 (Cologne: DuMont Buchverlag, 1994); *Definitions of Visual Culture II: Modernist Utopias—Postformalism and Pure Visuality*, edited by Christine Bernier (Montreal: Musée d'Art Contemporain de Montréal, 1996); and *Conceptual Art: A Critical Anthology*, edited by Alexander Alberro and Blake Stimson, pp. 546–49 (Cambridge, U.K.: Cambridge University Press, 1999).
"Two Kinds of Discrimination." *Yale Journal of Criticism* 6, no. 1, pp. 25–74. Reprinted in *Voicing Today's Visions: Writings by Contemporary Women Artists*, edited by Mara Witzling, pp. 286–308 (New York: Universe, 1994).
"Xenophobia and the Indexical Present II: Lecture." In *Place Position Presentation Public*, pp. 24, 136–57. The Hague: Jan Van Eyck Akademie and the Authors CIP-Gegevens Koninklijke Bibliotheek.

1995

"On 1980s Feminist Theorizing." *October* 71 (Winter): 35–36.

1996

"Dickinson's Charm." Letter. *New York Review of Books* 43, no. 15 (October 3): 57.
"Ian Burn's Conceptualism." Lecture transcript. *LIKE*, no. 1 (October): 42–53. Revised and edited version published in *Art in America* 85, no. 12 (December): 72–79, 106. Reprinted in *Conceptual Art: Theory, Myth and Practice*, edited by Michael Corris, pp. 342–58 (Cambridge, U.K.: Cambridge University Press, 2004).
"Mortal Remains." In *Mortal Remains*, edited by Ricardo Bloch and Don Celender. Minneapolis: Intermedia Arts Minnesota.
Out of Order, Out of Sight, vol. 1, *Selected Writings in Meta-Art, 1968–1992*. Cambridge, Mass.: MIT Press.
Out of Order, Out of Sight, vol. 2, *Selected Writings in Art Criticism, 1967–1992*. Cambridge, Mass.: MIT Press.
"Philip Morris' Artworld Fix." *Drama Review* 40, no. 4 (Winter): 5–6.
"Withdrawal Clarified." Letter. *Art in America* 84, no. 4 (April): 29.

1997

"Advice to Readers." Letter. *Art in America* 85, no. 4 (April): 27.
"Discussion with Marianne Brouwer, Martin Lucas and Adrian Piper." In *Voorbij ethiiek en esthetiek/ Beyond Ethics and Aesthetics*, edited by Ine Gevers and Jeanne van Heeswijk, pp. 42–79. Nijmegen: Uitgeverij SUN.

1998

"Xenophobia and the Indexical Present: Lecture." In *Disturbing the Peace: Radical Street Performance Around the World*, edited by Jan Cohen-Cruz, pp. 125–32. New York: Routledge.

2001

Excerpts from "Notes on Mythic Being." In *Double Life: Identity and Transformation in Contemporary Arts*, edited by Sabine Breitwieser, pp. 198–205. Exh. cat. Vienna: Generali Foundation.
"Whiteless." *Art Journal* 60, no. 3 (Winter): 63–65.

2002

"Letters: Adrian Piper on Black and White." *Art in America* 90, no. 1 (January): 25.
"I Answer This Request with Observations." In *Gloria: Another Look at Feminist Art in the 1970s*, p. 2. Exh. cat. New York: White Columns.

2003

"Adrian Piper." In *Occupying Space: Generali Foundation Collection*, pp. 427–64. Cologne: Verlag der Buchhandlung Walther König.

2004

"Corrections: Points of Clarification." *Art Papers* 28, no. 6 (November–December): 9.

2005

"The Memorial to the Murdered Jews of Europe." *Frieze*, no. 91 (May): 90–91.
"Letter to a Young Artist." *Art on Paper* 9, no. 6 (July–August): 36–37. Reprinted in *Letters to a Young Artist*, edited by Peter Nesbett and Sarah Andress, pp. 83–88 (New York: Darte, 2006).

2006

"Aspects of the Liberal Dilemma." In *Witness to Her Art*, edited by Rhea Anastas and Michael Brenson, pp. 83–84. Annandale-on-Hudson, N.Y.: Center for Curatorial Studies, Bard College; Ostfildern-Ruit, Germany: Hatje Cantz Verlag.
"Notes on Funk, I–II," 1983–85. Reprinted in *Participation: Documents of Contemporary Art*,

edited by Claire Bishop, pp. 130–34 (London: Whitechapel Ventures Limited).

2008

"Ideal Syllabus: Adrian Piper." *Frieze*, no. 16 (June–August): 38–39.

"Intuition and Concrete Particularity in Kant's Transcendental Aesthetic." In *Rediscovering Aesthetics: Transdisciplinary Voices from Art History, Philosophy, and Art Practice*, edited by Francis Halsall, Julia Jansen, and Tony O'Connor, p. 193. Palo Alto: Stanford University Press.

"Political Art and the Paradigm of Innovation." In *The Life and Death of Images: Ethics and Aesthetics*, edited by Diarmuid Costello and Dominic Willsdon, pp. 119–33. Ithaca: Cornell University Press; London: Tate. Reprinted in *The Idea of the Avant Garde–And What It Means Today*, edited by Marc Leger, pp. 4–11 (Manchester, U.K.: Manchester University Press, 2014).

"Response to Noel Carroll." In *The Life and Death of Images: Ethics and Aesthetics*, edited by Diarmuid Costello and Dominic Willsdon, pp. 110–18. Ithaca: Cornell University Press; London: Tate.

"To Sol Lewitt." Excerpted in *Bowery Artist Tribute*, edited by Ethan Swan, 1:20–21. New York: Isabel Asha Penzlien and New Museum of Contemporary Art.

2009

"Criticizing the Critics." Lecture followed by question and answer session with Jörg Heiser. In *Frieze Projects Frieze Talks, 2006–2008*, pp. 144–61. London: Frieze.

"Notes on Funk I-IV." In *Funkaesthetics*, pp. 91–110. Exh cat. Toronto: Justina M. Barnicke Gallery; Charlottetown, Prince Edward Island: Confederation Centre Art Gallery.

"The Unity of Sol LeWitt's Oeuvre." In *Sol LeWitt: 100 Views*, edited by Susan Cross and Denise Markonish, p. 89. North Adams: Massachusetts Museum of Contemporary Art; New Haven, Conn.: Yale University Press.

2010

"Questions of Style." *Artforum* 5, no. 1 (September): 269–70.

2011

"Political Self-Portraits." In *It Is Almost That*, edited by Lisa Pearson, pp. 10–15. Los Angeles: Siglio.

"To Hans." In *With Reference to Hans Haacke*, edited by Hans Dickel and Oliver Schwarz, pp. 68–69. Cologne: Verlag der Buchhandlung Walther König.

2012

"Artist's Favorites." *Spike Magazine* 5, no. 1 (March).

"Curating Curators." *Texte zur Kunst* 22, no. 86 (June): 42–62.

"Giotto's Kiss of Judas," *Frieze Masters Magazine* 5, no. 1 (October): 100.

"Introduction: Affirmative Actions of Power." In *The Reorder of Things*, edited by Roderick A. Ferguson, pp. 1–18. Minneapolis: University of Minnesota Press.

2013

"The Humming Room." In *Do It: The Compendium*, edited by Hans Ulrich Obrist and Kate Fowle, p. 309. New York: Distributed Art Publishers.

2014

"Political Art and the Paradigm of Innovation." In *The Idea of the Avant-Garde and What It Means Today*, edited by Marc Léger, pp. 4–11. Manchester, U.K.: Manchester University Press.

2017

"As a Matter of Fact." Letter to the editor. *Artforum* 55, no. 10 (Summer): 67–68.

"New Objectivity." Letter to the editor. *Artforum* 56, no. 4 (December): 26

SOLO EXHIBITION CATALOGUES AND BROCHURES

1980

Miller-Keller, Andrea, ed. *Matrix 56: Adrian Piper*. Hartford, Conn.: Wadsworth Atheneum.

1989

Farver, Jane, ed. *Adrian Piper: Reflections, 1967–1987*. New York: The Alternative Museum/John Weber Gallery.

Rifkin, Ned, ed. *Adrian Piper: What It's Like, What It Is #2*. Washington, D.C.: Smithsonian Institution, Hirshhorn Museum and Sculpture Garden.

Rinder, Lawrence, ed. *Matrix/Berkeley 130: Adrian Piper*. Berkeley: University of California, Berkeley Art Museum and Pacific Film Archive.

1990

Goldberg, Elyse, ed. *Adrian Piper: Pretend*. New York: John Weber Gallery.

Menaker, Deborah, ed. *Adrian Piper: Artworks*. Williamstown: Williams College Museum of Art.

1991

MacGregor, Elizabeth, ed. *Adrian Piper*. Birmingham, U.K.: Ikon Gallery; Manchester, U.K.: Cornerhouse.

Rubin, David S., ed. *Adrian Piper: Political Drawings and Installations, 1975–1991*. Cleveland: Cleveland Center for Contemporary Art.

Watkin, Mel, ed. *Adrian Piper: What It's Like, What It Is #1*. Washington, D.C.: Washington Project for the Arts.

1999

Berger, Maurice. *Adrian Piper: A Retrospective*. Baltimore: University of Maryland, Fine Arts Gallery.

2002

Breitwieser, Sabine, ed. *Adrian Piper: seit 1965; Metakunst und Kunstkritik*. With an introduction by Breitwieser and a preface by Dietrich Karner. Vienna: Generali Foundation; Cologne: W. König.

2003

Dávila, Mela, ed. *Adrian Piper: desde 1965*. With an introduction by Sabine Breitwieser. Barcelona: Museu d'Art Contemporani de Barcelona/Actar.

2017

Adrian Piper. The Probable Trust Registry: The Rules of the Game #1–3. Berlin: Hamburger Bahnhof–Museum für Gegenwart: Nationalgalerie Staatliche Museen zu Berlin.

Yasar, Begum, ed. *Adrian Piper*. New York: Lévy Gorvy.

GROUP EXHIBITION CATALOGUES AND OTHER BOOKS

1975

Kostelanetz, Richard, ed. *Essaying Essays: Alternative Forms of Exposition*. New York: Out of London Press.

1976

Lippard, Lucy. *From the Center: Feminist Essays on Women's Art*. New York: E. P. Dutton.

Serlis, Effie. "Adrian Piper." In *Interviews with Women in the Arts: Part 2*, edited by Joyce Kozloff, pp. 24–27. New York: School of Visual Arts Press.

1979

Goldberg, RoseLee. *Performance: Live Art, 1909 to the Present*. New York: Harry N. Abrams.

1981

Green, Ellen Renée. "Adrian Piper." In John T. Paoletti, *No title: [the collection of Sol Lewitt]*, pp. 82–84. Exh. cat. Middletown, Conn.: Wesleyan University; Hartford, Conn.: Wadsworth Atheneum.

1983

Roth, Moira. "Adrian Piper." In *The Amazing Decade: Women and Performance in America, 1970–1980*, edited by Moira Roth, pp. 122–23. Los Angeles: Astro Artz.

1984

Felshin, Nina. *Disarming Images: Art for Nuclear Disarmament*. Exh. cat. New York: Adama Books.

Lippard, Lucy. *Get the Message? A Decade of Art for Social Change*. New York: E. P. Dutton.

1985

The Art of Memory/The Loss of History. Exh. cat. New York: New Museum of Contemporary Art.

1988

Okun, Rob A., ed. *The Rosenbergs: Collected Visions of Artists and Writers*. Exh. cat. New York: Universe Books.

Sims, Lowery Stokes. "Aspects of Performance in the Work of Black American Women Artists." In *Feminist Art Criticism*, edited by Arlene Raven, Cassandra Langer, and Joanna Frueh, pp. 207–25. Ann Arbor: UMI Research Press.

1989

Steinbaum, Bernice. *American Resources: Selected Works of African American Artists*. Exh. cat. New York: Bernice Steinbaum Gallery.

Wilson, Judith. "Adrian Piper." In *Black Arts Annual, 1987–1988*, edited by Donald Bogle, pp. 40–41. New York: Garland.

Wooster, Ann-Sargent, and Judith E. Stein. "Making Their Mark." In *Making Their Mark: Women Enter the Mainstream, 1970–1985*, edited by Randy Rosen and Catherine C. Brawer, pp. 51–185. Exh. cat. New York: Abbeville Press.

1990

Coast to Coast: A Women of Color National Artists' Book Project. Exh. cat. Radford, Va.: Flossie Martin Gallery, Radford University.

Lippard, Lucy. *Mixed Blessings: New Art in a Multicultural America*. New York: Pantheon Books.

Ottmann, Klaus, ed. *Exotism*. Exh. broch. Middletown, Conn.: Ezra and Cecile Zilkha Gallery, Wesleyan University.

1991

Hixson, Kathryn. "AVA 10: 1991." In *Awards in the Visual Arts 10*, pp. 9–23. Exh. cat. Winston-Salem, N.C.: Southeastern Center for Contemporary Art.

Lippard, Lucy. "Intruders: Lynda Benglis and Adrian Piper." In *Breakthroughs: Avant-Garde Artists in Europe and America*, edited by John Howell, pp. 125–32. New York: Rizzoli.

Storr, Robert. *Devil on the Stairs: Looking Back on the Eighties*. Exh. cat. Philadelphia: Institute of Contemporary Art, University of Pennsylvania.

Storr, Robert, ed. *Dislocations*. Exh. cat. New York: The Museum of Modern Art.

1992

Berger, Maurice. "Black Skin, White Masks: Adrian Piper and the Politics of Viewing." In *How Art Becomes History: Essays on Art, Society, and*

Culture in Post-New Deal America, pp. 93–113. New York: Harper Collins.

1993

Berger, Maurice. "Displacements." In *Ciphers of Identity*, pp. 13–41. Exh. cat. Catonsville: Fine Arts Gallery, University of Maryland Baltimore County.

Bremner, Ann. "Black Box/White Box." In *Will/Power*, edited by Sarah J. Rogers, pp. 54–61. Exh. cat. Columbus: Wexner Center for the Arts, The Ohio State University.

Gaines, Charles. "The Theater of Refusal: Black Art and Mainstream Criticism." In *The Theater of Refusal: Black Art and Mainstream Criticism*, pp. 12–21. Exh. cat. Irvine: Fine Arts Gallery, University of California, Irvine.

Solomon-Godeau, Abigail. "Mistaken Identities." In *Mistaken Identities*, pp. 19–63. Exh. cat. Seattle: University of Washington Press.

1994

Pusch, Detlev. *Gewalt, Geschäfte: Eine Ausstellung zum Topos der Gewalt in der gegenwärtigen künstlerischen Auseinandersetzung*. Exh. cat. Berlin: NGBK.

Rugoff, Ralph. "Transformative Aesthetics." In *Transformers*, pp. 11–58. New York: Independent Curators Incorporated.

Storr, Robert. "Between a Rock and a Hard Place." *Paper #3*. Paper Series on the Arts, Culture and Society. New York: Andy Warhol Foundation for the Visual Arts.

———. "The Map Room: A Visitor's Guide." *Mapping*, pp. 5–23. Exh. cat. New York: The Museum of Modern Art.

Walker, Alexia. "Adrian Piper: Endless Loop Record/Erase." In *L'Hiver de l'amour*, pp. 72–73. Exh. cat. Paris: Musée d'art moderne de la ville de Paris.

1995

Ars 95: Näyttelyopas unställningsguide. Exh. cat. Helsinki: Museum of Contemporary Art, Finnish National Gallery.

Emenhiser, Karen. "Tactics of Shame." In *Adrian Piper: Cornered—Decide Who You Are*, pp. 40–42. Exh. cat. Buffalo: University at Buffalo Art Gallery.

Goldstein, Ann, and Anne Rorimer, eds. *Reconsidering the Object of Art: 1965–1975*. Exh. cat. Los Angeles: Museum of Contemporary Art; Cambridge, Mass.: MIT Press.

Lineker, Bruce, and Maurice Berger. *Civil Rights Now*. Exh. cat. Winston-Salem, N.C.: Southeastern Center for Contemporary Art.

Marks, Laura U. "The Blue Flame of Reason." In *Adrian Piper: Cornered—Decide Who You Are*, pp. 43–44. Exh. cat. Buffalo: University at Buffalo Art Gallery.

1996

Ameline, Jean-Paul, and Griselda Pollock. *Face à l'histoire 1933–1996: L'Artiste moderne devant l'événement historique*. Exh. cat. Paris: Flammarion/Centre Georges Pompidou.

Hunt, Ian. "Adrian Piper." In *Book Works: A Partial History and Sourcebook*, edited by Jane Rolo and Ian Hunt, pp. 122–24. London: Book Works.

1998

Patton, Sharon F. *African-American Art*. New York: Oxford University Press.

1999

Berger, Maurice. "Cornered." In *White Lies: Race and Myths of Whiteness*, pp. 159–63. New York: Farrar, Strauss, Giroux.

Global Conceptualism: Points of Origin, 1950s–1980s. Exh. cat. New York: Queens Museum of Art.

2001

Groos, Ulrike, Karen McCarthy, and Paul McCarthy. "Adrian Piper's 'Funk Lessons' and Other Works." In *Wiederaufnahme: Retake*, pp. 108–15. Exh. cat. Frankfurt: Revolver.

Rorimer, Anne. *New Art in the 60s and 70s: Redefining Reality*. London: Thames & Hudson.

2002

Drake, Jennifer. "Variations on Negation: Breaking the Frame with Lorna Simpson and Adrian Piper." In *Interfaces: Women/Autobiography/Image/Performance*, edited by Sidonie Smith and Julia Watson, pp. 211–39. Ann Arbor: University of Michigan Press.

Taylor, Simon. "The Women's Artist Movement from Radical to Cultural Feminism from 1969 to 1975." In *Personal and Political: The Women's Art Movement, 1969–1975*, by Simon Taylor and Natalie Ng, pp. 9–31. Exh. cat. East Hampton, N.Y.: Guild Hall Museum.

2003

Alberro, Alexander. *Conceptual Art and the Politics of Publicity*. Cambridge, Mass.: MIT Press.

Beyer, Melissa Brookheart, and Jill Dawsey. *Walking in the City: Spatial Practices in Art from the Mid-1960s to the Present*. Exh. brochure. New York: Apex Art.

Fogle, Douglas. *The Last Picture Show: Artists Using Photography, 1960–1982*. Exh. cat. Minneapolis: Walker Art Center.

Fusco, Coco, and Brian Wallis, eds. *Only Skin Deep: Changing Visions of the American Self*. New York: Harry N. Abrams.

Moten, Fred. "Resistance of the Object: Adrian Piper's Theatricality." In *In the Break: The Aesthetics of the Black Radical Tradition*, pp. 233–54. Minneapolis: University of Minnesota Press.

Phelan, Peggy. "Broken Symmetries: Memory, Sight, Love." In *The Feminism and Visual Culture Reader*, edited by Amelia Jones, pp. 105–14. New York: Routledge.

2004

Jackson, Shannon. *Professing Performance: Theatre in the Academy from Philology to Performativity*. Cambridge, U.K.: Cambridge University Press.

Saxenhuber, Hedwig, ed. *Erlauf Remembers*. Frankfurt: Revolver.

Zabunyan, Elvan. *Black Is a Color: Une histoire de l'art africain-américain contemporain*. Paris: Dis Voir.

2005

Burton, Johanna, Mark B. Godfrey, Boris Groys, and Donna De Salvo. *Open Systems: Rethinking Art c. 1970*. London: Tate.

Heiser, Jörg, ed. "Adrian Piper." In *Funky Lessons*, pp. 84–91. Interview. Frankfurt: Revolver.

Hoffmann, Jens, and Joan Jonas. *Perform*. London: Thames & Hudson.

Salazar, Erin. "Adrian Piper." In *Collection Remixed*, pp. 64–65. Bronx, N.Y.: Bronx Museum of the Arts.

Wood, William. "What Business Are You In?" In *What Business Are You In?* Exh. broch. Atlanta: Atlanta Contemporary Art Center.

2006

Alberro, Alexander, and Sabeth Buchmann. *Art after Conceptual Art*. Vienna: Generali Foundation; Cambridge, Mass.: MIT Press.

Franks, Pamela. "Conceptual Rigor and Political Efficacy, or, the Making of Adrian Piper." In *Witness to Her Art*, edited by Rhea Anastas and Michael Brenson, pp. 75–82. Annandale-on-Hudson, N.Y.: Center for Curatorial Studies, Bard College.

Wark, Jane. *Radical Gestures: Feminism and Performance Art in North America*. Montreal: McGill-Queen's University Press.

2007

Barber, Bruce. "Interview with Adrian Piper." In *Performance, [Performance] and Performer*, vol. 1, *Conversations*, edited by Marc James Léger. Toronto: YYZBOOKS.

Clausen, Barbara. "Documents between Spectator and Action." In *Live Art on Camera: Performance and Photography*, edited by Alice Maude-Roxby, pp. 68–78. Exh. cat. Southampton, U.K.: John Hansard Gallery.

Enwezor, Okwui. "Forms of Arrangement/Engagement: Josephine Meckseper's Displays of Political Pop." In *Josephine Meckseper*, edited by Marion Ackermann, pp. 48–54. Ostfildern-Ruit, Germany: Hatje Cantz Verlag.

Klotz, Elisabeth. "Adrian Piper, Seriation II (Now)." In *Multitasking—Synchronität als kulturelle Praxis*, pp. 78–79. Exh. cat. Berlin: Neue Gesellschaft für bildende Kunst.

Kotz, Liz. *Words to Be Looked At: Language in 1960s Art*. Cambridge, Mass: MIT Press.

Mayer, Rosemary, and Alice Maude-Roxby. "Art and Life." In *Live Art on Camera: Performance and Photography*, edited by Alice Maude-Roxby, pp. 79–82. Exh. cat. Southampton, U.K.: John Hansard Gallery.

Mende, Doreen. "Information/02.07.–20.09.1970, Museum of Modern Art, New York." In *Displayer 01*, pp. 31–40. Karlsruhe, Germany: Staatliche Hochschule für Gestaltung.

Peipon, Corrina. "Adrian Piper." In *WACK! Art and the Feminist Revolution*, edited by Cornelia Butler and Lisa Gabrielle Mark, pp. 282–83. Exh. cat. Cambridge, Mass.: MIT Press.

Platzker, David. "Adrian Piper Everything #10." In *Six Actions for New York City*, edited by Mark Beasley, pp. 11–12. New York: Creative Time Books.

Reeh, Peter. "Funky Lessons in Rock: Der Tanz als gesellschaftlicher Vermittler bei Dan Graham und Adrian Piper." In *Tanz, Sehen*, pp. 169–72. Exh. cat. Frankfurt: Revolver.

Svenungsson, Jan. *An Artist's Text Book*. Helsinki: Finnish Academy of Fine Arts.

2008

Brownlee, Andrea Barnwell, and Valerie Cassel Oliver, eds. *Cinema Remixed and Reloaded: Black Women Artists and the Moving Image since 1970*. Exh. cat. Atlanta: Spelman College Museum of Fine Art; Houston: Contemporary Arts Museum Houston; Seattle: University of Washington Press.

Carroll, Noel. "Response to Adrian Piper." In *The Life and Death of Images*, edited by Diarmuid Costello and Dominic Willsdon, pp. 134–38. London: Tate.

Kobena, Mercer, ed. *Exiles: Diasporas and Strangers*. London: Iniva, Insitute of International Visual Arts; Cambridge, Mass.: MIT Press.

Pichler, Michalis. *W.D.A.O.V.T.O.P.N.N.M.T.B.V.: Working Drawings and Other Visible Things on Paper Not Necessarily Meant to Be Viewed*. Chatou: Centre national édition art et image; Frankfurt: Revolver.

2009

Peter Eleey, ed. *The Quick and the Dead*. Exh. cat. Minneapolis: Walker Art Center.

Caruth, Nicole. "Adrian Piper." In *Racism: An American Family Value*, p. 30. Exh. cat. New York: Center for Book Arts.

Eichhorn, Maria, and Gerti Fietzek, eds. *The Artist's Contract*. Cologne: Verlag der Buchhandlung Walther König.

2010

Dezeuze, Anna. *The 'Do-It-Yourself' Artwork: Participation from Fluxus to New Media*.

Manchester, U.K.: Manchester University Press.

Lepecki, André. "Zones of Resonance: Mutual Formations in Dance and the Visual Arts Since the 1960s." In *Move: Choreographing You*, edited by Stephanie Rosenthal, pp. 152–63. Exh. cat. London: Hayward.

Lesage, Dieter, and Ina Wudtke. *Black Sound White Cube*. Vienna: Löcker Verlag.

2011

Bowles, John P. *Adrian Piper: Race, Gender and Embodiment*. Durham, N.C.: Duke University Press.

Hapgood, Susan, and Cornelia Lauf. *In Deed: Certificates of Authenticity in Art*. Exh. cat. Amsterdam: Roma Publications.

Jach, Aleksandra, Katarzyna Sloboda, Joanna Sokolowska. "Adrian Piper." In *Eyes Looking for a Head to Inhabit*, p. 55. Exh. cat. Łódź, Poland: Museum Sztuki.

Macel, Christine. "Adrian Piper." In *Danser sa vie: Art et danse de 1900 à nos jours*, edited by Christine Macel and Emma Lavigne pp. 274–75. Exh. cat. Paris: Éditions du Centre Pompidou.

Posner, Helaine. "Hot and Cool Feminist Art in Practice." In *The Deconstructive Impulse: Women Artists Reconfigure the Signs of Power, 1973–1991*, edited by Nancy Princethal, pp. 10–19. Exh. cat. Purchase, N.Y.: Neuberger Museum of Art; New York: DelMonico Books/Prestel.

Smith, Cherise, ed. *Enacting Others: Politics of Identity in Eleanor Antin, Nikki S. Lee, Adrian Piper, and Anna Deavere Smith*. Durham, N.C.: Duke University Press.

Witkowsky, Matthew S. *Light Years: Conceptual Art and the Photograph, 1964–1977*. Exh. cat. Chicago: Art Institute of Chicago; New Haven, Conn.: Yale University Press.

2012

Butler, Cornelia H., Sabeth Buchmann, and Pip Day. *From Conceptualism to Feminism: Lucy Lippard's Numbers Shows, 1969–1974*. London: Afterall Books.

Edlinger, Thomas. *Vollmilch: Der Bart als Zeichen*. Exh. cat. Linz, Austria: Lentos-Kunstmuseum Linz.

Enwezor, Okwui, Mélanie Bouteloup, and Frédéric Mittérand. *Intense Proximité: Guide de l'exposition*. Exh. cat. Paris: Centre national des arts plastiques/ Éditions Artlys.

Gassner, Hubertus, Annabelle Görgen, and Christoph Benjamin Schulz. *Alice im Wunderland der Kunst*. Exh. cat. Ostfildern-Ruit, Germany: Hatje Cantz Verlag; Hamburg: Hamburger Kunsthalle.

Kaasa, Nina Sundbeck-Arnäs. "Adrian Piper." In *I Wish This Was a Song: Music in Contemporary Art*, edited by Ingvild Krogvig, pp. 76–77. Exh. cat. Oslo: Nasjonalmuseet for kunst, arkitektur og design.

Kaiser, Phillip, and Miwon Kwon. *Ends of the Earth: Land Art to 1974*. Exh. cat. Los Angeles: Museum of Contemporary Art; Munich: Prestel.

Morineau, Camille, and Annalisa Rimmaudo. *Elles@centrepompidou: Women Artists in the Collection of the Musée national d'art moderne, Centre de création industrielle*. Exh. cat. Paris: Éditions du Centre Pompidou; Seattle: Seattle Art Museum.

Morris, Catherine, Vincent Bonin, and Julia Bryan-Wilson. *Materializing "Six Years": Lucy R. Lippard and the Emergence of Conceptual Art*. Exh. cat. Cambridge, Mass.: MIT Press; Brooklyn, N.Y.: Brooklyn Museum.

Simpson, Bennett, ed. *Blues for Smoke*. Exh. cat. Los Angeles: MoCA; Munich: Prestel.

2013

Boudou, Karima. *Ce lieu n'est pas la maison de Descartes*. Exh. cat. Amsterdam: Institut Français.

Enwezor, Okwui, and Rory Bester. *Rise and Fall of Apartheid: Photography and the Bureaucracy of Everyday Life*. New York: International Center of Photography; Munich: Prestel.

Falkenhausen, Susanne von. "Adrian Piper." In *Empire State*, edited by Alex Gartenfeld and Norman Rosenthal, pp. 157–59. Exh. cat. Milan: Skira.

Gareis, Sigrid, Georg Schöllhammer, and Peter Weibel. "Adrian Piper." In *Moments: Eine Geschichte der Performance in 10 Akten*, pp. 157–63. Exh. cat. Cologne: Verlag der Buchhandlung Walther König.

Krieger, Verena. *Brandschutz: Mentalitäten der Intoleranz*. Exh. cat. Jena, Germany: Friedrich Schiller Universität.

Meade, Fionn. *The Assistants*. Exh. cat. Milan: Mousse.

Phillpot, Clive. *Booktrek: Selected Essays on Artists' Books since 1972*. Zurich: JRP Ringier; Dijon: Les presses du reel.

Tamhane, Swapnaa, and Suzanne Titz. *In Order to Join—Politisch in einem historischen Moment*. Exh. cat. Mönchengladbach, Germany: Museum Abteiberg.

Volz, Jochen, and Lucia Pietroiusti, eds. *Serpentine Gallery: Memory Marathon*. Cologne: Verlag der Buchhandlung Walther König.

2014

Borja-Villel, Manuel J., Tamara Diaz, and Teresa Velázquez. *Playgrounds: Reinventing the Square*. Exh. cat. Madrid: Museo Nacional Centro de Arte Reina Sofía/Ediciones Siruela.

Burton, Johanna, and Anne Ellengood. *Take It or Leave It: Institution, Image, Ideology*. Exh. cat. Los Angeles: Hammer Museum; Munich: Prestel.

Cervenak, Sarah Jane. *Wandering: Philosophical Performances of Racial and Sexual Freedom*. Durham, N.C.: Duke University Press.

Fritz, Elisabeth. "Listening by Dancing: Adrian Piper, Funk Lesson (1982–1984)." In *Authentizität—Partizipation—Spektakel: Mediale Experimente mit "echten Menschen" in der zeitgenössischen Kunst*, pp. 96–108. Cologne: Böhlau Verlag.

Hudek, Anthony. *The Object: Documents of Contemporary Art*. London: Whitechapel Gallery; Cambridge, Mass.: MIT Press.

Knaup, Bettina, and Beatrice Ellen Stammer. *Re.act. feminism #2: A Performing Archive*. Nuremberg: Verlag für moderne Kunst; London: Live Art Development Agency.

Krasteva, Snejana, and Anastasia Mityushina. *Do It Moscow*. Exh. cat. Moscow: Garage Museum of Contemporary Art.

2015

Butler, Cornelia H. "What You See Is What You Get!" In *Scorched Earth: Mark Bradford*, pp. 9–37. Los Angeles: Hammer Museum; New York: DelMonico Books/Prestel.

Cuevas, Panera, and Francisco Javier. *This Is Not a Love Song: Video Art and Pop Music Crossovers*. Exh. cat. Istanbul: Pera Muzesi.

Manacorda, Francesco, Alex Farquharson, and Gregg Bordowitz, eds. *Glenn Ligon: Encounters and Collisions*. Exh. cat. London: Tate.

Marriott, David. "The Card Not Taken: Adrian Piper's Visitations." In *Whither Fanon?: Studies in the Blackness of Being*. Maryland: Johns Hopkins University Press.

McMillan, Uri. *Embodied Avatars: Genealogies of Black Feminist Art and Performance*. Sexual Cultures series. New York: New York University Press.

Miller, Dana, ed. *Whitney Museum of American Art: Handbook of the Collection*. New York: Whitney Museum of American Art.

Robinson, Hilary, ed. *Feminism-Art-Theory: An Anthology, 1968–2014*. West Sussex, U.K.: Wiley Blackwell.

2016

Ganz, Kate. *Drawing Then: Innovation and Influence in American Drawings of the Sixties*. Exh. cat. New York: Dominique Lévy.

9. Berlin Biennale für Zeitgenössische Kunst: The Present in Drag. Exh. cat. Berlin: Distanz Verlag.

2017

Gregory, Stamina, and Jeanne Vaccaro. "Canonical Undoings: Notes on Trans Art and Archives." In *Trap Door: Trans Cultural Production and the Politics of Visibility*, edited by Reina Gossett, Eric A. Stanley, and Johanna Burton, pp. 349–62. Cambridge, Mass.: MIT Press.

ARTICLES, ESSAYS, AND REVIEWS

1969

Kosuth, Joseph. "Art After Philosophy II." *Studio International* 178, no. 916 (November): 161.

Perreault, John. "Art." *Village Voice*, March 27, pp. 15–17.

———. "Art." *Village Voice*, May 1, pp. 14–15.

———. "Art." *Village Voice*, November 20, pp. 19, 34.

Plagens, Peter. "557, 087." *Artforum* 8, no. 3 (November): 67.

1970

Perreault, John. "Art." *Village Voice*, May 14, p. 16.

———. "Art." *Village Voice*, July 16, p. 31.

1971

Perreault, John. "Art." *Village Voice*, April 29, p. 31.

1972

Mayer, Rosemary. "Performance and Experience." *Arts* 47, no. 3 (December 1972–January 1973): 33–36.

1973

Perreault, John. "Art." *Village Voice*, February 8, p. 28.

1974

Crichton, Fennela. "London Newsletter." *Art International* 18, no. 6 (Summer): 42.

1975

Deak, Edit. "Pencil Moustache Makes Up." *Art-Rite* 11–12 (Winter 1975–76).

1976

Frank, Peter. "Performance Diary." *SoHo Weekly News*, April 1, p. 18.

Goldberg, RoseLee. "Public Performance, Private Memory." *Studio International* 192, no. 982 (July–August): 19–23.

———. "Recent Performance Work." *Studio International* 191, no. 980 (March–April): 288.

Howell, John. "Exegesis of the Phenomenon of Written Art by Women." *Art-Rite* 14 (Winter 1976–77).

Lippard, Lucy. "Women's Body Art: The Pains and Pleasures of Rebirth." *Art in America* 64, no. 3 (May–June): 73–82.

1978

Kingsley, April. "Art Goes Underground." *Village Voice*, October 16, p. 122.

Lippard, Lucy. "Caring: Five Political Artists." *Studio International* 193, no. 987 (May–June): 197–207.

1979

Litten, Laura. "Both Sides Now." *New Art Examiner* 7, no. 8 (April): 13–14.

1980

Kohn, Barbara. "Piper in Performance." *Dialogue*, September–October, pp. 9–10.

Kuspit, Donald. "Art of Conscience: The Last Decade." *Dialogue*, September–October, pp. 19–20.

Phillpot, Clive. "Arts Magazines and Magazine Art." *Artforum* 18, no. 6 (February): 52–54.

———. "Talking to Myself." *Art Journal* 39, no. 3 (Spring): 213-17.

1981

Barber, Bruce. "Adrian Piper: Western Front, Vancouver." *Parachute* 23 (Summer): 45-46.
———. "Performance as Social and Cultural Intervention: Interviews with Martha Rosler and Adrian Piper." *Parachute* 24 (Fall): 25-28.
Keziere, Russell. "Less Medium, More Message: Adrian Piper." *Vanguard* 10, no. 4 (May): 36-37.

1984

Borger, Irene. "Funk Lessons: A Guerrilla Performance." *L.A. Weekly*, March 28, pp. 63-64.
Buchanan, Nancy. "Collective Funk." *High Performance* 7, no. 4 (September): 69.
Remington, Judy. "Barbara Kruger and Adrian Piper." *WARM Journal* 5, no. 1.

1985

Olander, William. "Art and Politics: Of Arms and the Artist." *Art in America* 73, no. 6 (June).

1986

Borger, Irene. "The Funk Lessons of Adrian Piper." *Helicon Nine*, nos. 14-15 (Summer): 150-53.
Hess, Elizabeth. "Art Apocalypse." *Village Voice*, October 28, p. 94.

1987

Barr, Barbara. "Reply to Piper." *Women Artists News* 12, no. 2 (June): 6.
Brenson, Michael. "Adrian Piper." *New York Times*, May 1.
Hess, Elizabeth. "Ways of Seeing Adrian Piper." *Village Voice*, May 26, p. 100.
Kuspit, Donald. "Adrian Piper: Self-Healing Through Meta-Art." *Art Criticism* 3, no. 3 (September): 9-16.
McEvilley, Thomas. "Adrian Piper." *Artforum* 16, no. 1 (January): 128-29.
Tsatsos, Irene. "A Dialogue with Adrian Piper." *P-Form* 2, no. 2 (April-May): 22-25.

1988

Hammond, Marsha. "Adrian Piper." *Art Papers* 12, no. 2 (March-April): 40-41.
Langer, Cassandra L. "Autobiography: In Her Own Image." *Women Artists News* 13, no. 3 (Fall): 26-27.
"1987 in Review: Alternative Spaces." *Art in America Annual, 1988-89* 76, no. 78 (August): 53.
Raven, Arlene. "Colored." *Village Voice*, May 31, p. 92.
Thompson, Mildred. "Interview: Adrian Piper." *Art Papers* 12, no. 2 (March-April): 27-30.

1989

Als, Hilton. "Spotlight: Adrian Piper." *Flash Art*, Summer, pp. 142-43.
Failing, Patricia. "Black Artists Today: A Case of Exclusion?" *ARTnews* 88 (March): 124-31.
Morgan, Robert. "Adrian Piper." *Arts Magazine* 63, no. 10 (Summer): 99.
Raven, Arlene. "I to Eye." *Village Voice*, January 31, p. 86.
———. "In Tongues." *Village Voice*, May 30, p. 89.

1990

Als, Hilton. "Adrian Piper's Ways of Seeing." *Village Voice*, September 25: Arts section cover, pp. 55, 94-95.
Berger, Maurice. "The Critique of Pure Racism: An Interview with Adrian Piper." *Afterimage* 18, no. 3 (October): 5-9.
Brenson, Michael. "Adrian Piper's Head-On Confrontation of Racism." *New York Times*, October 26.
Checefsky, Bruce. "Ohio: Adrian Piper." *New Art Examiner* 18, no. 4 (December): 45.
Johnson, Ken. "Being and Politics." *Art in America* 78, no. 9 (September): 154-61.
Marks, Laura U. "Adrian Piper: Reflections, 1967-87." *Fuse*, Fall, pp. 40-42.
Sims, Lowery Stokes. "The Mirror the Other: The Politics of Esthetics." *Artforum* 28, no. 7 (March): 111-15.
Smith, Roberta. "Adrian Piper." *New York Times*, September 14.
Sterritt, David. "Watching TV Creatively—In a Video Installation." *Christian Science Monitor*, November 19.

1991

Bailey, David A. "Adrian Piper: Aspects of the Liberal Dilemma." *Frieze*, no. 1 (September-October): 14-15.
Barrie, Lita. "Shedding Her Male Identity." *Artweek*, March 14.
Bond, Ruth M. "Piper's Philosophy." *City Paper*, June 28, p. 38.
Chambers, Eddie. "Adrian Piper." *Art Monthly* 152 (December 1991-January 1992): 13-15.
Engberg, Kristen. "Marketing the (ad)just(ed) cause." *New Art Examiner* 18, no. 9 (May): 22-28.
Flam, Jack. "Armchair Activism at MoMA." *Wall Street Journal*, December 31.
Hayt-Atkins, Elizabeth. "'The Indexical Present: A Conversation with Adrian Piper." *Arts Magazine*, March, pp. 48-51.
Johnson, Ken. "'The Political Arm' at John Weber." *Art in America* 79, no. 6 (June): 48.
Knight, Christopher. "Looking Racism in the Face." *Los Angeles Times*, March 5.
Kuspit, Donald. "Art and the Moral Imperative." *New Art Examiner* 18, no. 5 (January): 18-25.
Ledes, Richard C. "Adrian Piper at John Weber." *Artscribe*, January-February, pp. 81-82.
Lewis, Jo Ann. "Images That Get Under the Skin; Artist Adrian Piper, Fighting Racism with 3 Exhibits." *Washington Post*, June 22.
Morrison, Ewan. "Vote/Emote: The Recent Work of Adrian Piper." *Variant* 10 (Winter): 22-23.
Schwendenwein, Jude. "Outtakes: Out of the Corner." *High Performance* 53 (Spring): 65, 67.
Smith, Roberta. "At the Modern, Works Unafraid to Ignore Beauty." *New York Times*, October 18.
Van Tuyl, Laura. "Artist Adrian Piper Mounts Urgent Challenge to Racism in Society." *Christian Science Monitor*, July 19, p. 10.
Walker, Maxine. "Maxine Walker in Conversation with Adrian Piper." *Autograph*, December.
Welish, Marjorie. "In This Corner, Adrian Piper's Agitprop." *Arts Magazine* 65, no. 7 (March): 43-47.
Wilson, Judith. "In Memory of the News and of Our Selves: The Art of Adrian Piper." *Third Text* 16-17 (Autumn-Winter): 39-64.

1992

Avgikos, Jan. "Adrian Piper: John Weber Gallery, Paula Cooper, Grey Art Gallery." *Artforum* 31, no. 4 (December): 91.
Bishton, Derek. "Fear of the Other." *Creative Camera*, February-March, pp. 48-49.
Bonami, Francesco. "Dislocations: The Place of Installation." *Flash Art*, January-February, p. 128.
Brandon, Dolores. "Dolores Brandon Interviews Adrian Piper (Highlights). Highlights excerpted from unpublished interview, October 7, 1992." At author's website, www.doloresbrandon.com/interviews/adrian-piper/.
Cotter, Holland. "Dislocating the Modern." *Art in America* 80, no. 1 (January): 100-107.
Cottingham, Laura. "Adrian Piper." *Journal of Contemporary Art*, Spring, pp. 88-136.
Deitcher, David. "Art on the Installation Plan." *Artforum* 30, no. 5 (January): 78-84.
Heartney, Eleanor. "New York—Dislocations: Museum of Modern Art." *ARTnews* 91, no. 1 (January).
O'Grady, Lorraine. "Olympia's Maid: Reclaiming Black Female Subjectivity." *Afterimage* 20, no. 1 (Summer): 14-15.
Stals, Jose Lebrero. "Adrian Piper—Convento de Santa Clara, Moguer, Spain." *Flash Art*, November-December, p. 135.
Verdino-Sullwood, Carla Maria. "Dislocations: Dialogue of Disparate Visions." *The Crisis* 99 (January): 7-8.

1993

Brumfield, John. "Marginalia: Life in a Day of Black L.A. or, the Theater of Refusal." *Art Issues* 29 (September-October): 24-27.
Dimling, Rebecca. "Review." *Art Papers*, January-February, pp. 58-59.
Fleming, Lee. "Galleries: Adrian Piper at Brody's." *Washington Post*, February 13.
Koniger, Maribel. "Adrian Piper." *Tema Celeste*, Spring, p. 94.
Metzger, Rainer. "Adrian Piper." *Kunstforum* 121, no. 435: 435-36.
Weil, Benjamin. "Art Still Has a Tremendous Political Potential: Interview with Adrian Piper." *Purple Prose* 3 (1993): 76-77.

1994

Giddings, Paula. "Black Males and the Prison of Myth." *New York Times*, September 11, 1994.
Hess, Elizabeth. "Visible Man." *Village Voice*, November 22, pp. 31, 33-34.
Raven, Arlene. "The Language of Virtue: What Makes Art Valuable?" *High Performance*, Fall, pp. 46-47.

1995

"Art: Piper Pulls Out of MOCA Show." *Los Angeles Times*, November 22.
Bhabha, Homi. "Focus: Black Male: Representations of Masculinity in Contemporary American Art." *Artforum*, February, p. 86.
Davenport, Kimberly. "Impossible Liberties: Contemporary Artists on the Life of Their Work over Time." *Art Journal* 54, no. 2 (Summer): 40-52.
Karmel, Pepe. "The Corner as Trap, Symbol, Vanishing Point, History Lesson." *New York Times*, July 21.
Nochlin, Linda. "Learning from 'Black Male.'" *Art in America* 83, no. 3 (March): 86-91.
Vogel, Carol. "Inside Art: Philip Morris Loses an Artist." *New York Times*, November 24.

1996

Joselit, David. "Object Lessons." *Art in America* 84, no. 2 (February): 68-71, 107.
Kimmelman, Michael. "In Los Angeles, the Making of a Better Mood." *New York Times*, January 14.
Kornblau, Gary. "1965-1975: Reconsidering the Object of Art." *Art Issues*, January-February, pp. 36-37.
Litten, Laura. "National Art News, Los Angeles: Artists Protest Sponsorship." *ARTnews*, February, p. 53.
Smith, Roberta. "The World Through Women's Lenses." *New York Times*, December 13.
Winston, Heidi. "Piper, Adrian: Out of Order, Out of Sight." *Library Journal* 121, no. 12 (July): 110, 112.

1997

Altschuler, Bruce. "Adrian Piper: Ideas into Art." *Art Journal* 56, no. 4 (Winter): 100-101.
Goodman, Jonathan. "Adrian Piper at John Weber." *Art in America* 85, no. 3 (March): 101.
Kester, Grant. "Adrian Piper in Concept." *The Nation*, February 3.
Maddex, Bobby. "Maximizing Clarity: An Interview with Conceptual Artist Adrian Piper." *Gadfly* 1, no. 2 (April): 22-25.
Mishlove, Robert. "Out of Order, Out of Sight." *New Art Examiner* 25, no. 1 (September): 71-72.
Schöllhammer, Georg. "Nan Goldin: I'll be your mirror/Adrian Piper: Ashes to Ashes." *Springer* 3, no. 1 (March/May): 73-74.

1998

Avgikos, Jan. "Adrian Piper: Thomas Erben Gallery." *Artforum* 36, no. 9 (May): 147–48.

Cotter, Holland. "In Boston, All Roads Lead to Museums." *New York Times*, August 7.

Schwendener, Martha. "Adrian Piper—The Mythic Being." *Time Out New York*, January 7–14.

Shatz, Adam. "Black Like Me." *Lingua Franca* 8, no. 8 (November): 39–54.

Sirmans, Franklin. "Fifteen Minutes with Adrian Piper: An Interview with Franklin Sirmans." *Nka Journal of Contemporary African Art*, no. 8 (Spring–Summer): 8–23.

———. "Letter from Milan: An Interview with Adrian Piper." Artnet.com, March 1998.

1999

Cotter, Holland. "Inside-Out Meditations on the Poison of Racism." *New York Times*, January 8.

2000

Brenson, Michael. "Split Personality." *New York Magazine*, November 13, pp. 80–81.

Cheng, Scarlet. "More Than an Academic Exercise." *Los Angeles Times*, August 13.

Johnson, Ken. "Adrian Piper." *New York Times*, November 17.

Perry, Weena. "I've Got Conceptual Art in My Identity Politics." *Afterimage* 28, no. 3 (November–December): 14.

Sirmans, Franklin. "The Beat Goes On." *Time Out New York*, November 23–30.

Wacks, Debra. "Antin and Piper." *Art Journal* 59, no. 1 (Spring): 103–6.

2001

Battista, Kathy. "Adrian Piper: A Retrospective." *Make Magazine*, March–April, p. 32.

Bowles, John P. "Blinded by the White: Art and History at the Limits of Whiteness." *Art Journal* 60, no. 4 (Winter): 38.

Camnitzer, Louis. "Adrian Piper, Yoko Ono: Conceptualism and Biographies." *ArtNexus* 41 (August–October): 82–85.

Franks, Pamela. "Adrian Piper." *Art Papers*, March–April, p. 45.

Heartney, Eleanor. "Blacks, Whites, and Other Mythic Beings." *Art in America* 89, no. 11 (November): 136–41.

Perkins, Glenn. "Mixed Feelings: Artist Adrian Piper Treats Race, Meaning, and Media." *Spectator*, October 11, p. 25.

Wark, Jane. "Conceptual Art and Feminism." *Women's Art Journal* 22, no. 1 (Spring–Summer): 44–50.

2002

Birnbaum, Daniel. "Artists Curate: Back at You." *Artforum* 40, no. 5 (January): 106–13.

Gau, Sønke. "Adrian Piper-Seit 1965: Metakunst und Kunstkritik." *Camera Austria International*, no. 79: 73–74.

Haase, Amine. "'Unsere Wunden heilen nicht' Ein Gespräch über die Documenta 11 und den Rassismus in den USA." Interview. *Kölner Stadt-Anzeiger*, June 16.

Heiser, Jörg. "Emotional Rescue." *Frieze*, no. 71 (November–December): 70.

Lillington, David. "Adrian Piper: Generali Foundation, Vienna." *Art Monthly* 30, no. 259 (September): 30–31.

Schöllhammer, Georg. "Adrian Piper, Generali Foundation, Vienna." *Artforum* 41, no. 2 (October): 151.

Stoll, Diana C. "Adrian Piper: Goodbye to Easy Listening." Interview. *Aperture* 166 (Spring): 38–47.

2003

Berlanga, Eduardo. "El Macba ofrece una selecciòn de las mejores obras de Adrian Piper." *El Mundo*, October 16.

Campbell, Clayton. "The Last White Art Show." *Flash Art*, October, pp. 59–61.

Fernández, Victor. "El Macba recoge el arte revindicativo surgido del Harlem de Adrian Piper." *La Razon*, October 1.

Guarnaccia, Matteo. "Tele dal gusto acido alla acoperta della realtà." *Alias (il Manifesto)* 6, no. 14 (April 5): 4–5.

Oliveras, Jaume Vidal. "Adrian Piper: El racismo que viene." *El Cultural*, October 30.

Poli, Francesco. "Adrian Piper." *Tema Celeste*, no. 96 (March–April): 99.

Scardi, Gabi. "Adrian Piper." *Flash Art*, no. 238 (February–March): 153.

Serra, Catalina. "Adrian Piper desmonta en el Macba los estereotipos del racismo." *El País*, October 16.

Zabunyan, Elvan. "Portraits: Adrian Piper." *Critique d'art* 22 (Fall): 112.

2004

Heiser, Jörg. "Questionnaire: Adrian Piper." *Frieze*, no. 87 (November–December): 126.

Phelan, Peggy. "Marina Abramović: Witnessing Shadows." *Theatre Journal* 56, no. 4 (December): 569–77.

Roediger, Dan R., Suka Ja Kang, and Tim Engles. "Mapping Mindsets: A Conversation with Adrian Piper." *Art Papers*, no. 5 (September–October): 34–39.

2005

Frascina, Francis. "Class, Conflict, Race, and Remembrance: Adrian Piper's Black Box/White Box, Greensboro, NC, 1 November 2001." *Oxford Art Journal* 28, no. 1 (March): 1–24.

Haffner, Hans-Jürgen. "Funky Lessons." *Camera Austria International* 89 (February–March): 80.

2006

Bollen, Claire. "Art in Review: Adrian Piper, Wayne Gonzales, Eric Baudelaire, Josephine Meckseper." *New York Times*, December 8.

Bowles, John P. "Adrian Piper as African American Artist." *American Art* 20, no. 3 (Fall): 108–117.

2007

Bannerman, Adelaide. "Shaivistic Reverberations: Exchanges between Adrian Piper and Adelaide Bannerman." Interview. *The International Review of African American Art* 21, no. 3 (March): 27–33.

Bowles, John P. "Acting Like a Man: Adrian Piper's Mythic Being and Black Feminism in the 1970s." *Signs: Journal of Women in Culture and Society* 32, no. 3 (Spring): 621–47.

Jancowicz, Mia. "Panic Attack!" *Frieze*, no. 110 (October): 295.

Lowenstein, Kate. "Adrian Piper's Latest Public Piece Puts a Face to a Message." *Time Out New York*, April 26.

Smith, Cherise. "Re-member the Audience: Adrian Piper's Mythic Being Advertisements." *Art Journal* 66, no. 1 (Spring): 46–58.

2008

Cotter, Holland. "The Topic Is Race; The Art Is Fearless." *New York Times*, March 30.

Gilbert, Alan. "Adrian Piper." *Modern Painters*, May, p. 89.

Jones, Amelia. "1970/2007: The Return of Feminist Art." *X-TRA Contemporary Art Quarterly* 10, no. 4 (Summer): 4–18.

O'Neill-Butler, Lauren. "Adrian Piper." *Artforum* 66, no. 9 (May): 378–79.

Pollack, Barbara. "Adrian Piper, Everything." *Time Out New York*, March 27–April 2.

Rosenberg, Karen. "Adrian Piper: Everything." *New York Times*, March 28.

Shaked, Nizan. "Critical Identity Politics." *X-TRA, Contemporary Art Quarterly* 11, no. 1 (Fall): 4–15.

Swenson, Kirsten. "Adrian Piper." *Art in America* 96, no. 6 (June–July): 194–95.

Zamudio, Paul. "Adrian Piper—Elizabeth Dee Gallery." *Flash Art*, May–June, p. 152.

2009

O'Grady, Lorraine. "The Black and White Show." *Artforum* 47, no. 9 (May): 190.

Pearlman, Alison. "Interactive Art for a Challenged Democracy." *X-TRA Contemporary Art Quarterly* 11, no. 3 (Spring): 4–15.

2010

"Adrian Piper." *New Yorker*, November 15.

Chong, Doryun. "Vanilla Nightmares." *The Last Register*, no. 3 (October 20): 3.

Cotter, Holland. "Adrian Piper: 'Past Time: Selected Works, 1973–1995.'" *New York Times*, November 19.

Heiser, Jörg. "Analyze This." *Frieze*, no. 133 (September): 96–102.

Troeller, Jordan. "Adrian Piper." *Artforum* website, November 17.

2011

Chambers, Christopher Hart. "Adrian Piper: Elizabeth Dee, New York." *Flash Art*, February, p. 95.

Gallo, Francesca. "L'autobiografia como tautologia: Il caso di Adrian Piper negli anni Settanta." *Avanguardia*, no. 46: 148–62.

Harris, Jane. "Adrian Piper." *Art in America* website, January 5.

Kazeem, Belinda. "1986 Adrian Piper. Belinda Kazeem 2011." *Der Standard*, October 15.

Richard, Frances. "Adrian Piper: Elizabeth Dee." *Artforum* 49, no. 6 (February): 227–28.

2013

Nelson, Crystal Am. "Scandal." *Brooklyn Rail* website, June 3.

Schmidt, Jason. "Work in Progress." *V Magazine* 86 (Winter): 46.

2014

"Adrian Piper My Calling (Card) #1 (for Dinners and Cocktail Parties); My Calling (Card) #2 (for Bars and Discos)." *Mousse* 46 (November): 96.

Wooden, Isaiah Matthew. "Shadows, Acts and Radical Presence." *Theater* 44, no. 3 (May): 68–73.

2015

Zabunyan, Elvan. "Did You Hear What They Said? Historicity and the Present in the Works by Adrian Piper and Renée Green." Translated by Olga Grlic. *Perspective* 2 (December 17). http://journals.openedition.org/perspective/6012.

2016

Black, Hannah. "The Identity Artist and the Identity Critic." *Artforum* 54, no. 10 (Summer): 338–39.

———. "9th Berlin Biennale." *Artforum* 55, no. 1 (September): 350–52.

Osterweil, Ara. "Fuck You! A Feminist Guide to Surviving the Art World." *Artforum* 54, no. 10 (Summer): 320–29.

2017

Canbaz, Melissa. "Adrian Piper: The Probable Trust Registry." *Art Monthly*, no. 406 (May): 26–27.

Speed, Mitch. "Adrian Piper." *Artforum* website, April 2017.

CHECKLIST OF THE EXHIBITION

* indicates works that will appear only at MoMA

1. *LSD Alice [Study for Alice Down the Rabbit Hole]*. 1965
Felt-tip pen, ballpoint pen, and pencil on paper
$11\frac{13}{16}$ × 9 in. (30 × 22.8 cm)
Collection Adrian Piper Research Archive Foundation Berlin
p. 96

2. *LSD Womb*. 1965
Acrylic on canvas
26 × 26 in. (66 × 66 cm)
Emi Fontana Collection
p. 99

3. *LSD Bloodstream*. 1965
Acrylic on canvas
12 × 12 in. (30.5 × 30.5 cm)
Collection Simona & Francesco Fantinelli
p. 102

4. *LSD Mirror Self-Portrait*. 1965
Charcoal and colored pencil on paper
22½ × 17¼ in. (57.2 × 43.8 cm)
Collection Liz and Eric Lefkofsky
p. 95

5. *LSD Abstraction*. 1965
Oil on canvas
16 × 16 in. (40.7 × 40.7 cm)
Collection Adrian Piper Research Archive Foundation Berlin

6. *Negative Self-Portrait*. 1966
Felt-tip pen on paper
$17\frac{11}{16}$ × 14¾ in. (45 × 37.5 cm)
Emi Fontana Collection
p. 97

7. *Over the Edge*. 1965
Oil on canvas
24⅝ × $18\frac{9}{16}$ in. (62.6 × 47.2 cm)
Collection Adrian Piper Research Archive Foundation Berlin
p. 98

8. *LSD Steve Shomstein*. 1966
Oil on canvas
36 × 48 in. (91.4 × 121.9 cm)
Collection Simona & Francesco Fantinelli

9. *LSD Void*. 1966
Acrylic on canvas
26 × 40 in. (66 × 101.6 cm)
Emi Fontana Collection
p. 100

10. *LSD Self-Portrait from the Inside Out*. 1966
Acrylic on canvas
40 × 30 in. (101.6 × 76.2 cm)
Emi Fontana Collection
p. 97

11. *LSD Self-Portrait with Tamiko*. 1966
Acrylic on canvas
$40\frac{9}{16}$ × $30\frac{5}{16}$ in. (103 × 77 cm)
Private collection
p. 101

12. *LSD Self-Portrait*. 1966
Pencil on paper
5½ × 8½ in. (13.9 × 21.6 cm)
Collection Adrian Piper Research Archive Foundation Berlin

* 13. *Phillip Zohn*. 1966
Charcoal on paper
21 × 17 in. (53.3 × 43.2 cm)
Collection Adrian Piper Research Archive Foundation Berlin
p. 226

14. *LSD Couple*. 1966
Oil on canvas
18⅛ × 23⅞ in. (46 × 60.7 cm)
Collection Adrian Piper Research Archive Foundation Berlin

15. *Alice in Wonderland: Alice and the Pack of Cards*. 1966
Tempera on canvas board
24 × 18 in. (61 × 45.7 cm)
Collection Konrad Baumgartner, Milan
p. 103

16. *Alice in Wonderland: The Mad Hatter's Tea Party*. 1966
Tempera on canvas board
24 × 18 in. (61 × 45.7 cm)
Collection Konrad Baumgartner, Milan
p. 103

17. *Alice in Wonderland: Alice Down the Rabbit Hole*. 1966
Tempera on canvas board
24 × 18 in. (61 × 45.7 cm)
Collection Konrad Baumgartner, Milan
p. 103

18. *LSD Alice sketch #1*. 1966
Rapidograph pen and ink on paper
8½ × 5½ in. (21.6 × 14 cm)
Collection Adrian Piper Research Archive Foundation Berlin
p. 33

19. *LSD Alice sketch #2*. 1966
Rapidograph pen and ink on paper
8½ × 5½ in. (21.6 × 14 cm)
Collection Adrian Piper Research Archive Foundation Berlin
p. 33

20. *LSD Alice sketch #3*. 1966
Rapidograph pen and ink on paper
8½ × 5½ in. (21.6 × 14 cm)
Collection Adrian Piper Research Archive Foundation Berlin
p. 33

* 21. *Self-Portrait at Age 5 with Doll*. 1966
Oil on canvas with doll
29¾ × 19¾ in. (75.5 × 50.2 cm)
Collection Adrian Piper Research Archive Foundation Berlin
p. 106

22. *Barbara Epstein and Doll*. 1966
Acrylic on canvas with doll
41⅝ × 41 in. (105.7 × 104.2 cm)
Collection Adrian Piper Research Archive Foundation Berlin
p. 107

23. *Untitled Planes Painting*. 1966
Acrylic on wood, mounted on acrylic on canvas
18 × 24 in. (45.7 × 61 cm)
Collection Adrian Piper Research Archive Foundation Berlin
p. 105

24. *Over the Edge 1 (Study)*. 1967
Pencil on notebook paper
4⅛ × 8½ in. (10.4 × 21.6 cm)
Collection Adrian Piper Research Archive Foundation Berlin
p. 104

25. *Over the Edge 2 (Study)*. 1967
Pencil on notebook paper
9 × $6\frac{15}{16}$ in. (22.8 × 17.6 cm)
Collection Adrian Piper Research Archive Foundation Berlin
p. 104

26. *Over the Edge 3 (Study)*. 1967
Pencil on notebook paper
11 × $8\frac{7}{16}$ in. (27.9 × 21.4 cm)
Collection Adrian Piper Research Archive Foundation Berlin
p. 104

27. *Untitled Self-Portrait*. 1967 (later signed "1968")
Pencil and charcoal on paper
11 × 8½ in. (27.9 × 21.6 cm)
Collection Sands and Robin Murray-Wassink, WASSINIQUE INC., Amsterdam
p. 111

28. *The Barbie Doll Drawings*. 1967
Rapidograph pen, ink, and/or pencil on thirty-five sheets of notebook paper
Each 8½ × 5½ in. (21.6 × 14 cm)
The Museum of Modern Art, New York. Acquired through the generosity of Catie and Donald Marron, The Friends of Education of The Museum of Modern Art, Carol and Morton Rapp, Richard S. Zeisler Bequest (by exchange), Committee on Drawings and Prints Fund, Riva Castleman Endowment Fund, John B. Turner Fund, and Monroe Wheeler Fund
pp . 108–10

29. *Drawings about Paper and Writings about Words #1*. 1967
Pencil on notebook paper
11 × 8½ in. (27.9 × 21.6 cm)
Collection Adrian Piper Research Archive Foundation Berlin
p. 112

30. *Drawings about Paper and Writings about Words #2*. 1967
Cut-and-pasted paper bag and pencil on notebook paper
11 × 8½ in. (27.9 × 21.6 cm)
Collection Adrian Piper Research Archive Foundation Berlin

31. *Drawings about Paper and Writings about Words #4*. 1967
Cut-and-pasted paper, pencil, and charcoal on notebook paper
11 × 8½ in. (27.9 × 21.6 cm)
Collection Adrian Piper Research Archive Foundation Berlin

32. *Drawings about Paper and Writings about Words #5*. 1967
Pencil and charcoal on notebook paper
11 × 8½ in. (27.9 × 21.6 cm)
Collection Louise Fishman
p. 113

33. *Drawings about Paper and Writings about Words #6*. 1967
Cut-and-pasted paper, pencil, charcoal, and pastel on notebook paper
11 × 8½ in. (27.9 × 21.6 cm)
Collection Adrian Piper Research Archive Foundation Berlin
p. 114

34. *Drawings about Paper and Writings about Words #8*. 1967
Cut-and-pasted paper and pencil on notebook paper
11 × 8½ in. (27.9 × 21.6 cm)
Collection Adrian Piper Research Archive Foundation Berlin
p. 115

35. *Drawings about Paper and Writings about Words #10*. 1967
Cut-and-pasted paper and pastel on notebook paper
11 × 8½ in. (27.9 × 21.6 cm)
Collection Adrian Piper Research Archive Foundation Berlin

36. *Drawings about Paper and Writings about Words #11*. 1967
Cut-and-pasted paper and pencil on notebook paper
11 × 8½ in. (27.9 × 21.6 cm)
Collection Adrian Piper Research Archive Foundation Berlin
p. 116

37. *Drawings about Paper and Writings about Words #12*. 1967
Cut-and-pasted paper and pencil on notebook paper
11 × 8½ in. (27.9 × 21.6 cm)
Collection Adrian Piper Research Archive Foundation Berlin

38. *Drawings about Paper and Writings about Words #13*. 1967
Pastel on notebook paper
11 × 8½ in. (27.9 × 21.6 cm)
Collection Adrian Piper Research Archive Foundation Berlin

39. *Drawings about Paper and Writings about Words #14*. 1967
Cut-and-pasted paper and pastel on notebook paper
11 × 8½ in. (27.9 × 21.6 cm)
Collection Adrian Piper Research Archive Foundation Berlin

40. *Drawings about Paper and Writings about Words #15*. 1967
Cut-and-pasted paper and pastel on notebook paper
11 × 8½ in. (27.9 × 21.6 cm)
Collection Adrian Piper Research Archive Foundation Berlin

41. *Drawings about Paper and Writings about Words #16*. 1967
Cut-and-pasted paper and pastel on notebook paper
11 × 8½ in. (27.9 × 21.6 cm)
Collection Adrian Piper Research Archive Foundation Berlin
p. 117

42. *Drawings about Paper and Writings about Words #17*. 1967
Cut-and-pasted paper and pencil on notebook paper
11 × 8½ in. (27.9 × 21.6 cm)
Collection Gregory R. Miller and Michael Wiener
p. 118

43. *Drawings about Paper and Writings about Words #18*. 1967
Pencil on notebook paper
11 × 8½ in. (27.9 × 21.6 cm)
Collection Adrian Piper Research Archive Foundation Berlin

44. *Drawings about Paper and Writings about Words #20*. 1967
Pencil on notebook paper
11 × 8½ in. (27.9 × 21.6 cm)
Collection Adrian Piper Research Archive Foundation Berlin

45. *Drawings about Paper and Writings about Words #21*. 1967
Pencil on notebook paper in plastic sleeve with crayon
11 × 8½ in. (27.9 × 21.6 cm)
Collection Adrian Piper Research Archive Foundation Berlin

46. *Drawings about Paper and Writings about Words #22*. 1967
Pencil on notebook paper
11 × 8½ in. (27.9 × 21.6 cm)
Collection Adrian Piper Research Archive Foundation Berlin

47. *Drawings about Paper and Writings about Words #23*. 1967
Colored felt-tip pen on graph paper
11 × 8½ in. (27.9 × 21.6 cm)
Collection Adrian Piper Research Archive Foundation Berlin

48. *Drawings about Paper and Writings about Words #24*. 1967
Felt-tip pen on graph paper
11 × 8½ in. (27.9 × 21.6 cm)
Collection Adrian Piper Research Archive Foundation Berlin
p. 119

49. *Drawings about Paper and Writings about Words #25*. 1967
Gouache on graph paper
11 × 8½ in. (27.9 × 21.6 cm)
Collection Adrian Piper Research Archive Foundation Berlin
p. 120

50. *Drawings about Paper and Writings about Words #26*. 1967
Felt-tip pen on graph paper
11 × 8½ in. (27.9 × 21.6 cm)
Collection Adrian Piper Research Archive Foundation Berlin

51. *Drawings about Paper and Writings about Words #27*. 1967
Gouache on graph paper
11 × 8½ in. (27.9 × 21.6 cm)
Collection Gregory R. Miller and Michael Wiener
p. 121

52. *Drawings about Paper and Writings about Words #28*. 1967
Gouache on graph paper
11 × 8½ in. (27.9 × 21.6 cm)
Collection Adrian Piper Research Archive Foundation Berlin

53. *Drawings about Paper and Writings about Words #29*. 1967
Gouache on partially sun-exposed graph paper
11 × 8½ in. (27.9 × 21.6 cm)
Collection Adrian Piper Research Archive Foundation Berlin

54. *Drawings about Paper and Writings about Words #31*. 1967
Cut-and-pasted paper, charcoal, and pencil on notebook paper
11 × 8½ in. (27.9 × 21.6 cm)
Collection Adrian Piper Research Archive Foundation Berlin

55. *Drawings about Paper and Writings about Words #32*. 1967
Pencil on notebook paper
11 × 8½ in. (27.9 × 21.6 cm)
Collection Adrian Piper Research Archive Foundation Berlin

56. *Drawings about Paper and Writings about Words #33*. 1967
Pencil on notebook paper
11 × 8½ in. (27.9 × 21.6 cm)
Collection Adrian Piper Research Archive Foundation Berlin
p. 122

57. *Drawings about Paper and Writings about Words #41*. 1967
Ink on notebook paper
11 × 8½ in. (27.9 × 21.6 cm)
Collection Dona Nelson

58. *Drawings about Paper and Writings about Words #42*. 1967
Pencil and pastel on notebook paper
11 × 8½ in. (27.9 × 21.6 cm)
Collection Adrian Piper Research Archive Foundation Berlin

59. *Drawings about Paper and Writings about Words #43*. 1967
Pencil and colored pencil on notebook paper
11 × 8½ in. (27.9 × 21.6 cm)
Collection Adrian Piper Research Archive Foundation Berlin

60. *Drawings about Paper and Writings about Words #44*. 1967
Cut-and-pasted paper and pencil on notebook paper
11 × 8½ in. (27.9 × 21.6 cm)
Collection Adrian Piper Research Archive Foundation Berlin

61. *Drawings about Paper and Writings about Words #45*. 1967
Pencil on notebook paper
11 × 8½ in. (27.9 × 21.6 cm)
Collection Adrian Piper Research Archive Foundation Berlin

62. *Drawings about Paper and Writings about Words #46*. 1967
Cut-and-pasted paper bag, charcoal, and pencil on notebook paper
11 × 8½ in. (27.9 × 21.6 cm)
The Museum of Modern Art, New York.
The Judith Rothschild Foundation Contemporary Drawings Collection Gift (purchase, and gift, in part, of The Eileen and Michael Cohen Collection)
p. 123

63. *Drawings about Paper and Writings about Words #47*. 1967
Pencil and charcoal on notebook paper
11 × 8½ in. (27.9 × 21.6 cm)
The Museum of Modern Art, New York.
The Judith Rothschild Foundation Contemporary Drawings Collection Gift (purchase, and gift, in part, of The Eileen and Michael Cohen Collection)
p. 124

64. *Drawings about Paper and Writings about Words #48*. 1967
Pencil on notebook paper in plastic sleeve with crayon
11 × 8½ in. (27.9 × 21.6 cm)
The Museum of Modern Art, New York.
The Judith Rothschild Foundation Contemporary Drawings Collection Gift (purchase, and gift, in part, of The Eileen and Michael Cohen Collection)
p. 126

65. *Drawings about Paper and Writings about Words #49*. 1967
Pastel on notebook paper
11 × 8½ in. (27.9 × 21.6 cm)
Collection Adrian Piper Research Archive Foundation Berlin
p. 125

66. *Drawings about Paper and Writings about Words #50*. 1967
Pencil on notebook paper
11 × 8½ in. (27.9 × 21.6 cm)
Collection Adrian Piper Research Archive Foundation Berlin

67. *Drawings about Paper and Writings about Words #51*. 1967
Pencil and pastel on notebook paper
11 × 8½ in. (27.9 × 21.6 cm)
Collection Adrian Piper Research Archive Foundation Berlin
p. 127

68. *Drawings about Paper and Writings about Words A*. 1967
Pencil, charcoal, and glue on notebook paper
11 × 8½ in. (27.9 × 21.6 cm)
Collection Adrian Piper Research Archive Foundation Berlin

69. *Drawings about Paper and Writings about Words B*. 1967
Pencil, charcoal, and glue on notebook paper
11 × 8½ in. (27.9 × 21.6 cm)
Collection Adrian Piper Research Archive Foundation Berlin

70. *Drawings about Paper and Writings about Words C*. 1967
Pencil, charcoal, and glue on notebook paper
11 × 8½ in. (27.9 × 21.6 cm)
Collection Adrian Piper Research Archive Foundation Berlin

71. *Drawings about Paper and Writings about Words D*. 1967
Cut-and-pasted paper and pencil on notebook paper
11 × 8½ in. (27.9 × 21.6 cm)
Collection Adrian Piper Research Archive Foundation Berlin

72. *Drawings about Paper and Writings about Words E*. 1967
Cut-and-pasted paper and pencil on notebook paper
11 × 8½ in. (27.9 × 21.6 cm)
Collection Adrian Piper Research Archive Foundation Berlin

73. *Drawings about Paper and Writings about Words F*. 1967
Cut-and-pasted paper and colored pencil on notebook paper
11 × 8½ in. (27.9 × 21.6 cm)
Collection Adrian Piper Research Archive Foundation Berlin

74. *Drawings about Paper and Writings about Words G*. 1967
Cut-and-pasted paper and colored pencil on notebook paper
11 × 8½ in. (27.9 × 21.6 cm)
Collection Adrian Piper Research Archive Foundation Berlin

75. *Drawings about Paper and Writings about Words H*. 1967
Cut-and-pasted paper and colored pencil on notebook paper
11 × 8½ in. (27.9 × 21.6 cm)
Collection Adrian Piper Research Archive Foundation Berlin

76. *Drawings about Paper and Writings about Words I*. 1967
Cut-and-pasted paper and pencil on notebook paper
11 × 8½ in. (27.9 × 21.6 cm)
Collection Adrian Piper Research Archive Foundation Berlin

77. *Drawings about Paper and Writings about Words K*. 1967
Cut-and-pasted paper and ink on notebook paper
11 × 8½ in. (27.9 × 21.6 cm)
Collection Adrian Piper Research Archive Foundation Berlin

78. *Nine-Part Floating Square*. 1967
Pencil and gesso on nine canvases, with pencil on wall
Each canvas 24½ × 24½ in. (62.2 × 62.2 cm); overall 66 × 66 in. (167.6 × 167.6 cm)
Collection Gregory R. Miller and Michael Wiener
p. 131

79. *Double Recess*. 1967
Masonite, wood frame, gesso, paint, and metallic paint (refabricated 2017)
36 × 60 × 6 in. (91.4 × 152.4 × 15.2 cm)
Collection Adrian Piper Research Archive Foundation Berlin
p. 129

* 80. *Protruded Rectangle Canvas*. 1967
Masonite on wooden frame (refabricated 2018)
72 × 36 in. (182.9 × 91.4 cm)
Collection Adrian Piper Research Archive Foundation Berlin

81. *Recessed Square*. 1967
Masonite on wood frame (refabricated 2017)
36 × 36 × 9 in. (91.4 × 91.4 × 22.9 cm)
Collection Adrian Piper Research Archive Foundation Berlin
p. 128

* 82. *Sixteen Permutations of a Nine-Part Floating Square*. 1968
Pencil on graph paper and tape
22 × 22 in. (55.9 × 55.9 cm)
Collection Gregory R. Miller and Michael Wiener
p. 130

83. *Here and Now*. 1968
Cardboard portfolio with text on graph paper and text on mimeographed paper taped to box; and text on sixty-four loose sheets of mimeographed paper
Each sheet 9 × 9 in. (22.9 × 22.9 cm)
Collection Alan Cravitz and Shashi Caudill
pp. 37, 135

84. *Sixteen Permutations of a Planar Analysis of a Square*. 1968
Mixed-medium installation. Photostat and wood model
Photostat 32⅞ × 21⅞ in. (83.5 × 55.5 cm); model: 10⅝ × 10⅜ × 8⅛ in. (27 × 26.4 × 20.6 cm)
Collection Adrian Piper Research Archive Foundation Berlin
pp. 136, 137

85. *3-2-1 Cube 3-2-1 Cube (Permutations on a Suspended Cube)*. 1968
Colored ink, colored pencil, and pencil on graph paper
15 × 22¼ in. (38.1 × 56.5 cm)
Collection Adrian Piper Research Archive Foundation Berlin
p. 134

* 86. *A Three-Dimensional Representation of Infinite Divisibility*. 1968
Pencil and colored pencil on graph paper
17½ × 22¼ in. (44.4 × 56.5 cm)
Collection Adrian Piper Research Archive Foundation Berlin
p. 132

87. *Infinitely Divisible Floor Construction*. 1968
Mixed-medium installation. Tape and particle board (refabricated 2002)
47¼ in. × 13 ft. 9⅜ in. (120 × 420 cm)
Collection Adrian Piper Research Archive Foundation Berlin
p. 133

88. *Five Unrelated Time Pieces (Meat into Meat)*. 1968
Notebook with typescript page, eight photographs, and text mounted on colored paper
Each page 9½ × 11½ in. (24.1 × 29.2 cm) or 11½ × 9½ in. (29.2 × 24.1 cm)
Collection Paul & Karen McCarthy
pp. 142, 143

89. *A Conceptual Seriation Arrested at Four Points in Time*. 1968
Notebook with six typescript pages; twenty-five photographs and text mounted on colored paper; and cut-and-pasted text on four sheets of colored paper
Each page 11 × 8½ in. (27.9 × 21.6 cm)
Collection Adrian Piper Research Archive Foundation Berlin

90. *Hypothesis: Situation #3 (for Sol LeWitt)*. 1968–69
Typescript on mimeographed paper;
gelatin silver prints and ink on graph paper;
and two photolithograph pages
11 × 8½ in. (27.9 × 21.6 cm); 11 × 33⅞ in. (27.9 × 86 cm); and each 11 × 8½ in. (27.9 × 21.6 cm)
Collection Adrian Piper Research Archive Foundation Berlin
pp. 144, 145

91. *Hypothesis: Situation #5*. 1968–69
Typescript on mimeographed paper;
gelatin silver prints and ink on graph paper;
and two photolithograph pages
11 × 8½ in. (27.9 × 21.6 cm); 11 × 33 ¾ in. (27.9 × 85.7 cm); and each 11 × 8½ in. (27.9 × 21.6 cm)
Generali Foundation Collection—Permanent Loan to the Museum der Moderne Salzburg

* 92. *Hypothesis: Situation #6*. 1968–69
Typescript on mimeographed paper;
gelatin silver prints and ink on graph paper;
and two photolithograph pages
11 × 8½ in. (27.9 × 21.6 cm); 11 × 18 in. (27.9 × 45.4 cm); and each 11 × 8½ in. (27.9 × 21.6 cm)
Walker Art Center, Minneapolis. T. B. Walker Acquisition Fund
pp. 146, 147

93. *Hypothesis: Situation #10*. 1968–69
Typescript on mimeographed paper;
gelatin silver prints and ink on graph paper;
and two photolithograph pages
11 × 8½ in. (27.9 × 21.6 cm); 11 × $17\frac{3}{16}$ in.
(27.9 × 43.6 cm); and each 11 × 8½ in. (27.9 × 21.6 cm)
Generali Foundation Collection—Permanent Loan to
the Museum der Moderne Salzburg
p. 35

94. *Utah-Manhattan Transfer*. 1968
Pencil and ballpoint pen on cut-and-pasted maps,
mounted on two pieces of foam core
First panel 13¼ × $14\frac{3}{16}$ in. (33.7 × 36 cm); second panel
12 × 12 in. (30.5 × 30.5 cm.)
Collection Adrian Piper Research Archive Foundation
Berlin
pp. 138, 139

95. *Parallel Grid Proposal for Dugway Proving Grounds Headquarters*. 1968
Two typescript pages; ink and colored ink on fourteen
sheets of paper; architectural tape on acetate over ink
on thirteen photostats; and ink on cut-and-pasted map,
mounted on colored paper
Twenty-five sheets each 8½ × 11 in. (21.6 × 27.9 cm); two
sheets each 8½ × $12\frac{11}{16}$ in. (21.6 × 32.2 cm);
three sheets each 11 × 8½ in. (27.9 × 21.6 cm)
Collection Beth Rudin DeWoody
pp. 140, 141

96. *Art-Sale Event*. 1968
Typescript page
11 × 8½ in. (27.9 × 21.6 cm)
Collection Adrian Piper Research Archive
Foundation Berlin
p. 155

* 97. *Two Recent Works*. 1968
Three typescript pages
Each 11 × 8½ in. (27.9 × 21.6 cm)
Collection Adrian Piper Research Archive
Foundation Berlin
p. 154

98. *Concrete Infinity 6 inch Square ["This square should be read as a whole . . ."]*. 1968
Typescript page in square mat
11 × 8½ in. (27.9 × 21.6 cm)
Collection Alan Cravitz and Shashi Caudill
p. 153

99. *Concrete 8" Square ["The sides of this square measure 8" . . ."]*. 1968
Ink and tape on graph paper, mounted on foam core;
and typescript page
21½ × 8½ in. (54.6 × 21.6 cm) and 11 × 8½ in.
(27.9 × 21.6 cm)
The Museum of Modern Art, New York. Gift of
Gilbert B. and Lila Silverman Instruction Drawing
Collection, Detroit
p. 152

100. *Seriation #1: Lecture*. 1968
Sound work. Audio, 00:29:17
Collection Adrian Piper Research Archive
Foundation Berlin

101. *Seriation #2: Now*. 1968
Sound work. Audio, 00:17:36
Collection Adrian Piper Research Archive
Foundation Berlin

Nineteen Concrete Space-Time-Infinity Pieces. 1968–69
Notebook with fifteen pageworks. Ring binder with
nineteen typescript pages in plastic sleeves
Each page 11 × 8 ½ in. (27.9 × 21.6 cm); binder
$11\frac{13}{16}$ × $10\frac{9}{16}$ × 1½ in. (30 × 26.8 × 3.9 cm)
Generali Foundation Collection—Permanent Loan
to the Museum der Moderne Salzburg

102. *Seriation #2 (Now) (November 11, 1968)* (1968),
in *Nineteen Concrete Space-Time-Infinity Pieces*
Typescript page
11 × 8½ in. (27.9 × 21.6 cm)
Generali Foundation Collection—Permanent Loan
to the Museum der Moderne Salzburg
p. 162

103. *Seriation #3 (November 14, 1968)* (1968), in
Nineteen Concrete Space-Time-Infinity Pieces
Typescript page
11 × 8½ in. (27.9 × 21.6 cm)
Generali Foundation Collection—Permanent Loan
to the Museum der Moderne Salzburg

* 104. *Untitled Statement ("My present work is involved . . .")* (1968), in *Nineteen Concrete Space-Time-Infinity Pieces*
Typescript page
11 × 8½ in. (27.9 × 21.6 cm)
Generali Foundation Collection—Permanent Loan
to the Museum der Moderne Salzburg

105. *Taped Lecture on Seriation (given November 7, 1968)* (1968), in *Nineteen Concrete Space-Time-Infinity Pieces*
Typescript page
11 × 8½ in. (27.9 × 21.6 cm)
Generali Foundation Collection—Permanent Loan
to the Museum der Moderne Salzburg
p. 156

* 106. *Taped Lecture on Seriation (given October 30, 1968)* (1968), in *Nineteen Concrete Space-Time-Infinity Pieces*
Typescript page
11 × 8½ in. (27.9 × 21.6 cm)
Generali Foundation Collection—Permanent Loan
to the Museum der Moderne Salzburg

107. *Untitled (Elements: Wristwatch A, Wristwatch B)* (1968), in *Nineteen Concrete Space-Time-Infinity Pieces*
Typescript page
11 × 8½ in. (27.9 × 21.6 cm)
Generali Foundation Collection—Permanent Loan
to the Museum der Moderne Salzburg

108. *Untitled ("If you are a slow reader . . . ")* (1968),
in *Nineteen Concrete Space-Time-Infinity Pieces*
Typescript page
11 × 8½ in. (27.9 × 21.6 cm)
Generali Foundation Collection—Permanent Loan
to the Museum der Moderne Salzburg
pp. 53, 157

109. *Untitled ("ENIL EHT . . .")* (1968), in *Nineteen Concrete Space-Time-Infinity Pieces*
Typescript page
11 × 8½ in. (27.9 × 21.6 cm)
Generali Foundation Collection—Permanent Loan
to the Museum der Moderne Salzburg

110. *Untitled ("The time needed to read a line . . .")* (1968), in *Nineteen Concrete Space-Time-Infinity Pieces*
Typescript page
11 × 8½ in. (27.9 × 21.6 cm)
Generali Foundation Collection—Permanent Loan
to the Museum der Moderne Salzburg
p. 158

111. *Untitled ("This piece stands in a ratio of 1:3 . . .")* (1968), in *Nineteen Concrete Space-Time-Infinity Pieces*
Typescript page
11 × 8½ in. (27.9 × 21.6 cm)
Generali Foundation Collection—Permanent Loan
to the Museum der Moderne Salzburg
p. 159

112. *Untitled ("The bottom surface area . . .")* (1968),
in *Nineteen Concrete Space-Time-Infinity Pieces*.
Recto of *Untitled ("The upper surface area . . .")*
Typescript page
11 × 8½ in. (27.9 × 21.6 cm)
Generali Foundation Collection—Permanent Loan
to the Museum der Moderne Salzburg
p. 160

113. *Untitled ("The upper surface area . . .")* (1968),
in *Nineteen Concrete Space-Time-Infinity Pieces*.
Verso of *Untitled ("The bottom surface area . . .")*
Typescript page
11 × 8½ in. (27.9 × 21.6 cm)
Generali Foundation Collection—Permanent Loan
to the Museum der Moderne Salzburg
p. 161

114. *Text of a Piece for Larry Wiener, 1/14/69* (1969),
in *Nineteen Concrete Space-Time-Infinity Pieces*
Three typescript pages; and ballpoint pen on
graph paper
11 × 8½ in. (27.9 × 21.6 cm)
Generali Foundation Collection—Permanent Loan
to the Museum der Moderne Salzburg
Note: This work was made for the artist
Lawrence Weiner.
p. 163

115. *0 to 9 (for Vito Acconci)* (1969), in *Nineteen Concrete Space-Time-Infinity Pieces*
Typescript page
11 × 8½ in. (27.9 × 21.6 cm)
Generali Foundation Collection—Permanent Loan
to the Museum der Moderne Salzburg
p. 170

116. *Three Untitled Projects [for 0 to 9]: Some Areas in the New York Area*. 1969
Three booklets of typescript pages, with paper bands
Each booklet, closed 11 × 8½ × ⅛ in. (27.9 × 21.6 ×
.3 cm); open 17 × 11 × ⅛ in. (43.2 × 27.9 × .3 cm)
The Museum of Modern Art Library, New York

Nine Abstract Space-Time-Infinity Pieces. 1968–69
Notebook with eight pageworks. Ring binder with
twenty-nine sheets in plastic sleeves
Each page 11 × 8½ in. (21.6 × 27.9 cm); binder
$11\frac{13}{16}$ × $10\frac{9}{16}$ × 1½ in. (30 × 26.8 × 3.9 cm)
Generali Foundation Collection—Permanent Loan
to the Museum der Moderne Salzburg

117. *Untitled ("First page following . . .")* (1969), in
Nine Abstract Space-Time-Infinity Pieces.
Typescript page; and cut-and-pasted paper on
onionskin paper over graph paper with text
11 × 8½ in. (27.9 × 21.6 cm)
Generali Foundation Collection—Permanent Loan
to the Museum der Moderne Salzburg

118. *Untitled ("The top side of the following page . . .")* (1969), in *Nine Abstract Space-Time-Infinity Pieces*
Typescript page
Each 11 × 8½ in. (27.9 × 21.6 cm)
Generali Foundation Collection—Permanent Loan to the Museum der Moderne Salzburg
p. 166

119. *Untitled ("The top side of the preceding page . . .")* (1969), in *Nine Abstract Space-Time-Infinity Pieces*
Typescript page
Each 11 × 8½ in. (27.9 × 21.6 cm)
Generali Foundation Collection—Permanent Loan to the Museum der Moderne Salzburg

120. *Untitled ("1. Maps representing four types . . .")* (1969), in *Nine Abstract Space-Time-Infinity Pieces*
Eleven typescript pages
Each 11 × 8½ in. (27.9 × 21.6 cm)
Generali Foundation Collection—Permanent Loan to the Museum der Moderne Salzburg

121. *Untitled ("1. Rectangles are located according to co-ordinate position . . .")* (1969), in *Nine Abstract Space-Time-Infinity Pieces*
Three typescript pages and felt-tip pen on seven photolithograph postcards
Each page 11 × 8½ in. (27.9 × 21.6 cm); each postcard
3½ × 5 in. (8.9 × 12.7 cm)
Generali Foundation Collection—Permanent Loan to the Museum der Moderne Salzburg

122. *Untitled ("Two Pieces for 600 ft. Tape . . .")* (1969), in *Nine Abstract Space-Time-Infinity Pieces*
Typescript on graph paper
11 × 8½ in. (27.9 × 21.6 cm)
Generali Foundation Collection—Permanent Loan to the Museum der Moderne Salzburg

123. *Untitled ("Proposal: to exhibit this piece . . .") (February 10, 1969)* (1969), in *Nine Abstract Space-Time-Infinity Pieces*
Typescript page
11 × 8½ in. (27.9 × 21.6 cm)
Generali Foundation Collection—Permanent Loan to the Museum der Moderne Salzburg
p. 168

124. *Untitled ("Maps schematizing different elements . . ."), 1-5/1969* (1969), in *Nine Abstract Space-Time-Infinity Pieces*
Colored felt-tip pen on six maps mounted on colored paper; and two typescript pages
Each 11 × 8½ in. (27.9 × 21.6 cm)
Generali Foundation Collection—Permanent Loan to the Museum der Moderne Salzburg
pp. 164, 165

125. *Untitled ("Street Works: Friday, April 18, 1969, 5-6 PM . . .")* (1969), in *Nine Abstract Space-Time-Infinity Pieces.*
Typescript page
11 × 8½ in. (27.9 × 21.6 cm)
Collection Adrian Piper Research Archive Foundation Berlin
pp. 54, 169

126. *Streetwork Streettracks I–II*. 1969
Two performance soundtracks. Audio, 00:55:15 and 00:47:13
Collection Adrian Piper Research Archive Foundation Berlin

127. *Untitled ("The area described by the periphery of this ad. . . .")/Area Relocation Series #2*. 1969
Advertisement appearing in the *Village Voice*, May 29, 1969. Newspaper page
Approx. 10¹⁵⁄₁₆ × 8⅝ in. (27.8 × 21.9 cm)
Collection Adrian Piper Research Archive Foundation Berlin
p. 171

128. *Untitled Map/Circle*. 1969
Five typescript pages, four photostats, and ink on paper
Each 11 × 8½ in. (27.9 × 21.6 cm)
Collection Adrian Piper Research Archive Foundation Berlin

129. *Untitled: Groups*. 1969
Seven black-and-white photographs and texts with pencil on colored paper
Each 11 × 8½ in. (27.9 × 21.6 cm)
Collection Adrian Piper Research Archive Foundation Berlin
pp. 174, 175

130. *Relocated Planes I: Indoor Series, 6/69*. 1969
Notebook with six typescript pages; ballpoint pen on four typescript pages; twelve photostats of architectural tape on acetate over photograph on paper; and cut-and-pasted text on twelve sheets of colored paper
Each page approx. 11 × 8½ in. (27.9 × 21.6 cm)
Generali Foundation Collection—Permanent Loan to the Museum der Moderne Salzburg
pp. 148, 149

131. *Relocated Planes II: Outdoor Series*. 1969
Notebook with six typescript pages; ballpoint pen on four typescript pages; twelve photostats of architectural tape on acetate over photograph on paper; and cut-and-pasted text on twelve sheets of colored paper
Each page approx. 11 × 8½ in. (27.9 × 21.6 cm)
Generali Foundation Collection—Permanent Loan to the Museum der Moderne Salzburg
pp. 150, 151

* 132. *World Work: One Event, Six Locations*. 1969–70
Carbon copy of typescript page on onionskin
11 × 8½ in. (27.9 × 21.6 cm)
Generali Foundation Collection—Permanent Loan to the Museum der Moderne Salzburg

133. *Groups*, in *Studio International*, March 1970. 1970
Four magazine pages
Each 12³⁄₁₆ × 20¹¹⁄₁₆ in. (31 × 52.5 cm)
The Museum of Modern Art Library, New York

* 134. *Context #6*. 1970
Two typescript pages; ink on typescript page; and ink and postage stamps on envelope
Each page 8½ × 11 in. (21.6 × 27.9 cm); envelope 9½ × 4³⁄₁₆ in. (24.1 × 10.6 cm)
Collection Adrian Piper Research Archive Foundation Berlin

135. *Context #7*. 1970
Seven ring binders with typescript page and ink, pencil, crayon, postage stamps, photographs, and sugar package on paper
Each binder 11¾ × 11 × 3 in. (29.8 × 27.9 × 7.6 cm)
Walker Art Center, Minneapolis. T. B. Walker Acquisition Fund
pp. 176, 177

136. *Context #8*. 1970
Binder with eighty-one flyers, mails, manifests, and postcards
Binder 11¹¹⁄₁₆ × 10¾ × 3 in. (29.7 × 27.3 × 7.6 cm)
Collection Adrian Piper Research Archive Foundation Berlin

137. *Context #9*. 1970
Binder with one typescript page and ballpoint pen and pencil on ninety-two sheets of paper
Binder 11¹¹⁄₁₆ × 10¾ × 3 in. (29.7 × 27.3 × 7.6 cm)
Collection Adrian Piper Research Archive Foundation Berlin

138. *Bach Whistled*. 1970
Sound work. Audio, 00:45:00
Collection Adrian Piper Research Archive Foundation Berlin

139. *Concrete Infinity Documentation Piece*. 1970
Handwritten text on notebook paper; and black-and-white photographs and handwritten text on fifty-six sheets of graph paper
Each sheet 10¾ × 8½ in. (27.3 × 21.6 cm)
The Museum of Contemporary Art, Los Angeles. Purchased with funds provided by the Drawings Committee
pp. 182, 185

140. *Catalysis III*. 1970
Documentation of the performance. Two gelatin silver prints and text mounted on colored paper
Overall 8½ × 11 in. (21.6 × 27.9 cm)
Photographs by Rosemary Mayer
Collection Thomas Erben, New York
p. 180

141. *Catalysis IV*. 1970
Documentation of the performance. Two gelatin silver prints and text mounted on colored paper
Overall 8½ × 11 in. (21.6 × 27.9 cm)
Photographs by Rosemary Mayer
Collection Thomas Erben, New York
pp. 77, 181

142. *Untitled Performance at Max's Kansas City*. 1970
Documentation of the performance. Four gelatin silver prints
Each 3⁹⁄₁₆ × 3⁹⁄₁₆ in. (9 × 9 cm)
Photographs by Rosemary Mayer
Collection Adrian Piper Research Archive Foundation Berlin
pp. 18, 178, 179

143. *Food for the Spirit*. 1971
Ring binder with fourteen gelatin silver prints and forty-four annotated pages torn from a paperback edition of Immanuel Kant's *Critique of Pure Reason*, mounted on colored paper, in plastic sleeves
Binder 11½ × 10 × 1½ in. (29.2 × 25.4 × 3.8 cm)
Collection Thomas Erben, New York
pp. 186–89

144. *Food for the Spirit*. 1971
Fourteen gelatin silver prints (reprinted 1997)
Each 14½ × 14¹³⁄₁₆ in. (37 × 37.7 cm)
The Museum of Modern Art, New York. The Family of Man Fund
pp. 190–93

145. *Infiltration, 6/71*. 1971
Carbon copies of two typescript pages on onionskin
Each 11 × 8½ in. (27.9 × 21.6 cm)
Generali Foundation Collection—Permanent Loan to the Museum der Moderne Salzburg
p. 56

* 146. *Phillip Zohn Catalysis*. 1972
Documentation of the performance. Audio, 01:26:25
Collection Adrian Piper Research Archive Foundation Berlin

147. *The Mythic Being, Village Voice Ads*. 1973–75
Advertisements appearing in the *Village Voice*.
Seventeen newspaper pages
Each 17 × 14 in. (43.2 × 35.6 cm)
The Museum of Modern Art, New York. Purchased with funds provided by Donald L. Bryant, Jr., Agnes Gund, Marlene Hess and James D. Zirin, Marie-Josée and Henry R. Kravis, Donald B. Marron, The Edward John Noble Foundation, Katherine Farley and Jerry Speyer, and Committee on Drawings Funds in honor of Kathy Fuld
Note: See "Pageworks," p. 333, for a full list of works.
pp. 194–98

148. *The Mythic Being*. 1973
Video excerpted from *Other Than Art's Sake* (1973), by Peter Kennedy. 16mm film transferred to video (black and white, sound), 00:08:00
Collection Adrian Piper Research Archive Foundation Berlin
p. 199

* 149. *The Mythic Being: I/You (Her)*. 1974
Gouache, tempera, and cut-and-pasted paper labels on ten black-and-white enlarged photographs
Each 8 × 5 in. (20.3 cm × 12.7 cm)
Walker Art Center, Minneapolis. T. B. Walker Acquisition Fund
pp. 200–4

150. *The Mythic Being Cycle I: 2/66*. 1974
Documentation of the performance rehearsal.
Audio, 00:14:00
Collection Adrian Piper Research Archive Foundation Berlin

151. *Stand-In #1: Rob*. 1974
Documentation of the interactive performance with Rob Rubin, with guitar composition by Adrian Piper. Audio, 00:23:00
Collection Adrian Piper Research Archive Foundation Berlin

152. *The Mythic Being: Dancing*. 1974
Fourteen gelatin silver prints
Each 10 × 8 in. (24.9 × 20.1 cm)
Collection Adrian Piper Research Archive Foundation Berlin
p. 205

153. *The Mythic Being: I Embody Everything You Most Hate and Fear*. 1975
Oil crayon on gelatin silver print
8 × 10 in. (20.1 × 24.9 cm)
Collection Thomas Erben, New York
p. 207

154. *The Mythic Being: Cruising White Women*. 1975
Documentation of the performance. Three gelatin silver prints
Each 8 × 10 in. (20.3 × 25.4 cm)
The Eileen Harris Norton Collection
pp. 212, 213

155. *The Mythic Being: Getting Back*. 1975
Five gelatin silver prints
Each 15¼ × 11¾ in. (38.7 × 29.8 cm)
Generali Foundation Collection—Permanent Loan to the Museum der Moderne Salzburg

* 156. *The Mythic Being: I Am the Locus #1–5*. 1975
Oil crayon on five gelatin silver prints
Each 8 × 10 in. (20.3 × 25.4 cm)
Smart Museum of Art, The University of Chicago. Purchase, gift of Carl Rungius, by exchange
pp. 208, 209

157. *The Mythic Being: Doing Yoga*. 1975
Six gelatin silver prints
Each 10 × 8 in. (25.4 × 20.3 cm)
Collection Margaret and Daniel S. Loeb

158. *The Mythic Being: It Doesn't Matter Who You Are*. 1975
Oil crayon on three gelatin silver prints
Each 10 × 8 in. (25.4 × 20.3 cm)
Spencer Museum of Art, University of Kansas. Museum Purchase: Helen Foresmen Spencer Art Acquisition Fund

159. *The Mythic Being: A 108*. 1975
Oil crayon on six gelatin silver prints
Each 25½ × 17¾ in. (64.7 × 45 cm)
Collection Candace King Weir
pp. 81, 210, 211

* 160. *The Mythic Being: Say It Like You Mean It*. 1975
Oil crayon on gelatin silver print
8 × 10 in. (20.1 × 24.9 cm)
Private collection

161. *Mythic Being: Look but Don't Touch (poster from Montclair State College)*. 1975
Photolithograph (recto and verso)
11 × 17 in. (27.9 × 43.2 cm)
Collection Adrian Piper Research Archive Foundation Berlin

162. *I/You/(Us)*. 1975
Photostats mounted on six pieces of foam core
Each 17 × 14 in. (43.2 × 35.5 cm)
Institut d'Art Contemporain, Rhône-Alpes
p. 206

163. *Some Reflective Surfaces*. 1975–76
Documentation of the audience-oriented performance at the Whitney Museum of American Art, New York, February 28, 1976. Two gelatin silver prints and 16mm film transferred to video (color, sound), 00:15:27
Prints 19½ × 15 in. (49.5 × 38.1 cm) and 15 × 19 ½ in. (38.1 × 49.5 cm)
Collection Adrian Piper Research Archive Foundation Berlin
pp. 52, 216

164. *Art for the Art World Surface Pattern*. 1976
Mixed-medium installation. Constructed wood environment, custom-printed wallpaper, stenciled text, audio, and naked light bulb
7 ft. × 60 in. × 60 in. (213.4 × 152.4 × 152.4 cm)
San Francisco Museum of Modern Art. Purchase through a gift of Shawn and Brook Byers
p. 215

165. *This Is Not the Documentation of a Performance*. 1976
Ink on screenprint of newspaper article
49 × 45 in. (124.5 × 114.3 cm)
Collection Lonti Ebers, New York
p. 214

166. *Aspects of the Liberal Dilemma*. 1978
Mixed-medium installation. Black-and-white photograph framed under Plexiglas, audio, and lighting
Photograph 18 × 18 in. (45.7 × 45.7 cm); installation dimensions variable
Source photography: Dick Durrance II/National Geographic (Cape Town, South Africa, 1977)
University of California, Berkeley Art Museum and Pacific Film Archive. Gift of the Peter Norton Family Foundation
pp. 84, 217

167. *Political Self-Portrait #1 (Sex)*. 1979
Photostat
29⅝ × 19⅝ in. (75.3 × 49.9 cm)
Collection Margaret and Daniel S. Loeb
p. 220

168. *Political Self-Portrait #2 (Race)*. 1978
Photostat
29⅝ × 19⅝ in. (75.3 × 49.9 cm)
Collection Richard and Ellen Sandor
p. 221

169. *Political Self-Portrait #3 (Class)*. 1980
Photostat
29⅝ × 19⅝ in. (75.3 × 49.9 cm)
Collection John Campione
p. 222

170. *Four Intruders Plus Alarm Systems*. 1980
Mixed-medium installation. Constructed wood environment, four photographs, light boxes, audio, and headsets
Dimensions variable
The Ohio State University. Courtesy Wexner Center for the Arts. Gift of the artist

171. *It's Just Art*. 1980
Documentation and video reconstruction of the performance at Allen Memorial Art Museum, Oberlin College, Oberlin, Ohio, Wednesday, April 23, 1980. Video (color, sound), 00:24:42; monitor, photolithograph; ink on notebook paper; ink and cut-and-pasted paper on fifteen gelatin silver prints; and ink and cut-and-pasted paper on three sheets of colored paper
Poster 14⅛ × 10¹³⁄₁₆ in. (35.9 × 27.5 cm); diagram 8 ½ × 11 in. (21.6 × 27.9 cm); each print 11¹³⁄₁₆ × 8¼ in. (30 × 21 cm); each collage 10 × 8 in. (25.4 × 20.3 cm)
Collection Adrian Piper Research Archive Foundation Berlin
pp. 218, 219

172. *Self-Portrait Exaggerating My Negroid Features*. 1981
Pencil on paper
10 × 8 in. (25.4 × 20.3 cm)
The Eileen Harris Norton Collection
pp. 83, 224

* 173. *$10.00/Hour Drawing of Pontus Hulten*. 1982
Pencil on paper
12 × 8⅞ in. (30.5 × 22.6 cm)
Collection Adrian Piper Research Archive Foundation Berlin
p. 227

174. *Portrait*. 1983
Photostat
40 × 30 in. (101.6 × 76.2 cm)
Private collection
p. 223

175. *Funk Lessons*. 1983–84
Documentation of the group performance at University of California, Berkeley, November 6, 1983. Video (color, sound), 00:15:17
Collection Adrian Piper Research Archive Foundation Berlin
p. 231

176. *Funk Lessons Direct Mail Advertisement*. 1983
Letterpress card with gold leaf
5¾ × 8¾ in. (14.6 × 22.2 cm)
Collection Adrian Piper Research Archive Foundation Berlin
p. 231

177. *Funk Lessons: A Collaborative Experiment in Cross-Cultural Transfusion*. 1984
Photolithograph
24 × 18 in. (61 × 45.7 cm)
The Museum of Modern Art Library, New York
pp. 60, 230

178. *Assorted Anti-Post-Modernist Artifacts*. 1984
Sound work. Audio, 00:10:00
Collection Adrian Piper Research Archive Foundation Berlin

* 179. *What Will Become of Me*. 1985–ongoing
Two framed texts, glass jars, shelf, hair, fingernails, and skin
Dimensions variable
The Museum of Modern Art, New York. Gift of Gwen and Peter Norton
pp. 234, 235

180. *A Tale of Avarice and Poverty*. 1985
Six texts and enlarged gelatin silver print
Each text 11 × 8½ in. (27.9 × 21.6 cm); photograph 37 ¼ × 25 ¼ in. (94.6 × 64.1 cm)
The Wadsworth Atheneum, Hartford, Connecticut. Purchased through the gift of James Junius Goodwin
pp. 232, 233

181. *My Calling (Card) #1 (Reactive Guerrilla Performance for Dinners and Cocktail Parties)*. 1986–90
Performance prop. Printed card
1⁵⁄₁₆ x 3½ in. (5 x 9 cm)
Davis Museum and Cultural Center, Wellesley College, Wellesley, Massachusetts. Museum purchase, The Dorothy Johnston Towne (Class of 1923) Fund
p. 246

182. *My Calling (Card) #2 (Reactive Guerrilla Performance for Bars and Discos)*. 1986–90
Performance prop. Printed card
1⁵⁄₁₆ x 3½ in. (5 x 9 cm)
Davis Museum and Cultural Center, Wellesley College, Wellesley, Massachusetts. Museum purchase, The Dorothy Johnston Towne (Class of 1923) Fund
p. 246

183. *My Calling (Card) #3 (Reactive Guerrilla Performance for Disputed Territorial Skirmishes)*. 2012
Performance prop. Printed card
1¹⁵⁄₁₆ × 3½ in. (5 × 9 cm)
Collection Adrian Piper Research Archive Foundation Berlin
p. 246

Exhibition note: Display of *My Calling (Card) #1*, *#2*, and *#3* includes a mixed-medium installation with pedestal, stenciled sign, and cardholders. The sign is in the collection of the Davis Museum and Cultural Center, Wellesley College, Wellesley, Massachusetts.

184. *Vanilla Nightmares #1*. 1986
Charcoal and oil crayon on newspaper
23⅝ × 13¹¹⁄₁₆ in. (60 × 34.8 cm)
Collection Adrian Piper Research Archive Foundation Berlin

185. *Vanilla Nightmares #2*. 1986
Charcoal and oil crayon on newspaper
22 × 28 in (55.8 × 71.1 cm)
Art Institute of Chicago. Margaret Fisher Endowment

186. *Vanilla Nightmares #3*. 1986
Charcoal and oil crayon on newspaper
25⅜ × 13⅞ in. (64.5 × 35.2 cm)
Walker Art Center, Minneapolis. T. B. Walker Acquisition Fund
p. 236

187. *Vanilla Nightmares #4a*. 1986
Charcoal on newspaper
23 × 13¾ in. (58.4 × 34.9 cm)
Sara M. and Michelle Vance Waddell

188. *Vanilla Nightmares #5*. 1986
Charcoal on newspaper
23¾ × 27¾ in. (60.3 × 70.5 cm)
The Heithoff Family Collection

189. *Vanilla Nightmares #6*. 1986
Charcoal on newspaper
23 × 13¾ in. (58.4 × 34.9 cm)
Collection Adrian Piper Research Archive Foundation Berlin
p. 237

190. *Vanilla Nightmares #9*. 1986
Charcoal and oil crayon on newspaper
22 × 13¾ in. (55.9 × 34.9 cm)
Walker Art Center, Minneapolis. T. B. Walker Acquisition Fund
p. 238

191. *Vanilla Nightmares #10*. 1986
Charcoal and oil crayon on newspaper
23 × 13½ in. (58.4 × 34.3 cm)
Walker Art Center, Minneapolis. T. B. Walker Acquisition Fund
p. 239

192. *Vanilla Nightmares #11*. 1986
Charcoal on newspaper
23⁷⁄₁₆ × 27⅜ in. (59.5 × 69.5 cm)
Collection Adrian Piper Research Archive Foundation Berlin

193. *Vanilla Nightmares #12*. 1986
Charcoal on newspaper
23½ × 13½ in. (59.7 × 34.3 cm)
The Museum of Modern Art, New York. Gift of Gwen and Peter Norton
p. 240

194. *Vanilla Nightmares #13*. 1986
Charcoal on newspaper
23⁷⁄₁₆ × 13⁹⁄₁₆ in. (59.6 × 34.5 cm)
Collection Adrian Piper Research Archive Foundation Berlin

195. *Vanilla Nightmares #14*. 1986
Charcoal on newspaper
23½ × 14 in. (59.7 × 35.6 cm)
Faulconer Gallery, Grinnell College Art Collection, Grinnell, Iowa
p. 241

196. *Vanilla Nightmares #16*. 1987
Charcoal on newspaper
21⅝ × 26⅜ in. (55 × 67 cm)
Collection Katharina Faerber
p. 242

197. *Vanilla Nightmares #17*. 1987
Charcoal and oil crayon on newspaper
22 × 14 in. (55.8 × 35.6 cm)
CS, NY

198. *Vanilla Nightmares #18*. 1987
Charcoal on newspaper
22³⁄₁₆ × 13¹¹⁄₁₆ in. (56.4 × 34.8 cm)
Williams College Museum of Art, Williamstown, Massachusetts. Gift of the American Academy and Institute of Arts and Letters, New York; Hassam, Speicher, Betts and Symons Funds
p. 243

199. *Vanilla Nightmares #19*. 1988
Charcoal on newspaper
22¼ × 27¼ in. (56.5 × 69.2 cm)
Collection Adrian Piper Research Archive Foundation Berlin
p. 244

200. *Vanilla Nightmares #20*. 1989
Charcoal on newspaper
23 × 13¾ in. (58.4 × 34.9 cm)
Hammer Museum, Los Angeles. Purchase
p. 245

* 201. *Close to Home*. 1987
Fifteen photographs with text, fifteen texts, and audio, 00:00:55
Each photograph with text 22 × 17 in. (55.8 × 43.1 cm) and each text 11 × 17 in. (27.9 × 43.1 cm)
Museum of Fine Arts, Houston. Museum purchase funded by Michael and Jeanne Klein

202. *An Open Letter to Donald Kuspit (Kuspit Extermination Fantasy)*. 1987
Pencil on paper
12 × 9 in. (30.4 × 22.8 cm)
University of Colorado Art Museum, Boulder. Gift of the artist
p. 228

203. *An Open Letter to Donald Kuspit (Kuspit Strangulation Fantasy)*. 1987
Pencil on paper
12 × 9 in. (30.4 × 22.8 cm)
University of Colorado Art Museum, Boulder. Gift of the artist
p. 229

204. *Think About It*. 1987
Mock-up for billboard design. Rephotographed newspaper images, transparent foil, text, and watercolor
14 × 17 in. (35.6 × 43.2 cm)
Sara M. and Michelle Vance Waddell

205. *Funk Lessons Meta-Performance*. 1987
Documentation of the participatory performance and discussion. Video (color, sound), 00:42:00
Collection Adrian Piper Research Archive Foundation Berlin

206. *Colored People*. 1987
Artist's book
Publisher: Book Works, London, 1991
The Museum of Modern Art Library, New York

207. *My Calling (Card) #1 Meta-Performance.* 1987–88
Documentation of the participatory performance and discussion. Video (color, sound), 00:58:00
Collection Adrian Piper Research Archive Foundation Berlin

208. *A Conversation with Kinshasha Conwill.* 1988
Documentation of the discussion. Audio, 01:22:24
Collection Adrian Piper Research Archive Foundation Berlin

209. *Merge.* 1988
Video of Times Square LED billboard. Video (color, silent), 00:00:56, endless loop
Collection Adrian Piper Research Archive Foundation Berlin
p. 247

* 210. *The Big Four Oh.* 1988
Video installation. Video (color, sound), 00:47:32, with monitor, ring binder with 153 blank sheets, two pages of handwritten text, forty baseballs, disassembled plastic coat of armor in fourteen pieces, and five bottles each containing blood, sweat, tears, piss, or vinegar
Dimensions variable
Walker Art Center, Minneapolis. T. B. Walker Acquisition Fund
p. 249

211. *Cornered.* 1988
Video installation. Video (color, sound), 00:17:00, with monitor, birth certificates, table, and chairs
Dimensions variable
Museum of Contemporary Art, Chicago. Bernice and Kenneth Newberger Fund
p. 248

* 212. *Ur-Mutter #2: We Made You.* 1989
Screenprinted text on black-and-white photograph, mounted on foam core
40 × 23 in. (101.6 × 58.4 cm)
Source photography: Peter Turnley/Newsweek
Mount Holyoke College Art Museum, South Hadley, Massachusetts. Purchase with the Eleanor H. Bunce (Class of 1926) Art Acquisition Fund
p. 251

213. *Ur-Mutter #8.* 1989
Screenprinted text on black-and-white photograph, mounted on foam core
36 × 59½ in. (91.4 × 151.1 cm)
Source photography: Sonnabend Gallery/Artforum; Peter Turnley/Newsweek
Collection Adrian Piper Research Archive Foundation Berlin
p. 252

214. *Free #2.* 1989
Screenprinted text on two black-and-white photographs, mounted on foam core
48 × 31 in. (121.9 × 78.7 cm) and 38 × 53 in. (96.5 × 134.6 cm)
Collection Adrian Piper Research Archive Foundation Berlin
p. 250

* 215. *Why Guess #2.* 1989
Screenprinted text on two black-and-white photographs, mounted on foam core
Each 36 × 30 in (91.5 × 76.2 cm)
Collection Adrian Piper Research Archive Foundation Berlin

216. *Safe #1–4.* 1990
Mixed-medium installation. Screenprinted text on four black-and-white photographs, mounted on foam core and affixed to the corners of a room, with audio
30¼ × 42 in. (76.8 × 106.7 cm); 24⅝ × 39 ¼ in. (62.5 × 99.7 cm); 30⁷⁄₁₆ × 24¹⁵⁄₁₆ in. (77.3 × 63.3 cm); and 44⁵⁄₁₆ × 39 in. (112.6 × 99.1 cm)
Source photography: Ebony; Ebony/General Fords Corp.; Parsons School of Design; AT&T
Collection Adrian Piper Research Archive Foundation Berlin
pp. 256, 257

* 217. *Pretend #1.* 1990
Screenprinted text on eight black-and-white photographs, mounted on foam core
Six prints each 12 × 8 in. (30.4 × 20.3 cm) and two prints each 12 × 12 in. (30.4 × 30.4 cm)
The New School Art Collection, New York
p. 253

218. *Pretend #2.* 1990
Screenprinted text on three black-and-white photographs, mounted on foam core
44 × 22 in. (111.7 × 55.8 cm); 44 × 35 in. (111.7 × 88.9 cm); and 44 × 31 in. (111.7 × 78.7 cm)
Brooklyn Museum, New York. Purchased with funds given by the Daniel and Joanna S. Rose Fund
pp. 254, 255

219. *Pretend #3.* 1990
Screenprinted text on four photographs, mounted on foam core; one photograph of pencil drawing on graph paper
42½ × 63 ¾ in. (108 × 161.9 cm); 11⅝ × 28 ¼ in. (29.5 × 71.8 cm); 66¾ × 28¼ in. (169.5 × 71.8 cm); 17½ × 36¼ in. (44.5 × 92.1 cm); 30 in. × 6 ft. 3 in. (76.2 × 190.5 cm)
The Eileen Harris Norton Collection

* 220. *Pretend #5.* 1990
Screenprinted text on nine photographs, mounted on foam core
Each 24 × 24 in. (61 × 61 cm)
Siemens Fotosammlung, Pinakothek der Moderne

221. *Please, God.* 1991
Video (color, sound), 01:01:00
Collection Adrian Piper Research Archive Foundation Berlin

222. *Vote/Emote.* 1990
Mixed-medium installation. Four wood booths with swinging doors, four notebooks with preprinted pages, pens, four photographs, light boxes, and framed windows
7 ft. × 13 ft. 8½ in. × 48 ¾ in. (213.4 × 417.8 × 123.8 cm)
Source photography: Kristine Larsen, Village Voice (1988; Brooklyn, NY); Dick Durrance II, National Geographic (1977; Cape Town, South Africa); Bruce Davidson–Magnum, Newsweek (August 29, 1963; Washington, D.C); Alon Reininger–Village Voice (January 14, 1980)
Collection Adrian Piper Research Archive Foundation Berlin

223. *What It's Like, What It Is #3.* 1991
Video installation. Video (color, sound), constructed wood environment, four monitors, mirrors, and lighting
Dimensions variable
The Museum of Modern Art, New York. Acquired in part through the generosity of Lonti Ebers, Marie-Josée and Henry Kravis, Candace King Weir, and Lévy Gorvy Gallery, and with support from The Modern Women's Fund
pp. 85, 258, 259

224. *Black Box/White Box.* 1992
Video installation. Video (color, sound), 00:30:00, with two constructed wood environments, monitor, four photographs, light box, audio, chairs, tables, tissue boxes, and trash baskets
Dimensions variable
Generali Foundation Collection—Permanent Loan to the Museum der Moderne Salzburg
pp. 268, 269

225. *Decide Who You Are #1: Skinned Alive.* 1992
Screenprinted images and text on three sheets of paper, mounted on foam core
72 × 42 in. (182.8 × 106.7 cm); 72 × 63 in. (182.8 × 160 cm); and 72 × 42 in. (182.8 × 106.7 cm)
Collection Margaret and Daniel S. Loeb
pp. 260, 261

226. *Decide Who You Are #6: You'r History.* 1992
Screenprinted images and text on seven sheets of paper, mounted on foam core
72 × 42 in. (182.8 × 106.7 cm); 9 ¾ × 7 in. (24.8 × 17.8 cm); 24 × 7 ¼ in. (61 × 18.4 cm); 24 × 29 in. (61 × 73.7 cm); 22 × 32 in. (55.9 × 81.3 cm); 20 × 24 ¾ in. (50.8 × 62.9 cm); and 72 × 42 in. (182.8 × 106.7 cm)
Mott-Warsh Collection, Flint, Michigan
pp. 262, 263

227. *Decide Who You Are #15: You Don't Want Me Here.* 1992
Screenprinted images and text on three sheets of paper, mounted on foam core
72 × 42 in. (182.8 × 106.7 cm); 61 ¾ × 36 in. (156.9 × 91.4 cm); and 72 × 42 in. (182.8 × 106.7 cm)
Collection Marilyn and Larry Fields
pp. 264, 265

* 228. *Decide Who You Are #21: Phantom Limbs.* 1992
Screenprinted images and text on four sheets of paper, mounted on foam core
72 × 42 in. (182.8 × 106.7 cm); 24 × 43 in. (61 × 109.2 cm); 15 × 13 in. (38.1 × 33 cm); and 72 × 42 in. (182.8 × 106.7 cm)
Source photography: Russell Harbour; David Clendenen/U.S. Fish and Wildlife Service; Acey Harper/People
Collection Adrian Piper Research Archive Foundation Berlin
pp. 266, 267

229. *Decide Who You Are, Right-Hand (Constant) Panel Text.* 1992
Sound work. Audio, 00:52:24
Collection Adrian Piper Research Archive Foundation Berlin
pp. 76, 77

230. *I Am Some Body, The Body of My Friends #1–18.* 1992–95
Fifteen color photographs and three black-and-white photographs
Each 8 × 12 in. (20.3 × 30.5 cm)
Collection Adrian Piper Research Archive Foundation Berlin

231. *Art Talk: Xenophobia and the Indexical Present.* 1993
Documentation of the lecture. Video (color, sound), 01:22:00
Collection Adrian Piper Research Archive Foundation Berlin

232. *Self-Portrait as a Nice White Lady*. 1995
Oil crayon on black-and-white photograph
10 × 8 in. (30.4 × 20.3 cm)
The Studio Museum in Harlem, New York.
Museum purchase made possible by a gift from
Barbara Karp Shuster, New York
p. 225

233. *Ashes to Ashes*. 1995
Enlarged black-and-white photograph, two enlarged color photographs, and text
48 × 30 in. (121.9 × 76.2 cm); 48 × 24 in. (121.9 × 61 cm); 18 × 30 in. (45.7 × 76.2 cm); and 24 × 30 in. (61 × 76.2 cm)
Collection Adrian Piper Research Archive Foundation Berlin
pp. 270, 271

234. *Philosophy Talk: A Kantian Analysis of Xenophobia*. 1996
Documentation of the lecture. Video (color, sound), 01:24:52
Collection Adrian Piper Research Archive Foundation Berlin

235. *Self-Portrait 2000*. 2001
Text and image on computer monitor
Dimensions variable
Collection Adrian Piper Research Archive Foundation Berlin

236. *The Color Wheel Series, First Adhyasa: Annomayakosha #8*. 2000
Photostat mounted on foam core with laminate
56 × 36 in. (142 × 91 cm)
Collection Adrian Piper Research Archive Foundation Berlin

237. *The Color Wheel Series, First Adhyasa: Annomayakosha #10*. 2000
Photostat mounted on foam core with laminate
56 × 36 in. (142 × 91 cm)
Collection Adrian Piper Research Archive Foundation Berlin

238. *The Color Wheel Series, First Adhyasa: Annomayakosha #15*. 2000
Photostat mounted on foam core with laminate
56 × 36 in. (142 × 91 cm)
Collection Adrian Piper Research Archive Foundation Berlin

Artist's note: in The Color Wheel Series, the artist assigns a different combination of Pantone colors for each viewing occasion, whether in print reproduction, a gallery or museum setting, or projections for talks.

239. *Das Gebetsrad Quadriert*. 2001
Sound work. Audio, 00:32:57
Collection Adrian Piper Research Archive Foundation Berlin

240. *You/Stop/Watch: A Shiva Japan*. 2002
Documentation of the performance. Video (color, sound), 00:42:26
Collection Adrian Piper Research Archive Foundation Berlin
p. 274

241. *Everything #2.1*. 2003
Photograph photocopied on graph paper and sanded with sandpaper, with printed text
8½ × 11 in. (21.6 × 27.9 cm)
Stephen Schiffer

242. *Everything #2.3*. 2003
Photograph photocopied on graph paper and sanded with sandpaper, with printed text
8½ × 11 in. (21.6 × 27.9 cm)
Private collection
p. 276

243. *Everything #2.5*. 2003
Photograph photocopied on graph paper and sanded with sandpaper, with printed text
11 × 8 ½ in. (27.9 × 21.6 cm)
Private collection
p. 277

244. *Everything #2.6*. 2003
Photograph photocopied on vellum over inkjet print, with printed text, combined in plastic sleeve
8½ × 11 in. (21.6 × 27.9 cm)
Collection Adrian Piper Research Archive Foundation Berlin

245. *Everything #2.7*. 2003
Photograph photocopied on graph paper and sanded with sandpaper, with printed text
8½ × 11 in. (21.6 × 27.9 cm)
Private collection
p. 278

246. *Everything #2.8*. 2003
Photograph photocopied on graph paper and sanded with sandpaper, with printed text
8 ½ × 11 in. (21.6 × 27.9 cm)
Private collection
p. 279

247. *Everything #2.9*. 2003
Photograph photocopied on graph paper and sanded with sandpaper, with printed text
11 × 8½ in. (27.9 × 21.6 cm)
Private collection. Courtesy Flow Advisory
p. 280

248. *Everything #2.10*. 2003
Photograph photocopied on graph paper and sanded with sandpaper, with printed text
11 × 8½ in. (27.9 × 21.6 cm)
Rothier Faria Collection
p. 281

249. *Everything #2.11a*. 2003
Photograph photocopied on graph paper and sanded with sandpaper, with printed text
8½ × 11 in. (21.6 × 27.9 cm)
Private collection

250. *Everything #2.11b*. 2003
Photograph photocopied on graph paper and sanded with sandpaper, with printed text
8½ × 11 in. (21.6 × 27.9 cm)
Collection Elizabeth Dee Gallery, New York

251. *Everything #2.12a*. 2003
Photograph photocopied on paper and sanded with sandpaper, with printed text
8½ × 11 in. (21.6 × 27.9 cm)
Collection J-E Van Praet
p. 282

252. *Everything #2.12b*. 2003
Photograph photocopied on graph paper and sanded with sandpaper, with printed text
8½ × 11 in. (21.6 × 27.9 cm)
Private collection

253. *Everything #2.13*. 2003
Photograph photocopied on graph paper and sanded with sandpaper, with printed text
8½ × 11 in. (21.6 × 27.9 cm)
Collection Lonti Ebers, New York
p. 283

254. Everything #2.14. 2003
Photograph photocopied on vellum over inkjet print, with printed text, combined in plastic sleeve
8½ × 11 in. (21.6 × 27.9 cm)
Private collection
p. 284

255. *Everything #2.15*. 2003
Photograph photocopied on graph paper and sanded with sandpaper, with printed text
8½ × 11 in. (21.6 × 27.9 cm)
Collection Lonti Elbers, New York
p. 285

256. *Everything #3*. 2003
Sandwich-board performance
Collection Adrian Piper Research Archive Foundation Berlin
p. 286

257. *Everything #4*. 2004
Engraved mirror, gold leaf, and wood frame
13 × 10 in. (33 × 25.4 cm)
Collection Adrian Piper Research Archive Foundation Berlin
p. 287

Exhibition note: Display includes two from an edition of eight

258. *Everything #5.1*. 2004
Engraved Plexiglas and gold leaf, inserted into wall
48 × 24 in. (121.9 × 61 cm)
Collection Adrian Piper Research Archive Foundation Berlin
p. 288

259. *Everything #6*. 2004
Six digital prints on wallpaper
Each print 24 × 24 in. (61 × 61 cm)
Source photography: Portraits of Abraham Lincoln, Medgar Evers, John F. Kennedy, Malcolm X, Martin Luther King, Jr., and Robert F. Kennedy
Collection Adrian Piper Research Archive Foundation Berlin

260. *Shiva Dances with the Art Institute of Chicago*. 2004
Documentation of the participatory performance-lecture. Video (color, sound), 01:43:18
Collection Adrian Piper Research Archive Foundation Berlin
pp. 67, 275

261. *Passing beyond Passing*. 2004
Documentation of the screening, lecture, and discussion. Video (color, sound), 01:38:07
Collection Adrian Piper Research Archive Foundation Berlin

262. *Construct Madrid*. 2005
Sound work. Four audio tracks, each 00:10:15
Collection Adrian Piper Research Archive Foundation Berlin

263. *Unite (Part I of The Pac-Man Trilogy)*. 2005
Animated video (color, silent), 00:43:37
Collection Adrian Piper Research Archive Foundation Berlin
p. 294

264. *The Spurious Life-Death Distinction (Part II of The Pac-Man Trilogy)*. 2006
Animated video (color, silent), 00:09:22
Collection Adrian Piper Research Archive Foundation Berlin
p. 89, 294

265. *Bait-and-Switch (Part III of The Pac-Man Trilogy)*. 2008
Animated video (color, silent), 00:04:48
Collection Adrian Piper Research Archive Foundation Berlin
p. 294

266. *Philosophy Talk: Intellectual Intuition in Kant's First Critique and Samkhya Philosophy*. 2007
Documentation of the lecture and discussion. Video (color, sound), 01:20:33
Collection Adrian Piper Research Archive Foundation Berlin

267. *Everything #19.1*. 2008
White vinyl text on wall with 10% gray paint
Dimensions variable
Collection Adrian Piper Research Archive Foundation Berlin
p. 292

268. *Everything #19.2*. 2007
Video (black and white, silent), 00:04:45
Collection Adrian Piper Research Archive Foundation Berlin
p. 293

269. *Adrian Moves to Berlin*. 2007
Documentation of the street performance. Video (color, sound), 01:02:42
Video by Robert Del Principe
Collection Adrian Piper Research Archive Foundation Berlin
p. 304

270. *Philosophy Interview: Telling Time—Adrian Piper*. 2007
Interview by Lynn Tjernan Lukkas. Video (color, sound), 01:35:20
Collection Adrian Piper Research Archive Foundation Berlin

271. *Adrian Piper Interview: Rationality and the Structure of the Self*. 2007–10
Interview by Robert Del Principe. Video (color, sound), 01:01:43
Collection Adrian Piper Research Archive Foundation Berlin

* 272. *Everything #10*. 2007
Participatory group performance
Commissioned by Creative Time, New York
Collection Adrian Piper Research Archive Foundation Berlin
p. 289

273. *Everything #17.2*. 2007
Extensive-form decision tree. Vinyl wall print
Dimensions variable
Collection Adrian Piper Research Archive Foundation Berlin
pp. 290, 291

274. *Vanishing Point #2*. 2009
Pencil and ballpoint pen on expense report sanded with sandpaper
11 × 8½ in. (27.9 × 21.6 cm)
Annette Gentz and Pascal Decker Collection
p. 296

275. *Vanishing Point #3*. 2009
Pencil on credit application sanded with sandpaper
11 × 8½ in. (27.9 × 21.6 cm)
Collection Adrian Piper Research Archive Foundation Berlin
p. 297

276. *Vanishing Point #4*. 2009
Pencil, colored pencil, and ballpoint pen on employment application sanded with sandpaper
11 × 8½ in. (27.9 × 21.6 cm)
Collection Adrian Piper Research Archive Foundation Berlin
p. 298

277. *Vanishing Point #5*. 2009
Ballpoint pen and pencil on employment application sanded with sandpaper
11 × 8½ in. (27.9 × 21.6 cm)
Collection Adrian Piper Research Archive Foundation Berlin
p. 299

278. *Vanishing Point #6.1*. 2009
Ballpoint pen, crayon, and pencil on weekly expense-report form sanded with sandpaper
11 × 8½ in. (27.9 × 21.6 cm)
Collection Adrian Piper Research Archive Foundation Berlin
p. 300

279. *Vanishing Point #6.2*. 2009
Ballpoint pen, crayon, and pencil on weekly expense-report form sanded with sandpaper
11 × 8½ in. (27.9 × 21.6 cm)
Collection Adrian Piper Research Archive Foundation Berlin
p. 301

280. *Vanishing Point #7*. 2009
Ballpoint pen and colored pencil on inventory form sanded with sandpaper
11 × 8½ in. (27.9 × 21.6 cm)
Collection Adrian Piper Research Archive Foundation Berlin
p. 302

281. *Vanishing Point #8*. 2011
Colored ink, ballpoint pen, pencil, and colored pencil on inventory form
11 × 8½ in. (27.9 × 21.6 cm)
Collection Adrian Piper Research Archive Foundation Berlin
p. 303

* 282. *Mauer*. 2010
Video installation. Thirty-six monitors, videos with randomly programmed images, and fresh roses
Dimensions variable
Collection Adrian Piper Research Archive Foundation Berlin

283. *Everything #21*. 2010–13
Chalk on four vintage blackboards in lacquered wood frames, each covered with the handwritten sentence "Everything will be taken away" and mounted on the wall at eye-level
Each 47¼ in. × 8 ft. 2⁷⁄₁₆ in. (120 × 250 cm)
Rennie Collection, Vancouver
p. 295

284. *The Humming Room*. 2012
Voluntary group performance. Full-time museum guard, empty room equipped to echo, and two text signs, one above the door and one adjacent
Dimensions variable
Collection Adrian Piper Research Archive Foundation Berlin

285. *Mokshamudra Progression*. 2012
Nine lithographs
Each 16 × 9 in. (40.6 × 22.9 cm)
Printer: Poligrafa Obra Grafica, Barcelona
Edition of 20
Collection Adrian Piper Research Archive Foundation Berlin

286. *Thwarted Projects, Dashed Hopes, A Moment of Embarrassment*. 2012
Digital file
Dimensions variable
Collection Adrian Piper Research Archive Foundation Berlin
pp. 15, 306

287. *The Probable Trust Registry: The Rules of the Game #1–3*. 2013
Installation and participatory group performance. Embossed gold vinyl text on three walls with 70% gray paint, three circular gold reception desks with stools, computer system, contracts, registry of contact data for signatories, three administrators, and self-selected members of the public
Each desk 6 ft. ¹⁄₁₆ in. (183 cm) diam. × 53 in. (160 cm) high; installation dimensions variable
Hamburger Bahnhof–Museum fur Gegenwart, Nationalgalerie, Staatliche Museen, Berlin
pp. 20, 308, 309

288. *Imagine [Trayvon Martin]*. 2013
Photolithograph
10⁷⁄₁₆ × 10¾ in. (26.5 × 27.3 cm)
Collection Adrian Piper Research Archive Foundation Berlin
Artist's note: This work can be downloaded for free at www.adrianpiper.de/art/.
pp. 69, 307

289. *Second Wave Feminism: Unfinished Business*. 2014
Documentation of the lecture and discussion. Video (color, sound), 01:49:41
Collection Adrian Piper Research Archive Foundation Berlin

290. *Howdy #6 [Second Series]*. 2015
Ceiling-mounted light projection, closed and locked door, and darkened hallway
Projection 36 × 36 in. (91.4 × 91.4 cm)
Collection Adrian Piper Research Archive Foundation Berlin
p. 310

291. *Never Forget*. 2016
Wall print
31 × 33 in. (78.7 × 83.8 cm)
Collection Adrian Piper Research Archive Foundation Berlin
p. 311

PHOTOGRAPH CREDITS

In reproducing the images contained in this publication, The Museum of Modern Art, New York, obtained the permission of the rights holders whenever possible. In those instances where the Museum could not locate the rights holders, notwithstanding good-faith efforts, it requests that any contact information concerning such rights holders be forwarded so that they may be contacted for future editions.

All works © Adrian Piper Research Archive Foundation Berlin except the following and as noted below: © Generali Foundation and Adrian Piper Research Archive Foundation Berlin: 35, 53, 54, 107, 148–51, 156–70, 268, 269; and © Adrian Piper Research Archive Foundation Berlin and Fondazione La Biennale di Venezia–Archivio Storico delle Arti Contemporanee; photograph by Andrea Avezzù: 293

© 2018 Vito Acconci: 19

Photograph by David Allison: 123, 124, 126

Photograph by Larry Andrews: 313

Artforum: 252

© 2018 Estate of Marcel Broodthaers /Artists Rights Society (ARS), New York / SABAM, Brussels: 22

Photograph by Emily Assiran: 131

© 2018 BBC: 74

Installation view of *The Present in Drag*, 9th Berlin Biennale, June 4–September 18, 2016: 310

Photograph by bpk Bildagentur/Hamburger Bahnhof-Museum fur Gegenwart, Nationalgalerie, Staatliche Museen, Berlin, Germany / David von Becker: pp. 308–9

© Fondazione La Biennale di Venezia–Archivio Storico delle Arti Contemporanee; photograph by Andrea Avezzù: 324

Photograph by Ben Blackwell; courtesy Museum of Modern Art San Francisco: 215

© Mel Bochner: 41

Photograph by Yvette Brackman: 321

Courtesy Brooklyn Museum: 254–55

Photograph by Peter Butler: 118, 121, 130

Photograph by David Campos: 258, 259

© CNAC/MNAM/Dist. Grand Palais / Art Resource, NY; photograph by Jacques Faujour, Bibliotheque Kandinsky/Musee National d›Art Moderne/Centre Pompidou: 316

Courtesy Creative Time: 247

Courtesy Elizabeth Dee Gallery: 20, 249; installation view of *Adrian Piper: Everything*, Elizabeth Dee Gallery, New York, March 1–April 19, 2008: 294; installation view of *Est. 2002*, Elizabeth Dee Gallery, New York, June 29–August 15, 2012: 249

Photograph by Phillip Dixon: 230

Photograph by Dick Durrance II / National Geographic (1977, Cape Town, South Africa): 84

Courtesy Ebony: 256

Photograph by R. Ferdon; courtesy New Directions Publishers: 74

Photograph by Étienne Frossard: 20, 249

Installation view of *Adrian Piper seit 1965*, Generali Foundation, Vienna, May 17–August 18, 2002: 268–69

© Mark Gerson / National Portrait Gallery, London: 75 (bottom)

Getty Images, Bettman Archive; © 2005 Ned Otter; photograph by Robert Otter: 314 (top)

© 2017 Gilbert & George, Courtesy Sonnabend Gallery: 42

Photograph by James Gutmann: 52, 205, 212, 213

Courtesy Hammer Museum, Los Angeles: 245

Installation view of *January 5–31, 1969*: 38

© 2017 The Donald Judd Estate / Artists Rights Society (ARS), New York, courtesy the Wexner Center for the Arts; photograph by Lynette Molnar: 41

Photograph by Werner Kaligofsky: 148–49, 150–51, 268–69

© Dmitri Kasterin: 75 (top)

Photograph by Nathan Keay; ©MCA Chicago: 248

Photograph by Boris Kirpotin: 101

Photograph by Paul Laster: 286

Courtesy Lévy Gorvy, New York; photograph by Elisabeth Bernstein: 76, 266–67; Installation view of *Adrian Piper*, Lévy Gorvy, New York, September 14-October 21, 2017; photograph by Ralph Neri: 218–19

Installation view of *Drawing Then: Innovation and Influence in American Drawings of the Sixties*, at Lévy Gorvy, January 27–March 26, 2016: 108

© 2017 The LeWitt Estate / Artists Rights Society (ARS), New York/ LeWitt Collection, Chester, Connecticut, USA: 63

© 2017 The LeWitt Estate / Artists Rights Society (ARS), New York; photograph by RJ Phil: 46

Courtesy Matthew Marks Gallery; photograph by Bill Orcutt: 95

Photograph by André Moin: 206

Courtesy Mott-Warsh Collection: 262–63

Courtesy Museum of Contemporary Art, Los Angeles: 182, 183, 184, 185

The Museum of Modern Art, New York, Department of Imaging Services; photograph by Peter Butler: 59, 108, 109–10, 194, 195, 196, 197, 198: photograph by Robert Gerhardt: 81, 210, 211; photograph by Jonathan Muzikar: 17, 186–93, 234–35; photograph by John Wronn: 37, 135, 240

The New York Times / Paul Hosefros, Jim Wilson and Dan Miller; Danny Lyon, Jack Levine; Bruce Davidson / Magnum Photos; Black Star / Flip Schulke; Bruce Davidson: 317

Courtesy The Eileen Harris Norton Collection: 52, 83, 212, 213, 224

Photograph by Timo Ohler: 18, 53, 104–6, 112, 127–29, 132, 136–39, 154, 155, 171, 178–79, 226, 227, 250, 252, 270–71, 287, 313

Photograph by Allen Phillips / Wadsworth Atheneum: 232–33

Photograph by Lia Mir Pileggi: 228, 229

Photograph by Adrian Piper: 174, 175, 319

Photograph by Daniel R. Piper: 315

© 2017 Estate of Ad Reinhardt / Artists Rights Society (ARS), New York, courtesy David Zwirner, New York, London: 47

Photograph by Alan Seabright: 13

© Bob Sheff: 25

Photograph by Warren Silverman: 216; © Art Media Holdings, LLC, New York. Reprinted by permission: 318

Photograph © 2017 courtesy The David and Alfred Smart Museum of Art, The University of Chicago: 208, 209

Sonnabend Gallery: 252

Photograph by Peter Turnley / Newsweek: 251, 252

Courtesy University of California at Berkeley: 23

Courtesy Walker Art Center: 146–47, 176, 177, 200–4, 236, 238, 239

Photograph by the Weatherspoon Art Museum at The University of North Carolina at Greensboro: 83

Courtesy Williams College Museum of Art: 243

Published in conjunction with the exhibition *Adrian Piper: A Synthesis of Intuitions, 1965–2016*, at The Museum of Modern Art, New York, March 31–July 22, 2018. Organized by Christophe Cherix, The Robert Lehman Foundation Chief Curator of Drawings and Prints, The Museum of Modern Art; Cornelia H. Butler, Chief Curator, Hammer Museum, Los Angeles; and David Platzker, former Curator, The Department of Drawings and Prints, The Museum of Modern Art; with Tessa Ferreyros, Curatorial Assistant, Department of Drawings and Prints, The Museum of Modern Art

The exhibition will travel to:

Hammer Museum, Los Angeles
September 30, 2018–January 6, 2019

Haus der Kunst, Munich
April 12–September 22, 2019

Hyundai Card

The exhibition is made possible by Hyundai Card.

Major support is provided by The Modern Women's Fund and Lannan Foundation.

Generous funding is provided by The Friends of Education of The Museum of Modern Art, Marilyn and Larry Fields, and by Marieluise Hessel Artzt.

Additional support is provided by the Annual Exhibition Fund.

Produced by the Department of Publications, The Museum of Modern Art, New York
Christopher Hudson, Publisher
Don McMahon, Editorial Director
Marc Sapir, Production Director

Edited by Emily Hall
Designed by IN-FO.CO
Production by Hannah Kim
Color separations by t'ink, Brussels
Printed and bound by Graphius—New Goff, Belgium

This book is typeset in Media77, Alternate Gothic, and Atlas Grotesk.
The paper is 150 gsm Magno Matt.

Published by The Museum of Modern Art, New York
11 West 53 Street
New York, New York 10019
www.moma.org

Distributed in the United States and Canada by
ARTBOOK | D.A.P.
155 Sixth Avenue, 2nd floor
New York, New York 10013
www.artbook.com

Distributed outside the United States and Canada by Thames & Hudson Ltd.
181A High Holborn
London WC1V 7QX

ISBN: 978-1-63345-049-3
Library of Congress Control Number: 2018934969

Printed in Belgium

Cover:
Decide Who You Are: Right-Hand (Constant) Panel. 1992
Screenprinted text on paper, mounted on foam core
72 × 42 in. (182.8 × 106.7 cm)
Various public and private collections

Back cover:
Drawings about Paintings and Writings about Words #5. 1967
Pencil and charcoal on notebook paper
11 × 8½ in. (27.9 × 21.6 cm)
Collection Louise Fishman